Signed Language and Gesture Research in Cognitive Linguistics

Cognitive Linguistics Research

Editors
Dirk Geeraerts
Dagmar Divjak

Honorary editors
René Dirven
Ronald W. Langacker

Volume 67

Signed Language and Gesture Research in Cognitive Linguistics

Edited by
Terry Janzen and Barbara Shaffer

DE GRUYTER
MOUTON

ISBN 978-3-11-221371-1
e-ISBN (PDF) 978-3-11-070378-8
e-ISBN (EPUB) 978-3-11-070389-4
ISSN 1861-4132

Library of Congress Control Number: 2023934705

Bibliographic information published by the Deutsche Nationalbibliothek
The Deutsche Nationalbibliothek lists this publication in the Deutsche Nationalbibliografie;
detailed bibliographic data are available on the internet at http://dnb.dnb.de.

© 2025 Walter de Gruyter GmbH, Berlin/Boston
This volume is text- and page-identical with the hardback published in 2023.
Typesetting: Integra Software Services Pvt. Ltd.
Printing and binding: CPI books GmbH, Leck

www.degruyter.com

For Sherman

Acknowledgements

First and foremost, this book would not be what it is without the thoughtful and enthusiastic work of all of our chapter authors, so thank you. We also appreciate the careful work of all the chapter reviewers. There are also many others who have helped us out, in big and small ways, and we thank you all: Tasheney Francis, Liz Janzen, Gudrun Kendon, Lorraine Leeson, Christine Monikowski, Anna-Lena Nilsson, Barbara Pennacchi, Bruno Pinto Silva, Daz Saunders, Haaris Sheikh, Susan Tompkins, Paul Twitchell, Martin Watkins, and Terry Wu.

We are especially indebted to Brigitte Garcia and Paola Pietrandrea for agreeing to become co-authors with our good friends Elena Antinoro Pizzuto (Brigitte) and Tommaso Russo (Paola) to complete these two manuscript drafts, both of which came to us not too long before their passing, and which we have been holding for a chance to publish. We are so pleased that both of these chapters were able to be completed and included here. We thank Adam Kendon too who, even though he was already not well, never wavered in his enthusiasm in being a contributing author.

We are grateful to Anke Beck, who was the original editor at de Gruyter Mouton who encouraged us and helped us envision this project, and Birgit Sievert and Kirstin Börgen, our editors now at de Gruyter Mouton for guiding us through the process of putting the book together. Thanks too, to Dirk Geeraerts and Dagmar Divjak, the series editors for Cognitive Linguistics Research, where we are so pleased that we are able to place this work.

Contents

Acknowledgements —— VII

Cornelia Müller
Foreword —— XIII

Terry Janzen and Barbara Shaffer
Introduction: Examining signed language and gesture research within the domain of cognitive linguistics —— 1

I Guiding principles for signed and spoken language research

Penny Boyes Braem and Virginia Volterra
Through the signed language glass: Changing and converging views in spoken and signed language research —— 23

Elena Antinoro Pizzuto and Brigitte Garcia
Coming back to the issue of the graphic representation of signed language discourse in signed language linguistics —— 49

Paola Pietrandrea
What is a language? A socio-semiotic approach to signed and spoken languages —— 75

II Iconicity in spoken and signed language

Ronald W. Langacker
Structure, iconicity, and access —— 105

Corrine Occhino
When hands are things and movements are processes: Cognitive iconicity, embodied cognition, and signed language structure —— 127

III Multimodality

Eve Sweetser
Gestural meaning is in the body(-space) as much as in the hands —— 157

Laura Ruth-Hirrel
A Place for joint action in multimodal constructions —— 181

Terry Janzen, Barbara Shaffer, and Lorraine Leeson
What I know is here; what I don't know is somewhere else: Deixis and gesture spaces in American Sign Language and Irish Sign Language —— 211

Darren Saunders and Anne-Marie Parisot
Insights on the use of narrative perspectives in signed and spoken discourse in Quebec Sign Language, American Sign Language, and Quebec French —— 243

IV Blending and metaphor

Anna-Lena Nilsson
Exploring Real Space blends as indicators of discourse complexity in Swedish Sign Language —— 275

Tommaso Russo and Paola Pietrandrea
Metaphors and blending in Italian Sign Language discourse: A window on the interaction of language and thought —— 303

V Grammatical constructions

Elisabeth Engberg-Pedersen
The mouth shrug and facial consent in Danish Sign Language —— 329

Erin Wilkinson, Ryan Lepic, and Lynn Hou
Usage-based grammar: Multi-word expressions in American Sign Language —— 357

André Nogueira Xavier and Rocío Anabel Martínez
Possibility modals in Brazilian Sign Language and Argentine Sign Language: A contrastive study —— 389

Sara Siyavoshi
The semantics of relative clause constructions in Iranian Sign Language —— 417

VI Concluding commentary

Adam Kendon
Language in the light of sign and gesture —— 443

Index —— 463

Cornelia Müller
Foreword

Language and the body – Dynamic relations between gestures and signed language

In the spring of 2007 a cognitive linguistic conference took place in Lille, a university town in the north of France announcing a remarkable topic: "Typology, Gesture and Sign". It was the second conference of the French Association for Cognitive Linguistics (AFLiCo) and it was the second linguistics conference that invited two communities of researchers to listen to each other that hitherto had not had much chance to do so: signed language linguists and gesture researchers. It was on that historic occasion that I first met Sherman and Phyllis Wilcox. Phyllis was one of the speakers in a theme session on "Metonymy in Gesture" that I co-organized with Irene Mittelberg. Phyllis's talk was called "Metonymic conceptualizations in ASL", Silva Ladewig's was "Metonymic bases of a recurrent polysemous gesture", and I gave a talk on "Gestural modes of representation as metonymic resources of gesture creation". In a sense, we were all seeking to understand some of the developmental processes underlying the stabilization and codification of visible bodily actions that result in conventionalized forms in spoken and in signed languages.

Gesture researchers were looking at recurrent and emblematic gestures within spoken languages as mirroring different stages in the conventionalization process of co-speech gestures (Ladewig 2014a, 2014b; Müller 2014b, 2017) and signed language linguists were interested in the development of lexical and grammatical signs (Wilcox 2005). Mandel's paper on "Iconic Devices in ASL" (Mandel 1977) and Kendon's work on signed languages of Papua New Guinea (Kendon 1980a, 1980b, 1980c) and "Sign Languages of Aboriginal Australia" (1988b) inspired signed language linguists as well as gesture researchers (Müller 2014a). For all of us, the iconicity of visible bodily actions played a core role as a semiotic base for gestures and for signs (Armstrong, Stokoe and Wilcox 1995; Mittelberg 2014; Müller 1998; Taub 2001; P. Wilcox 2000). Metonymy as a cognitive principle addressed the iconicity of gestures and signs as a cognitive and semiotic principle (Mittelberg 2019).

Sherman followed the panel with acute attention and the participants profited greatly from his open-minded comments on their respective research agendas. Everybody thoroughly enjoyed Sherman's exceptional expertise on these issues. It was clear that he was framing his comments against the backdrop of decades of his thinking about such questions. The subject matter had been at the core of his reflections about signed languages for a very long time: the publication of *Gesture and the Nature of Language* in 1995, co-written with David Armstrong and William

Stokoe, marked a milestone in exploring relations between gestures and signing from a linguistic point of view.

An important element of Sherman's contributions to the discussions on the occasion of the 2007 AFLiCo panel continues to surface in my own ongoing reflections on processes of stabilization in co-speech gestures. This element is his more recent work on lexicalization and grammaticalization in signed languages. "Routes from Gesture to Language" appeared in 2005 and discussed how gestures that are "not a conventional unit in the linguistic system" develop into signs with grammatical functions (Wilcox 2005: 12; see also Janzen and Shaffer 2002). In his paper, Wilcox distinguishes two routes from gesture to grammatical items within signed language: one in which gestures evolve into lexical units that then develop into grammatical forms (lexical to grammatical is well known from grammaticalization processes in spoken languages). "The first route, by which signed words develop out of nonwords and further to grammatical morphemes, begins with a gesture that is not a conventional unit in the linguistic system. This gesture becomes incorporated into a signed language as a lexical item. Over time, these lexical signs acquire grammatical function" (Wilcox 2005: 12). The other developmental route is where grammatical expression bypasses a lexical stage and evolves from gesture to prosody to grammatical morphology:

> The second route proceeds along quite a different path. In this route, the source gesture is one of several types including the manner of movement of a manual gesture or sign, and various facial, mouth, and eye gestures. I claim that this second route follows a path of development from gesture to prosody/intonation to grammatical morphology. ... Notably, the second route bypasses any lexical stage. (Wilcox 2005: 13)

The first route is noteworthy for gesture researchers, since it allows us to identify similarities and differences between gestures and signs, while we do see conventional gestural expression that one could describe as forms of lexicalization (Kendon 1988a; Müller 2018). For example, the ring gesture is an expression of perfection and excellence, or is a gesture for "okay", but we are *not* seeing gestures used along with spoken constructions within grammaticalization processes. Albeit, this appears not surprising, but it is still interesting to note.

Wilcox's second route alludes to processes of decomposition that we see in hybrid forms of recurrent gestures, where a stable formational and functional core, for example the ring-shape, can be used with variable movement patterns, orientations, and locations in the gesture space when used to express the preciseness of co-articulated arguments (Müller 2017). When, however, the ring-gesture becomes fully conventionalized—as when it is used to express perfection and excellence—all aspects of kinesic form are stable (Müller 2014b, forthcoming). What we see here, in my view, are proto-forms of lexicalization processes. It would be of interest to carry out research on gestures that are used along with signed language to see if similar processes can be observed. However, this is only one of the manifold relations that remain to be explored for students interested in the dynamic relations that characterize language as emerging from the body and, more specifically, from the mundane practices of our bodily interactions with the world.

Sherman Wilcox saw early on how valuable a cognitive linguistic framework would be for an understanding of signed language, because it offers a pathway for a view of language as being grounded in, and going along with, embodied experiences as we sign, speak and gesture (Bressem 2021; Ladewig, 2020; Müller 2018).

The present book brings together a wealth of contributions that elucidate fascinating aspects of signed language and gesture research that, notably, only appear on stage once we allow ourselves to look—and *see*—Sherman's stance on visible bodily actions as language. It honors Sherman Wilcox's kind, lucid, pioneering thoughts in the best possible manner – it carries them forward.

References

Armstrong, David F., William C. Stokoe & Sherman E. Wilcox. 1995. *Gesture and the Nature of Language*. Cambridge: Cambridge University Press.

Bressem, Jana. 2021. *Repetitions in Gesture: A Cognitive and Usage-based Perspective*. Berlin/Boston: De Gruyter Mouton.

Janzen, Terry & Barbara Shaffer. 2002. Gesture as the substrate in the process of ASL grammaticization. In Richard P. Meier, David Quinto-Pozos & Kearsy Cormier (eds.), *Modality and Structure in Signed and Spoken Languages*, 199–223. Cambridge: Cambridge University Press.

Kendon, Adam. 1980a. A description of a deaf-mute sign language from the Enga Province of Papua New Guinea with some comparative discussion. Part I: The formational properties of Enga signs. *Semiotica* 32. 1–34.

Kendon, Adam. 1980b. A description of a deaf-mute sign language, etc. Part II: The semiotic functioning of Enga signs. *Semiotica* 32. 81–117.

Kendon, Adam. 1980c. A description of a deaf-mute sign language, etc. Part III: Aspects of utterance construction. *Semiotica* 32. 245–313.

Kendon, Adam. 1988a. How gestures can become like words. In Fernando Poyatos (ed.), *Crosscultural Perspectives in Nonverbal Communication*, 131–141. Toronto: C. J. Hogrefe.

Kendon, Adam. 1988b. *Sign Languages of Aboriginal Australia: Cultural, Semiotic and Communicative Perspectives*. Cambridge: Cambridge University Press.

Ladewig, Silva H. 2014a. The cyclic gesture. In Cornelia Müller, Alan Cienki, Ellen Fricke, Silva H. Ladewig, David McNeill & Jana Bressem (eds.), *Body – Language – Communication: An International Handbook on Multimodality in Human Interaction*, Vol. 2, 1605–1618. Berlin/Boston: De Gruyter Mouton.

Ladewig, Silva H. 2014b. Recurrent gestures. In Cornelia Müller, Alan Cienki, Ellen Fricke, Silva H. Ladewig, David McNeill & Jana Bressem (eds.), *Body – Language – Communication: An international*

Handbook on Multimodality in Human Interaction, Vol. 2, 1558–1575. Berlin/Boston: De Gruyter Mouton.

Ladewig, Silva H. 2020. *Integrating Gestures. The Dimension of Multimodality in Cognitive Grammar*. Berlin/Boston: De Gruyter Mouton.

Mandel, Mark. 1977. Iconic devices in American Sign Language. In Lynn A. Friedman (ed.), *On the Other Hand: New Perspectives on American Sign Language*, 57–107. New York: Academic Press.

Mittelberg, Irene. 2014. Gestures and iconicity. In Cornelia Müller, Elle Fricke, Silva H. Ladewig, David McNeill & Jana Bressem (eds.), *Body – Language – Communication: An International Handbook on Multimodality in Human Interaction*, Vol. 2, 1712–1731. Berlin/Boston: De Gruyter Mouton.

Mittelberg, Irene. 2019. Visuo-kinetic signs are inherently metonymic: How embodied metonymy motivates form, function and schematic patterns in gesture. *Frontiers in Psychology* 10.

Müller, Cornelia. 1998. Iconicity and gesture. In Serge Santi (ed.), *Oralité et Gestualité: Communication Multimodale, Interaction*, 321–328. Montréal: L'Harmattan.

Müller, Cornelia. 2014a. Gestural modes of representation as techniques of depiction. In Cornelia Müller, Alan Cienki, Ellen Fricke, Silva H. Ladewig, David McNeill & Jana Bressem (eds.), *Body – Language – Communication: An International Handbook on Multimodality in Human Interaction*, Vol. 2, 1687–1702. Berlin/Boston: De Gruyter Mouton.

Müller, Cornelia. 2014b. Ring-gestures across cultures and times: Dimensions of variation. In Cornelia Müller, Alan Cienke, Ellen Fricke, Silva H. Ladewig, David McNeill & Jana Bressem (eds.), *Body – Language – Communication: An International Handbook on Multimodality in Human Interaction*, Vol. 2, 1511–1522. Berlin/Boston: De Gruyter Mouton.

Müller, Cornelia. 2017. How recurrent gestures mean: Conventionalized contexts-of-use and embodied motivation. *Gesture* 16(2). 277–304.

Müller, Cornelia. 2018. Gesture and sign: Cataclysmic break or dynamic relations? *Frontiers in Psychology* 9:1651. 1–20.

Müller, Cornelia. (forthcoming). A toolbox of methods for gesture analysis. In Alan Cienki (ed.), *Handbook of Gesture Studies*. Cambridge: Cambridge University Press.

Taub, Sarah F. 2001. *Language from the Body: Iconicity and Metaphor in American Sign Language*. Cambridge: Cambridge University Press.

Wilcox, Phyllis Perrin. 2000. *Metaphor in American Sign Language*. Washington DC: Gallaudet University Press.

Wilcox, Sherman. 2005. Routes from gesture to language. *Revista da ABRALIN*, 4(1–2). 11–45.

Terry Janzen and Barbara Shaffer
Introduction: Examining signed language and gesture research within the domain of cognitive linguistics

1 Introduction

This introductory chapter outlines some critical work to date in the field of cognitive linguistics on signed languages and gesture, along with relevant and related topics such as multimodality, iconicity, and the use of space in signed language discourse. Special attention is paid to the work of Sherman Wilcox, a longstanding and prominent researcher in these areas as well as regarding gestural theories of language evolution: this volume stands as a tribute to his many contributions to the fields of language origins, cognitive linguistics, and signed language structure within the cognitive linguistics framework. The second half of the chapter introduces readers to the chapters in this volume. Themes that emerge from the collection of researchers and their contributed chapters are highlighted.

2 The influence of Sherman Wilcox's research within cognitive linguistics

Sherman Wilcox began his research career in linguistics in the mid-1980s, and came into prominence around the time that the 1995 International Cognitive Linguistics Association conference (ICLC 4) was hosted by the University of New Mexico, organized by Sherman, where he was an Associate Professor. He had already been developing his theory of language origins and in 1995 published *Gesture and the Nature of Language* with David Armstrong and William Stokoe, which has become standard reading in the debate surrounding the origins of human language. Beyond this, Sherman, along with many of his like-minded colleagues, has brought to light the many reasons why linguistic analyses need to place signed languages alongside spoken languages. For Sherman, this was within the domain of cognitive linguistics. He and Phyllis Perrin Wilcox summarize this endeavor as follows:

Terry Janzen, Department of Linguistics, University of Manitoba, Canada,
e-mail: terry.janzen@umanitoba.ca
Barbara Shaffer, University of New Mexico, USA, e-mail: bshaffer@unm.edu

> The analysis of signed languages permits linguists and cognitive scientists to address important questions about the nature of grammaticalization, metaphor, iconicity, and metonymy.... Because signed languages are visually perceived, they extend the linguist's scope of study by adding the capability of triangulating optical with acoustic data and observing first-hand how material that starts its life outside of the linguistic system becomes conventionalized, lexicalized, and grammaticalized. (Wilcox and Perrin Wilcox [2010] 2015: 863)

In the sections below, we look at some critical areas of Sherman's research, namely, language origins, iconicity, multimodality and gesture, linguistic modality, and his more recent work on space and Place.

2.1 Language origins

From very early on in his career, Sherman was intrigued with Neisser's (1967) view that "all language whether spoken or signed is articulatory gesturing" (Wilcox 1996a: 182), adopting this view along with his colleagues William Stokoe and David Armstrong, who altogether proposed a gestural model of language evolution (Armstrong, Stokoe and Wilcox 1994, 1995; Armstrong and Wilcox 2007). They argued that "the primary sensory adaptation of primates is visual. Consequently... language-cum-syntax may have come naturally from an analysis of visible gesture" (Armstrong, Stokoe and Wilcox 1995: 18), and that the "earliest linguistic units may have been either visible or vocal gestures or, quite likely, both" (Armstrong, Stokoe and Wilcox 1995: 19). The question, then, was not one of whether language originated as vocalization or manual gesturing, but of how these two systems might have evolved together given that there were advantages to vocalization as the human vocal tract evolved, along with advantages as the physiology of human arms and hands evolved. Add to this developing human cognitive affordances and the visual components of sociality, and the stage is set for the emergence of language.

2.2 Iconicity

Sherman's view of language origins ties directly to his writings on iconicity in signed language. Iconicity has been a theme in his writing throughout his career, perhaps stemming from the view that if something can be efficiently iconically represented in language, there may be no rational reasoning to abandon it for something more arbitrary. Here Sherman draws on Hockett in his review (1996a) of Barbara King's (1994) book *The Information Continuum: Evolution of Social Information Transfer in Monkeys, Apes, and Hominids*. In his review, Sherman notes that Hockett frames his discussion of signed versus spoken languages as a difference in dimensionality:

The difference of dimensionality means that signages can be iconic to an extent to which [spoken] languages cannot ... Now, while arbitrariness has its points, ... it also has its drawbacks, ... so that it is perhaps more revealing to put the difference the other way around, as a limitation of spoken languages. Indeed, the dimensionality of signing is that of life itself, and it would be stupid not to resort to picturing, pantomiming, or pointing whenever convenient ... But when a representation of some four-dimensional hunk of life has to be compressed into the single dimension of speech, most iconicity is necessarily squeezed out. (Hockett 1978: 274–275)

Without question, iconicity is present in signed language discourse. Many signs appear to have evolved from gestural sources, the importance of which varies from sign to sign. Frishberg (1975) shows that historically, ASL signs that evolve from gestural roots tend to diminish in iconic significance over time in favor of more arbitrary forms, which seemingly supports the notion that linguistic forms—words, essentially—are necessarily arbitrary forms. While space does not permit a more extensive discussion of iconicity in signed language here, it is most certainly the case that iconicity remains as a distinguishing feature of many signed forms as imagic iconicity as well as in the structure of constructions as diagrammatic iconicity, the analysis of which has been further buoyed by the increasing awareness of iconicities at play in spoken language (Bybee 1985; Haiman 1983, 1985; Simone 1995, and others; for a current analysis, see Langacker, this volume). Wilcox (2004) suggests in particular that while it may be the case that some elements of iconicity may submerge in the signed language discourse context, others emerge anew, illustrating that iconicity in language has a dynamic presence, far from being a historical artifact.

2.3 Multimodality and gesture

At the onset of Sherman's interest in gesture was a fascination with historical perspectives on relationships among spoken language, signed language, and gesture, and how this has impacted mid to late 20th century thinking, especially regarding the legitimacy of signed language. He points specifically to the Second International Congress on Education of the Deaf in Milan, Italy, in 1880, where arguments supporting speech (as more Godly) and against signing (as base and unable to engender thought) prevailed.[1] In a (1996b) manuscript entitled "Hands and bodies, minds and souls: Or, how a sign linguist learned to stop worrying and love gesture", which was published as Wilcox (2004c) under a somewhat different title, Sherman argues that the Milan congress had a profound influence on attitudes toward signed language

---

[1] For a closer look at the 1880 Milan congress, see Lane (1984), Baynton (2002); for extensive discussion on mind-body dualism, see Varela, Thompson and Rosch (1991); Lakoff and Johnson (1999).

moving forward, but at the same time a similar disparity had been occurring in the development of modern linguistics pertaining to the gulf between true language and gesture. This is summed up as three overarching assumptions: 1) language is speech but not gesture; 2) signs are gestures but not language; and 3) speech is of the mind, whereas signs are of the body (Wilcox 1996b: 4). In the latter part of the 1900s and on into the 2000s, however, gesture research has grown significantly, leading Wilcox and Xavier to describe multimodality in this way:

> Language and gesture are dynamic, emergent systems, the product of a human expressive ability that is grounded in embodied cognitive abilities. . . . [D]etermining whether a unit is language or gesture may ultimately be futile. It will depend on the expressive unit's occurrence in a particular usage event, by a particular individual, who is communicating in a particular context, who knows and uses particular languages. Even then, because these systems are in constant interaction and undergo constant change, what is gesture today may be tomorrow's language. (Wilcox and Xavier 2013: 107–108)

2.3.1 Grammaticalization and gesture

Sherman's early claims on the primary role of gesture in the evolution of language (Armstrong, Stokoe and Wilcox 1994, 1995) are extended to his research on grammaticalization in signed languages. Drawing on work on grammaticalization in ASL (Janzen 1998, 1999; Shaffer 2000; Janzen and Shaffer 2002; and others), Sherman distills two routes of grammaticalization that begin with gestural sources, one that includes an intermediate lexical stage (gesture > lexical > grammatical) and a second where no lexical stage mediates (gestural > prosodic/grammatical) (e.g., Wilcox 2007).

Sherman's view on the role of gesture in language has pervaded his many publications on the nature of language, which has taught us much about how language has evolved, the most significant understanding of which is that language for the modern human hominid remains a composite of vocalization and gesture, predicable from his original gestural theory of language, carefully articulated in his writings not only on gesture and signed language, but also on more global statements of his view that both spoken and signed language can be seen as a unified human phenomenon, where modality (signed or spoken) is largely inconsequential (e.g., Wilcox 2002, 2004b; Wilcox and Xavier 2013).

2.4 Modality

Prior to Sherman and Phyllis Wilcox's chapter on modality in ASL, which appeared in Joan Bybee and Suzanne Fleischman's (1995) volume *Modality in Grammar and*

Discourse, there had only been occasional and brief mentions of the category (e.g., Fischer and Gough 1978; Padden 1988; Ferreira Brito 1990 for Brazilian Sign Language), without any real discussion of the function or meaning of modal verbs. Wilcox and Wilcox's answer to this was to explicate root and epistemic modality differences in terms of iconic features of strength, for example the single, sharp movement of MUST as strong obligation, and the shorter, repeated movement of SHOULD as weak obligation, when otherwise the articulatory features of the two signs (handshape, orientation, location) are identical. They propose that this iconic relationship holds across modal categories in ASL, as increased strength of condition or commitment is represented by more gestural substance (i.e., sharper movement), while decreased strength of condition or commitment is represented by reduced gestural substance (i.e., shorter, softer movement).

Sherman subsequently supervised two doctoral dissertations on modality in signed languages: A Syntactic, Pragmatic Analysis of the Expression of Necessity and Possibility in American Sign Language (Barbara Shaffer 2000), and The Expression of Modality in Iranian Sign Language (ZEI) (Sara Siyavoshi 2019), and went on to explore more aspects of modality along with his students (e.g., Wilcox and Shaffer 2006 on ASL; Xavier and Wilcox 2014 on Brazilian Sign Language [Língua Brasileira de Sinais, or Libras]; Shaffer, Jarque and Wilcox 2011 on ASL and Catalan Sign Language [Llengua de signes catalana, or LSC]).

In all of this research on modality, with Sherman as a central figure, it became increasingly clear that expression of modality is multimodal in nature, and that multiple viable iconicities are apparent cross-linguistically.

2.5 Space and Place

More recently, Sherman has begun to explore the notion of Place in signed language discourse as a way to understand the role of space in referential constructions. Sherman and his colleagues base their discussion of placing and pointing (Wilcox and Occhino 2016; Martínez and Wilcox 2019; Wilcox and Martínez 2020) on Clark's (2003) observations, where pointing and placing are two forms of gestural indicating. In pointing, the addressee's attention is directed toward a thing of interest, whereas in placing, a thing is located so as to be within the addressee's focus of attention. Within the context of signed languages, Sherman and colleagues extend the notion of placing to, firstly, spatially placed signs themselves. Secondly, they suggest that placing has two functions, *create-placing*, which creates a new Place, and *recruit-placing*, which recruits an existing Place that has previously been created. Place is a symbolic structure where the phonological pole is a location either in the signer's current visible space or is a schematic location, and the semantic pole profiles a schematic thing, which is instantiated in an actual discourse context (Wilcox and Occhino 2016). Responding to suggestions that spatial location of deictic pointing may be gestural and not linguistic in signed languages, thereby representing a referential domain that differs from direct linguistic expression (e.g., Liddell and Metzger 1998; Liddell 2000, 2003), Wilcox and Martínez's (2020: 14) main claim is that, significantly, "Places unify deixis and anaphor. Rather than representing two distinct domains of reference, we suggest that they are ends of a symbolic continuum that varies in terms of subjectification" (see Cooperrider and Mesh 2022 for further discussion of deictic pointing).

3 The rising presence of signed language and gesture in cognitive linguistics

Prior to 2004 the journal *Cognitive Linguistics* does not list any articles by title that focus on signed language research, although in 1998 (volume 9, issue 3) Scott Liddell's article entitled "Grounded blends, gestures, and conceptual shifts" appeared, which applies these relatively new ideas within the theory of Mental Spaces (Fauconnier 1994, and later, Conceptual Integration Theory, Fauconnier and Turner 2002) to speakers' gestures and ASL signers. Here Liddell introduces the term "Real Space" to a cognitive linguistics audience, which labels the "mental representation of one's immediate surroundings [that] constitutes a mental space" (Liddell 1998: 290), following Lakoff (1987).

In 2004 a special issue of *Cognitive Linguistics* appeared on signed languages (volume 15, issue 2) featuring five articles by prominent and upcoming cognitive linguists, guest edited by Sherman Wilcox and Terry Janzen. In their introduction, they comment that:

> Signed languages are vitally important to linguists who wish to explore the cognitive dimensions of human language. Because they are produced in space by the hands and body of their users and rely on vision for reception, signed languages bring a unique set of characteristics to cognitive linguistics not shared by spoken languages. Issues such as iconicity, metaphor, metonymy, and gesture take on new relevance when they are manifest in the world's signed languages. (Wilcox and Janzen 2004: 113)

This special issue was meant as a response to the virtual absence of a presence of signed language research in the journal to date.

In this special issue, Paul Dudis's article "Body partitioning and real-space blends" shows how a signer's body has partitionable zones such that two entities can be represented simultaneously, for example the signer's face and right hand representing one entity and the left hand a second entity, and how the two can then interact. Over the years, this has been seen as explanatory for much simultaneity in signers' enactments, and it has taken hold in gesture research as well (see Sweetser, this volume).

Following Phyllis Wilcox's (2000) ground-breaking book *Metaphor in American Sign Language,* her article "A cognitive key: Metonymic and metaphoric mappings in ASL" sets out to show that everyday ASL discourse is rife with metaphor, metonymy and iconicity, which had not been fully recognized before this time. Phyllis's careful and enlightening analyses of metaphor and metonymy has subsequently influenced researchers in this area, one result of which has been her guest-edited issue of *Sign Language Studies* (2005), a cross-linguistic collection of articles continuing and extending her work.

With few notable exceptions (e.g., Ferreira Brito 1990; Wilcox and Wilcox 1995), little work on grammatical modality in signed languages—and especially within the domain of cognitive linguistics—had been done prior to Barbara Shaffer's (2000) dissertation and following studies such as the one in this 2004 journal issue. In "Information ordering and speaker subjectivity: Modality in ASL" Shaffer examines both agent-oriented and epistemic modal constructions and shows the interplay between the (lexical) modal sign and facial gestures that together indicate highly subjective aspects of each construction. Further, contrary to earlier claims that the choice of preverbal or clause-final modal did not affect meaning (Aarons et al. 1995), Shaffer shows that in ASL a preverbal modal has scope over the verb whereas an utterance-final modal has scope over the utterance as a whole.

Terry Janzen's article "Space rotation, perspective shift, and verb morphology in ASL" was the first in a series of publications that looked at perspective-taking within a usage-based model of language. He notes that rather than the often described notion of "body shifts" in space that accompany shifts in the taking of perspective of story characters in narratives, the signers in his conversational ASL corpus decidedly did not do this, and instead appeared to mentally rotate the story scene space such that various characters whose perspective the signer wished to portray came into alignment with the signer's own central (or "neutral") stance. Thus no body shift to another space was needed, and in later research it was shown that mentally-rotated alignment for perspective taking characterized narrative discourse and body-shifted alignment occurred more frequently with comparative spaces discourse (Janzen 2012).

Finally, Sherman Wilcox's contribution to this special issue is entitled "Cognitive Iconicity: Conceptual spaces, meaning, and gesture in signed language". Set within a Cognitive Grammar framework (Langacker 1987, and numerous publications following, including this volume), Wilcox defines cognitive iconicity as "a special case where the phonological and semantic poles of a symbolic structure reside in the same region of cognitive space" (Wilcox 2004: 119), in other words, it is a relationship between two cognitive spaces rather than just a relationship between the form a sign has and its reference to something in the real world. The phonological pole, Wilcox claims, also resides in conceptual space because the pronunciation of the sign is equally conceptualized by the signer as is its meaning. While arbitrariness in language had long before this been posited as (in Wilcox's terms) the phonological and semantic poles of a structure residing in very different regions of conceptual space (a foundational notion of duality of patterning: Hockett [1963] 1966; cf. Pietrandrea, this volume), bringing these two poles together in the same region of space results in (cognitive) iconicity. Wilcox then works through a number of cogent examples in ASL especially in the areas of temporal relations and aspect marking, and concludes by inviting linguists working on signed languages to reconsider iconicity as not only concerning form-meaning pairings, but something more central in the embodied conceptualization of language form and meaning as a whole (see also Langacker, this volume).

As mentioned, prior to this 2004 collection of cognitive linguistic articles on signed language there had been only a single signed language-related article published in the journal. After 2004 it would take another five years until the next such publication (Taub, Galvan and Piñar 2009), but from that point to 2022, there have been fifteen additional articles on signed language in the journal. This still represents a fraction of the research published in *Cognitive Linguistics*, but it demonstrates growing interest, and is perhaps reflective of Sherman's call for linguists to place signed languages alongside spoken languages in the arena of linguistic investigation.

Elsewhere, the field of cognitive linguistics can be seen to influence researchers' approaches to signed languages. At least three grammars of signed languages have been written based on tenets of cognitive linguistics: Trevor Johnston and Adam Schembri's (2007) *Australian Sign Language: An Introduction to Sign Language Linguistics*, which the authors describe as adopting a "broadly cognitive-functionalist" (Johnston and Schembri 2007: 282) framework, although they describe their work as not presented from within any one specific theory; and Lorraine Leeson and John Saeed's (2012) *Irish Sign Language: A Cognitive Linguistic Account*. Leeson and Saeed ground their description of Irish Sign Language in cognitive linguistic theory, especially in terms of iconicity, metaphor and metonymy, mental models of space, body partitioning and simultaneous constructions, and gesture. Ultimately, four principles underpin their analysis: "that linguistic knowledge is encyclopaedic and non-autonomous; that linguistic meaning is perspectival; that linguistic meaning is dynamic and flexible; and that linguistic knowledge is based on usage and experience" (Leeson and Saeed 2012: 5–6). The third such volume is Virginia Volterra, Maria Roccaforte, Allessio Di Renzo, and Sabina Fontana's (2022) volume

Italian Sign Language from a Cognitive and Socio-semiotic Perspective, which takes a usage-based, socio-pragmatic approach, informed by cognitive semantics. As well, a good number of cognitive linguistically-oriented articles and chapters have appeared in journals and edited volumes, too many to mention specifically in this brief introduction, but one example is Wilcox and Occhino's chapter "Signed Languages" in Barbara Dancygier's (2017) *The Cambridge Handbook of Cognitive Linguistics*.

Cognitive linguistics has also made inroads in the field of gesture research, perhaps in part because cognitive linguistics tends more and more to be usage-based in nature and, with the growing ease of capturing linguistic data with video, researchers are acknowledging that visible body actions, following Kendon (2004; see also Enfield 2009), continuously and consistently play a role in utterance meaning. It comes as no surprise, then, that cognitive linguistically-oriented signed language and gesture researchers have come together symbiotically, united by a heightened awareness of the importance of signers' and speakers' bodies in the use of language. Janzen (2017) outlines some of the history of controversies over gesture in signed language research (e.g., that signed languages are linguistic and not simply elaborate gesture systems), while Müller (2018) takes us through the development of an awareness of signed languages from the perspective of gesture researchers, and proposes a synergistic and dynamic view of gesture and signed language, suggesting that both are fundamental to the study of language.

Gesture research has become more prominent in cognitive science and linguistics in the last number of years, exemplified by the dedicated journal *Gesture* (Benjamins), which has attracted researchers interested in multimodality across spoken and signed languages. In this serial and elsewhere, we are seeing a rise in the number of research reports of cognitive linguistically-oriented work, with few early examples such as Liddell and Metzger (1998), and more recent works, for example, Johnston (2013), Janzen (2017), Ferrara and Hodge (2018), Hodge and Johnston (2018), Cooperrider and Mesh (2022), and de Vos et al. (2022). It is fitting, therefore, that a unified approach to signed language and gesture research characterizes the present volume.

4 An introduction to the book sections and chapters

The volume is organized along five main themes: some overarching guiding principles for research on signed and spoken language; iconicity in signed and spoken language; multimodality; blending and metaphor; and grammatical constructions, with the themes frequently intersecting. The volume was conceived as having two main intentions, the first being the desire to assemble a collection of current work on signed language and gesture in cognitive linguistics, and second, to bring authors together in the spirit of honoring Sherman Wilcox and his body of work, some of whom are Sherman's closest, longstanding peers, and others are his past graduate students who now also count themselves as having joined his circle of peers.

Part 1: Guiding principles for signed and spoken language research

Penny Boyes Braem and Virginia Volterra lead this first section by noting that as linguists began examining signed languages, they did so using models of spoken language, which both influenced how they saw signed languages and resulted in publications that assumed such a model. Their aim in this chapter is to examine how theories of signed language have evolved over the last several decades, and to present a view of the theoretical landscape as it exists today. To accomplish this, they focus on three areas: the view of language as a form of action; the attention to multimodal behaviors; and the recognition of the role of iconicity at all levels of language. The result is an in-depth exploration of a wide scope of literature on spoken language, signed language, and gesture that is increasingly convergent, which is leading us to understand signed languages more clearly, not just through a rubric of what spoken languages are like, and furthermore, it leads to an emerging unified view of language altogether. These new models of language, Boyes Braem and Volterra suggest, necessarily depend on the face-to-face multimodal discourse of both spoken and signed language users. The study of signed languages, they say, which necessarily consists of face-to-face interactions, has been instrumental in pushing us to understand all of language in terms of multimodality.

The chapter by Elena Antinoro Pizzuto and Brigitte Garcia is a revision of some of Elena's earlier work prior to her passing in 2011. We are grateful to Brigitte, a close friend and colleague of Elena's, for bringing the manuscript to its current form. This chapter outlines the idea of, and issues with, the graphic representation of signed languages and efforts of the team at the Sign Language Laboratory (SLL) in Rome. Signed language researchers know well how difficult it is to represent a signed language graphically, either for the purpose of linguistic transcription or as a written form of the language. Transcription has most often hinged on glosses – written words from the surrounding community's language, which Antinoro Pizzuto and Garcia claim is not a transcription at all because glosses do not represent any form features of signs, nor are they annotations. While a few transcription systems have been designed, e.g., the Berkeley Transcription System, they have not taken hold widely, and the authors here remark that it is surprising that a solution to the problem of transcription has not maintained a primary focus in the research community, as a standard system would be of benefit to researchers crosslinguistically. In terms of both a writing system and a system of transcription, the SLL has had some success in adapting SignWriting for LIS, and this may have continued, Antinoro Pizzuto and Garcia suggest, had the project been able to continue.

The final chapter in this section, by Paola Pietrandrea, considers the enduring question: "what is a language?", taking a broadly socio-semiotic approach and considering both signed and spoken languages. Pietrandrea argues that definitions of language in the theories put forward by Charles F. Hockett, André Martinet, and Noam Chomsky regarding "openness", recursion, and arbitrariness in language, which are largely structural in scope, are inadequate in accounting for the inter-related cognitive, social, iconic, and gestural elements of signed languages and ultimately, of the linguistic abilities of all language users regardless of modality. Pietrandrea instead proposes a view in the socio-semiotic tradition of Tullio de Mauro's definition of language as a semiotic system that includes both functionally and formally relevant elements, the entire mass of its speakers, time, and the full network of socio-pragmatic and historical-cultural evolving relationships it is situated within. Applied to signed languages, Pietrandrea finds much compatibility between de Mauro's ideas and the nature of signed language expression *and* that of spoken language, accounting for contiguity among action gestures, signs, and speech.

Part 2: Iconicity in spoken and signed language

Opening this section, Ron Langacker's chapter "Structure, iconicity, and access" continues his exploration of Cognitive Grammar, expanding on where iconicity is found in language. While Langacker does not deal specifically with either signed language or gesture, his detailed view of iconicity is clearly germane to both fields. The chapter begins with the claim that structure and iconicity are non-distinct, in the sense that iconicity suggests similarity between two phenomena, and structures display similarity between their formal properties (which could be form and/or meaning) and the processing activity that constitutes them, with this overlap facilitating their co-activation. Iconicity, then, can not only be understood as form-meaning iconicity, but also form-form and meaning-meaning iconicity. This theory is developed with respect to both substantive and diagrammatic iconicity, for which categorization plays a key role, as it resides in processing activity, and is based on resemblance. The analysis here suggests that Langacker's characterization of iconicity is such that it applies throughout all aspects of linguistic organization, based on the view that structure resides in assemblies of connected elements, with this view accommodating the roles of similarity, overlap, categorization, and paths of access.

In the second chapter in this section, Corrine Occhino takes the ideas of *things* and *processes* from Cognitive Grammar, applying them to hand configurations (as things) and movements of signs (as processes), and the connections between such elements of form and meaning as iconic assemblies. Occhino draws on William Stokoe's work on semantic phonology and Sherman Wilcox's theory of Cognitive Iconicity, where the relation between the phonological pole and semantic pole (in Cognitive Grammar) is seen as aligning closely in conceptual space in an iconic relationship, and here she develops the idea of an embodied account of grammar across signed and spoken language. Occhino suggests that signers have access to meaningful parts of the structure of signs, e.g., a meaningful handshape, location, or movement, and exploit these to profile certain aspects of meaning when they wish to, or not when they don't wish to, and spoken language speakers may at times have access to parts of constructions in similar ways. Occhino notes that form is not experienced without meaning, and that in situated instantiations of use, signers and speakers exploit variabilities of form to create these meanings. The mapping of meaningful experience to the body, Occhino claims, is at the very core of our semiotic repertoire.

Part 3: Multimodality

Eve Sweetser begins this section of four chapters with her exploration of gestural meaning and the body within a gestural space, taking the point of view that rather than beginning with features of a gesture itself to find meaning, the meaning of the gesture emerges from the naturally occurring meaning of the body within a gestural space. This leads us to understand that what the hands are doing gesturally changes in terms of meaning depending on how they relate to what the body is doing, and this takes place both in co-speech gestures and in signed languages. Therefore the beginning point of understanding gestural meaning is with the experiential bodily presence. Sweetser suggests that the body has meaning even before communication occurs because of, for example, front/back asymmetry in visual perception and physical aspects of human interaction, such that our attention is most often directed toward the space immediately in front of the body. Sweetser discusses this in terms of iconicity, metaphor and metonymy, our enacting of characters in narratives, and Real-Space blends in jointly shared communicative space. Sweetser concludes that the body and the surrounding space constitute shared meaning, which in turn acts as a meaningful frame for articulatory communicative activity.

The chapter that follows is Laura Ruth-Hirrel's examination of multimodal joint action and the idea of Place in the discourse of American English speakers, drawing on Wilcox and Occhino's (2016) definition of Place as a symbolic structure for spatially placing a meaningful element in signed languages, so that the Place itself becomes a meaningful location. Akin to what signers do, Ruth-Hirrel proposes that positioning a gesture at a salient spatial location within an interlocutor's focus of attention can evoke a Place structure. Set within a Cognitive Grammar analysis, Ruth-Hirrel sees Place structures in gesturers' interpersonal space as both phonologically and semantically dependent: a Place must be elaborated by a conceptually more autonomous structure that specifies the referent, whether in the speech or meaningful gestures of the speaker/gesturer, shown in examples taken from talk show host and guest conversations. Interpersonal Place structures are analyzed as joint-action projects, where Interpersonal Place schematically profiles an interactional "thing", which is elaborated when a conventionalized Place is recruited through an act of placing. Ruth-Hirrel proposes that this specific type of placing construction functions to indicate a joint action in American English.

Terry Janzen, Barbara Shaffer, and Lorraine Leeson show how gesture spaces in American Sign Language and Irish Sign Language reflect the CONCEPTUAL DISTANCE IS SPATIAL DISTANCE metaphor in that things that are conceptually close occupy spaces proximal to the signer and those that are conceptually distant as occupying more distal spaces. Further, things placed proximally in front of the signer tend to be known, experienced, or better understood, and those placed in distal "other" spaces are things not known or understood, not experienced (yet). This embodied conceptual view, the authors argue, has its basis in signers' experiences of the physical world where, for example, something being examined is held directly in view in front of the signer, whereas something not being directly experienced, or not within the signer's immediate consciousness, is not in view, but is somewhere else. The analysis begins with basic examples that map a perceived physical space relationship onto articulation space, and progresses to examples involving a higher level of conceptualized closeness or distance, having to do with temporality, affinity, or involvement. Janzen, Shaffer, and Leeson also include examples of spoken language where speaker/gesturers exhibit similarly differentiated gesture spaces, suggesting that the same CONCEPTUAL DISTANCE IS SPATIAL DISTANCE metaphor is cognitively operational in both modalities.

In the final chapter in this section, Darren Saunders and Anne-Marie Parisot examine the intricate shifts of perspective accompanying enactments in Quebec Sign Language, American Sign Language, and spoken Quebec French. Enactments (elsewhere: depiction; constructed action/speech) take place when the signers or speakers assume the role of an actant within a discourse segment such as a narrative in order to illustrate what the actant has done or said. Saunders and Parisot outline various markers and forms of enactment, and show how the integration of lexical material and gestures produce both simple perspective shifts as well as more complex constructions where two perspectives are produced simultaneously, that is, the perspectives of the narrator and the actant in the story. Including gestural aspects of enactment in linguistic models often presents challenges for theoretical approaches, but Langacker's Cognitive Grammar, the authors suggest, enables such an integration analysis. They show that enactments can be complete, when every aspect of the signer's or speaker's face and body represents an actant, or partial, and that enactments take place more frequently for L1 LSQ and ASL signers than for L2 LSQ signers and French speakers.

Part 4: Blending and metaphor

Using Fauconnier and Turner's theory of conceptual integration, Anna-Lena Nilsson explores Real Space blends in Swedish Sign Language monologic discourse with an aim to identify markers of discourse complexity. Real Space blends occur when elements within conceptual spaces are grounded in, or connect to, the actual spatial environment surrounding the signer, which serves as an additional input space to create the blend. Discourse complexity is determined by the number and type of discourse features, such as which perspective the signer chooses; switching between perspectives, and if so, the frequency of such switches; the identity, location, and type of blended entities; the number of blended entities; whether the entities are introduced explicitly and whether they reoccur; and which linguistic expressions are used to identify or describe entities. Nilsson operationalizes the emerging picture of discourse complexity through Real Space blend tables, which then serve as a rubric for formalizing the dynamicity of complexity as the signer moves through connected segments of the monologic text. The result is that discourse complexity is seen to be quite variable, dependent on the number of Real Space blends and the blended entities they contain, and crucially on whether the signer maintains narrator perspective or switches perspective to one or more discourse entities.

The second chapter in this section represents the second manuscript that was drafted by a researcher before their passing, in this case, Tommaso Russo Cardona, who died in 2007. The manuscript was taken up by Paola Pietrandrea and completed, and we are grateful to be able to include it in this collection. This chapter addresses metaphors in Italian Sign Language (LIS) and the ways that Blending Theory can model the interaction between, and cross-mapping of, the source and target domains of metaphors in signed languages. It is also useful in comparisons between signed language and spoken language metaphor. A critical feature of signed languages in general, and of metaphors in particular, is iconicity. The hypothesis that iconic devices are "linguistic traces" of the nondiscrete, analogic conceptualization processes taking place during language production and comprehension leads to Russo and Pietrandrea's analysis of iconic phenomena apparent in LIS. They find numerous examples of iconic-metonymic and iconic-metaphorical mappings in their LIS database, and ultimately argue that it is not just the case that some features of the source domain are generically mapped onto the signed form, but rather, iconicity provides a mapping between the signed form and semantic features of *both* the source and target domains that are projected in the blend. Their analysis of metaphors and iconic devices in LIS is therefore an important contribution to the study of interactions between language-independent conceptual processes and language-specific structures.

Part 5: Grammatical constructions

Elisabeth Engberg-Pedersen opens this section on grammatical constructions by looking at two recurring facial expressions in Danish Sign Language (DTS), the mouth shrug, which is an emblem that is commonly in use in Danish society, and facial consent, consisting of a raised upper lip and possibly wrinkling of the nose, the origin of which is unknown. These two facial expressions are not produced simultaneously with signs expressing a proposition, but occur with anaphors of the proposition, interjections, or on their own. The present analysis is based on recorded conversations between four dyads of native DTS signers, who were tasked with discussing how to deal with a hypothetical, demanding situation, designed to elicit expressions of doubt. Findings reveal that the mouth shrug is generally understood to be an epistemic signal of doubt, although various meanings were identified in this study. Predominantly, it is a backchannel signal, sometimes co-occurring with other gestures such as the palm up, open hand gesture. It was found to have meanings of, among others, uncertainty, the rejection of an interlocutor's idea, an introspective gesture of one's own doubt, or a mitigation of a rejection. The facial consent expression is also a backchannelling device, indicating agreement with an interlocutor.

Wilkinson, Lepic, and Hou take a usage-based approach to the analysis of multi-word expressions in American Sign Language (ASL), arguing that the notion of recycling of sequential units provides a useful template for analyzing signed language data. They define a multi-word expression as a sequence of identifiable words that also functions as a holistic unit, and discuss four case studies comprised of sequential constructions that fall on a continuum from more flexible expressions to more highly fixed expressions. Wilkinson, Lepic, and Hou see linguistic patterns as being shaped and reshaped by continuing experience with language, such that structures that are frequently encountered by signers serve as the foundation for a dynamic knowledge of a language: recurring structures are also recycled structures, used in new ways. Findings show that ASL constructions are recycled as structured units displaying various levels of fixedness and complexity, and at multiple levels of schematization. These constructions participate in emergent networks of relatively fixed, conventionalized constructions and are repurposed having more specialized grammatical functions in wider contexts, repackaged as increasingly holistic units. The result, the authors suggest, is that in individual signers and collectively across signers, these processes ultimately cause the structure of language to shift continuously and dynamically over time.

The next study of grammatical constructions, by André Nogueira Xavier and Rocío Anabel Martínez, is on possibility modals in Brazilian Sign Language (Libras) and Argentine Sign Language (LSA) (two unrelated languages), which are analyzed contrastively, following van der Auwera and Plungian's (1998) framework for modal constructions. Libras and LSA are two relatively understudied languages, so Xavier and Martínez draw from more in-depth studies of modals in other languages such as American Sign Language to inform their study. They find that the possibility modal systems of both Libras and LSA cover the full range of non-epistemic meanings proposed by van der Auwera and Plungian. They also show that the possibility modals in both languages are highly polysemous but that there are other modals with more limited meanings. The study outlined in this chapter helps to advance our knowledge of the expression of modality in Libras and LSA, which can be added to the growing body of knowledge about modality in signed languages crosslinguistically, including the tendency for negative modals to be historically unrelated to their positive counterparts. Xavier and Martínez conclude that the polysemy they see in Libras and LSA modals is a by-product of grammaticization processes, consistent with what has been found in other languages.

The final chapter in this section is Sara Siyavoshi's study of relative clause constructions in Iranian Sign Language (ZEI), using Cognitive Grammar as her framework, in particular Langacker's view that relative clauses are a type of reference-point construction where one entity serves as a reference point for establishing mental contact with another. Important in this regard is how relative clauses are conceptualized in terms of both structure and function. Siyavoshi focuses on three prominent relative clause markers: a manual marker (pointing), and two facial markers (raised eyebrows and squinted eyes) that occur simultaneously with the signed construction. Pointing, Siyavoshi claims, is an obligatory manual marker of ZEI relative clauses, which has a directing force to establish a mental contact with the entity indicated by the head noun, and pointing also indicates the head noun's definiteness. The nominal head as the reference point in the relative clause is marked by raised eyebrows, which are held through the entire relative clause, and raising the eyebrows and then returning them to their neutral position indicates the boundary between the relative and matrix clauses. In this way the relative clause and the main clause are construed to be in relation to one another.

Part 6: Concluding commentary

The final chapter in the volume was written by Adam Kendon, which may be one of his last remaining works. We were saddened by his passing in late 2022 but honored to have this chapter to remember him by. Adam was deeply committed to learning about the relationship between language and gesture, and in his later years expressed his growing view that using the terms "language" and "gesture" implied a separation, which he did not believe existed. He was also a researcher who welcomed the discussion of signed language into the mix, and was eager to learn how the visible bodily actions of gesturers and signers compared. And so his essay here on language in the light of sign and gesture is a fitting conclusion to this collection of research. It is in part a recollection of how we have arrived at a current understanding of spoken language, signed language and gesture, and in part a commentary on such questions as: Are the bodily movements of speakers a part of language? And, since these bodily expressions of speakers are often similar in function (and sometimes also in form) to those used by signers, does this have implications for understanding signed languages in relation to spoken languages? Kendon walks us through a host of issues and past arguments about language as a bounded, arbitrary system and the importance of duality of patterning, and the resistance of researchers to allow any sort of extralinguistic material to be considered as part of the formal system. However, the increasing tide of gestural and signed language evidence bringing the whole body of the language user into the picture cannot be discounted; Kendon takes us on the journey of reconsidering the very essence of what language is, highlighting many significant publications that give us a new view of language that, like each of the authors in this volume attest, is a bodily enterprise with a multiplicity of means with which to construct utterances. Kendon's vision of language, so thoughtfully brought to life in this chapter, is thoroughly instructive.

References

Armstrong, David F., William C. Stokoe & Sherman E. Wilcox. 1994. Signs of the origin of syntax. *Current Anthropology* 35(4). 349–368.

Armstrong, David F., William C. Stokoe & Sherman E. Wilcox. 1995. *Gesture and the Nature of Language*. Cambridge: Cambridge University Press.

Armstrong, David F. & Sherman E. Wilcox. 2007. *The Gestural Origin of Language*. Oxford: Oxford University Press.

Aarons, Deborah, Ben Bahan, Judy Kegl & Carol Neidle. 1995. Lexical tense markers in ASL. In Karen Emmorey & Judy Reilly (eds.), *Language, Gesture, and Space*, 225–253. Hillsdale, NJ: Lawrence Erlbaum.

Baynton, Douglas C. 1996. *Forbidden Signs: American Culture and the Campaign Against Sign Language*. Chicago: University of Chicago Press.

Bybee, Joan L. 1985. *Morphology: A Study of the Relation Between Meaning and Form*. Amsterdam/Philadelphia: John Benjamins.

Bybee, Joan & Suzanne Fleischman (eds.). 1995. *Modality in Grammar and Discourse*. Amsterdam/Philadelphia: John Benjamins.

Clark, Herbert H. 2003. Pointing and placing. In Satoro Kita (ed.), *Pointing: Where Language, Culture, and Cognition Meet*, 243–268. Mahwah, NJ: Lawrence Erlbaum.

Cooperrider, Kensy & Kate Mesh. 2022. Pointing in gesture and sign. In Aliyah Morgenstern & Susan Goldin-Meadow (eds.), *Gesture in Language: Development Across the Lifespan*, 21–46. Berlin/Boston: De Gruyter Mouton. https://doi.org/10.1515/9783110567526

Dancygier, Barbara. 2017. *The Cambridge Handbook of Cognitive Linguistics*. Cambridge: Cambridge University Press.

de Vos, Connie, Marisa Casillas, Tom Uittenbogert, Onno Crasborn & Stephen C. Levinson. 2022. Predicting conversational turns: Signers' and nonsigners' sensitivity to language-specific and globally accessible cues. *Language* 98(1). 35–62.

Dudis, Paul G. 2004. Body partitioning and real-space blends. *Cognitive Linguistics* 15(2). 223–238.

Enfield, N. J. 2009. *The Anatomy of Meaning: Speech, Gesture, and Composite Utterances*. Cambridge: Cambridge University Press.

Fauconnier, Gilles. 1994. *Mental Spaces: Aspects of Meaning Construction in Natural Language*. Cambridge: Cambridge University Press.

Fauconnier, Gilles & Mark Turner. 2002. *The Way We Think: Conceptual Blending and the Mind's Hidden Complexities*. New York: Basic Books.

Ferrara, Lindsay & Gabrielle Hodge. 2018. Language as description, indication, and depiction. *Frontiers in Psychology* 9:716, 1–15. doi:10.3389/fpsyg.2018.00716

Ferreira Brito, Lucinda. 1990. Epistemic, alethic, and deontic modalities in a Brazilian Sign Language. In Susan D. Fischer & Patricia Siple (eds.), *Theoretical Issues in Sign Language Research, Volume 1: Linguistics*, 229–260. Chicago: University of Chicago Press.

Fischer, Susan D. & Bonnie Gough. 1978. Verbs in American Sign Language. *Sign Language Studies* 18. 17–48.

Frishberg, Nancy. 1975. Arbitrariness and iconicity in American Sign Language. *Language* 51. 696–719.

Haiman, John. 1983. Iconic and economic motivation. *Language* 59. 781–819.

Haiman, John (ed.). 1985. *Iconicity in Syntax*. Amsterdam/Philadelphia: John Benjamins.

Hockett, Charles F. 1966 [1963]. The problem of universals in language. In Joseph H. Greenberg (ed.), *Universals of Language*, 2nd edn., 1–29. Cambridge, MA: The MIT Press.

Hockett, Charles F. 1978. In search of Jove's brow. *American Speech* 53(4). 243–313.

Hodge, Gabrielle & Trevor Johnston. 2014. Points, depictions, gestures and enactment: Partly lexical and non-lexical signs as core elements of single clause-like units in Auslan (Australian Sign Language). *Australian Journal of Linguistics* 34(2). 262–291.

Janzen, Terry. 1998. *Topicality in ASL: Information Ordering, Constituent Structure, and the Function of Topic Marking*. Albuquerque: University of New Mexico dissertation.

Janzen, Terry. 1999. The grammaticization of topics in American Sign Language. *Studies in Language* 23(2). 271–306.

Janzen, Terry. 2004. Space rotation, perspective shift, and verb morphology in ASL. *Cognitive Linguistics* 15(2). 149–174.

Janzen, Terry. 2012. Two ways of conceptualizing space: Motivating the use of static and rotated vantage point space in ASL discourse. In Barbara Dancygier & Eve Sweetser (eds.), *Viewpoint in Language: A Multimodal Perspective*. 156–174. Cambridge: Cambridge University Press.

Janzen, Terry. 2017. Composite utterances in a signed language: Topic constructions and perspective-taking in ASL. *Cognitive Linguistics* 28(3). 511–538.

Janzen, Terry & Barbara Shaffer. 2002. Gesture as the substrate in the process of ASL grammaticization. In Richard P. Meier, Kearsy Cormier & David Quinto-Pozos (eds.), *Modality and Structure in Signed and Spoken Languages*, 199–223. Cambridge: Cambridge University Press.

Johnston, Trevor. 2013. Towards a comparative semiotics of pointing actions in signed and spoken languages. *Gesture* 13(2). 109–142.

Johnston, Trevor & Adam Schembri. 2007. *Australian Sign Language: An Introduction to Sign Language Linguistics*. Cambridge: Cambridge University Press.

Kendon, Adam. 2004. *Gesture: Visible Action as Utterance*. Cambridge: Cambridge University Press.

King, Barbara J. 1994. *The Information Continuum: Evolution of Social Information Transfer in Monkeys, Apes, and Hominids*. Santa Fe, NM: SAR Press.

Lakoff, George. 1987. *Women, Fire, and Dangerous Things: What Categories Reveal about the Mind*. Chicago: University of Chicago Press.

Lakoff, George & Mark Johnson. 1999. *Philosophy in the Flesh: The Embodied Mind and its Challenge to Western Thought*. New York: Basic Books.

Lane, Harlan. 1984. *When the Mind Hears: A History of the Deaf*. New York: Random House.

Leeson, Lorraine & John I. Saeed. 2012. *Irish Sign Language*. Edinburgh: Edinburgh University Press.

Liddell, Scott K. 1998. Grounded blends, gestures, and conceptual shifts. *Cognitive Linguistics* 9(3). 283–314.

Liddell, Scott K. 2000. Indicating verbs and pronouns: Pointing away from agreement. In Karen Emmorey & Harlan Lane (eds.), *The Signs of Language Revisited: An Anthology to Honor Ursula Bellugi and Edward Klima*, 303–320. Mahwah NJ: Lawrence Erlbaum.

Liddell, Scott K. 2003. *Grammar, Gesture, and Meaning in American Sign Language*. Cambridge: Cambridge University Press.

Liddell, Scott K. and Melanie Metzger. 1998. Gesture in sign language discourse. *Journal of Pragmatics* 30. 657–697.

Martínez, Rocío & Sherman Wilcox. 2019. Pointing and placing: Nominal grounding in Argentine Sign Language. *Cognitive Linguistics* 30(1). 85–121.

Müller, Cornelia. 2018. Gesture and sign: Cataclysmic break of dynamic relations? *Frontiers in Psychology* 9:1651.

Neisser, Ulric. 1967. *Cognitive Psychology*. New York: Appleton-Century-Crofts.

Padden, Carol A. 1988. *Interaction of Morphology and Syntax in American Sign Language*. New York: Garland Publishing.

Shaffer, Barbara. 2000. *A Syntactic, Pragmatic Analysis of the Expression of Necessity and Possibility in American Sign Language*. Albuquerque: University of New Mexico dissertation.

Shaffer, Barbara. 2004. Information ordering and speaker subjectivity: Modality in ASL. *Cognitive Linguistics* 15(2). 175–195.

Shaffer, Barbara, Maria Josep Jarque & Sherman Wilcox. 2011. The expression of modality: Conversational data from two signed languages. In Márcia Teixeira Nogueira & Maria Fabíola Vasconcelos Lopes (eds.), *Modo e Modalidade: Gramática, Discurso e Interação* [Mood and Modality: Grammar, Discourse, and Interaction], 11–39. Fortaleza, Brazil: Edições UFC.

Siyavoshi, Sara. 2019. *The Expression of Modality in Iranian Sign Language (ZEI)*. Albuquerque: University of New Mexico dissertation.

Simone, Raffaele (ed.). 1995. *Iconicity in Language*. Amsterdam/Philadelphia: John Benjamins.

Taub, Sarah, Dennis Galvan & Pilar Piñar. 2009. The role of gesture in crossmodal typological studies. *Cognitive Linguistics* 20(1). 71–92.

Varela, Francisco J., Evan Thompson & Eleanor Rosch. 1991. *The Embodied Mind: Cognitive Science and Human Experience*. Cambridge MA: MIT Press.

Volterra, Virginia, Maria Roccaforte, Allesio Di Renzo & Sabina Fontana. 2022. *Italian Sign Language from a Cognitive and Socio-semiotic Perspective*. Amsterdam/Philadelphia: John Benjamins.

Wilcox, Phyllis Perrin. 2004. A cognitive key: Metonymic and metaphorical mappings in American Sign Language. *Cognitive Linguistics* 15(2). 197–222.

Wilcox, Sherman. 1996a. Not from Jove's brow. *Language & Communication* 16(2). 179–192.

Wilcox, Sherman. 1996b. Hands and bodies, minds and souls: Or, how a sign linguist learned to stop worrying and love gesture. University of New Mexico manuscript.

Wilcox, Sherman. 2002. The gesture-language interface: Evidence from signed languages. In Rolf Schulmeister & Heimo Reinitzer (eds.), *Progress in Sign Language Research*, 63–81. Hamburg: Signum-Verlag.

Wilcox, Sherman. 2004a. Cognitive Iconicity: Conceptual spaces, meaning, and gesture in signed language. *Cognitive Linguistics* 15(2). 119–147.

Wilcox, Sherman. 2004b. Gesture and language: Cross-linguistic and historical data from signed languages. *Gesture* 4(1). 43–75.

Wilcox, Sherman. 2004c. Hands and bodies, minds and souls: What can signed languages tell us about the origin of signs?" In Morana Alač & Patrizia Violi (eds.), *In the Beginning: Origins of Semiosis*, 137–167. Turnhout, Belgium: Brepols.

Wilcox, Sherman. 2007. Routes from gesture to language. In Elena Pizzuto, Paola Pietrandrea & Raffaele Simone (eds.), *Verbal and Signed Languages: Comparing Structures, Constructs and Methodologies*, 107–131. Berlin/New York: Mouton de Gruyter.

Wilcox, Sherman & Terry Janzen. 2004. Introduction: Cognitive dimensions of signed languages, *Cognitive Linguistics* 15(2). 113–117.

Wilcox, Sherman & Rocío Martínez. 2020. The conceptualization of space: Places in signed language discourse. *Frontiers in Psychology* 11:1406. doi:10.3389/fpsyg.2020.01406

Wilcox, Sherman & Corrine Occhino. 2016. Constructing signs: Place as a symbolic structure in signed languages. *Cognitive Linguistics* 27(3). 371–404.

Wilcox, Sherman & Barbara Shaffer. 2006. Modality in American Sign Language. In William Frawley (ed.), *The Expression of Modality*, 207–237. Berlin: Mouton.

Wilcox, Sherman & Phyllis Wilcox. 1995. The gestural expression of modality in ASL. In Joan Bybee & Suzanne Fleischman (eds.), *Modality in Grammar and Discourse*, 135–162. Amsterdam/Philadelphia: John Benjamins.

Wilcox, Sherman & Phyllis Perrin Wilcox. 2015 [2010]. The analysis of signed languages. In Bernd Heine & Heiko Narrog (eds.), *The Oxford Handbook of Linguistic Analysis*, 2nd edn., 843–863. Oxford: Oxford University Press.

Wilcox, Sherman & André Nogueira Xavier. 2013. A framework for unifying spoken language, signed language and gesture. *Todas as Letras*, 15(1). 88–110.

Xavier, André Nogueira & Sherman Wilcox. 2014. Necessity and possibility modals in Brazilian Sign Language. *Linguistic Typology* 18(3). 449–488.

I **Guiding principles for signed and spoken language research**

Penny Boyes Braem and Virginia Volterra
Through the signed language glass: Changing and converging views in spoken and signed language research

1 Introduction

Looking back over our own several decades of working in the field of signed language research, we've observed that increasingly many signed and spoken language researchers are expressing similar views on several topics, a moving together which has influences on evolving underlying linguistic theories.[1] We began thinking more generally about past and current signed and spoken language research after reading Guy Deutscher's (2010) book that intrigued us both: *Through the Language Glass: Why the World Looks Different in Other Languages*. As an historical linguist, Deutscher takes the reader through centuries of raging academic wars in which different theories for observed phenomena are proposed, dominate for a while, followed by changed or expanded theories.

Deutscher's historical review of changing assumptions about spoken languages motivated us to look at evolving views of language also 'through the signed language glass'. Many of the views we will be looking at are, of course, not all that recent. Liddell, for example, wrote several years ago that

> ...it is much more likely that spoken and signed languages both make use of multiple types of semiotic elements in the language signal, but that our understanding of what constitutes language has been much too narrow. (Liddell 2003: 362)

Several researchers have already pointed out that most of the first, and many of the still current, descriptive models of signed languages have been based on assumptions derived from models of spoken languages. Individual characteristics which never quite fit into early models were typically discussed in terms of oddities stem-

---

[1] We would like to acknowledge the helpful comments of the reviewers as well as of two outside readers, Rachel Sutton-Spence and Mary M. Fox. This work was partially supported by a grant from the Italian Ministry for Research and University (MUR, PRIN 20177894ZH).

Penny Boyes Braem, Forschungszentrum für Gebärdensprache (Center for Sign Language Research) FZG, Switzerland, e-mail: boyesbraem@gmail.com
Virginia Volterra, Istituto di Scienze e Tecnologie della Cognizione (Institute of Cognitive Sciences and Technologies) CNR, Italy, e-mail: virgi.volterra@gmail.com

https://doi.org/10.1515/9783110703788-002

ming from signed languages' use of a modality of production and perception that is different from that of spoken languages. What we have found additionally interesting, however, is that in recent years some linguists have begun discussing characteristics of language as it is spoken (versus as it is written) in a way very similar to how signed language researchers have for years described the elements which they viewed as being uniquely relevant to visual-gestural languages. This has included, for example, considering to be linguistically important the factor of iconicity and the arbitrariness of gradient categories (e.g., Dingemanse et al. 2015; Clark 2016, 2019) as well as discrete linguistic categories (e.g., Langacker 2008; Albano Leoni 2009, 2022; Wilcox and Occhino 2017). These more recent views also bring into question the traditional dichotomy between elements that have been considered to be "linguistic" and those that had often been seen as "paralinguistic" or "non-linguistic".

Some researchers from both within the field of signed language research and beyond have already called for new models and paradigms to better accommodate these more recent views, as Cienki (2017) comments:

> Whereas we started with a model of language that, in the traditional view, had a clear boundary, we might sketch an alternative model in which the spoken words and grammar, the intonation patterns, the non-lexical sounds, and the gestures each are categories with fuzzy boundaries that overlap in dynamic ways. (Cienki 2017: 175)

What we also find interesting is the fact that rarely have researchers from other disciplines mentioned the work contemporaneously being done in signed language research as being relevant to their areas. An exception has been Dan Slobin, a psycholinguist specializing in acquisition and cross-linguistic research, who has explicitly pointed out that moving towards a new understanding of language has been pushed by signed language research:

> Sign language linguists have begun to create tools with which to arrive at a deeper and more comprehensive understanding of human language, human cognition, and human social interaction. Indeed, old paradigms are fading, and revolutionary new ideas are growing up across disciplines, languages, and countries. The habitual molds are being broken and new molds are beginning to be formed. (Slobin 2008: 129)

To review all the evolving theories is beyond the scope of this contribution. Our aim here is simply to focus a light on three areas, which seem to be especially relevant in this pushing towards new models and paradigms by linguistic researchers, not only of signed and spoken language, but also researchers of gesture and symbolic development. These are:

1. The view of language as a form of action
2. The attention to multimodal behaviors
3. The recognition of the role played by iconicity at all levels of language and in major linguistic activities

While we will discuss these areas and related issues separately, we fully recognize that they are, of course, deeply interrelated. Although it clearly would be impossible to review *all* the literature that addresses these points, we will try to give relevant examples of these ideas for each area.

2 Areas of evolving theory

2.1 Area 1: The origin of language acquisition in action

At the beginning of research on signed languages in the 1960s and 1970s, we, like many other early signed language researchers, tried to show in our early descriptions of the signed languages we were documenting that the linguistic sign was something far from a simple motor action or gesture.

However, in that same period, our research on language acquisition of hearing children was taking us in a completely different direction.[2] We were finding that all infants already in their first year of life start to perform a series of motor actions in their explorations and manipulations of objects in their world. Then, thanks to the environment around them and especially to those who interact with them, these motor actions acquire a symbolic meaning and are then progressively used as communicative gestures to represent an object or an event even outside the communicative context in which they had been originally produced. These studies on gesture used by young hearing children in different cultures (Australian, British, English Canadian, Italian, Japanese), show how gesture functions as meaningful action in relationship to speech (Pettenati et al. 2012; Marentette et al. 2016; Cattani et al. 2019). Action, gesture, and word combinations contribute to the general meaning of the first crossmodal (gestures and words) utterances at both the semantic and pragmatic levels and pave the way to multi-word sentences (e.g., Capirci et al. 1996; Capirci and Volterra 2008; Iverson et al. 2008; Sparaci and Volterra 2017; Volterra et al. 2017, 2018).

The strong relationship between action-gestures performed by infants and the first words that they comprehend and then produce has also received strong support from neuroscientists exploring the role of mirror neurons, which confirms a neural

---

2 For a review, see Volterra et al. (2005).

substrate common to gesture and speech. Research on the early stages of child development has thus supported the hypothesis that these neural bases are part of the human genetic makeup (see Arbib 2012). Today, there is a growing recognition among researchers from several disciplines (e.g., Arbib 2020) that this "origin in action" is not something specific to signed languages, although it is more visible in this form of language.

The presence and relevance of gestures do not disappear in the spoken communications of children as they grow older and become adults. The psycholinguist David McNeill (2012) has clarified the role of gesture not only in the process of what Slobin (1987) has called "thinking for speaking", that is in the transition from thought to linguistic units, but has also looked at the possibility of expressing more than one meaning through the simultaneous production of gesture and word. Gesture used by speakers can reinforce meaning expressed vocally, or it can express a further meaning that is not expressed in speech, or it can further specify a concept that is expressed vocally only in vague way (see also Alibali, Flevares and Goldin-Meadow 1997; Goldin-Meadow 2003).

Adam Kendon (2004) in his book *Gesture: Visible Action as Utterance* was one of the first gesture researchers to stress the continuity and similarity between co-verbal gestures and signs in signed languages, showing how both speakers and signers use semiotic strategies that involve categorical as well as gradient aspects. For some researchers in both gesture and signed language research, however, an earlier view remains that there is a "cataclysmic break" between the status of gesture and language, based in part on the assumption that gradient aspects of signs are gesture (Singleton, Goldin-Meadow and McNeill; Goldin-Meadow and Brentari 2017). Other researchers (Emmorey and Herzig 2003; Occhino and Wilcox 2017) have countered this claim by arguing that rather than a cataclysmic break, we should view language (signed or spoken) as not wholly categorical, and view gesture as not wholly gradient. Kendon (2015, 2017) has proposed a new terminology which rejects the opposition of "gesture" vs. "sign" by referring to both as "visible action as utterance", a formulation that makes clear the relationship between action, gesture, and sign. Some spoken language linguists, for example the Italian linguist De Mauro (2008), have long taken the view that not only voice, but all our speaking, understanding, and knowing of language is rooted in all our body, a view which, although coming from a different European linguistic tradition, is very close to the "embodied language" approach taken today by cognitive linguistics.

Important for the action-gesture language continuum are the symbolic representational strategies used by children, which are grounded in basic embodied motor acts. These four basic strategies are: (a) the person's own body enacting the action and/or the character; (b) the hand enacting how an object is held or manipulated; (c) the hands becoming/representing an object; or (d) the hands representing the size/shape of an object.

The same basic strategies have been reported in studies in several disciplines – spoken and signed language acquisition, symbolic development, and gestures as well as in descriptions of signed languages (e.g., Marentette et al. 2016; Volterra et al. 2018). Researchers in these different fields, however, have used different terminology for strategies of symbolic representation (see Table 1). These strategies will look very familiar to researchers of different signed languages who sometimes refer to them with such varying terminology.[3]

Table 1: Terminology that has been used in the developmental, gesture and signed language literature for the four strategies of symbolic representation reported.[4]

	Strategy	Terms in studies of gestures of adults and children	Terms in studies of signed languages	Examples
A	The whole body represents the action or the character	– own-body – personification – mime/ pantomime – action gesture – character viewpoint	– constructed action – role-playing – body classifier – enactment – person transfer	
B	The hands assume a grasping configuration recalling the action	– hand as hand – handling – manipulation – action gesture – function gesture – character viewpoint	– constructed action – handling classifier – manipulator – person transfer	
C	The hands represent the object	– hand as object – modelling – form gesture – function gesture – observer viewpoint	– whole entity classifier – instrument classifier – polycomponential signs – substitutor – situation transfer – form transfer	
D	The hands trace the shape or the size	– size and shape – drawing – delimitation – observer viewpoint	– size and shape specifier – tracing – form or shape transfer	

---

[3] For example, the same symbolic strategies have been used to produce what has been called by American researchers "classifiers" (Frishberg 1975), "polycomponential signs" (Slobin et al. 2003), "productive signs" or "constructed actions" (Cormier, Smith, and Sevcikova-Sehyr 2016; Schembri, Jones and Burnham 2005), "depicting constructions" (Liddell 2003), by Norwegian researchers, "depicting signs" and "enactments" (Ferrara and Halvorsen 2017), by French researchers, "highly iconic structures" (Cuxac and Sallandre 2007), and by German researchers, "image-creating techniques" (Langer 2005).

[4] Table 1 is adapted from Volterra et al. (2022).

The choice of which symbolic strategy to use is determined by different factors, for example by the nature of the referent and the context. In many signed languages, both the object 'hammer' and the action of 'hammering' involve a hand-as-manipulator strategy of grasping of the instrument and showing the action of hammering. In the sign for 'scissors' in many signed languages, it's not the action but rather the V-shape of the object itself that is represented using a hand-as-object strategy. Age is another potential factor in the choice of strategy, although in spoken language acquisition, the question is still insufficiently researched of whether children use different strategies at different stages of their language acquisition (Volterra et al. 2019; Tomasuolo et al. 2020). Different preferences for strategies have been found between hearing persons' gestures and signers' signs. For example, Sutton-Spence and Boyes Braem (2013) found in their study comparing the data from the same task done by American hearing mimes who had no knowledge of any signed language and British deaf signing poets, that the gestures of the hearing mimes most frequently involved the "hand-as-hand" strategy and only very rarely the "hand-as-object" strategy, whereas the deaf signing poets used an abundance of both strategies. Signed languages also seem to differ in their preference for using one strategy over another (Padden et al. 2015).

The continuity and dynamic relation between action, gesture, and word/sign so evident in language acquisition by children and in adult communication is also at the core of the study of language philogeny. This deep interconnection is linked to our evolutionary history with the hypothesis of gestural origins of language gaining support thanks to several studies (among many others, Haiman 1998; Armstrong 1999; Armstrong, Stokoe, and Wilcox 1995; Armstrong and Wilcox 2007; Corballis 2003; Tetel Andresen 2014; Arbib 2020). The theory that a form of integrated speech-gesture communication preceded the dominance of both spoken languages and signed languages is further supported by the possible development from gestures not only of lexical items but also of grammatical elements of signed languages (e.g., Janzen and Shaffer 2002; Janzen, Shaffer, and Leeson 2016; Wilcox 2004a, 2007, 2009; Wilcox and Wilcox 1995; Wilcox, Rossini, and Antinoro Pizzuto 2010). As Müller (2018) points out, this historical process involves no cataclysmic break, no sudden rupture transforming gesture into sign from one moment to another.

To sum up this first area, a more integrated perspective has been emerging that views the language faculty as manifesting itself in both the visual-gestural and phonic-acoustic channels (see e.g., Perniss, Özyürek, and Morgan 2015). As has been widely supported by the gestural studies literature, the linguistic act can be achieved by gesture as well as by spoken words, which can interact in dynamic ways based on the intention of the speaker. This opens the way to linguistic or semiotic models, which consider multimodality as one of the fundamental aspects of human languaging.

2.2 Area 2: Multimodality

As we have discussed in the previous section, hearing infants are clearly able to communicate with their environment long before they are able to use spoken language, in that they are already able to produce several gestural and vocal modes of communication, which pave the way to the emergence of spoken words and sentences. Communication, including languaging, is thus from the very beginning, multimodal. Many researchers have come to the view that what has been called "linguistic" comprehension and production in fact entails many kinds of elements (including gestures, facial expression, head and body movements, prosody, intonation, etc.). Adults as well as children can continuously communicate using channels and modes in addition to that of speech, means which have traditionally been called non-verbal communication.

Because of these developing views, the prosodic and gestural behaviors produced simultaneously with speech are now considered by many researchers to be truly linguistic phenomena and should be integral parts of the description of spoken languages. In the past, researchers and scholars from other disciplines interested in the study of human language were not able to observe and describe in detail such characteristics. Thanks to continued technological development, especially of video recordings, the prevalence of these phenomena has become clearer and fully visible. These elements in the past were relegated to a kind of limbo along with other phenomena considered "nonlinguistic", partly because they could not always be analyzed as discrete elements, which hampered their categorization and classification.

On the signed language side, the level of basic units was considered by many very early researchers to involve mainly manual components (i.e., only the hands). Some of us when looking back at the very early days of signed language research can even remember discussing whether the head and face needed to be in the picture frame. Again, aided by evolving recording technology, the recognition grew quickly over the succeeding decades that not only must the behaviors of the hands be considered as basic linguistic components, but also different parts of the body such as the positions of the torso, shoulders, head, elements of facial expression and oral components such as mouth gestures and mouthing, as well as direction of eye gaze (e.g., Dudis 2004). The concept of multimodality and multi-channels became the topic of more research in both signed and spoken languages. Linguists interested in speech began devoting more attention to gestures and prosody (e.g., Magno Caldognetto and Poggi 1997) and linguists interested in signed language began more studies of oral elements such as mouthings (e.g., Boyes Braem and Sutton-Spence 2001).

Research on signed languages began documenting the important roles these non-manual elements play not only at the lexical level, but also at the levels of syntax and discourse. No longer considered merely "non-manual" elements, these visible and often gradient components are now considered to be formal elements in descriptions of signed language by many researchers (e.g., Wilbur 2000; Aristodemo and Geraci 2017; Lepic and Occhino 2018; Dotter 2018; Perniss 2019; Sandler 2018).

These non-manual elements have been found to be more difficult to master. Early studies of the acquisition of non-manual morphology in American Sign Language (ASL) found that "once children are producing multi-signed utterances, we see a consistent, developmental patterns in which manual signs take developmental precedence over non-manual behavior... Deaf children use a linear, lexical strategy before they tackle the complex simultaneous facial morphology" (Reilly and Andersen 2002: 179). In recent Italian Sign Language (Lingua dei Segni Italiana, or LIS) studies involving sentence repetition tasks, the non-manual components were also found to be more difficult for deaf signing children to acquire and execute than were the manual components (Rinaldi et al. 2018). The inclusion of these non-manual components in this study thus put a focus on a developmental factor that had not been considered in most sentence repetition tasks with children conducted up to that time. Finally, non-manuals are not only difficult to master by children, but also by adults learning a signed language (as educators of signed language interpreters have often informally reported to us).

For both spoken as well signed languages, the problem has been how to describe and transcribe such behavior, the features of which could not easily be broken down into discrete components, were often continuous and gradient, and usually were produced simultaneously with behavior in other channels. Most of the expressive gestural aspects, along with prosodic variations, remain almost completely outside the sphere of graphic reproduction in written representations of the languages, not only due to the difficulty of their categorization and classification, but also because their simultaneous productions are complicated to capture in the linearity of most written forms (see Antinoro Pizzuto and Garcia, this volume). One of the most striking features of visual multimodal behaviors is that they can be simultaneously produced by different articulators. Slonimska and her colleagues have called this the linearization problem: "... an event that occurs simultaneously in the world that has to be split in language to be organized on a temporal scale" (Slonimska, Özyürek, and Capirci 2020: 14). Not only can the facial, head, body and manual behaviors occur simultaneously, but the three-dimensional space around the signer can also simultaneously give information enriching what is being communicated.

Fortunately, in more recent years many of these problems have been mitigated by the development of new technology for tagging video media in which written annotations could be directly linked to the raw videotaped data. Software such as the free application ELAN,⁵ developed for other kinds of research and for all computer platforms by the Max Planck Institute in Nijmegen became widely used by signed language researchers for annotating longer signed texts. However, while having the raw data always available is helpful, it does not really solve the problem of giving different glosses to the same sign by different researchers in different projects at different times. One technological attempt to overcome this problem is the iLex software developed at the University of Hamburg (Hanke and Storz 2008; Konrad 2011). The iLex tagging technology is like that of ELAN but has the additional advantage of linking the same written gloss in all corpus files to the same sign lemma in a central lexicon.

The development of media tagging technology has thus meant that large corpora of multimodal data can now be in a form that makes possible the discovery and analyses of new kinds of research questions in all kinds of contexts, signed by different types of users. One of the first, and to date the largest signed language corpora, is the long term (2009–2024) project for documenting the "everyday" lexicon of German Sign Language (Deutsche Gebärdensprache, or DGS), drawing data from a wide variety of users and contexts (Prillwitz and Zienert 1990).

For signed languages, these advances in methodologies have involved not only a growing recognition of the importance of the wide variety of communities of users but also the increased involvement of these users in the collection of data collected and the methods of analyses. Deaf signers researching their own language often begin to change their assumptions about it, often adopting some of the *academic* norms – their *metalinguistic* awareness is awakened and enlarged. In many countries (such as Italy and Switzerland), these changing assumptions about their language get transmitted to the larger community of signers. Then, the community of users themselves, with changed assumptions, can in turn begin to influence how the language they use changes (Fontana et al. 2015).

Signed languages have traditionally been "transcribed" primarily by using spoken word-labels (called glosses) as a primary representation tool (for overviews see, e.g., van der Hulst and Channon 2010; Boyes Braem 2012). Glosses using written words run into the danger, however, of misrepresenting the meaning and the structure of signed languages (see Pizzuto, Rossini, and Russo 2006). In response to signed language researchers' need to be able to document the phonological features of these languages, several notation systems have been developed for lexical items.⁶

---

5 http://www.lat-mpi.eu/tools/elan/
6 Among the most widely-used notation systems are Stokoe notation (Stokoe 1960), the Hamburg Notation System or HamNoSys (Prillwitz and Zienert 1990), and Signfont (Newkirk 1987). The Berkeley Transcription System (Slobin et al. 2001) was developed for notating morphemes. Valerie Sutton adapted a system of choreographic notation for signs to create SignWriting in 1981. SignWriting

In early signed language linguists' attempts to show that signed languages have a grammar and syntax, comparisons were usually made not just to the models based on written forms of spoken languages, but also mostly to the models of Indo-European languages. These attempts often resulted in trying to find formal distinctions, for example, between nouns and verbs, or to identify a fixed order of elements in the sentence based on categories such as subject, object, and verb. At the same time, it often involved neglecting sign structures that were too different and not often easily analyzable with the instruments available from spoken languages, such as role-taking, productive structures involving classifier handshapes with simultaneous components, and using the space around the signer for linguistic purposes. Even the signed language research pioneer William Stokoe in his later years began trying to convince people to be careful about making too rigid classifications of signed languages, underscoring how a single sign could already represent enactment indicating the agent, the action, and the object of an event. Slobin (2006, 2013) as well as Schembri et al. (2018) have pointed out the fundamental mistake of trying to put signed languages typologically in an inappropriate class of languages. Slobin has argued that signed languages, due to their manual/visual multimodality are more like head-marking languages (like those of native Americans, parts of the Caucasus, the Far East, and Oceania) than they are like dependent-marking languages (Indo-European languages) with overt morphological marking of syntactic relations. Signed languages are more verb-framed as opposed to satellite-frame, topic prominent as opposed to subject prominent. Slobin notes that spoken languages also have access to the simultaneous channels of gesture, gaze direction, and facial expression in face-to-face communication, i.e., they are multimodal. The effect of recognizing this multimodality has added to a demand for new language models, a need which Perniss (2018) has expressed as:

> The conception that 'language' is that which is linguistic, while communication is something different. . .is not given by necessity. As such, it is time to reconceptualise our object of study and to usher in a new paradigm of language theory, a paradigm that focuses on multimodal language, that aligns with the real world use of language and focuses on *doing language*. (Perniss 2018: 2, italics in original)

To conclude this discussion of multimodality, one could say that the facial, gestural, and other prosodic behaviors produced simultaneously with either speech or signing had traditionally usually been relegated to a kind of limbo with other phenomena that were considered "paralinguistic" or "nonlinguistic". They were

---

also uses symbols and graphic representations for representing many multi-channel (hands, face, head, trunk) behaviors, which can greatly facilitate crosslinguistic research (Petitta et al. 2013; https://www.signwriting.org).

not easily decomposable into discrete components, which hampered their categorization within the linguistic models being used. Multimodal elements, including gradient ones, are now considered by many researchers to be relevant linguistic phenomena.[7] This changing view has contributed to more diverse typologies being considered in the analyses of both spoken and signed languages. This process has been greatly aided by evolving computer and media technologies in these years, particularly in the development of usage corpora for both signed and spoken languages.

2.3 Area 3: Iconicity

Although most early researchers recognized there were some aspects of signed languages that had representational, iconic aspects, these were thought not to be important for the linguistic structure of a proper language. Also in this regard, early researchers wished to demonstrate that signed languages should not be understood as mere loose gesturing and pantomime, forms of communication that were not true or full languages. To be like spoken languages, signed languages should have elements which were not only discrete and categorical, but also arbitrary, based on the tenet that arbitrariness of a small set of subcomponents makes it possible for their recombination into new elements with different meanings.

The concept of arbitrariness has often been conflated with the concept of iconicity, where the form of an element has some connection to its meaning. Many early signed language studies reinforced this bias against iconicity. Historical research comparing old French and historically-related modern ASL signs concluded that the iconic nature of lexical items became more arbitrary over time (Frishberg 1975; Woodward and Erting 1975). Regular grammatical processes that one finds in spoken languages, such as verbal and nominal inflections, were viewed as contributing to this weakening importance of iconic elements in ASL (see e.g., Bellugi and Klima 1976; Bellugi 1980). Other studies found that iconic aspects of signs played little role in the rapid processing of lists of signs or in memory (Bellugi, Klima and Siple 1975.)

In his 1960 pioneering book on ASL, *Sign Language Structure*, Willian Stokoe coined the term "cheremes" to refer to discrete basic units of signed languages, analogous to phonemes in spoken language phonology. However, it became more and more evident that sign cheremes can have meaning, i.e., can be polysemous in referring to more than one meaning and that combinations of cheremes from

---

7 See e.g., the overview in Müller et al. 2014.

different parameters contribute to the global meaning of the sign. For example, the fist handshape can convey the idea of strength and power, but also a specific kind of grasping or the shape of a small, solid, round object. The signer can play with the polysemous phonological units to create new signs or creatively modify existing signs for poetic purposes (e.g., Bauman 2003; Sutton-Spence 2005). Stokoe himself (1991) later proposed a "semantic phonology" in which semantic dimensions are present in the articulation. This moving away from his original view of arbitrary cheremes, however, presents a challenge to Hockett's (1960) design feature of duality of patterning, in which arbitrariness is a necessary characteristic of the sublexical level of linguistic structure (see e.g., Armstrong 1999).

The idea of duality of patterning itself also came under criticism from spoken language linguists for several reasons. One of these reasons was that not all phonological elements even of spoken languages are easily analyzable into meaningless, discrete, separate categories. The Italian linguist Albano Leoni (2009, 2022), among others, has shown how in spoken communication, speakers do not usually perceive and produce words as discrete categories but rather as wholes or gestalts. Various other experiments (e.g., Albano Leoni and Maturi 1992) have shown that sound segments do not have a single identical physical realization, but one can perceive them within the context of the sentence.

Some early signed language studies approached the problem of iconicity by asking the question of "how really iconic are signs?" by looking at how much non-signers understand their meanings from just seeing their forms. Hoemann (1975) found the meanings of only 30% of 200 very common ASL signs were correctly identified by hearing non-signers. Bellugi and Klima (1976) found that hearing non-signers performed no better than chance at guessing a sign's meaning. For LIS, Grosso (1997) also found that Italian hearing non-signers guessed correctly only approximately 22% of the signs shown them. These studies seem to verify the opinion that iconicity isn't all that important in signs.

Several other early researchers focused more broadly on iconicity in individual signed languages, among them in ASL (e.g., Friedman 1975; Mandel 1977; DeMatteo 1977; Boyes Braem 1981), and British Sign Language (Brennan 1990). In her early study of Danish Sign Language (dansk tegnsprog), Engberg-Pedersen wrote that the space around the signer is "semantically loaded from the moment the signer starts signing" (Engberg-Pedersen 1993:78). A decade later, Wilcox (2004b) also began to look at iconicity within the framework of cognitive grammar, culminating in an article discussing cognitive iconicity in French, American and Italian signed languages.

In the following years, a great many more studies found that iconicity plays a role in the modulation of signs to express space, location, quantity, quality, modality, aspect, as well as agentivity. Russo (2004) suggests that iconicity, and especially dynamic iconicity, is in part related to some structural features of signs (i.e., in coarticulation and simultaneous syntax) and factors in the dimension of variability versus standardization, as well as in relation to different discourse registers. In their overview of much of this research Meir et al. (2013) write that grammar does not necessarily suppress iconicity but also, different types of iconicity can play active roles in the structuring of grammars. Van der Hulst (2022) points out in his history of sign phonology that the various approaches he reviews "share the idea that iconicity and phonology are not incompatible, and this view is gaining more support within the field" (van der Hulst 2022: 37). These expanding views of iconicity have resulted in models such as that proposed by Cogill-Koez (2000a, 2000b) which attempts to account for both more visual and more linguistic types of representation in signed languages.

In spoken language linguistics, although Roman Jakobson wrote as early as 1966 that "the representation by likeness is superior to the use of arbitrary signs" (Jakobson 1966: 348), linguists using more current theoretical perspectives have often downplayed iconicity, usually noting that it is a phenomenon found in only a small number of lexical items. There were, however, linguists who did not take this view. Reviews of the different ways iconicity has been viewed for spoken languages (e.g., Perniss, Thompson, and Vigliocco 2010; Perniss and Vigliocco 2014; Dingemanse et al. 2015), describe the many kinds of iconicity that have been reported, especially in descriptions of non-Western European languages which were already beginning to be done in the mid-19th century.

Some spoken language researchers have been viewing iconicity and arbitrariness as co-existing in a relationship in which a similarity is created corresponding with an extralinguistic acoustic reality. Beyond the well-known examples of the different sounds that are ascribed to a given animal, such as a cow or a pig, in different languages, there are also iconic effects of the phonological properties of some verbs, including length and reduplication, which have been shown to have interpretive effects relating to verbal aspect as duration and iterativity (Haiman 1980, 2008; Dingemanse 2015; Kuhn and Aristodemo 2017). In many languages, the superlative adjective is longer than the neutral form (e.g., in the Italian words for good and very good: *bene* vs. *benissimo*). Iconicity is even more evident when the plural is formed through reduplication, a phenomenon found in many languages of the world (e.g., in Sumerian, sheep *udu* vs. many sheep *udu-udu*).

An important fact to note here, however, is that each language's choice of sound is arbitrary in the sense that it will use a sound-iconic representation from within its language-specific repertoire of phonology, which might differ from that of other languages. The decision of which iconic strategy to use for representing a meaning seems, among other things, to depend on conventional agreement within the community of users. A meaningful relationship between form (of sign, word, or gesture) and referent becomes more conventional as it becomes an established cultural feature for the community of users, who can be from a specific geographic or cultural community, or from a deaf community.

To look at how differences in culture and hearing status can interact in ways that influence how people attribute meaning to signs, Corazza and Volterra (1988) showed deaf LIS signers and Italian hearing non-signers the same picture story, "The Snowman", signed in two regional dialects of LIS (Trieste and Rome), in another European signed language (Danish), and in a non-European signed language (Chinese). The attribution of meaning revealed three groups of signs: (a) those understood by everybody, indicating there are some language- and culture-free, presumably universal highly iconic, often pantomimic, features like 'looking-out-from the-window'; (b) those understood more by deaf signers of any signed languages than by hearing non-signers, indicating there are potentially more linguistically encoded universals, often classifier-based elements such as 'light falling of snowflakes on the ground' which probably obey similar organizational principles across different signed languages; and (c) entirely language-specific elements understood only by deaf signers and only when encoded in their own signed language, such as a lexical sign for 'mother'.

In a follow-up study, Pizzuto and Volterra (2000) explored the comprehensibility of LIS lexical items by hearing and deaf subjects belonging to six different national cultures and twelve language communities (both signed and spoken) in Denmark, The Netherlands, England, Switzerland, Spain, and Portugal. None of these participants knew LIS. The items for which the participants had to guess the meaning were 20 LIS signs whose meaning was determined to be transparent, in that they had been guessed correctly by at least 50% of the Italian hearing non-signers in the Grosso (1997) study mentioned earlier, together with 20 signs defined as non-transparent, as no subjects (or at most one Italian hearing non-signer) had guessed the correct meaning. The results of the Pizzuto and Volterra (2000) study confirmed the earlier Corazza and Volterra (1988) results. It also added the finding that some signs were guessed more correctly by both hearing and deaf non-signing Italians compared to guesses of deaf and hearing members sharing other cultures, indicating the existence of some culture-specific factors that both deaf and hearing non-signers share.

In signed languages, very often iconicity is expressed through visually-based metaphoric or metonymic relationships in which the sign extends its form to other meanings. For example, the LIS sign for 'university' is represented by showing the form of the traditional academic hat of the Italian university student. Studies looking at metaphoric/metonymic iconicity in signed languages began early on by some researchers. Among these are Boyes Braem (1981, 1983), Brennan (1990), P. Wilcox (1993, 2000, 2004, 2007), Taub (2001), and Meir (2010). Overviews of studies on iconic metaphors, for which an adequate overview would be a chapter in itself, can be found in Cuxac (2000), Pietrandrea and Russo (2007), Cuccio and Fontana (2012, 2017), Meir and Cohen (2018), and Russo and Pietrandrea (this volume). A study by Occhino et al. (2017) found that signers who learned ASL or DGS as their first language, saw signs from their own language as more iconic than those from other signed languages. A possible explanation for the fact that unrelated signed languages often have similar signs for abstract concepts has been hypothesized by Napoli (2017) to be the result of the use of common chains of mappings from different perceptual systems into visual realizations with a semantic sense.

The gestures made by hearing persons have also been found to have meaningful sub-components (see an early study of French co-speech gestures in Calbris 1990). Many of these sub-components are like those of signed languages. For example, the results of the cross-cultural study of Pizzuto and Volterra (2000) were later further analyzed to look at the metaphors which seem to underlie the meanings which the hearing and deaf participants of different European countries ascribed to the LIS signs (Boyes Braem, Pizzuto, and Volterra 2002). This study suggests that the signers seem to attribute different meanings than do the non-signers to these items partly because of (a) focusing on different parameters, i.e., location, handshape, or movement and (b) the tendency to attribute different types of meaning, i.e., the hearing non-signers focusing on the action itself, and the deaf signers seeing action as a reference to an object. For example, the LIS sign meaning 'to drink' is an outstretched thumb moving toward the upper body and was attributed the meaning of 'drinking' by many hearing non-signers. Some hearing non-signers, however, seemed to focus only on the movement toward the body, seeing this as pointing generally to the self and attributed the meaning 'I/me'. Most deaf signers seemed to focus on the movement toward the mouth, but attributed not only meanings like 'drinking', but unlike the non-signers, also meanings of objects which metaphorically/metonymically are associated with drinking, such as 'beer', beer bottle', 'water', or 'baby'.

The role of metaphor in perception and production of gestures by hearing persons has been the subject of other many gestural studies (e.g., P. Wilcox 2007; Cienki and Müller 2008, 2014; Russo 2008; McNeill 2014; Ruth-Hirrel and Wilcox 2018). Some of these focus on gestures used in special professions. For example, a study of gestures used by orchestral conductors (Boyes Braem and Bräm 2000) found a repertoire of metaphors used by orchestral conductor for musical messages, for example making a "pulling out" movement with a "pincher" handshape to elicit a high thin sound from an oboe, and the same movement but with a rounded palms-up handshape to elicit a fuller sound from a horn.

The issue of iconicity is also involved in the general ability of human beings to express themselves in both spoken and signed languages through the devices of pointing, describing, and depicting (e.g., Ferrara and Hodge 2018). Pointing allows the locating of a given referent in space. It is possible to describe or label various meanings through conventionalized words or signs of the lexicon, while depiction shows more directly what one is expressing. The assumption could be made that the modality of spoken languages makes it more attuned to describing, while the visual signed languages are more likely to use depicting. Most observers of signed languages have in fact noted that its users make a transition between description and depicting rapidly, subtly, and very often (e.g., Ferrara and Halvorsen 2017). Studies of spoken communication are also re-discovering iconic depicting (Clark 2016, 2019; Dingemanse et al. 2015). One example of many kinds of iconic depiction in spoken language is the lengthening of a word making it assume a depicting function, such as producing the English words 'grand' and 'big' as 'graaaande' or 'biiig', evoking the concept of something really large.

These views of iconicity have relevance for general linguistic theory. Dingemanse et al. (2015) not only note that there is evidence from studies of both signed and spoken language that seem to indicate that iconicity is not a binary property but comes in different types and degrees but they also make the following interesting more general observations:

> A fully arbitrary vocabulary is unlikely to be a stable feature of natural languages, because form-to-meaning correspondences are shaped by cultural evolutionary processes which favour not just discriminability but also learnability and communicative utility. An upheaval is underway in current thinking about the arbitrary nature of linguistic signs. The longstanding view that the form of a word has an essentially arbitrary relation to the meaning of the word is giving way to a perspective that recognizes roles for both arbitrariness and non-arbitrariness in language. (Dingemanse et al. 2015: 603)

Summing up this section, it has been impressive to witness the great proliferation of studies related to iconicity (of which only a very small sample could be cited here) that have found significant iconic alongside arbitrary phenomena in all forms of languaging – signed and spoken language as well in gestures. Signs and words can at the same time be both motivated and conventional, having an original, and sometimes still active—or re-activable—iconic motivation, which is the result of a potentially arbitrary cultural/community choice.

3 Concluding thoughts

Inspired by Deutscher's (2010) "through the language glass" discussion of historically changing theoretical views, we have attempted here to focus on three areas where the views of an increasing number of researchers from different disciplines (including signed and spoken languages as well as gestures) seem throughout the past several decades to be moving together. The specific topics of these areas concern the origin of language in action, the comprehension of language as a multimodal system, and the importance of gradient along with discrete components in languages.

We have discussed research which has indicated that an "origin in action" can be found not only in the gestures used by adults, but also in the acquisition of languages by hearing and deaf children. We have pointed out that for both spoken and signed languages, the segments, which the linguist posit in an analysis, don't seem to be the same kinds of discrete units that are produced or perceived by the speaker or signer in actual multimodal discourse. We have also discussed some of the evidence for the presence of both arbitrariness and non-arbitrariness as co-existing features in these forms of human communication.

All of this has contributed to a push for outlining new models for describing languages, be they spoken or signed, arising from descriptions of what happens between users of face-to-face communication systems. The proponents of these new models will no doubt need to consider a revision of the traditional concept of duality of patterning, impelled by viewing basic linguistic units as not all being meaningless but involving more than one modality or channel, allowing for gradient elements to coexist with discrete and segmental elements.

Researchers of signed languages have played an especially important part in these views, as we've been compelled from the onset to deal with these three phenomena due to the visual, bodily, multimodal nature of the face-to-face form of communication we've all been trying to describe – we couldn't avoid it.

One of the signed language researchers who has from the very beginning of his long career recognized and addressed almost all these factors is Sherman Wilcox, who, together with his wife, Phyllis Perrin Wilcox, and his colleagues, has investigated routes from gestures to language, the role of iconicity and metaphor, language multimodality, and has constantly pointed out the need for new models and paradigms. These researchers have, for years, been at the forefront of leading us all to...

> ...a framework for unifying spoken language, signed language and gesture...a human expressive ability ... based on the need of moving creatures to comprehend their environment, resulting in a conceptual system embodied in perceptual and motor systems. (Wilcox and Nogueira Xavier 2013: 88)

References

Albano Leoni, Federico. 2009. *Dei suoni e dei sensi. Il volto fonico delle parole* [Sounds and Senses. The Phonic Face of Words]. Bologna: Il Mulino.

Albano Leoni, Federico. 2022. Some remarks on orality and the antinomy between writing and speaking in western linguistic thought. In Andrea Ercolani & Laura Lulli (eds.), *Rethinking Orality 1: Codification, Transcodification, and Transmission of 'Cultural Messages'*, 52–71. Berlin/Boston: De Gruyter.

Albano Leoni, Federico & Pietro Maturi. 1992. Per una verifica pragmatica dei modelli fonologici [Towards a pragmatic testing of phonological models]. In Giovanni Gobber (ed.), *La linguistica pragmatica* [Pragmatic Linguistics], 39–49. Rome: Bulzoni.

Alibali, Martha, Lucia Flevares & Susan Goldin-Meadow. 1997. Assessing knowledge conveyed in gesture: Do teachers have the upper hand? *Journal of Educational Psychology* 89(1). 183–193.

Arbib, Michael A. 2012. *How the Brain Got Language: The Mirror System Hypothesis*. Oxford: Oxford University Press.

Arbib, Michael A. (ed.). 2020. *How the Brain Got Language – Towards a New Road Map*. Amsterdam/Philadelphia: John Benjamins.

Aristodemo, Valentina & Carlo Geraci. 2017. Visible degrees in Italian Sign Language. *Natural Language & Linguist Theory* 36(3). 685–699. http://doi 10.1007/s11049-017-9389-5

Armstrong, David F. 1999. *Original Signs: Gesture, Sign, and the Sources of Language*. Washington, DC: Gallaudet University Press.

Armstrong, David F., William C. Stokoe & Sherman E. Wilcox. 1995. *Gesture and the Nature of Language*. Cambridge: Cambridge University Press.

Armstrong, David F. & Sherman E. Wilcox. 2007. *The Gestural Origin of Language*. Oxford/New York: Oxford University Press.

Bauman, H-Dirksen L. 2003. Redesigning literature: The cinematic poetics of American Sign Language poetry. *Sign Language Studies* 4(1). 34–47.

Bellugi, Ursula. 1980. Clues from the similarities between signed and spoken language. In Ursula Bellugi & Michael Studdert-Kennedy (eds.), *Signed and Spoken Language: Biological Constraints on Linguistic Form*, 115–140. Weinheim: Verlag Chemie.

Bellugi, Ursula & Edward S. Klima. 1976. Two faces of sign: Iconic and abstract. In Stevan R. Harnad, Horst D. Steklis & Jane Lancaster (eds.), *The Origins and Evolution of Language and Speech*, 514–538. New York: N.Y. Academy of Sciences.

Bellugi, Ursula, Edward S. Klima & Patricia Siple. 1975. Remembering in signs. *Cognition* 3(2). 93–125.

Boyes Braem, Penny. 1981. *Significant Features of the Handshape in American Sign Language*. Berkeley: University of California, Berkeley dissertation.

Boyes Braem, Penny. 1983. Studying sign language dialects. In Virginia Volterra & William Stokoe (eds.), *Sign Language Research '83, Proceedings of the III. International Symposium on Sign Language Research*, 247–253. Silver Spring, MD: Linstok Press.

Boyes Braem, Penny. 2012. Evolving methods for written representations of signed languages of the deaf. In Andrea Ender, Adrian Leemann & Bernhard Wälchli (eds.), *Methods in Contemporary Linguistics*, 411–438. Berlin/Boston: De Gruyter Mouton.

Boyes Braem, Penny & Thüring Bräm. 2000. A pilot study of the expressive gestures used by classical orchestra conductors. In Karen Emmorey & Harlan Lane (eds.), *The Signs of Language Revisited: An Anthology to Honor Ursula Bellugi and Edward Klima*, 143–155. Mahwah, NJ: Lawrence Erlbaum.

Boyes Braem, Penny, Elena Pizzuto & Virginia Volterra. 2002. The interpretation of signs by (hearing and deaf) members of different cultures. In Rolf Schulmeister & Heimo Reinitzer (eds.) 2002. *Progress in Sign Language Research: In Honor of Siegmund Prillwitz*, 187–219. Hamburg: Signum.

Boyes Braem, Penny & Rachel Sutton-Spence (eds.). 2001. *The Hands are the Head of the Mouth*. Hamburg: Signum.

Brennan, Mary. 1990. Productive morphology in British Sign Language: Focus on the role of metaphors. In Siegmund Prillwitz & Tomas Volhaber (eds.), *Current Trends in European Sign Language Research: International Studies on Sign Language and Communication of the Deaf*, 205–228. Hamburg: Signum.

Calbris, Geneviève. 1990. *The Semiotics of French Gestures*. Bloomington: Indiana University Press.

Capirci, Olga, Jana M. Iverson, Elena Pizzuto & Virginia Volterra. 1996. Gestures and words during the transition to two-word speech. *Journal of Child Language* 23(3). 645–673.

Capirci, Olga & Virginia Volterra. 2008. Gesture and speech: The emergence and development of a strong and changing partnership. *Gesture* 8(1). 22–44.

Cattani, Allegra, Caroline Floccia, Evan Kidd, Paola Pettenati, Daniela Onofrio & Virginia Volterra. 2019. Gestures and words in naming: Evidence from crosslinguistic and crosscultural comparison. *Language Learning* 69(3). 709–746. http:// doi: 10.1111/lang.12346.

Cienki, Alan. 2017. *Ten Lectures on Spoken Language and Gesture from the Perspective of Cognitive Linguistics*. Leiden & Boston: Brill.

Cienki, Alan & Cornelia Müller (eds.). 2008. *Metaphor and Gesture*. Amsterdam/Philadelphia: John Benjamins.

Cienki, Alan & Cornelia Müller. 2014. Ways of viewing metaphor in gesture. In Cornelia Müller, Alan Cienki, Ellen Fricke, Silvia Ladewig, David McNeill & Jana Bressem (eds.), *Body –Language – Communication: An International Handbook on Multimodality in Human Interaction. Volume 2*, 1766–1778. Berlin/Boston: De Gruyter Mouton.

Clark, Herbert H. 2016. Depicting as a method of communication. *Psychology Review* 123(3). 324–347. http://doi: 10.1037/rev0000026.

Clark, Herbert H. 2019. Depicting in communication. In Peter Hagoort (ed.), *Human Language: From Genes and Brains to Behavior*, 235–247. Cambridge, MA: MIT Press.

Cogill-Koez, Dorothea. 2000a. Signed language classifier predicates: Linguistic structures or schematic visual representation? *Sign Language & Linguistics* 3(2). 153–207.

Cogill-Koez, Dorothea. 2000b. A model of signed language classifier predicates as templated visual representation. *Sign Language & Linguistics* 3(2). 209–236.

Corazza, Serena & Virginia Volterra. 1988. La comprensione di lingue dei segni straniere [Comprehension of foreign sign languages]. In Tullio De Mauro, Stefano Gensini & Maria Emanuela Piemontese (eds.), *Dalla parte del ricevente: Percezione, comprensione, interpretazione. Atti del XIX Congresso Internazionale SLI*, 73–82. Rome: Bulzoni.

Corballis, Michael C. 2003. *From Hand to Mouth: The Origins of Language*. Princeton/Oxford: Princeton University Press.

Cormier, Kearsy, Sandra Smith & Zed Sevcikova-Sehyr. 2016. Rethinking constructed action. *Sign Language & Linguistics* 18(2). 167–204. https://doi.org/10.1075/sll.18.2.01cor.

Cuccio Valentina & Sabina Fontana. 2013. Metaphor use in sign systems: A two-step model for the understanding of metaphor and metonymy. In Elisabetta Gola & Francesca Ervas (eds.), *Metaphor in Focus: Philosophical Perspectives on Metaphor Use*, 155–179. Newcastle: Cambridge Scholars Publishing.

Cuccio, Valentina & Sabina Fontana. 2017. Embodied simulation and metaphorical gestures. In Francesca Ervas, Elisabetta Gola & Maria Grazia Rossi (eds.), *Metaphor in Communication, Science and Education*, 77–91. Berlin/Boston: De Gruyter Mouton.

Cuxac, Christian. 2000. La Langue des Signes Français (LSF) – *Les voies de l'iconicité. Faits de langues* 15/16. Paris: Ophrys.

Cuxac, Christian & Marie-Anne Sallandre. 2007. Iconicity and arbitrariness in French Sign Language: Highly iconic structures, degenerated iconicity and diagrammatic iconicity. In Elena Pizzuto, Paola Pietrandra & Simone Raffaele (eds.), *Verbal and Signed Languages: Comparing Structures, Constructs and Methodologies*, 13–33. Berlin/New York: Mouton de Gruyter.

De Mauro, Tullio. 2008. *Il linguaggio tra natura e storia* [Language Between Nature and History]. Milano: Mondadori Università.

DeMatteo, Asa. 1977. Visual imagery and visual analogues in American Sign Language. In Lynn A. Friedman (ed.), *On the Other Hand: New Perspectives on American Sign Language*, 109–136. New York: Academic Press.

Deutscher, Guy. 2010. *Through the Language Glass: Why the World Looks Different in Other Languages*. London: Penguin/Random House.

Dingemanse, Mark. 2015. Ideophones and reduplication: Depiction, description, and the interpretation of repeated talk in discourse. *Studies in Language* 39(4). 946–970. http://doi 10.1075/sl.39.4.05din.

Dingemanse, Mark, Damián E. Blasi, Gary Lupyan, Morten H. Christiansen & Padraic Monaghan. 2015. Arbitrariness, iconicity, and systematicity in language. *Trends in Cognitive Science* 19(10). 603–615. http://doi: 10.1016/j.tics.2015.07.013

Dotter, Franz. 2018. Most characteristic elements of sign language texts are intricate mixtures of linguistic and non-linguistic parts, aren't they? *Colloquium: New Philologies* 3(1). 1–62. http://doi:10.23963/cnp.2018.3.1.1

Dudis, Paul G. 2004. Body partitioning and real-space blends. *Cognitive Linguistics* 15(2). 223–238.

Emmorey, Karen & Melissa Herzig. 2003. Categorical versus gradient properties of classifier constructions in ASL. In Karen Emmorey (ed.), *Perspectives on Classifier Constructions in Sign Languages*, 221–246. Mahwah, NJ: Lawrence Erlbaum.

Engberg-Pedersen, Elisabeth. 1993. *Space in Danish Sign Language: The Semantics and Morphosyntax of the Use of Space in a Visual Language*. Hamburg: Signum.

Ferrara, Lindsay & Rolf Piene Halvorsen. 2017. Depicting and describing meanings with iconic signs in Norwegian Sign Language. *Gesture* 16(3). 371–395.

Ferrara, Lindsay and Gabrielle Hodge. 2018. Language as description, indication, and depiction. *Frontiers in Psychology* 9:716. 1–15. http://doi:10.3389/fpsyg.2018.00716

Fontana, Sabina, Serena Corazza, Penny Boyes Braem & Virginia Volterra. 2015. Language research and language community change: Italian Sign Language 1981–2013. *International Journal of Sociolinguistics* 236. 1–30.

Friedman, Lynn A. 1975. Space, time, and person reference in American Sign Language. *Language* 51(4). 940–961.

Frishberg, Nancy. 1975. Arbitrariness and iconicity: Historical changes in American Sign Language. *Language* 51(3). 696–719.

Goldin-Meadow, Susan. 2003. *Hearing Gesture: How Our Hands Help Us Think*. Cambridge, MA: Harvard University Press.

Goldin-Meadow, Susan & Diane Brentari. 2017. Gesture, sign, and language: The coming of age of sign language and gesture studies. *Behavioral and Brain Sci*ence 40:e46. http://doi: 10.1017/S0140525X15001247

Grosso, Barbara. 1997. Gli udenti capiscono i segni dei sordi? [Do hearing people understand the signs of the deaf?]. In Maria Cristina Caselli & Serena Corazza (eds.), *LIS, Studi, esperienze e ricerche sulla Lingua dei Segni in Italia*, 79–86. Pisa: Edizioni Del Cerro.
Haiman, John. 1980. The iconicity of grammar: Isomorphism and motivation. *Language* 56(3). 515–540.
Haiman, John. 1998. The metalinguistics of ordinary language. *Evolution of Communication* 2(1). 117–135.
Haiman, John. 2008. In defense of iconicity. *Cognitive Linguistics* 19(1). 35–48.
Hanke, Thomas & Jakob Storz. 2008. iLex – A database tool for integrating sign language corpus linguistics and sign language lexicography. Poster, 3rd Workshop on the Representation and Processing of Sign Languages, 6th International Conference on Language Resources and Evaluation, LREC 2008, Marrakech. Paris: ELRA.
Hockett, Charles F. 1960. The origin of speech. *Scientific American* 203. 88–111.
Hoemann, Harry W. 1975. The transparency of meaning of sign language gestures. *Sign Language Studies* 7. 151–161.
Iverson, Jana M., Olga Capirci, Virginia Volterra & Susan Goldin-Meadow. 2008. Learning to talk in a gesture-rich world: Early communication in Italian vs. American children. *First Language* 28(2). 164–181.
Jakobson, Roman. 1971. Quest for the essence of language. In *Selected Writings, Vol. 2: Word and Language*. The Hague: Mouton. 345–359.
Janzen, Terry & Barbara Shaffer. 2002. Gesture as the substrate in the process of ASL grammaticization. In Richard P. Meir, Kearsy Cormier & David Quinto-Pozos (eds.), *Modality and Structure in Signed and Spoken Languages*, 199–223. Cambridge: Cambridge University Press.
Janzen, Terry, Barbara Shaffer & Lorraine Leeson. 2016. The proximity of gesture to grammar: Stance-taking in American Sign Language and Irish Sign Language constructions. Symposium on multimodal stance-marking in signed and spoken languages, International Society for Gesture Studies (ISGS) 7, Sorbonne Paris 3, Paris, France, July 18–22, 2016.
Kendon, Adam. 2004. *Gesture: Visible Action as Utterance*. Cambridge: Cambridge University Press.
Kendon, Adam. 2015. Gesture and sign: Utterance uses of visible bodily action. In Keith Allen (ed.), *The Routledge Handbook of Linguistics*, 33–46. London and New York: Routledge. doi/10.4324/9781315718453.ch3
Kendon, Adam. 2017. Languages as semiotically heterogenous systems. *Behavioral and Brain Sciences* 40:e59. doi:10.1017/S0140525X15002940
Konrad, Reiner. 2011. *Die lexikalische Struktur der DGS im Spiegel empirischer Fachgebärdenlexikographie. Zur Integration der Ikonizität in ein korpusbasiertes Lexikonmodell* [The lexical structure of DGS in the mirror of empirical technical terms lexicography: Towards the integration of iconicity in a corpus-based lexicon model]. Tübingen: Narr Verlag.
Kuhn, Jeremy & Valentina Aristodemo. 2017. Pluractionality, iconicity, and scope in French Sign Language. *Semantics & Pragmatics* 10(6). 1–49. https://doi.org/10.3765/sp.10.6.
Langacker, Ronald. 2008. *Cognitive Grammar: A Basic Introduction*. Oxford: Oxford University Press.
Langer, Gabriele. 2005. Bilderzeugungstechniken in der Deutschen Gebärdensprache. [Image Creation Techniques in German Sign Language]. *Das Zeichen* 70. 254–270.
Lepic, Ryan & Corinne Occhino. 2018. A construction morphology approach to sign language analysis. In Geert Booij (ed.), *The Construction of Words: Advances in Construction Morphology*, 141–172. Berlin: Springer.
Liddell, Scott K. 2003. *Grammar, Gesture and Meaning in American Sign Language*. Cambridge: Cambridge University Press.

Magno Caldognetto, Emanuela & Isabella Poggi. 1997. Micro- and macro-bimodality. In Christian Benoît & Ruth Campbell (eds.), *ESCA Workshop on audio-Visual Speech Processing (AVSP'97)*, Rhodes, Greece, September 26–27, 1997. 33–36. https://www.isca-speech.org/archive_open/avsp97/

Mandel, Mark A. 1977. Iconic devices in American Sign Language. In Lynn A. Friedman (ed.), *On the Other Hand: New Perspectives on American Sign Language*, 57–107. New York: Academic Press.

Marentette, Paula, Paola Pettenati, Arianna Bello & Virginia Volterra. 2016. Gesture and symbolic representation in Italian and English-speaking Canadian 2-year-olds. *Child Development* 87(3). 944–961.

McNeill, David. 2012. *How Language Began: Gesture and Speech in Human Evolution*. Cambridge: Cambridge University Press.

McNeill, David. 2014.The emblem as metaphor. In Mandana Seyfeddinipur & Marianne Gullberg (eds.), *From Gesture in Conversation to Visible Action as Utterance: Essays in Honor of Adam Kendon*, 75–94. Amsterdam/Philadelphia: John Benjamins.

Meir, Irit. 2010. Iconicity and metaphor: Constraints on metaphorical extension of iconic forms. *Language* 86(4). 865–896.

Meir, Irit & Arien Cohen. 2018. Metaphor in sign languages. *Frontiers in Psychology* 9:1025. 1–13. doi:10.3389/fpsyg.2018.01025

Meir, Irit, Carol Padden, Mark Aronoff & Wendy Sandler. 2013. Competing iconicities in the structure of languages. *Cognitive Linguistics* 24(2). 309–943. http://doi: 10.1515/cog-2013-0010

Müller, Cornelia. 2018. Gesture and sign: Cataclysmic break or dynamic relations? *Frontiers in Psychology* 9:1651. 1–20. http///doi:10.3389/fpsyg.2018.01651

Müller, Cornelia, Alan Cienki, Ellen Fricke, Silva H. Ladewig, David McNeill & Jana Bressem (eds.). 2014. *Body – Language – Communication: An International Handbook on Multimodality in Human Interaction, Volume 2*. Berlin/Boston: De Gruyter Mouton.

Napoli, Donna Jo. 2017. Iconicity chains in sign languages. In Claire Bowern, Laurence Horn & Raffaella Zanuttini (eds.), *On Looking into Words (and Beyond)*, 517–546. Berlin: Language Science Press.

Newkirk, Don E. 1987. *Architect: Final Version, SignFont Handbook*. San Diego, CA: Emerson & Stern Associates.

Occhino, Corrine, Benjamin Anible, Erin Wilkinson & Jill P. Morford. 2017. Iconicity is in the eye of the beholder: How language experience affects perceived iconicity. *Gesture* 16(1). 99–125.

Occhino, Corrine & Sherman Wilcox. 2017. Gesture or sign? A categorization problem. *Behavioral and Brain Sciences* 40:e66. http://doi:10.1017/S0140525X15001247

Padden, Carol A., So-One Hwang, Ryan Lepic & Sharon Seegers. 2015. Tools for language: Patterned iconicity in sign language nouns and verbs. *Topics in Cognitive Science* 7(1). 81–94. https://doi.org/10.1111/tops.12121

Perniss, Pamela. 2018. Why we should study multimodal language. *Frontiers in Psychology* 9.1109. https://doi.org/10.3389/fpsyg.2018.01109

Perniss, Pamela, Robin L. Thompson & Gabriella Vigliocco. 2010. Iconicity as a general property of language: Evidence from spoken and signed languages. *Frontiers in Psychology* 1.227. 1–15. http://doi: 10.3389/fpsyg.2010.00227

Perniss, Pamela & Gabriella Vigliocco. 2014. The bridge of iconicity: From a world of experience to the experience of language. *Philosophical Transactions of The Royal Society B* 369: 20130300. 1–13. http://doi: 10.1098/rstb.2013.0300

Perniss, Pamela, Asli Özyürek & Gary Morgan. 2015. The influence of the visual modality on language structure and conventionalization: Insights form sign language and gesture. *Topics in Cognitive Science* 7(1). 2–11. http://doi: 10.1111/tops.12127

Pettenati, Paola, Kazuki Sekine, Elena Congestrì & Virginia Volterra. 2012. A comparative study on representational gestures in Italian and Japanese children. *Journal of Nonverbal Behavior* 36(2). 149–164. http://doi: 10.1007/s10919-011-0127-0

Petitta, Giulia, Alessio Di Renzo, Isabella Chiari & Paolo Rossini. 2013. Sign language representation: New approaches to the study of Italian Sign language (LIS). In Laurence Meurant, Aurélie Sinte, Mieke Van Herreweghe & Myriam Vermeerbergen (eds.), *Sign Language Research, Uses and Practices: Crossing Views on Theoretical and Applied Sign Language Linguistics*, 137–158. Boston/Berlin: De Gruyter Mouton and Nijmegen: Ishara Press.

Pietrandrea, Paola & Tommaso Russo. 2007. Diagrammatic and imagic hypoicons in signed and verbal languages. In Elena Pizzuto, Paola Pietrandrea & Raffaele Simone (eds.), *Verbal and Signed Languages: Comparing Structures, Constructs and Methodologies*, 35–56. Berlin/New York: Mouton De Gruyter.

Pizzuto, Elena & Virginia Volterra. 2000. Iconicity and transparency in sign languages: A cross-linguistic cross-cultural view. In Karen Emmorey & Harlan Lane (eds.), *The Signs of Language Revisited: An Anthology to Honor Ursula Bellugi and Edward Klima*, 261–286. Mahwah, NJ: Lawrence Erlbaum.

Pizzuto, Elena, Paolo Rossini & Tommaso Russo. 2006. Representing signed languages in written form: Questions that need to be posed. In Chiara Vettori (ed.), *Proceedings of the 2nd Workshop on the Representation and Processing of Sign Languages, LREC-2006*, 1–6. Pisa: ILC-CNR.

Prillwitz, Siegmund & Heiko Zienert. 1990. Hamburg Notation System for sign language: Development of a sign writing with computer application. In Siegmund Prillwitz & Tomas Vollhaber (eds.), *Current Trends in European Sign Language Research*, 355–379. Hamburg: Signum.

Reilly, Judy & Diane Anderson. 2002. FACES: The acquisition of non-manual morphology in ASL. In Gary Morgan & Bencie Woll (eds.), *Directions in Sign Language Acquisition*, 159–181. Amsterdam/Philadelphia: John Benjamins.

Rinaldi, Pasquale, Maria Cristina Caselli, Tommaso Lucioli, Luca Lamano & Virginia Volterra. 2018. Sign language skills assessed through a sentence reproduction task. *Journal of Deaf Studies and Deaf Education* 23(4). 408–421. https://doi.org/10.1093/deafed/eny021

Russo, Tommaso. 2004. Iconicity and productivity in sign language discourse: An analysis of three LIS discourse registers. *Sign Language Studies* 4(2). 164–197.

Russo, Tommaso. 2008. Metaphors in sign languages and in co-verbal gesturing. *Gesture* 8(1). 62–81.

Ruth-Hirrel, Laura & Sherman Wilcox. 2018. Speech-gesture constructions in cognitive grammar: The case of beats and points. *Cognitive Linguistics* 29(3). 453–493. https://doi.org/10.1515/cog-2017-0116

Sandler, Wendy. 2018. The body as evidence for the nature of language. *Frontiers in Psychology* 9:1782. http://doi: 10.3389/fpsyg.2018.01782

Schembri, Adam, Caroline Jones & Denis Burnham. 2005. Comparing action gestures and classifier verbs of motion: Evidence from Australian Sign Language, Taiwan Sign Language, and nonsigners' gestures without speech. *Journal of Deaf Studies and Deaf Education* 10(3). 272–290. https://doi.org/10.1093/deafed/eni029

Schembri, Adam, Jordan Fenlon, Kearsy Cormier & Trevor Johnston. 2018. Sociolinguistic typology and sign language. *Frontiers in Psychology* 9:200. https://doi.org/10.3389/fpsyg.2018.00200

Singleton, Jenny L., Susan Goldin-Meadow & David McNeill. 1995. The cataclysmic break between gesticulation and sign: Evidence against a unified continuum of gestural communication. In Karen Emmorey & Judy Reilly (eds.), *Language, Gesture, and Space*, 287–311. Hillsdale, NJ: Lawrence Erlbaum.

Slobin, Dan I. 1987. Thinking for speaking. *Proceedings of the Thirteenth Annual Meeting of the Berkeley Linguistics Society (1987)*. 435–445.

Slobin, Dan I. 2006. Issues of linguistic typology in the study of sign language development of deaf children. In Brenda Schick, Marc Marschark & Patricia Elizabeth Spencer (eds.), *Advances in the Sign Language Development of Deaf Children*, 20–45. Oxford: Oxford University Press.

Slobin, Dan I. 2008. Breaking the molds: Signed languages and the nature of human language. *Sign Language Studies* 8(2). 114–130.

Slobin, Dan I. 2013. Typology and channel of communication: Where do signed languages fit in? In Balthasar Bickel, Lenore A. Grenoble, David A. Peterson & Alan Timberlake (eds.), *Language Typology and Historical Contingency: In Honor of Johanna Nichols*, 47–67. Amsterdam/Philadelphia: John Benjamins.

Slobin, Dan I., Nini Hoiting, Michelle Anthony, Yael Biederman, Marlon Kuntze, Reyna Lindert, Jennie Pyers, Helen Thumann & Amy Weinberg. 2001. Sign language transcription at the level of meaning components: The Berkeley Transcription System (BTS). *Sign Language & Linguistics* 4(1/2). 63–104.

Slobin, Dan I., Nini Hoiting, Marlon Kuntze, Reyna Lindert, Amy Weinberg, Jennie Pyers, Michelle Anthony, Yael Biederman & Helen Thumann. 2003. A cognitive/functional perspective on the acquisition of "classifiers". In Karen Emmorey (ed.), *Perspectives on Classifier Constructions in Sign Languages*, 271–296. Mahwah, NJ: Lawrence Erlbaum.

Slonimska, Anita, Asli Öyzürek & Olga Capirci. 2020. The role of iconicity and simultaneity for efficient communication: The case of Italian Sign Language (LIS). *Cognition* 200:104246. 1–20. http://dx.doi.org/10.1075/tsl.104.02slo

Sparaci, Laura & Virginia Volterra. 2017. Hands shaping communication: From gestures to signs. In Marta Bertolaso & Nicola Di Stefano (eds.), The *Hand: Perception, Cognition, Action*, 29–54. Cham, Switzerland: Springer.

Stokoe, William C. 1960. *Sign Language Structure: An Outline of the Visual Communication Systems of the American Deaf. Studies in Linguistics, Occasional Papers 8*. Buffalo: New York.

Stokoe, William C. 1991. Semantic phonology. *Sign Language Studies* 71. 107–114.

Supalla, Ted. 1986. The classifier system in America Sign Language. In Colette Craig (ed.), *Noun Classes and Categorization*, 181–214. Amsterdam/Philadelphia: John Benjamins.

Sutton-Spence, Rachel. 2005. *Analysing Sign Language Poetry*. Houndmills: Palgrave Macmillan.

Sutton-Spence, Rachel & Penny Boyes Braem. 2013. Comparing the products and the processes of creating sign language poetry and pantomimic improvisations. *Journal of Nonverbal Behavior* 37(4). 245–280. http://doi 10.1007/s10919-013-0160-2

Taub, Sarah. 2001. *Language From the Body: Iconicity and Metaphor in American Sign Language*. Cambridge: Cambridge University Press.

Tetel Andresen, Julie. 2014. *Linguistics and Evolution: A Developmental Approach*. Cambridge: Cambridge University Press.

Tomasuolo, Elena, Chiara Bonsignori, Pasquale Rinaldi & Virginia Volterra. 2020. The representation of action in Italian Sign Language. *Cognitive Linguistics* 31(1). 1–36.

van der Hulst, Harry. 2022. The (early) history of sign language phonology. In B. Elan Dresher & Harry van der Hulst (eds.), *The Oxford History of Phonology*, 284–306. Oxford: Oxford University Press.

van der Hulst, Harry & Rachel Channon. 2010. Notation systems. In Diane Brentari (ed.), *Sign Languages*, 151–172. Cambridge: Cambridge University Press.

Volterra, Virginia, Maria Cristina Caselli, Olga Capirci & Elena Pizzuto. 2005. Gesture and the emergence and development of language. In Michael Tomasello & Dan I. Slobin (eds.), *Beyond Nature-Nurture: Essays in Honor of Elizabeth Bates*, 3–40. Mahwah, NJ: Lawrence Erlbaum.

Volterra, Virginia, Olga Capirci, Maria Cristina Caselli, Pasquale Rinaldi & Laura Sparaci. 2017. Developmental evidence for continuity from action to gesture to sign/word. *Language, Interaction and Acquisition* 8(1). 13–41.

Volterra, Virginia, Olga Capirci, Pasquale Rinaldi & Laura Sparaci. 2018. From action to spoken and signed language through gesture: Some basic issues for a discussion on the evolution of the human language-ready brain. *Interaction Studies*. 19(1-2). 216–238.

Volterra, Virginia, Maria Roccaforte, Alessio Di Renzo & Sabina Fontana. 2019. *Descrivere la lingua dei segni italiana. Una prospettiva cognitiva e sociosemiotica* [Describing Italian Sign language: A Cognitive and Sociosemiotic Perspective]. Bologna: Il Mulino.

Volterra, Virginia, Maria Roccaforte, Alessio di Renzo and Sabina Fontana. 2022. *Italian Sign Language from a Cognitive and Socio-Semiotic Perspective: Implications for a General Language Theory*. Amsterdam/Philadelphia: John Benjamins.

Wilbur, Ronnie B. 2000. Phonological and prosodic layering of nonmanuals in American Sign Language. In Karen Emmorey & Harlan Lane (eds.), *The Signs of Language Revisited: An Anthology to Honor Ursula Bellugi and Edward Klima*, 215–244. Mahwah, NJ: Lawrence Erlbaum.

Wilcox, Phyllis. 1993. *Metaphorical Mapping in American Sign Language*. Albuquerque, New Mexico: University of New Mexico dissertation.

Wilcox, Phyllis Perrin. 2000. *Metaphor in American Sign Language*. Washington, DC: Gallaudet University Press.

Wilcox, Phyllis Perrin. 2004. A cognitive key: Metonymic and metaphorical mappings in ASL. *Cognitive Linguistics* 15(2). 197–222.

Wilcox, Phyllis Perrin. 2007. Constructs of the mind: Cross-linguistic contrast of metaphor in spoken and signed languages. In Elena Pizzuto, Paola Pietrandrea & Raffaele Simone (eds.), *Verbal and Signed Languages: Comparing Structures, Constructs and Methodologies*, 251–272. Berlin/New York: Mouton de Gruyter.

Wilcox, Sherman. 2004a. Gesture and language: Cross-linguistic and historical data from signed languages. *Gesture* 4(1). 43–73. https://doi.org/10.1075/gest.4.1.04wil

Wilcox, Sherman. 2004b. Cognitive iconicity: Conceptual spaces, meaning, and gesture in signed languages. *Cognitive Linguistics* 15(2). 119–147.

Wilcox, Sherman. 2007. Routes from gesture to language. In Elena Pizzuto, Paola Pietrandrea & Raffaele Simone (eds.), *Verbal and Signed Languages: Comparing Structures, Constructs and Methodologies*, 107–131. Berlin/New York: Mouton de Gruyter.

Wilcox, Sherman. 2009. Symbol and symptom: Routes from gesture to signed language. *Annual Review of Cognitive Linguistics* 7. 89–110.

Wilcox, Sherman & Corrine Occhino. 2017. Signed languages. In Barbara Dancygier (ed.), *The Cambridge Handbook of Cognitive Linguistics*, 99–117. Cambridge: Cambridge University Press.

Wilcox, Sherman, Paolo Rossini & Elena Antinoro Pizzuto. 2010. Grammaticalization in sign languages. In Diane Brentari (ed.), *Sign languages*, 332–354. Cambridge: Cambridge University Press.

Wilcox, Sherman & Phyllis Wilcox. 1995. The gestural expression of modality in ASL. In Joan Bybee & Suzanne Fleischman (eds.), *Modality in Grammar and Discourse*, 135–162. Amsterdam/Philadelphia: John Benjamins.

Wilcox, Sherman & André Nogueira Xavier. 2013. A framework for unifying spoken language, signed language and gesture. *Revista Todas as Letras* 15(1). 88–110.

Woodward, James & Carol Erting. 1975. Synchronic variation and historical change in American Sign Language. *Language Sciences* 37. 9–12.

Elena Antinoro Pizzuto and Brigitte Garcia

Coming back to the issue of the graphic representation of signed language discourse in signed language linguistics

1 Introduction

The graphic representation of discourse in signed language linguistics[1] has been the unifying theme of the deaf and hearing team, the Sign Language Laboratory (SLL), which Elena Antinoro Pizzuto created at the ISTC-CNR in Rome in the early 2000s, and daily animated for a decade. She insisted that the work of the SLL, in particular that of its deaf members, who were striving to provide Italian Sign Language (Lingua dei Segni Italiana, or LIS) with a written form, had been the crucible of her reflections on these subjects. May this team be thus fully associated with the contents developed here.[2]

This chapter is based on this team's works, as well as the numerous discussions held between the authors, and the writings of the second author. We shared the ideas presented here to such an extent that the "we" used in this paper is no convenience of writing; it is deeply implicated. The second author however takes full responsibility for the wording and would like to specify that, given the developments in the field over the last ten years, updating the content is of course hers alone.

The growing number of projects aiming at creating "modern" signed language corpora, especially since the early 2000s, has given rise to many debates, mainly methodological. In these debates, two issues have most often been overlooked, namely the question of the medium used as a basis for the representation of signed language discourse—the written form of the spoken language—and, loosely

---

1 We warmly thank the editors Terry Janzen and Barbara Shaffer, as well as our three reviewers.
2 That is, Paolo Rossini, Alessio Di Renzo, Gabriele Gianfreda, Luca Lamano, Tommaso Lucioli, Barbara Pennachi, Fabrizzio Borgia, Claudia Savina Bianchini and Giulia Petitta. Also associated are those who collaborated with Elena Antinoro Pizzuto in key publications linked to the issues addressed here: Tommaso Russo, Paola Pietrandrea, Isabella Chiari, Christian Cuxac, Marie-Anne Sallandre, and Erin Wilkinson.

Elena Antinoro Pizzuto, ISTC-CNR Roma, Italy
Brigitte Garcia, UMR 7023 SFL (University Paris 8 & CNRS), France, e-mail: Brigitte.garcia@univ-paris8.fr

https://doi.org/10.1515/9783110703788-003

related, the question of transcription (as opposed to annotation). The objective here is to expose at least some of the facets of these nodal questions.

We begin by pointing out the atypical nature of the most common representations of signed language discourse, i.e., the "gloss-based annotations" in Section 2. We then expose the following paradox: despite the unique situation of signed languages in relation to writing, the question of transcription is rarely addressed by signed language linguists, while it remains an issue on its own in spoken language linguistics, in Section 3. Next, in Section 4, we discuss the biases linked to these most common graphic practices, and especially the epistemological circularity they reveal. We finally describe the experiment on SignWriting conducted within the SLL for more than ten years in Section 5, before concluding (Section 6).

2 Common graphic representations in signed language linguistics: an atypical procedure

Pizzuto and Pietrandrea (2001) question very head-on the common graphic practices in signed language linguistics, which are presented as "annotations" of discourse. They demonstrate how these practices are, at the very least, atypical, compared to those prevailing in spoken language linguistics. Indeed, for spoken languages, there are two successive levels of graphic representation. First, there is transcription, that is, a primary graphic representation of the signifying form of the utterance, through a (more or less adapted) orthographic standard (provided the studied language has a written form) or through the International Phonetic Alphabet (IPA). Second, there is annotation, which uses a written form of a spoken language (the linguist's spoken language or an international spoken language, primarily English), the function of which is to express linguistic analysis of the signifying forms, for which the transcription has provided a representation. What is labeled *annotation* is thus dependent on the prior existence of a representation to which it relates.

The following example, adapted from Givón (1978: 327), illustrates these practices. This is an utterance from a Rwandan corpus, transcribed and then annotated through glosses and abbreviations (specific to the particular linguistic analysis).
1. umugabo, nhi-ya-mu-boonye [=forms of the language]
2. man, NEG-he-him-saw [=gloss and annotation by the researcher]
3. 'The man, he didn't see him' DEF, TOP [=translation and annotation][3]

---

[3] This line includes two abbreviations that imply linguistic categories not discussed here: DEF (definite) and TOP (topicalization).

In spoken language linguistics, transcription can fulfill various functions. In linguistic work on a discourse corpus, transcription is used to bring out the elements relevant to the analysis, according to the intended purpose and level of detail required. In this case, transcription has an obvious heuristic value, as it is the only way to identify regularities in a large corpus. This is the essence of Slobin et al.'s (2001: 64) words:

> The most basic aim of every system of notation of behavior is to help researchers see patterns in the data—that is, to facilitate their human pattern-recognition devices. The task of transcription and subsequent data summaries is to present information in various forms, so that one may identify regularities that may not be evident while directly observing the behavior in question.

But for any linguist, transcription also serves to communicate with the research community. Its purpose is thus to render visible the linguistic description itself—the correlations the researcher established between elements of form (transcription) and linguistic values (annotation)—thereby rendering them available for questions and evaluation. In order to enable effective communication with the research community, transcription must allow an acceptable reconstruction of the signifying form of the utterance under analysis.

The key point Pizzuto and Pietrandrea (2001) highlight is that in signed language linguistics, unlike spoken language linguistics, the first level of representation is directly the sequence of words from the surrounding spoken language. Figure 1 below provides an illustration of this type of graphic representation. This is an extract from the typological study of signed languages proposed by Zeshan (2008: 684; her examples (5a–c)).

```
1.   IX1 CHILD-pl EXIST
2.   'I have children.'

1.   IX1 CHILD-pl THREE
2.   'I have three children.' (lit. 'My children are three.')

                    y/n
1.   IX2 CHILD-pl EXIST?
2.   'Do you have children?'
```

Figure 1: Example of Zeshan's (2008: 684) transcription of an utterance in Indo-Pakistani Sign Language.

However, such sequences of spoken language words cannot be claimed to have the status of a transcription, as they do not enable the reconstruction of the signifying form of the data. As a result, these conventions do not make visible the correlation the linguist has established between a particular aspect of the signal and its linguistic value: that is the point. This graphic reality cannot be considered as annotation either, since annotation is intended to apply to an initial representation of the signifying form of the data. Neither corresponding to what, for spoken languages is considered a transcription, nor to what is defined as an annotation, their status appears to be hybrid at best.

Signed languages are languages for which no written form has ever emerged in a way comparable to what was for spoken languages the (very) progressive constitution of written language, based on diverse writing systems (see among others, Olson 1998). Almost all signed language notation systems in the last 50 years are derived from William Stokoe's first modern proposal (e.g., Miller 2001). They are mono-linear systems,[4] showing manual aspects of the visual signifying form of decontextualized lexical signs. Their inability to provide a valid representation of signed language discourse was soon taken for granted by signed language linguists (e.g., Stokoe 1987; Johnston 1991; Miller 2001), therefore leading to so-called "gloss-based notation". What is noteworthy is that the atypicality of this practice has not been seen as problematic, with the exception of the Miller (2001) article. This is all the more surprising since, as far as spoken languages are concerned, the issue of transcription still produces many publications. The following section discusses this point.

3 Transcription of signed language discourse: an oddly minimized question

3.1 Spoken language linguistics: Transcription as an issue in its own right

Of course, in spoken language linguistics, no naivety is conceivable regarding the idea of a neutral transcription. A multitude of works has addressed this topic, particularly since Ochs' (1979) seminal work. Spoken language linguists know that any transcription rests on choices regarding the material to be transcribed and the methods of transcription, choices based partly on the transcriber's theoretical hypotheses and partly on the specific analytical foci. Other factors are involved,

---

[4] SignWriting is exceptional with respect to mono-linearity (Sutton 1999). The next two sections address only specialized notations that have been used in signed language linguistics, which is not the case for SignWriting. Section 5 addresses this system in more detail.

which remove any illusion of neutrality, such as the involuntary filtering of data based on semantic prevalence. This aspect is emphasized by Antinoro Pizzuto, Chiari and Rossini (2008: 151), following Chiari (2007): "Transcribers' errors are, to a certain extent, unavoidable, following regular patterns of substitution, deletion, insertion and inversion typically semantically-driven." In addition to this prevalence of meaning, the filtering of data comes from the fact that the transcribing linguist, as a scholar, is specifically conditioned by the written language, which strongly influences what he or she "believes" to be hearing (e.g., Pontecorvo 1997; Blanche-Benveniste 1997, 2000).

The issue of transcription took on a particular significance among spoken language linguists aiming at working on oral data *per se* (e.g., Halliday 1985; Blanche-Benveniste 1997). These linguists face the paradox of having to account for the structures and segmentations of oral forms while resorting to written forms. This is the case with standard spelling, which therefore requires a series of adjustments, raising the question of transcription standards. This is also the case with the IPA and other phonetic transcription systems. Far from being reflections of a phonetic reality, these systems would probably not have been historically possible (or even operational) if they had not inherited alphabetic writing systems. This is shown by various early, and more recent, works that have questioned the phonetic nature of these transcription systems. According to them, these systems derive rather from the segmentations imposed by the letters, themselves conditioned by the phonological structure of the (few) particular languages for which these alphabets were originally forged (see, for example, Lüdtke 1969; Cao 1985; Manfrellotti 2001; Port 2007). IPA transcription poses other types of problems, notably the readibility of large corpora, which explains their use of standard spelling. These various issues are currently under discussion, especially in the context of the development of multimedia annotation software and annotation schemes (see Antinoro Pizzuto, Chiari and Rossini 2008: 151–153).

The discussions have expanded with the emergence of more specific work focusing on analysis of interactions and, more broadly, capturing the multimodality of direct face-to-face communication in spoken languages (e.g., Mondada 2008). In this domain in particular, annotation methods are treated as an issue *per se*, that first requires the transcription of co-speech gesture. It should be noted that the transcription of co-speech gestures would also benefit from improvements in transcribing signed languages.

Finally, two points should be underlined concerning the transcription and annotation of spoken language corpora. First, the principle of distinguishing transcription and annotation remains undisputed, especially for rare and under-described spoken language corpora (e.g., Mettouchi, Vanhove and Caubet 2015). Second, in spoken language linguistics, problems related to transcription are still frequently addressed: the impact the selected transcription software has on the image of the data; the processing conventions of existing systems and their limits; the principles of segmentation and delimitation of units to different levels of analysis (and many others, Gadet 2017; Mondada 2008).

Yet, spoken language transcription manages to some extent to fulfil the functions described above, which are the basis of the linguistic description. For phonetic aspects, at the very least, it enables indeed an acceptable reconstruction of the signifying form of the data examined. This is possible only since the systems of transcription benefit from a long history of adjustment between audio-vocal and visual-graphic modalities, proven over the centuries for all types of spoken languages. Above all, they benefit from the deep assimilation of their language graphic representations by speakers from writing societies (to which linguists clearly belong).

Since signed languages do not have such a long specific written tradition, transcribers do not have the benefit of such experience in matching visuo-gestural and visual-graphic modalities. This is the main difference between signed and spoken languages—including those without a written form—and what makes signed languages unique with respect to writing (see Garcia 1997, 2010). In light of this uniqueness, it is paradoxical that the question of transcription has generated so little discussion in signed language linguistics, as we will see next.

3.2 Transcription in signed language linguistics: A dodged or (considered) outdated issue

The attempts to develop specialized notation systems were essentially limited to the 1970s and 1980s and they only rarely attest a semio-graphic creativity.[5] Even the number of studies addressing methodological and epistemological questions raised by the "gloss" principle is quite limited (e.g., Friedman 1977; Stokoe 1991; Johnston 1991; Jouison 1995; Brennan 1990, 2001; Cuxac 1996, 2000; Garcia 1997, 2016; Pizzuto and Pietrandrea 2001 and related articles by Antinoro Pizzuto and her team; Slobin 2006, 2013; Slobin et al. 2001; Leeson 2008). Moreover, these scarce reflections have generated little response from signed language linguists, and even less debate about practices. Aside from a very few exceptions, the question of signed language discourse transcription has not been raised in recent years, despite the rapid development of large machine-readable signed language corpora. If it is brought up, it is to cast doubt on its significance: transcription can be presented as

---

5 On the latter two aspects, an exception is the work done this past decade around the Typannot transcription system (e.g., Doan et al. 2019). See also the very promising proposal by Filhol (2020).

an outdated issue for signed language research, given the recent possibilities for the representation and treatment of data and annotations provided by advanced technologies. Thus, the integration of video data with annotation frames in tools such as ELAN and especially the possibility to synchronize the annotations with the video signal would render superfluous any need for a transcription of the signifying form (e.g., Johnston 2001, 2010, 2019). Johnston (2019: 6) thus writes:

> Multi-media annotation software makes it is possible to gain instant and unambiguous access to the actual form of the signs being annotated—the raw data of the video recording—because annotations and media are time aligned. Provided there are spoken or written documentary recordings of a language which are available and accessible to the researcher, this eliminates the necessity for linguists to transcribe language data first before they are able to share data or commence a range of investigations into the lexicon and grammar.

Indubitably, the integration of video and the possibility of synchronizing annotations directly to the video signal have been a major step forward for both spoken and signed languages. Nevertheless, understanding this point as an argument against transcription indicates a confusion of its proper functions (as noted in 1 above) with those of the video signal. As stated by Mondada (2008: 79, translation and emphasis ours):

> [. . .] loin de remplacer [l'enregistrement], la transcription n'a de sens qu'autant qu'elle y renvoie comme instance de vérification, *et qu'elle en permet une consultation outillée*. La transcription et l'enregistrement s'éclairent en effet mutuellement : *la première permet un accès au second qui en augmente l'intelligibilité et l'analysibilité* ; le second donne à la première son caractère d'évidence.

> [. . .] far from replacing [the recording], transcription has no meaning aside from a verification, *and allowing equipped consultation*. Transcription and recording clarify each other: *the first allows access to the second, which adds intelligibility and analyzability*; the second establishes the evidential nature of the first.

What spoken language linguist would be satisfied with an audio or audiovisual recording as a substitute for transcription? Moreover, in these modern "machine-readable" corpora, requests do not operate on the recorded signal. Consequently, these recordings are not the basis for the analyses and generalizations that anchor or validate linguistic modeling. In addition, the uniqueness of signed language rests on the multi-linearity of the signifying form: how then can the form-meaning correlations be clearly established between the video signal and the information in the annotations? The function of the integrated video signal, however important, is quite distinct to that of a transcription.

Another way to avoid the question of transcription is to alter it. Thus, the true question would not be that of the spoken language "gloss" as such (the only solution due to the absence of a satisfactory transcription system) but its "consistency", i.e., the internal coherence of the tags used to gloss (e.g., Johnston 2008, 2019). Consistency of glosses necessitates that the language be subjected to a lemmatization process, which requires the establishment of a consistent lexical database constituted by the systematic assignment of so-called ID-glosses[6] to lemmas. The need for such lemmatization is undeniable. However, one must first ask *what is first taken into consideration* in the elaboration of such lemmatization, that is what is retained by/in these gloss-based annotations. This is what is at stake in the next two sections.

3.3 The main limitations of "word-tags" . . .

Pizzuto and Pietrandrea (2001) list many biases, generated by labeling conventional signs using the researcher's spoken language (or an international spoken language), that affect both the representation and the analysis. The central problem is the exogenic segmentation imposed by the use of a written spoken language both on the form level and the sense level, since signed language, like any other language, has its own organizational principles, with no necessary correspondence to the words of the surrounding spoken language. Moreover, as pointed out by the authors, the segmentation differs depending on whether the annotation is in Italian or in English, for example. In addition, the annotated signed language unit is overlaid with morphosyntactic information associated with the spoken language word (e.g., category, inflection), which may also differ depending on the annotation language.

Cuxac (1996, 2000: 319–327) highlighted the same biases. In his pioneering linguistic analysis of French Sign Language (langue des signes française, or LSF), based on a large discourse corpus recorded in situ, he endeavoured to make its linguistic description explicit, a demand that led him to develop an original procedure. For the same reasons as the others, he avoided using existing specialized notations. Moreover, having taken into account all manual and non-manual parameters from the outset, he was one of the first to opt for a multi-linear representation, long before the invention of annotation software. Cuxac's transcription system provides one line for each of the following parameters: right hand (MD),[7] both hands (D et G),

---

6 According to Johnston (2019: 13), who pioneered the use of this term for signed language corpora: "It is imperative that signed units of the same type are consistently and uniquely identified: each token of a type should have the same identifying gloss which is unique to that type. A gloss which uniquely identifies a lexical sign is called an ID-gloss."
7 The abbreviations in parentheses (MD, MG, etc.) are those that appear in the first column of Figure 2. These abbreviations refer to the French "main droite", "droite et gauche", "main gauche", "corps", "visage", "regard", and "mimique faciale" respectively.

left hand (MG), body (C), face (V), gaze (R) and facial expression (MF), as shown in Figure 2. On this basis, he disassociated the notation of those elements he considered relevant (i.e., the transcription) from the notation of the meaning or linguistic values he assigned them, that is, strictly speaking, the annotation in the bottom half of Figure 2. This led him to a four-level graphic representation: (i) notation of functional elements considered pertinent; (ii) the linguistic value and meaning associated with each retained and numbered element; (iii) an "approximate translation" of the established meaning, each element retrieved through the numbering in (ii); (iv) a literal translation in French, as close as possible to the "approximate translation". Figure 2 below shows the notation of the first three seconds of the corpus under consideration. The conventions of notation (for (i) as well as for (ii)) are of course multiple and extremely precise and it is not possible to state them in detail here.[8] By way of illustration, here is the way it works for the elements noted as "1" and "2" in Figure 2. "1. Interaction avec le public" ['Interaction with the public] is coded by the absence of any indication on line R (eye gaze) in Figure 2: by convention indeed, the gaze directed towards the addressee is coded by a non-indication. "2. POINT modalo énonciatif" refers to what, on the MD line (right hand), is transcribed as "Pointage" ['Pointing sign']. This type of pointing at the very beginning of an interaction, which is characterized by a weakly extended index finger directed towards the addressee, is regularly associated with a phatic value. Thus, 1, which simply initiates taking the floor by means of the shared gaze, is rendered literally by the interjection "Eh bien" ['Well'], and the phatic value of 2 is translated by "disons que" ['let's say']. Another point to emphasize is the distinction that is made between lexical units, noted in small capitals between square brackets,[9] and non-conventional units, noted in lower case (see "borne temporelle", 'temporal milestone'). The dotted lines in the upper half of the figure indicate maintaining the formal element noted, whether it is gaze (IX............I)[10] or, in the example of the time bound, handshape.

As the author notes, phase (i) runs parallel to the limits of using spoken language "glosses", and does not enable a reconstruction of the signifying form of the data described. The author highlights that the image given of a signed language through these methods is necessarily distorted, even for a careful linguist, and that the risks of a biased analysis remain. Yet the point is that this particularly time-consuming

---

8 For detailed conventions, see Cuxac (2000: 319–327).
9 This is the case for [REVENIR EN ARRIÈRE] ('go backwards').
10 "X" means that the gaze is directed (cataphorically) toward locus X, in this case the location where the handshape that marks the "temporal boundary" (in this case the I-proform) is to be performed (deictic function of the gaze).

four-step procedure fulfills an essential function of transcription, namely *the explicitness of the descriptive work* through the distinction and correlation that is made between (i) and (ii).

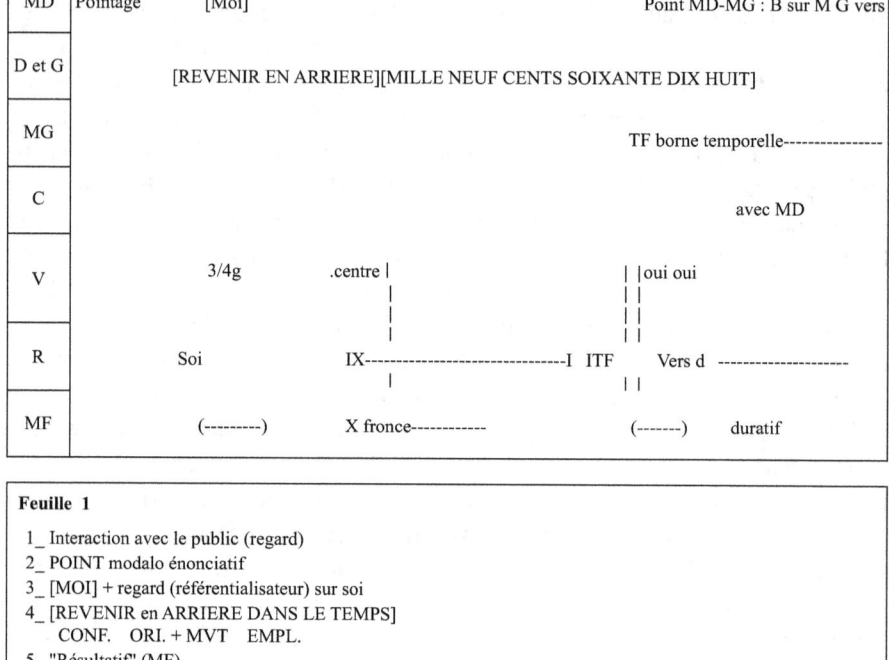

Figure 2: Transcription and annotation used by Cuxac (2000: 328–329).

Slobin et al. (2001: 66) similarly list the risks associated with the use of spoken language words, and more generally deplore what Slobin (2008: 123) called "the tyranny of glossing". They conclude as follows: "[...] on the linguistic level, it all too often leads the analyst to treat the sign language in terms of the written language used in glossing, rather than in its own terms". Their alternative proposal, the Berkeley Transcription System (BTS), is a mono-linear graphic symbolization, on the morpheme rather than the sign level. The BTS, originally designed for ASL and NGT (Nederlandse Gebarentaal, or Sign Language of the Netherlands), and related to the CHILDES system (MacWhinney 2000), aims to enable the transcription of all signed languages. Slobin provides a particularly interesting illustration of the BTS, that of a morphologically complex ASL sign whose approximate meaning is 'walk forward': Pm'TL-pst'ERC-pthF-mvt'WIG. This sign is considered as made up of four parts, "[t]he system uses what we call a property marker (what has misleadingly come to be called a 'classifier' in sign language linguistics), abbreviated TL for 'two legs.' This property marker is in a particular posture, abbreviated ERC for 'erect.' There is a path, indicated by F for 'forward.' There is also an internal movement indicated by WIG for 'wiggling'" (Slobin 2008: 123).

The principle of approaching notation directly through meaning, starting at the morpheme level, is a particularly relevant way of avoiding the filtering induced by the use of spoken language written words. It seems to us, however, that the BTS is not a transcription in the sense that we have specified above. It is rather a coding that mixes morphological categories proposed by the linguist (like Pm, in this example, meaning property marker) with partial articulatory descriptions of manual parametric components (like ERC or WIG). Most critically, as argued by Antinoro Pizzuto, Chiari and Rossini (2010: 16): "Since the forms of the language are NOT represented, there is no way to assess the appropriateness of the analyses performed. In other words, the description provided is, in a deep sense, unfalsifiable."

The fact is that word-tags (ID-glosses or not), which map a lexical/conventional signed language sign to a spoken language written word, remain the backbone of the most common signed language annotations. Only a few authors (e.g., Johnston 2008, 2010, 2019; Pizzuto and Pietrandrea 2001; Pizzuto, Rossini, and Russo 2006; Brennan 2001; Cuxac 1996, 2000; Slobin et al. 2001; Slobin 2008) have pointed out the issues raised by the annotation of what is not a "conventional unit", i.e., complex non-conventional constructions, currently termed as "classifier constructions", "productive signs" or "depicting signs" on the one hand, and "role shifts" or "constructed action/dialogue", on the other. These non-conventional constructions cannot simply be mapped onto a single spoken language word, or even sequences of two or three words. This topic is discussed below.

4 ... And highlighting a problematic epistemological circularity

Two main epistemological perspectives have existed in signed language linguistics nearly since its establishment, which some have described as "assimilationist" versus "non-assimilationist" (Vermeerbergen 2006; and for discussion, Pizzuto, Pietrandrea, and Simone 2007; Cuxac and Antinoro Pizzuto 2010; Garcia and Sallandre 2014). The "assimilationist" perspective, which has long been largely dominant, has focused explicitly on types of data or features that suggest that signed languages and spoken languages are fundamentally not typologically different. The "non-assimilationist" approach prevailed in the description of LSF carried out within the theoretical framework now known as the "Semiological Approach" (e.g., Cuxac 1985, 1999; Cuxac and Sallandre 2007; Cuxac and Antinoro Pizzuto 2010; Garcia and Sallandre 2014, 2020), as well as in the study of LIS (Russo 2004, 2005; Pizzuto 2007; Antinoro Pizzuto, Chiari and Rossini 2008), and is also found in the study of other signed languages, in somehow different theoretical frameworks (among others, Friedman 1977; Brennan 1992, 2001; Armstrong, Stokoe and Wilcox 1995; Wilcox 2004; Wilcox and Janzen 2004; Occhino 2017).

A central point is precisely, depending on the perspective adopted, the difference in treatment of the above-mentioned non-conventional units. The currently dominant perspective views "signs" ("conventional signs", that is, mainly lexical units) as the only fully linguistic units of signed languages. In contrast, in accordance with the Semiological Approach, we consider so-called non-conventional constructions as the grammatical core of signed languages. For details on this theoretical framework, the reader is referred to the articles mentioned above. Here, we only outline some aspects that are relevant for the present discussion.

Garcia and Sallandre (2020) summarize critical aspects of Cuxac's work on this topic as follows. Beginning with meaning and working to understand what conveys it, as seen above, Cuxac's initial corpus-driven description considers both manual and non-manual articulators, with particular focus on the role of eye-gaze. Very early on, he noted a high frequency of constructions for which the traditional criteria defining lexical signs cannot be used. Although they consisted of the same manual components as did lexical units, such constructions were iconic and gradient, and thus did not meet the criteria then used to define "verbal". Because of this, Cuxac established that they stem from a small set of linguistic structures or "patterns", which he referred to as *transfer structures* (Cuxac 1985). These patterns enabled him to account for numerous highly iconic constructions in discourse, which he termed *transfer units*. The main transfer structures are:

(i) the "Size and Shape Transfer" (SST), which allows one to show the entity's shape and/or size;
(ii) the "Situational Transfer" (ST), which shows an actant on the dominant hand, moving with respect to a stable locative typically articulated on the non-dominant hand, all of which is represented as a global view (i.e., an external point of view); and
(iii) the "Personal Transfer" (PT), wherein the signer takes on the role of the entity being discussed, showing, from an internal point of view, the actions performed or suffered.

These units are characterized formally by a break in the signer's gaze to the addressee.[11]

A key point here is that any transfer unit (SST, ST or PT) involves both non-manual and manual parameters simultaneously. This means that what are described as classifier constructions or depicting signs only match the *manual* component of the transfer units. As for role shifts or constructed action/dialogue, these correspond more or less to PT. However, PT is precisely defined by specific patterns of non-manual parameters and in particular eye-gaze, which is no longer toward the addressee.[12]

With regard to descriptions made within the Semiological Approach, Sallandre (2003) found that transfer units account for an average of 70% of narrative discourse in LSF and between 30% and 50% in other discourse genres. According to Antinoro Pizzuto, Chiari and Rossini (2008), transfer units constitute the major mode of anaphoric expression in LSF, LIS and ASL (80–95%). Analyses in other theoretical frameworks confirm the high frequency of non-conventional units in various signed languages (among many others, Liddell 1995, 2003 and Winston 1995 for ASL; Brennan 1992, 2001 for BSL; Johnston and Schembri 1999, 2007 for Auslan). And yet, despite their omnipresence in signed language discourse, and the central role they play particularly in discourse cohesion (e.g., Engberg-Pedersen 1993, 2003; Winston 1991; Liddell 2003), these non-conventional constructions are somehow relegated, both in terms of their transcription/annotation and in terms of their status in the language, to something nonlinguistic. Although they have aroused growing interest since the 1990s (see, among many others, Liddell 2003; Cormier, Smith and Sevcikova-Sehyr 2015; Hodge, Ferrara and Anible 2019), particularly

---

[11] For a more detailed description, refer to Cuxac and Sallandre (2007) and Garcia and Sallandre (2020).

[12] For detailed mappings of the units and structures proposed in the Semiological Approach to those proposed in other types of signed language descriptions, see Sallandre (2003), Meurant (2008) and, more specifically on the mapping to Liddell's concepts, see Garcia and Sallandre (2014, 2020).

among those who reject formalist approaches, these types of constructions are still often considered to be only partially (or not at all) integrated into signed language grammars. Indeed, the analyses proposed over the last twenty-five years by and after Liddell (e.g., 2003), although explicitly from an anti-formalist perspective, consider non-conventional units as only partly linguistic or nonlinguistic[13] (for discussion on these still-debated questions, see Pizzuto 2007; Garcia and Sallandre 2014; and more recently, Goldin-Meadow and Brentari 2017; Occhino and Wilcox 2017).

We now return to one of the characteristics of these units that may explain, even if indirectly, their long-held designation in the signed language linguistic literature and the ever-present difficulty of giving them a fully linguistic status, that is, the fact that they cannot be directly mapped onto an annotating spoken language word (or even two or three). "Transfer units most often have the same format as lexical units (they coincide overwhelmingly with a 'minimum unit of realization') and involve the same types of parametric components" (Garcia and Sallandre 2020: 6). Cuxac (2013: 78, translation ours) referred to these two main types of signed language discourse units as "multi-track body matrices with relevant cells that are more or less filled in (gaze, posture, facial expressions, manual parameters) depending on the structure achieved".[14] But unlike lexical units, which manually convey a concept of the same type as a spoken language lexical unit, a transfer unit, which simultaneously involves manual and non-manual parameters, may be equivalent in conceptual content to a spoken language proposition or even a clause. An ST unit, for example, could amount to something like 'a long, thin, vertical shape moving slowly towards a fixed, horizontal ovoid shape'. The conceptual content conveyed by the different types of transfer units on the one hand and lexical units on the other matches the whole spectrum of conceptual content conveyed at the various levels of spoken language linguistic analysis (phrase, clause/utterance, text/discourse, morpheme/lexeme), from the infra-conceptual with the SST (e.g., 'flat shape with a pointed edge'), to the content of a proposition or a clause for PT or ST units.

In short, word-tags can only retain what is structurally similar to the labeling spoken language, that is "conventional signs"—which are still frequently referred to in the literature as "words". One can then notice that this graphic filtering coincides with the ever-dominant perspective in signed language research, according to which word-signs constitute the only fully-linguistic/symbolic/verbal units. By contrast, what word-tags cannot capture coincides precisely with what is considered as

---

[13] Let us say, at least, not having a "grammatical" status.
[14] Original: "(. . .) matrices corporelles multipistes à cases pertinentes plus ou moins remplies (regard, posture, MF [mimique faciale], paramètres manuels) en fonction de la structure réalisée."

non- or only partly grammatical or linguistic. It may also be that the lesser attention in the literature to non-manual parameters for defining non-conventional units, such as was noted earlier in comparing classifiers/depicting signs with transfer units, is partly due to this historical focus on lexical signs (that is, manual signs). At the very least, this seems to fall into Slobin et al.'s (2001: 66) warning, noted above: "the danger is to treat the sign language in terms of the written language of the surrounding speech community". From our point of view, this attests to a dependence of signed language linguistics on spoken language linguistics, and even more so on the linguistics of the written forms of just a few spoken languages.

Johnston (e.g., 1991, 2008, 2010, 2019) is unquestionably the signed language linguist who has been most concerned with these issues and, in particular, with how to consider the graphic representation of non-conventional units. His *Auslan Corpus Annotation Guidelines* (Johnston 2019, in particular p. 31–46, 59–63) attests to his ongoing search to account as accurately as possible for what he calls "partly-lexical" signs (including "depicting signs") on the one hand and "constructed actions/dialogs" on the other. This undeniably represents a considerable step forward in taking into account and streamlining the analysis (and annotation) of these types of units. However, this may not be the only issue. A recurrent argument of Johnston's against the value and interest of any research on the transcription of signed language discourse is the considerable amount of time it requires, when technology should finally allow us to make serious progress in linguistic research on signed languages: "Detailed phonetic or phonological transcription has consumed the efforts of many research teams over a considerable period of time yet have resulted in relatively modest texts that still lack the identification of type-like units at any other level of linguistic organization beyond the individual sign" (Johnston 2019: 4). Are we sure that our primary concern should be speed, and that quantitative research, which only modern corpora allow, should always prevail over the more artisanal and "old-fashioned" qualitative analysis? If Cuxac had not spent the very long time needed to transcribe his corpus frame by frame, according to his demanding four-level grid (cf. Figure 2), he could not have highlighted the constituent patterns of the transfer structures. These represent an alternative segmentation and modeling that should subsequently be possible to validate or invalidate. It is unclear whether this could be achieved by using an annotation system that focuses first on conventional units and only then takes into account other types of units.

Di Renzo et al. (2009) point out how representing a sequence of signed language discourse simply by a sequence of spoken language words would result in making the signed language being represented look like gibberish. For spoken language, the ethical and political question of the images conveyed by transcription has been posed, as well as whether respect is maintained for those whose languages are graphically represented (cf. Ochs 1979; Bucholtz 2000; Gadet 2008; Baude 2006).

These questions, however, have not been asked for signed languages. We must not minimize the socio-linguistic effects of gloss-based annotations.

Since the 18th century, glossing has been employed in a long tradition of signed language *exo-grammatisation*, in the sense of Auroux (1994), through so-called "sign language dictionaries" in written forms of a spoken language (beginning with Ferrand [ca. 1784] 2008). Largely reinforced by educational practices, this tradition of one unilateral spoken language word/one signed language sign matching has probably contributed to linguists focusing on the most salient structural similarities between the two languages (i.e., the lexical units). Furthermore, the impact on the image that signers have of their own language, such as the importance given to the lexicon over other specific structural aspects, and the evaluation of the richness of their language through this parameter alone (that is, a "poor" lexicon that should be enriched), are not insignificant (see Cuxac and Antinoro Pizzuto 2010).

As a culmination, we briefly present in the next section the long-term work on SignWriting carried out by the team of deaf and hearing people in Rome (SLL) led by Elena Antinoro Pizzuto, in light of the various linguistic, epistemological, ethical, and sociolinguistic issues raised so far.

5 The SignWriting experience: Significance and contribution of the SLL

Numerous publications and conferences have addressed the original work of the NRC-ICLS Sign Language Laboratory (SLL) (e.g., Di Renzo et al. 2006; Pizzuto, Rossini, and Russo 2006; Antinoro Pizzuto et al. 2008, Di Renzo et al. 2009, Antinoro Pizzuto, Chiari, and Rossini 2010; Petitta et al. 2013) regarding the possibility of writing and transcribing LIS through the SignWriting system (Sutton 1999). We can, of course, only briefly outline here some of the main results and observations of this attempt to scripturize a signed language, carried out over ten years by a team composed mainly of deaf LIS signers. For details, we refer the reader to the above mentioned works. It is a one of a kind experience because of its concreteness and its motivation to seek constructive alternatives. This experience forms the basis and context that feed into and legitimize the critical points set out in the previous sections.

Several general observations emerge from the SLL experimentation with SignWriting. First of all, it is worth noting the ease and speed with which the team's deaf signers were able to master this system (on this particular aspect, see Bianchini et al. 2011; Bianchini 2012). The same is true of the fact that SignWriting allowed them an easy and readable representation of the co-articulation between manual and non-manual traits. It should also be noted that the signers used the system from the outset not only to *transcribe* but also to *write*, i.e., to communicate between themselves in writing. In addition, every signer in the SLL familiar with SignWriting could "read aloud", that is, to fairly quickly reconstruct a text in written LIS that he has not produced himself, or a transcribed text of LIS the source of which he hasn't seen. The indisputable ergonomics of SignWriting for deaf signers and the possibility it offered them to represent the form-meaning patterns of their language in a way that resonated with them, allowed the signers to adopt an authentically metalinguistic posture. It also provided them with the unprecedented experience of writing in their own language, and so, of comparing writing and transcribing. They were indeed able to experience the distinction between "face-to-face LIS" via the transcription of their corpora of LIS exchanges, and written LIS, i.e., LIS used directly and exclusively for remote communication. The extensive corpus of transcribed and written LIS they finally developed has led to many linguistic observations.

First of all, the two types of units discussed above both turn out to be easily representable. Moreover, there are numerous transfer units and, notably, they are just as numerous in the transcriptions as in the SignWriting writings. Another important observation with respect to the two types of units is that the deaf writers/transcribers systematically indicate both manual and non-manual components, the latter appearing practically in every SignWriting vignette, thus echoing the expression "multi-track body matrices" used by Cuxac (see above) to qualify the discourse units.

The table in Figure 3 illustrates the different points and provides a first look at the possibilities offered by SignWriting for signed language corpus documentation, respecting the distinction between transcription and annotation similar to that practiced in spoken language research.

Column (2a) includes various codes: LU (lexical unit) and HIS (Highly Iconic Structures, that is, transfer structures/units) correspond to the two types discussed above, as described in the Semiological Approach. The degree of granularity in the representation of forms and the analogical mode of representation of the signifying (manual and non-manual) multi-linearity that characterize SignWriting are precisely the features that enable the writers/transcribers to identify and categorize these units.[15] These same characteristics enable the accurate tracking of the referential functions of these two types across long texts (written and transcribed). In the table, "deict" (for "deictic") indicates a unit that corresponds to a first intro-

---

15 On the motivation for this identification (direction of eye gaze, body posture), see Antinoro Pizzuto, Chiari, and Rossini (2010: 25). See also Petitta et al. (2013: 8–12).

(1)	(2)	(2a)
 ☺☒	there-is	LU
 ☺	(a) man	LU, deict
(...)	(...)	
 ☺	the man pouch / put-inside-pouch[pears]	HIS, ana/rm
(....)		
 ☺	the man holding-pouch / holding-ladder-bar gets-down	HIS, ana/rm
 ☺	the man holding-pouch / turns-around	HIS, ana/rm

(3) 'there is a man (...) [the man] puts [the pears] inside the pouch (...) [he] comes down the ladder holding the pouch with one hand and the ladder with the other hand, he gets down and, still holding the pouch, turns around'

Figure 3: Excerpt from a SignWriting-encoded written LIS text showing column (1) the LIS signs, (2) English glosses, (2a) coding, and (3) a translation in English (from Antinoro Pizzuto, Chiari, and Rossini 2010, their Table 9–4).

duction of the referred entity, "ana" and "rm" correspond to anaphoric reference and maintained reference (not distinguished in this context). Systematic analysis of this aspect in written and transcribed LIS (Di Renzo et al. 2009) has shown that transfer units constitute 77–95% of expressions used for anaphoric and maintained reference. These observations illustrate a kind of analysis that only an accurate representation of the signifying form of signed language discourse can provide. The articles mentioned above provide further illustrations, showing, for example, how direct experimentation with signed language scripturization through such a system can heuristically address the nodal issue of segmentation: should this particular portion of the discourse be represented by one or more vignettes[16]?

---

16 See on this point Di Renzo et al. (2006); Antinoro Pizzuto, Chiari, and Rossini (2008: 154–155).

6 Conclusion

We do not claim SignWriting to be the solution, nor the answer to the various criticisms raised in this chapter. The system poses various problems (for details, see Bianchini 2012; Bianchini, Borgia and Castelli 2021), in particular, for its implementation in multimedia annotation software like ELAN. Another difficulty highlighted by Antinoro Pizzuto, Chiari and Rossini (2008, 2010) is the computerized composition of texts. The databases and software developed for the storage, retrieval and search of data in SignWriting (e.g., SignPuddle, SignBank) have in fact been designed starting from decontextualized lexical signs. As a result, composing the diverse types of units, symbol by symbol (that is, in their manual and non-manual pluriparametric reality), poses various technical problems and remains a particularly time-consuming task. Undoubtedly, these various problems could have been solved if the SLL experiment had continued[17].

Nevertheless, the very substantial and encouraging set of results and observations that the SignWriting experiment has yielded suggest at the very least a complementary route to the current practices of signed language discourse representation, as demanding as this may be in time. But there is more. The SignWriting experiment is the daily work over a long period of time of a team primarily composed of deaf LIS signers, struggling with a representation of their own language and using a notation system that is not filtered by the dominant written spoken language. In this respect, this experimentation fully responds to the sociolinguistic issues mentioned above. Grounded on the idea that the "scripturization" of a language is essential to metalinguistic awareness, it echoes the conception of a Bébian or a Berthier in the 19th century according to which writing is the vector of social and intellectual emancipation of the Deaf.

References

Antinoro Pizzuto, Elena, Isabella Chiari & Paolo Rossini. 2008. The representation issue and its multifaceted aspects in constructing sign language corpora: questions, answers, further problems. In Onno Crasborn, Eleni Efthimiou, Thomas Hanke, Ernst Thoutenhoofd & Inge Zwitserlood (eds.), *Proceedings of the 3rd Workshop on the Representation and Processing of Sign Languages: Construction and Exploitation of Sign Language Corpora*, LREC 2008, Marrakech, May 27–June 1, 2008. 150–158. Paris: ELRA.

---

[17] The trauma caused by the sudden and premature passing of Elena, followed by the retirement of Paolo Rossini, historical figurehead of the group of deaf signers, probably explains why this experience, so demanding in terms of time and follow-up, was interrupted rather abruptly.

Antinoro Pizzuto, Elena, Isabella Chiari & Paolo Rossini. 2010. Representing sign language: Theoretical, methodological and practical issues. In Massimo Pettorino, Antonella Giannini, Isabella Chiari & Francesca Dovetto (eds.), *Spoken Communication*, 205–240. Newcastle on Tyne: Cambridge Scholars Publishing.

Antinoro Pizzuto, Elena, Paolo Rossini, Marie-Anne Sallandre & Erin Wilkinson. 2008. Deixis, anaphora and highly iconic structures: Cross-linguistic evidence on American (ASL), French (LSF) and Italian (LIS) Signed Languages. In Ronice Quadros de Muller (ed.), *Sign Languages: spinning and unraveling the past, present and future. TISLR9, forty-five papers and three posters from the 9th Theoretical Issues in Sign Language Research Conference*, Florianopolis, Brazil, December 2006, 475–495. Petrópolis/RJ, Brazil: Editora Arara Azul. http://www.editora-arara-azul.com.br/EstudosSurdos.php.

Auroux, Sylvain. 1994. *La Révolution technologique de la grammatisation : Introduction à l'histoire des sciences du langage* [The Technological Revolution of Grammaticization: An Introduction to the History of Language Sciences]. Brussels: Mardaga.

Armstrong, David F., William C. Stokoe & Sherman E. Wilcox. 1995. *Gesture and the Nature of Language*. Cambridge: Cambridge University Press.

Baude, Olivier. 2006. *Corpus oraux. Guide de bonnes pratiques* [Oral Corpora: A Guide to Best Practices]. Paris: CNRS éditions.

Bianchini, Claudia Savina. 2012. *Analyse métalinguistique de l'émergence d'un système d'écriture des Langues des Signes : SignWriting et son application à la Langue des Signes Italienne (LIS)* [Metalinguistic Analysis of an Emerging Writing System for Sign Languages: SignWriting and its Implementation to Italian Sign Language (LIS)]. Paris: University Paris 8/Università degli Studi di Perugia/ISTC-CNR Roma dissertation.

Bianchini, Claudia S., Fabrizio Borgia & Margherita Castelli. 2021. L'appropriation et les modifications de SignWriting (SW) par des locuteurs de la Langue des Signes Italienne (LIS) [The adoption and modification of SignWriting (SW) by Italian Sign Language (LIS) speakers]. In Catherine Collin & Fabienne Toupin (eds.), *Transcrire, Écrire, Formaliser 2* [Transcribe, Write, Formalize 2], 99–116. Renne, France: Presses Universitaires de Renne.

Bianchini, Claudia S., Gabriele Gianfreda, Alessio Di Renzo, Tommaso Lucioli, Giula Petitta, Barbara Pennacchi, Luca Lamano & Paolo Rossini. 2011. Écrire une langue sans forme écrite: Réflexions sur l'écriture et la transcription de la Langue des Signes Italienne (LIS) [Writing a language without a written form: Reflections on the writing and transcription of Italian Sign Language (LIS)]. In Gilles Col & Sylvester N. Osu (eds.), *Transcrire, Écrire, Formaliser 1* [Transcribe, Write, Formalize 1]. 71–89. Rennes, France: Presses Universitaires de Rennes.

Blanche-Benveniste, Claire. 1997. The unit in written and oral language. In Clotilde Pontecorvo (ed.), *Writing Development: An Interdisciplinary View*, 21–45. Amsterdam/Philadelphia: John Benjamins.

Blanche-Benveniste, Claire. 2000. *Approches de la langue parlée en français* [Approaches to Spoken French]. Paris: Ophrys.

Brennan, Mary. 1990. Productive morphology in British Sign Language. In Siegmund Prillwitz & Tomas Vollhaber (eds.), *Sign Language Research and Application: Proceedings of the International Congress on Sign Language Research and Application, Hamburg '90*, 205–228. Hamburg: Signum Press.

Brennan, Mary. 1992. The visual world of British Sign Language: An introduction. In David Brien (ed.), *Dictionary of British Sign Language/English*, 1–133. London: Faber and Faber.

Brennan, Mary. 2001. Encoding and capturing productive morphology. *Sign Language & Linguistics* 4(1/2). 47–62.

Bucholtz, Mary. 2000. The politics of transcription. *Journal of Pragmatics* 32(10). 1439–1465.

Cao, Xuan Hao. 1985. *Phonologie et Linéarité. Réflexions critiques sur les postulats de la phonologie contemporaine* [Phonology and Linearity: Critical Reflections on the Assumptions of Contemporary Phonology]. Paris. SELAF.

Chiari, Isabella. 2007. Redundancy elimination: The case of artificial languages. *Journal of Universal Language* 8(2). 7–38.

Cormier, Kearsy, Sandra Smith & Zed Sevcikova-Sehyr. 2015. Rethinking constructed action. *Sign Language & Linguistics* 18(2). 167–204.

Cuxac, Christian. 1985. Esquisse d'une typologie des langues des signes [Outline of a typology of sign languages]. In Christian Cuxac (ed.), *Autour de la langue des signes, Journées d'Études 10* [Concerning sign language: Proceedings of the 10th Symposium, Paris, 4 June 1983], 35–60. Paris: UFR de linguistique générale et appliquée, University René Descartes.

Cuxac, Christian. 1996. *Fonctions et structures de l'iconicité des langues des signes : analyse descriptive d'un idiolecte parisien de la langue des signes française* [Functions and Structures of the Iconicity of Sign Languages: Descriptive Analysis of a Parisian Idiolect of French Sign Language]. Paris: University of Paris 5 Habilitation dissertation.

Cuxac, Christian. 1999. The expression of spatial relations and the spatialization of semantic relations in French Sign Language. In Catherine Fuchs & Stéphane Robert (eds.), *Language Diversity and Cognitive Representations*, 123–142. Amsterdam/Philadelphia: John Benjamins.

Cuxac, Christian. 2000. *La Langue des Signes Française (LSF). Les voies de l'iconicité* [French Sign Language (LSF): Pathways to iconicity]. *Faits de Langues* [Language Facts] 15/16. Paris: Ophrys.

Cuxac, Christian. 2013. Langues des signes : une modélisation sémiologique [Sign languages: Semiological modeling]. In Andrea Benvenuto & Didier Séguillon (eds.), *Surdités, langues, cultures, identités : recherches et pratiques* [Deafness, Languages, Cultures, Identities: Research and Practice] (special issue), *La Nouvelle Revue de l'adaptation et de la scolarisation* 64, 65–80.

Cuxac, Christian & Elena Antinoro Pizzuto. 2010. Émergence, norme et variation dans les langues des signes : vers une redéfinition notionnelle [Emergence, norms and variation in signed languages: Towards a notional redefinition]. *Langage et Société* 131. 37–53.

Cuxac, Christian & Marie-Anne Sallandre. 2007. Iconicity and arbitrariness in French Sign Language: Highly Iconic Structures, degenerated iconicity and diagrammatic iconicity. In Elena Pizzuto, Paola Pietrandrea & Raffaele Simone (eds.), *Verbal and Signed Languages: Comparing Structures, Constructs and Methodologies*, 13–33. Berlin/New York: Mouton de Gruyter.

Di Renzo, Alessio, Gabriele Gianfreda, Luca Lamano, Tommaso Lucioli, Barbara Pennacchi, Paolo Rossini, Claudia Savina Bianchini, Giulia Petitta & Elena Antinoro Pizzuto. 2009. Representation – Analysis – Representation: Novel approaches to the study of face-to-face and written narratives in Italian Sign Language (LIS). Paper presented at the Colloque International sur les langues des signes (CILS), Palais des Congrès de Namur, Belgique, 16–20 November 2009.

Di Renzo, Alessio, Luca Lamano, Tommaso Lucioli, Barbara Pennacchi & Luca Ponzo. 2006. Italian Sign Language (LIS): Can we write it and transcribe it with SignWriting? In Chiara Vettori (ed.), *Proceedings of the LREC 2006 Second Workshop on the Representation and Processing of Sign Languages: Lexicographic Matters and Didactic Scenarios*, 11–16. Genoa: ELRA (European Language Resources Association).

Doan, Patrick, Dominique Boutet, Claudia Savina Bianchini, Claire Danet, Morgane Rébulard, Jean-François Dauphin, Léa Chèvrefils, Chloé Thomas & Mathieu Reguer. 2019. Handling sign language handshapes annotation with the Typannot typefont. *CogniTextes* 19. 1–24.

Engberg-Pedersen, Elisabeth. 1993. *Space in Danish Sign Language: The Semantics and Morphosyntax of the Use of Space in a Visual Language*. Hamburg: Signum Press.

Engberg-Pedersen, Elisabeth. 2003. How composite is a fall? Adults' and children's descriptions of different types of falls in Danish Sign Language. In Karen Emmorey (ed.), *Perspectives on Classifier Constructions in Sign Languages*, 311–332. Mahwah, NJ: Lawrence Erlbaum.

Ferrand, Jean. 2008 [ca. 1784]. *Dictionnaire à l'usage des sourds et muets* [Dictionary for the Deaf and Mute]. Archives de la langue des signes française. Limoges, France : Lambert-Lucas.

Filhol, Michael. 2020. A human-editable sign language representation inspired by spontaneous productions...and a writing system? *Sign Language Studies* 21(1). 98–136. doi:10.1353/sls.2020.0030

Friedman, Lynn (ed.). 1977. *On the Other Hand: New Perspectives on American Sign Language*. New York: Academic Press.

Gadet, Françoise. 2017. L'oralité ordinaire à l'épreuve de la mise en écrit : ce que montre la proximité [Ordinary orality put to the test of writing: What proximity shows]. *Langages* 208(4). 113–126.

Garcia, Brigitte. 1997. Enjeux d'une écriture de la langue des signes : un dialogue intersémiotique [Issues in writing a signed language: An intersemiotic dialogue]. *LIDIL – Revue de linguistique et de didactique des langues* 15, 31–51.

Garcia, Brigitte. 2010. *Sourds, surdité, langue(s) des signes et épistémologie des sciences du langage. Problématiques de la scripturisation et modélisation des bas niveaux en Langue des Signes Française (LSF).* [Deaf people, deafness, signed language(s) and the epistemology of language sciences. Problems in scripturizing LSF, and modeling of low language levels in French Sign Language (LSF)]. Paris: University Paris 8 Habilitation dissertation.

Garcia, Brigitte. 2016. Scripturisation, grammatisation et modélisation linguistique à la lumière du cas des langues des signes [Scripturization, grammatization and linguistic modeling in light of the case of sign languages]. *Dossiers d'HEL* (SHESL): *Écriture(s) et représentations du langage et des langues* 9. 238–253.

Garcia, Brigitte & Marie Perini. 2010. Normes en jeu et jeu des normes dans les deux langues en présence chez les sourds locuteurs de la Langue des Signes Française (LSF) [Norms in play and playing with norms in the two languages cognitively present among deaf signers of French Sign Language (LSF)]. *Langage et Société* 131. 75–94.

Garcia, Brigitte & Marie-Anne Sallandre. 2014. Reference resolution in French Sign Language (LSF). In Patricia Cabredo Hofherr & Anne Zribi-Hertz (eds.), *Crosslinguistic Studies on Noun Phrase Structure and Reference*, 316–364. Leiden/Boston: Brill.

Garcia, Brigitte & Marie-Anne Sallandre. 2020. Contribution of the Semiological Approach to deixis – Anaphora in sign language: The key role of eye-gaze. *Frontiers in Psychology* 11:583763. doi:10.3389/fpsyg.2020.583763

Givón, Talmy. 1978. Definiteness and referentiality. In Joseph H. Greenberg, Charles A. Ferguson & Edith A. Moravcsik (eds.), *Universals of Human Language, Volume 4: Syntax*, 291–330. Stanford, CA: Stanford University Press.

Goldin-Meadow, Susan & Diane Brentari. 2017. Gesture, sign and language: The coming of age of sign language and gesture studies. *Behavioral and Brain Sciences* 40, e46. 1–60. doi:10.1017/S0140525X15001247

Halliday, M. A. K. 1985. *Spoken and Written Language*. Victoria, Australia: Deakin University.

Hodge, Gabrielle, Lindsay N. Ferrara & Benjamin D. Anible. 2019. The semiotic diversity of doing reference in a deaf signed language. *Journal of Pragmatics* 143. 33–53.

Johnston, Trevor. 1991. Transcription and glossing of sign language texts: Examples from Auslan (Australian Sign Language). *International Journal of Sign Linguistics* 2(1). 3–28.

Johnston, Trevor. 2001. The lexical database of Auslan (Australian Sign Language). *Sign Language & Linguistics* 4(1/2). 145–169.

Johnston, Trevor. 2008. Corpus linguistics and signed languages: No lemmata, no corpus. In Onno Crasborn, Eleni Efthimiou, Thomas Hanke, Ernst Thoutenhoofd & Inge Zwitserlood (eds.), *Proceedings of the 3rd Workshop on the Representation and Processing of Sign Languages: Construction and Exploitation of Sign Language Corpora*, LREC 2008, Marrakech, May 27–June 1, 2008, 82–87. Paris: ELRA.

Johnston, Trevor. 2010. From archive to corpus: Transcription and annotation in the creation of signed language corpora. *International Journal of Corpus Linguistics* 15(1). 106–131.

Johnston, Trevor. 2019. *Auslan Corpus Annotation Guidelines.* https://www.academia.edu/40088269/Auslan_Corpus_Annotation_Guidelines_August_2019_version (accessed 5 July 2020).

Johnston, Trevor & Adam Schembri. 1999. On defining lexeme in a sign language. *Sign Language & Linguistics* 2(2). 115–185.

Johnston, Trevor & Adam Schembri. 2007. *Australian Sign Language (Auslan): An Introduction to Sign Language Linguistics.* Cambridge: Cambridge University Press.

Jouison, Paul. 1995. *Écrits sur la Langue des Signes Française* [Writings on French Sign Language]. (Edition prepared by Brigitte Garcia). Paris: L'Harmattan.

Leeson, Lorraine. 2008. Quantum leap – Leveraging the Signs of Ireland Digital Corpus in Irish Sign Language/English Interpreter Training. *The Sign Language Translator and Interpreter* 2(2). 149–176.

Liddell, Scott K. 1995. Real, surrogate, and token space: Grammatical consequences in ASL. In Karen Emmorey & Judy S. Reilly (eds.), *Language, Gesture and Space*, 19–41. Hillsdale, NJ: Lawrence Erlbaum.

Liddell, Scott K. 2003. *Grammar, Gesture, and Meaning in American Sign Language.* Cambridge: Cambridge University Press.

Lüdtke, Helmut. 1969. Die Alphabetschrift und das Problem der Lautsegmentierung [The alphabet and the problem of sound segmentation]. *Phonetica* 20. 147–176.

Macwhinney Brian. 2000. *The CHILDES Project: Tools for Analyzying Talk (3rd edition). Vol 1: Transcription Format and Programs* (3rd edn.). Hillsdale, NJ: Lawrence Erlbaum.

Manfrellotti, Olga. 2001. The role of literacy in the recognition of phonological units. *Italian Journal of Linguistics/Rivista di linguistica* 13(1). 85–98.

Mettouchi, Amina, Martine Vanhove & Dominique Caubet (eds.). 2015. *Corpus-based Studies of Lesser-described Languages. The CorpAfroAs Corpus of Spoken AfroAsiatic Languages.* Amsterdam/Philadelphia: John Benjamins.

Meurant, Laurence. 2008. *Le regard en langue des signes. Anaphore en langue des signes française de Belgique (LSFB) : morphologie, syntaxe, énonciation* [Eye Gaze in Signed Language. Anaphora in French Belgian Sign Language (LSFB): Morphology, Syntax, Utterance]. Namur: Presses Universitaires de Namur, Rennes: Presses Universitaires de Rennes.

Miller, Christopher. 2001. Some reflections on the need for a common sign notation. *Sign Language & Linguistics* 4(1/2). 11–28.

Mondada, Lorenza. 2008. La transcription dans la perspective de la linguistique interactionnelle [Transcription from the perspective of interactional linguistics]. In Mireille Bilger (ed.), *Données orales. Les enjeux de la transcription* [Oral Data: Transcription Issues], 78–109. Perpignan: Presses Universitaires Perpignan.

Occhino, Corrine. 2017. An introduction to embodied cognitive phonology: Claw5 handshape distribution in ASL and Libras. *Complutense Journal of English Studies* 25. 69–103.

Occhino, Corrine & Sherman E. Wilcox. 2017. Gesture or Sign? A categorization problem. *Behavioral and Brain Sciences* e66. 36–37. doi:10.1017/S0140525X15003015

Ochs, Elinor. 1979. Transcription as theory. In Elinor Ochs & Bambi B. Schieffelin (eds.), *Developmental Pragmatics*, 43–72. New York: Academic Press.

Olson, David R. 1998. *L'univers de l'écrit. Comment la culture écrite donne forme à la pensée* [The World of Writing: How Written Culture Shapes Thought]. Paris: Retz.

Petitta, Giulia, Alessio Di Renzo, Isabella Chiari & Paolo Rossini. 2013. Sign language representation: New approaches to the study of Italian Sign language (LIS). In Laurence Meurant, Aurélie Sinte, Mieke Van Herreweghe & Myriam Vermeerbergen (eds.), *Sign Language Research, Uses and Practices: Crossing Views on Theoretical and Applied Sign Language Linguistics*, 137–158. Boston/Berlin: De Gruyter Mouton/Ishara Press.

Pizzuto, Elena. 2007. Deixis, anaphora and person reference in signed languages. In Elena Pizzuto, Paola Pietrandrea & Raffaele Simone (eds.), *Verbal and Signed Languages: Comparing Structures, Constructs and Methodologies*, 275–308. Berlin/New York: Mouton De Gruyter.

Pizzuto, Elena & Paola Pietrandrea. 2001. The notation of signed texts: open questions and indications for further research. In Brita Bergman, Penny Boyes-Braem, Thomas Hanke & Elena Antinoro Pizzuto (eds.), *Sign Language and Linguistics, (Special Volume – Sign Transcription and Database Storage of Sign Information)*, 4(1/2). 29–43.

Pizzuto, Elena, Paola Pietrandrea & Raffaele Simone (eds.). 2007. *Verbal and Signed Languages: Comparing Structures, Constructs and Methodologies*. Berlin/New York: Mouton De Gruyter.

Pizzuto, Elena, Paolo Rossini & Tommaso Russo. 2006. Representing signed languages in written form: Questions that need to be posed. In Chiara Vettori (ed.), *Proceedings of the LREC 2006 Second Workshop on the Representation and Processing of Sign Languages: Lexicographic Matters and Didactic Scenarios*, 1–6. Genoa: ELRA (European Language Resources Association).

Pontecorvo, Clotilde (ed.). 1997. *Writing Development: An Interdisciplinary View*. Amsterdam/Philadelphia: John Benjamins.

Port, Robert 2007. The graphical basis of phones and phonemes. In Ocke-Schwen Bohn & Murray J. Munro (eds.). *Language Experience in Second Language Learning: In Honor of James Emil Flege*, 349–365. Amsterdam/Philadelphia: John Benjamins.

Russo, Tommaso. 2004. Iconicity and productivity in sign language discourse: An analysis of three LIS discourse registers. *Sign Language Studies* 4(2). 164–197.

Russo, Tommaso. 2005. A crosslinguistic, cross-cultural analysis of metaphors in two Italian Sign Language (LIS) registers. *Sign Language Studies* 5(3). 333–359.

Sallandre, Marie-Anne. 2003. *Les unités du discours en Langue des Signes Française. Tentative de catégorisation dans le cadre d'une grammaire de l'iconicité* [Discourse Units in French Sign Language: An Attempt at Categorization Within the Framework of a Grammar of Iconicity]. Paris: University Paris 8 dissertation.

Slobin, Dan I. 2006. Review of S. Liddell, *Grammar, Gestures* [sic], *and Meaning in American Sign Language. Language* 82. 176–179.

Slobin, Dan I. 2008. Breaking the molds: Signed languages and the nature of human language. *Sign Language Studies* 8(2). 114–130.

Slobin, Dan I. 2013. Typology and channel of communication: Where do signed languages fit in? In Balthasar Bickel, Lenore A. Grenoble, David A. Peterson & Alan Timberlake (eds.), *Language Typology and Historical Contingency: In Honor of Johanna Nichols*, 47–67. Amsterdam/Philadelphia: John Benjamins.

Slobin, Dan I., Nini Hoiting, Michelle Anthony, Yael Biederman, Marlon Kuntze, Reyna Lindert, Jennie Pyers, Helen Thumann & Amy Weinberg. 2001. Sign language transcription at the level of meaning components: The Berkeley Transcription System (BTS). *Sign Language & Linguistics* 4(1/2). 63–104.

Stokoe, William C. 1987. Sign writing systems. In John V. Van Cleve (ed.), *Gallaudet Encyclopedia of Deaf People and Deafness*, vol. 3, 118–120. New York: McGraw-Hill.

Stokoe, William C. 1991. Semantic phonology. *Sign Language Studies* 71. 107–114.
Sutton, Valerie. 1999 [1995]. *Lessons in SignWriting. Textbook & Workbook*, 2nd edn. La Jolla, CA: Deaf Action Committee for Sign Writing.
Vermeerbergen, Myriam. 2006. Past and current trends in sign language research. *Language and Communication* 26(2). 168–192.
Wilcox, Sherman E. 2004. Cognitive iconicity: Conceptual spaces, meaning, and gesture in signed languages. *Cognitive Linguistics* 15(2). 119–147.
Wilcox, Sherman E. & Terry Janzen. 2004. Introduction: Cognitive dimensions of signed languages. *Cognitive Linguistics* 15(2). 113–117.
Winston, Elizabeth A. 1991. Spatial referencing and cohesion in an American Sign Language text. *Sign Language Studies* 73. 397–410.
Winston, Elizabeth A. 1995. Spatial mapping in comparative discourse frames. In Karen Emmorey & Judy S. Reilly (eds.). *Language, Gesture, and Space*, 87–114. Hillsdale, NJ: Lawrence Erlbaum.
Zeshan, Ulrike. 2008. Roots, leaves and branches – The typology of sign languages. In Ronice Muller de Quadros (ed.), *Sign Languages: Spinning and Unraveling the Past, Present and Future. TISLR9, Forty-five Papers and Three Posters from the 9th Theoretical Issues in Sign Language Research Conference, Florianopolis, Brazil, December 2006*, 671–695. Petrópolis/RJ, Brazil: Editora Arara Azul. http://www.editora-arara-azul.com.br/EstudosSurdos.php (accessed 5 July 2020).

Paola Pietrandrea
What is a language? A socio-semiotic approach to signed and spoken languages

> It all depends on how we define human language.
> And that in turn depends on how we define human.
> Sherman Wilcox (1996: 179)

1 Introduction

Sherman Wilcox spent his life as a linguist—one of his many lives—to show that language evolution must be regarded as a gradual and continuous process (Armstrong, Stokoe, and Wilcox 1995), that gestures and speech are contiguous activities (Wilcox 2005), and that language must be conceived as a radically social activity arising from "information donation" (Wilcox 1996: 181). This approach led Sherman to reconsider, theoretically, the impact that often neglected phenomena such as iconicity (Wilcox 2004; Wilcox and Wilcox 1995), and more in general social, cognitive, and semiotic factors (Wilcox and Wilcox 2013) have on linguistic structures. And, as we know, he wished to put forward a unified framework for analyzing gestures, signed languages, and spoken languages (Wilcox 2013; Wilcox and Xavier 2013).[1,2]

But what exactly is a "language"?

The entire intellectual and scientific activity of Sherman Wilcox has this question as a motivation. Linguists, however, as noted by David Crystal ([1987] 2010), rarely attempt to define what a language is.

---

[1] Virginia Volterra, Penny Boyes Braem, Paolo Ramat, and Luisa Corona read a previous version of this chapter and provided, as usual, invaluable insights. I wish to thank Terry Janzen and Barbara Shaffer for their warm professionalism, as well as the three anonymous reviewers for their extremely helpful suggestions. A special thanks goes to my son Marco Guerrini, with whom I discussed many issues addressed in this chapter. I dedicate this work to the memory of Elena Antinoro Pizzuto, Tullio De Mauro, and Tommaso Russo Cardona.
[2] It is a great privilege and an immense pleasure to contribute this chapter to the volume in honor of my mentor and old time friend, Sherman Wilcox: my reflection on signed languages has enormously benefited from our conversations.

Paola Pietrandrea, Université de Lille & CNRS UMR STL 8163, France,
e-mail: paolapietrandrea@gmail.com

In this chapter I examine three important and well-known responses that Charles F. Hockett, André Martinet, and Noam Chomsky have given to this question (Sections 2 to 4). As we will see, these three scholars maintain that a language is defined by its openness, and in so doing, they shift the problem to attempting to define precisely what the openness of a linguistic system means, and what enables it to be this way (Section 5).

I argue that the attempts made by Hockett and Martinet to explain the openness of linguistic systems via duality of patterning and arbitrariness is not theoretically compatible with the linguistic status of signed languages (Section 6). Chomsky's hypothesis that the openness of linguistic systems rests on the capacity for recursion realized by an autonomous, innate, and uniquely human component of the nervous system does not explain the contiguity between, on one hand, action, gesture, and language, and on the other hand, cognitive, social, and linguistic abilities (Sections 7 and 8). Chomsky's definition is therefore equally inadequate (Section 9). I then present an alternative definition of language put forward in the Italian tradition of Tullio De Mauro (Section 10). I suggest that such a definition, which is socio-semiotic, i.e., based on the social, cognitive, and communicative abilities of humans rather than structural features, accounts simultaneously for the linguistic status of both spoken and signed languages and provides a theoretical justification for an empirical, social, cognitive analysis of language (Section 11). I conclude this chapter with some thoughts on the impact that the adoption of such a definition of language may have for the work of linguists, and in particular, for the work of signed language linguists.

2 Hockett's sixteen design features

In a series of influential papers appearing in the 1950s and 1960s, Hockett (1958, 1959, 1960, [1963] 1966, but also 1978) proposed a *design features* model for the classification of communication systems, which was originally intended to contrast animal communication systems with human language. After a number of revisions of his model, Hockett ([1963] 1966: 6) proposed a list of 16 features "found in every [human] language on which we have reliable information, and [. . .] lacking in at least one known animal communicative system":

1. *Use of the vocal-auditory channel.*
2. *Directional reception of acoustic signals.*
3. *Rapid fading of acoustic signals.*
4. *Interchangeability* between the transmitter and the receiver of linguistic signals.
5. *Complete feedback,* i.e., the reception by transmitters of their own messages.

6. *Specialization of linguistic signals.*
7. *Semanticity*, i.e., the capacity to have a denotation of linguistic signals.
8. *Arbitrariness*, i.e., the non-resemblance between (the form of) a meaningful element of the language and its denotation.
9. *Discreteness*, i.e., the fact that the possible messages in any language constitute a discrete rather than a continuous repertory.
10. *Displacement*, i.e., the possibility to refer to denotations remote in time or space, or both, from the site of communication.
11. *Openness*, i.e., the possibility to easily and freely coin new linguistic messages. According to Hockett this crucial property reflects two separate facts:
    (a) *"in a language, new messages are freely coined by blending, analogizing from, or transforming old ones...* This says that every language has grammatical patterning" (Hockett [1963] 1966: 11, italics in original).
    (b) *"in a language, either new or old elements are freely assigned new semantic loads by circumstances and context...* This says that in every language new idioms constantly come into existence" (Hockett [1963] 1966: 11, italics in original).
12. *Tradition*, i.e., the transmission of the conventions of a language through teaching and learning.
13. *Duality of patterning*, i.e., the existence of both a cenematic sub-system, i.e., a phonological sub-system comprising "empty" units, having a uniquely distinctive function, and a plerematic sub-system, i.e., a subsystem comprising "full" units having a morphological, semantic function.
14. *Prevarication*, i.e., the possibility to produce false and meaningless messages.
15. *Reflexiveness*, i.e., the possibility of communicating about communication.
16. *Learnability*, i.e., a user of one language can learn another language.

According to Hockett, human language is a communication system defined by the necessary presence of these 16 features.

3 Martinet's duality of patterning

In parallel, in the French tradition, André Martinet (1960) argued that two properties are to be considered as defining features of human language:
1. *Use of the vocal auditory channel.*
2. *Duality of patterning*, or more precisely, *double articulation.*

According to Martinet, who builds on Humboldt's ([1836] 1999) original proposal, duality of patterning, which Hockett considered a distinctive feature of both human and primate language, is essential for the economy of linguistic systems: it allows humans to combine a finite number of meaningless, phonological, linguistic units to encode a potential infinite number of meanings.

4 Chomsky's recursion

More recently, in a widely debated paper on the faculty of language, Hauser, Chomsky, and Fitch (2002: 1570) propose to define language not as a communication system, but rather as "an internal component of the mind/brain system" assuming that this internal component "is the primary object of interest for the study of the evolution and function of the language faculty". In their model, the language faculty as a whole is composed of the components of the human nervous system recruited in the use of language; among these components it is possible to distinguish:

1. A number of systems which are necessary but not sufficient for language, such as the sensory-motor and conceptual-intentional systems, and memory, respiration, digestion, circulation, etc., called the *faculty of language - broad sense (FLB)*.
2. An essential component, consisting in "an abstract linguistic computational system [...] independent of the other systems with which it interacts and interfaces" (Hauser, Chomsky, and Fitch 2002: 1571), called the *faculty of language - narrow sense (FLN)*.

FLN is defined as "a computational system (narrow syntax) that generates internal representations and maps them into the sensory-motor interface by the phonological system, and into the conceptual-intentional interface by the (formal) semantic system" (Hauser, Chomsky, and Fitch 2002: 1571). Chomsky and colleagues add that "a core property of FLN is recursion, attributed to narrow syntax in the conception just outlined. FLN takes a finite set of elements and yields a potentially infinite array of discrete expressions [...] each of these discrete expressions is then passed to the sensory-motor and conceptual-intentional systems, which process and elaborate this information in the use of language" (Hauser, Chomsky, and Fitch 2002: 1571). And further, "the core recursive aspect of FLN currently appears to lack any analog in animal communication and possibly other domains as well" (Hauser, Chomsky, and Fitch 2002: 1571).

Importantly, as mentioned above, Chomsky and colleagues denied that FLN, and more generally, a language, is "properly regarded as a system for communication". They write: "The question is whether particular components of the functioning of FLN are adaptations for language, specifically acted upon by natural selection—or, even more broadly, whether FLN evolved for reasons other than communication" (Hauser, Chomsky, and Fitch 2002: 1574).

This passage alludes, as highlighted by Pinker and Jackendoff (2005), to Chomsky's well-known position according to which language would not be properly regarded as a system of communication, but rather as a system whose main function is expressing thought (Chomsky 2002: 75). We will return to this highly controversial point in Section 8.3.

To sum up, according to Chomsky and colleagues, language is defined as a uniquely human, potentially infinite abstract computational "system of sound-meaning connections" designed for thought expression rather than having emerged via adaptation to communication needs; the capacity of recursion in syntax, which is regarded as independent of any other biological system, is presented as a condition for the potential infiniteness of language.

5 The relevance of openness

It should be noted that in spite of their differences, Hockett's, Martinet's, and Chomsky's definitions of language agree on an important point: openness is a key property of human language. The three definitions slightly diverge, though, on the exact meaning of openness and the identification of the properties that they consider necessary for openness.

While Martinet and Chomsky propose a strict definition of openness, in which this property is regarded as coinciding with the capacity of generating potentially infinite new expressions, Hockett suggests that the openness of linguistic systems rests on three capacities: (1) the capacity to generate potentially infinite new expressions (of course), but also (2) the capacity of semantic organization of grammatical patterning: *"new messages are freely coined by blending, analogizing from, or transforming old ones"* (Hockett [1963] 1966: 11, italics in original), and (3) the semantic plasticity of linguistic elements: *"new or old elements are freely assigned new semantic loads by circumstances and context"* (Hockett [1963] 1966: 11).

This larger characterization of openness by Hockett is quite crucial; we will return to it in Section 8.1.

Let us focus for now on what we could call openness *stricto sensu*, i.e., the capacity to generate potentially infinite new expressions, which Hockett regards as *one* of the key factors for openness and Chomsky and Martinet as *the* key factor for openness. It should be noted that while Martinet and Hockett consider the capacity to generate potentially infinite new expressions as resting on duality of patterning, Chomsky attributes it to the recursive character of syntax.

6 When the definitions of language meet signed languages

As mentioned above, two of the three traditional definitions of language were elaborated in the 1950s and 1960s. In those years, signed language linguistics was on the rise and signed language linguists were busy demonstrating the linguistic status of signed languages. The peculiarities of signed languages, especially those going against the traditional definition of language were cause for embarrassment, such as the use of the visuo-gestual rather than vocal-auditory channel, the absence of a clear duality of patterning, and the presence of iconicity. As we will see in the next sections, in an initial phase of signed language linguistics, attempts were made to minimize these. But things changed: the linguistic status of signed languages was increasingly taken for granted by the linguistic community. At that point the differences between signed and spoken languages led to some reconsideration and redefinition of language in general. We next examine the crucial steps of this long debate in detail.

6.1 The irrelevance of the vocal-auditory channel

The first macroscopic difference between spoken and signed languages concerns the channel used to convey messages: signed languages do not use the vocal-auditory channel, which is considered as a defining feature of language by both Martinet and Hockett.

Martinet did not address this specific point in the brief essay acknowledging the impact that signed languages had on his own definition of language (Martinet 1996).[3] Hockett, who was also aware of the difficulties raised by these languages, quite surprisingly and quite circularly, argued in 1978 that signed languages are identical to spoken languages with the exception of the use of the vocal-auditory channel and a reduced presence of arbitrariness (Hockett 1978). In a sense, the

---

[3] I am infinitely grateful to the anonymous reviewer who brought to my attention this essay by Martinet.

importance of the vocal-auditory channel, which is also absent in writing, was somehow reconsidered without great argumentation.

6.2 The problem posed by duality of patterning

As observed by Wilcox (1995), the importance given to duality of patterning by Martinet and Hockett led linguists who were trying to prove the linguistic status of signed languages to search for a finite sub-system of empty "cenematic" units that could be infinitely recombined, i.e., a phonology.

The essence of William Stokoe's (1960) analysis was to show that "signs consist of analyzable units of sublexical structure" (Wilcox 2015: 669). Each sign of a signed language is, according to Stokoe, analyzable into three so-called "cheremes": (1) handshape, i.e., the configuration that the hand makes when producing the sign; (2) location, the place where the sign is produced; and (3) the movement made by the signer's hands in producing the sign. For each of these cheremes, Stokoe identified a finite number of possible realizations. This organization of sublexical units was, according to Stokoe (1960), reminiscent of the organization of phonemes within words: the signs of signed languages were indeed analyzable as composed of a finite number of smaller meaningless and contrastive units that could be relatively freely recombined. Showing the existence of phoneme-like units, Stokoe intended to prove the existence of duality of patterning in signed languages, and by consequence, that signed languages are full-fledged languages. In Martinet's (1996) essay on signed languages, he fully embraced this view.

In spite of Stokoe's remarkable results, along with efforts made by other linguists to further analyze and characterize signed language sublexical systems (Battison 1978; Liddell 1984; Padden and Perlmutter 1987; Brentari 1998; Sandler 1999), it became rapidly clear that there exist important differences in the organization of spoken and signed languages. Penny Boyes-Braem was the first researcher who courageously highlighted these differences in her 1981 pioneering work on iconicity. Boyes-Braem (1981) observed that handshapes in signed languages are often associated with precise meanings, for example a flat hand (a so-called B configuration) conveys a flat surface, as is the case for the B handshape in the Italian Sign Language (Lingua dei Segni Italiana, or LIS) sign for FLOOR represented in Figure 1. This entails that cheremes are not always purely contrastive.

In an analysis of the LIS lexicon (Pietrandrea 1995, 1998, 2002), I quantified the presence of meaningful sublexical (minimal) units, calculating that 50% of occurrences of handshapes and 67% of occurrences of body locations *were* meaningful. That is, they not only had a distinctive, phonological function, but also a morphological, semantic function.

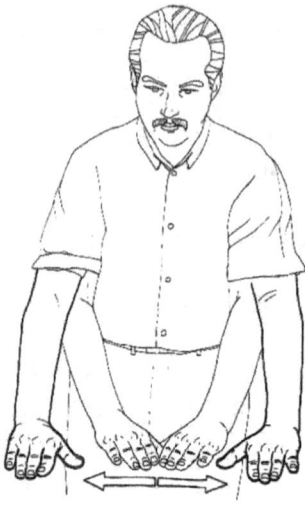

Figure 1: The LIS sign for FLOOR (from Radutzky (ed.) 1992, Figure 156.2, used with permission).

6.3 The redefinition of arbitrariness

Penny Boyes-Braem's (1981) dissertation not only showed that cheremes are meaningful, but also showed that cheremes often present an iconic relation with the meaning they convey; this is the case, once again, for the sign for FLOOR in Figure 1 where the flatness of the hand mirrors the flatness of the surface of the represented object.

Iconicity in signed languages, whether strictly viewed as the reflection of extralinguistic reality in linguistic structures, or more generally as the influence exerted by the human body (cognitive abilities included) on linguistic structures, is indeed quite evident.

For a long time, linguists considered iconicity and arbitrariness as antonyms: a semiotic system in their view could not be iconic and arbitrary at the same time. By consequence, the presence of iconicity in the sublexical organization of signed languages was considered as at odds, not only with duality of patterning, but also with the arbitrariness that Hockett, following a long tradition we can trace back to Saussure, had considered as defining of natural languages.

As mentioned in 6.1, Hockett (1960) was aware of the problem, posed by the presence of iconicity, for the inclusion of signed languages in the inventory of full-fledged languages. He simply stated that signed languages are like other languages in spite of the presence of diminished arbitrariness. Hockett's early iteration of this argument is in fact in line with the conclusion reached by contemporary signed language linguistics after decades of tortured and tormented debates.

In its earliest days, signed language linguistics tried to explain iconicity away. In studies conducted on American Sign Language (ASL), Bellugi and Siple (1975) observed that iconicity does not play a role in the memorization of signs by deaf native signers. Frishberg (1975) argued that iconicity tends to diminish diachronically. Bellugi and Klima (1976) and Klima and Bellugi (1979) found that, for people unfamiliar with ASL, iconicity only partially facilitates the comprehension of individual signs and that even the iconicity recognizable in individual signs turns out to be undetectable when those signs are produced in discourse. In the cultural context, dominated a few years later by the rediscovery of iconicity as a crucial conceptual construct in functional linguistics (Bybee 1985; Haiman 1985; Simone 1995), the iconicity in signed languages became considered as something of a special interest.

Many studies explored the presence of, and the role played by, iconicity in grammatical processes in ASL (Wilcox and Wilcox 1995), in the sublexical organization of the semantic domain of spatio-temporal relations in LIS (Pizzuto et al. 1995), in the cross-cultural, crosslinguistic comprehension of signed languages (Pizzuto and Volterra 2000), and in the LIS lexicon (Pietrandrea 2002) and poetry (Russo 2000, 2004a, 2004b; Russo, Giurana and Pizzuto 2001; Russo and Pietrandrea, this volume).

Cuxac and Antinoro Pizzuto (2010) showed that while it was somehow possible to reconsider the presence of iconicity at the lexical level, it is impossible to describe the discursive structures of signed languages without also taking into account their iconic properties. Wilcox (2004) introduced the concept of cognitive iconicity. Building on Stokoe's (1991) notion of semantic phonology, he proposed that signs, as well as the reality they represent, occupy conceptual space. He defined iconicity:

> not as a relation between the form of a sign and its real world referent, but as a distance relation within a multidimensional conceptual space between the phonological and semantic poles of symbolic structures. Greater distance in conceptual space between a symbolic unit's semantic and phonological poles creates arbitrariness. When the phonological and semantic poles of a sign lie more closely together in conceptual space, iconicity is increased. (Wilcox 2010: 675)

I have argued in Pietrandrea (2002) and jointly with Tommaso Russo (Pietrandrea and Russo 2007) that far from being incompatible properties, imagic iconicity and arbitrariness can co-exist.[4] While iconicity concerns the vertical relation between a referent and a sign, or to put it in cognitive iconicity terms, between the phonological and semantic poles of symbolic structures, the "radical" arbitrariness that according to Saussure is a necessary condition for language is better described in terms of "emancipation" of language from reality.

---

4 On this point see also Langacker (this volume).

> The Saussurean principle of Radical Arbitrariness has often been understood as stating that the linguistic signs must not be iconic, i.e., that they cannot display perceptual features of their referents (see Givón 2002). We claim instead that this principle basically states that languages obey systematic formal constraints which are autonomous, i.e. arbitrary, to the extent that they fulfil [sic] two distinct requirements: (a) they are not predictable on the grounds of external reality and (b) they do not exhaustively determine utterance meaning, allowing pragmatic interpretation and, consequently, semantic variability (see also Russo 2004b: ch. 6). Iconic features can thus characterize linguistic signs to the extent that they do not contrast with these two requirements. (Pietrandrea and Russo 2007)

Pietrandrea and Russo put forward two characteristics regarding the radical arbitrariness of signed languages:
1. Given an articulatory unit, it is not possible to predict if and with what iconic meaning a handshape, location, or movement will be used (Pietrandrea 2002).
2. The repertoire of articulation units remains limited to the forms within a paradigm defined by the linguistic system which, independent of iconicity, is organized as bundles of oppositions similar to paradigms of articulatory elements of spoken languages (Martinet 1955; Pietrandrea and Russo 2007).

To explain therefore this coexistence of iconicity and arbitrariness, Russo and I proposed that rather than considering iconicity and arbitrariness as antonyms, we must accept the existence of semiotic systems as radically arbitrary and still characterized by an important presence of iconicity (Pietrandrea and Russo 2007).

7 The need for a new definition

In contemporary linguistics, despite the modality of signed languages, despite the meaningfulness of their minimal units, and despite their iconicity, no one seriously doubts the linguistic status of signed languages anymore. Signed languages are indeed open communication systems capable of freely expanding, adapting old and new elements to new contexts, and coining new messages. If this is not due to the vocal-auditory channel, nor duality of patterning, nor the traditional notion of arbitrariness, the question arises of what human abilities and which properties of linguistic systems (in both spoken and signed languages) make this openness possible.

Which definition of language, then, is able to accommodate both spoken and signed languages? Is Chomsky's definition of language as a uniquely human, independent, innate, biological system, capable of recursion, a good candidate? I don't think so. Let's consider recursion.

8 The limits of recursion

As shown above, Chomsky hypothesized that language rests on (and ultimately coincides with) a capacity for recursion. This capacity is realized as a computational system, integrated in a uniquely human component of the nervous system that is autonomous from any other system.

We acknowledge the vast literature that, since Everett's (2005) paper on Pirahã, contests the hypothesis that recursion necessarily characterizes every language, but here we just mention that a lack of syntactic embedded structures, and by consequence a lack of a clear manifestation of recursion, also seems to characterize at least some village-level signed languages (Meir et al. 2010).

Even without entering into the details of, and taking a position on, this long *querelle*, it is clear that Chomsky and colleagues' proposal poses problems at least at three levels:
1. Recursion does enable openness *stricto sensu*, however it does not seem at play in the linguistic creativity which is responsible for the diachronic extension of the meanings of signs; by consequence, recursion alone cannot explain the complexity of linguistic openness.
2. The alleged independence of FLN from any other biological system is at odds with what we now know about the contiguity between action, gesture and language.
3. The hypothesis that FLN is not designed for communication is theoretically incompatible with the roles that sociality and interaction seem to play in the emergence of language from action.

In the next sections I examine these issues in detail.

8.1 Recursion does not enable openness

As noted by Tomalin (2007: 1799), among others, the word recursion has many senses in the formal sciences and its use by Chomsky and colleagues is extremely vague. The most widely accepted interpretation concerns constituent structures, "in that recursion consists of embedding a constituent in a constituent of the same type" (Pinker and Jackendoff 2005: 211). I add, along with Levelt (2008) and Evans and Levinson (2009) that recursion may also be defined over dependency structures, since "it is equally possible to have recursive structures that employ dependency relations rather than constituency structures" (Evans and Levinson 2009: 442).

If this interpretation is correct, the recursion to which Chomsky and colleagues allude is an ability to produce a potentially infinite number of embedded sentences and constituents, rather than an ability to indefinitely adapt language to changing situations through grammaticality and semantic plasticity. In this sense, Chomsky's notion of openness coincides strictly with potential infiniteness.

Diachronic linguistics has now clarified that the semantic openness of linguistic systems is enabled by the fact that new meanings basically arise in discourse through the use of already existing words, while "speakers and writers experiment with uses of words and constructions in the flow of strategic interaction with addressees" (Traugott and Dasher 2002: i; see also Wilkinson, Lepic, and Hou, this volume).

Potential infiniteness, as I argue below, is a property shared by other nonlinguistic systems such as arithmetic (see Section 10.1), and is therefore not a uniquely linguistic peculiarity. It does not suffice to explain this kind of openness, which was highlighted by Hockett ([1963] 1966), and seems to be responsible for the real semiotic power of linguistic systems.

8.2 Action, gesture, and language are contiguous

According to Hauser, Chomsky, and Fitch (2002), the computational system responsible for language is clearly autonomous and independent of any other cognitive or sensory motor system. This postulate is at odds, however, with a growing body of research that provides support for the early hypotheses put forward by Étienne Bonnot de Condillac, Giambattista Vico, and Johann Gottfried Herder, that gestures and language are contiguous. In the past decades, it has been shown indeed that there are ontogenetic, semiotic, neural, and (possibly) phylogenetic and cognitive links between action, gestures, and language (see Kendon 2016 for a thorough review).

From an ontogenetic standpoint, as shown by, among others, the numerous works by Virginia Volterra and colleagues (e.g., Capirci and Volterra 2008; Sparaci and Volterra 2017; Volterra et al. 2017; Volterra et al. 2018, Volterra et al. 2019), there is a tight link between the acquisition of motor actions, gestures, and (signed) languages. As Volterra et al. synthetize it:

> Infants, already in their first year of life, start to perform a series of motor actions in their exploration and manipulation of objects. Thanks to the social context that surrounds the infants and in particular to the adults who interact with them, these actions take on a symbolic meaning and are then progressively used as communicative gestures to represent an object or an event even outside the communicative context in which they had been originally produced. (Volterra et al. 2022: 168)

From a semiotic standpoint, Marentette et al. (2016) and Volterra et al. (2018) note that communicative gestures express four basic strategies of symbolic representation:

1. mimicry (the whole body represents the referent);
2. manipulation (the hands represent grasping the referent);
3. hands as objects (the hands take the shape of the referent);
4. shape and size (the hands trace the shape or indicate the size of the referent).

Interestingly enough, these strategies are also found in the symbolic representation of signed languages (Pizzuto and Volterra 2000; Boyes Braem, Pizzuto, and Volterra 2002; Volterra et al. 2019), showing a semiotic commonality between gestures and signed languages.

The hypothesis of contiguity between action and gestures has been corroborated by the discovery of mirror neurons. This discovery, which would lead to Arbib's (2012) mirror neurons hypothesis about the origins of language, suggested that the neurological system responsible for actions is also responsible for symbolic gestures (Gallese et al. 1996; Rizzolatti et al. 1996). This research indicates that monkey brains contain certain neurons, called mirror neurons, which are associated with the manipulation of objects. These neurons are highly congruent: that is, they fire only in the presence of a meaningful (goal-oriented) action and not after a generic movement; they do not fire for example when the object is simply presented without manipulation. Some of these neurons are highly selective in that some fire only when an object is grasped; others when the object is held, for example. Significantly, these neurons fire both when a monkey performs an action and when observing a conspecific performing this action. According to Arbib and Rizzolatti (1996) these neurons are also present in humans.

Rizzolatti and Arbib (1998) and Arbib (2012) suggest that mirror neurons may be implicated in the emergence of language. These neurons have motor properties, thus in the observer of a manipulation, the internal action of the neurons' firing can produce a movement. This, then, may have been a critical evolutionary link that causes the performer and observer to become sender and receiver of a communicative message. This involuntary movement in the receiver may cause the sender to become more aware that their action has been recognized and therefore could influence the receiver's behavior. The sender may then deliberately use a pantomime of the action in order to bias the receiver's behavior. At this point a sort of gestural communication would be established (see Pietrandrea 2002 for a more detailed summary, and implications for iconicity in signed language).

This hypothesis would confirm not only the contiguity between action and gestures, but also the radically social nature of any symbolic activity, which needs at least two participants to attribute meaning to body movements. From a cognitive point of view, Armstrong, Stokoe, and Wilcox's (1995) volume and Sherman Wilcox's subsequent work put forward one of most recent and groundbreaking theories of contiguity between action, gesture, and (both signed and spoken) language. Wilcox and colleagues build on two basic tenets of Stokoe's (1991) semantic phonology and cognitive grammar. As Wilcox (2009) wrote in his commemoration of William Stokoe:

> Semantic phonology suggests that visible gestures, whether the common everyday gestures we make when we speak or the conventionalized gestures that are the signs of natural signed languages, are primordial examples of self-symbolization. It is the twist in the Möbius strip. The phonological pole of gestures and signs consists of something that acts and its action. Hands are objects that move about and interact energetically with other objects. Hands are prototypical nouns and their actions are prototypical verbs. Hands and their actions manifest archetypal grammatical roles. A hand can act transitively on another hand, transmitting energy to the impacted object. Or, a hand can act intransitively, as when we trace the path of an object that has moved. (Wilcox 2009: 402)

Cognitive grammar claims that both semantic and phonological structures reside within the same conceptual space. On this ground, Wilcox and colleagues propose that visible gestures are to be considered as both objects in the world and objects about the world: visible gestures are at the same time symbolic and non-symbolic, or in other words, they are self-symbolic.

> Like the Roman god Janus, *visible gestures simultaneously face in two directions*: toward the perceived world of objects and events and toward the conceived world of grammar. Visible gestures are instrumental actions in the world that are recruited as communicative actions about the world. They are capable of serving as motivated signs for objects and events in the physical world, and in their internal structure they exhibit the properties of grammatical categories and relations. Visible gestures unite the represented world of objects and events and the representing world of language. (Wilcox 2009: 403; italics added)

In order to explain theoretically the symbolic power of gestures, Wilcox argues:

> The phonological and semantic poles of linguistic symbols reside in the same, broadly conceived semantic space. Because of this, it is possible to compare the regions in conceptual space occupied by the semantic and phonological poles of symbolic structures. The typical case for language is that the semantic pole and the phonological pole of a symbolic structure reside in vastly different regions of conceptual space. . . . However, the semantic and phonological poles of linguistic symbols may occupy regions of conceptual space that are not so distant. Sometimes the poles occupy regions that are quite close. . . . In fact, as a limiting case, the two poles of a linguistic symbol may occupy the same conceptual space; they may be put into correspondence with each other and become self-symbolizing or self-referential. (Wilcox 2009 : 401–402)

Wilcox (2009: 403) goes on to conclude: "Semantic phonology thus answers the question of how gestures came to represent the world, but the answer also comes with a twist: they never didn't."

The contiguity between actions and gestures can easily be extended to speech, as "beautifully" proposed by Wilcox (1996: 187) in his review of Barbara King's (1994) book. He writes:

> I am not suggesting that information transfer switched from gesture to speech. In fact, I am proposing just the opposite: there was no Great Switch from gesture to speech. I am suggesting that there was a gradual realignment of information transmission from a holistic gestalt of channels in which the optical (visible gesture) initially played a critical role to one in which the acoustic (vocal tract gesture) became predominant. Initially gesture carried the burden of information donation, even though vocal communication was present. Today speech carries the burden of information donation even though gesture remains.

All in all, an important body of evidence shows that actions, gestures, language, and speech are better regarded as different aspects of one and the same underlying motoric, neural, cognitive, social activity. The contiguity between action, gesture and language is too robust to be dismissed by the simple postulate that language *must* be independent of any other biological system. As I will show, this aspect of the analysis of language is also closely related to the function of language, which according to Chomsky's hypothesis is not communication.

8.3 Language is a communication system

Pinker and Jackendoff (2005) is a thorough criticism of Chomsky's denial of the "truism that language is properly regarded as system of communication" (Pinker and Jackendoff 2005: 224), showing the fragility of Chomsky's arguments. These are mainly based on:

1. The higher frequency of inner speech over dialogue.
This fact, according to Pinker and Jackendoff, cannot suffice to prove that language is not designed to communicate: as they put it "the key question in characterizing a biological function is not what a trait is typically *used* for but what it is *designed* for" (Pinker and Jackendoff 2005: 224; italics in original) and, as suggested by Paolo Ramat (personal communication), the exaptation of the oropharynx to language is a case in point.

2. An alleged perfection of language in the mapping between sound and meaning.
As Pinker and Jackendoff observe, this representation of language structures does not seem to match with the existence of multiple formal devices, often deployed redundantly, to convey meaning.

3. An alleged lack of the redundancy that typically characterizes communication systems.

Pinker and Jackendoff (2005: 228) show that redundancy does characterize linguistic systems, as it can be identified in "idioms, semiproductive derivational morphology, and families of irregular forms". I would add that redundancy is also identifiable in the Zipfian distribution of lexicon, lexical meanings, and lexical forms in linguistic systems, including signed language lexical systems, as I show in Pietrandrea (1995, 1998, 2002).

8.4 A summary

I contest, on the basis of the evidence outlined in this section, the following: 1) the insistence by Chomsky and colleagues to consider recursion as an autonomous and independent, uniquely human, uniquely linguistic ability, 2) the vagueness of this notion altogether, and 3) the hypothesis that language is not designed for communication. However, I suggest in Section 12 below that recursion can indeed play a major role in the emergence of language.

9 In search of a comprehensive definition of language

Openness, which distinguishes human languages from other communication systems and is responsible for their semiotic power, does not depend on duality of patterning and nor does it depend on recursion. This is evident from the absence of clear and consistent duality of patterning in signed languages (and the fragility of Chomsky and colleagues' proposal).

This leaves us with the need to identify a definition of language capable of accounting for the openness of language. Such a definition should not consecrate duality of patterning as the semiotic defining feature of language, and it should be able to account for the contiguity between action, gesture, and language that is evident in spoken as well as signed languages. It should also consider the relevance that the social and communicative dimension of language may have for the emergence of language from gestures and ultimately from action.

10 De Mauro's socio-semiotic definition of language

Building on de Saussure's ([1922] 1967) social definition of the linguistic sign, in the 1970s and 1980s (primarily) Italian linguist Tullio De Mauro developed a socio-semiotic definition of language that he synthetizes in his most recent studies as follows: "A language is not just a semiotic system. Or to put it better, a language is a semiotic system that includes functional and formally relevant elements, the mass of speakers, the time, as well as the network of socio-pragmatic, historical-cultural relationships in which [. . .] it is located and evolves" (De Mauro 2018: 113).[5]

De Mauro's definition of language was not grounded in an abstract characterization of language as a product. Rather, it focuses on the specificity of the cognitive, sensorimotor, and social and cultural human behaviors that enable the use and the acquisition of language (see Wacewicz and Zywiczynski 2015 for this distinction) and it motivates, on these grounds, its properties. In his first essay on semantics he noted: "It is erroneous to claim that words or sentences signify something: it is only humans in reality, who signify, through sentences and words" (De Mauro 1965: 31–32). Humans, he observes in De Mauro (1982: 101), signify by keeping an attitude of "tolerance upon the fields" (see also Lenneberg 1971).[6] They are able to presuppose and to "tolerate" that variability as an inherent property of the signs of a system and therefore they are able to accept that a linguistic sign that is recognized as "the same" sign may have different phonological realizations across different speakers, uses, and times, and that a word may have different meanings across different speakers, uses, and times.

By presupposing and tolerating this inherent variability, humans introduce in language a particular form of indeterminacy that De Mauro calls in his first studies "vagueness" and in his later studies "plasticity".

---

5 See also other works by De Mauro (e.g., 1965, 1982, 1991, 2000). Translations of quotes taken from De Mauro's Italian texts are mine.
6 Lenneberg (1971: 12, italics in original) formalized this notion as follows: "Because words map only onto ill-defined fields, the interpretation of words between speakers can never be exact. We know with only varying degrees of certainty what our interlocutor means by the words he is using. The efficiency of communication is not vitally affected by this sloppiness as long as the variance in denotation between the two speakers is not too great. In other words, we can *tolerate* a certain degree of shifting and fuzziness of the fields. This notion could be formalized, and the *tolerance upon the fields* could, at least in theory, be defined with some rigor".

10.1 The plasticity of linguistic signs

Plasticity, which uniquely characterizes human languages, should not be confused with the polyvalence that characterizes both human languages and other communication systems, for example, arithmetic.

The polyvalence of signs within a system is the property that makes it possible for a single sign to have more than one referent (by polysemy or homonymy, or metaphorical, metonymic extension) and, vice versa, for a single referent to be signified by more than one sign (by synonymy). Polyvalence also allows the meaning of a sign at a broader level of generality to be applied to a referent that would be further divisible and specifiable (Devos 2003, among others).

Polyvalence is not only typical of linguistic systems; other semiotic systems are also characterized by it. Arithmetic, for example, has polyvalence when we think that, at least in certain respects, 12 and 6+6 may signify the same referent, i.e., are synonyms. What differentiates linguistic polyvalence from that identifiable in a system such as arithmetic is the fact that the latter, but not the former, is calculable.

Given an arithmetic sign, say 12, we can 1) calculate its various formal values; 2) calculate the (albeit potentially infinite) signs that can be considered, in certain respects, its synonyms, for example 6+6, 8+4, 12-0, etc.; and 3) identify exclusionary referents; we can for example exclude 10+3 (as synonymous with 12).

By contrast, the polyvalence of linguistic signs, which are plastic, cannot be calculated: "We cannot decide on the basis of formal considerations if, once the referent is known and the expression is known, the expression is always or never applicable to the referent" (De Mauro 1982: 99). For example, we could not have decided sixty years ago that the word *mouse* would never be applicable to an electronic pointer.

10.2 Plasticity, openness and human cognition

From a strict semiotic point of view, plasticity manifests itself in what De Mauro (1982, 2000, 2018) calls the *borderlessness* of linguistic signifiers and linguistic meanings. Signs are loosely articulated and meanings are constantly oscillating. This looseness and oscillation are what allow a constant adaptation of the meanings of linguistic signs to new senses (through contextual specification, and also through bleaching and metaphorical and metonymic extensions).

From a cognitive point of view, it is important to highlight that the semantic extension of linguistic signs is driven by the tendency within human cognition to categorize concepts (and therefore signs) radially: the new senses of a linguistic sign have a "family resemblance" (see Wittgenstein 1953) with pre-existing senses. Humans apply the same cognitive strategy of categorization to both reality and to linguistic signs, as suggested by Armstrong, Stokoe, and Wilcox (1995). Since human cognition allows for the widespread conceptualization of entities and events in reality *and* signs in language, human languages are potentially open, which, according to De Mauro, is enabled by a constant tolerance towards the continuous readjustment of meanings (and forms, at least to an extent).

Like the other scholars who have dealt with the definition of language, De Mauro considered openness as a key element. He did not dismiss the necessity of a capacity for the potentially infinite generation of new expressions to do this, but he did not limit his definition of openness to this property. He argued instead that this capacity is not specific to linguistic systems (e.g., note arithmetic) and like Hockett, De Mauro observed that openness also includes the capacity to freely assign new meanings to old and new elements alike. According to De Mauro, it is plasticity that enables exactly the latter capacity via tolerance for the intrinsic variability of linguistic signs, making it possible to extend and reassign new semantic senses.

10.3 Plasticity, reflexiveness, and the social dimension of language

Interestingly, De Mauro highlighted that semantic extensions enabled by plasticity are inextricably intertwined with two other characteristics of linguistic systems: reflexiveness and the social dimension of language.

The plasticity of linguistic signs can, potentially, compromise mutual understanding as it can give way, as De Mauro (p.c.) put it, to a *schizoide* ('schizoid') system, where signs can signify whatever a speaker intends to signify. Paradoxically, a correction to this possible consequence of plasticity resides in plasticity itself. The plasticity of linguistic signs indeed allows the speaker to extend the meaning of a sign to the point where a sign is used to signify itself. Linguistic signs can, therefore, be self-referring: they can be used metalinguistically to indicate themselves. This property entails reflexiveness, which, according to Hockett's ([1963] 1966: 9) definition, is "the possibility in a language of communicating about communication". Reflexiveness therefore allows the users of a language to negotiate the meaning of a sign in any context. See, for example, (1):

(1) A : I am a rock
    B : What do you mean by "rock"?

Through this negotiation, the semantic extension of a sign is socially and contextually determined; mutual understanding becomes possible, and the linguistic community, not just a single speaker, drives the linguistic system. In this sense the plasticity of a sign is inherently intertwined with the radically social nature of linguistic signs. As De Mauro put it:

> When we reflect on vagueness we are forced to explicitly reintroduce a reference to users as concrete subjects more or less aware of what they communicate and how they communicate about it. (De Mauro 1982: 99)

> A linguistic system can only be described in connection with the uses and beliefs that are current at a precise time between concrete groups of users. While other semiotic systems admit good analyses at a zero time and for zero users, the time and the speaker are internal factors of a linguistic system, as pointed out by de Saussure. (De Mauro 1982: 102)

10.4 Plasticity and arbitrariness

It is worth noting that plasticity is crucially related to arbitrariness: only arbitrary signs can be freely reinterpreted, can freely extend and adapt their meanings. We have shown in Pietrandrea and Russo (2007) that it is radical arbitrariness (see 6.3 above), i.e., the autonomy of a linguistic sign vis-à-vis the representation of reality that is a prerequisite for plasticity.

This point leads us toward an assessment of the compatibility of signed languages with De Mauro's definition, or better, the other way around, toward an assessment of De Mauro's definition in light of signed languages. So, is De Mauro's definition in fact compatible with what we currently know about signed languages?

11 When De Mauro's definition of language met signed languages

The reader will forgive me for adding a brief personal note here. Not far from De Mauro's office in Rome was the historical Tommaso Silvestri Institute for deaf children in Via Nomentana. In the same years De Mauro elaborated his theoretical definition of language, Virginia Volterra led a group of researchers in conducting the first scientific analysis of Italian Sign Language, critically involving deaf people in this monumental research. This environment constituted a privileged observatory to test the soundness of De Mauro's theoretical definition. It was indeed possible to observe how the increased use of LIS, and the interaction between LIS signers along with the metalinguistic reflection and negotiation triggered by their linguistic research enabled the development, stabilization, and enrichment of this language.

In the early 1990s, De Mauro suggested that Tommaso Russo and myself, who were his students at that time, join the group working in Via Nomentana and focus our own first linguistic analyses on LIS.

We witnessed the dynamic of a linguistic community that was acquiring, through linguistic analysis and discussions about the language, a stronger metalinguistic awareness. This contributed to consolidating and stabilizing the language. Virginia Volterra told us that when she first approached the Roman deaf community in the 1970s, their metalinguistic awareness was so limited that, when questioned, they denied having a language. But then, they immediately turned to each other and began to sign. Twenty years later LIS was being used on TV and in a number of educational projects. It was clear that Roman deaf people had by this time developed a solid metalinguistic awareness. They were teaching courses in their language and were always keen to engage in passionate discussions about the creation and diffusion of neologisms, on the meaning of particular structures, on etymology, and on the variants of certain forms. In other words, by joining the Roman deaf community we could concretely witness the metamorphosis of the language through metalinguistic negotiation as theorized by De Mauro.

Tommaso and I conducted analyses of the structure and the redundancy of the LIS lexicon (Pietrandrea 1995, 1997, 1998, 2002), LIS poetry and discourse (Russo 2000, 2004a, 2004b; Russo, Giurana and Pizzuto 2001), iconicity in LIS (Pietrandrea 2000, 2002; Russo 2000, 2004a, 2004b; Russo, Giurana and Pizzuto 2001; Pietrandrea and Russo 2007; Russo and Pietrandrea, this volume).

We learned from Sherman Wilcox, who had multiple institutional exchanges with Via Nomentana, how to reframe our observations and analyses in the context of cognitive linguistics and studies of language evolution, which helped us further ground the socio-semiotic definition of language that we were testing.

After a few years of beautiful and passionate scientific teamwork, De Mauro (2000) could put forward that LIS is a communication system characterized by openness and reflexiveness, whose signs (not necessarily non-iconic) are radically arbitrary and plastic: his definition of language had passed the test of signed languages.

12 Conclusion

Building on the common ground established between Sherman Wilcox's cognitive approach to language, and our own Roman socio-semiotic approach, I revisit De Mauro's definition of language in this chapter. Thus, language can be defined as a particular type of semiotic system, in which the capacity of its users to accept limitless variability of the signs determines an inherent plasticity of the system. Plasticity enables open creativity and, being a pre-condition for reflexiveness, it also enables social control of this creativity. Time, speakers, and culture are all internal factors of this unique and uniquely human semiotic system. This definition, which focuses on the specificity of human behavior that enables the acquisition and use of language rather than on supposed inherent structural properties, has the merit of readily accommodating both spoken and signed languages. It is also theoretically compatible with all that we know about the contiguity between action gestures, signs, and speech.

This definition, though, comes at the cost of great scientific responsibility. Beginning with a theoretical point of view, it is necessary to identify and formalize which cognitive abilities allow humans to handle the plasticity of linguist systems (on this point see Tomasello 2003, among others). In particular, it is imperative to understand the exact relationship between plasticity and reflexiveness. We may hypothesize that plasticity is not simply *regulated* by reflexiveness, as proposed by De Mauro, rather that plasticity fundamentally rests on reflexiveness. This hypothesis would allow us to posit a tighter link between De Mauro's definition of language and Wilcox and colleagues' hypothesis that gestures are self-referring actions. As observed by Wilcox (2009), this would in turn lead to reconsidering the role played by recursion, this time intended not in the linguistic sense, but in the more general Gödelian sense of reflexivity (Gelernter 1998), in language emergence.

From a methodological point of view, an awareness that linguistic systems cannot be approached without taking into account speakers as internal factors in the system entails that the linguist must acquire and use the appropriate methodological instruments to conduct extended empirical inquires of languages. This is both challenging and critically necessary for signed language research, as shown by Wilcox and Morford (2007). Regarding signed languages, an appropriate system of written representation is a minimal requirement for a sound empirical analysis, as repeatedly argued by Elena Antinoro Pizzuto and colleagues who proposed a representation system of LIS based on Sutton's ([1995] 1999) SignWriting (Pizzuto and Pietrandrea 2001; Antinoro Pizzuto, Chiari and Rossini 2008, 2010; Gianfreda et al. 2009; Cuxac and Antinoro Pizzuto 2010).

From a social and educational point of view, by accepting the fact that the description of a language cannot be separate from the description of the linguistic community, and that this has an important impact on that linguistic community, linguists commit to describing languages in each of these extensions. Thorough analyses of the entire repertory of discourses are necessary, which may be especially difficult (but even more necessary) for signed languages.

In this sense, as pointed out by Schembri and Johnston (under review), the analysis of language in general, and of signed languages in particular, can benefit enormously from the rise of cognitive sociolinguistics, a new field of linguistic inquiry at the interface between cognitive linguistics, sociolinguistics, discourse analysis, and corpus linguistics (Kristiansen and Dirven 2008; Geeraerts, Kristiansen, and Peirsman 2010), which is poised to provide a unified framework to deal with the inescapable complexity of what constitutes a language.

References

Antinoro Pizzuto, Elena, Isabella Chiari & Paolo Rossini. 2008. The representation issue and its multifaceted aspects in constructing sign language corpora: Questions, answers, further problems. In Onno Crasborn, Eleni Efthimiou, Thomas Hanke, Ernst D. Thoutenhoofd & Inge Zwitserlood (eds.), *3rd Workshop on the Representation and Processing of Sign Languages: Construction and Exploitation of Sign Language Corpora*, LREC 2008, Marrakech, May 27–June 1, 2008. 150–158, Paris: ELRA.

Antinoro Pizzuto, Elena, Isabella Chiari & Paolo Rossini. 2010. Representing sign language: Theoretical, methodological and practical issues. In Massimo Pettorino, Antonella Giannini, Isabella Chiari & Francesca Dovetto (eds.), *Spoken Communication*, 205–240. Newcastle on Tyne: Cambridge Scholars Publishing.

Arbib, Michael A. 2012. *How the Brain Got Language: The Mirror System Hypothesis.* Oxford: Oxford University Press.

Arbib, Michael A. & Giacomo Rizzolatti. 1996. Neural expectations: A possible evolutionary path from manual skills to language. *Communication & Cognition* 29(3/4). 393–424.

Armstrong, David F., William C. Stokoe & Sherman E. Wilcox. 1995. *Gesture and the Nature of Language.* Cambridge: Cambridge University Press.

Battison, Robbin. 1978. *Lexical Borrowing in American Sign Language.* Silver Spring, MD: Linkstok Press.

Bellugi, Ursula, Edward S. Klima & Patricia Siple. 1975. Remembering in signs. *Cognition* 3(2). 93–125.

Bellugi, Ursula & Edward Klima. 1976. Two faces of sign: Iconic and abstract. In Stevan Harnad, Horst D. Steklis & Jane Lancaster (eds.), *The Origins and Evolution of Language and Speech,* 514–538. New York: N.Y. Academy of Sciences.

Boyes Braem, Penny. 1981. *Significant Features of the Handshape in American Sign Language.* Berkeley: University of California, Bekeley dissertation.

Boyes Braem, Penny, Elena Pizzuto & Virginia Volterra. 2002. The interpretation of signs by (hearing and deaf) members of different cultures. In Rolf Schulmeister & Heimo Reinitzer (eds.), *Progress in Sign Language Research: In Honor of Siegmund Prillwitz,* 187–219. Hamburg: Signum Press.

Brentari, Diane. 1998. *A Prosodic Model of Sign Language Phonology.* Cambridge, MA: The MIT Press.

Bybee, Joan. 1985. *Morphology: A Study of the Relation Between Meaning and Form.* Amsterdam/Philadelphia: John Benjamins.

Capirci, Olga & Virginia Volterra. 2008. Gesture and speech: The emergence and development of a strong and changing partnership. *Gesture* 8(1). 22–44.

Chomsky, Noam. 2002. On Nature and Language. New York: Cambridge University Press.

Crystal, David. 2010 [1987]. *The Cambridge Encyclopedia of Language,* 3rd edn. Cambridge: Cambridge University Press.

Cuxac, Christian & Elena Antinoro Pizzuto. 2010. Émergence, norme et variation dans les langues des signes : vers une redéfinition notionnelle [Emergence, norms and variation in signed languages: Towards a notional redefinition]. *Langage et Société* 131. 37–53.
De Mauro, Tullio. 1965. *Introduzione alla semantica* [Introduction to Semantics]. Bari: Laterza.
De Mauro, Tullio. 1982. *Minisemantica dei linguaggi non verbali e delle lingue* [Minisemantics of Non-verbal and Verbal Languages]. Bari: Laterza.
De Mauro, Tullio. 1991. Ancora Saussure e la semantica [Saussure and semantics revisited]. *Cahiers Ferdinand de Saussure* 45. 101–109.
De Mauro, Tullio. 2000. Vocalità, gestualità, lingue segnate e non segnate [Vocality, gestures, signed and nonsigned languages]. In Caterina Bagnara, Giampaolo Chiappini, Maria Pia Conte & Michela Ott (eds.), *Viaggio nella città invisibile* [Journey to the Invisible City], 17–25. Pisa: Edizioni del Cerro.
De Mauro, Tullio. 2018. *L'Educazione Linguistica Democratica* [Democratic linguistic education]. Bari: Laterza.
de Saussure, Ferdinand. 1967 [1922]. *Corso di linguistica generale* [Course in general linguistics] edited and translated by Tullio de Mauro. Bari: Laterza.
Devos, Filip. 2003. Semantic vagueness and lexical polyvalence. *Studia Linguistica* 57(3). 121–141.
Evans, Nicholas & Stephen C. Levinson. 2009. The myth of language universals: Language diversity and its importance for cognitive science. *Behavioral and Brain Sciences* 32. 429–492.
Everett, Dan. 2005. Cultural constraints on grammar and cognition in Pirahã. *Current Anthropology* 46(4). 621–646.
Frishberg, Nancy. 1975. Arbitrariness and iconicity: Historical change in American Sign Language. *Language* 51(3). 696–719.
Gallese, Vittorio, Luciano Fadiga, Leonardo Fogassi & Giacomo Rizzolatti. 1996. Action recognition in the premotor cortex. *Brain* 119. 593–609.
Geeraerts, Dirk, Gitte Kristiansen & Yves Peirsman, (eds.), 2010. *Advances in Cognitive Sociolinguistics*. Berlin/New York: De Gruyter Mouton.
Gelernter, David. 1998. *Machine Beauty: Elegance and the Heart of Technology*. New York: Basic Books.
Gianfreda, Gabriele, Giulia Petitta, Claudia Bianchini, Alessio Di Renzo, Paolo Rossini, Tommaso Lucioli & Luca Lamano. 2009. Dalla modalità faccia-a-faccia ad una lingua scritta emergente: nuove prospettive su trascrizione e scrittura della Lingua dei Segni Italiana (LIS) [From a face-to-face modality to an emerging written language: New perspectives on the transcription and writing of Italian Sign Language (LIS)]. In Carlo Consani, Cristiano Furiassi, Francesca Guazzella & Carmela Perta (eds.), *Atti del 9° Congresso Internazionale di Studi dell'Associazione Italiana di Linguistica Applicata (AItLA)*, 413–437. Perugia: Guerra Edizioni.
Givón, T. 2002. *Biolinguistics: The Santa Barbara Lectures*. Amsterdam/Philadelphia: John Benjamins.
Haiman, John.1985. *Natural Syntax: Iconicity and Erosion*. Cambridge: Cambridge University Press.
Hauser, Marc D., Noam Chomsky & W. Tecumseh Fitch. 2002. The faculty of language: What is it, who has it, and how did it evolve? *Science* 298(5598). 1569–1579.
Hockett, Charles F. 1958. *A Course in Modern Linguistics*. New York: Macmillan.
Hockett, Charles F. 1959. Animal "languages" and human language. *Human Biology* 31(1). 32–39.
Hockett, Charles F. 1960. The origin of speech. *Scientific American* 203(3). 88–96.
Hockett, Charles F. 1966 [1963]. The problem of universals in language. In Joseph H. Greenberg (ed.), *Universals of Language*, 2nd edn., 1–29. Cambridge, MA: The MIT Press.
Hockett, Charles F. 1978. In search of Jove's brow. *American Speech* 53(4). 243–313.

Humboldt, Wilhelm von. 1999 [1836]. *Ueber die Verschiedenheit des menschlichen Sprachbaus und ihren Einfluss auf die geistige Entwicklung des Menschengeschlechts*. [On Language. On the Diversity of Human Language Construction and Its Influence on the Mental Development of the Human Species]. Cambridge: Cambridge University Press.

Kendon Adam. 2016. Reflections on the "gesture-first" hypothesis of language origins. *Psychonomic Bulletin & Review* 24. 163–170.

King, Barbara J. 1994. *The Information Continuum: Evolution of Social Information Transfer in Monkeys, Apes, and Hominids*. Santa Fe, NM: School of American Research Press.

Klima, Edward S. & Ursula Bellugi. 1979. *The Signs of Language*. Cambridge, MA: Harvard University Press.

Kristiansen, Gitte & René Dirven (eds.). 2008. *Cognitive Sociolinguistics: Language Variation, Cultural Models, Social Systems*. Berlin/New York: De Gruyter Mouton.

Lenneberg, Eric H. 1971. On language knowledge, apes, and brains. *Journal of Psycholinguistic Research* 1. 1–29.

Levelt, Willem J.M. 2008. *Formal Grammars in Linguistics and Psycholinguistics*. Amsterdam/Philadelphia: John Benjamins.

Liddell, Scott K. 1984. THINK and BELIEVE: Sequentiality in American Sign Language. *Language* 60(2). 372–399.

Marentette, Paula, Paola Pettenati, Arianna Bello & Virginia Volterra. 2016. Gesture and symbolic representation in Italian and English-speaking Canadian two-year-olds. *Child Development* 87(3). 944–96.

Martinet, André. 1955. *Economie des changements phonétiques: Traité de phonologie diachronique* [Economy of Phonetic Changes: Treatise on Diachronic Phonology]. Bern: Francke AG Verlag.

Martinet, André. 1960. *Éléments de linguistique générale* [Elements of General Linguistics]. Paris: Armand Colin.

Martinet, André. 1996. Preface. In Nève François-Xavier, *Essai de grammaire de la langue des signes Française* [An Essay on French Sign Language Grammar]. Genève: Droz.

Meir, Irit, Wendy Sandler, Carol Padden & Mark Aronoff. 2010. Emerging sign languages. In Marc Marschark & Patricia Elizabeth Spencer (eds.), *The Oxford Handbook of Deaf Studies, Language, and Education*, Volume 2, 268–280. Oxford: Oxford University Press.

Padden, Carol A. & David M. Perlmutter. 1987. American Sign Language and the architecture of phonological theory. *Natural Language & Linguistic Theory* 5(3). 335–375.

Pietrandrea, Paola. 1995. *Analisi semiotica dei dizionari della Lingua Italiana dei Segni* [A Semiotic Analysis of the Lexicon of Italian Sign Language]. Rome: Università La Sapienza thesis.

Pietrandrea, Paola. 1997. I dizionari della LIS: analisi qualitative e quantitative [LIS dictionaries: Qualitative and quantitative analyses]. In Maria Cristina Caselli & Serena Corazza (eds.), *LIS, Studi, esperienze e ricerche sulla lingua dei segni in Italia* [LIS: Studies, Experiences, and Research on Sign Language in Italy], 255–259. Pisa: Edizioni del Cerro.

Pietrandrea, Paola. 1998. Sublexical regularities and linguistic economy in Italian Sign Language: A quantitative analysis. In Catie Berkenfield, Dawn Nordquist & Angus Grieve-Smith (eds.), *Proceedings of the First Annual High Desert Linguistics Society Conference*, 69–80. Albuquerque: University of New Mexico.

Pietrandrea, Paola. 2000. L'interazione complessa di iconicità e arbitrarietà nel lessico LIS [The complex interplay of iconicity and arbitrariness in the LIS lexicon]. In Caterina Bagnara, Giampaolo Chiappini, Marie Pia Conte & Michela Ott (eds.), *Viaggio nella città invisibile* [Journey to the Invisible City], 38–49. Pisa: Edizioni del Cerro.

Pietrandrea, Paola. 2002. Iconicity and arbitrariness in Italian Sign Language. *Sign Language Studies* 2(3). 296–321.
Pietrandrea, Paola & Tommaso Russo. 2007. Diagrammatic and imagic hypoicons in signed and verbal languages. In Elena Pizzuto, Paola Pietrandrea & RAffaele Simone (eds.), *Verbal and Signed Languages: Comparing Structures, Constructs and Methodologies*, 35–56. Berlin/New York: Mouton de Gruyter.
Pinker, Steven & Ray Jackendoff. 2005. The faculty of language: What's special about it? *Cognition* 95(2). 201–236.
Pizzuto, Elena, Emanuela Cameracanna, Serena Corazza & Virginia Volterra. 1995. Terms for spatio-temporal relations in Italian Sign Language. In. Raffaele Simone (ed.), *Iconicity in Syntax*, 237–257. Amsterdam/Philadelphia: John Benjamins.
Pizzuto, Elena & Paola Pietrandrea. 2001. The notation of signed texts: Open questions and indications for further research. *Sign Language & Linguistics* 4(1/2). 29–45.
Pizzuto, Elena & Virginia Volterra. 2000. Iconicity and transparency in sign languages: A cross-linguistic cross-cultural view. In Karen Emmorey & Harlan Lane (eds.), *The Signs of Language Revisited: An Anthology in Honor of Ursula Bellugi and Edward Klima*, 261–286. Mahwah, NJ: Lawrence Erlbaum.
Radutzky, Elena (ed.). 1992. *Dizionario bilingue elementare della lingua italiana dei segni* [Elementary Bilingual Dictionary of Italian Sign Language]. Roma: Edizioni Kappa.
Rizzolatti, Giacomo & Michael A. Arbib. 1998. Language within our grasp. *Trends in Neurosciences* 21. 188–194.
Rizzolatti, Giacomo, Luciano Fadiga, Massimo Matelli, Valentino Bettinardi, Eraldo Paulesu, Daniela Perani & Ferrucio Fazio. 1996. Localization of grasp representations in humans by PET: 1. Observation versus execution. *Experimental Brain Research* 111. 246–252.
Russo, Tommaso. 2000. *Iconicità e Metafora nella LIS* [Iconicity and Metaphor in LIS]. Palermo: Università degli Studi di Palermo dissertation.
Russo, Tommaso. 2004a. Iconicity and productivity in sign language discourse: An analysis of three LIS discourse registers. *Sign Language Studies* 4(2). 164–197.
Russo, Tommaso. 2004b. *La mappa poggiata sull'isola. Iconicità e metafora nelle lingue dei segni e nelle lingue vocali* [The map laid down upon the island: Iconicity and metaphor in sign languages and vocal languages]. Rende: Centro Editoriale e Librario, Università della Calabria.
Russo, Tommaso, Rosaria Giurana & Elena Pizzuto. 2001. Italian Sign Language (LIS) poetry: Iconic properties and structural regularities. *Sign Language Studies* 2(1). 84–112.
Sandler, Wendy. 1999. Review: *A Prosodic Model of Sign Language Phonology*. *Phonology* 16(3). 443–447.
Schembri, Adam & Trevor Johnston. (Under Review). Usage-based grammars and sign languages: Evidence from Auslan, BSL and NZSL.
Simone, Raffaele (ed.). 1995. *Iconicity in Language*. Amsterdam/Philadelphia: John Benjamins.
Sparaci, Laura & Virginia Volterra. 2017. Hands shaping communication: From gestures to signs. In Marta Bertolaso & Nicola Di Stefano (eds.), *The Hand: Perception, Cognition, Action*, 29–54. Cham, Switzerland: Springer.
Stokoe, William C. 1960. *Sign Language Structure: An Outline of the Visual Communication Systems of the American Deaf, Studies in Linguistics, Occasional Papers 8*. Buffalo, NY.
Stokoe, William C. 1991. Semantic phonology. *Sign Language Studies* 71. 107–114.
Sutton, Valerie. 1999 [1995]. *Lessons in SignWriting: Textbook and Workbook*, 2nd edn. La Jolla, CA: Deaf Action Committee for Sign Writing.
Tomalin, Marcus. 2007. Reconsidering recursion in syntactic theory. *Lingua* 117. 1784–1800.
Tomasello, Michael. 2003. *Constructing a Language: A Usage-Based Theory of Language Acquisition*. Cambridge, MA: Harvard University Press.

Traugott Elizabeth C. & Richard B. Dasher. 2002. *Regularity in Semantic Change*. Cambridge: Cambridge University Press.

Volterra, Virginia, Olga Capirci, Maria Cristina Caselli, Pasquale Rinaldi & Laura Sparaci. 2017. Developmental evidence for continuity from action to gesture to sign/word. *Language, Interaction and Acquisition* 8(1). 13–41.

Volterra, Virginia, Olga Capirci, Pasquale Rinaldi & Laura Sparaci. 2018. From action to spoken and signed language through gesture: Some basic developmental issues for a discussion on the evolution of the human language-ready brain. *Interaction Studies* 19(1/2). 216–238.

Volterra, Virginia, Maria Roccaforte, Alessio Di Renzo & Sabina Fontana. 2019. *Descrivere la lingua dei segni italiana. Una prospettiva cognitiva e sociosemiotica* [Describing Italian Sign Language: A cognitive and socio-semiotic perspective]. Bologna: Il Mulino.

Volterra, Virginia, Maria Roccaforte, Alessio Di Renzo & Sabina Fontana. 2022. *Italian Sign Language from a Cognitive and Socio-semiotic Perspective: Implications for a General Language Theory*. Amsterdam/Philadelphia: John Benjamins.

Wacewicz, Sławomir & Przemysław Żywiczyński. 2015. Language evolution: Why Hockett's design features are a non-starter. *Biosemiotics* 8(1). 29–46.

Wilcox, Sherman. 1996. Not from Jove's brow. *Language & Communication* 16(2). 179–192.

Wilcox, Sherman. 2004. Cognitive iconicity: Conceptual spaces, meaning, and gesture in signed languages. *Cognitive Linguistics* 15(2). 119–147.

Wilcox, Sherman. 2005. Routes from gesture to language. *Revista Da ABRALIN* 4(1/2). 11–45.

Wilcox, Sherman. 2009. William C. Stokoe and the gestural theory of language origins. *Sign Language Studies* 9(4). 398–409.

Wilcox, Sherman. 2010. Signed languages. In Dirk Geeraerts & Hubert Cuyckens (eds.), *The Oxford Handbook of Cognitive Linguistics*, 1113–1136. Oxford: Oxford University Press.

Wilcox, Sherman. 2013. Language in motion: A framework for unifying spoken language, signed language, and gesture. *Anuari de Filologia. Estudis de Lingüística* [Yearbook of Philology: Linguistic Studies] 2. 49–57.

Wilcox, Sherman. 2015. Signed languages. In Ewa Dąbrowska & Dagmar Divjak, *Handbook of Cognitive Linguistics*, 668–689. Berlin/Boston: De Gruyter Mouton. https://doi.org/10.1515/9783110292022-034

Wilcox, Sherman & Jill Morford. 2007. Empirical methods in signed language research. In Monica Gonzalez-Marquez, Irene Mittelberg, Seana Coulson & Michael J. Spivey (eds.), *Methods in Cognitive Linguistics*, 171–200. Amsterdam/Philadelphia: John Benjamins.

Wilcox, Sherman & André N. Xavier. 2013. A framework for unifying spoken language, signed language and gesture. *Revista Todas as Letras* 15(1). 88–110.

Wilcox, Sherman & Phyllis Wilcox. 1995. The gestural expression of modality in ASL. In Joan Bybee & Suzanne Fleischman (eds.), *Modality in Grammar and Discourse*, 135–162. Amsterdam/Philadelphia: John Benjamins.

Wilcox, Sherman & Phyllis P. Wilcox. 2013. Cognitive linguistics and signed languages. *International Journal of Cognitive Linguistics* 3(2). 127–151.

Wittgenstein, Ludwig. 1953. *Philosophical Investigations*. New York: Macmillan.

Zipf, George. 1935. *The Psychobiology of Language: An Introduction to Dynamic Philology*. Boston: Houghton-Mifflin.

II **Iconicity in spoken and signed language**

Ronald W. Langacker
Structure, iconicity, and access

1 Structure as activity

Given that language effects the pairing of forms and meanings, to what extent is their connection motivated rather than arbitrary? The classic principle of *l'arbitraire du signe* (de Saussure 1916) is simplistic even in the case of lexemes, and fares even worse if extended to grammar. A basic tenet of Cognitive Grammar (Langacker 1987, 1991, 2008) is that lexicon, grammar, and even discourse reside in a continuum of form-meaning pairings. In all but the simplest expressions, iconicity proves to be a major factor. Wilcox (2004) has argued (in regard to signed languages) that arbitrariness and iconicity coexist in linguistic structure as manifestations of a deeper cognitive basis. I will take this one step further, suggesting that structure and iconicity are actually non-distinct, in that both are manifestations of overlapping activity.

Cognitive Grammar posits just three broad kinds of structures. A *semantic* structure (the meaning part of a form-meaning pairing) can be any sort of conception or experience. "*Phonological*" structures (the form part) include not only sounds but other observable modes of expression (notably gestures). A *symbolic* structure resides in the association of a semantic and a phonological structure—its *poles*—such that either serves to activate the other. Linguistic structure is *dynamic*, consisting in interactive processing activity, so time is a basic dimension of organization at either pole. It is also dynamic in the sense of being learned, maintained, and modified through language *use* in context. Through *entrenchment* (for individuals) and *conventionalization* (in social groups), recurring patterns of activity give rise to established *units* employed in subsequent usage events.

As an abstract characterization, I say that *structure* consists in *elements* being *connected* in a certain way (through association, influence, or overlap). Connected elements adapt to one another. They constitute a *grouping*: a distinct *higher-order element*, with its own internal structure and the potential to participate in further connections. In Figure 1(a), a dashed-line ellipse represents the grouping effected by the connection of elements (x) and (y). A grouping achieves *structural significance* to the extent that it exploits its connective potential; its role in larger groupings is its *function* (cf. Harder 2010). In Figure 1(b), the grouping ((x)—(y)) is significant owing to its role in the grouping (((x)—(y))—(z)).

Ronald W. Langacker, University of California, San Diego, USA, e-mail: rlangacker@ucsd.edu

https://doi.org/10.1515/9783110703788-005

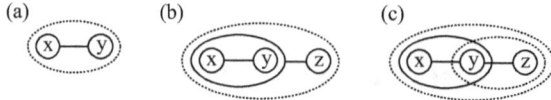

Figure 1: Structure as elements, connections, and groupings.

An element within a grouping can participate in further connections, resulting in groupings that cross-cut one another. In Figure 1(c), (y) is already grouped with (x), but then connects with (z), resulting in the cross-cutting groupings ((x)—(y)) and ((y)—(z)). These are themselves connected, by overlap, to form a still larger grouping. For instance, a verb like *turn on* connects with its object in two ways: as a whole (e.g. *turn on the lights*); or via its verbal subpart (*turn the lights on*), in which case the groupings *turn on* and *turn the lights* cross-cut one another. But in either case *turn on* is a lexical grouping, where *turn* and *on* adapt to one another as facets of its composite meaning.

The basic phenomena in Figure 1 give rise to structures of unlimited complexity and variety. Since these are not reducible to any single type of configuration (like a "tree"), I say that a structure (of any size) comprises an *assembly* of connected elements (Langacker 2021). Cognitive Grammar posits just three general kinds of structures: semantic, phonological, and symbolic (residing in the association of the other two). Lexicon, grammar, and discourse consist in assemblies of symbolic structures.

Linguistic structure is non-material, consisting in organized activity of various sorts (e.g. neural, psychological, physical, perceptual, interactive). It is therefore inherently *dynamic*, unfolding through time in a certain manner. A structure (of any kind or size) can be described informally as a *pattern* of activity. A speaker's grasp of a language resides in a vast assembly of patterns—referred to as *units*—with varying degrees of entrenchment and conventionality. This overall assembly is never static, but has sufficient stability for its role in thought and communication. The expression employed in a particular *usage event* constitutes a limited, transient assembly comprising both activated units and any structures induced by their co-activation in that context. Even for a simple expression, this processing activity runs concurrently in separate domains, at multiple levels, and on different time scales. On a given time scale, we can posit processing windows of a certain rough duration, within which connections are made and structure emerges.[1]

---

[1] Owing to concurrent processing, an expression's structure does not consist in a single linear sequence, nor can its time course be reduced to a single "left-to-right" pass through it. Also involved are such phenomena as recall, backtracking, interruption, reconceptualization, anticipation, afterthought, and ellipsis.

While assemblies have no specific form, certain *basic configurations* (Figure 2) are both discernible in their organization and highly prevalent. In *hierarchy* (Figure 2a), a grouping established at one level of organization functions as a whole—effectively as a single element—in a higher-level grouping. It is a matter of *composition*, substantive *component* structures being grouped to form a *composite* structure that functions as a component at the next higher level. In *seriality* (Figure 2b), elements occur in sequence, adjacent elements being connected by temporal contiguity. These connections result in groupings that overlap in chain-like fashion, as in Figure 1(c). While such a grouping may achieve significance by functioning as a whole for some higher-level purpose, that is not inherent to this mode of organization. *Layering* (Figure 2c) involves an asymmetry between a substantive *core* and its *elaboration*, at successive levels, by elements of lesser substance (Langacker 2016a). While the core is *autonomous* (i.e. capable of independent manifestation, like a vowel), elaborating elements are usually *dependent* on one with greater substance (e.g. consonants depend on the sonority provided by vowels). Hence they can also be viewed as operations connecting one autonomous structure to the next.

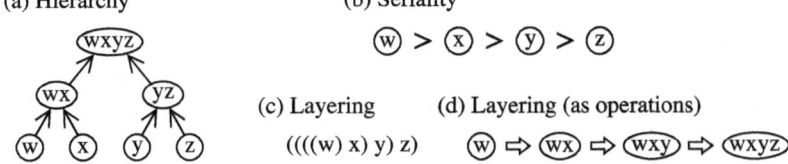

Figure 2: Basic structural configurations.

These configurations are all discernible in expressions of even modest complexity, as shown for *carefully* in Figure 3. The horizontal arrow labeled T is *processing time*, which functions as the time of both conception (cc) and expression (ex).[2] Four kinds of connection figure in this assembly. The first is symbolization (Σ): each morpheme is a minimal symbolic grouping in which a semantic and a phonological structure—its two poles—are connected by association; each is able to activate the other, thereby making it accessible. The assembly exhibits seriality, for at either pole the basic elements occur sequentially (*care* > *ful* > *ly*). It also exhibits hierarchy, in that *care* and *ful* form the grouping *careful*, which in turn is one component of *carefully*. Though closely related to hierarchy, layering represents an additional factor, since hierarchy per se is neutral as to whether the connected structures are

---

[2] These are really not distinct, in that sound, gesture, and other expressive means are included in conception by virtue of being apprehended (Langacker 1987, section 2.2.1, beginning p. 76).

autonomous or dependent. Nesting of the larger boxes indicates that *care* is the substantive core (innermost layer), with outer layers consisting in successive elaboration by *ful* and *ly*.

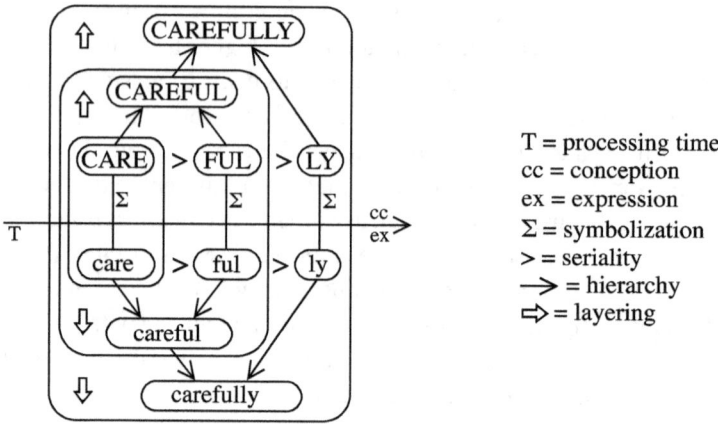

Figure 3: An assembly with parallelism along multiple paths of access.

In each configuration, elements are connected at multiple levels of organization, i.e., a grouping established at one level can participate in further connections. The configurations are thus dynamic in that the connections define a *path of access* represented by arrows (>, →, or ⇒).[3] Its origin and direction are based on different factors: temporal sequencing for seriality, composition for hierarchy, and autonomy for layering. A key point is that these and other access paths tend to co-align, thereby minimizing processing effort. Note in particular that the upper and lower paths in Figure 3 mirror one another; e.g., movement along the semantic path (CARE) > (FUL) > (LY), and along the phonological path (care) > (ful) > (ly), proceed in parallel. Given formulaically in (1), this parallelism (‖) is a main factor in the expression's morphological regularity and represents a basic kind of iconicity.

(1) a. **Seriality:** CARE > FUL > LY ‖ care > ful > ly
 b. **Hierarchy:** {CARE, FUL} → CAREFUL; {CAREFUL, LY} → CAREFULLY ‖ {care, ful} → careful; {careful, ly} → carefully
 c. **Layering:** CARE ⇒ CAREFUL ⇒ CAREFULLY ‖ care ⇒ careful ⇒ carefully

---

[3] In the case of hierarchy, the access path is *complex*, with branches converging from multiple origins. It should be evident that assemblies are not equivalent to the classical notion of constituency, which is viewed in Cognitive Grammar as being neither fundamental nor essential (Langacker 1997).

2 Iconicity as overlap

The term *iconicity* implies some kind of similarity between two phenomena. This raises a fundamental question to be addressed in what follows: "Where does iconicity stop and structure begin?". I make the general assumption that structures are similar by virtue of overlap in the processing activity constituting them, and that this facilitates their co-activation. Iconicity is thus a natural consequence of the tendency for dynamic processing systems to gravitate toward low-energy states (Feldman 2006).[4] If it is just a matter of similarity, it is utterly pervasive in language; note, for instance, that parallelisms like those in (1) constitute abstract similarities. In this broad sense there may be little in language that is not iconic to some degree.

What might be a case of total non-iconicity? An obvious candidate is a simple lexeme like *tree*, often cited to illustrate *l'arbitraire du signe*, there being no evident resemblance between the expression's form and meaning. It is *unanalyzable*, i.e., it cannot be decomposed into smaller symbolic structures (and is thus a morpheme). Though complex, its semantic and phonological poles participate only as wholes in the symbolic relationship, and supposedly they are wholly dissimilar. If accepted as an instance of complete non-iconicity (zero resemblance), this represents one end of a continuum in regard to form-meaning similarity. At the opposite extreme are cases of *self-symbolization*, where an observable structure functions simultaneously as the two poles of a symbolic relationship. A common example is the expression *aaaah* used by doctors, as in (2a). It amounts to self-symbolization because its form and meaning are identical: the conception symbolized by the sound sequence is nothing other than that sequence itself.

(2) a. *Stick out your tongue and say "Aaaah".*
     b. *A cat says "Meow", but a dog goes "Woof".*

Full arbitrariness and complete identity are both atypical, with most cases falling in between. The self-symbolization of *aaaah* shades off into *imitative* expressions like those in (2b), where the perceived resemblance need not be very strict. Arbitrary symbolization is thus a matter of degree. If only by chance, many words are bound to have phonological properties which vaguely resemble certain facets of their meanings. To the extent that these have some cognitive and linguistic status, we speak of elements like *phonesthemes*. For instance, the insubstantial nature of

---

[4] Seeing it from this perspective would seem to obviate the issue of iconic vs. economic motivation (Haiman 1983), e.g., whether iconicity based on size or distance is motivated by similarity or by the efficiency of using a compact expression to symbolize a more evident notion.

[ɪ] resonates with semantic features of words like *bit, pin, tip, sip, dim, rip, flimsy*, etc. Likewise, [fl] is suggestive of the rapid motion described by words like *fly, flow, flip, flutter, flick, flux*, and *flurry*. Phonesthemes are just the more obvious cases of resemblance. One can argue that fully arbitrary symbolization, hence the total absence of form-meaning iconicity, is rare (see Pietrandrea, and Russo and Pietrandrea, this volume, for their discussion of iconicity and arbitrariness across signed and spoken language).

If iconicity resides in the similarity of structures, simple *form-meaning* iconicity is not the only kind. We will also note cases of both *form-form* and *meaning-meaning* iconicity, where the resemblance holds between different aspects of the structure at either pole. Along another axis, we can distinguish between *substantive* and *diagrammatic* iconicity, depending on whether it pertains to the actual phonological and conceptual substance of individual elements, or more abstractly, to configurations defined by the relations among such elements. While they are useful, these distinctions do not amount to an adequate classificatory scheme, as they are matters of degree, and multiple kinds of resemblance figure in actual cases. In short, an account of iconicity is not just a matter of a simple taxonomy, or of attaching descriptive labels to particular examples, but presupposes a detailed structural analysis of the expressions involved.

An expression's structure comprises an assembly of connected elements. Because these reside in patterns of activity, their connection involves some kind of influence or interaction. This may just be a matter of *association*, whereby one structure tends to activate another; bidirectional influence of this sort is the essential feature of symbolization. A stronger kind of connection, *overlap*, is essential for grammar and is the basis for iconicity. Consisting in the partial sharing of processing activity, overlap facilitates co-activation of the structures involved, which is more efficient than the separate activation of disjoint patterns. There are kinds and degrees of overlap. The overlapping portions of two structures need not be self-contained or sharply defined, but are often diffuse and hard to pin down. It is common for one structure to be wholly included in another. As a special case, the included structure can be schematic for the other, abstracting away from its fine-grained details. The full identity of two structures represents the limiting case of overlap.

Extent of overlap correlates with the nature and degree of form-meaning similarity, as sketched in Figure 4. There may be no resemblance at all, in which case we can speak of an arbitrary pairing. If there is some resemblance (r in Figures 4b and c), it may be diffuse or hard to pin down; for instance, while the word *elephant* seems vaguely appropriate for its meaning, no individual subpart is suggestive of any particular semantic feature. By contrast, the phonestheme [fl] is readily discernible even though it represents just a portion of a word's form and meaning. The extreme case of overlap, form-meaning identity (i in Figure 4d), is the basis for self-symbolization (e.g. *aaaah*), where the functions of conception and expression are conflated.⁵

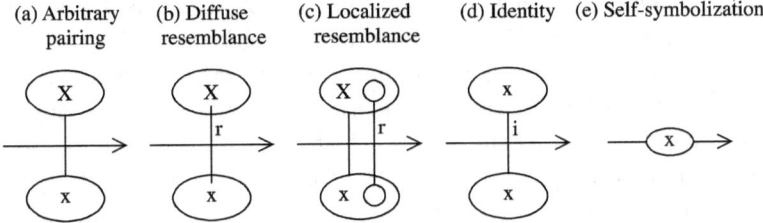

Figure 4: Degrees of form-meaning overlap.

The notion that iconicity is based on similarity raises a fundamental question: "What is similar to what?". The answer is neither simple nor straightforward. For one thing, it has to cover both substantive and diagrammatic iconicity. Nor can it be limited to form-meaning iconicity between an expression's two poles. A further issue is whether iconicity is "internal" to linguistic structure or holds between language and something "external" to it. Of course, this distinction is both simplistic and problematic, as there is no precise boundary between "linguistic" and "extra-linguistic" structures. We need to clarify the nature of their relationship, and the key to that is *categorization*.

As an aspect of cognition, categorization resides in processing activity and exemplifies the characterization of structure in terms of connections, groupings, and assemblies. Because it is based on resemblance, categorization is itself a matter of overlap, involving the co-activation of a categorizing structure (the "standard") and the structure being categorized (the "target"). The relation is asymmetrical, in that the former provides the basis for apprehending the latter, which in that sense is accessed through it (Langacker 1987). Categorizations represent a basic dimension of organization in linguistic assemblies, comprising what is known as *paradigmatic* (rather than *syntagmatic*) structure (Langacker 2008: 171). An initial act of categorization effects the transient grouping of the standard and target. When established as a unit through entrenchment, this becomes a stable grouping with the potential to be activated whenever needed.⁶

---

5 Recall that conception and expression are non-distinct (footnote 2), so the same structure can function in both capacities.
6 A basic tenet of cognitive linguistics is that a category is usually *complex*, comprising a network (or field) of variants (Langacker 2006). Complex categories can be characterized as assemblies in

Our concern is with the role of categorization in linguistic meaning. We employ expressions to describe conceived situations; the one currently under discussion is called the *descriptive target* (DT).[7] Figure 5(a) depicts a particular usage event, in which an expression (X) describes some facet of DT, represented as (X'). I refer to this as *coding* (Langacker 1987: 77). It is a matter of categorization: due to some resemblance, (X) is invoked for the apprehension of (X'), which is thereby categorized as an instance of (X). Being a kind of connection, this effects the grouping of (X) and (X'), yielding a higher-order structure in which (X) organizes the conception of (X'). In Figure 5(b) this grouping is given as ((X) X'), indicating that (X') is *apprehended as* an instance of (X). An essential point is that ((X) X') is a distinct structure not equivalent to either (X) or (X') alone. Nor are these precisely the same as they appear in isolation, since connected elements influence and adapt to one another.

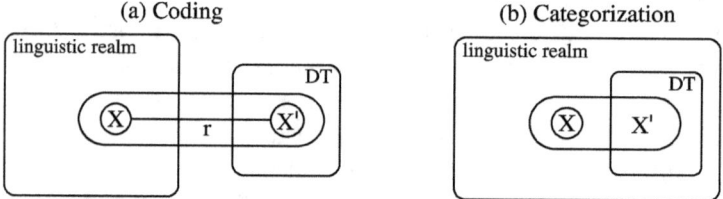

Figure 5: Linguistic categorization as the apprehension of overlap.

Suppose I see a large, woody plant that might either be a tree or a bush and decide to call it a *tree*. (TREE) is then the semantic pole of the lexeme as usually understood (its conventional semantic value), (TREE') is what I am trying to describe (the plant as I actually see it), and ((TREE) TREE') represents the lexeme's interpretation in this context—its contextually determined linguistic meaning (Langacker 2008: 464).

Sketched in Figure 6(a), this use of *tree* exemplifies a general kind of iconicity inherent even in supposedly non-iconic expressions: the resemblance that motivates the application of linguistic units to facets of DT. If a target is extralinguistic to begin with, coding brings it into the linguistic realm, connecting it (if only momentarily) to the vast assembly comprising the structure of a language. The direct connection of (tree) with (TREE), the lexeme's conventionally established meaning, mediates its connection with ((TREE) TREE'), its contextually determined linguistic meaning. So granted that the symbolic association of (TREE) and (tree) is

---

which particular categorizations are connected via overlap ("family resemblance"). As such, they represent a higher level of organization in the paradigmatic plane.

7 Importantly, DT is thus conceptual in nature: rather than belonging to the "outside world" as such, it is mentally constructed (Fauconnier 1997).

basically arbitrary, using (tree) in reference to (TREE') is nonetheless motivated by the latter's similarity to (TREE). If considered iconic, this is not a case of form-meaning iconicity, but rather meaning-meaning iconicity, as the resemblance (r) holds between two conceptions.

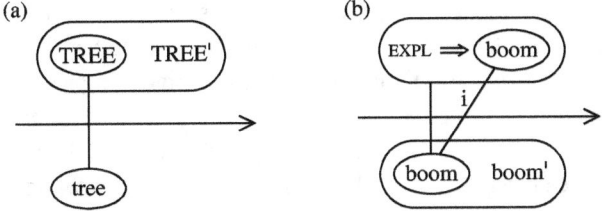

Figure 6: Simple cases of meaning-meaning and form-form iconicity.

By contrast, expressions like *meow, woof, boom, clang,* and *hiss* are conventionally established instances of form-form iconicity. As shown for *boom* in Figure 6(b), these are imitative in that the phonological structure, (boom), is perceived as being similar to an abstracted sound image, (boom'), representing an open-ended set of auditory experiences, e.g., an explosion. The notation ((boom) boom') indicates that, despite the evident discrepancy, the former is invoked as the basis for categorizing such experiences—they are equivalent in the sense that (boom) can be taken as a faint imitation of any of them. An imitative expression is also iconic in that the phonological structure as such is central to its meaning.[8] For this reason (boom) is depicted twice in 6(b), as both the symbolizing phonological structure and part of the symbolized conception. These are identical ('i'), just two roles of the same structure. Still, the semantic and phonological poles are distinct because the former is more inclusive, e.g., it includes the specification that the sound is caused by an explosion (EXPL) or some comparable event.

We can note a family resemblance among the types of form-meaning iconicity surveyed in this section: imitative expressions share with phonesthemes the feature of a localized form-meaning resemblance (Figure 4(c)), and with self-symbolization, the feature of a phonological structure also serving as the symbolized conception (Figure 4(e)). Their variety shows that answering the question "What is similar to what?" requires a detailed structural analysis. This is especially obvious when we turn to substantive vs. diagrammatic iconicity.

---

8 It is in fact the *profile* (conceptual referent) when the expression is used as a noun.

3 Diagrammatic iconicity

Substantive iconicity pertains to the phonological and conceptual content of individual elements. With diagrammatic iconicity the similarity is more abstract, residing in the relations among substantive elements.[9]

Figure 7(a) represents a *symbolization path*, in which the association of semantic and phonological structures results in their being activated in the same sequence (and roughly simultaneously). This is a fundamental kind of form-meaning iconicity inherent in the very nature of language structure. It is said to be *diagrammatic* because the similarity does not pertain to individual semantic and phonological elements (whose association can perfectly well be arbitrary), but to the *configurations* of these elements at the two poles. The formula in 7(b) indicates that these configurations are parallel in two respects. At each pole, the connections are based on successive activation in processing time, so that elements occur in a particular sequence. And crucially, this ordering is coordinated, so that symbolically associated elements occupy analogous positions in the two sequences.

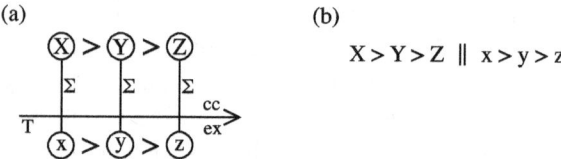

Figure 7: The diagrammatic iconicity of a symbolization path.

As an ever-present aspect of linguistic organization, ubiquitous and essentially automatic, symbolization paths tend to be taken for granted. Discussions of diagrammatic iconicity usually focus on more elaborate cases. Often cited as examples are sentences like (3), in which the events described are conceived as occurring in the order of their expression.

(3) *He won the lottery and quit his job.*

Figure 8(a) shows the basic elements and connections: 'E' is an event, 'e' is its symbolization, and '>' indicates temporal sequencing. For each event, the substantive elements E and e are connected by symbolic association (Σ); there need be no resemblance between them. The iconicity resides in connections, the relationship

---

9 For an extensive psychological treatment, see the "structure-mapping" theory of analogical processing (e.g., Gentner 1983; Gentner and Hoyos 2017).

E1 > E2 being analogous to e1 > e2. Figure 8(b) further indicates symbolic groupings as well as those effected at either pole.[10] Recall that connected elements constitute a higher-order element capable of participating (as a whole) in further connections. In this case, connection via temporal adjacency results in both the conceptual grouping (E1 > E2) and the phonological grouping (e1 > e2). The iconic resemblance (r) is shown as holding between these two higher-level elements. Thus connected, they in turn form a grouping which can function as a single element for subsequent purposes (Figure 1). Figure 8(c) represents the schematic form-meaning overlap comprising this type of iconicity. (E1 > E2) and (e1 > e2), analogous in that both are instances of temporal sequencing, are identical (i) when viewed in abstraction from their substantive content.

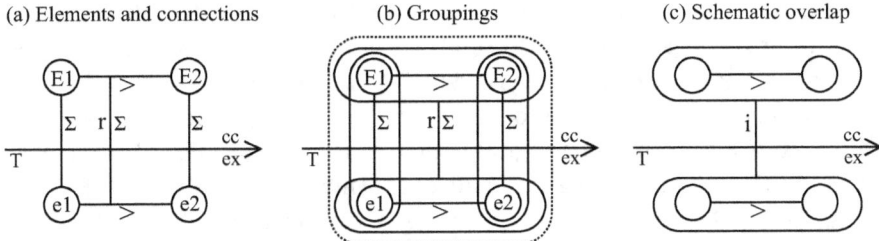

Figure 8: Groupings and overlap in a symbolization path.

As it stands, Figure 8 is insufficient regarding the question "What is similar to what?". It fails to distinguish the structures given in Figure 5 as (X) and (X'): the expression's semantic structure, as a linguistic entity, and the descriptive target, the objective situation under discussion. In terms of these notations, Figure 8 merely indicates that (e1 > e2) mirrors the sequence of event *conception*, i.e., (E1 > E2). To indicate that it also mirrors the sequence of event *occurrence*, (E1' > E2'), we must expand 8(a) to include the descriptive target (DT), as shown in Figure 9(a). Observe that sequence of conception and sequence of occurrence are very different matters involving distinct roles of time: whereas events are conceived (and symbolized) through processing time (T), their conceived occurrence unfolds through *conceived time* (t), i.e., time as an aspect of the target situation (DT). So while the conceptual sequence (E1 > E2) is activated at the current moment (the time of speaking), the target sequence (E1' > E2') is described in (3) as occurring in the past.

---

10 A typical assembly is too complex for all facets of it to be represented in a single readable diagram. Practicality dictates the use of multiple diagrams or the omission of certain details.

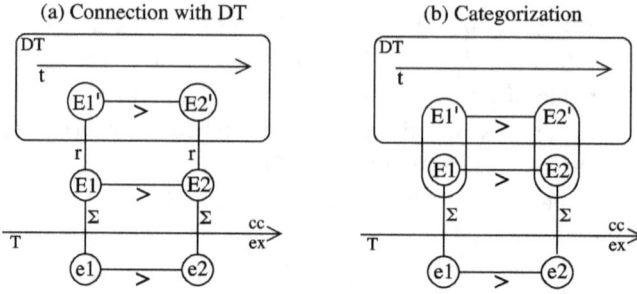

Figure 9: Categorization as a facet of diagrammatic iconicity.

An external target enters the linguistic realm through coding (categorization by linguistic structures), as in Figures 5(b) and 9(b). The semantic structures (E1) and (E2) categorize the target events (E1') and (E2'), so that the latter are apprehended as instances of the former: ((E1) E1') and ((E2) E2'). Since DT is part of the supporting conceptual substrate, these groupings constitute the linguistic meanings of the clausal expressions. The phonological structures (e1) and (e2) directly symbolize (E1) and (E2), and in so doing they indirectly symbolize ((E1) E1') and ((E2) E2'). What, then, is the phonological sequence (e1 > e2) similar to? There are several options: (E1 > E2), (E1' > E2'), and ((E1) E1') > ((E2) E2'). We might therefore recognize the four-way parallelism in (4a). But since the first two options are implicit in the third, (4a) is equivalent to the more compact representation in (4b).

(4) a. e1 > e2 || E1 > E2 || E1' > E2' || ((E1) E1') > ((E2) E2')
    b. e1 > e2 || ((E1) E1') > ((E2) E2')

Cases of this type of iconicity can be of any length, e.g., the four-event sequence in (5). In dynamic terms, the successive event descriptions can thus be viewed as steps in a path of access through DT. Characterizing longer sequences is not, however, just a matter of adding more steps, as it involves other kinds of overlap representing higher-levels of organization.

(5) a. *He won the lottery, quit his job, moved to Hawaii, and learned to surf.*
    b. e1 > e2 > e3 > e4 || ((E1) E1') > ((E2) E2') > ((E3) E3') > ((E4) E4')

This is indicated in Figure 10(a), representing the four-step path in (5). Boxes in 10(a) delimit higher-level groupings consisting of successive pairs of event descriptions. (Observe that each such grouping corresponds to the dotted-line box in Figure 8(b)—a grouping comprising the entire configuration at that level.) At a higher level still, these groupings are themselves connected to form an overall grouping (outer box) which, based on their individual grammatical roles, functions as a complex clausal predicate. Two kinds of overlap, one local and the other global, figure in their connection. Locally, they combine in chain-like fashion, the final element of one being the initial element of the next. Globally, they are connected via their common schematic core, shown in Figure 10(b).[11]

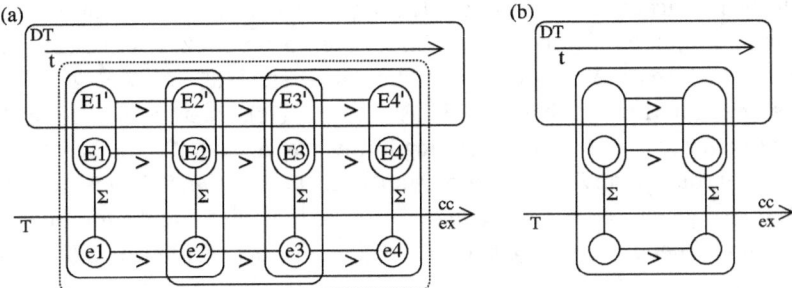

Figure 10: Groupings and overlap in a complex example.

The construction in (5) illustrates some general points in regard to the question "What is similar to what?". One is the fact that diagrammatic iconicity commonly involves configurations based on different relationships; for instance, the parallelism in (5) involves temporal sequencing in two distinct realms, language processing and the descriptive target. The second point is the essential role of the descriptive target. Important here is the nature of DT, which is not equated with "reality" or the "external world", but is rather a conception representing some facet of our mental universe. As such, it reflects the same cognitive abilities evident in semantic structure. So when the iconicity pertains to time, what counts as temporal ordering is subject to construal. For example, we have the ability to mentally access a series of events in a sequence opposite to that of their occurrence. This sort of reversal is often overtly indicated, e.g., by expressions like *after* and *because*. But it can also be covert, tacitly invoked as part of the conceptual substrate. A plausible example is (6), where each event description prompts the speaker to recall the event leading up to it.

(6) *He's living in Hawaii. He moved there from Chicago. The bad weather was ruining his health.*

---

11 These features are characteristic of a broad family of serial constructions in English (Langacker 2011, 2020), not limited to either coordination or temporal iconicity. Nested locatives (discussed below) involve neither.

Is this a case of iconicity? Not if that requires the strict parallelism represented abstractly in (7a), where the order of symbolized event descriptions (X > Y > Z), in T, follows the sequence of described events in t (X' > Y' > Z'). Instead we have the non-parallelism in (7b), where the linguistic presentation runs counter to the sequence of events in the target. But does it? The presumption that it does ignores the fact that DT is mentally constructed, so that ordering in t can be superseded at a higher-level of conceptual organization. The target in (6) can thus be analyzed as a multi-level conception in which the baseline sequence X' > Y' > Z' gives rise to the higher-level structure Z' < Y' < X' by an operation of reversal (X' > Y' > Z' ⇒ Z' < Y' < X').[12] The expression thus involves the full assembly in (7c), where '<' can be read as 'follows in t' (or 'precedes when scanning in reverse through t'). And based on the higher-level conception Z' < Y' < X', which answers the question "What is similar to what?", (6) is indeed iconic. This further illustrates the point that diagrammatic iconicity can hold between configurations based on distinct relationships (in this case, '>' vs. '<').

(7) a. X' > Y' > Z' ‖ X > Y > Z ‖ x > y > z
    b. X' > Y' > Z' ∦ Z > Y > X ‖ z > y > x
    c. X' > Y' > Z' ⇒ Z' < Y' < X' ‖ Z > Y > X ‖ z > y > x

This is still more evident from the construction in (8), where a series of locative expressions specify an entity's location in more and more detail (Langacker 2020). It comes in two varieties, which can be described impressionistically as either "zooming in" to smaller and smaller regions or—less commonly—as "zooming out" to successively larger ones. In either variant, the semantic structures X, Y, and Z represent these locations, which are conceived as being related by spatial inclusion in the target situation: X' ⊃ Y' ⊃ Z'. The zooming-in variant is thus an instance of diagrammatic iconicity based on an abstract similarity between the spatial configuration X' ⊃ Y' ⊃ Z', in DT, and the temporal configuration X > Y > Z (as well as x > y > z), in T. These configurations are of course quite different in terms of the relationships involved—spatial inclusion is not the same as temporal sequencing.[13]

---

[12] Their relationship is an instance of layering, analogous to the morphological layering discussed earlier in regard to *carefully*. (For the prevalence and importance of this type of organization, see Langacker 2016a.)

[13] To be sure, temporal sequencing lurks in the background, since expressions like (8a) would typically be used to specify a path (physical or mental) to be followed step-by-step through time in order to "reach" the entity in question. But in terms of the actual linguistic expression, the parallelism holds between spatial and temporal configurations.

They are however analogous, in that the locations in DT and the linguistic structures describing them occupy corresponding positions in the two series.

(8) a. *The flour is in the pantry, on the bottom shelf, next to the sugar.* [zooming in]
     X' ⊃ Y' ⊃ Z' ‖ X > Y > Z ‖ x > y > z
  b. *The flour is next to the sugar, on the bottom shelf, in the pantry.* [zooming out]
     X' ⊃ Y' ⊃ Z' ⇒ Z' ⊂ Y' ⊂ X' ‖ Z > Y > X ‖ z > y > x

Motivated by the everyday experience of trying to reach or find something, the zooming-in variant reflects the natural strategy of following a path of access through successively smaller areas. By contrast, the zooming-out variant starts with the smallest area and proceeds in the opposite direction. It therefore manifests an alternate strategy based on a different spatial relationship: expansion (⊂) rather than inclusion (⊃). This is another case of layering (cf. (7c)), in which the baseline configuration X' ⊃ Y' ⊃ Z' gives rise to the inverse sequence Z' ⊂ Y' ⊂ X' at a higher level of conceptual organization.[14] When applied to this higher-level conception, expressions like (8b) are iconic.

While temporal ordering offers an obvious basis for diagrammatic iconicity, the key factor in its abstract characterization—that associated elements occupy analogous positions in complex structures—can be observed in other sorts of configurations. A prime example is metaphor, in which elements associated via metaphorical mappings occupy corresponding positions in a shared "image-schematic" configuration (Lakoff 1990). Another case, illustrated by the response in (9), is the English pattern of indicating the *informational focus* by means of unreduced stress.

(9) **A:** *Which dress should I wear?* **B:** *The* BLUE *dress.*

This is an instance of form-meaning iconicity internal to language, holding between the semantic and phonological poles of a complex expression. It does not pertain to the temporal sequencing of the elements involved (in this case *blue* and *dress*), as these can occur in either order and need not even be adjacent. The configurations in question are based instead on other relations representing distinct structural domains. Informational focusing is a matter of *informativeness* as determined by the prior discourse. In (9), the prior context establishes the semantic relationship BLUE ⊃ DRESS, where '⊃' indicates higher position on a scale. At the phonologi-

---

14 The requisite operation reflects another cognitive ability: a kind of reverse engineering, such that starting from a specific location, we can figure out what path we might have taken to get there. Moving step by step along the inverse path is a matter of successively expanding the scope of awareness (zooming out) until it encompasses a known point of origin.

cal pole, the analogous configuration is based on *amplitude*, only *blue* being fully accented. However, this is not assessed in relation to the prior discourse, but to the surrounding elements in the current expression. We thus have the following parallelism: BLUE ⊃ DRESS ∥ BLUE ⊃ dress. It constitutes diagrammatic iconicity in that the semantic structures and the symbolizing phonological structures occupy corresponding scalar positions, albeit with respect to different scales.[15]

Perhaps less obviously, we can recognize a case of form-form iconicity in the tendency (at least in English) for the syllables and morphemes of a complex word to coincide. In the word *carefully*, for example, the same sequence of forms function as both syllables (s) and symbolizing structures (σ). So in purely phonological terms, there is full iconicity (identity) between the two modes of organization: $care_s > ful_s > ly_s \parallel care_\sigma > ful_\sigma > ly_\sigma$.[16] The difference does not reside in the sequence itself—it is the same sequence, as part of the same assembly—but in which facets of the assembly are being considered. When the elements are viewed as morphemes, what matters is their symbolizing function; that they constitute a word (w) can be ignored, as indicated in Figure 11(a). But when they are viewed as a word, their status as such overshadows their semantic contributions, as indicated in Figure 11(b).

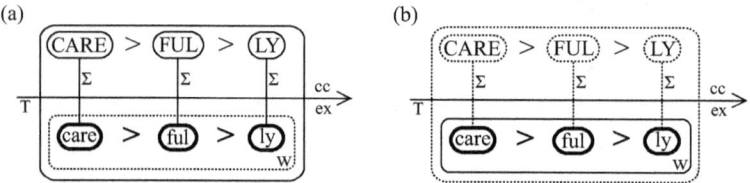

Figure 11: The form-form iconicity of syllables and morphemes in a word.

It might be objected that the foregoing characterization of iconicity is overly broad—so much so, that it applies to virtually any aspect of linguistic organization. But that is precisely my basic point. Attempts at explicit analysis suggest that there is no non-arbitrary boundary between iconicity and non-iconicity, nor between linguistic and extralinguistic structure. A unified account is thus envisaged based on a

---

15 Since these scales are abstractly similar (both involving magnitude), this also qualifies as an instance of substantive iconicity, as well as metaphor (informativeness being understood in terms of amplitude). These characterizations are perfectly consistent, amounting to different perspectives on the same assembly.

16 By contrast, the word *morpheme* exhibits a discrepancy between the two sequences: $mor_s > pheme_s \not\parallel morph_\sigma > eme_\sigma$. It is presumably less efficient because these configurations are non-congruent.

dynamic view of structure that is both general (residing in assemblies of connected elements) and accommodates the basic role of factors like similarity, overlap, categorization, and paths of access.

4 Iconicity and structure

The limited but varied range of examples considered suggest that any aspect of linguistic structure can exhibit iconicity. Here I propose that structure and iconicity are actually non-distinct, representing different "takes" on the same assemblies. Both are manifestations of overlapping activity: structure is primarily based on overlap (hence iconic in a broad sense), and iconicity can be seen as a dimension of the structures involved (rather than a separate phenomenon).[17] For example, an intrinsic structural feature of complex expressions is a symbolization path (see Figure 7): an instance of diagrammatic iconicity in which corresponding semantic and phonological structures are activated in the same sequence and roughly simultaneously. The semantic and phonological configurations, (X) > (Y) > (Z) and (x) > (y) > (z), participate in two kinds overlap based on full inclusion: they are abstractly similar, in that each elaborates the schematic configuration ( ) > ( ) > ( ); and both are facets of the symbolic configuration (X/x) > (Y/y) > (Z/z).

More generally, the co-alignment of access paths is an important aspect of structural regularity. Recall the discussion of *carefully*, a parade example of the non-distinctness of structure and iconicity. A main factor in its being recognized as regular is that its semantic and phonological structures are precisely analogous (showing up in Figure 3 as mirror images). The structures at the two poles are parallel in regard to the basic configurations of seriality, hierarchy, and layering. Each configuration, at either pole, represents an access path whose direction reflects an inherent asymmetry (based on temporal sequencing, composition, or autonomy). A key point is that these and other access paths tend to co-align, thereby minimizing processing effort. There is parallelism not only across the two poles (form-meaning iconicity), but also, at either pole, across the three configurations: *care* is accessed at the initial step in all three, and *ly* as the final step. This similarity across configurations constitutes diagrammatic iconicity (both form-form and meaning-meaning) at a higher level of organization.

---

[17] This is not at odds with the standard notion that many structures are non-iconic, since only certain kinds of overlap are traditionally recognized as iconicity. The suggestion here is merely that *some* kind of iconicity figures in a given structure, not every potential kind.

Not every expression rivals *carefully* in its degree of regularity and iconicity. Assemblies become more flexible and loosely integrated as we move along the spectrum from morphology to syntax to discourse. They form a gradation regarding the relative importance of *descriptive* vs. *discursive* organization (Langacker 2015a, 2016b). These are not separate "components" or discrete levels of representation, but coexisting aspects of the structure of a given expression. The terms allude to the primary function of *describing* conceived situations, by means of substantive conceptual and phonological content, vs. the subsidiary task of cogently *presenting* that content in a coherent discourse.[18] Presentational factors fall under three broad headings: *sequencing, prominence*, and *packaging*. Because these obtain at either pole, they participate in symbolic relations, which are often based on the same factor and are thus iconic. A symbolization path is an example of iconicity based on sequencing. Likewise, informational focusing is a case in which accentual prominence symbolizes a certain kind of discursive prominence.

An example based on packaging is the "classical" notion of grammatical constituency (Langacker 1997). Packaging is the grouping and selection of content for presentation in a processing window on a certain time scale. This occurs at both poles—each phonological package symbolizing a semantic one—so constituents are both symbolic and iconic. Since processing unfolds on multiple time scales, it commonly results in hierarchy, as groupings effected at one level are themselves packaged in a single window on a larger time scale. In addition to packaging, essential features of classical constituency are thus hierarchy (represented by bracketing or trees) as well as temporal sequencing. Though inadequate as a general model of grammatical structure, it is not inappropriate for the descriptive content of straightforward expressions reasonably considered "basic", as in (10).

(10) (((the)-(dog))-((ate)-((my)-(homework))))

In Cognitive Grammar, constituency of this sort is merely a kind of organization often discernible in assemblies. The constituents in (10) represent the packaging of descriptive content in windows on different time scales. They consist in the symbolic association of conceptual and phonological groupings, each of which is cohesive and coherent at either pole. Semantically, each grouping implements a particular function (e.g., nominal reference for *the dog*) and involves some kind of prominence (e.g., profiling). Phonologically, each comprises a continuous segmental sequence involving both prominence (e.g., accent) and cohesiveness (e.g., rhyth-

---

18 Descriptive vs. discursive organization is thus a special case of the Cognitive Grammar notion of *content* vs. *construal*.

mic grouping). Hence all three presentational factors—packaging, sequencing, and prominence—figure in canonical instances of classical constituency. Such expressions thus illustrate the intermixture of descriptive and discursive organization, even in basic grammar.

At the phonological pole, these factors amount to *prosody*, which figures in yet another kind of iconicity. Each constituent in (10)—be it a word, a phrase, or a clause—is a *prosodic grouping* on some time scale. For instance, the main constituents in (10) also function as the highest-level prosodic groupings: (*the dog*)-(*ate my homework*). Based on canonical examples of such structures, we can speak of *word-*, *phrase-*, or *clause-sized* windows. Conventional occurrence in windows of a certain size is an inherent aspect of basic grammatical constructions.[19] But prosody is not always in the service of description. It has its own rationale, one pertaining to effective presentation, an aspect of discursive organization. For constituents and prosodic groupings to coincide is therefore natural but contingent, a baseline situation (Langacker 2016a) from which deviations are common. When it does obtain, their congruence—a matter of overlap—represents a kind of *descriptive-discursive iconicity*. Departures from this baseline are usual in expressions of any complexity, e.g. (11), which is non-iconic in that basic constituents and salient prosodic groupings cross-cut one another.

(11) (*she gave to the prosecutors*)-(*the key to a safe-deposit box*)-(*containing a whole host*)-(*of very incriminating documents*)

Even if we abstract away from specific content and view them as schematic patterns, prosodic groupings have conceptual import residing in their function: that of framing and grouping an array of content by presenting it in a single processing window. Patterns on different time scales have additional import related to their presentational function. In particular, special significance attaches to word-sized and clause-sized groupings. At least canonically, a word has enough phonological substance (at least one syllable) and enough conceptual substance (being built around a lexeme) to be produced, perceived, and considered meaningful in isolation; hence its characterization by Bloomfield (1933: 178) as a "minimum free form". The clause-sized groupings in (11) exemplify what Chafe (1994) called "intonation units" (their being identified by phonological properties) and I have

---

19 Of course, the correspondence is only prototypical. Based on rate of speech and other factors, we have the flexibility to package a given expression in windows of different sizes (e.g., *the dog* would normally occur in a single word-sized window).

referred to as "attentional frames" (Langacker 2001). These were aptly described by Chafe as representing the amount of information we can hold in mind at one time.

Minimally, then, prosodic groupings have the semantic effect of momentarily highlighting the conceptual content they express. This goes unnoticed when they coincide with descriptive groupings, in which case the effect is merely one of reinforcement. As a typical feature of basic grammatical constructions, their coincidence represents a pervasive kind of descriptive-discursive iconicity. On the other hand, the effect of non-coincidence is to differentiate descriptive and discursive groupings, so that alternate symbolization paths figure in the same assembly. This is unproblematic (cross-cutting groupings being a hallmark of assemblies), but since attention is a limited resource, the salience of either path diminishes that of the other. As a competing alternative, non-congruent prosodic grouping tends to background the descriptive organization on which it supervenes.

5 Conclusion

This investigation has centered on two basic questions in regard to iconicity. I have suggested that answering the first question, "What is similar to what?", is prerequisite to any cogent analysis but less straightforward than it might appear. As for the second question, "Where does iconicity stop and structure begin?", I have suggested that ultimately they are non-distinct: both are manifestations of overlapping activity, and reside in overlapping facets of the same assemblies.

Both questions hinge on assumptions about the extent and nature of language structure. Cognitive Grammar has an expansive view of structure because it posits gradations rather than sharp boundaries (e.g., between semantics and pragmatics, grammar and connected discourse, even form and meaning). However, it does not extend indefinitely, since structures count as linguistic units only due to *entrenchment* (by individuals) and *conventionalization* (in a speech community). With the avoidance of artificial boundaries comes the possibility of *unification*, as the many dimensions and levels of linguistic organization inhere in a vast assembly of semantic, phonological, and symbolic structures. Seemingly very different phenomena are sometimes just a matter of perspective (different "takes" on the same structures) or how they function as part of larger configurations.

Since iconicity is neither separate and distinct nor self-contained, I have not proposed a serious classification: owing to diversity, complexity, and intermediate cases, no particular taxonomy can claim to be exhaustive or "correct". Analyzing iconicity instead requires the detailed description of a broad and varied range of cases, including a reasonably explicit characterization of the conceptual structures they involve. Decades of research in cognitive linguistics has elucidated many aspects of conceptual semantics and demonstrated that its investigation can be carried out in a principled and revealing manner (Lakoff 1987; Talmy 2000a, 2000b; Fauconnier and Turner 2002; Langacker 2015b).

Despite their obvious limitations, the analyses of iconicity presented here illustrate a central claim of Cognitive Grammar: that explicit conceptual description is prerequisite to understanding grammar, which consists in the structuring and symbolization of semantic content. They further provide a specific way of interpreting the insightful comment by Wilcox cited at the outset: that arbitrariness and iconicity coexist in linguistic structure as manifestations of a deeper cognitive basis.

References

Bloomfield, Leonard. 1933. *Language*. New York: Holt.
Chafe, Wallace. 1994. *Discourse, Consciousness, and Time: The Flow and Displacement of Conscious Experience in Speaking and Writing*. Chicago & London: University of Chicago Press.
de Saussure, Ferdinand. 1916. *Cours de linguistique générale*. Paris: Payot.
Fauconnier, Gilles. 1997. *Mappings in Thought and Language*. Cambridge: Cambridge University Press.
Fauconnier, Gilles & Mark Turner. 2002. *The Way We Think: Conceptual Blending and the Mind's Hidden Complexities*. New York: Basic Books.
Feldman, Jerome A. 2006. *From Molecule to Metaphor: A Neural Theory of Language*. Cambridge, MA & London: MIT Press.
Gentner, Dedre. 1983. Structure mapping: A theoretical framework for analogy. *Cognitive Science* 7(2). 155–170.
Gentner, Dedre & Christian Hoyos. 2017. Analogy and abstraction. *Topics in Cognitive Science* 9(3). 672–693.
Haiman, John. 1983. Iconic and economic motivation. *Language* 59(4). 781–819.
Harder, Peter. 2010. *Meaning in Mind and Society: A Functional Contribution to the Social Turn in Cognitive Linguistics*. Berlin/New York: De Gruyter Mouton.
Lakoff, George. 1987. *Women, Fire, and Dangerous Things: What Categories Reveal about the Mind*. Chicago & London: University of Chicago Press.
Lakoff, George. 1990. The invariance hypothesis: Is abstract reason based on image-schemas? *Cognitive Linguistics* 1(1). 39–74.
Langacker, Ronald W. 1987. *Foundations of Cognitive Grammar*, vol. 1, *Theoretical Prerequisites*. Stanford: Stanford University Press.
Langacker, Ronald W. 1991. *Foundations of Cognitive Grammar*, vol. 2, *Descriptive Application*. Stanford: Stanford University Press.
Langacker, Ronald W. 1997. Constituency, dependency, and conceptual grouping. *Cognitive Linguistics* 8. 1–32.
Langacker, Ronald W. 2001. Discourse in Cognitive Grammar. *Cognitive Linguistics* 12(2). 143–188.
Langacker, Ronald W. 2006. On the continuous debate about discreteness. *Cognitive Linguistics* 17(1). 107–151.

Langacker, Ronald W. 2008. *Cognitive Grammar: A Basic Introduction*. New York: Oxford University Press.
Langacker, Ronald W. 2011. Conceptual semantics, symbolic grammar, and the *day after day* construction. In Patricia Sutcliffe, William J. Sullivan & Arle Lommel (eds.), *LACUS Forum 36: Mechanisms of Linguistic Behavior*, 3–24. Houston: LACUS.
Langacker, Ronald W. 2015a. Descriptive and discursive organization in Cognitive Grammar. In Jocelyne Daems, Eline Zenner, Kris Heylen, Dirk Speelman & Hubert Cuyckens (eds.), *Change of Paradigms—New Paradoxes: Recontextualizing Language and Linguistics*, 205–218. Berlin/Boston: De Gruyter Mouton.
Langacker, Ronald W. 2015b. Construal. In Ewa Dąbrowska & Dagmar Divjak (eds.), *Handbook of Cognitive Linguistics*, 120–143. Berlin/Boston: De Gruyter Mouton.
Langacker, Ronald W. 2016a. Baseline and elaboration. *Cognitive Linguistics* 27(3). 405–439.
Langacker, Ronald W. 2016b. Toward an integrated view of structure, processing, and discourse. In Grzegorz Drożdż (ed.), *Studies in Lexicogrammar: Theory and Applications*, 23–53. Amsterdam / Philadelphia: John Benjamins.
Langacker, Ronald W. 2020. Nested locatives: Conceptual basis and theoretical import. In Wander Lowie, Marije Michel, Audrey Rousse-Malpat, Merel Keijzer & Rasmus Steinkrauss (eds.), *Usage-based Dynamics in Second Language Development*, 207–223. Bristol, UK: Multilingual Matters.
Langacker, Ronald W. 2021. Functions and assemblies. In Kazuhiro Kodama & Tetsuharu Koyama (eds.), *The Forefront of Cognitive Linguistics*, 1–54. Tokyo: Hituzi Syobo.
Talmy, Leonard. 2000a. *Toward a Cognitive Semantics*, vol. 1, *Concept Structuring Systems*. Cambridge, MA & London: MIT Press.
Talmy, Leonard. 2000b. *Toward a Cognitive Semantics*, vol. 2, *Typology and Process in Concept Structuring*. Cambridge, MA & London: MIT Press.
Wilcox, Sherman. 2004. Cognitive iconicity: Conceptual spaces, meaning, and gesture in signed languages. *Cognitive Linguistics* 15(2). 119–147.

Corrine Occhino
When hands are things and movements are processes: Cognitive iconicity, embodied cognition, and signed language structure

1 Introduction

Things and *processes* are well-known constructs of Cognitive Grammar (Langacker 1987, 1991, 2008). Roughly, things, used here in Langacker's technical sense, denote regions in conceptual space (often entities bounded in space and time, united through reification), while processes, also used in a technical sense, denote events (that unfold in space and time) (Langacker 2008). Things and processes, and the relationships between them, are conceptualizations abstracted and extracted from our experiences in the world. At the heart of the human linguistic endeavor is explaining 1) the existence, movement, action, and interaction of (especially animate) entities in space, and 2) the actions, states, positions, and relationships they undergo. What is language if not a reflection of human perceptions and perspectives of the world around them?

Central to cognitive linguistics is the idea that grammars encode conceptual organization and are thus a reflection of it (Langacker 1987; Bybee 2001). Grammar emerges from language use as we make sense of our world by encoding and enregistering our conceptualizations of things, processes, and relations. These conceptualizations map onto the pragmatic functions of referring, predicating, and modifying, which represent universal ways of conceptualizing experience for the purpose of communicating (Croft 2001). Central to a cognitive perspective is that language and language faculties are not separate from other domains of knowledge. Language is not mere mathematical manipulation but is instead grounded in both procedural and declarative knowledge along with embodied experiences in the world.

Acknowledgement: I would like to thank Sherman Wilcox, for whom this book is dedicated. Sherman opened many intellectual doors for me and asked me to walk through them. A consummate scholar and thoughtful advisor, he modeled reading broadly and emphasized making connections between linguistics and fields such as philosophy, physics, and music theory. I owe much of my own linguistic theorizing to hours of lively debate with Sherman over coffee and croissants. I am forever grateful to him for teaching me that it is the linguist's job to uncover how speakers and signers categorize linguistic expressions, and describe that to the best of our abilities.

Corrine Occhino, Syracuse University, USA, e-mail: cmocchin@syr.edu

We use language to talk about, and make sense of, the world and in doing so, give rise to structure that reflects our conceptualizations.

In a similar way that we construe language, then, we construe things and processes in the real world, and further, we construe our bodies and bodily articulations as things and processes. It is in this very way that "hands make good things and movements make good processes" (p.c. Sherman Wilcox, 2012). Wilcox (2004) has argued that signers' ability to construe their articulators as objects allows the articulators to be conceptualized within semantic space. Articulations are thus subject to the same cognitive operations performed on other conceptualized objects. The hands (and of course other active articulators) are thus recruited by signers to "be" things that enact or represent. That signers can conceptualize their articulators and imbue them with meaning is the central claim of Wilcox's (2004) Cognitive Iconicity.

In this paper, I discuss the rise of Cognitive Iconicity from linguistic observations through the lenses of Cognitive Grammar (Langacker 1987, 1991) and Semantic Phonology (Stokoe 1991). Despite the seemingly radical nature of their work at the time, Cognitive Iconicity fits easily within a larger emergentist framework, e.g., Usage-based Phonology (Bybee 2001); dynamic systems approaches to language (Beckner et al. 2009); connectionist theories of acquisition (Bates and Elman [1993] 2002); and it anticipated contemporary views of embodied cognition (Gibbs 2006; Marghetis and Bergen 2014; Varela, Thompson and Rosch 2016). I then show how recent research into the distribution and functions of articulatory parameters in signed languages supports the construct of Cognitive Iconicity. I discuss how construction-based approaches (Goldberg 1995, 2006; Lepic 2016a, 2016b; Lepic and Occhino 2018; Wilcox and Occhino 2016) help us understand the relationships between form and meaning at the level of the sign and the level of grammar. Finally, I discuss how considering Cognitive Iconicity alongside both usage-based phonology and embodied cognition helps us develop an embodied account of grammar for spoken and signed languages.

1.1 Setting the stage

Cognitive Iconicity is the theoretical notion that "the phonological and the semantic poles of a symbolic structure reside in the same region of conceptual space" (Wilcox 2004: 119). Simply put, it proposes that "the phonological pole of signs involves objects moving in space as viewed from a certain vantage point: hands moving in space as viewed by the signer and the observer" (2004: 119). That is, objects (handshapes and orientations) move (movement) in space (location).

To understand Cognitive Iconicity (Wilcox 2004; Wilcox, Wilcox and Jarque 2004), we must note that it was built on the foundation of Cognitive Grammar (Langacker

1987, 1991, 2008), grounded in the importance of language use (Bybee 2001), and situated within an encyclopedic view of semantics (Langacker 1987; Fillmore 1982). For Langacker, "[m]eaning is equated with conceptualization" (1986: 1) and "grammatical structure can only be understood in relation to the conceptual organization it embodies and expresses" (Langacker 2008: 405). Viewing grammar as symbolic, where form is not merely abstract structure but is itself meaningful, opens the door for investigations of language that view form and meaning as complementary facets reinforced by and reinterpreted through one another. In other words, form and meaning are two sides of the same coin.

Within Cognitive Grammar, the phonological pole is the speaker's construal of form, and the semantic pole is the speaker's construal of meaning (Langacker 1987). The combination of a phonological pole and a semantic pole creates a symbolic structure (Langacker 1987, 2008, this volume). A symbolic structure is any pairing of form and meaning, also known as a "construction" in other construction-based views of language (Kay and Fillmore 1999; Croft 2001; Goldberg 1995, 2006). Within Cognitive Grammar, grammar is meaningful, it is not separate from either the lexicon or semantics, and phonological space resides in conceptual space. On this, Wilcox (2004: 122) notes that the "the phonological pole reflects our conceptualization of pronunciations." And as Langacker (this volume) has suggested, "[a] structure (of any kind or size) can be described informally as a *pattern* of activity" (p. 106, italics his) and these patterns of activity "are similar by virtue of overlap in the processing activity constituting them, and that this facilitates their co-activation" (p. 109). Why this is important will be clarified below, but let us for now discuss why we need the construct of Cognitive Iconicity in the first place.

1.2 The St. Louis Arch and the meaningful parts of signs

When asking an English speaker why a word means what it means, you might be given a 'real' or a 'folk' etymology, having to do with the meaning of the compositional parts. For example, a knowledgeable person might tell you that 'disaster' comes from Latin *dis-* + *aster* meaning ill-starred.[1] They are able to decompose the word into constituent parts that hold a stable form-meaning mapping. If you ask an ASL signer why a given sign means what it means, you may get a slightly different kind of answer, one that focuses on the reason behind the formal properties of the sign.[2] The sign

---

[1] Often referred to as "star-crossed" as in Shakespeare's *Romeo and Juliet*, as pointed out by one reviewer.
[2] While etymological explanations (folk or otherwise) do occur, as when ASL signers explain that the sign GIRL is derived from bonnet strings (see for example, Shaw and Delaporte 2015), signers

ST. LOUIS (Figure 1a) is articulated with an S-handshape (closed-fist) changing to an L-handshape (extended pointer and thumb at a 90-degree angle), as the dominant hand makes a high arc from the non-dominant shoulder to the wrist. This sign was first shown to me with the unsolicited explanation, "because S, L, and St. Louis Arch," as the signer slowly demonstrated the sign as seen in Figure 1a, with the Gateway Arch shown in 1b. The sign was created by selecting a visually salient landmark in the city that falls with a semantic frame (Fillmore 1982) of "things about St. Louis".[3]

(a) ST. LOUIS (b) St. Louis Arch

Figure 1a: ASL sign ST. LOUIS (Sign1News 12.14.18; https://www.youtube.com/watch?v=QlWYfiGhL08); Figure 1b: The Gateway Arch in St. Louis, MO (https://commons.wikimedia.org/wiki/Category: Gateway_Arch).

That signers tend to give explanations of lexical forms by describing the contributions of component parts of signs suggests evidence of signs having analyzable internal structure. But signs are also structured gestalts in that the whole is not equal to the sum of its parts. Adding the component parts together does not guarantee being able to predict the meaning of the whole. Signers are often aware of why signs mean what they mean, and they exploit such form-meaning mappings in everyday conversation along with storytelling and poetry.

Cognitive Iconicity grew from the observation that signers' interactions with signs sometimes makes the component parts of signs more explicit, or more accessible to them, than do interactions between spoken language users and the words they produce.

---

often ascribe the contributions of individual articulation features to the meaning of the sign.

3 Note also that this more abstract pattern of a movement arc from shoulder to forearm along with a handshape change, is also a more general name sign pattern (for people), prevalent in the Southern United States (p.c. Joseph Hill, 2020).

1.3 Spiders, arbitrariness of the sign, and duality of patterning

Why does *spider* mean 'spider'? Why are spoons called spoons? The answer is found in the argument behind the *arbitrariness of the sign* in the Saussurean sense. Linguists often teach their students that the string d-o-g and the meaning of "dogness" is solely based on convention, and perhaps historical accident. Duality of patterning, then, is the idea that "the meaningful units of language – words or morphemes – are made up of meaningless units – phonemes or features – whose only function is to distinguish the meaningful units from one another" (Ladd 2012: 261) is, according to Hockett (1960), a central tenet of what makes language uniquely. But if signed languages have motivated mappings at the phonemic or feature levels, does this mean they do not in fact have duality of patterning?

In 1960 William Stokoe observed that all signs are composed of handshape, movement, and location.[4] However, there is still considerable debate about the status of these components within the signed language linguistics community. In some theoretical circles, these components are considered phonological building blocks, analogous to structuralist models of spoken languages (Sandler 1989; Corina and Sandler 1993; Brentari 1998). In this view, signs can be broken down into discrete meaningless segments consisting of even smaller feature units. One segment can be replaced by another to create what have been called "minimal pairs" (Klima and Bellugi 1979). Figure 2 gives an example of two ASL signs, ONION and APPLE, which differ only in their location.

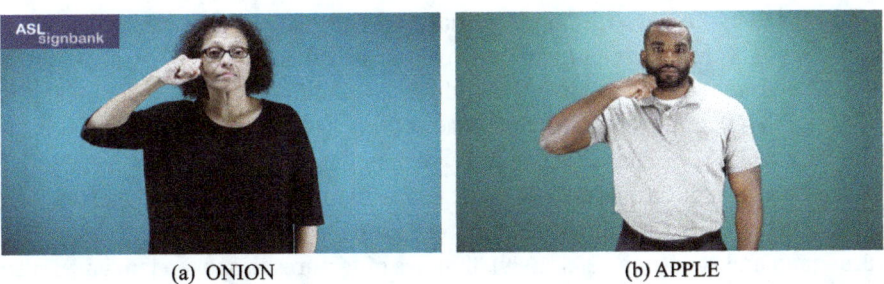

(a) ONION (b) APPLE

Figure 2: ASL minimal pair differing only in location; (a) ASL ONION and (b) APPLE (ASL Signbank 2021).[5]

---

4 Palm orientation and the number of hands involved in sign production are considered by some to be "minor parameters" (Klima & Bellugi 1979: 45; see also Mandel 1981) as they distinguish a limited number of signs.
5 All figures from ASL Signbank are used with permission of Hochgesang, Crasborn and Lillo-Martin (2021).

Thus, in the same way that the English word *spider* can be broken down into five sequential segments /s/ /p/ /aj/ /d/ /r/, which can be further broken down into articulatory features (/s/ = voiceless alveolar fricative, /p/ = unreleased voiceless bilabial stop, etc.), the two-handed ASL sign SPIDER (Figure 3) can be broken down into handshapes (both Claw-5 in this sign), location (neutral space), palm orientation (downward), and movement (finger-wiggle and path movement away from body), which can further be broken down into features (selected fingers (5), flexion of joints (yes), contact (dominant hand's wrist contacting non-dominant hand's wrist), etc.

Figure 3: ASL sign SPIDER produced with wiggling fingers and a forward movement (ASL Signbank 2021).

A difference in these two examples is that in the English word *spider* the articulatory content is produced sequentially, while the articulatory content of the ASL sign SPIDER is produced with all features articulated simultaneously. For example, it is not possible for a movement to take place without either a handshape or a location for it. Thus, if we consider phonology segmentally, signed language articulation seems very different from spoken language articulation where segments follow one another temporally. On the other hand, from an Articulatory Phonology perspective (Browman and Goldstein 1986, 1989), bundles of features in spoken languages also occur simultaneously and are dependent on one another. For example, one can't make a nasal stop without both closing the velum, producing a pulmonic egression, and forcing that air through the nasal cavity while keeping the lips closed. Nasality tends to persist across several articulatory units thereby creating simultaneous articulatory gestures that get re-timed when speech becomes routinized (Bybee 2001, 2010). It may be, then, that distinguishing the articulation of spoken language and signed language words on the basis of sequentiality and simultaneity is not entirely possible.

What is actually quite different about these two examples is that for the English word, there is nothing particularly spidery about /spajdr/,[6] However in ASL, SPIDER clearly evokes an image of a spider and how it moves around (Figure 4). This observation forces us to consider phonological and featural units in signed languages, as potentially meaning bearing which is seemingly at odds with arbitrariness and duality of patterning as they are traditionally understood.

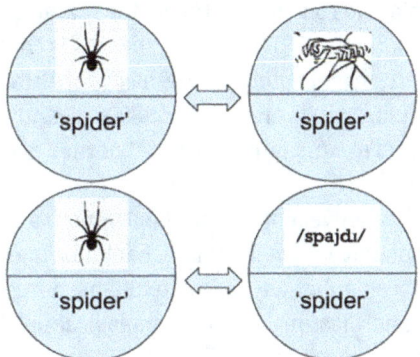

Figure 4: Graphic representation of the phonological and semantic poles (the symbolic units) of SPIDER in ASL (top row) and 'spider' in English (bottom row) from Occhino (2016).

Considering the examples of SPIDER (Figure 3) and ST. LOUIS (Figure 1), then, should we call such pieces of form "phonemes"? Understanding that signs have analyzable internal structure has opened the door to claims by some that phonemes are in fact meaningless building blocks of signs (Nijen Twilhaar and van den Bogaerde 2016; Meir and Sandler 2008). But can we say, despite the apparent ease of analyzability and the ability to replace a component part to get a minimal pair, that these "phonemes" are truly devoid of meaning?

According to many dominant phonological theories, the answer is "yes" (Sandler 1986, 1989; Corina and Sandler 1993; Brentari 1998). In these theories, handshape, movement, location, orientation, and any additional phonological parameters are governed by phonotactic rules of well-formedness and are void of meaning. But to make such a claim work, one must be willing to build extra theoretical machinery to account for the lexicon. Brentari and Padden (2001), for example, have claimed a "core-foreign" sign distinction, meaning that some signs (and by extension some of

---

6 Although see Kemmerer (2015: 274) for an explanation of why concepts such as *banana* are grounded in several sensory perceptual systems (and not completely amodal) following the Grounded Cognition Model.

their parameters), are not held to the same rules as signs in the core of the grammar. Regarding iconic forms, placing these signs outside the "core" positions them theoretically outside its scope, and thus they are not subject to phonological scrutiny.

With the remaining "well-behaved" signs (i.e., in the core), which fit into prescribed phonological rules, claims that phonological parameters are arbitrary are taken at face value, despite visual evidence to the contrary. Looking again at SPIDER and ST. LOUIS, any vestige of iconic form-meaning mapping would be considered an artifact of the visual domain and said to play no role in structuring the grammar of the language (Frishberg 1975; Klima and Bellugi 1979). However, the fact is that signers, both first and second language users, *see meaning* in the forms of these signs (Wilcox 2004; Occhino 2016, 2017; Occhino, Anible, and Morford 2020). So how can it be both that the phonological parameters are meaningless, but that they also have meaning? The simple answer is, it can't.

How, then, should we deal with this conflict between theoretical machinery and experiential knowledge? If signed languages do have phonology, is it that it just does not work like spoken language phonology? I argue that we have actually been mistaken about the relationship between form and meaning at the phonological level for *both* signed and spoken languages. By accepting arbitrariness as the default and duality of patterning as a necessity of human language, we have overlooked the role of language specific systematicity, the pressure for grammars to encode cognitive motivation at all levels of complexity, and the human drive to find and make meaning.

2 Revisiting signed language phonology

It is important to keep in mind that research on signed language phonology arose largely from adaptations of popular linguistic theories designed to account for spoken language phonology. These theories, which dominated the field from the mid-1970s until the early 2000s, were invested in capturing contrastive structure, uncovering underlying forms, finding universal units of form, and designing hierarchical representations of segmental timing units (Sandler 1989, 2012; Brentari 1998). Assimilationist approaches viewed language as a singular construct, therefore, signed languages would have little new to show us about the nature of language since their structures must be akin to those of spoken languages (Wilcox 2001; Cuxac and Sallandre 2007).

Early descriptions of ASL emphasized that signs had analyzable internal structure (Stokoe 1960; Stokoe, Casterline and Croneberg 1965). Stokoe named these units "cheremes" (Greek: cher/chir = hand), analogous to phonemes but based on production by the hand rather than regarding sounds. However, over time the majority of linguists gravitated to referring to these form units as "phonemes" and the study of them as "phonology".

Armstrong and Wilcox (2009), like Stokoe before them, found value in considering these units as phonological, but they challenge us to rethink what it means for a unit to *be* phonological. This line of reasoning underlies Cognitive Iconicity (Wilcox 2004) and later, Embodied Cognitive Phonology (Occhino 2016, 2017), that is, signs can exhibit analyzable phonological structure, but these structures can be either partially or fully motivated, or abstract and arbitrary.

2.1 Putting meaning back into form

In response to the growing theoretical complexities in signed language phonology exemplified in Sandler (1989, 1993), Brentari and Goldsmith (1993), and Brentari (1998) and to the disregard for analyses that iconicity is inherent to signed language structure (e.g., Cuxac and Sallandre 2007; see also Pietrandrea, this volume), Stokoe revised many of his claims about the sublexical structure of ASL ([1991] 2001). He was disillusioned with the state of phonological analyses, suggesting that researchers were overcomplicating issues to fit current popular theories. He recommended getting back to the basics of describing signed language usage as it naturally occurs and suggested starting with "the physiological basis (which is the place phonology began and sign phonology ought never to have left)" (Stokoe 2001: 436). Stokoe proposed a new way of thinking about signs[7], asking researchers to consider them as "simply a marriage of a noun and a verb" (2001: 434). In other words, signs are like *agent-verb* constructions. He explained, "when a signer of American Sign Language signifies 'yes,' the sign agent (i.e. the signer's active arm including the hand) flexes at the wrist; it is intransitive, it has no object, it acts on no patient" (Stokoe 2001: 434). In this case, while the closed-fist handshape nods up and down, the gloss equivalent is YES (Figure 5), but the proposition is more akin to something along the line of a solid roundish object moves up and down repeatedly, like a head nodding. In other words, signs, even signs thought to be "lexicalized"[8] (often glossed as having simplex English translations such as 'yes') can encode a full proposition, including actors/agents, events/verbs, and recipients/patients. Stokoe put meaning back into

---

7 Although Stokoe used examples from ASL, his semantic phonology proposal was not specific to any particular signed language.
8 See Lepic (2019) for why lexicalization is a problematic concept and a proposal for an alternative theoretical construct for understanding what have traditionally been considered frozen and classifier signs.

the "phonological" pieces of signs, instead analyzing what was on the surface, and walking back the theoretical compositionality of the sign itself.

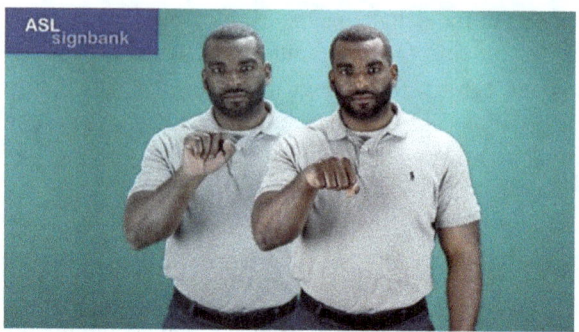

Figure 5: The ASL sign glossed YES, with an S-handshape and a wrist flexion movement (ASL Signbank 2021).

Stokoe was not alone in recognizing meaning in the sublexical structures of signed languages. During the early 1990s, researchers were documenting sublexical form-meaning correspondences across a variety of signed languages. Despite the phonemic status of these sublexical parameters, researchers were using terms such as "morphological" and "morphophonological" as they grappled with describing their data (Brennan, Colville and Lawson 1984; Deuchar 1984; Kyle and Woll 1985 for British Sign Language; Wilcox 1993; Klima and Bellugi 1979 for ASL; Engberg-Pederson 1993 for Danish Sign Language (dansk tegnsprog); Wallin 1990 for Swedish Sign Language (svenskt techenspråk, or STS); Pizzuto and Corazza 1996 for Italian Sign Language (Lingua dei Segni Italiana).

Despite this growing descriptive catalog showing that handshape, location, movement, orientation, and even contact could indeed encode meaning, Wilcox (2001) and Armstrong and Wilcox (2009) report that Stokoe's departure from linguistic cannon was met with resistance. Some thought that Stokoe's treatise implied that signed languages did not have duality of patterning, and that his 1991 article and the co-authored book *Gesture and the Nature of Language* (Armstrong, Stokoe and Wilcox 1995) rejected duality of patterning for signed languages all together. Thompson, Emmorey and Gollan (2005) argued against Semantic Phonology, suggesting that if there were in fact no arbitrary form-meaning mappings in signed languages, then "tip of the fingers" phenomena, which they had observed, should not be predicted (2005: 858). Armstrong and Wilcox pushed back, stating that "[e]vidence for 'phonological' decomposition of some signs by signers is not necessarily evidence for duality [of patterning] as strictly defined since duality has to do with a lack of semantic penetration of the basal layer of linguistic units" (Armstrong and Wilcox 2009: 414).

Several years later, Stokoe and his colleagues' assertions were supported in a special issue of *Language and Cognition* where several spoken language linguists questioned the necessity of duality of patterning altogether. In this issue, Blevins (2012) makes the following claim about duality of patterning generally:

> [A]n alternative interpretation, explored in this article, is that duality, like other proposed linguistic universals, is a statistical *tendency* reflecting a complex set of factors, and most centrally, the need for some minimal number of basic units that can recombine to yield a potentially infinite set of form-meaning correspondences. If this is the essence of duality, then we expect: languages where duality is not a central component of grammar; languages where most, but not all, utterances are decomposable into meaningless phonological units; and different types of phonological building blocks in different languages. (Blevins 2012: 275; italics added)

In the same issue, Ladd (2012) contends that while signed language phonologists have claimed that signed languages do in fact have duality of patterning, "it seems fair to say that researchers' attention has been directed to these issues precisely because of the force of the sceptics' argument that, if sign phonology lacks linear structure, then signed languages must be different in some essential way from spoken languages. Implicitly, that is, everyone accepts that linearity is a crucial property of phonology" (Ladd 2012: 269). That is to say, to legitimize these languages in the eyes of the larger linguistic community, the effort to prove that duality of patterning exists in signed languages was a bit of a red herring. If we reconsider duality of patterning as a statistical tendency, as Blevins suggests, and not as a design feature of language (Hockett 1960), we can explore the phonological properties of signed languages unencumbered, to better understand how they are structured and organized in the minds of signers.

While Stokoe did not in fact imply that signed languages do not have arbitrariness or duality of patterning, his proposal did open the door for a new way of thinking about signs and signed language phonology. Semantic Phonology, and later Cognitive Iconicity as proposed by Wilcox (2004), offered theoretical tools for understanding signers' ability to encode semantic information into the smallest units of form.

3 Putting meaning back into phonology

Returning to Stokoe's example of the ASL sign YES (Figure 5), if we recognize that the nodding motion of the wrist is not *just* a movement, and that the fist is not *just* a handshape, we can begin to see why a construction-based analysis that considers form *and* meaning is necessary. Analyzing YES as a construction allows us to identify the form-meaning mappings inherent to the sign. Following Stokoe (2001), this includes 1) the raised forearm (elbow bent at 45 degrees), 2) the closed-fist handshape (S-handshape), and 3) a nodding movement (wrist flexion), which in turn moves the S-handshape up and down, connecting it with the sense of 'head nods up and down'. It is the constellation of articulatory features that creates the sign, with the interconnected nature of these features being important in understanding the complexity of the form-meaning mapping. Segmenting isolated parts of a sign's form may be a convenient exercise for the linguist and the lexicographer, but a segmental approach to phonology obscures both the articulatory complexity of signs and the fact that the meaning of a sign is often more than the sum of arbitrary formal parts. This is not to say that in YES, the handshape means 'head' or that nodding means 'nodding', but it is to say that the use of these units within the larger constellation of features making up the sign creates this meaning. The pieces are therefore not arbitrary, which is also evidenced by the participation of such a sign in its larger constructional families (Lepic 2019, 2021).

It would be one thing for signers to know that the sign YES has meaningful form-meaning mappings by virtue of the fact that the arm and fist are construed as the neck and head and for the iconicity to stop there in a sort of one-off idiosyncratic form. However, other signs also make use of this same form-meaning mapping, which can be formalized in the constructional pattern [[fist::head] [arm::neck] [movement::movement]].[9] The systematicity of this pattern within the ASL lexicon both reinforces the form-meaning mapping through multiple instantiations across separate but related constructions, and also makes the construction productive in that the pattern can be extended. The ASL signs HEAD-BACK 'blown away' and BORNs 'to be born' (my translations) in Figure 6 can also be seen as part of the more schematic construction of "head movement signs" glossed in Hochgesang, Crasborn and Lillo-Martin's (2021) ASL Signbank as DS_s (seen in Figure 7), which represents the more abstract concept of 'solid roundish object (head) moves.'

This form-meaning mapping occurs across a variety of constructions that encode 'movement of the neck and head,' but it is more complicated because these head-neck movements can take on new meanings through metonymic extension. In some signs the head-neck movement is no longer physical movement, but instead encodes pragmatic function, emotions, or feelings indexed by the specific movement. In YES, the meaning is not just a head nodding but is 'nodding the head in agreement' due to

---

9 The notation [X::Y] is used to denote a construction in which the left side of the [::] refers to the form and the right side refers to the meaning. Smaller constructions can reside within a larger construction leading to the formalization [[x::x] [y::y] [z::z]].

(a) HEAD-BACK (b) BORNs

Figure 6: ASL sign HEAD-BACK (a) translated as 'blown away'; BORNs (b) (ASL Signbank).

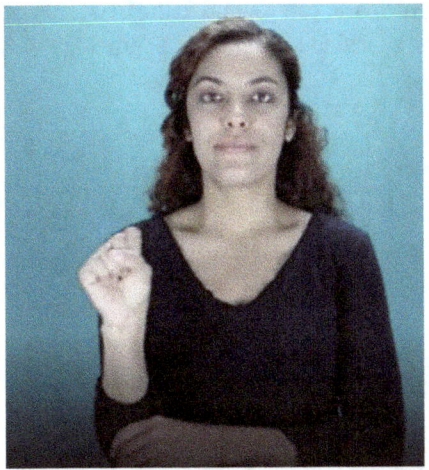

Figure 7: Depicting sign (DS_s) with an S-handshape (ASL Signbank).

the conventional gesture of head-nodding as a sign of agreement. Signers know the relationship between YES and head-nodding because they also know *other* signs that make use of the same constructional schema. In the sign HEAD-BACK (sometimes glossed as BLOWN-AWAY, as in being shocked by something), the raised-arm/fist is executed with a sharp-backwards wrist bend (and often elbow bend). The literal meaning is 'head/neck moves sharply and stiffly back', which can be used metonymically and metaphorically for psychologically or emotionally reacting abruptly to an external force (Talmy 1988, 2000; Occhino 2023). Ultimately, this sort of pattern only emerges when we look at groups of signs that share similar form-meaning mappings, not by looking at form alone or meaning alone. To understand the systematicity of this type of iconicity within the grammars of signed languages we must take a broadly construction-based approach.

Recent work on construction-based approaches to signed languages has begun to lay the groundwork for these types of analysis (Lepic 2015, 2016a, 2016b, 2019; Lepic and Occhino 2018; Wilcox and Occhino 2016). Lepic (2015), for example, provides helpful visualizations for understanding how groups of signs share relationships between form and meaning. As Figure 8 shows, the ASL sign FIGURE-OUT (itself a construction), with two K handshapes, has shared form-meaning relationships with other signs in the same constructional family. Importantly, these signs share the same movement and location, produced in neutral space as a two-handed sign, with the hands making a brushing contact. These parameters can be said to be the "fixed" parts of the construction. The handshape parameter, however, is schematic and can be one of the handshapes: K (the default), M, A, T, C, or G, which also correspond to the first letter of the English word (except K), depending on the specified referent (see Figure 8).

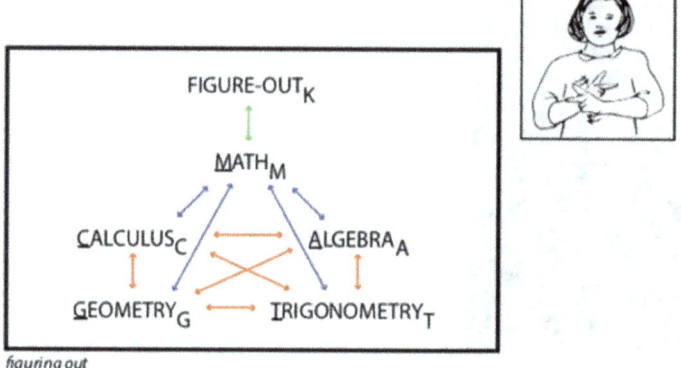

figuring out

Figure 8: The relationship between FIGURE-OUT and other signs that share similar movement and location but which differ in handshape. Used with permission from Lepic (2015).

ASL signers make use of the productive word-formation mechanism of "initializing" signs, where handshapes from the English manual alphabet form the handshape of the sign, to expand specialized vocabulary, in this case mathematical fields, and create dense constructional networks of signs related in both form and meaning (see Lepic 2021).

Another example is given in Figure 9a, which shows the sign TASTE, while Figure 9b illustrates what Lepic (2015) describes as the constructional families in which TASTE participates. On one hand TASTE (articulated with an open-8 handshape, with the extended middle finger pad contacting the chin) participates in the [open-8 handshape::sensation] construction that shares this handshape and its mapping to sensation with other signs like FEEL and TOUCH. On the other hand, the sign is articulated with contact at the chin, so it also participates in the [chin_location::mouth activity] construction where a group of signs share this place of articulation and its mapping to mouth activity (or mouth movement), for example signs like SAY and EAT.

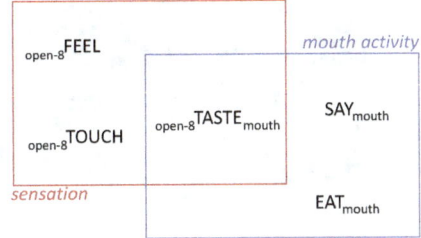

(a) TASTE (with 'open-8' handshape)   (b) Lepic's Constructional Families

Figure 9: (a) is the ASL sign TASTE (ASL Signbank); (b) shows the overlapping constructional families of 'sensation' and 'mouth activity', of which TASTE is a member (used with permission from Lepic 2015).

Lepic's analysis, which focuses on signs as constructions and as members of constructional families, provides a useful lens through which we can understand the organization of a signed language grammar. Signers build these constructional families from usage-events. Signers encounter signs as usage-events, subconsciously comparing each new usage to past instances of use, and in doing so build patterns of use of various form-meaning combinations. Wilcox and Occhino's (2016) claim that the extraction of these patterns takes place at the phonological level is explained by Wilcox's (2004) Cognitive Iconicity.

Based on these types of embodied form-meaning abstractions, Occhino (2016, 2017) therefore proposes a framework for understanding the emergence and organization of phonological structures in signed (and spoken) languages. Figure 10 is an example of form-meaning schemas extracted at the phonological level for the CUT sign family in ASL, in which the handshape is fixed as is the path movement, but the schematic path-extent (i.e., length of the path movement) and body location are not. While the A-handshape stays fixed across various instantiations of the CUT construction, the location parameter (of the incision) is abstracted from various bodily locations of possible cuts: here forehead, cheek, and hand. Signers extract such a schema from their experiences of bodily cuts and incisions in the real world. Importantly, Sweetser suggests that the "meaningfulness of gesture starts with the naturally meaningful spatial existence of the body – gestures emerge *relative* to that," (this volume: 157; italics in original).

In the next section I extend this construction-based analysis to the ASL sign HIT and show how it participates in a network of related constructional schemas. Multiple specific parameters and schematic parameters can be identified, filtered through experiential domains related to entities, movement, and force.

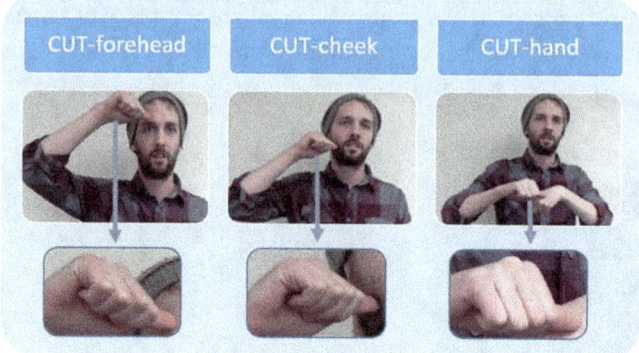

Figure 10: Extracted phonological schema for the construction CUT: [A-handshape::cutting instrument] and [location::location] (Occhino 2016).

3.1 The [2-handed NDH-1::transitive] family of constructions

Taking a broad definition of construction as a pairing of form and meaning, regardless of the degree of schematicity or complexity, we can begin to compare form-meaning pairings across similar constructions to determine whether a symbolic unit is an example of an existing schema or that a new schema be created. In the ASL sign HIT (Figure 11), the non-dominant hand articulates a vertical 1-handshape, while the dominant hand articulates a closed-fist S-handshape that makes contact with the non-dominant index finger via a straight path movement.

Figure 11: The ASL sign HIT (ASL Signbank 2021).

When the sign is isolated, it may seem to be a simple monomorphemic verb. However, signers may recognize that there are other constructions that share the same non-dominant 1-handshape, and that are articulated in neutral space with a short path movement of the dominant hand resulting in contact with the non-dominant 1-handshape. In these signs, the dominant handshape however, may or may not be the S-handshape and is a schematic or variable slot in this construction. For example, the variable slot can take the form of a B-handshape, palm up, thumb extended. This sign is glossed as CONVINCE (Figure 12) and shares much of its form with HIT.

Figure 12: ASL sign CONVINCE (ASL Signbank 2021).

We begin to see a pattern of interaction between the dominant and non-dominant hands in these two constructions. We can see this pattern with the construction schematic [form::function], introduced in footnote 15 above, and note that both the form and function can be either specific or schematic. Here, we might summarize the HIT and CONVINCE constructional patterns as 1) [non-dominant 1-handshape::patient], and 2) [dominant hand [X]-handshape::agent], where X is a schematic handshape slot. These two patterns can then be combined to make a constructional schema representing the simultaneous articulation of the two handshapes in a transitive construction, which can be written as:

[[non-dominant 1-handshape::patient] [dominant hand [X]-handshape::agent]]

The "non-dominant hand" can be abbreviated as NDH, "dominant hand" as DH, and "handshape" as HS, so that the schematic representation is:

[[NDH 1-HS::patient] [DH [X]-HS::agent]]

This construction can be schematized further to profile the transitive meaning inherent in each case as:

[2-handed NDH-1::transitive]

Other signs that share the schematic properties of [[NDH 1-HS::patient] [DH [X]-HS::agent]] are seen in Figure 13.

(a) REMIND   (b) CAPTURE   (c) CAJOLE

Figure 13: Some additional signs participating in the transitive construction: (a) REMIND; (b) CAPTURE; (c) CAJOLE (ASL Signbank 2021).

These constructions can be interpreted as interactions between the dominant and the non-dominant hands as agent-patient entities. Force Dynamics (Talmy 1985; 1988) is a cognitive semantics theory of how languages encode information about the interactions between agents and patients, and provides an ideal theoretical backdrop by which to interpret these patterns of form-meaning relationships between the dominant and non-dominant hands. In the [2-handed NDH-1::transitive] construction, the non-dominant hand encodes the patient, and the dominant hand encodes the agent (or agonist and antagonist in Force Dynamic terms). The movement (path), force of movement (manner), and contact (related to manner but also to a definitive endpoint to the path movement) all encode information about the force of the interaction between the agonist and antagonist. In Table 1, I attempt to schematize different instantiations of the [2-handed NDH-1::transitive] construction in ASL, using the examples of HIT (Figure 11), REMIND (Figure 13a), CAPTURE (Figure 13b) and CAJOLE (Figure 13c). Formal parameters of the signs are listed in column 1, while individual sign features are listed in columns 2-5. Columns 6-7, in grey, represent the form-meaning schema of the construction. Note the similarity in the form of the non-dominant hand and the path movement, the contact (either individual or repeated) made by the dominant hand (in various handshapes), and the various manners of movement.

Table 1: Schematic representation of signs in the [2-handed NDH-1::Transitive] construction in ASL.

Parameter					Constructional Schema	
	HIT	REMIND	CAPTURE	CAJOLE	Form Schema	Meaning Schema
Dominant Hand (DH)	S	Bent-B	Claw-5 > S	Open-B	Dominant Hand	(Agent)
Non-dominant Hand (NDH)	1	1	1	1	1	Patient
Path movement	direct path	direct path	direct path	direct path	(movement toward NDH)	(agent acting on patient)

Table 1 (continued)

Parameter					Constructional Schema	
Manner movement	single	repeated	single	repeated		
Force movement	forceful	soft	soft	soft	(manner of articulation)	(aspectual meaning)
Contact	Single knuckles on NDH-1	Repeated fingertips on NDH-1	Single knuckles on NDH-1	Alternate flat plane fingers front to back	(schematic contact DH on NDH)	(schematic outcome of force dynamic interaction)
Location	Neutral Space	Neutral Space	Neutral Space	Neutral Space	Neutral Space	(3-D space for interaction)

Much in the spirit of Stokoe's (2001) Semantic Phonology, evoking the tenets of Force Dynamics to understand the semantic aspects of the NDH-1 Transitive construction allows us to see how the formal components of the signs encode aspects of the semantics of transitive interactions. Cognitive Iconicity (Wilcox 2004) helps us to explain how one hand's movement relative to the other, the manner, force, and contact can all be mapped onto construals of how objects in the real world move. Without Cognitive Iconicity, we are unable to unite these patterns, and we are unable to understand how the systematicity of such patterns within the language encode grammatical concepts.

3.2 Emergence of form-meaning mappings

But where do these constructions come from? And do they constrain productivity in signed languages? To tackle the first question, we need to look at usage-based approaches to language (Langacker 1988) and to usage-based phonology in particular (Bybee 2001). As we experience usage events (Langacker 2008), the relationship of a communicative intent paired with a specific gestural utterance becomes entrenched (Bybee 2001). From these fully contextualized utterances, children can detect statistical patterns of combinations of form and meaning, along with how the two form associations (Bybee 2001, 2010).

Regardless of the formal complexity (e.g., size of the linguistic unit), form is not experienced without meaning, is not extracted without meaning, and is not stored without meaning (Bybee 2001). Children start with a big picture and slowly carve linguistic signals into smaller and smaller pieces as they detect language internal structure. Research has shown that pattern detection is at the core of linguistic development and that children who are better at detecting patterns, regardless of modality, are better at identifying grammatical patterns (Kidd and Arciuli 2016). Infants exploit statistical properties of usage events to make hypotheses about probabilistic tendencies of language and to detect distributional patterns in language input (Kuhl 2000; Bybee 2001).

Usage-based approaches have also shown that language use itself changes perception of linguistic units. As with other dynamic systems, language acquisition and language change are influenced by language users' experience (Thelen and Smith 1994; Beckner et al. 2009). Language learners continually make statistical hypotheses about what items pattern together, and update their understanding of relationships between linguistic units as they encounter more forms (Gershkoff-Stowe and Thelen 2004). When language users are exposed to usage events, the units do not have labels attached to them telling speakers what they *are*. It is up to the language user to discover form units of various sizes, based on repetition, within given social, linguistic, and temporal contexts (Wilcox and Occhino 2016; Occhino 2017), which varies across speakers. What counts as gesture for one, may be a sign for another; what counts as a morpheme for one, might count as a phoneme for another; what is meaningful for one, might be overlooked by another (Occhino and Wilcox 2017). This discovery process holds for linguistic units at all levels of meaning and complexity, from prosodic patterns to phonetic cues, and from syntactic constructions to phonological contrast. In the end, as Langacker suggests, a "speaker's grasp of a language resides in a vast assembly of patterns—referred to as *units*—with varying degrees of entrenchment and conventionality" (Langacker, this volume: 106).

But we have still not answered the question of whether this mapping of articulatory form to meaning constrains productivity in signed languages. While deterministic views of language and cognition have been rejected in cognitive linguistics, it seems many linguists now accept that language does influence how we think about the world. Our conceptual metaphors and semantic frames shape the way we think about basic conceptual units such as space, time, relationships, movement, emotions, possession, among other things (Johnson 1987; Lakoff and Johnson 1980; Lakoff 1987).

Such is the case with signed languages too. For example, in a language like ASL, where the sign FLY evokes the concept of flapping wings (Figure 14a), English metaphors about time flying have been shown to not translate well (Meir 2010). One ASL time metaphor, built on the idea of time moving quickly and encoded with respect to space, is ZOOM-OFF, which represents an object getting smaller as it moves toward the horizon (Figure 14b).

So, in the sense that languages are, in general, informed by their constructional repertoire, signed languages are no different from spoken languages. Individual motivated mappings may opportunistically be co-opted by signers in systematic

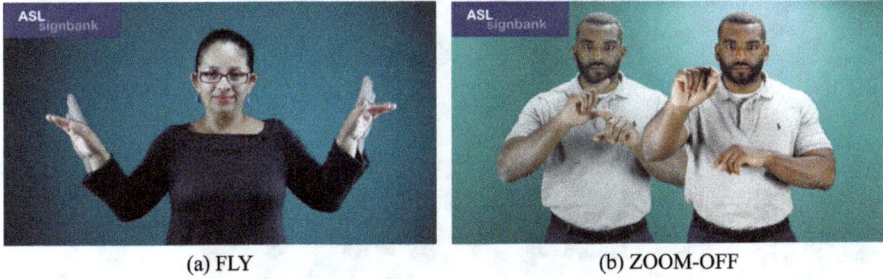

Figure 14: ASL sign FLY in (a), also used for wings and flapping; ASL sign ZOOM-OFF in (b) (ASL Signbank 2021).

and regular ways, but they in no way determine that the visual language then obligatorily uses that particular mapping from then on. Each signed language is mediated via its socio-cultural, linguistic, and communicative norms. For example, many signed languages have a metonymic sign meaning 'chicken' that evokes a physical or behavioral characteristic of chickens, namely the shape of its beak or pecking the ground (Figure 15a–c). Chatino Sign Language (San Juan Quiahije Chatino Sign Language) in Oaxaca, Mexico, has a sign that "depicts the action of sawing a machete into the chicken's head, which is a local custom for killing chickens" (Hou 2018: 585, see also Hou 2016), shown in Figure 16. Thus while different cultures co-opt similar salient features for metonymic signs, culturally salient practices or ways of being in the world can also motivate the form of the sign.

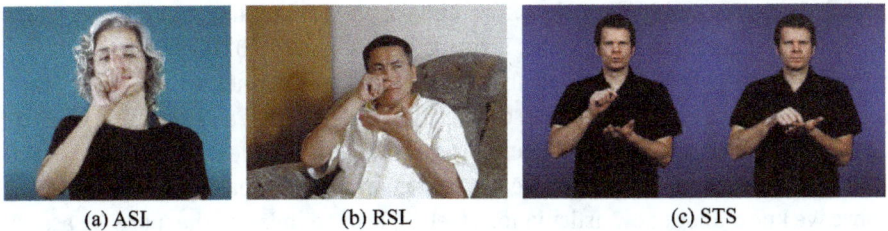

Figure 15: 'Chicken' in three signed languages, denoting the beak or pecking. One variant of the sign CHICKEN in ASL is in (a) (ASL Signbank 2021); one variant of the Russian Sign Language (Russkii Zhestovyi Yazyk) sign for 'chicken' is in (b) (Burkova 2015); one variant of the STS sign for 'chicken' is in (c) (Wallin and Mesch 2014).[10]

---

[10] Permission statement: Swedish Sign Language Lexicon by the Department of Sign Language, Department of Linguistics, Stockholm University is licensed under a Creative Commons Attribution-NonCommercial-Share Alike 4.0 International (CC BY-NC-SA 4.0). Based on a work at www.ling.su.se.

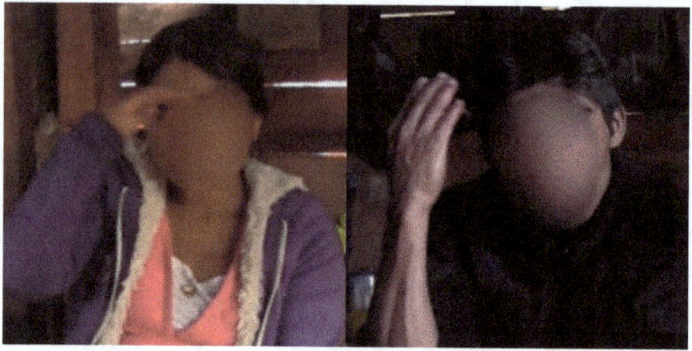

Figure 16: Two signers of Chatino Sign Language demonstrating their sign for 'chicken' that indexes a machete chopping the head of the chicken (Hou 2016).

Idiosyncratic iconic strategies for creating form-meaning has been referred to as "patterned iconicity" (Padden et al. 2013, 2015; Hwang et al. 2017), and described as the "recurring use of one or more *iconic strategies* across signs in a particular semantic category" (Padden et al. 2015: 82, italics in original). It seems once signers begin using an iconic strategy for encoding a semantic category, other signs within that semantic domain gravitate toward the same form-meaning mapping. Hwang et al. (2017) showed that personification was the preferred strategy cross-linguistically for encoding signs for animals.[11] The researchers point out that what is interesting about identifying patterned iconicity is "not that signs for 'bird' look similar or different in any two sign languages, but that (i) signs for 'bird' are likely to share an iconic strategy with other signs for animals, and (ii) broadly, sign languages use similar strategies to organize their lexicons" (Hwang et al. 2017: 598–599).

Finally, how we feel and think about objects and how we interact and engage with a concept has direct effects on our construal of phonological and semantic content. Individual construals also have an important role to play in the way we organize and understand language. The more we use particular signs for particular concepts, the more we know about how articulations feel, look, or sound. And the more we associate those forms with our individual construals of the meaning, the more we solidify our own mental representations of form and meaning. Recent work has shown that experience influences perception of iconicity and that iconicity is thus not an objective property of signs but a subjective mapping imbued on the construction (Occhino

---

Permission for the use of Russian Sign Language from Svetlana Burkova, Russian Sign Language Corpus. http://rsl.nstu.ru/ (Accessed 10/20/2021).
11 In an elicitation task, personification occurred in the majority of signs for animals: 67% in Central Taurus Sign Language, 65% in ASL, and 68% in Japanese Sign Language.

et al. 2017; Occhino, Anible and Morford 2020). This is not surprising given that the construal of form and of meaning are the foundation of symbolic units within a cognitive framework (Langacker 1987 and elsewhere). The fact that language users can (and do) reflect on perceptual elements of the formal properties of signs is one of the bases for Cognitive Iconicity. In signed languages, because the articulators are always perceptually available, signers are able to capitalize on their ability to construe handshapes, movements, and articulatory locations as having meaning (Wilcox 2004; Occhino 2016, 2017).

4 Toward an embodied grammar

As noted in Section 3 above, Sweetser suggests that the "meaningfulness of gesture starts with the naturally meaningful spatial existence of the body – gestures emerge *relative* to that" (this volume: 157). She goes on to say that this is "most obvious with respect to the hands, since they are the articulators most mobile in 3-D space with respect to the rest of the body, and most able to perform varied shapes and motions that are different from their functional non-communicative uses" (this volume: 157). So, the mapping of meaningful experience (with the body) *to the body* is at the very core of our semiotic repertoire as human beings. Recently, signed language linguists have added a considerable amount of experimental support for this view. Rigorous studies on the distribution and function of articulatory forms within the grammars of multiple signed languages have all found articulatory parameters to cluster around stable semantic patterns, including handshape (Cabeza-Pereiro 2014; Hwang et al. 2017; Occhino 2017; Occhino, Anible and Morford 2020); two-handed signs (Börstell, Lepic and Belsitzman 2016; Lepic et al. 2016); the location of signs on the body (Cates et al. 2013; Östling, Börstell and Courtaux 2018). Usage-based constructional theoretical frameworks such as Cognitive Construction Grammar (Goldberg 1995, 2006), Cognitive Grammar (Langacker 2008), Radical Construction Grammar (Croft 2001), Usage-based Phonology (Bybee 2001), Cognitive Iconicity (Wilcox 2004), and more recently Embodied Cognitive Phonology (Occhino 2016, 2017) provide tools that allow for rigorous investigations of form-meaning mappings at all levels of formal complexity, from feature-level phenomena to syntactic and prosodic structures. Visual similarity judgements can be made between articulatory forms and objects. Just as one object can be understood in terms of another via a metaphorical extension, so too can a given articulatory form be understood in terms of an emerging or established semantic domain.

As principles of embodied cognition become more accepted within mainstream linguistics, we are able to make substantive comparisons between signed and spoken languages. By focusing on the role of the body in the emergence of form and in the making of meaning, usage-based and embodied frameworks help us develop an account of grammar, including phonology, that can describe the structure and processing of language, again both spoken and signed. Interestingly, focusing on theories of semantics (e.g., Force Dynamics, Talmy 1985; Frame Semantics, Fillmore 1982; Simulation Semantics, Barsalou 2003) may expand our ability to describe the grammars of signed languages, and the ways in which signed languages develop formal parameters to encode what signers mean. What is clear is that usage-based approaches that consider the role of the body and seek to understand how general cognitive mechanisms interact with modality-specific sensory-motor pressures will show us the way forward.

References

Armstrong, David F., William C. Stokoe & Sherman E. Wilcox. 1995. *Gesture and the Nature of Language*. Cambridge: Cambridge University Press.

Armstrong, David F. & Sherman E. Wilcox. 2009. Gesture and the nature of semantic phonology. *Sign Language Studies* 9(4). 410–416.

Barsalou, Louis. 2003. Situated simulation in the human conceptual system. *Language and Cognitive Processes* 18(5/6). 513–562.

Bates, Elizabeth A. & John L. Elman. 2002 [1993]. Connectionism and the study of change. In Mark H. Johnson, Munakata Yuko & Rick O. Gilmore (eds.), *Brain Development and Cognition: A Reader*, 420–440. Oxford: Blackwell Publishers.

Beckner, Clay, Richard Blythe, Joan L. Bybee, Morton H. Christiansen, Willian Croft, Nick C. Ellis, John Holland, Jin Yun Ke, Diane Larsen-Freeman & Tom Schoenemann. 2009. Language is a complex adaptive system: Position paper. *Language Learning* 59. 1–26.

Blevins, Juliette. 2012. Duality of patterning: Absolute universal or statistical tendency? *Language and Cognition* 4(4). 275–296. https://doi.org/10.1515/langcog-2012-0016

Börstell, Carl, Ryan Lepic & Gal Belsitzman. 2016. Articulatory plurality is a property of lexical plurals in sign language. *Lingvisticæ Investigationes* 39(2). 391–407. https://doi.org/10.1075/li.39.2.10bor

Brennan, Mary, Martin D. Colville & Lillian K. Lawson. 1984. *Words in Hand: A Structural Analysis of the Signs of British Sign Language*. Edinburgh: Edinburgh BSL Research Project.

Brentari, Diane. 1998. *A Prosodic Model of Sign Language Phonology*. Boston, MA: MIT Press.

Brentari, Diane & John Goldsmith. 1993. Secondary licensing and the non-dominant hand in ASL phonology. In Geoffrey R. Coulter (ed.), *Current Issues in ASL Phonology*, 19–42. New York: Academic Press.

Brentari, Diane & Carol A. Padden. 2001. Native and foreign vocabulary in American Sign Language: A lexicon with multiple origins. In Diane Brentari (ed.), *Foreign Vocabulary in Sign Language: A Crosslinguistic Investigation of Word Formation*, 87–119. Mahwah, NJ: Lawrence Erlbaum.

Browman, Catherine P. & Louis Goldstein. 1986. Towards an articulatory phonology. *Phonology* 3. 219–252.

Browman, Catherine P. & Louis Goldstein. 1989. Articulatory gestures as phonological units. *Phonology* 6(2). 201–251. https://doi.org/10.1017/S0952675700001019

Burkova, Svetlana. 2015. Russian Sign Language: general information. Russian Sign Language Corpus. Novosibirsk, 2012–2015. Project leader: Svetlana Burkova. http://rsl.nstu.ru/site/signlang. Accessed 10/20/2021.

Bybee, Joan L. 2001. *Phonology and Language Use*. Cambridge: Cambridge University Press.

Bybee, Joan L. 2010. *Language, Usage and Cognition*. Cambridge: Cambridge University Press.

Bybee, Joan L. & David Eddington. 2006. A usage-based approach to Spanish verbs of 'becoming'. *Language* 82(2). 323–355.

Cabeza-Pereiro, Carmen. 2014. Metaphor and lexicon in sign languages: Analysis of the hand-opening articulation in LSE and BSL. *Sign Language Studies* 14(3). 302–332.

Cates, Deborah, Eva Gutiérrez, Sarah Hafer, Ryan Barrett & David Corina. 2013. Location, location, location. *Sign Language Studies* 13(4). 433–461.

Corina, David & Wendy Sandler. 1993. On the nature of phonological structure in sign language. *Phonology* 10(2). 165–207.

Croft, William. 2001. *Radical Construction Grammar: Syntactic Theory in Typological Perspective*. Oxford: Oxford University Press.

Cuxac, Christian & Marie-Anne Sallandre. 2007. Iconicity and arbitrariness in French Sign Language: Highly iconic structures, degenerated iconicity and diagrammatic iconicity. In Elena Pizzuto, Paola Pietrandrea & Raffaele Simone (eds.), *Verbal and Signed Languages: Comparing Structures, Constructs and Methodologies*. Berlin/New York: Mouton de Gruyter.

Deuchar, Margaret. 1984. *British Sign Language*. New York: Routledge.

Engberg-Pedersen, Elisabeth. 1993. *Space in Danish Sign Language: The Semantics and Morphosyntax of the Use of Space in a Visual Language*. Hamburg: Signum.

Fillmore, Charles J. 1982. Frame semantics. In The Linguistic Society of Korea (ed.), *Linguistics in the Morning Calm: Selected Papers from SICOL-1981*, 111–137. Seoul: Hanshin.

Frishberg, Nancy. 1975. Arbitrariness and Iconicity: Historical Change in American Sign Language. *Language* 51(3). 696–719.

Gershkoff-Stowe, Lisa & Esther Thelen. 2004. U-shaped changes in behavior: A dynamic systems perspective. *Journal of Cognition and Development* 5(1). 11–36. https://doi.org/10.1207/s15327647jcd0501_2

Gibbs, Raymond W. Jr. 2006. *Embodiment and Cognitive Science*. Cambridge: Cambridge University Press.

Goldberg, Adele. 1995. *Constructions: A Construction Grammar Approach to Argument Structure*. Chicago: Chicago University Press.

Goldberg, Adele. 2006. *Constructions at Work: The Nature of Generalization in Language*. Oxford: Oxford University Press.

Hochgesang, Julie A., Onno Crasborn & Diane Lillo-Martin. 2021. *ASL Signbank*. New Haven, CT: Haskins Lab, Yale University. https://aslsignbank.haskins.yale.edu/

Hockett, Charles F. 1960. The origin of speech. *Scientific American* 203(3). 88–96.

Hou, Lynn Yong-Shi. 2016. *"Making Hands": Family Sign Languages in the San Juan Quiahije Community*. Austin: University of Texas at Austin dissertation.

Hou, Lynn. 2018. Iconic patterns in San Juan Quiahije Chatino Sign Language. *Sign Language Studies* 18(4). 570–611. doi:10.1353/sls.2018.0017

Hwang, So-One, Nozomi Tomita, Hope Morgan, Rabia Ergin, Deniz İlkbaşaran, Sharon Seegers, Ryan Lepic & Carol Padden. 2017. Of the body and the hands: Patterned iconicity for semantic categories. *Language and Cognition* 9(4). 573–602. https://doi.org/10.1017/langcog.2016.28

Johnson, Mark. 1987. *The Body in the Mind: The Bodily Basis of Meaning, Imagination, and Reason.* Chicago: University of Chicago Press.

Kay, Paul & Charles J. Fillmore. 1999. Grammatical constructions and linguistic generalizations: The *What's X doing Y?* construction. *Language* 75(1). 1–33.

Kemmerer, David. 2015. *Cognitive Neuroscience of Language.* New York/London: Psychology Press.

Kidd, Evan & Joanne Arciuli. 2016. Individual differences in statistical learning predict children's comprehension of syntax. *Child Development* 87(1). 184–193. DOI: 10.1111/cdev.12461

Klima, Edward S. & Ursula Bellugi. 1979. *The Signs of Language.* Cambridge, MA: Harvard University Press.

Kuhl, Patricia K. 2000. A new view of language acquisition. *Proceedings of the National Academy of Sciences* 97(22). 11850–11857. DOI: 10.1073/pnas.97.22.11850

Kyle, James G. & Bencie Woll. 1985. *Sign Language: The Study of Deaf People and Their Language.* Cambridge: Cambridge University Press.

Ladd, D. Robert. 2012. What *is* duality of patterning, anyway? *Language and Cognition* 4(4). 261–273. https://doi.org/10.1515/langcog-2012-0015

Lakoff, George. 1987. *Women, Fire, and Dangerous Things: What Categories Reveal about the Mind.* Chicago: University of Chicago Press.

Lakoff, George & Mark Johnson. 1980. *Metaphors We Live By.* Chicago: University of Chicago Press.

Langacker, Ronald W. 1986. An introduction to Cognitive Grammar. *Cognitive Science* 10. 1–40.

Langacker, Ronald W. 1987. *Foundations of Cognitive Grammar: Theoretical Prerequisites*, Vol. 1. Stanford, CA: Stanford University Press.

Langacker, Ronald W. 1988. A usage-based model. In Brygida Rudzka-Ostyn (ed.), *Topics in Cognitive Linguistics*, 127–161. Amsterdam/Philadelphia: John Benjamins.

Langacker, Ronald W. 1991. *Foundations of Cognitive Grammar: Descriptive Application*, Vol. 2. Stanford, CA: Stanford University Press.

Langacker, Ronald W. 2008. *Cognitive Grammar: A Basic Introduction.* Oxford/New York: Oxford University Press.

Lepic, Ryan. 2015. Motivation in Morphology: Lexical Patterns in ASL and English. San Diego: University of California, San Diego dissertation.

Lepic, Ryan. 2016a. The great ASL compound hoax. In Aubrey Healey, Ricardo Napoleão de Souza, Pavlina Pešková & Moses Allen (eds.), *Proceedings of the 11th High Desert Linguistics Society Conference*, 227–250. Albuquerque, NM: University of New Mexico.

Lepic, Ryan. 2016b. Lexical blends and lexical patterns in English and in American Sign Language. *Mediterranean Morphology Meetings* [Online] 10, 98–111. https://doi.org/10.26220/mmm.2728

Lepic, Ryan. 2019. A usage-based alternative to "lexicalization" in sign language linguistics. *Glossa: A Journal of General Linguistics* 4(1). 1–30. https://doi.org/10.5334/gjgl.840

Lepic, Ryan. 2021. From letters to families: Initialized signs in American Sign Language. In Hans C. Boas & Steffen Höder (eds.), *Constructions in Contact: Language Change, Multilingual Practices, and Additional Language Acquisition*, 267–305. Amsterdam/Philadelphia: John Benjamins. https://doi.org/10.1075/cal.30.09lep

Lepic, Ryan, Carl Börstell, Gal Belsitzman & Wendy Sandler. 2016. Taking meaning in hand: Iconic motivations in two-handed signs. *Sign Language & Linguistics* 19(1). 37–81. https://doi.org/10.1075/sll.19.1.02lep

Lepic, Ryan & Corrine Occhino. 2018. A Construction Morphology approach to sign language analysis. In Geert Booij (ed.), *The Construction of Words*, 141–172. Cham: Springer. https://doi.org/10.1007/978-3-319-74394-3_6

Marghetis, Tyler & Benjamin K. Bergen. 2014. Embodied meaning, inside and out: The coupling of gesture and mental simulation. In Cornelia Müller, Alan Cienki, Ellen Fricke, Silva H. Ladewig, David McNeill & Sedinha Teßendorf (eds.), *Body – Language – Communication. An International Handbook on Multimodality in Human Interaction*, Vol. 2. Berlin/Boston: Mouton de Gruyter.

Meir, Irit. 2010. Iconicity and metaphor: Constraints on metaphorical extension of iconic forms. *Language* 86(4). 865–896.

Meir, Irit & Wendy Sandler. 2008. *A Language in Space: The Story of Israeli Sign Language*. New York: Lawrence Erlbaum.

Nijen Twilhaar, Jan & Beppie van den Bogaerde (eds). 2016. *Concise Lexicon for Sign Linguistics*. Amsterdam/Philadelphia: John Benjamins.

Occhino, Corrine. 2016. *A Cognitive Approach to Phonology: Evidence from Signed Languages*. Albuquerque: University of New Mexico dissertation.

Occhino, Corrine. 2017. An introduction to Embodied Cognitive Phonology: Claw-5 handshape distribution in ASL and Libras. *Complutense Journal of English Studies* 25. 69–103.

Occhino, Corrine. 2023. Force dynamic constructions in ASL. In Fuyin Thomas Li (ed.), *Handbook of Cognitive Semantics*, 20–56. Leiden/Boston: Brill.

Occhino, Corrine, Benjamin Anible & Jill P. Morford. 2020. The role of iconicity, construal, and proficiency in the online processing of handshape. *Language and Cognition* 12(1). 114–137. https://doi.org/10.1017/langcog.2020.1

Occhino, Corrine, Benjamin Anible, Erin Wilkinson & Jill P. Morford. 2017. Iconicity is in the eye of the beholder: How language experience affects perceived iconicity. *Gesture* 16(1). 100–126. https://doi.org/10.1075/gest.16.1.04occ

Occhino, Corrine & Sherman Wilcox. 2017. Gesture or sign? A categorization problem. *Behavioral and Brain Sciences* 40, e66. https://doi.org/10.1017/S0140525X15003015

Östling, Robert, Carl Börstell & Servane Courtaux. 2018. Visual iconicity across sign languages: Large-scale automated video analysis of iconic articulators and locations. *Frontiers in Psychology* 9:725. 1–17. https://doi.org/10.3389/fpsyg.2018.00725

Padden, Carol, Irit Meir, So-One Hwang, Ryan Lepic, Sharon Seegers & Tory Sampson. 2013. Patterned iconicity in sign language lexicons. *Gesture* 13(3). 287–308.

Padden, Carol, So-One Hwang, Ryan Lepic & Sharon Seegers. 2015. Tools for language: Patterned iconicity in sign language nouns and verbs. *Topics in Cognitive Science* 7. 81–94.

Pizzuto, Elena & Serena Corazza. 1996. Noun morphology in Italian Sign Language (LIS). *Lingua* 98(1–3). 169–196. https://doi.org/10.1016/0024-3841(95)00037-2

Sandler, Wendy. 1986. The spreading hand autosegment of American Sign Language. *Sign Language Studies* 50. 1–28.

Sandler, Wendy. 1989. *Phonological Representation of the Sign: Linearity and Nonlinearity in American Sign Language*. Berlin/New York: De Gruyter Mouton.

Sandler, Wendy. 1993. Linearization of phonological tiers in ASL. In Geoffrey R. Coulter (ed.), *Current Issues in ASL Phonology*, 103–129. San Diego, CA: Academic Press.

Sandler, Wendy. 2012. The Phonological organization of sign languages. *Language and Linguistics Compass* 6(3). 162–182. https://doi.org/10.1002/lnc3.326

Shaw, Emily & Yves Delaporte. 2015. *A Historical and Etymological Dictionary of American Sign Language: The Origin and Evolution of More than 500 Signs*. Washington, DC: Gallaudet University Press.

Stokoe, William C. 1960. *Sign Language Structure: An Outline of the Visual Communication Systems of the American Deaf* (Studies in Linguistics Occasional Papers 8). Buffalo, NY: University of Buffalo.

Stokoe, William C. 2001 [1991]. Semantic phonology. *Sign Language Studies* 1(4). 434–441. https://doi.org/10.1353/sls.2001.0019.

Stokoe, William C., Dorothy C. Casterline & Carl G. Croneberg. 1965. *A Dictionary of American Sign Language on Linguistic Principles*. Washington, DC: Gallaudet College Press.

Svenskt teckenspråkslexikon. 2021. Svenskt teckenspråkslexikon. Sign Language Section, Department of Linguistics. Stockholm: Stockholm University. teckensprakslexikon.ling.su.se

Talmy, Leonard. 1985. Force dynamics in language and thought. In William H. Eikfont, Paul D. Kroeber & Karen L. Peterson (eds.), *Papers from the Twenty-first Regional Meeting of the Chicago Linguistic Society* 21(2). 293–337. Chicago: Chicago Linguistic Society.

Talmy, Leonard. 1988. Force Dynamics in language and cognition. *Cognitive Science* 12. 49–100.

Talmy, Leonard. 2000. *Toward a Cognitive Semantics, Vol 2, Typology and Process in Concept Structuring*. Cambridge, MA: MIT Press.

Thelen, Esther & Linda B. Smith. 1994. *A Dynamic Systems Approach to the Development of Cognition and Action*. Cambridge, MA: MIT Press.

Thompson, Robin L., Karen Emmorey & Tamar H. Gollan. 2005. "Tip of the fingers" experiences by deaf signers: Insights into the organization of a sign-based lexicon. *Psychological Science* 16(11). 856–860.

Varela, Francisco J., Evan Thompson & Eleanor Rosch. 2016 [1991]. *The Embodied Mind: Cognitive Science and Human Experience*. Cambridge MA: MIT Press.

Wallin, Lars. 1990. Polymorphemic predicates in Swedish Sign Language. In Ceil Lucas (ed.), *Sign Language Research: Theoretical Issues*, 133–148. Washington, DC: Gallaudet University Press.

Wallin, Lars & Johanna Mesch. 2014. Annoteringskonventioner för teckenspråkstexter, Version 5. Sign Language Section, Department of Linguistics, Stockholm University. http://www.ling.su.se/teckensprakskorpus

Wilcox, Phyllis. 1993. *Metaphorical Mapping in American Sign Language*. Albuquerque: University of New Mexico dissertation.

Wilcox, Phyllis Perrin. 2000. *Metaphor in American Sign Language*. Washington, DC: Gallaudet University Press.

Wilcox, Sherman. 2001. Searching for language: Process, not product. *Sign Language Studies* 1(4). 333–343. https://doi.org/10.1353/sls.2001.0021

Wilcox, Sherman. 2002. William C. Stokoe and the gestural theory of language origins. In David F. Armstrong, Michael A. Karchmer & John Vickrey Van Cleve (eds.), *The Study of Signed Languages: Essays in Honor of William C. Stokoe*, 118–130. Washington, DC: Gallaudet University Press.

Wilcox, Sherman. 2004. Cognitive iconicity: Conceptual spaces, meaning, and gesture in signed language. *Cognitive Linguistics* 15(2). 119–147. https://doi.org/10.1515/cogl.2004.005

Wilcox, Sherman. 2014. Moving beyond structuralism: Usage-based signed language linguistics. *Lingua de Señas e Interpretación*. 5–97.

Wilcox, Sherman & Corrine Occhino. 2016. Constructing signs: Place as a symbolic structure in signed languages. *Cognitive Linguistics* 27(3). 371–404. https://doi.org/10.1515/cog-2016-0003

Wilcox, Sherman & Phyllis Wilcox. 1995. The gestural expression of modality in American Sign Language. In Joan Bybee & Suzanne Fleischman (eds.). *Modality in Grammar and Discourse*, 135–162. Amsterdam/Philadelphia: John Benjamins.

Wilcox, Sherman, Phyllis Perrin Wilcox & Maria Josep Jarque. 2004. Mappings in conceptual space: Metonomy, metaphor, and iconicity in two signed languages. *Jezikoslovlje* [Linguistics] 4(1). 139–156.

III Multimodality

Eve Sweetser
Gestural meaning is in the body(-space) as much as in the hands

1 Introduction

In the study of co-speech gesture, the primary elements being transcribed are usually the shape, motion and location of the hands (first of all), followed by changes in gaze, head direction, facial expression, and bodily posture. This situation generally persists in both gesture and signed language studies, despite broader approaches such as that laid out in Bressem (2014).[1] However, it has long been noted that the same hand and handshape may carry different meaning depending on the location relative to the body, perhaps the most-studied contrast being that of the dominant-hand vs. non-dominant-hand sides of the body (Casasanto 2009, Casasanto and Jasmin 2010). A layer of locational and orientational meaning is thus added to the patterns of shape, motion path, etc.

My suggestion is that to a significant extent, we should reverse this ontology. The meaningfulness of gesture starts with the naturally meaningful spatial existence of the body – gestures emerge *relative* to that. This is most obvious with respect to the hands, since they are the articulators most mobile in 3-D space with respect to the rest of the body, and most able to perform varied shapes and motions that are different from their functional non-communicative uses. Fingerspelling[2], for

---

[1] It is manifestly impossible to transcribe every aspect of a gestural sequence; and apparent "inconsistencies" and gaps in transcriptions are often due to researchers' different needs and goals. I am not here devaluing transcripts or analyses focusing on manual gesture, but suggesting a framework in which we might differently contextualize them.
[2] Fingerspelling is a system of hand-configurations used in many signed languages to represent alphanumeric characters and thus "spell" written language forms. The American Manual Alphabet used by American Sign Language (ASL) users (different from the British Sign Language system), may be readily found online, including on Wikipedia. Many gesture researchers have used fingerspelling labels for handshapes in gesture, thus a gesture researcher may say "B hand" to mean a flat hand with fingers together, since that's the shape of AMA "B"; similarly, a "5 hand" is a flat hand with fingers separated. It happens that "D" and the number "1" are fingerspelled with the same hand form in AMA: an extended index finger with the three other fingers pulled back to touch the thumb. Since gesture researchers are only labeling handshape (regardless of variation in location and orientation), "D hand" typically refers in gesture research simply to this handshape, and the label "1 hand" would not contrast with it.

Eve Sweetser, University of California, Berkeley, USA, e-mail: sweetser@berkeley.edu

https://doi.org/10.1515/9783110703788-007

example, is far more different from object-directed functional hand actions than the possibilities for gaze-direction or body-posture in communication are different from non-communicative gaze and posture.[3]

A "D" or "B" or "5" handshape on its own has no stable meaning. Does the flat hand of a B mime a surface? Mime cutting through something? Mime pushing away something? Does a "D" deictically enact a point (index finger pointing towards what?)? or does the index finger of the D handshape iconically (Taub 2001, Wilcox 2004) represent a long, thin object (or one kind of such object, a numeric digit 1)? There are many different iconic, metaphoric, and metonymic mappings involved in such readings. But what I shall try to do here is lay out the layers of meaning which I see in the gesture spaces within which multimodal communication is embedded. These layers of construal provide the motivating *background* against which we experience individual handshapes, motions, postural shifts, and gesture in general as iconically, metaphorically, metonymically and deictically meaningful.

At one level, this recapitulates understandings of language and thought such as those of Merleau-Ponty (1962) or Bühler ([1934] 2011); in particular, I agree with them that experiential bodily presence is deeply important to meaning, and that we can't give meaning to body and space separately and independently. I am also clearly inspired by Johnson's (1987, 2007) and Shuman and Young's (2018) understanding of the meaning of the body, and by Müller's (2014) general semiotic view of gesture. But in particular, I am striving to build an ontology of co-speech gestural meaning, starting with what patterns gesture analysts have observed, and what we now know about the neural systems involved in action and gesture. This ontology includes hypothesized dependence relationships between aspects of the bodily/gestural meaning system. That is, I need to have the basic ego-centered bodily self/space described in section 2, as a prerequisite for deictically meaningful gesture which depends on it, or for iconic uses of gesture space; and I have to be working with deictic and iconic bodily meanings, to go on to the interpersonal, narrative and discourse uses of gesture space.

To take an example: A palm-outwards flat ("B") hand gesture which means "don't interrupt" certainly exploits (1) *deictic* aspects of body space, since its meaning depends on its being directed away from the body and towards the interlocutor. This gesture also makes use of (2) our *iconic* capacity, in representing the visual shape of a flat barrier, force-dynamically and muscularly directed outwards in space, so as to resist something approaching the body. This outward-facing

---

3 Posture and gaze are always *potentially* communicative in the sense that they are always possible input to mind-reading by conspecifics (See section 3). However, posture and gaze are essential in our moving about the environment, whether or not conspecifics are present to "read" them.

barrier is (3) *metaphorically* interpreted via COMMUNICATION IS OBJECT EXCHANGE (Taub 2001 describes a parallel structure in ASL) as an attempt to deter the interlocutor's speech, which the literal physical hand-barrier is powerless to do. And the communicative point of the gesture in context is very likely (4) *discourse regulation*: a good gloss of an English speaker's use of this gesture is often, "(Wait, please) don't interrupt."

Without the basic deictic and iconic strata, the metaphoric construal would not be possible: that is, I first need to be able to construe this hand as an outward-directed physical barrier, in order to metaphorically construe it as a metaphoric "barrier" to communicative exchange. And the discourse-regulatory function depends in turn on the metaphoric interpretation: a raised hand is not a literal, physical barrier to the interlocutor's speech.

Once we have in place this multi-layered model of gestural-spatial bodily meaning, it becomes (usefully, in my view) clear that we cannot put gestures into either-or compartments as iconic, or metaphoric, or discourse-regulating. All these aspects of the body's meaningful affordances in space are available simultaneously, in ontologically layered relationship with each other, and they jointly contribute to meaning, often within the same gesture.[4]

This model also opens up added questions for cross-linguistic and cross-cultural examination of gesture systems. Shared human bodily existence in space may give all humans some of the same range of physical gesture abilities, and we also share meaning-construction affordances (including deixis, iconicity, metonymy, and mental-space blends such as metaphor). But that does not mean we necessarily use those affordances the same way. Particular languages' systems of deixis or metaphor are different from each other (Levinson and Wilkins 2006; Hanks 1990), and so are systems of co-speech gesture (Enfield 2009; Núñez and Sweetser 2006; Kita 2003). However, there seem to be more constraints on the structure of deictic systems in language, and wider variation in linguistic metaphor systems (Gaby and Sweetser 2017; Dancygier and Sweetser 2014); similarly, gestural systems could show sub-areas of greater or lesser cross-cultural variation. Whatever aspects of bodily presence and experience are in fact cross-culturally shared (we share the experience of peripersonal space with fellow apes at least), those would be likely grounds for cross-culturally shared aspects of gesture systems.

I certainly don't mean to suggest by this metaphor of "layers" that in actual communication, speakers are processing these layers in some *temporal* order, start-

---

[4] I won't here address the relationship of this kind of ontological dependency to questions of evolution of language systems from gesture (e.g., Armstrong and Wilcox 2007; Corballis 2003), though I hope this work may relate to theirs.

ing with egocentric deixis and then adding other aspects of interpretation. It is possible that there is some relationship between these ontological dependencies and order of acquisition: children certainly become capable of pointing long before they understand metaphor. But I don't address this issue here. In communicative understanding, all the relevant aspects of gestural meaning operate simultaneously and in concert.

2 Underlying gesture: The bodily space of ego-centered affordances

To a speaker/gesturer, bodily space—or perhaps better, the body in space, the "extended body" (Froese and Fuchs 2012)—has meaning independent of communication. The term *extended body* emphasizes that we never experience body-adjacent accessible space as just "space," but carry along with us the specific matrix (matrices) of coordinates which our presence imposes on it; nor of course do we experience our *body* as a thing independent of those adjacent-space affordances. Being a human in a body is being embodied within a spatial matrix. Location and direction are naturally parts of our basic physical experience of space; this includes—not only, but centrally—location and direction relative to Ego. For example, whether or not we're present in the relevant rooms, we may have knowledge of what objects are located in what room, knowledge which does not consist of a single viewpointed imagining. But once inside a room, we are necessarily experiencing the accessible objects in egocentric coordinates.

Neuroscience has identified neural systems that establish a contrast between *peripersonal space* (experienced immediate bodily space) and *extrapersonal space* (Rizzolatti et al. 1997). The former (at least for the upper body) bears a clear relationship to *personal gesture space*, while the latter refers to the rest of the space around us. You will experience a buzzing bug, for example, quite differently depending on whether it is inside or outside your peripersonal space. Interestingly, peripersonal space can be sensorily expanded by expanding practical interactional affordances; with no tool in their hand, a primate's peripersonal space extends no farther than their unaided reach, but extending the reach with a tool also extends the region of felt peripersonal space. Social affordances also have an effect on peripersonal space (Pellencin et al. 2018). Further, we are aware of conspecifics' (and some other animals') spatial affordances: a Beta chimp will not reach for the food item if they can see that it's within the Alpha chimp's reach (Tomasello 1999, 2008).

To these we may add the inherent front-back asymmetry in the affordances of human visual perception and manual interaction: we are not octopods who can grasp equally well in many directions, or owls whose heads turn 270 degrees. There is also the basic up/down asymmetry of the gravitic environment we live in, which combines with our bodies' up/down asymmetry; our anatomy fits us not only to stand erect on our feet rather than on our heads, but also to reach most effortlessly for objects in the height range in front of our trunk, rather than at our feet or over our heads.

All this gives rise a to a (well-known to signed language and gesture researchers) virtual quarter-sphere in front of the upper body, which is the optimal space of the individual's attention and manual interaction (see also Janzen, Shaffer, and Leeson, this volume). Further, the lateral asymmetry of handedness dominance creates natural *preferences* within that space; particularly for some manual affordances, the dominant-side half of the quarter-sphere is optimal. I want my tea-mug and my pen to be on my dominant-hand side within the optimal manual/visual space, while written notes are more equally visually accessible on either side of it. This is a neural phenomenon, with most humans having a pronounced lateral dominance, with about 90% of them being right-dominant. The relevant affordance issues are apparently very symmetric, that is the field of access is pretty much flipped but not radically changed in other ways between right-dominant and left-dominant humans. So it is no surprise that signed language and gesture patterns also "flip" mirror-symmetrically across the center-line depending on hand-dominance. We will get back to this in sections 6 and 7. Some major differences do appear when human-built artifacts (including writing systems) or social conventions (hand-shaking) are structured asymmetrically specifically for the right-handed majority, so that left-handed people cannot simply mirror but may need to adapt to the right-handed structures.

These parameters collectively contribute to build up an ego-centered Deictic space, where the Here (locus of the communicator's Self, or consciousness) is centered either in the upper body or in the core peripersonal space in front of the upper body, and further focused in the dominant side of that space. This is opposed to "There" locations in the extrapersonal space. One thing I am *not* trying to do here—others, including Merleau-Ponty (1962), have made more useful contributions to that—is to reflect on the ontogenesis of consciousness. But it's clear that consciousness and self-consciousness are deeply intertwined with the experiential placement of Self and "here-ness." Consciousness also involves "now-ness", and in our here-and-now, the two are correlated.

In addition to this, we add on other basic experiential correlations (some of which we will return to later as bases for Primary Metaphors). Our motor and vision systems are evolved for us to competently walk forwards, not backwards. Our back and behind space is physically relevant and meaningful in a different way than our fore-space, therefore: we aren't drawn to attend, as we walk, to the space a meter behind our body, while we are attending to the space a meter in front of our body. Our peripersonal space contracts behind us, as we move out of earlier locations; and expands in front of us, as we move into new locations. Further, when in motion, we experience the spaces behind us on our path as correlated with Past times, and locations ahead of us as correlated with expected Future times, while our current bodily location is naturally correlated with the Present moment (Lakoff and Johnson 1999; Moore 2014; Núñez and Sweetser 2006).

In everyday activities, we also develop correlations in experience between scenes or *frames*,[5] which make spatial phenomena *around us* meaningful. A young mammal being hugged by a care-giving mammal experiences social nurturance simultaneously with the physical warmth a baby needs, and social intimacy simultaneously with physical proximity. These frame-correlations make basic spatial *inter*actions meaningful beyond the purely physical locational (or thermal) aspects. Similarly, a child pouring liquid or dealing with liquid in containers will experience the correlation between greater quantity of liquid in a container, and *higher level* of the liquid column. These are *situational* correlations in a human's (a young child's) regular experience. More liquid does not always mean a higher level, if the liquid is spilled on the floor for example; but in the context of the same container, the correlation is predictable. Since we are much better at estimating height than 3-D quantity/volume, the experience of changes in the height of contained liquid are *valid cues* for volume, and physically meaningful via this correlation. Such frame correlations have been labeled Primary Scenes (Grady 1997, 1998; Johnson 1997; Lakoff and Johnson 1999) and hypothesized to give rise to Primary Metaphors (see section 5).

Personal Bodily Space and bodily experiences, which pre-exist co-speech gesture, are *meaningful*. Meaning emerges from experienced correlations and affordances that allow us to structure our actions. In Sweetser (2012), I commented on some of the above—the bodily affordances which give rise to the asymmetries of Ego-centered experiential space—as constitutive elements of embodied viewpoint. Below, I will attempt to lay out systematic ways in which this physical body-in-space (at least significant aspects of which are shared with apes and some with other animals) allows the emergence of uniquely human communicative gesture structures.

---

[5] I am here using the concept of *frame* developed by Charles Fillmore (1982, 1985). Specifically, a frame is a structured chunk of cognitively processed experience, which has gestalt character: the whole is not just the sum of its parts, but the parts have meaning relative to the whole (try explaining *Monday* without previously explaining the larger frame of Week) and the parts evoke the whole (seeing a menu lets us know the whole Restaurant frame is in place). Containment is such a frame, involving roles for Container and Contents.

3 Gesture: Real Space and deictic viewpoint

The experiential "extended body" in space, which is to some extent shared with other animals, is the necessary backdrop for human meaningful gesture. And (no surprise here) the quarter-sphere of core affordances and presence is precisely the space which is often labeled *gesture space* (or *signing space*).

But systematic *communicatively* meaningful gesture seems to be a human phenomenon; by hypothesis, it relies significantly not just on the individual action affordances discussed above, but on shared attention. As Tomasello (1999, 2008) and others have shown, humans as a species are uniquely predisposed to share, and prompt the sharing of attention. And gesture space is not only the gesturer's "own" space most rich in affordances, it is also the part of our bodily space which is most *visibly accessible* to an interlocutor who is face-to-face with us and making regular eye contact. It naturally invites shared attention, which in turn makes *deictic* use of gesture, posture, and gaze possible.

The pre-established experiential ego-centered deictic space is the underlying basis for the meaningful nature of deictic points. But deictic pointing needs more: a point creates or prompts a vector to *direct* shared attention, whether within or beyond the immediate reach of the gesturer. We can thus not only share attention in Real Space, but prompt and direct it. (I use Liddell's (1998) term Real Space to refer to the communicator/gesturer's cognitive and perceptual construal of their physically present surroundings.) Non-human great apes don't point or respond to points in the same way humans do. Without the intent and ability to direct shared attention, regular symbolic communication is impossible: so deictic points are part of the deepest stratum of communicative gesture. Even before children point deictically, they follow caregiver gaze, and they learn that caregivers will follow theirs. From observing the trajectory of a gaze and gazing in the same direction, we progress to amplifying the trajectory with, for example, a manual pointing gesture which again is intended to set up a trajectory for the interlocutor's gaze. And at this point, yes, gaze as well as posture and manual gesture become communicative, whether passively (that is, we "mind-read" others' attention states by observing their gaze even when they are unaware of this)[6] or actively, when gaze is actively communicating and sharing our attention.

This is only a tiny fraction of an account of deixis in gesture. There is huge cross-cultural variation in actual pointing phenomena (cf. Kita 2003; Enfield 2009)

---

6 In Sir Arthur Conan Doyle's "The Resident Patient" (1893), Sherlock Holmes goes one better, deducing Watson's entire thought chain by observing his attentional shifts among objects in the room which are associated with various subjects.

and too little attention has been paid to the nonmanual manifestations of deixis. Also (see section 6) deixis is incorporated into depictional *blends*,[7] that is, once a gesturer is enacting a character, her deictic field *represents* that of the character rather than her own. In the blend, she "is" the character. Deixis itself does not "do" representation, although it is definitely possible for the same gesture to have both iconic and deictic components (like that "don't interrupt" palm-out hand). An English speaker's standard deictic point with an index finger (D-hand) does not tell us anything about the nature of the thing pointed at, only about where to look. So we need iconicity, to account for depiction and enactment.

4 Real Space blends and representation, stage 1: Iconicity

The representational functions of communication are more necessary and more powerful when the content is not intersubjectively present in physical space. Deictic pointing can take us a long way in referring to objects which we can both see and touch. But referring to a lion, a car, or a mango when none is present requires representation, and one way into representation is the human capacity for iconicity.

Although chimpanzees don't process deictic pointing, they do *mime* initial stages of desired action routines (Tomasello 1999, 2008); a youngster may make grabbing motions at desired food and the mother may respond by sharing food, or a youngster may make clambering motions on a mother's back, and then be allowed to climb onto the back. This kind of representation is a very interesting combination of the current Real Space situation with intentionality about a desired event in an immediate future (still irrealis) space; the desired event is desired to happen right here and now, and involve the currently interacting participants. One might imagine this kind of "depiction" as a potential bridge between realis and irrealis mental space depictions, even though the irrealis space of chimp "miming" is tightly tied to the realis one in physical space, time and causation. The question would be to what extent it is *representational* and iconic, as opposed to *constituting* preparatory action for the intended resulting event.

What we do *not* think chimpanzees do is gesturally depict far-distant or imagined events not closely tied to Real Space. But all humans regularly do this both in language and in gesture (it is one of the standard metrics for a full human

---

[7] Blends is a term from Mental Spaces Theory, developed in Fauconnier and Turner 2002. It will be brought up in more detail in later sections of the paper.

language that it can describe non-present and non-real situational meanings). The representational, as opposed to deictic, dimensions of gesture are further shaped by our ability to imaginatively construe non-present situations and use the Real Space (both peripersonal and extrapersonal) to represent those situations *iconically*, where iconicity means a representation with a relationship of structured similarity to the represented entity. Gestures which have their basis in physical interaction routines (Streeck 2008 and elsewhere) are clear examples of this; humans iconically gesture grabbing objects, holding telephones, manipulating steering-wheels, and more. These may be akin in motivation to the young chimp's food-grabbing gesture, but they are very different in mental space structure: as a human, I can *descriptively* represent grabbing or hammering or typing in gesture, as I talk about distant past or fictional mental-space scenarios. And in making such a depictive gesture, I certainly need not have any intent to bring the depicted events about in the Real Space (unlike young chimps' mimes, which always involve such intent). And even if I did have such an intent, it might be another kind of communicative act such as a directive to someone else to hammer, not an announcement of desire/intent to start hammering.

In short, human depictive gestures bring about Real-Space iconic blends (Liddell 1998; Dudis 2004), i.e., blended mental spaces (in the sense of Fauconnier and Turner 2002). That is, there are two *inputs* (two spaces that are systematically blended in construal), one of which is the real physical surroundings, while the other is a non-present space being represented by that physical input. When a subject gestures forwards with two empty hands to mime throwing an object as she says *Granny throws the cat out the window* (McNeill 1992; Özyürek 2002), she is not doing any actual throwing in the Real Space, but she is engaging in a successful *iconic representation* of throwing. This is possible because both she and her interlocutor have the relevant neural capacity to construct and comprehend mime. Non-human great apes do not show mirror-neuron responses to miming actions; their manual-action mirror neurons are activated by seeing a human or ape grab an actual object (Rizzolatti et al. 1997; Rizzolatti, Fogassi, and Gallese 2001; Umiltà et al. 2001) but not by the miming of grasping. Humans on the other hand do respond to iconic mime representations of action. They mentally "complete" the grasping action to include a grasped object. That is, they construct a representational blend between the empty-handed Real Space and an imagined space of grasping. Humans do this kind of completion in metaphoric gesture as well as literal iconic gesture (Wilson and Gibbs 2007).

A crucial added point: we know that iconic representation is not restricted to one modality of imagery. Auditory iconicity is common; auditorily iconic spoken-language forms such as *ding-dong* or *meow* are labeled phonosymbolism, sound symbolism or onomatopoeia. In the case of the "don't interrupt" palm-out hand, visual input also frame-metonymically evokes at least muscular force-dynamic imagery of resistance, as well as the direct visual imagery of a flat surface.

Iconic depiction is mostly highly *schematic*, by which I mean it is not fully elaborated, but presents only "skeletal" shared structure between the icon and the intended referent.[8] We have our human body at our disposal for gestural iconicity; it is not always the same shape as the depicted object, nor can we always depict all the details of a depicted action. This is also the case, unsurprisingly, with ASL (or any signed language) signs. The ASL sign TREE uses the dominant-side fore-arm directed straight upwards with fingers extended (5 hand); but it is not a sign for a thick-trunked straight tree with exactly five branches, it is a sign for any tree, regardless of details such as the number of branches or the degree of bentness of the trunk. Similarly, an English gesturer might gesture running with two forefingers "running" on an imagined surface, or by "being" the runner and miming arm motions of effortful running. Neither of these options, exemplifying the classic Observer-Viewpoint and Participant-Viewpoint depiction options as defined in McNeill (1992; see also Parrill 2009) attempts to iconically represent the whole runner, legs and arms and body. This is for good reason: these partial representations are far more economical of effort than actually running, as the gesture accompanying linguistic reference to running.[9]

These gestural representations are also *partitioned*, in the sense of Dudis' (2004) work on ASL. That is, in watching the "running fingers" of the gesturing hand as runner, we do not wonder what the rest of the speaker/gesturer's body is representing. Only the hand is (schematically and partially) representing the described runner. Partitioning is useful in other ways when we are describing a situation involving two participants, since we have only one body with which to perform our gestural representation. Dudis cites an ASL storyteller representing someone hitting someone else, by using one fist to hit his own face. We will address this further in section 6.

Why do these blends occur? At least a partial explanation may lie in neural patterns. Since "neurons that fire together wire together", the neurons that recognize the motor motions involved in grasping may activate the (often co-activated) pattern of recognizing the full action of grasping an object.

To sum up, iconic gesture consists of gestural blends between the Real Space of the gesturer and the depicted space. These blends naturally depend on the speak-

---

[8] Mittelberg (2018) is a detailed analysis of schematicity and iconicity in gesture.
[9] As one reviewer percipiently noted, iconically representing the "whole" action would never be complete – you might need to accurately represent pace, path, running technique, etc., of the specific action referred to.

er's pre-existing personal space structure, and (given articulatory affordances) they are typically both schematic and partitioned.

5 Real Space blends, stage 2: Metonymy and metaphor

The interpretation of iconic depiction, however, is not as simple as reference to a bodily action enacted, or an object shape embodied by the gesture (a fist clenched to indicate a rock, a vertical finger for a standing human). Often an iconic gesture is instead interpreted *frame-metonymically*, that is, the gesture iconically represents some element from a larger scenario or frame (in Fillmore's 1982, 1985 terms) which evokes the whole larger frame. That larger frame or some element in it is the actual referent. Streeck (2008) has examples of a speaker/gesturer gesturing "scraping plaster with a plaster-scraper" while talking about that activity; subsequently the same speaker also does little "plaster-scraping" gestures when mentioning the tool used in that action-frame. The speaker's hand-motion does not depict the tool, but depicts the activity-routine or frame within which the tool is normatively used, which metonymically refers to the tool. This compares with ASL signs DRIVE and CAR, both of which involve the "hands on driving-wheel" position. DRIVE thus iconically represents not "putting your hands on a steering-wheel" but the full activity of driving which includes that (distinctive) hand-positioning. And the noun CAR is not an iconic depiction of a car, but of a distinctive aspect of a driver's functional interaction with a car. The speaker/gesturer's gesture is so distinctive that a viewer can often readily identify "driving" content from the video of gesture alone without the voice sound-track. There is no space here for a full treatment of gestural metonymy, though Mittelberg's (2006, 2014; also Mittelberg and Waugh 2014 and elsewhere) work has given a complex picture of aspects of the relationship between metonymy, iconicity and gesture.[10]

This brings us to the next stage: depictive iconic gestural representations can be understood metaphorically rather than literally. Humans are apparently also the only species to engage in regular metaphoric mappings. Sweetser (1998), Cienki (1998), Dancygier and Sweetser (2014), and others have argued that the relationship here is a basic one: metaphoric gesture is *iconic gesture depicting the source domain of the metaphor, but referring ultimately to the target domain.* More specifi-

---

10 See also Dancygier and Sweetser's (2014) treatment of frame metonymy, and Wilcox's (2004) discussion of similar metonymy in ASL.

cally, Dancygier and Sweetser argue (following Sullivan 2013) that what is mapped is not large, amorphous "domains", but actually specific *frames*. The source frame is the frame overtly referred to; the target frame is the one which is metaphorically meant, which is being understood in terms of the source frame. Thus, when an English speaker says *You got your point across to the audience* they are using the source frame of Object Exchange to conceptualize and refer to the target frame of Communication.

These metaphoric mapping relationships build mental space blends of another kind, that is, they build a systematic relationship whereby one mental space (structured by one frame) is understood as another. In the blend, words and gestures normally meaning one thing mean something else; moving upwards, for example, *is* increasing in quantity.

English speakers (and speakers of many other languages) consistently gesture upwards when talking about increase in quantity, and downwards when mentioning decrease in quantity. Sometimes this co-occurs with verbal metaphor, sometimes not, as Cienki (1998) initially observed: a speaker may gesture upwards when saying *high grade*, but also when saying *good grade*, and downwards when saying *low grade* or *bad grade*. A downwards gesture accompanying verbal *bad grade* does not directly depict "badness", but it does depict motion downwards or low position, and in context we understand this as meaning "bad". Whether we interpret this iconic gesture metaphorically via a MORE IS UP, LESS IS DOWN mapping, or a GOOD IS UP, BAD IS DOWN one (Lakoff and Johnson 1980), the result is the same since numerically greater course grades (unlike golf scores) are also better.

Primary metaphors in particular (Grady 1997, 1998; Johnson 1997) involve a Primary Scene as described in section 2, an experiential correlation between the source and target frames. And in many cases, this correlation happens precisely within the bodily affordance space or the shared communicative space (see below). It is as I drink from or pour liquid into a mug that I experience the regular correlation between an increased or diminished quantity of liquid and a changing vertical location of the upper surface of the liquid in the container, giving rise plausibly to the metaphor MORE IS UP. Similarly, as small children are communicating with caregivers, there are frequent exchanges of physical objects back and forth between them, so there is an actual correlation of the palm-up-open-hand configuration with literal giving or displaying of objects (the palm-up position being adapted to object-holding or display) and communicative interaction. This plausibly gives rise to COMMUNICATION IS OBJECT EXCHANGE (sometimes called the Conduit Metaphor, after Reddy (1979), where IDEAS ARE OBJECTS which I may "give" you via verbal communication.

Some of these correlations have been tested in the lab, for example Williams and Bargh (2008) have shown a relationship between physical warmth (hot coffee vs. a cold drink) of a beverage given to a subject, and the assessed social "warmth" and likeability of someone the subject is asked to encounter. This would show a correlational basis for the AFFECTION IS WARMTH primary metaphor, plausibly motivated (Johnson 1997; Grady 1997) by the mammalian baby's inevitable association between caregiver bodily warmth and positive social relationship. Also relevant here are the observations of Pellencin et al. (2018) about the relationship between social comfort/intimacy and physically perceived peripersonal space, mentioned in section 2: experiential correlation is the potential basis for Primary Metaphor again, in this case INTIMACY IS CLOSENESS.

The contrasting meanings emerging from palm direction and force dynamics are also inputs to metaphor, as mentioned above. The palm-out open hand "wait" iconically represents an *outward-directed* barrier resisting potential motion toward ego, while other palm-directions do not mean this.[11] This is because palm-outwards is force-dynamically appropriate to pushing away; we cannot as effectively push back-handed, although pulling something towards us usually involves the palm positioned inward towards the body. One could certainly make a case for this being input to a plausible primary metaphor set. REJECTION IS PUSHING AWAY, ACCEPTANCE OR WELCOME IS PULLING TOWARDS EGO. And indeed, small children often make pushing gestures of rejection even when the phenomenon being rejected is social rather than physical; adults also will push outwards not only to "fend off" interruption but also to "ward off" imagined misfortune or bad future eventualities.

We have earlier discussed the correlation between front-back bodily asymmetry and temporal relevance of surrounding spaces to the body in motion. We do experience time without engaging in goal-directed bodily motion, but motion is inevitably experienced in time and is correlated with it in regular ways. If the back of a *moving* body is meaningfully related to the past,[12] then PAST IS BEHIND EGO and FUTURE IS IN FRONT OF EGO are metaphoric mappings based closely in basic bodily meaning (cf. Moore 2014).

As will be discussed in sections 7 and 8, social or emotional preferences towards topics will also naturally result in lateral contrasts in gesture, whatever the reason for the social preference. Gestural references to the current topic (as opposed to some other contrasting topic) and preferred option (as opposed to a dispreferred one) are well-recognized to be enacted not by different gesture shapes but by loca-

---

11 This is also true in ASL; cf. Taub (2001).
12 This temporal correlation does not hold in the same way for a static body outside of a motion situation. See Núñez and Sweetser (2006), Sweetser and Gaby (2017), Gaby and Sweetser (2017), or Cooperrider, Núñez and Sweetser (2014) for a discussion of time metaphors which result from other mappings.

tion on the dominant vs. non-dominant side (cf. Casasanto 2009 and elsewhere; this is also a long-recognized generalization about ASL).

The literature on gestural metaphor is extensive, and bears on the issue (raised by Müller 2008) of how cognitively activated conventional metaphors may be. Núñez and Sweetser (2006), for example, used gesture to argue for the cognitive presence of metaphoric mappings in time metaphors. Stickles (2016) has given evidence of the relationship between metaphorically interpreted iconic gesture and syntactic constructions. Gibbs (1994, 2006) gives evidence for the cognitive presence of the source domain in the use of highly conventional metaphors, and Bergen (2012) gives a useful review of some of the issues involved in arguing for the neural representation of metaphoric mappings. And Sweetser (2000) examines the ways in which both literal iconic depiction and metaphoric use of depiction can be used *performatively*: enactment of a metaphoric gestural ritual (such as the Eucharistic meal, metaphorically consuming Christ's body) can be understood as bringing about changes in the actor's social world.

6 Real-Space blends, stage 3: Enacting characters in narrative

The very best iconic representation of an acting and communicating human body is, unsurprisingly, a human body. Once we add that level of iconic representation to our Real-Space blends, it is natural that a human should be capable of understanding a communicator's language and gesture as *representing* (in the blended construal, as *being*) those of another actor, that is, attributing the observed language and gesture to the represented speaker rather than to the current one. This phenomenon is definitely not evidenced in other species, whereas role-playing is a very basic and pervasive behavior of humans, regularly evidenced even among small children.

In what might be described as a "meta-blend", humans are also fully capable of imagining a speaker/gesturer's body (like a signer's body) as suddenly rotated 180 degrees with respect to its imagined surroundings (see Janzen 2004, 2012 for the ASL parallel).[13] Suddenly, the Real Space body represents/enacts a different person's body in the narration space. This creates a new blended space, and new

---

[13] Compare this with shot/countershot technique in film, where the camera alternates between two characters in a conversation, and the viewer fuses the depiction into a single event.

affordances. What is particularly interesting is that we seem capable of maintaining both blended spaces at once. A speaker enacting a disapproving official holding a document (Figure 1(a)) can then switch to using face and voice to enact the playing-innocent person talking to the official (Figure 1(b)), while still keeping hands in the "document-holding" position (Sweetser 2013; Sweetser and Stec 2016).

Figure 1: Two blended spaces resulting in a "meta-blend".

Alternatively, English narrators also adopt a strategy closely parallel to the well-known ASL-style 20-degree rotation away from the speaker-hearer line to enact a character, and then if necessary rotating 20 degrees in the opposite direction to enact the first character's interlocutor. Thus, a speaker telling a story about interaction between her (shorter) past self and her (taller) boyfriend may alternate between rotating 20 degrees to one side and looking up (Figure 2(a)) while enacting the past self, and rotating 20 degrees to the other side and looking down (Figure 2(b)) while enacting the boyfriend's reply (Sweetser 2013; Sweetser and Stec 2016).

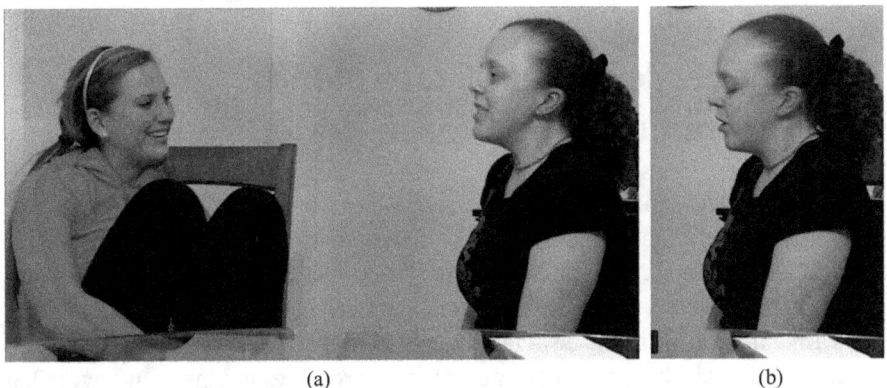

Figure 2: A 20-degree rotation between story characters.

Based on physical articulatory restrictions of production, there is no reason not to enact narrative characters in the space directly facing the interlocutor. Nor is there any reason to switch back and forth between two different character spaces. It would be less physically effortful always to use the 180-degree virtual rotation for character-switching, and also remain in line with the interlocutor while narrating; this would not involve any displacement of the speaker/gesturer. But the space directly face-to-face with the interlocutor is "taken" as we shall discuss below; it is *meaningfully* occupied by the Real-Space communicative interaction. And in the back-and-forth 20-degree switches between one character and another in an enacted conversation, each of the two sub-spaces takes on a meaningful association with the relevant character, becoming that character's space, and not the other's.

"Deferred pointing" (Haviland 2000) is another kind of character/gesturer blend. As discussed in Sweetser (2012), I might say to you, *as you come into my office, the light switch is here*, and gesturally point to my left at torso-level (perhaps even hooking my fingers as if to access a light switch). Assuming we are not near my office, my interlocutor, far from looking for a light switch in the air near my gesturing fingers, will assume that when standing in the doorway of my office, they will find the light switch on the wall to their left. That is, they will successfully *blend* the Real Space of the gesturer with the imagined space of a character standing in the doorway of the office and looking for the light switch.

Via Real-Space blends, the Real Space of the gesturer thus successfully represents, both deictically and iconically, the gestural and deictic spaces of imagined characters. This inherits metaphoric blending as well, that is, a gesturer enacting a narrative character's gestures can still gesture upwards for "more", downward for "less", and this will be understood as representing (via the blend) the character's gestures and not the narrator's own.

7 Yet higher-level Real-Space blends: Joint communicative space

Where we do *which* enactments is crucial, as we can see from the character spaces in the discussion of narrative above. As humans, we are incapable of ignoring or being unaffected by conspecifics' affordances as well as our own. As soon as another person is in the room, their visual, manual, etc., affordance spaces are present to us as are our own. This may be at least partly because of mirror neuron responses which make us sensitive to motor and pre-motor routines in others. But overall, it makes sense to say that we experience conspecifics' body-space as well as our own (I discussed this issue earlier in Sweetser 2012 and 2013).

Therefore, in communicative interaction, the *joint* communicative-attentional space builds yet another layer of meaning onto the meaningful spatial structures involved in deixis and representation. The speaker-addressee line now also determines gestural meaning, e.g., a palm-out-open-hand (POOH) gesture along this line directed towards the addressee counts as a regulatory interactional gesture, while a POOH directed sideways would not (cf. Sweetser and Sizemore 2008; Wehling 2010, 2018).

This is also relevant for iconic representation. As Özyürek (2002) has shown, gesturers hesitate to perform some iconic gestures directly in the inter-speaker space, between the two speakers' personal gesture spaces, which is reserved for interactive gesture (cf. Sweetser and Sizemore 2008; Laparle 2020). Özyürek's subjects tended to enact a character throwing a cat out the window by gesturing in a direction that didn't seem to put the imagined cat into the Real-Space addressee's lap. Though the cartoon character threw the cat directly forwards from her body space, some speaker/gesturers recounting the cartoon story went so far as to gesture throwing the cat out the window backwards over their shoulders if there were two Real-Space listeners and thus no "unclaimed" space in front of the speaker. Such an unclaimed extrapersonal space, i.e., space that is neither the speaker's nor addressee's personal space, nor the interpersonal space between the two personal spaces, is ideal for such representation. Partial rotations allow this: by rotating the body slightly when inhabiting character roles in recorded discourse, the communicator avoids the risk of blending the addressed character (in the depicted scene) with the actual addressee in Real Space.

8 Reinscribing meaning over time: The discourse space record

The discourse record of communicative interaction itself adds further meaning to bodily space. In co-speech gesture, it is recognized that (somewhat as in signed language; see Liddell 2003), loci are established for different entities referred to; these are stable over current discourse. In a speaker's comparison of Chicago and New York, for example, references to each city are likely to have a defined gestural locus; points to those stable loci will refer meaningfully to the two subjects (cf. Parrill and Sweetser 2004). The two loci may be unrelated to the Real-Space relative locations of Chicago and New York, often one locus will be on the speaker's right, and the other on the left, very possibly with the locus on the speaker's dominant-hand side being assigned to the city more positively evaluated, or more directly under discussion. Thus the spatial "conversational topic record" establishes another layer of meaningful bodily spatial structure, which lasts over stretches of interaction. (This temporal stability is also true of physical deictic meaning: a deictic point to a colleague's now-vacant seat may accompany a reference to the person in question.)

Unlike the long-term dominant-side preference, more specific referential associations with gesture-space sub-areas are temporary, but have continued meaning within an ongoing interaction. As a result, manipulation of this meaningful space can result in changes to the topic structure. As observed by Laparle (2020; see also Laparle and Jones 2020), topic-changing particles such as *anyway* may be accompanied by gestures of brushing or moving away objects from the gesture-space (cf. Müller, Bressem and Ladewig 2014). That is, our discourse record is meaningfully tied to the space around us, and gestural acting in that space accompanies changes in the discourse record.

9 Conclusions

Basically, then, the body and the surrounding space give each other shared meaning, and then the meaningful bodily space in turn gives a meaningful frame to articulatory activity in communication. Interestingly, one might speculate that this complex bodily/communicative space is based significantly on cross-culturally accessible parameters—or at any rate, on parameters which vary only with distinct cultural construals of the body itself—whereas the choice of a handshape, even with iconic motivation, might be much more language/culture-specific. But at any rate, the capacities for deixis, iconicity, metaphor, and communicative aspects of bodily space must be shared.

I will not here address the interaction of facial expression, gaze, or attention with this space, except to say that speakers do use attention both to maintain speaker-addressee connection and also to direct shared attention to parts of the bodily space or the communicative space. Handshape is quite orthogonal to these built-in spatial structures, but nonetheless does take meaning from them, as we saw with the open hand, where orientation with respect to the communicative space is what allows the interactional meaning of "don't interrupt".

But I would like to make two final points. The first is about compositionality. To the extent that there is orthogonality between these various components of the body-in-space structure and its added layers of meaning, gesture is necessarily compositional. This is something that the field has been converging on for some time, but modern gesture studies has been founded in McNeill's (1992, 2005) oppositions between linguistic compositionality and the more gestalt character of gesture. But the more we look at gesture, the more we find some of the same compositional structure that ASL signs/constructions have. In the "don't interrupt now" palm-out hand gesture, it is clear that the direction towards the interlocutor is what contributes discourse-interactional meaning and allows it to be interpreted as discourse-regulating. The shape and force-dynamic structure of the outwards-pushing palm-out hand are what we interpret as meaning a barrier, which is then metaphorically interpreted as an objection to verbal input. If instead, the speaker reached out with a pointing "D" hand towards the interlocutor, the directionality would still make the gesture discourse-interactional, but the new handshape component would be more likely to mean an attempt to claim the floor or make a point (Sweetser and Sizemore 2008).

The same is true with partitioned gesture structures. In the case of Figure 1 above where the speaker simultaneously enacts her faux-naïve past self's face and words, while still using her hands to represent the past self's interlocutor's bodily holding of a document, each of those two components comes together to create parts of a larger scene, involving the two participants. This is definitely compositional. Dudis's ASL story where the signer's trunk and left hand represent the person being hit, while the right fist represents the hitter, shows similar compositional structure.

And finally, I return to the issue of cross-cultural differences and typology of gesture. If there is really a causal dependence relationship between aspects of gestural meaning, then (just as chimps show "pre-iconic" gestures but not deixis or metaphor) this should give us some idea of which aspects of gestural meaning are more likely to be shared across human cultures, and which are more culture-specific. We know how culture-specific emblems (lexical gestures) can be, and how different that is from deictic gesturing, even though handshapes and other aspects of deictic gesture vary significantly.

As an example, consider archeologists' interpretive stance towards a carved mammoth-ivory plaque depicting a human with arms raised upward on each side of the head (no details of hands are visible), about 35,000-40,000 years old, found in the Geissenklösterle cave in the Swabian Jura near Blaubeuren, Germany.[14] The lifted arms are clearly not an unmarked, relaxed position; a viewer must impute some reason for this posture/gesture. But what? The object has been labeled "The Adorant" (Dutkiewicz, Wolf, and Conard 2017)), presumably because raised arms were culturally related to prayer in older Greco-Roman tradition. Depictions of Greco-Roman prayer show the supplicant addressing the gods and physically looking/reaching upwards towards their high location (in the sky/heavens, on Mount Olympus). This appears to be a discourse-regulating gesture within the joint inter-

---

14 See photos on Wikipedia under "Adorant from the Geissenklösterle Cave."

action space, reaching hands upwards towards the interlocutor, given the higher location of the divine addressees.

But the Adorant plaque is not in fact a Greco-Roman or Christian artifact. We know nothing of the religious beliefs or practices of the Upper-Paleolithic makers of the plaque. In some modern Euro-American Christian cultures, the praying position involves kneeling with upwards-pointed palm-together hands in front of the torso. Modern Americans might even interpret the Adorant carving's posture as resembling "hands up" when threatened with shooting. Yet the time gap (less than 2,000 years) between Greco-Roman culture and ours is much smaller than that between Upper Paleolithic cultures and the Greco-Roman world. Just because the Greco-Roman "ancient" world is documented and more accessible to us, that does not mean we should project its gestural patterns back another 30,000-plus years.

It is not obvious, therefore, that we can readily predict the meaning of gesture or gestural depictions from our general human capacities for gestural meaning. The field is open for researchers to examine what aspects of gestural meaning may be shared or culturally determined, and how. My hope is that this future research can be fruitfully conducted in the context of the framework I have outlined, in relation to those general human capacities.

Acknowledgments: Although errors in this piece are all my own, anything useful in it owes much to a community. My biggest thanks go to Sherman Wilcox, for whom this paper is written. Always far ahead of the curve as a researcher, heroically generous as a colleague and mentor, and committed and thoughtful as an organizer, Sherman has been such a huge builder of the current productive gesture studies community, that it's now almost hard to remember the *very* different pre-1995 academic landscape. It's mostly Sherman's fault (along with David McNeill and Adam Kendon) that I went into gesture studies. His 1995 LSA Linguistic Institute in Albuquerque was a communal watershed point, after which I personally could no more go back into the non-multimodal "box" than flow upstream. Terry Janzen and Barbara Shaffer have been brilliantly stimulating and supportive fellow-travelers on the "viewpoint trail" ever since. Thanks to Phyllis Wilcox, Fey Parrill, Kashmiri Stec, Irene Mittelberg, Cornelia Müller, Barbara Dancygier, and Schuyler Laparle for their enlightening viewpoints. Past and present members of the Berkeley Gesture and Multimodality Group have given me invaluable multidisciplinary intellectual input. Special thanks to Katharine Young for always bringing us back to embodiment, and to Elise Stickles and Vito Evola for insightful and very last-minute comments on this manuscript.

References

Armstrong, David F. & Sherman E. Wilcox. 2007. *The Gestural Origin of Language*. Oxford: Oxford University Press.

Bergen, Benjamin. 2012. *Louder than Words*. New York: Basic Books.

Bressem, Jana. 2014. Transcription systems for gestures, speech, prosody, postures and gaze. In Cornelia Müller, Alan Cienki, Ellen Fricke, Silva Ladewig, David McNeill & Jana Bressem (eds.), *Body – Language – Communication: An International Handbook on Multimodality in Human Interaction*, Volume 2 (HSK 38.2), 1037–1059. Berlin/Boston: De Gruyter Mouton.

Bühler, Karl. 2011[1934]. *The Theory of Language: The Representational Function of Language*. Translated by Donald Fraser Goodwin. Amsterdam/Philadelphia: John Benjamins.

Casasanto, Daniel. 2009. Embodiment of abstract concepts: Good and bad in right- and left-handers. *Journal of Experimental Psychology: General* 138(3), 351–367.

Casasanto, Daniel & Kyle Jasmin. 2010. Good and bad in the hands of politicians: Spontaneous gestures during positive and negative speech. *PLoS ONE* 5(7), e11805. doi:10.1371/journal.pone.0011805

Cienki, Alan. 1998. Metaphoric gestures and some of their relationships to verbal metaphoric counterparts. In Jean-Pierre Koenig (ed.), *Discourse and Cognition: Bridging the Gap*, 189–205. Stanford, CA: CSLI Publications.

Cooperrider, Kensy, Rafael Núñez & Eve Sweetser. 2014. The conceptualization of time in gesture. In Cornelia Müller, Alan Cienki, Ellen Fricke, Silva Ladewig, David McNeill & Jana Bressem (eds.), *Body – Language – Communication: An International Handbook on Multimodality in Human Interaction*, Volume 2 (HSK 38.2), 781–1788. Berlin/Boston: De Gruyter Mouton.

Corballis, Michael C. 2003. From hand to mouth: The gestural origins of language. In Morton H. Christiansen & Simon Kirby (eds.), *Language Evolution*, 201–218. Oxford: Oxford University Press.

Dancygier, Barbara and Eve Sweetser. 2014. *Figurative Language*. Cambridge: Cambridge University Press.

Doyle, Arthur Conan. 1893. *The Memoirs of Sherlock Holmes*. London: George Newnes.

Dudis, Paul G. 2004. Body partitioning and real-space blends. *Cognitive Linguistics* 15(2), 223–238.

Dutkiewicz, Ewa, Sibylle Wolf & Nicholas J. Conard. 2017. Early symbolism in the Ach and Lone valleys of southwestern Germany. *Quaternary International* 491, 30–45.

Enfield, Nick J. 2009. *The Anatomy of Meaning: Speech, Gesture, and Composite Utterances*. Cambridge: Cambridge University Press.

Fauconnier, Gilles & Mark Turner. 2002. *The Way We Think: Conceptual Blending and the Mind's Hidden Complexities*. New York: Basic Books.

Fillmore, Charles J. 1982. Frame semantics. In The Linguistic Society of Korea (ed.), *Linguistics in the Morning Calm*. Seoul: Hanshin Publishing Company.

Fillmore, Charles J. 1985. Frames and the semantics of understanding. *Quaderni di semantica* 6(2), 222–253.

Froese, Tom & Thomas Fuchs. 2012. The extended body: A case study in the neurophenomenology of social interaction. *Phenomenology and the Cognitive Sciences* 11, 205–235.

Gaby, Alice & Eve Sweetser. 2017. Linguistic patterns of space and time vocabulary. In Barbara Dancygier (ed.) *The Cambridge Handbook of Cognitive Linguistics*, 625–634. Cambridge: Cambridge University Press.

Gibbs, Raymond W. 1994. *The Poetics of Mind: Figurative Thought, Language, and Understanding*. Cambridge: Cambridge University Press.

Gibbs, Raymond W. 2006. *Embodiment and Cognitive Science.* Cambridge: Cambridge University Press.

Grady, Joseph. 1997. THEORIES ARE BUILDINGS revisited. *Cognitive Linguistics* 8(4), 267–290.

Grady, Joseph. 1998. The "Conduit Metaphor" revisited: A reassessment of metaphors for communication. In Jean-Pierre Koenig (ed.), *Discourse and Cognition: Bridging the Gap*, 205–218. Stanford CA: CSLI Publications.

Hanks, William F. 1990. *Referential Practice: Language and Lived Space in a Maya Community.* Chicago: University of Chicago Press.

Haviland, John B. 2000. Pointing, gesture spaces, and mental maps. In David McNeill (ed.), *Language and Gesture*, 13–46. Cambridge: Cambridge University Press.

Janzen, Terry. 2004. Space rotation, perspective shift, and verb morphology in ASL. *Cognitive Linguistics* 15(2), 149–174.

Janzen, Terry. 2012. Two ways of conceptualizing space: Motivating the use of static and rotated vantage point space in ASL discourse. In Barbara Dancygier and Eve Sweetser (eds.), *Viewpoint in Language: A Multimodal Perspective*, 156–174. Cambridge: Cambridge University Press.

Johnson, Christopher R. 1997. Metaphor vs. conflation in the acquisition of polysemy: The case of see. In Masako K. Hiraga, Chris Sinha & Sherman Wilcox (eds.), *Cultural, Typological and Psychological Issues in Cognitive Linguistics: Selected Papers from the Biannual ICLA meeting in Albuquerque, July 1995*, 155–169. Amsterdam/Philadelphia: John Benjamins.

Johnson, Mark. 1987. *The Body in the Mind: The Bodily Basis of Meaning, Imagination and Reason.* Chicago: University of Chicago Press.

Johnson, Mark. 2007. *The Meaning of the Body: Esthetics of Human Understanding.* Chicago: University of Chicago Press.

Kita, Sotaro. 2003. *Pointing: Where Language, Culture and Cognition Meet.* Mahwah NJ: Lawrence Erlbaum.

Lakoff, George & Mark Johnson. 1980. *Metaphors We Live By.* Chicago: University of Chicago Press.

Lakoff, George & Mark Johnson. 1999. *Philosophy in the Flesh: The Embodied Mind and its Challenge to Western Thought.* New York: Basic Books.

Laparle, Schuyler. 2020. Multi-modal QUD management: Case studies of topic-shifting. Presentation at Sinn und Bedeutung 25, Special Session: Gestures and Natural Language Semantics. University College London and Queen Mary University of London. September. Retrieved from osf.io/7v9q5

Laparle, Schuyler & Kelly Jones. 2020. Gesture space as discourse space: Spatial topic-shifting and the conduit metaphor. Presentation at Researching and Applying Metaphor Conference. Inland Norway University of Applied Sciences, Hamar, Norway.

Levinson, Stephen C. & David P. Wilkins (eds.). 2006. *Grammars of Space.* Cambridge: Cambridge University Press.

Liddell, Scott K. 1998. Grounded blends, gestures and conceptual shifts. *Cognitive Linguistics* 9(3), 283–314.

Liddell, Scott K. 2003. *Grammar, Gesture and Meaning in American Sign Language.* Cambridge: Cambridge University Press.

McNeill, David. 1992. *Hand and Mind: What Gestures Reveal about Thought.* Chicago: University of Chicago Press.

McNeill, David. 2005. *Gesture and Thought.* Chicago: University of Chicago Press.

Merleau-Ponty, Maurice. 1962[1945]. *The Phenomenology of Perception.* Translated by Colin Smith. London: Routledge and Kegan Paul.

Mittelberg, Irene. 2006. *Metaphor and metonymy in language and gesture: Discourse evidence for multimodal models of grammar.* Ithaca, NY: Cornell University dissertation.

Mittelberg, Irene. 2014. Gestures and iconicity. In Cornelia Müller, Alan Cienki, Ellen Fricke, Silva H. Ladewig, David McNeill & Jana Bressem (eds.), *Body – Language – Communication: An International Handbook on Multimodality in Human Interaction*, Volume 2, 1712–1732. Berlin/Boston: De Gruyter Mouton.

Mittelberg, Irene. 2018. Gesture as image schemas and force gestalts: A dynamic systems approach augmented with motion-capture data analyses. *Cognitive Semiotics* 11(1), pp. 20180002. https://doi.org/10.1515/cogsem-2018-0002

Mittelberg, Irene & Linda R. Waugh. 2014. Gestures and metonymy. In Cornelia Müller, Alan Cienki, Ellen Fricke, Silva H. Ladewig, David McNeill & Jana Bressem (eds.), *Body – Language – Communication: An International Handbook on Multimodality in Human Interaction*, Volume 2 (HSK 38.2.), 1747–1755. Berlin/Boston: De Gruyter Mouton.

Moore, Kevin E. 2014. *The Spatial Language of Time: Metaphor, Metonymy and Frames of Reference*. Amsterdam/Philadelphia: John Benjamins.

Müller, Cornelia. 2008. *Metaphors Dead and Alive, Sleeping and Waking: A Dynamic View*. Chicago: University of Chicago Press.

Müller, Cornelia. 2014. Gestures as a medium of expression: The linguistic potential of gestures. In Cornelia Müller, Alan Cienki, Ellen Fricke, Silva Ladewig, David McNeill & Jana Bressem (eds.), *Body – Language – Communication: An International Handbook on Multimodality in Human Interaction*, Volume 2 (HSK 38.2), 202–217. Berlin/Boston: De Gruyter Mouton.

Müller, Cornelia, Jana Bressem & Silva H. Ladewig. 2014. Towards a grammar of gestures: A form-based view. In Cornelia Müller, Alan Cienki, Ellen Fricke, Silva Ladewig, David McNeill & Jana Bressem (eds.), *Body – Language – Communication: An International Handbook on Multimodality in Human Interaction*, Volume 2 (HSK 38.2), 707–733. Berlin/Boston: De Gruyter Mouton.

Núñez, Rafael & Eve Sweetser. 2006. With the future behind them: Convergent evidence from Aymara language and gesture in the crosslinguistic comparison of spatial construals of time. *Cognitive Science* 30(3), 401–450.

Özyürek, Asli. 2002. Do speakers design their co-speech gestures for their addressees? The effects of addressee location on representational gestures. *Journal of Memory and Language* 46(4), 688–704. doi: 10.1006/jmla.2001.2826

Parrill, Fey. 2009. Dual viewpoint gestures. *Gesture* 9(3), 279–281.

Parrill, Fey & Eve Sweetser. 2004. What we mean by meaning: Conceptual integration in gesture analysis and transcription. *Gesture* 4(2), 197–219.

Pellencin, Elisa, Maria Paola Paladino, Bruno Herbelin & Andrea Serino. 2018. Social perception of others shapes one's own multisensory peripersonal space. *Cortex* 104, 163–179.

Reddy, Michael. 1979. The conduit metaphor: A case of frame conflict in our language about language. In Andrew Ortony (ed.), *Metaphor and Thought*, 284–324. Cambridge: Cambridge University Press.

Rizzolatti, Giacomo, Luciano Fadiga, Leonardo Fogassi & Vittorio Gallese. 1997. The space around us. *Science* 277(5323), 190–191. doi: 10.1126/science.277.5323.190

Rizzolatti, Giacomo, Leonardo Fogassi & Vittorio Gallese. 2001. Neuropsychological mechanisms underlying the understanding and imitation of action. *Nature Neuro-science Reviews* 2, 661–70.

Shuman, Amy & Katharine Young. 2018. The body as medium: A phenomenological approach to the production of affect in narrative. In Zara Dinnen & Robyn Warhol (eds.), *The Edinburgh Companion to Contemporary Narrative Theories*. 399–416. Edinburgh: Edinburgh University Press.

Stickles, Elise. 2016. *The interaction of syntax and metaphor in gesture: A corpus-experimental approach*. Berkeley, CA: University of California, Berkeley dissertation.

Streeck, Jürgen. 2008. *Gesturecraft: The Manu-facture of Meaning*. Amsterdam/Philadelphia: John Benjamins.
Sullivan, Karen. 2013. *Frames and Constructions in Metaphoric Language*. Amsterdam/Philadelphia: John Benjamins.
Sweetser, Eve. 1998. Regular metaphoricity in gesture: bodily-based models of speech interaction. In *Actes du 16ᵉ Congrès International des Linguistes* (CD-ROM), Elsevier.
Sweetser, Eve. 2000. Blended spaces and performativity. *Cognitive Linguistics* 11(3/4), 305–333.
Sweetser, Eve. 2012. Introduction: viewpoint and perspective in language and gesture, from the Ground down. In Barbara Dancygier & Eve Sweetser (eds.), *Viewpoint in Language: A Multimodal Perspective*, 1–22. Cambridge: Cambridge University Press.
Sweetser, Eve. 2013. Creativity across modalities in viewpoint construction. In Mike Borkent, Barbara Dancygier & Jennifer Hinnell (eds.), *Language and the Creative Mind*, 239–254. Stanford, CA: CSLI Publications.
Sweetser, Eve & Alice Gaby. 2017. Space-time mappings beyond language. In Barbara Dancygier (ed.), *Cambridge Handbook of Cognitive Linguistics*, 635–650. Cambridge: Cambridge University Press.
Sweetser, Eve & Marisa Sizemore. 2008. Personal and interpersonal gesture spaces: Functional contrasts in language and gesture. In Andrea Tyler, Yiyoung Kim & Mari Takada (eds.), *Language in the Context of Use: Cognitive and Discourse Approaches to Language*, 25–51. Berlin/New York: Mouton de Gruyter.
Sweetser, Eve & Kashmiri Stec. 2016. Maintaining multiple viewpoints with gaze. In Barbara Dancygier, Wei Lun Lu & Arie Verhagen (eds.), *Viewpoint and the Fabric of Meaning: Form and Use of Viewpoint Tools across Languages and Modalities*, 237–257. Berlin/Boston: de Gruyter Mouton.
Taub, Sarah. 2001. *Language from the body: Metaphor and iconicity in American Sign Language*. Cambridge: Cambridge University Press.
Tomasello, Michael. 1999. *The Cultural Origins of Human Cognition*. Cambridge, MA: MIT Press.
Tomasello, Michael. 2008. *Origins of Human Communication*. Cambridge, MA: MIT Press.
Umiltà, Maria Alessandra, Evelyne Kohler, Vitorio Gallese, Leonardo Fogassi, Luciano Fadiga, Christian Keysers & Giacomo Rizzolatti. 2001. I know what you are doing. A neurophysiological study. *Neuron* 31(1),155–165.
Wehling, Elisabeth. 2010. Argument is gesture war: Function, form and prosody of discourse structuring gestures in political argument. In *Proceedings of the 35th Annual Meeting of the Berkeley Linguistics Society*, 54–65. Berkeley, CA: Berkeley Linguistics Society.
Wehling, Elisabeth. 2018. Discourse management gestures: An embodiment account of gesture pragmatics in face-to-face discourse. *Gesture* 16(2), 245–276.
Wilcox, Phyllis Perrin. 2004. A cognitive key: Metonymic and metaphorical mappings in American Sign Language. *Cognitive Linguistics* 15(2), 197–222.
Williams, Lawrence E. & John A. Bargh. 2008. Experiencing physical warmth promotes interpersonal warmth. *Science* 322(5901). 606–607.
Wilson, Nicole L. & Raymond W. Gibbs. 2007. Real and imagined body movement primes metaphor comprehension. *Cognitive Science* 31(4), 721–731.

Laura Ruth-Hirrel
A Place for joint action in multimodal constructions

1 Introduction

Language in interaction is a highly collaborative orchestration of individual actions. Conversational participants manage to coordinate their individual actions much of the time to achieve joint action (Clark 1996). In order to successfully carry out joint actions, we need conventional ways to let our interlocutors know when we are seeking collaboration or participating as collaborators. For example, a prototypical use of a question form conventionally signals an invitation for the addressee to participate in some communicative task or project. If I were at the supermarket with my mother in front of a fruit display and I asked, "Which pineapple should we get?" I would be signaling that I want her to collaborate with me on a task.

Language is not the only mechanism that can be used to indicate participation in a joint action. Building on the example above, suppose my mother inspected a particular pineapple and then placed it in the cart. I would interpret this non-linguistic action as an indication that my mother had made a decision. Clark (2003) calls actions such as these "placing" acts and suggests that they draw another person's attention to the placed object.

This chapter focuses on American English speakers' use of a particular location in space where the hands are routinely placed while gesturing in conversation. The location of interest is a region of space that, in many face-to-face interactions, falls approximately midway between two interlocutors' bodies, in line with the head and torso. In the context of gesturing, Sweetser and Sizemore (2008) refer to this spatial region as "interpersonal space", finding that American English speakers' use of interpersonal space is functionally motivated. Wilcox and Occhino (2016) call spatial locations that are used meaningfully in signed languages *Place* structures, recognizing that they are meaningful structures in their own right. I build on their terminology in examining "interpersonal space", which I will refer to as "Interpersonal Place" when highlighting its use as a meaningful structure in the gestural modality. Figure 1 provides an example of a manual gesture that incorporates Interpersonal Place as a meaningful component.

Laura Ruth-Hirrel, California State University, Northridge, USA, e-mail: laura.hirrel@csun.edu

Figure 1: Interpersonal Place in co-speech gesture ("This is your second baby?").[1]

In this example, talk show host Stephen Colbert asks actor John Krasinski a confirmation-seeking question, "This is your second baby?" with the question type signaled prosodically. With the onset of the question form, Colbert extends his arm out toward the space between him and Krasinski. Colbert's palm faces up, his index and middle fingers are extended and held close together, and the third finger and pinky are curled in toward the palm. The hand is held in this location until Krasinski confirms in the following turn (not shown) that the proposition on which Colbert seeks confirmation is accurate. The manual gesture shown in Figure 1 is a symbolically complex gestural expression that integrates at least two symbolic components: Interpersonal Place and a meaningful handshape.[2] Colbert uses an emblematic handshape expressing the numeral concept 'two', which is clearly related to the descriptive content of the word "second" expressed in his speech. As this symbolically complex gestural expression is integrated with speech, it serves as a component of a multimodal expression.

In the current study, I examine cases in which American English speakers place their hands in interpersonal space while gesturing in interaction. This chapter has two primary objectives. First, it aims to expand understanding of the functional properties associated with Interpersonal Place by examining the contexts in which it is used with speech. Based on these analyses, I propose that Interpersonal Place is used to signal a speaker's commitment to participate in a joint action, which I interpret within Clark's (1996, 2006) framework that identifies language use as a form of joint action. Second, I will illustrate processes through which Interpersonal

---

[1] All figures in this chapter are permissible under 17 U.S.C §107 (Limitations on exclusive rights: Fair use). https://www.govinfo.gov/content/pkg/USCODE-2010-title17/html/USCODE-2010-title17-chap1-sec107.htm

[2] The upward orientation of the palm is also likely to be functionally relevant.

Place may be symbolically integrated into a multimodal (gesture-speech) expression using descriptive tools from Cognitive Grammar.

This chapter is organized as follows. Section 2 introduces the concept of "symbolic structure" within the framework of Cognitive Grammar and discusses research proposing that Place is a type of symbolic structure. Section 3 presents evidence from existing research to support the claim that interpersonal space functions as a Place structure in gesture. Section 4 provides an analysis of cases in which Interpersonal Place is integrated with speech and two other meaningful structures in gesture—Palm Up Open Hand (Müller 2004; Kendon 2004) and the Cyclic gesture (Hirrel 2018; Ladewig 2011, 2014).[3] Insights gained from this analysis are used to propose a schematic function for placing constructions involving Interpersonal Place. The final section of the chapter provides a fine-grained analysis of a specific case where a speaker makes use of Interpersonal Place. Using the theory of Cognitive Grammar, this final analysis demonstrates how meaningful units that are co-articulated with Interpersonal Place may elaborate its meaning in specific usage events.

2 Symbolic structures in Cognitive Grammar

In the theory of Cognitive Grammar, grammar is not treated as an autonomous formal system that exists independently of meaning (Langacker 1987, 1991). Instead, grammatical knowledge is argued to emerge through processes of schematization and categorization of form-meaning structures that occur in linguistic expressions. As Cognitive Grammar is a usage-based theory, the only structures permitted in the description of grammar are those that are present in linguistic expressions and those mediated by basic, domain-general cognitive processes. This is known as the *content requirement* (Langacker 2008: 24–25). The content requirement restricts "elements ascribable to a linguistic system" to three types of structures: semantic, phonological, and symbolic structures (Langacker 2008: 24–25). *Semantic structures* are conceptualizations that are recruited for the expression of meaning in language. *Phonological structures* are perceptible linguistic forms. *Symbolic structures* are pairings of meaning and form, created through an associative link between phonological structures and semantic structures. This link is bidirectional "such that one is able to evoke the other" (Langacker 2008: 5).

A symbolic structure is described as "bipolar" because it integrates phonological structure and semantic structure (Langacker 2008:15). In elaborating this

---

[3] Labels given to meaningful structures are capitalized.

spatial metaphor, phonological structures (i.e., forms) are described as residing at the *phonological pole* and semantic structures (i.e., meanings) as residing at the *semantic pole*. Crucially, the distinction between linguistically encoded meaning and contextual knowledge in Cognitive Grammar is a graded one rather than categorical. The semantic pole includes the contextualized meaning of an expression, "not only what is said explicitly but also what is inferred, as well as everything evoked as the basis for its apprehension" (Langacker 2008: 457–458). The pairing of a phonological structure and a semantic structure gives rise to a symbolic structure. Of course, we need more than a simple pairing of semantic structure and phonological structure to use language successfully. Linguistic expressions typically integrate multiple symbolic structures. Symbolically complex expressions are called *symbolic assemblies* (Langacker 2008: 161, see also Langacker, this volume).

2.1 Expressive and conceptual channels

At each pole of a symbolic structure, there are multiple channels. At the phonological pole, several expressive channels interact in the physical manifestation of meaningful expressions (Langacker 2001: 145–146). In spoken language, there are segmental and intonational expressive channels. In signed languages and gesture, the manual channel is employed whenever meaning is expressed using the hands. Non-manual expressive channels also exist, such as facial movements (e.g., involving the eyebrows, eyes, and mouth), eye-gaze, and head, torso, and shoulder positioning. Any of these expressive channels can be recruited to convey meaning and thus form a symbolic structure.

At the semantic pole, the conceptualization channels described by Langacker are objective content, information structure, and speech management (Langacker 2008: 461–462). The objective content channel relates to the descriptive, substantive meanings evoked by linguistic expressions. The information structure channel is tied to meanings that are typically evoked by more symbolically complex expressions, such as clauses, utterances, and discourse strings. Langacker (2001: 146) describes this channel as accommodating a variety of functions, such as emphasis, discourse topic, and information status (i.e., givenness). Speech management is associated with functions such as holding the floor and taking a turn. I have previously proposed an additional conceptualization channel I called "interactional function" (Hirrel 2018: 173–174; see Figure 2). The interactional function channel corresponds to speech acts and stancetaking.

Figure 2 depicts channels associated with both the phonological and semantic poles for spoken language, signed language, and gesture. The number of expressive channels shown goes beyond those discussed by Langacker (2001, 2008). Lan-

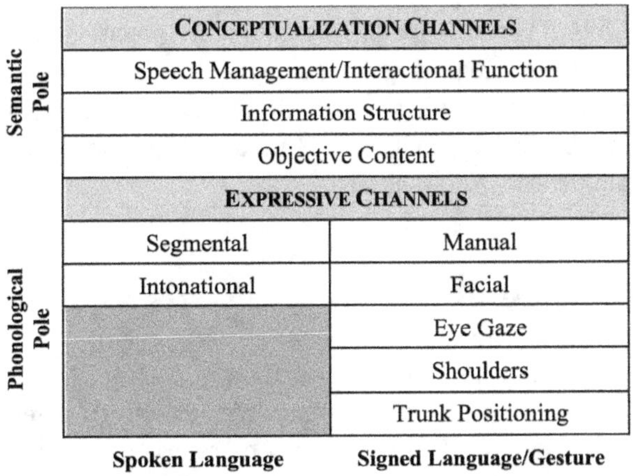

	CONCEPTUALIZATION CHANNELS	
Semantic Pole	Speech Management/Interactional Function	
	Information Structure	
	Objective Content	
	EXPRESSIVE CHANNELS	
Phonological Pole	Segmental	Manual
	Intonational	Facial
		Eye Gaze
		Shoulders
		Trunk Positioning
	Spoken Language	Signed Language/Gesture

Figure 2: Channels of expression and conceptualization.

gacker describes a single gesture channel, which includes manual gestures, facial gestures, and bodily posture. I have previously suggested that there are multiple channels within the visual modality (Hirrel 2018). The expressive channels on the right side of Figure 2 reflect a working hypothesis that is motivated by both formal and functional properties. First, for a body part to be considered a channel it must be relatively autonomous phonologically. The hands, and the face, can move independently of one another, as can the eyes, shoulders, head, and trunk of the body. Second, each posited channel must also be available for the expression of meaning in signed languages and/or gesture. For example, the shoulders are included as a channel because they are relatively autonomous phonologically and because research suggests they can be used meaningfully (Debras and Cienki 2012). Head movements have been found to be used for a wide range of functions across languages (McClave et al. 2007).

The expressive channels shown in Figure 2 likely represent an incomplete list. The facial channel may need to be broken up into multiple channels, such as eyebrows, eye aperture, and mouth. These structures have a moderate degree of phonological autonomy and can individually contribute meaning to linguistic expressions (Siyavoshi 2019). As we continue to learn more about the ways other parts of the body contribute meaning in language use, channel divisions for the visual modality will likely need to be revised.

Importantly, channels should not be thought of as autonomous modules or components in the expression of language. Rather, symbolic assemblies simultaneously incorporate multiple expressive channels and evoke meanings across each of the conceptual channels. However, particular expressive channels may be more salient to a given expression due to linguistic and contextual factors. Including channels in semantic analyses has the benefit of allowing for a more precise analysis of semantic composition processes, recognizing that symbolic structures may be evoked through expressive channels that linguists have traditionally excluded from analysis. Considering conceptualization channels allows us to reframe meaning altogether to include more than just propositional meaning.

2.2 Symbolic structures in gesture

Many gesture researchers have tended to adopt the position of McNeill (1992: 21) that manual gestures are unanalyzable, holistic structures. However, when researchers describe meaningful units in gesture, they may be referring to handshapes (Kendon 1995; Seyfeddinipur 2004), movements (Ladewig 2011), manners of movement (McNeill 1992), locations (Sweetser and Sizemore 2008), or combinations of those properties (Bressem and Müller 2014). Phonologically, handshapes, movements, manners of movement, and locations are components within a single gesture, so it logically follows that a gesture has the potential to be symbolically complex. I have made this argument in earlier work (Hirrel 2018; Ruth-Hirrel and Wilcox 2018) and will not expand upon it here due to space limitations.

What is important to the current study is that unlike symbolically complex expressions in spoken language, manual gestural expressions can simultaneously incorporate symbolic structures that are expressed through the same channel at the phonological pole (cf. the example shown in Figure 1). A manual gesture can, all at once, integrate a handshape, movement, and location, all of which are meaningful. Like symbolically complex spoken expressions, the meanings of symbolic assemblies in gesture are not expected to be fully predictable from the meanings of the component structures that comprise them.

2.3 The symbolic structure of Place

The symbolic structure in gesture that is the focus of this chapter is phonologically expressed as location in space. Wilcox and Occhino (2016) provide the term Place to describe meaningful locations in space in signed languages. The term is capitalized to emphasize its technical usage as a type of symbolic structure. In order for a Place structure to be incorporated into an expression, it needs to be evoked by a more autonomous structure. One strategy for evoking a Place structure and incorporating it into an expression is pointing to a location in space (the phonological pole of the Place). Pointing is a symbolically complex act that minimally incorporates two symbolic structures, a pointing device and a Place structure (Wilcox and

Occhino 2016). The pointing device (e.g., hand, finger, eye gaze, lips, or head) and movement towards the phonological pole of Place schematically functions to direct attention (conceptual and sometimes visual attention) to a Place structure. Wilcox and Occhino propose that, schematically, a Place structure *profiles* (i.e., designates) a *thing* at the semantic pole. Thing is a technical term in Cognitive Grammar that describes a "product of grouping and reification" (Langacker 2008: 105). A thing can emerge in any domain, whether it is tangible (e.g., a dog) or abstract (e.g., a plan of action).

Martínez and Wilcox (2019) identify another strategy for evoking Place structures in signed languages, which they term *placing*, adopted from Clark (2003). Clark notes that language users can place an object in a person's focus of attention for communicative purposes, however, placing an object as such does not direct specific attention to the Place, as it does with the pointing strategy. Clark describes placing (and pointing) as a type of *indicating strategy* in gesture. For example, a person might place a plate of food in front of another person to indicate that it is time to eat. This act renders the spatial location meaningful (i.e., a Place), at least temporarily. If the plate of food was suddenly taken away from the location while the person went to get a glass of water, they might point toward the location where the plate was previously placed while asking what had happened to the food.

For signed languages, Martínez and Wilcox (2019: 86) propose two types of placing. In the first type, called *Placing-for-Creating* (or "create-placing"), a new Place structure is created when a manual sign is articulated (placed) at a location in space. Through that placing act, a Place structure is created. Martínez and Wilcox provide an example in which a signer of Argentine Sign Language (Lengua de Señas Argentina, or LSA) produces the sign meaning 'person' in a region of space to the right of the body. This symbolic act creates a Place. The location at which the manual sign is produced is the phonological pole of the Place structure. The semantic pole of the Place structure is elaborated by the semantic pole of the sign PERSON. In other words, the "thing" at the semantic pole of the Place structure is specified as 'person'.

The second type of placing that Martínez and Wilcox (2019: 86) discuss is called *Placing-by-Recruiting* (or "recruit-placing"). Once a Place has been established through an act of pointing or create-placing, a signer can make use of the previously established Place structure by producing a new lexical sign at the phonological pole of the Place structure. Recruit-placed signs establish an associative link between the conceptual content the newly placed lexical sign profiles and the semantic pole of the Place structure previously established. Building on the example given for create-placing, the signer may recruit the Place structure previously associated with 'person' when articulating lexical signs that describe attributes of the referenced person. This recruit-placing act would create a semantic association between the attributes and the referent of the 'person' profiled in the previously established Place structure.

Place structures are phonologically and semantically dependent. The location (phonological pole) of a particular Place structure is in existence on its own. But in order for a location to be evoked as a salient entity within the interlocutors' focus of attention, a language user's hand(s) must be moved to that location in space. At the semantic pole, a Place structure requires elaboration by a conceptually more autonomous structure to specify the reference of the thing that is instantiated in a particular construal. In signed languages, this semantic elaboration is achieved when a sign is placed in the location, as was shown in the LSA examples.

Extending Martínez and Wilcox's insights to gestures used with speech, I propose that placing a manual gesture at a salient spatial location in an interlocutor's focus of attention can evoke a Place structure.

3 Interpersonal space as Place

Wilcox and Occhino's (2016) recognition that locations in space can be symbolic structures has revealed important insights into the grammar of signed languages. Other researchers have discussed motivated uses of space in signed languages (Cormier, Fenlon and Schembri 2015; Engberg-Pedersen 1993; Liddell 2003) and in gesture (Parrill and Stec 2017; Stec and Huiskes 2014; Sweetser and Sizemore 2008). While space can be used as a meaningful resource in co-speech gesture, gestures are often produced in front of a speaker's torso in "central gesture space" (McNeill 1992: 82), which is a default, less salient region of gesture space.[4]

Sweetser and Sizemore (2008) have identified at least three meaningful divisions in gesture space in American English based on conversational data: personal, interpersonal, and extrapersonal space (see also Sweetser, this volume). They characterize personal gesture space as the region immediately in front of a speaker's head and torso. In physical arrangements where interlocutors are not positioned in extremely close proximity to one another, interpersonal gesture space is the space existing between two interlocutors' personal gesture spaces. Extrapersonal or "unclaimed" gesture space refers to all other regions of gesture space, such as out to the sides of the body (assuming interlocutors are not sitting side-by-side). Sweetser and Sizemore found that extrapersonal space is used for gestures expressing descriptive linguistic content (see also Özyurek 2000). Contrastively, interpersonal space is used for func-

---

[4] Although note that there may be high degrees of individual variation in the use of certain dimensions of space (Priesters and Mittelberg 2013).

tions such as floor-claiming, introducing new discourse topics, and signaling solidarity. Sweetser and Sizemore (2008) assess that when American English speakers make an excursion out of personal space and into interpersonal space, they are regulating the spoken interaction in some way and highlighting that act of regulation.

Sweetser and Sizemore also observe that gestural handshapes appear to be important to functional differences in the use of interpersonal space. While they do not systematically explore this variable, they find that when a gesture is located in interpersonal space using the handshape prototypically associated with acts of pointing (i.e., the index finger extended), the gesture is used for floor-claiming functions. By contrast, when the palm is open but facing downward, the gestures occur in the context of topic changes.

Because interpersonal space has been found to be used in meaningful ways for particular types of interactional functions in English, it can be identified as a conventionalized symbolic structure. Following Wilcox and Occhino's (2016) proposal, I identify it as a type of Place structure, and describe this in more detail in Section 4 below.

4 Interpersonal Place in American English

In this section, I analyze cases in which Interpersonal Place is integrated with speech and with other symbolic structures in gesture. The analysis specifically examines the interactional functions speakers perform while gesturing in Interpersonal Place.

The first gestural symbolic structure that is examined in terms of its integration with Interpersonal Place is the Palm Up Open Hand (henceforth PUOH) gesture.[5] This gestural structure is characterized by a relatively open hand and an upward-facing (supinating) palm. PUOH gestures have been described as a gesture family (Kendon 2004; Müller 2004). Different formal realizations of PUOH, such as its position in gesture space, have been shown to correspond to distinct functions in language use. Müller (2004) argues that these variants of PUOH are united by a core meaning characterized as 'transfer of an entity'. This transfer can be construed as either offering or receiving: Müller suggests that the sources of PUOHs are the physical actions of giving, receiving, or requesting concrete objects (Müller 2004: 236).

The second symbolic structure examined in this chapter in terms of its integration with Interpersonal Place is the "cyclic" gesture. Cyclic gestures are phonologi-

---

5 Kendon (2004: 264) alternatively uses the term Open Hand Supine (OHS) for this hand configuration.

cally expressed as a circular rotation of the wrist (or elbow). In German, they have been found to be used during word searches, when describing ongoing events, and when making certain types of requests (Ladewig 2011, 2014). Ladewig argues that cyclic-type gestures are a gesture family that is linked by the core meaning 'cyclic continuity'. In English, circular rotational gestures have been found to be used for various functions, such as for the expression of path and manner of motion (Zima 2014), with word searches (Sweetser 1998), with particular aspectual construals (Hinnell 2018), and with epistemic evaluations (Hirrel 2018).

The case study presented in Sections 4.1–4.3 examines how American English speakers use Interpersonal Place in two types of gestural expressions co-occurring with speech. First, I examine cases in which Interpersonal Place and PUOH are integrated. Then, I turn to cases in which Interpersonal Place is integrated with the cyclic gesture. Two separate gestural expression types involving Interpersonal Place are considered to better understand the functional-semantic properties of Interpersonal Place as a component structure.

4.1 Data and methods

The cases selected come from a larger corpus collected from American talk show episodes. The corpus (at the time of writing) includes a total of 135 tokens of Interpersonal Place used in multimodal expressions. The larger corpus included 77 tokens of Interpersonal Place used with PUOH and 58 tokens of Interpersonal Place used with cyclic gestures. The examples included in the present analysis were selected because they illustrate different linguistic and interactional contexts in which each gestural expression is used, and they were representative of the larger corpus.

Segmentation of the component structures in gesture (i.e., Interpersonal Place, PUOH, and cyclic) and annotations of the co-occurring speech were performed using ELAN software.[6] To operationalize that a speaker-gesturer was using a location in interpersonal space with a PUOH or cyclic gesture, aspects of the speaker-gesturer's arm positioning were used as cues. The primary cue was shoulder flexion in the gesturing arm. Visual cues of this flexion included the elbow of the gesturing arm being pulled in front of the body (away from the sides of the body) and being extended to an angle of 45 degrees or less. If interlocutors were seated side-by-side, then any reach out in the direction of an interlocutor while talking was considered to be a use of interpersonal space. Eye gaze was an additional cue. In the larger

---

6 (Version 5.8) Nijmegen: Max Planck Institute for Psycholinguistics, The Language Archive. https://archive.mpi.nl/tla/elan

corpus, the speaker-gesturer's eye gaze was always found to be directed toward the addressee when gesturing in interpersonal space, and the addressee's gaze almost always met the gesturer's gaze. The spoken utterances, occurring immediately before, during, and after the gestural expressions, were transcribed and analyzed for interactional function (speech act or stancetaking function).

4.2 Interpersonal Place/PUOH assemblies

This section discusses cases in which speakers use Interpersonal Place/PUOH gestural assemblies. In these examples, the speaker-gesturer is engaging in at least one of the following functions: 1) asking a question; 2) attempting to shift topic; 3) indicating their alignment with a stance expressed by the interlocutor; and 4) inviting the interlocutor to align with their stance. Sections 4.2.1 through 4.2.3 discuss each function and provide specific examples from the data. Functions (3) and (4) are grouped together as components of a broader act of stancetaking in 4.2.3.

4.2.1 Asking a question

Example (1) shows an Interpersonal Place/PUOH assembly while the speaker-gesturer is asking a question.[7] Temporal alignment of the gesture in relationship to speech is indicated with curly brackets, marking the onset of the gestural excursion to interpersonal space and the onset of the retraction of the gesture from interpersonal space. Prior to the dialogue shown in (1), Stephen Colbert and actor John Krasinski had been discussing a recent dinner that Colbert, Krasinski, and their spouses had shared together. Colbert makes a humorous remark to which Krasinski responded with laughter, lasting approximately 1.5 seconds. Krasinski's laughter is interrupted by the question forms Colbert expresses in (1). Colbert seems to interpret Krasinski's laughter as signaling an appropriate end to the previous discourse topic because the first question in the turn (line 1) shifts to a new topic of discussion.

(1) 1 COLBERT: {How is your lovely wife?
    2   **You just had a baby,**
    3   [right?] (0.45)}
    4   KRASINSKI: [We ju]st had a} baby. Yes.

---

7 Transcription conventions are adapted from Du Bois, Schuetze-Coburn and Paolino (1993). See Appendix 1.

At the same time that Colbert begins to express the first question form in speech (line 1), he extends his arm out to interpersonal space using a PUOH. The resulting Interpersonal Place/PUOH assembly is shown in Figure 3. Note that Colbert does not wait for Krasinski to respond to the first question form before expressing a second question form, suggesting that the first question functions primarily as a move to shift the topic (as opposed to it being a genuine question). The second question (lines 2–3) is a tag question that seeks confirmation that the proposition asserted in the clause preceding the tag is true (i.e., "You just had a baby"). Interestingly, Colbert holds the Interpersonal Place/PUOH assembly for his entire turn and into Krasinski's turn. It is as if Colbert is waiting for Krasinski to confirm the propositional content in the tag—the expected response—before he retracts his hand from interpersonal space.

Figure 3: An Interpersonal Place/PUOH construction with a question/topic shift (example 1).

4.2.2 Shifting topics

Example (2) it taken from an interaction between talk show host Jimmy Kimmel and actor Issa Rae. During two different moves to shift the topic (line 11 and line 21), the two interlocutors perform a series of Interpersonal Place/PUOH assemblies. In total there are three Interpersonal Place/PUOH assemblies performed in (2).

The interaction in (2) starts immediately after Rae walks on stage for the interview segment. Rae performs an Interpersonal Place/PUOH construction (line 11) with an expressive speech act (ie., "Thank you..."). As in example (1), the Interpersonal Place/PUOH construction is preceded by a laugh from the interlocutor. The phatic expression "thank you" conventionally carries the expectation of a response, acknowledging the act of thanking. In this context, it also serves as an attempt to shift topic from the previous line of talk about Rae's clothes. Rae's Interpersonal Place/PUOH gesture starts higher up in interpersonal gesture space, during the first part of her turn (line 11). Rae then lowers her hand (fingers lax and curved), palm still facing upward, when expressing the reason for the expression of gratitude (line 12). Rae holds this lax PUOH low in interpersonal space until Kimmel responds and finishes his turn (and slightly beyond). Rae's lowered gesture is shown in the first image (on the left) in Figure 4.

(2) 1   KIMMEL: I love this- (0.5)
     2   What would you call this outfit?
     3   Is this a jumpsuit?
     5   RAE: Uh yeah jumpsuit.
     6   I call it orange blossom.
     7   KIMMEL: Oh.
     8   [Alright.]
     9   RAE: [I just n]amed it right now.
    10   KIMMEL: ((laughs))
    11   RAE: **{Thank you**
    12   **for giving me boom operator credit by the way.**
    13   **Nobody's ever done that**
                  [before.]
    14   KIMMEL: **[Well I]** **am uh nothing if not thorough.**
    15   RAE: **((laughs))}** ((continues laughter))
    16   KIMMEL: I really scoured your Wikipedia page.
    17   RAE: ((laughs))
    18   KIMMEL: Yeah you do everything on your show.
    19   RAE: Barely. Everything, something.
    20   KIMMEL: Everything and something, yeah.
    21   **{Congratula}**tions on your Emmy nomination.
    22   **{It was your first}** Emmy nomination.

The second and third Interpersonal Place/PUOH gestural expression in (2) occur as a part of the same turn, which starts on line 20. This time it is Kimmel who performs the gestures. Kimmel's first Interpersonal Place/PUOH expression is shown in the second image (on the right) in Figure 4. In the first gesture Kimmel performs, similar to that of Rae's, the speaker-gesturer's PUOH hand reaches out into interpersonal space at the start of a construction performing an expressive speech act (line 21). The spoken content ("congratulations") carries the expectation of a response from the interlocutor (conventionally "thank you"). In this context, it also establishes a move to shift topic from Rae's work on her television show to her Emmy nomination.

Unlike Rae's gesture, these two gestural expressions (lines 21 and 22) involve two excursions to interpersonal space with immediate retractions once the apex is reached. Additionally, both of Kimmel's gestures integrate a beat into the symbolic gestural assembly. A beat is a forceful, biphasic manner of movement. Beats are a type of symbolic structure that are used to emphasize meanings elaborated by speech (Ruth-Hirrel and Wilcox 2018).[8]

Figure 4: An Interpersonal Place/PUOH construction with topic shift (example 2).

In line 22, Kimmel asserts that it was Rae's first nomination for an Emmy award and performs a second Interpersonal Place/PUOH assembly (not shown). By doing so, he elaborates on the situation introduced in the previous utterance, adding knowledge to the shared ground. The spoken expression occurring with this Interpersonal Place/PUOH (plus beat) construction also strengthens Kimmel's move for a topic shift by introducing salient information about the proposed topic. These examples suggest that topic-shifts may be relevant to the use of Interpersonal Place/ PUOH assemblies in American English.

4.2.3 Stancetaking

Example (3) is from an interaction between Jimmy Kimmel and actor Tiffany Haddish. In this example, Haddish performs an Interpersonal Place/PUOH assembly (line 10) while verbally expressing alignment with Kimmel's epistemic evaluation in the previous turn. This evaluation is an act of stancetaking. Du Bois (2007: 141) explains that "the act of taking a stance necessarily invokes an evaluation at one level or another,

---

[8] For discussion of beats, see McNeill (1992, 2008), McNeill, Levy and Duncan (2015), and Hirrel (2018), among others.

whether by assertion or inference". Evaluations occur when a stancetaker "orients to an object of stance" (the target of the evaluation) and "characterizes it as having some specific quality or value" (Du Bois 2007: 143). When a person expresses an evaluation (e.g., "That's fantastic!"), they position themselves in relation to the object of stance and potentially in relation to other stancetakers' evaluations toward that same stance object. An act of alignment may show positive, negative, or partial alignment with an already expressed stance.

(3) 1   HADDISH: I said okay cool.
     2   Since y'all got dinner last night,
     3   Ima get y'all Groupons.
     4   Don't worry,
     5   everything on me.
     6   (1.1)
     7   So,
     8   HADDISH AND KIMMEL: ((extended laughter))
     9   KIMMEL: That seems fair.
     10 HADDISH: **{Yeah that's fair.}**

At the start of this example, Haddish is narrating the circumstances of a humorous situation she had recently experienced. After a period of shared laughter by the interlocutors, Kimmel, who is the stancetaker, makes the evaluation "That seems fair" toward an object of stance (line 9). The object of stance is the state of affairs Haddish had described in her previous turn (lines 2–5). Immediately following Kimmel's evaluation, Haddish takes a turn in which she affirms and reasserts an unhedged version of Kimmel's evaluation: "Yeah that's fair". Haddish reaches out into interpersonal space using PUOH while performing this act of stance alignment (shown in Figure 5).

Figure 5: An Interpersonal Place/PUOH construction with stance alignment (example 3).

4.3 Interpersonal Place/cyclic assemblies

Here I describe a single case of the Interpersonal Place/cyclic gestural assembly. Every Interpersonal Place/cyclic token in the larger corpus (58 tokens) occurs when a speaker-gesturer is requesting information from an addressee, most often using a question form. This contrasts with the Interpersonal Place/PUOH assemblies discussed in the previous section, which were shown to be used with spoken expressions that function for multiple interactional purposes.

In example (4), a speaker-gesturer uses an Interpersonal Place/cyclic gesture when trying to elicit information from an interlocutor. In this interaction, actor Russel Brand is discussing his experiences with sobriety and his work with others who are seeking sobriety (lines 1–8). One of the hosts, Rosie Perez, asks the polarity question, "Do you struggle with it?" regarding his experience with sobriety (lines 12–13). Perez performs a cyclic gesture in interpersonal space while asking this question. Figure 6 shows an image of this gestural display. Perez is seated second from the right. Perez's blurred hand is a visual cue that the hand is in motion.

Another host of the show, Rosie O'Donnell, attempts to take a turn at the same time as Perez, asking Brand a confirmation-seeking tag question that overlaps with Perez's question (lines 14–15). Interestingly, O'Donnell performs an Interpersonal Place/PUOH assembly with the statement that precedes the tag. O'Donnell is seated furthest to the right in Figure 6.

(4) 1 BRAND: If anyone at all with a drug or alcohol problem,
     2   says Russell I want to get clean,
     3   I have to help them.
     4   It's like a mandatory obligation.
     5   And sometimes I want to go,
     6   Nuh!
     7   Ahh,
     8   I have to.
     9 EVERYONE: ((laughter))
    10 O'DONNELL: Yeah.
    11   You have to.
    12 PEREZ: {Do you
    13   s[truggle with it?]} (Interpersonal Place/cyclic)
    14 O'DONNELL: {[And it's been]
    15   like eleven years} for you, right? (Interpersonal Place/PUOH)

Figure 6: An Interpersonal Place/cyclic construction (Perez, second from right) (example 4).

4.4 Conclusions for data on Interpersonal Place/PUOH and Interpersonal Place/cyclic assemblies

The Interpersonal Place/PUOH assemblies shown in the cases discussed above occur with spoken expressions that serve several functions: asking a question, attempting to shift the line of talk, and stancetaking. The Interpersonal Place/cyclic gestural assemblies (example 4 above, and all others in the corpus) are used when a speaker is requesting information from their interlocutor. What the examples of Interpersonal Place/PUOH and Interpersonal Place/cyclic assemblies have in common is that they all occur when a speaker-gesturer is either initiating or responding to a conversational move that requires action from both interlocutors to complete.

In the next section, I use a framework that recognizes language as a type of joint action (Clark 1996) to interpret the results of this case study. I propose a schematic meaning for placing acts in American English that make use of Interpersonal Place. I argue that when a speaker-gesturer places their hands in interpersonal space to gesture, they are indicating to their interlocutor that they are making a contribution toward an act of joint action.

4.5 Interpersonal Place and joint action

Language frequently occurs in the context of activities that require the cooperation of more than one participant to accomplish, such as ordering food or seeking advice (Clark 1996). Participants engage in various pursuits together that unfold through discourse. Clark calls these pursuits "joint projects". A joint project is defined as "a joint action projected by one of its participants and taken up by the others" (Clark

1996: 191). In this section, I argue that the meaning of Interpersonal Place is tied to component acts that comprise a basic-level joint project.

A joint project can be of any size. If you ask someone a question and they provide an answer, you have established a *minimal joint project* (Clark 1996: 201). That minimal project might end abruptly if you or someone else in the conversation makes a move for a new joint project after the question-answer pair is completed. If you continue with the same topic of talk that is conceptually related to the question-answer sequence, it will grow into an extended joint project (i.e., continuing beyond two individual coordinated actions). Clark (2006) calls the strategy we use to achieve a minimal joint project a *projective pair*. A projective pair is formed through two components, a *proposal* and an *uptake*. Clark (2006: 132) defines a proposal as "any signal that raises the possibility, at any strength, of a joint action or position by the initiator and addressees" while an uptake is "any action that addresses the proposed possibility". A few examples of proposals are greetings, questions, and pointing gestures. Parallel examples of uptakes are returned greetings, answers, and attention directed to the location referenced in an act of pointing. When one participant's uptake aligns with another participant's proposal (e.g., answering a question), a minimal joint project is established.

In the cases discussed above, the spoken language expressions with which Interpersonal Place/PUOH and Interpersonal Place/cyclic assemblies were performed function either as the proposal or uptake of a projective pair. When a person asks a question, requests information, or makes a move to shift topic, they are putting forth a proposal and marking their intention to initiate a joint project. They are also expecting that the addressee will recognize their intention and choose to uptake that proposal through some action, leading to a joint action. Alternatively, when a speaker makes an evaluation that shows some degree of alignment (positive or negative) with another interlocutor's evaluation, it is because they have recognized it as a proposal to join them in the evaluation of that object of stance. These are the joint actions in which Interpersonal Place/PUOH and Interpersonal Place/cyclic assemblies are used in the cases discussed above. The structure that links these assemblies is Interpersonal Place.

American English speakers gesture in interpersonal space during conversations when making a proposal or responding to a proposal for joint action. I claim then that this placing act that incorporates Interpersonal Place schematically functions to indicate a move for joint action. Clark suggests that placing (an indicating act) "exploits a preexisting indexing site and connects object *o* with it" (Clark 2003: 250). This is compatible with Wilcox and Occhino's (2016) proposal that a Place structure schematically profiles a thing. The "object" (*o*) Clark refers to is comparable to a specific instantiation of a Place structure, where the thing profiled at the semantic pole of the Place structure is elaborated by some more autonomous symbolic structure. Clark's characterization of placing shares similarities with recruit-placing, one of the two placing strategies that Martínez and Wilcox (2019) propose. Recall that recruit-placed signs use a previously established Place structure to create an associative link between the semantic pole of that Place structure and the profile of the newly placed lexical sign.

The use of Interpersonal Place in American English shares similarities with recruit-placing. By performing a gestural expression in interpersonal space, the semantic pole of the manual gesture becomes associated not with the semantic pole of a Place previously established in the discourse but with the semantic pole of a conventionalized Place structure. Data from this study suggest that American English speakers use Interpersonal Place Placing constructions to indicate that they are engaging in a move toward joint action. The thing profiled by the Place structure is then some type of joint action. Whether it is a proposal or uptake and what the specific function of that move is (e.g., to shift to a new joint project or to align with a stance) is elaborated by the semantic pole of the co-expressed spoken expression (cf. Section 4.6).

Figure 7 shows the phonological and semantic structure of a placing strategy that integrates Interpersonal Place as the Place structure. Interpersonal Place is phonologically expressed as a location, specifically the region of gesture space between interlocutors. Interpersonal Place phonologically requires a more autonomous gesture in the manual gestural channel to be evoked: the placed hand. This dependency is indicated by the bold arrow. The manual gesture is necessary for the realization of an act of placing, as indicated by the square box that includes both the autonomous and dependent structures at the semantic poles. The meaning of Interpersonal Place Placing construction resides in the interactional function channel. At the semantic pole, it indicates a move for joint action (i.e., proposal or uptake).

4.6 Symbolic assemblies and Interpersonal Place

In this section, I analyze a specific instantiation of Interpersonal Place found in an Interpersonal Place/PUOH assembly using the theory of Cognitive Grammar. This theory is especially appropriate for studying interactions between gesture and speech because it recognizes that gestures are symbolic and can reflect conceptualizations along with the speech. This analysis demonstrates how PUOH and conceptual content that is evoked through spoken symbolic assemblies can elaborate the meaning of an Interpersonal Place placing construction by specifying the nature of the joint action.

The example shown in (5) comes from an interaction between talk show host Ellen DeGeneres and then U.S. presidential candidate Hillary Clinton in 2016. In the

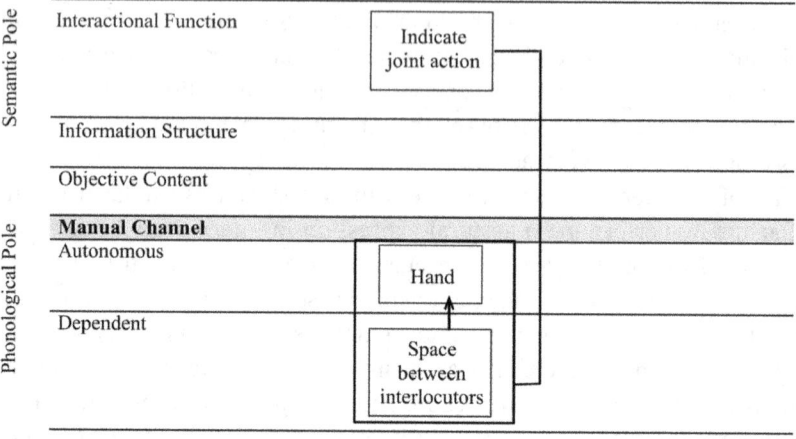

Figure 7: Placing strategy and Interpersonal Place.

discourse preceding (5), DeGeneres quotes then U.S. presidential candidate Donald Trump as saying that he "will be good for women". DeGeneres asks Clinton, "What do you think about that?". Clinton then expresses her skepticism that Trump will in fact be good for women, in a turn of nearly one minute. Clinton completes her turn saying, "There's just no evidence that he has an understanding of what women's lives are like today". DeGeneres then initiates a turn, which is shown in example (5).

(5) 1 DEGENERES: **{He's**
    2   **(0.2)**
    3   **gonna be the nominee.**
    4   **I mean,**
    5   **did you ever think you would get to this point where}**
    6   (0.2)
    7   you're gonna be
    8   (0.9)
    9   up against Trump?

DeGeneres begins her turn by making an assertion about Donald Trump (lines 1–3), a previously established topical referent. DeGeneres then asks Clinton a question (lines 5–9) that elaborates the assertion that Trump is "gonna be the nominee". As DeGeneres begins the turn, she performs an Interpersonal Place/PUOH assembly, which is shown in Figure 8. The gestural expression is held in interpersonal space throughout the asserted content, across the stance marking expression "I mean" and through a portion of the question form. To account for the use of this Interpersonal Place/PUOH token, it is important to consider meanings expressed using the intonation channel.

Figure 8: The Interpersonal PLACE/PUOH assembly in example (5).

Prosodic properties associated with example (5) suggest that DeGeneres is incredulous that Donald Trump is expected to be the presidential nominee for the Republican Party.[9] The first word in DeGeneres's turn ("He's") forms a prosodic unit. It is offset by the pause that may function to mitigate the assertion that follows. The final syllable of "nominee" (line 3) rises sharply from a low tone. This contour pattern has been found to contribute to a general meaning of contrast (Watson, Tanenhaus and Gunlogson 2008). Here, the contrast is not with respect to something previously stated, but rather, it implicates DeGeneres's prior expectations (i.e., Trump would not get the nomination) and contrasts them with the state of affairs at the time of speaking (i.e., Trump receiving the nomination is imminent). While DeGeneres makes an assertion in the segmental (speech) channel (lines 1–3), she is simultaneously expressing her affective evaluation of incredulity toward the asserted proposition using the intonational channel.

The prosodic properties associated with speech in lines 4–9 are more complex, but the meaning conveyed through the intonational channel can be summarized as expressing a contrast between the propositional content of the question (i.e., Clinton will be up against Trump) and what DeGeneres assumes Clinton expected (i.e., Clinton will not be up against Trump). Interestingly, what DeGeneres signals to be the expected stance of Clinton is parallel to her own stance. When DeGeneres asks Clinton the question (line 5–9), it does not act merely as a request that Clinton answer as yes or no. The segmental and intonational channels together suggest that DeGeneres is inviting Clinton to align with her disbelief about a state of affairs (i.e., Trump becoming the Republican Party nominee). As this is a proposal for a joint

---

9 Thank you to Caroline Smith for her insights on the prosodic patterns in this example.

action, it is unsurprising that DeGeneres integrates an Interpersonal Place/PUOH assembly into the multimodal expression.

With respect to the gestural assembly, there are at least three component symbolic structures that are integrated: 1) PUOH; 2) Interpersonal Place; and 3) a hold (actively maintaining the hand in a position in space). Figure 9 shows the schematic functions I propose for each of these symbolic structures across conceptualization channels and for the act of placing. Arrows indicate that a symbolic structure is phonologically dependent on another structure for instantiation. Interpersonal Place is dependent on a handshape/orientation and the gesture hold is dependent on both a location in space and the handshape/orientation.

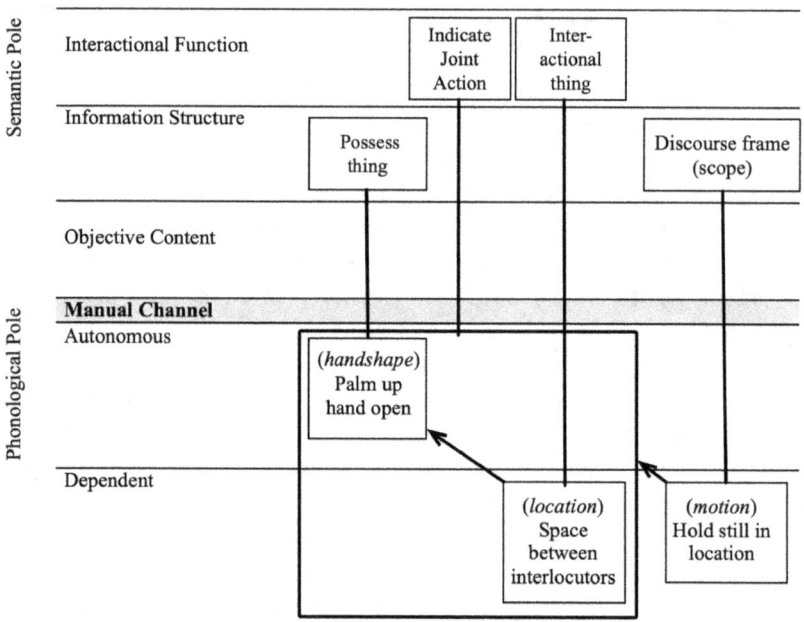

Figure 9: Symbolic components in the Interpersonal PLACE/PUOH assembly in example (5).

Phonologically, the PUOH consists of an open hand, oriented upward. Conceptually, I categorize this hand configuration as schematically evoking a relationship between a thing (in the technical sense) and a possessor within the information structure channel. This characterization is based on previous research that has found PUOH variants used to signal offers or requests involving abstract discourse entities (Kendon 2004; Müller 2004). With offers, the possessor of the discursive entity/thing is the speaker-gesturer. With requests, the speaker intends to become the possessor of the thing (e.g., new knowledge supplied by the interlocutor).

Interpersonal Place is realized phonologically as a location between interlocutors, which is schematically characterized as an "interactional thing" in the interactional channel. The Place is evoked through a placing act (placing the hand(s) at the phonological pole of interpersonal space). This act of placing at interpersonal space, which requires both an autonomous and dependent structure (hand and location), gives rise to the schematic meaning 'indicate joint action'. Note that the movement required to hit the target of Interpersonal Place is an articulatory gesture that occurs as a part of the preparation phase and does not contribute meaning in this expression. In preparation phases, the hand is moved away from a position of rest to the spatial location where the primary meaning-bearing phase is performed (Kendon 1980).

Finally, the gesture hold is a feature of movement, but here it is the lack of movement that is meaningful. The function of gestural holds most closely aligns with the channel of information structure. Holding a manual gesture in a period of stasis at a location shows that the gesture is relevant to the speech with which it temporally aligns (Harrison 2010; McNeill 1992). In Figure 9, the term "discourse frame" describes this function. A discourse frame is "the scope of concern at a given stage of the discourse" (Langacker 2008: 281).

Figure 10 shows the composite Interpersonal Place/PUOH placing assembly (G_1) that DeGeneres uses. While the component symbolic structures (S_1–S_3) evoke meanings in multiple channels (c.f. Figure 9), the meaning of the composite structure G_1 resides in the interactional channel. I characterize the meaning profiled by G_1 as 'offer joint action'. The 'possession of a thing' associated with the PUOH is metonymically interpreted as an offer when PUOH is integrated with Interpersonal Place. The hold indicates that the meaning has relevance across successive clauses in speech.

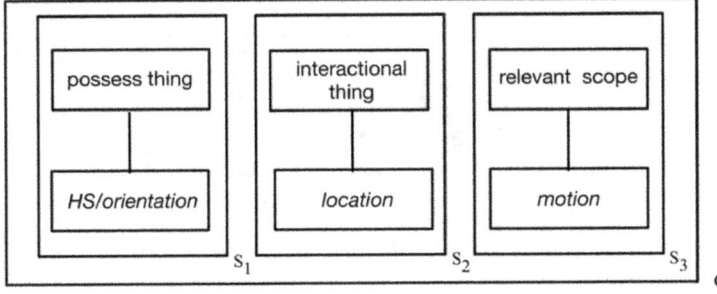

Figure 10: The composite Interpersonal Place/PUOH placing assembly in example (5).

Figure 11 shows the integration of symbolic assemblies across the spoken and gestural modalities in example (5). The elements that are most salient to the current discussion are bolded. While it excludes complexity of the usage event, it draws attention to conceptual structures evoked in speech that elaborate the schematic meaning of the G_1. Arrows point toward structures that conceptually elaborate other relevant structures at the semantic pole. The symbolic structures expressed in speech (S_1–S_4) are organized by intonational groupings (i.e., intonation units). These assemblies of symbolic structures or "attentional frames" function to parse discourse into manageable and coherent "windows of attention" (Langacker 2001: 154–155). This function is not represented for simplicity.

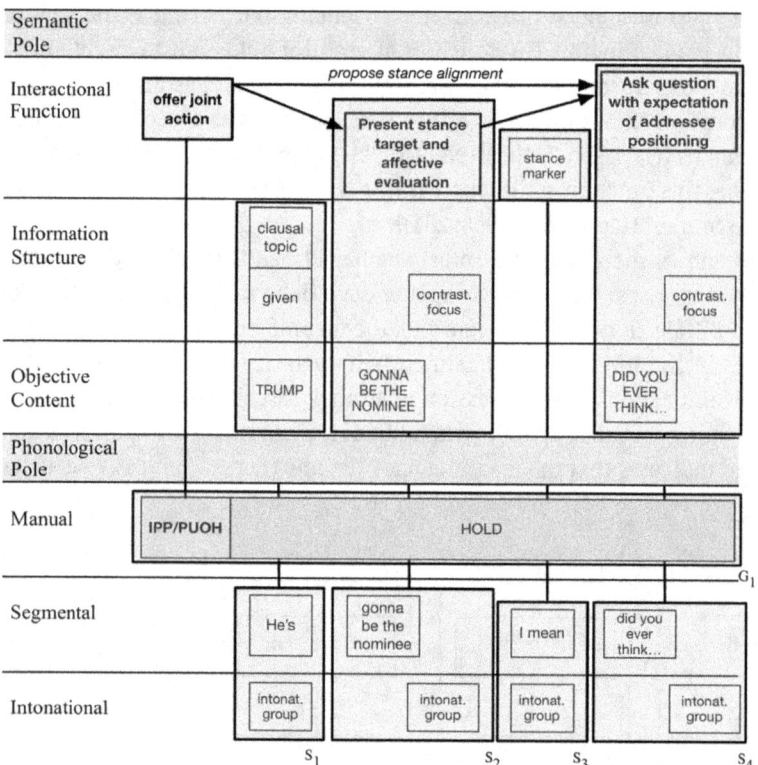

Figure 11: Multimodal symbolic assemblies for example (5).

The first two attentional frames (S_1 and S_2) elaborate the offer evoked at the semantic pole of the Interpersonal Place/PUOH placing expression (G_1) by establishing the specific topic the speaker wants to offer for joint activity (i.e., Trump will be the Republican nominee). Through the situated use of contrastive focus in the intonational channel, S_2 further specifies DeGeneres's affective stance (i.e., incredulity) toward the propositional content. The segmental content in S_1 and S_2 provides the target of the evaluation (i.e., "He's gonna be the nominee") while the conceptual content evoked through the intonation channel locates this assertion as a stance-taking act.

The attentional frame (S_3) that follows, prefaces an upcoming stance act, perhaps providing a coherence link between two stance-related attentional frames. The final attentional frame with which G_1 is symbolically integrated (via the hold) is S_4. This symbolic structure elaborates S_2 by specifying what DeGeneres wants done with the topic established in S_1–S_2. The question form elaborates that DeGeneres wants Clinton to comment on the topic. It also provides a more specific characterization of the joint action in G_1: as a question, it characterizes it as a proposal. Finally, the conceptual content expressed through the intonational channel in S_4 further elaborates the nature of the joint action indicated by G_1 by characterizing it as a proposal for stance alignment. With S_4, the indeterminate aspects of G_1 as an offer of joint action are specified as a proposal for Clinton to share in DeGeneres's own surprise about Trump's nomination.

This analysis of example (5) highlights that G_1 is a complex symbolic assembly with multiple meaningful components. When unified through an act of placing it gives rise to the schematic meaning 'offer a joint action'. It also shows that conceptual content evoked through the segmental and intonational channels in speech can elaborate the meaning of an Interpersonal Place/PUOH assembly in the gestural modality. Importantly, the meaning of G_1 is schematic without considering its relationship to the spoken expressions that elaborate it.

5 Conclusions

When American English speakers gesture in interpersonal space, they are making a public, on-the-record commitment to participate in a jointly coordinated action. The cases examined here show that speaker-gestures use placing constructions in interpersonal space when proposing a joint project of talk and during uptake of an interlocutor's proposal to engage in a joint action. Following this observation, I have proposed that Interpersonal Place is a symbolic structure that schematically profiles an interactional "thing". That thing is elaborated when this conventional Place is recruited through an act of placing. I have proposed that this specific type of placing construction in American English schematically functions to indicate a joint action. As was shown in the previous section, the schematic function of this placing construction is elaborated by symbolic assemblies expressed in speech to specify the type and purpose of the joint action. Other symbolic structures in the manual gestural channel may also elaborate the meaning of the gestural expression (e.g., PUOH specifying it as an offer for joint action).

The proposals I have made in this chapter will need to be tested across a larger number of tokens produced by different speakers to determine whether adjustments made to the schematic characterization of the semantic pole of Interpersonal Place and Interpersonal placing are necessary. The characterization of Interpersonal Place ideally should accurately capture its use within different construction types. I have suggested that this placing construction in American English shares similarities with recruit-placing (Martínez and Wilcox 2019), but there are important differences that should be explored in future research. In gesture, an associative link is created between the semantic pole of the Place structure and the semantic pole of the co-expressed speech, whereas in Argentine Sign Language, the associative link was found between the semantic pole of Place and the semantic pole of the placed sign. Future research may explore whether placing of this type in speech is functionally equivalent and appropriately characterized as recruit-placing.

Interestingly, the use of the Interpersonal Place placing construction in gesture is not required to perform a proposal or uptake in American English. Perhaps the use of these gestural expressions increases the likelihood that a proposal for joint action will be successful by minimizing the chance of it being misunderstood for something else. A speaker's overt move for joint action using elements of the physical ground may invite an addressee to uptake. With respect to an action of uptake, placing the hand(s) in interpersonal space may interact with participant engagement in the interaction or degrees of solidarity/familiarity between the interlocutors. Interactions between contextual, social, and cultural factors and the use of this placing construction should be explored in future research.

Cognitive Grammar is a theory that offers conceptual unification of language phenomena across different modalities: spoken, signed, and gestural. The construct of channels allows for fine-grained analyses of the phonological and semantic integration of symbolic structures that are evoked in different expressive channels and that have meanings associated with different conceptualization channels. Applying this theory to gesture has helped to reveal symbolic complexity that exists in the gestural channel, something that has traditionally been overlooked in gesture research. In this chapter, Cognitive Grammar has been used to illustrate how meaningful structures in gesture and speech may be symbolically integrated and give rise to higher-level interactional meanings.

Transcription conventions:

Gestural expressions – General	Text that is bolded and underlined shows where Interpersonal PLACE/PUOH or Interpersonal PLACE/cyclic assemblies overlap with speech.
Gestural expressions – Endpoints	The left curly bracket indicates the onset of the manual movement toward Interpersonal Place and the right curly bracket indicates the retraction of the manual movement from Interpersonal Place.
Speech overlap	Marked by square brackets.
Pauses	Marked by parentheses containing numbers that indicate pause length in seconds.
Word truncation	Marked by hyphen.
Terminative intonation	Marked by a period.
Continuative intonation	Marked by a comma.

References

Bressem, Jana & Cornelia Müller. 2014. The family of away gestures: Negation, refusal, and negative assessment. In Cornelia Müller, Alan Cienki, Ellen Fricke, Silva H. Ladewig, David McNeill & Jana Bressem (eds.), *Body – Language – Communication: An International Handbook on Multimodality in Human Interaction, Volume 2*, 1592–1604. Berlin/Boston: De Gruyter Mouton.

Clark, Herbert H. 1996. *Using Language*. Cambridge: Cambridge University Press.

Clark, Herbert H. 2003. Pointing and placing. In Sotaro Kita (ed.), *Pointing: Where Language, Culture, and Cognition Meet*, 243–268. Mahwah, NJ: Lawrence Erlbaum.

Clark, Herbert H. 2006. Social actions, social commitments. In N. J. Enfield & Stephen C. Levinson (eds.), *Roots of Human Sociality: Culture, Cognition and Interaction*, 126–150. Oxford/New York: Berg.

Cormier, Kearsy, Jordan Fenlon & Adam Schembri. 2015. Indicating verbs in British Sign Language favour motivated use of space. *Open Linguistics* 1(1). 684–707. https://doi.org/10.1515/opli-2015-0025

Debras, Camille & Alan J. Cienki. 2012. Some uses of head tilts and shoulder shrugs during human interaction, and their relation to stancetaking. *Proceedings of the ASE/IEEE International Conference on Social Computing*. 932–937.

Du Bois, John W., Stephan Schuetze-Coburn, Susanna Cumming & Danae Paolino. 1993. Outline of discourse transcription. In Jane A. Edwards & Martin D. Lampert (eds.), *Talking Data: Transcription and Coding in Discourse Research*, 45–89. Hillsdale, NJ: Laurence Erlbaum.

Du Bois, John W. 2007. The stance triangle. In Robert Englebretson (ed.), *Stancetaking in Discourse: Subjectivity, Evaluation, Interaction*, 139–182. Amsterdam/Philadelphia: John Benjamins.

Engberg-Pedersen, Elisabeth. 1993. *Space in Danish Sign Language: The Semantics and Morphosyntax of the Use of Space in a Visual Language*. Hamburg: SIGNUM.

Harrison, Simon. 2010. Evidence for node and scope of negation in coverbal gesture. *Gesture* 10(1). 29–51.

Hinnell, Jennifer. 2018. The multimodal marking of aspect: The case of five periphrastic auxiliary constructions in North American English. *Cognitive Linguistics* 29(4). 773–806.

Hirrel, Laura. 2018. *Cyclic Gestures and Multimodal Symbolic Assemblies: An Argument for Symbolic Complexity in Gesture*. Albuquerque: University of New Mexico dissertation. https://digitalrepository.unm.edu/ling_etds/57/

Kendon, Adam. 1980. Gesticulation and speech: Two aspects of the process of utterance. In Mary R. Key (ed.), *The Relationship of Verbal and Nonverbal Communication*, 207–227. The Hague: Mouton.

Kendon, Adam. 1995. Gestures as illocutionary and discourse structure markers in Southern Italian conversation. *Journal of Pragmatics* 23(3). 247–279.

Kendon, Adam. 2004. *Gesture: Visible Action as Utterance*. Cambridge: Cambridge University Press.

Ladewig, Silva H. 2011. Putting the cyclic gesture on a cognitive basis. *CogniTextes* 6. http://cognitextes.revues.org/406

Ladewig, Silva H. 2014. The cyclic gesture. In Cornelia Müller, Alan Cienki, Ellen Fricke, Silva H. Ladewig, David McNeill & Jana Bressem (eds.), *Body – Language – Communication: An International Handbook on Multimodality in Human Interaction, Volume 2*, 1592–1604. Berlin/Boston: De Gruyter Mouton.

Langacker, Ronald W. 1987. *Foundations of Cognitive Grammar: Volume I, Theoretical Prerequisites*. Stanford, CA: Stanford University Press.

Langacker, Ronald W. 1991. *Foundations of Cognitive Grammar: Volume 2, Descriptive Application*. Stanford, CA: Stanford University Press.

Langacker, Ronald W. 2001. Discourse in cognitive grammar. *Cognitive Linguistics* 12(2). 143–188.

Langacker, Ronald W. 2008. *Cognitive Grammar: A Basic Introduction*. Oxford/New York: Oxford University Press.

Liddell, Scott K. 2003. *Grammar, Gesture, and Meaning in American Sign Language*. Cambridge: Cambridge University Press.

Martínez, Rocío & Sherman Wilcox. 2019. Pointing and placing: Nominal grounding in Argentine Sign Language. *Cognitive Linguistics* 30(1). 85–121.

Müller, Cornelia. 2004. Forms and uses of the palm up open hand: A case of a gesture family? In Roland Posner & Cornelia Müller (eds.), *The Semantics and Pragmatics of Everyday Gestures*, 233–256. Berlin: Weidler Buchverlag.

McClave, Evelyn, Helen Kim, Rita Tamer & Milo Mileff. 2007. Head movements in the context of speech in Arabic, Bulgarian, Korean, and African-American Vernacular English. *Gesture* 7(3). 343–390.

McNeill, David. 1992. *Hand and Mind: What Gestures Reveal about Thought*. Chicago: University of Chicago Press.

McNeill, David. 2008. *Gesture and Thought*. Chicago: University of Chicago Press.

McNeill, David, Elena T. Levy & Susan D. Duncan. 2015. Gesture in discourse. In Deborah Tannen, Heidi E. Hamilton & Deborah Schiffrin (eds.), *The Handbook of Discourse Analysis*, 262–289. Hoboken, NJ: Wiley Blackwell.

Özyurek, Asli. 2000. The influence of addressee location on spatial language and representational gestures of direction. In David McNeill (ed.), *Language and Gesture*, 64–83. Cambridge: Cambridge University Press.

Parrill, Fey & Kashmiri Stec. 2017. Gestures of the abstract: Do speakers use space consistently and contrastively when gesturing about abstract concepts? *Pragmatics & Cognition* 24(1). 33–61.

Priesters, Matthias A. & Irene Mittelberg. 2013. Individual differences in speakers' gesture spaces: Multi-angle views from a motion-capture study. *Proceedings of the Tilburg Gesture Research*. 1–4. http://tiger.uvt.nl/pdf/papers/priesters.pdf

Ruth-Hirrel, Laura & Sherman Wilcox. 2018. Speech-gesture constructions in cognitive grammar: The case of beats and points. *Cognitive Linguistics* 29(3). 453–493.

Seyfeddinipur, Mandana. 2004. Meta-discursive gestures from Iran: Some uses of the 'Pistolhand'. In Roland Posner & Cornelia Müller (eds.), *The Semantics and Pragmatics of Everyday Gestures*, 205–266. Berlin: Weidler Buchverlag.

Siyavoshi, Sara. 2019. Hands and faces: The expression of modality in ZEI, Iranian Sign Language. *Cognitive Linguistics* 30(4). 655–686.

Stec, Kashmiri & Mike Huiskes. 2014. Co-constructing referential space in multimodal narratives. *Cognitive Semiotics* 7(1). 31–59.

Sweetser, Eve. 1998. Regular metaphoricity in gesture: Bodily-based models of speech interaction. In *Actes du 16e Congrès International des Linguistes* (CD-ROM). Oxford: Elsevier.

Sweetser, Eve & Marisa Sizemore. 2008. Personal and interpersonal gesture spaces: Functional contrasts in language and gesture. In Andrea Tyler, Yiyoung Kim & Mari Takada (eds.), *Language in the Context of Use: Discourse and Cognitive Approaches to Language*, 25–51. Berlin/New York: Mouton de Gruyter.

Watson, Duane G., Michael K. Tanenhaus & Christine A. Gunlogson. 2008. Interpreting pitch accents in online comprehension: H* vs. L+H*. *Cognitive Science*s 32(7). 1232–1244.

Wilcox, Sherman & Corrine Occhino. 2016. Constructing signs: Place as a symbolic structure in signed languages. *Cognitive Linguistics* 27(3). 371–404.

Zima, Elisabeth. 2014. English multimodal motion constructions. A construction grammar perspective. *Papers of the Linguistic Society of Belgium 8*, 14–29. Linguistic Society of Belgium.

Terry Janzen, Barbara Shaffer, and Lorraine Leeson
What I know is here; what I don't know is somewhere else: Deixis and gesture spaces in American Sign Language and Irish Sign Language

1 Introduction

When signers talk about things they know, they position those things directly in front of them in a central space. But when they talk about things they don't know—things unknown, in unknown locations, about unspecified referents, things in the future—these are relegated to other spaces (Shaffer, Leeson, and Janzen 2017). And so a pattern emerges: spaces associated with the here and now, the known, and past experience, contrasting with spaces associated with the unknown, the distant, and the future. Related to this, Janzen (2019) has considered the CONCEPTUAL DISTANCE IS SPATIAL DISTANCE metaphor as describing how things that are conceptually close occupy spaces proximal to the signer and those that are conceptually distant as occupying more distal spaces.[1]

In this study, we examine a number of schematized phenomena in American Sign Language (ASL) and Irish Sign Language (ISL) that contrast the spatially-articulated difference between things that are known versus things that are unknown or not fully specified, and the effects appear to be regularized. Jacobowitz and Stokoe (1988), we note, postulated that ASL has future tense marking, which positions verbs

---

[1] We would like first to acknowledge the participants in our study who have shared their languages with us. Ethics approvals were received from the Universities of Manitoba and New Mexico, which allowed for image use, but not recognition by participant name. Research ethics approval at Trinity College Dublin facilitates naming participants, therefore our thanks go to Fiona Ennis-Regan, Mary O'Connor, Frankie Berry, and Fergus Dunne. Thanks to those at the International Society for Gesture Studies conference in Cape Town, South Africa (2018), and especially comments by Daz Saunders, Eve Sweetser, and Cornelia Müller. Thanks too to others who have supported and inspired our work: Kyra Zimmer, Sarah Rabu, Marge Pettypiece, Denise Sedran, Erin Wilkinson, and Rick Zimmer.

Terry Janzen, Department of Linguistics, University of Manitoba, Canada,
e-mail: terry.janzen@umanitoba.ca
Barbara Shaffer, University of New Mexico, USA, e-mail: bshaffer@unm.edu
Lorraine Leeson, Trinity College Dublin, Ireland, e-mail: leesonl@tcd.ie

https://doi.org/10.1515/9783110703788-009

in an upward and outward space, even though the analysis of this as a tense marker has not been further substantiated. Nonetheless, it is common in signed languages for irrealis categories, such as future (Shaffer and Janzen 2016), to be articulated in an "other" space. Likewise, Shaffer (2012) has demonstrated that reported speech evidentials (see section 4) in ASL are semblances of interactions with unspecified others. The spaces these semblances occupy are frequently off-center in a likewise "other" space, perhaps reflecting the non-specificity of the "other" even if that entity is, at times, given unquestioned authority. And in a study on motivated spaces for pronoun use in both ISL and ASL, Leeson, Janzen, and Shaffer (2012) examined complex pronoun spatial placement that showed that conceptually remote referents were increasingly articulated toward locations more distal from a front and center space.

Here we analyze these occurrences as contributing collectively to, and building a distinction between, what is known or what is in focus, thus what is presented to the addressee in a central shared space, in opposition to what is of the "other"—distant, unimportant, unknown, or irrelevant—and so relegated to more distal spaces. In short, in this way deictic spaces are schematized at a complex, discourse level of information organization, such that the use of these systematic and schematized spaces contributes to the intersubjectively shared understanding of the significance of discourse elements by virtue of where they are positioned in signers' gesture space.

In section 2 we begin our exploration of conceptualization and spatial mapping, including the idea of neutral space and arbitrary choices of spatial location, claiming that these notions do not fit with our examples of spatial positioning in ASL and ISL. We also look at space as perspectivized. In section 3 we introduce the CONCEPTUAL DISTANCE IS SPATIAL DISTANCE metaphor, and discuss a number of examples from ASL and ISL that show how the use of proximal and distal spaces exemplify the metaphor. Evidential constructions as examples of epistemological stance-taking are given in section 4. In section 5 we show how similar uses of space appear in speaker/gesturers' discourse, which suggests that CONCEPTUAL DISTANCE IS SPATIAL DISTANCE is a conceptual metaphor employed by both signers and speakers in their gestures. Section 6 offers some conclusions.

2 The conceptualization and use of space in signed languages

How space is used in the articulation of a signed language has, for obvious reasons, been fundamental in the description of signs themselves and in analyses of signed discourse. Friedman (1975) gives an early description of "signing space":

The space in which the language is articulated mainly extends over the area delimited by an approximate rectangle, the perimeters of which are:
a. A line above the head, to which the arms can extend when loosely bent at the elbows (approximately 6 inches above the head).
b. Lines extending downward from the upper line, parallel to the sides of the body, which the arms describe when lax.
c. A horizontal lower line, parallel to the waist. (Friedman 1975: 944–945)

While Friedman describes a two-dimensional plane, focusing just on the outer boundaries of the plane, Klima and Bellugi's (1979) description is three-dimensional and includes the signer's body. With respect to the place of articulation of signs, these occur at "particular locations and areas on and around the body within a delimited region we call the signing space" (Klima and Bellugi 1979: 51), with the hollow of the neck as "the articulatory center of the signing space" (1979: 73). This conceptualization of space is further elaborated in Uyechi's (1996) geometry of visual phonology model of local, global, and discourse signing spaces. "Signing space" has predominated as the term used to refer to the space within which signed language articulation takes place (e.g., Barberà Altimira 2015: 14; Liddell 2003: 8; Oomen and Kimmelman 2019), but it is sometimes referred to as articulation space (Friedman 1975: 945; Janzen 2004, 2012, 2019), and some authors have used both terms interchangeably (e.g., Leeson and Saeed 2012).

2.1 Neutral space

In Stokoe's ([1960] 2005) and Stokoe, Casterline, and Croneberg's (1965) seminal description of the structure of signs in ASL, spatial location is one phonetic ("cheremic" in their terms) category labeled the tab (tabula), along with the categories of dez (designator, or handshape) and sig (signation, or movement). Stokoe (2005) lists a "zero tab" in his tab category defined as the "space in front of the signer's body where movement is easy and natural" (Stokoe 2005: 34). Stokoe et al. (1965: x) refer to this as "the neutral place where the hands move", contrasting this with all other locations that contact the body, without distinguishing any regional differentiations in the signing space and not defining the space in terms of its outer boundaries. Liddell (2003) points out that Stokoe saw the space in front of the signer as altogether one neutral location on purely phonological grounds, as a single articulatory location listable along with locations contacting the body, because he had no evidence of minimal pairs distinguished solely by spatial positioning.

The idea of a "neutral space directly in front of the signer's body" (Friedman 1975: 943) is often an assumption made by signed language researchers, as in Meir et al. (2007), who refer to signs not articulated on the body as occurring in neutral space. Neutral space as a default space is assumed by Lillo-Martin and Gajewski, who state that "[m]any signs are simply specified for production in 'neutral space', such as the ASL sign HOUSE" (Lillo-Martin and Gajewski 2014: 393). It appears that neutral space is conceptualized in two ways depending on whether the discussion is phonological or semantic in nature. Phonologically, neutral space is a kind of default space where, barring discourse or pragmatic effects, signs are regularly articulated. Engberg-Pedersen's (1993) description of the relationship between phonological and semantic space in Danish Sign Language (dansk tegnsprog) is as follows:

> *Neutral space* is an area from a little above the signer's waist to her throat. Signs that have neutral space as their place of articulation are made at lexically determined heights. Two-handed signs are usually made in the space at the middle of the signer's body; one-handed signs usually displace the hand a little to the ipsilateral side. Neutral space should be kept distinct from the *signing space*, which is an area from a little above the signer's head to a little below her waist; its depth corresponds approximately to the length of the lower arm to the sides and forward from the body. Signs which have neutral space as their place of articulation can change meaningfully so that they are no longer made with the hands in neutral space, but the hands stay inside the signing space in unmarked signing." (Engberg-Pederson 1993: 36–37; italics in original)

Whereas Engberg-Pedersen uses descriptive terms to set neutral space as a region within signing space as a whole, Winston (1995) contrasts neutral space with leftward- and rightward-oriented spaces as a function of discourse. Winston's subject, when giving a lecture, positions the "art of poetry" in the leftward space and the "science of poetry" in the rightward space in what Winston calls a "comparative frame" (1995: 100). However, for the subject's evaluative comments on the comparative spatial mapping of art and science he returns to "neutral space" (1995: 105). In Winston's case, a neutral space is assumed when the signer is not referencing a space that is aligned with a specific concept; when the signer breaks from such an alignment, he returns to articulation within a centrally-located space. Thus for Winston, this space is contrastive semantically.

Neutral space from a phonological perspective, therefore, is considered when signs are located in space, off the body, where no alignment takes place with localized entities or events positioned somewhere in the signing space. From a semantic point of view, neutral space is considered in contrast to such localized entities or events when reference to the entity or event is not intended.

We claim that the central space in front of the signer is not rightly termed a "neutral" space. While detailed analysis of such a concept is left for further analysis overall, this frontal, proximal space in our examples consistently represents elements conceptually close to the signer, therefore the space is not in any way neutral. Second, the use of this space appears to be tied to the signer's presentation of ideas to the addressee, such that it is a *shared* discourse space (see, for example, Janzen 2019), which is seen most explicitly in our epistemic example of evidential space in section 4. We return to these issues in our discussion below.

2.2 Arbitrary locations in space

A somewhat related concept to neutral space is that of arbitrarily-chosen locations within articulation space. Lillo-Martin and Gajewski refer to these as such: "For non-present referents, arbitrary locations in signing space are set up as associated with those referents" (Lillo-Martin and Gajewski 2014: 393). Nominal loci, then, are "placed in arbitrary locations in the horizontal plane in front of the signer" (Kuhn 2016: 452). The idea of locating entities (semantically) or noun phrases (syntactically) at arbitrarily chosen points in articulation space has long been accepted in signed language structure (e.g., Emmorey, Corina, and Bellugi 1995; Sandler and Lillo-Martin 2006: 25) although there may be motivating factors that make location choice nonarbitrary. De Vos and Pfau (2015) claim that arbitrary loci can be seen in some signed languages such as Sign Language of the Netherlands (Nederlandse Gebarentaal) but not always in rural signed languages like Kata Kolok. Some researchers differentiate between "topographical" space and "syntactic" space. For example, in British Sign Language (BSL) Sutton-Spence and Woll (1998) state that when signers conceptualize space as topographical, it reflects or maps onto some real-world space such that the spatial arrangements that are articulated in BSL are motivated by, and so "copy" the real-world arrangement as an analogical correspondence (DeMatteo 1977; see also Emmorey et al. 1995 for ASL). Syntactic space, on the other hand, reflects only syntactic elements in BSL structure, therefore "the referent is the location – and the location is the referent" (Sutton-Spence and Woll 1998: 130), and these locations are arbitrary. Others, for example Emmorey et al. (1995) use the term "referential" space.

Liddell (1990, 1995), however, makes the point that even abstract entities that have no associated inherent spatial connections may still have topographical significance in signed discourse. Liddell claims that such abstract entities may be positioned in space not in an arbitrary way but in a conceptualized spatial relation to other entities, and may be manipulated in and around the space. Winston's (1995) example of a signer comparing the art of poetry with the science of poetry—all abstract notions—by choosing two relationally significant spaces demonstrates that this cannot be considered simply an arbitrary choice. Of this, Liddell states: "If signers are able not only to point toward but also to manipulate conceptual entities in the space ahead of them, then we are not dealing with meaningless loci in a syntactic space" (Liddell 1995: 37). Further, Leeson, Shaffer and Janzen (2018) demonstrate that when two things, whether abstract or real, are being compared, they are rarely of equal status. They find that relatively consistently, ASL and ISL signers position the item that is the point of comparison in a space contralateral to the dominant hand, and they frequently do this firstly. In contrast, they find that signers position the item that is the focus of comparison in a space ipsilateral to the dominant hand, articulating it secondly. This indicates a further dimension of non-arbitrariness in the spatial positioning of entities.

2.3 Perspectivizing space

The entry for COMPARE in Long's 1918 dictionary of early 20th century ASL shows a non-arbitrary use of space, with the signer's hands positioned with palms at a 45 degree angle, more or less facing the signer. The signer looks at the palms as if comparing them, Long's description says, thereby showing the signer has a perspectivized view of these spaces. This also holds for Irish Sign Language. The descriptive entry for COMPARE in the 1847 *Dictionary of the Methodic Irish Sign Language* reads, "place the hands together and look first at one, then at the other as if comparing them" (Foran 1994: 25).[2] These dictionary descriptions from the mid 1800s and early 1900s are early indications that the "signing space" is not an objective space in front of the signer, but that at least sometimes the signer is a participant in what takes place within that space. These are early indications that the signer is not just physically present in articulation space, but is conceptually present as well.

Descriptions of perspective-taking in signed languages have frequently focused on two orientations, character perspective and observer perspective (Perniss 2007a), although characterization of, and nomenclature for, these differs somewhat across the research. For example, Liddell (1995, 2003) refers to surrogate space and token space (see Nilsson, this volume, for detailed analysis of surrogates in a Swedish Sign Language (svenskt teckenspråk) text). For character perspective, the signer acts within a character role, interacting with other conceptualized entities as life-sized. For observer perspective, the signer views the scene from the "perspective of an external observer... constructing the event on a reduced scale in the area of space in front of the body" (Perniss 2007a: 1316–1317). Perniss (2007b, 2007c) identifies double-perspective constructions in German Sign Language (Deutsche

---

2 See de Jorio ([1832] 2000:135–137; translated by Adam Kendon) for a description of comparative gestures in Neapolitan antiquity that also use the two hands to represent two elements being compared.

Gebärdensprache) where a character perspective and an observer perspective are blended in a simultaneous construction through body partitioning (Dudis 2004). Character and observer perspectives have also been proposed and analyzed in gesture studies (e.g., McNeill 1992; Parrill 2012).

Another aspect of perspectivizing space concerns interactions being retold as narratives, which primarily entail character perspective. Traditionally, researchers have claimed that signers reposition their body at or toward some locus in articulation space associated with one entity and orient their discourse from the physical perspective of that locus, as constructed action (Metzger 1995), toward another space. Lillo-Martin (1995) refers to this as a point of view predicate. However, Janzen (2004, 2005, 2012) has shown that in narratives, ASL signers treat space as "mentally rotated", that is, they align and realign the perspectives of story characters with their own view on the space, rather than locating these entities in the space around them, and physically aligning their body with those spatial locations. Janzen (2012) argues that a "static" space, where entities are spatially positioned with the signer physically moving or leaning toward that space, is reserved for comparative discourse frames (see also Winston 1995). Emmorey, Klima and Hickok (1998) make the observation that spatial scenes are most often described from the signer's perspective in ASL, which necessitates that the viewer mentally rotate the spatial dimension of the scene 180° from the signer's to their own perspective in order to understand the description (e.g., of an apartment layout). The seeming preference for this orientation implies both that signers tend not to accommodate the viewer's perspective, and that viewers do the work of mental rotation, thus empathizing with the signer's point of view on the space.

Mental rotation, therefore, takes place for both signer and addressee, but in somewhat different ways. The signer's own mentally-rotated space stems from a particular conceptualization of space within narrative events by rotating the visual scene to bring various characters' visual perspectives into alignment with their own. The addressee, on the other hand, as Emmorey, Klima, and Hickok (1998) have shown, mentally rotates their own visual conceptualization of the scene to that of the signer, that is, they then follow the signer's perspective alignments.

Overall, the perspectivization of space is an important aspect of the examples we discuss below, in that the signers' deictic positioning of conceptualized elements in the space around them is not immediately meaningful without taking into account the signer's perspective on that spatial position. This is examined further in the next section on the CONCEPTUAL DISTANCE IS SPATIAL DISTANCE metaphor in both ASL and ISL.

3 The CONCEPTUAL DISTANCE IS SPATIAL DISTANCE metaphor

The CONCEPTUAL DISTANCE IS SPATIAL DISTANCE metaphor,[3] discussed in Janzen (2019), is exemplified by signers' positioning elements in the space surrounding them not as literal, topographical spatial mappings, but as metaphorical. When an element, which could be a physical entity or a more abstract notion, is conceptualized as somehow close to the signer, it tends to be positioned in a space proximal to the signer's body. It is no accident that possessive markers in signed languages are frequently articulated close to, or contacting, the body. Long (1918: 26) lists HAVE/POSSESS as "Cross the open hands in front, palms to self and then draw them up against the breast" as in Figure 1a.[4] In ISL one form of HAVE (possession), shown in Figure 1b, is a dominant-hand "flat O" moving so the fingertips rest on the non-dominant open palm. In this figure the sign is positioned more distally from the signer, but concerns another individual's being in possession of an item, conceptualized by the signer as the referent occupying a rightward space contiguous with the sign. This appears to be an older sign, referenced in the 1847 dictionary of ISL and described there as, "Put into the hand. Shut it" (Foran 1994)[5]. A second ISL form of HAVE (possession) (Figure 1c) is an open "5" handshape, upward facing palm that moves downwards, and closes to a fist, held proximal to the body, borrowed into ISL from BSL. In this instance of use both hands articulate the sign although today, we more regularly see a one-handed sign. This second type of possessive marker is a grasping metaphor. For the two forms of ISL HAVE it appears that the more strongly the possessor (e.g., first person) is profiled in the possessor-possessed relationship, the more proximal the sign position to the signer's body.

There also appear to be instances of spatial positioning following the CONCEPTUAL DISTANCE IS SPATIAL DISTANCE metaphor where a location is more distal to the signer, representing an entity that is conceptually distant in some way. In this chapter we explore especially how such proximal and distal spaces are associated with known, lesser known, and unknown concepts and entities in both ASL and ISL. We propose that these are cognitively regularized, entrenched and schematized metaphorical uses of the signer's body and space (cf. Wilcox and Occhino 2016 on Place).

---

3 See Wilcox and Wilcox (2015) for an overview of metaphor in signed languages.
4 In modern ASL, HAVE is similar although the hands do not overlap and only the fingertips contact the chest.
5 This variant of HAVE seems to appear more frequently in the phrasal modal HAVE-TO in ISL today.

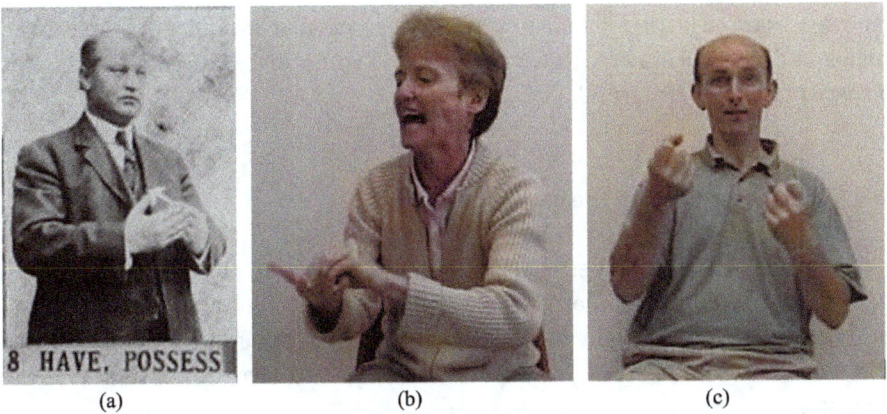

Figure 1: a) Old ASL HAVE/POSSESS in Long (1918: 24); b) HAVE in ISL, dominant hand acting on the non-dominant hand; c) HAVE in ISL, a two-handed version, final handshape.

3.1 Perspectivizing physical and conceptual spaces

In this section, we describe a range of uses of space in both ASL and ISL. In each of the instances illustrated below the space directly in front of the signer's body corresponds to an entity or concept that is "known", with a high degree of perceived *reality* on the part of the signer, while entities that are unknown or displaced, either temporally or conceptually (and sometimes both), are referenced in "other", more distal spaces not directly in front of the signer's body. Lakoff and Johnson (1980: 20) list among their "orientation metaphors" both UNKNOWN IS UP (e.g., "That's *up in the air*"), and KNOWN IS DOWN ("The matter is *settled*") which, they note, is experientially-based along with UNDERSTANDING IS GRASPING. Phyllis Wilcox (2000) adds the point that in ASL, metaphorical grasping and selecting occur in the space directly in front of the signer such that the grasping or selecting handshape/hand movement brings the thing being understood into the signer's central visible space.

The sense of "known/unknown" referred to here has to do with the signer's own subjective conceptualization, and not necessarily whether knowledge is shared among interlocutors, as in "old" versus "new" information (Givón 1984), "given" information (Prince 1981), or information that is "active" in the minds of both speaker and addressee at some specific point in the discourse (Chafe 1994). We return to this discussion in section 6 below regarding perceivability and the inferences interlocutors may make based on gesture space positioning.

As mentioned above, we suggest that this is a regularized, entrenched, and schematized use of the signers' body and space and that it is used deictically to index a relationship between the signer and some aspect of "knowledge". In 3.1.1 we consider how space is used in a very literal way, mapping spaces that are either proximal to the signer or directly behind the signer, to real world spaces and spatial relationships as experienced in the real world.

3.1.1 The motorbike and the garden hose

A very literal use of an "other" space appears in Fiona's ISL narrative about riding a motorbike, where a space located behind the signer references an unknown physical entity. She recounts how she feels that something isn't quite right and glances behind her, shown in Figure 2. She doesn't see anything awry, so continues on her journey.

Figure 2: Fiona looks behind her but sees nothing awry.

Then, a lorry catches up with her and they both come to a stop at a set of traffic lights. At this point Fiona, as narrator, shifts perspective to the lorry driver's point of view, enacting how he gestures to her to 'look behind', using a thumb-point gesture back over his shoulder, shown in Figure 3b, with Fiona's utterance structure in (1).

(1) MAN SAY PRO.2 SEE 'behind shoulder'(thumb) PRO.2
'The lorry driver said, "Look behind you" (from lorry driver's perspective).'

This prompts Fiona as past-self story character to physically look behind her, still on her motorbike (Figure 4). Now she discovers the cause for the lorry driver's persistence: a 30ft garden hose caught in her back wheel.

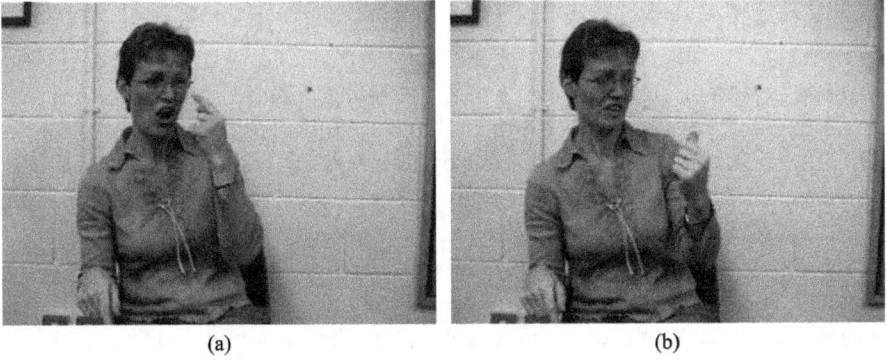

Figure 3: a) SEE; b) 'behind' (thumb towards location behind Fiona).

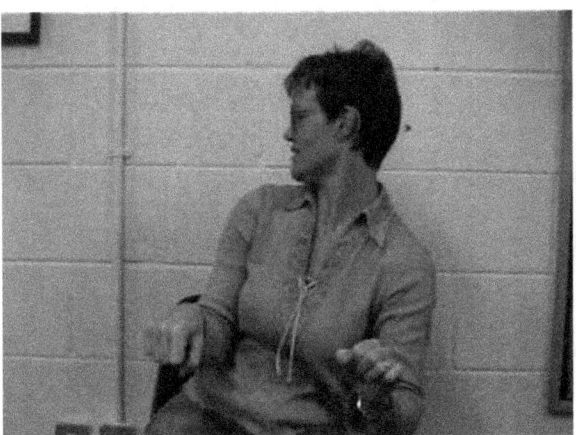

Figure 4: Fiona looks behind her to where the lorry driver has gestured.

This example illustrates the literal use of gesture space to represent something unknown, at the moment the lorry driver gestures to Fiona, which is the embodied physical basis for the metaphor UNSEEN IS UNKNOWN. Fiona is oblivious to the garden hose, as it is outside her visual field; in other words it is "somewhere else", thus the title of this chapter. In this example, the garden hose eventually becomes a known entity; later in the text Fiona coils it up and takes it with her to work. In the next section, however, we consider an example where something more distant from the signer is first not known or understood, but becomes known, and it changes how the signer represents this in her use of space.

3.1.2 Is it really snow?

This next example, also regarding a physical, topographical scene, illustrates that something quite distant may be difficult to comprehend, and thus is less "knowable", but once it is experienced more closely, it becomes "knowable". In this narrative, positioning within the signer's space reflects an unknown/distal versus known/proximal difference.

Mary, an ISL signer, tells of a holiday experience with her husband in Norway. As the narrative begins, they are at a lower altitude where it's warm and sunny, but they can see what seems to be snow high up on a mountain to their right. Mary's husband is certain that it cannot be snow because the sun is shining and the temperature is quite high. Determined to investigate further, they trek up up the mountain to verify the information visually. The distal location, from their lower altitude perspective, is shown in Figure 5a.

(a)   (b)

Figure 5: a) Index toward locus for the snow on signer's upper right; b) Index towards locus for the sun on signer's upper left.

(2) PRO.1 SEE(rt+high) CANNOT REAL S-N-O-W. MOUNTAIN WEATHER HOT INDEX(lt+high) . . .
'It seemed to me that there was snow on the mountain, but we wondered if that could be true given that the sun was so hot.'

This example, similar to the garden hose example, illustrates the physical, experiential basis for the metaphor CONCEPTUAL DISTANCE IS SPATIAL DISTANCE where physical distance serves as the source domain while knowledge is the target domain. The trek up the mountain gives them visual confirmation that it is in fact snow. From this new perspective, Mary now indexes what had been a distal element in the gesture space directly in front of her. Shown in Figure 6, what was previously distal and unknown to them is now something proximal and known. Mary's husband confirms this, by saying SEE BELIEVE 'Now that I can really see it, I believe it'.

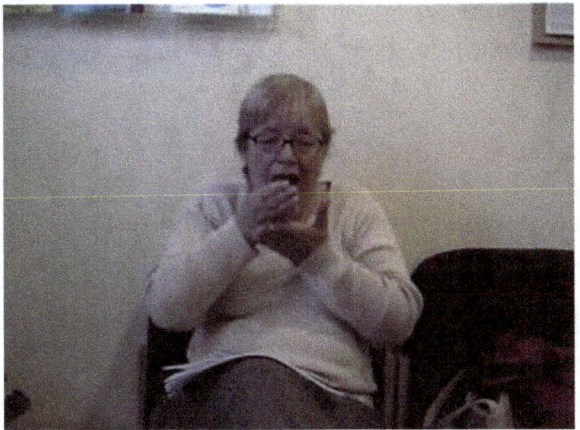

Figure 6: ARRIVE 'We arrived [at the top]' signed in a close proximal location.

This example, perhaps even more so than the previous example, suggests that elements that are not within our direct experience are not likely to be positioned in a front and center gesture space. These examples regard physical objects, but they are also conceptualizations in the way that everything the human mind deals with amounts to some sort of conceptualization. The physical proximity in experienced events such as in these examples form the embodied basis for more abstract examples of the CONCEPTUAL DISTANCE IS SPATIAL DISTANCE metaphor. In the next section we explore examples that begin to move away from the metaphor's physical experiential basis. The narrative about the mechanics in 3.1.3 seems an intermediate step in this direction.

3.1.3 The mechanics: Further distal spaces as more unknown

In the last example where the snow was eventually positioned in a proximal space once it became a known entity, and in those to follow in sections below, known concepts are very often profiled and positioned front and center in the signer's space. The signer's perspective is privileged here (Leeson and Saeed 2012) but we note that a signer may select to rotate their point of view to present an equally profiled, centralized view from another person's perspective, as in this next example. Here in an ISL narrative, Fergus first tells of checking the engine of his car, using a centrally-oriented space, shown in

Figure 7a. But, he needs to take it to a professional mechanic. Through this narrative, Fergus references a total of four mechanics, some known to him directly, and others who are recommended to him. This corresponds to varying degrees of knowledge which, from his subjective point of view, are mapped onto differing gesture spaces. The first mechanic Fergus enlisted for help (mechanic 1) was initially indexed in a contralateral gesture space, as in (3) below, and illustrated in Figure 7b.

(3) PRO.1 SEE PRO.3(rt) PRO.1 FRIEND HAVE PRO.3(rt) EXPERT ABOUT CAR REPAIR DIFFERENT++ POSS.3(rt)
'I went to see a friend of mine who is very skilled in terms of car repair. He has worked with lots of different [models].'

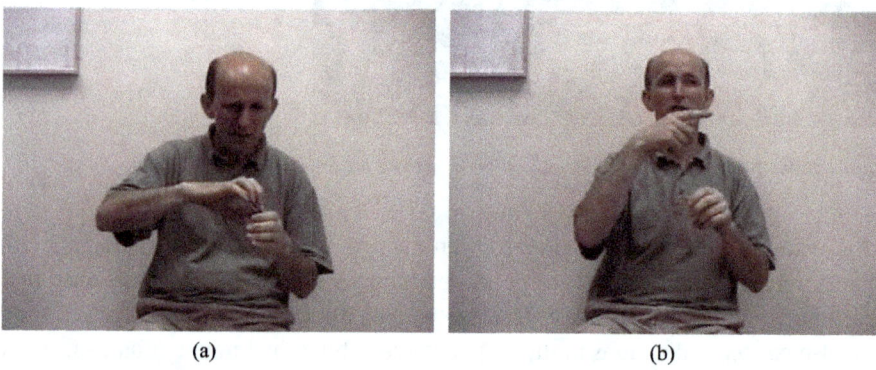

(a)   (b)

Figure 7: Fergus's viewpoint in (a) and indexing mechanic 1 in a contralateral space in (b).

Fergus then mentally "rotates" the space so that the same central space is used to enact his mechanic checking out the engine.[6] This is shown in Figure 8. The mechanic is well known to Fergus, and his viewpoint is centrally focused as Figure 8 shows.

However, mechanic 1 is unable to do the job, and refers Fergus to mechanic 2 for a quote. Mechanic 2 is also indexed proximally, but in an ipsilateral gesture space (Figure 9a). Fergus indicates this proximal space as PRO.3(lt) in (4). Unfortunately the quote was too high.

(4) BUT HAVE OTHER PRO.3(lt) GARAGE G-A-R-A-G-E PRO.3(lt), ENTER . . . EXPENSIVE
'but there was another garage. I went in. . . .[but it was] very expensive. . .'

---

[6] This perspective realignment also takes place in ASL narrative discourse (Janzen 2004, 2005, 2012) as described above in section 2.3.

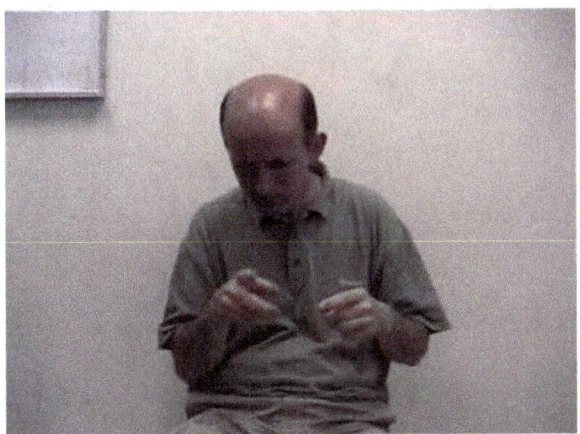

Figure 8: The perspective of mechanic 1 inspecting the engine.

Then Fergus remembers a friend, mechanic 3, in Wexford, a distant location from his home in Dublin. Mechanic 3 is indexed at a high ipsilateral gesture space, reflecting the relative distance and direction of travel from Fergus's Dublin home. This point is seen in Figure 9b, and in (5).

(5) PRO.3(rt+high) IN LIVE IN W-E-X-F-O-R-D
'[He] lives in Wexford.'

Mechanic 3 tells Fergus that the engine can't be fixed and a new one is needed. He suggests that his brother (mechanic 4), who Fergus doesn't know, may be able to find him a reconditioned engine. Mechanic 4 is also indexed distally relative to Fergus, but proximal to Mechanic 3's location in gesture space, shown in Figure 9c, with a possessive pronoun (in other words '*his* brother'). Mechanics 3 and 4 are closely aligned in the distal space because of their close affiliation (Engberg-Pedersen 1993).

Why are both mechanic 3 and 4 indexed at such a height in the signer's space? Mechanic 4 is known to Fergus only tangentially via his association with mechanic 3, so while the use of space here is complex in relation to two conceptualized points of view, we can say that the choice of this fourth mechanic's space represents a temporally, spatially, and conceptually dislocated entity in the discourse. Mechanic 3, however, is someone Fergus once knew, but who may not have been within his immediate consciousness, so the location indexed is an interesting, and most likely motivated, choice.

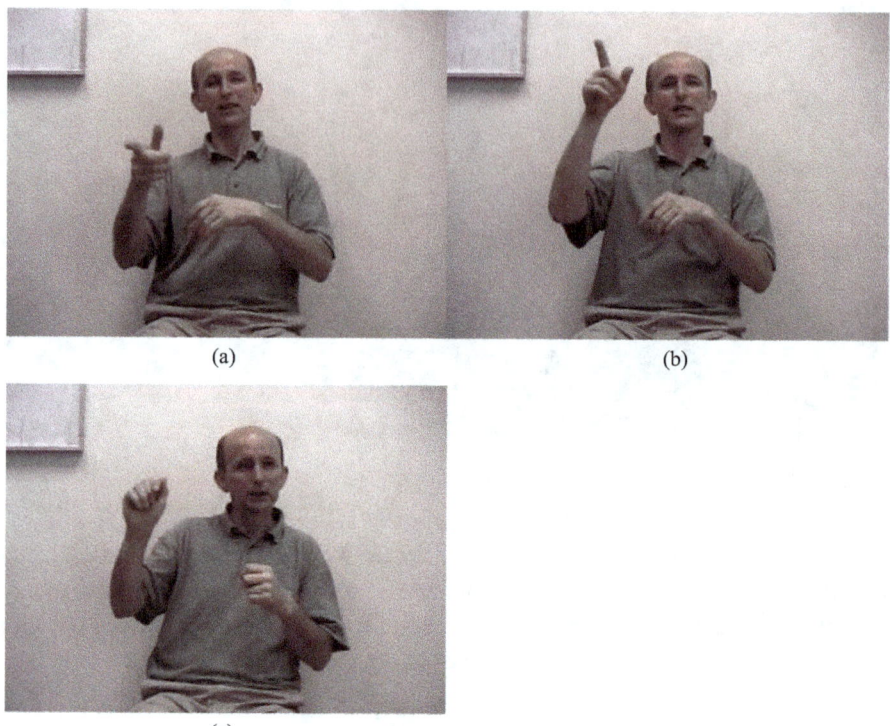

Figure 9: Spatial placement of (a) Mechanic 2; (b) Mechanic 3; (c) Mechanic 4.

3.1.4 The past is somewhere else

Janzen (2019) describes an ASL signer telling a story as part of a conversation about her family going to a camp in another province (Ontario) when she was much younger. This is how she begins the narrative. In Figure 10 she indexes Ontario in an upward and extended distal space, while maintaining eye gaze with her addressee. As with Wexford in the example above, there is no topographic reason to locate the Ontario camp at such a height. Instead, we suggest that both the distance of the place from her present location along with the event taking place in the distant past motivate this location in her articulation space: she conceptualizes the location and time of the event as something not within her present-day experience, thus as an "other" space, and she is emphasizing its remoteness spatially. It is significant in this regard that the signer begins her narrative by placing the event well away from her eye gaze to the addressee. But she has a specific story to tell, and soon she brings this distant location into view. First, as shown in Figure 11a, she shifts eye gaze to the distal

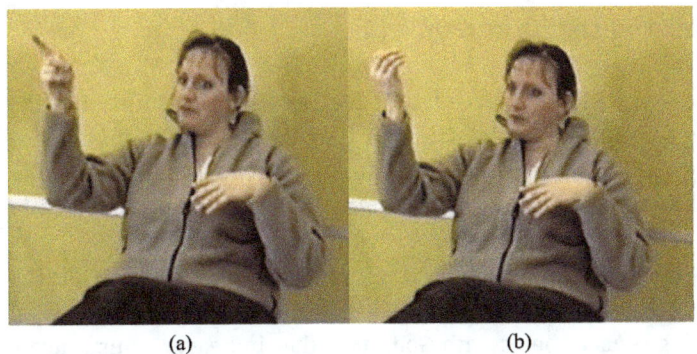

Figure 10: The signer's distal point to a past and distant location in (a); identifying the location with the NP ONTARIO in (b).

space, which indicates that it is something accessible, and then she begins the story of her father cooking dinner outside on a grill by enacting a character viewpoint of her father chopping mushrooms in Figure 11b. She has now brought the scene into a proximal, central space. It is a memory of an event presented as visible to both signer and addressee in the present narrative context, something entirely knowable.

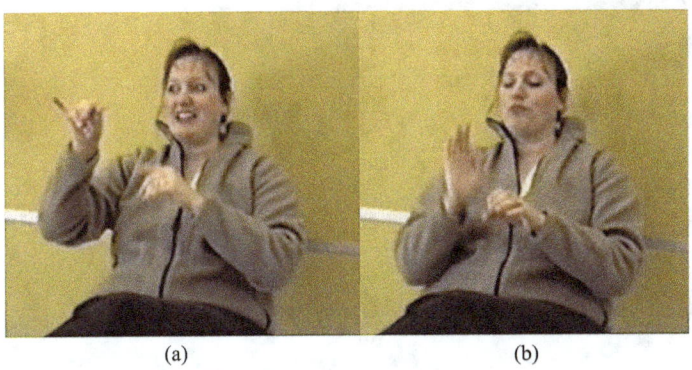

Figure 11: The signer looks at the past and distant location in (a); the signer expressing a character viewpoint in (b).

The contrast between the conceptualized distant "other" space and the proximal "knowable" space in this example is striking, but so is the fact that signers can leverage spaces to suggest a degree of knowability. Our examples show that proximal and distal spaces provide a schema expressing this aspect of conceptualization in a robust way, exemplifying the metaphor SEEING IS KNOWING. The next example further illustrates this use of space.

3.2 Conceptualizing the unknown

Around 1913 a sermon by Robert P. McGregor, a deaf lay pastor, was filmed by the National Association of the Deaf.[7] In it, McGregor first discusses the importance of Jesus' words found in the Scriptures, and second, the world becoming a smaller place as travel and communication advances bring people closer together. In each, we see examples of the CONCEPTUAL DISTANCE IS SPATIAL DISTANCE metaphor.

In the first instance, illustrated in Figure 12, McGregor signs JESUS POSS.3 WORD+ 'Jesus' words', positioning the possessive pronoun in an upward distal space, acknowledging Jesus as being with God the Father in heaven, thus conceptually distant, removed from the world. Heaven is a place not easily understood, at least not by earthly mortals until after death. It is unsurprising, then, that McGregor indexes Jesus in this distal space as in Figure 12a. However, Jesus' words are more tangible: they are written in the Scriptures, which can be held and read, and are thus entirely knowable. In Figure 12b, McGregor positions WORD+ in a proximal, accessible location that indicates their conceptual closeness to him (recall Lakoff and Johnson's KNOWN IS DOWN metaphor). Wherever Jesus himself might be, his words are well known, perceivable and tangible, held in the hand.

(a)   (b)

Figure 12: An upward distal reference to Jesus in heaven in (a); the proximal position of Jesus' words in the Scriptures as an accessible, known entity in (b).

McGregor goes on to describe the past when people couldn't connect with their spiritual brothers and sisters because the world was simply too big, and people were too far away. He makes multiple references to the vast distances in the world, repeating the sign FAR, shown in Figure 13a and b. It is significant that in Figure 13b the

---

7 hsldb.georgetown.edu/films/

signer is turned away from the distal location of FAR, further increasing the sense of inaccessibility (Figure 13c and d are discussed below).

Eye gaze itself, however, does not indicate the knowability of something distal. In Figure 14 the signer describes her family driving on the highway toward some sort of incident taking place far ahead of them. She signs WHAT'S.UP (i.e., 'what's happening?') while continuing to gaze toward the distal location. Thus, looking at a distal space where some entity has been conceptualized as located does not entail knowledge or understanding of it.

Figure 13: The world as a vast, unknowable entity in (a) and (b); in (b) McGregor accentuates this unknowable vastness with his eye gaze diverted away from the spatial position of the sign FAR. In (c) he indicates the modern world is shrinking until in (d) it is smaller, knowable, proximal.

In McGregor's sermon, after describing the far reaches of the world as unknowable places, he goes on to say, that in more recent times the ease of travel and advances in communication mean that the world is shrinking (Figure 13c), resulting in a much smaller world, (Figure 13d). Here the world is represented as small, and close: McGregor positions it directly in front of himself, perceivable and knowable. He says that now they can know their once-far brothers and sisters in Christ.

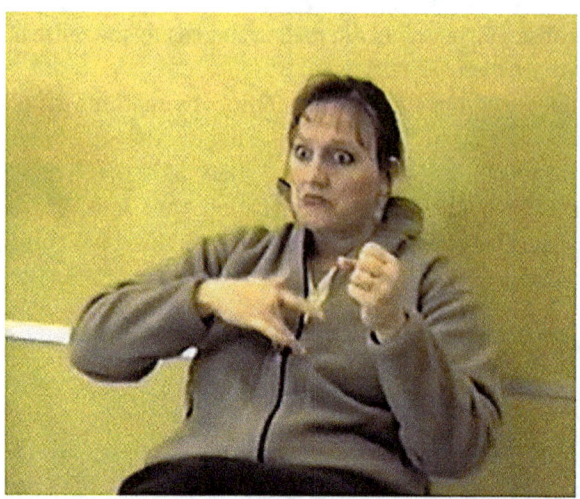

Figure 14: Eye gaze toward a distal spatial location. At this point in the narrative the signer has no idea what is taking place in that distal location.

3.3 From distal to proximal: The unknown becomes known

Summing up, we have now seen several examples that not only contrast a distal unknown space with a proximal knowable space, demonstrating that these linguistic metaphors are emblematic of the conceptual metaphor CONCEPTUAL DISTANCE IS SPATIAL DISTANCE. But more than this, in these cases, what has been unknown becomes known. In the narrative about Ontario, the signer begins with a distinctly distal location, but as the actual story begins with her father as the central character, she brings the past event into a proximal, character-viewpointed space. In McGregor's case, the once vast unknowable world is also brought into his immediate proximal space as a now knowable thing. This suggests a subjective construal of ideas and their positioning within the signer's articulation space, and also that signers can leverage this construal as once-unknown things become known to them.

4 Epistemological stance-marking

Epistemological stance-marking encompasses evidentials, epistemics, and other linguistic devices conveying attitudes toward the status of knowledge (Chafe and Nichols 1986). Here we focus on evidentials. Regardless of the language under investigation, evidentials could be argued to index a prior situation, making them deictic in nature (cf. Schlichter 1986). Importantly, evidentials denote the relative distance between the speaker and the propositional content, for example an indirect evidential might be used for something taking place outside the speaker's deictic sphere (e.g., I heard (from someone else) that it's going to rain) whereas a direct evidential would be used for something within the deictic sphere (e.g., I hear rain (myself)) (de Haan 2005). In the expression of reported speech evidentials, signers make frequent use of constructed discourse as described by Dudis (2004) and others, with their bodies as a deictic center from which to situate the content they report.

Shaffer (2012) describes how signers make use of space and their bodies to report on the stance of others. Using conceptual integration theory (Fauconnier and Turner 1996, 1998; see also Dudis 2004), she describes how ASL signers indicate the source of the evidence they have for claims they make in their discourse. An evidential is any of the set of devices in a given language used to indicate the nature of evidence for a statement and, more broadly, how a speaker chooses to mark the veracity of that statement (Chafe and Nichols 1986).

Signers create complex mental space blends (Fauconnier 1985; Fauconnier and Turner 1996, 1998, 2002) to, in essence, visually reconstruct the act of acquiring information in a physical space, along with their reaction to this new information in the following way. They shift their eye-gaze to an imagined physical space that is somewhere off-center, thus temporarily disengaging from the discourse with their interlocutor. This off-center exchange, given fully in (6), from Shaffer (2012: 142; her example 6, adapted slightly here) and shown in Figure 15b, indexes the indirect evidence, which she then brings back to the centrally located discourse as an assertion, that is, something that has now become known. The example we give here is just one of many in this data, and we see similar examples in ISL. The conceptual basis for this is brought forward in Lazard (2001):

> The opposition is not direct vs. indirect knowledge, old vs. new knowledge, or assimilated vs. unassimilated knowledge. Rather, it is an opposition at the morphosyntactic level between forms indicating nothing about the source of the information and forms referring to the source of the information without specifying it. 'Ordinary', non-evidential forms state the facts purely and simply. Evidential forms, on the other hand, point to the speaker's *becoming aware* of the facts. In the case of inference it implies 'as I infer'; in the case of unexpected perception it implies 'as I see'. The speaker is somehow split into two persons, the one speaking and the one who has heard, inferred, or perceived. (Lazard 2001: 362; italics in original)

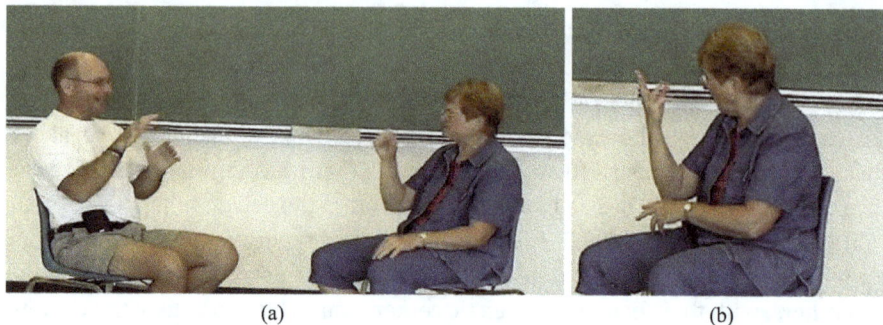

Figure 15: Direct face-to-face interaction in (a); a positional shift, including eye-gaze, to the right in (b).

(6) YES AND PRO.1 HEAR (eye-gaze shifts away from addressee) $_3$SIGN.TO$_1$ (leans forward toward right side) [#WHAT]-EMPH
(eye-gaze returns to addressee; spatial position returns to center) V-R-S (nod) START CUT.SCISSORS-lh CUT.SCISSORS-rh CUT.SCISSORS-lh
[HAPPEN SEE NAME]-TOP [KNOW WHO]-TOP
CUT.SCISSORS REFUSE ANSWER
[WHY]-TOP SOMETIMES SIT NAKED BODY, SECOND BAD SWEAR VARIOUS [TRUE]-Y/N
'Yes, and I heard, well, I was told, and was shocked to hear, that the VRS (companies) are starting to disconnect calls. If they see a name that they know they don't answer, because sometimes people have answered naked, or used profanity. Is that true?'

In (6) the signer and her addressee are discussing the use of video relay services (VRS).[8] She signs PRO.1 HEAR 'I heard...', and shifts her eye-gaze from the addressee off to the right. This off-center constructed conversation that constitutes the evidential is thus signed in an 'other' space outside her deictic sphere, following which the idea is brought back into the present, central discourse space. While the 'other' space in this example is not so much a distal space, it contrasts with the centrally-located proximal space we show as associated with known information. In the signer's perspective of the constructed dialog positioned in the off-center space, the evidential information is at first not known, but then becomes known. The change in status of the information (not known to known) corresponds to a change in spatial location.

---

8 Video relay service (VRS) is a telephone service provided to deaf individuals. The deaf person has a video camera that connects to an interpreter, who then interprets between the deaf person and hearing standard telephone users.

5 CONCEPTUAL DISTANCE IS SPATIAL DISTANCE seen in gesture

We have examined a number of examples of ISL and ASL signers' deictic referencing by positioning known elements in a close proximal space, and unknown, less known, or difficult to understand elements in a distal space. The evidential example in section 4 illustrates too that some elements that are other than the main present discourse event are positioned off to the side, away from the central discourse space. In the following sections we show that speaker/gesturers conceptualize deictic elements in ways similar to ASL and ISL signers, which are reflected in the resulting gesture spaces (see Kendon 2004, 2014).

5.1 Evidential distancing and gesture spaces

Example (7) is from a recording of a witness testifying at the West Kingston Truth Commission, which investigated an incident in the Jamaican community in 2010 (Francis 2019). According to Francis, the cross-examining counsel had asked whether the person who was the focus of the inquiry, Christopher "Dudus" Coke, had distributed treats in the local community. The Jamaican Creole multimodal response from this witness in (7) is significant in terms of the spatial positioning of her gestures.

(7) ye mi ier se chiit kiip fi di komyniti [*raised and extended hand*]
'yes I hear that treats are held for the community'

...

a jos ier mi ier [*hand moves close to speaker's body*]
'I really just hear'

In this example, the speaker refers to the community (which ostensibly she is a part of) with a raised and distally extended gesture, seen in Figure 16a. However, Francis notes that the witness distances herself from the event both by the evidential of only just having heard about it and by the accompanying gesture close to her body, shown in Figure 16b. Whether the witness was actually present when treats were given is not known but what she says and what she gestures conceptually distances herself from that community event.

The distal gesture (community event involving Dudus) and the proximal gesture (me) clearly distinguish the two aspects of the event and emphasize the speaker's claim of non-involvement.

Figure 16: A raised and extended gesture of the hand in (a); a gesture close to the body in (b) (Francis 2019, with permission).

5.2 O'Briain's wall

In a brilliant demonstration of a gesture space representing something unknowable, the Irish comedian Dara O'Briain gestures to his far right, slightly behind him, as part of his comedy sketch.[9] This text was used as one of two English texts in a study that looks at how simultaneous interpreters conceptualize the incoming (source) text as they interpret it into another language (Janzen, Shaffer and Leeson 2016; Leeson, Janzen and Shaffer 2016).

O'Briain is discussing "the wall", but his comedy sketch centers around what isn't known and in fact can't be known—he is attempting to explain electricity but can only come up with the idea that you plug things into the wall; what makes appliances actually run is just not knowable to him. Significantly, he gestures to the wall—the unknowable function of it, actually—in a distal space that he is decidedly looking away from, as in Figure 17a. But as in some of our previous examples, directing eye gaze toward the unknowable thing doesn't make it any more knowable (Figure 17b). He never does come to know how it works; perhaps staring at it will help him understand, but it does not.

Interestingly, many of the interpreters in the simultaneous interpreting study also gestured to the unknowable function of the wall in the same way, shown in Figure 17c (interpreting into Navajo) and 17d (interpreting into Spanish). Whether they were coming to this conceptualization and corresponding gesture on their own or taking their cue from O'Briain is not known.

---

9 https://www.youtube.com/watch?v=BVxOb8-d7Ic

Figure 17: Dara O'Briain gesturing to his right in (a), and looking at the gesture space in (b) (used by permission). In (c) and (d) two interpreters in the study also gesture to the rightward space as they interpret the sequence.

5.3 Chris Hadfield's son moves to China

In the same simultaneous interpreting study, the second source language text is an interview with Canadian astronaut Chris Hadfield on CBC's *The Hour*.[10] In the interview Hadfield talks about his family and at one point says, "my son moved all the way to China", which is accompanied by the gesture seen in Figure 18a. While his hands are only partly visible, we can see that he has positioned them in a proximal space in front of him (the interviewer is positioned slightly to his right; Hadfield's eye gaze shifts back and forth between the interviewer and the proximal space in front of his torso). The motivation for this proximal gesture might be that China is not an unfamiliar place to him. He has been to China and has visited his son who lives there, and while on the International Space Station he would have been able to see China as he circled the earth. Like the world for McGregor, it is a small, knowable thing.[11]

---

10 https://www.cbc.ca/strombo/videos/chris-hadfield-full-interview-strombo
11 Space does not permit further discussion of Hadfield's orientation toward his gesture space, but it appears that this is different from the type of "other" space seen in the example in Figure 15 above.

On the other hand, the ASL interpreter[12] shown in Figure 18b has indexed a high distal space for China, and her facial gestures accentuate its conceptual distance. The difference in spatial positioning for the same concept is striking, dependent on experientially-based conceptualizations of the event, illustrating different aspects of the CONCEPTUAL DISTANCE IS SPATIAL DISTANCE metaphor. That is, Hadfield's known space is proximal to him, whereas the interpreter's space reflects a lack of experiential knowledge and is distal.

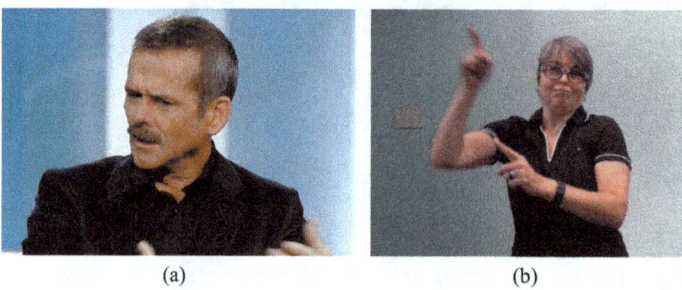

(a)   (b)

Figure 18: Canadian astronaut Chris Hadfield gesturing proximally on the talk show *The Hour* (CBC) in (a);[13] an ASL interpreter gesturing to a raised distal space as she interprets Hadfield's interview in (b).

6 Conclusions

The examples we have given of signers and gesturers indexing elements in various spaces illustrate the CONCEPTUAL DISTANCE IS SPATIAL DISTANCE metaphor. We began with examples that on a basic level map a perceived physical space relationship onto articulation space, and progressed to examples that involve a higher level of conceptualized closeness or distance, having to do with time, affinity, or involvement.

Spatial positioning in signed languages has been shown to be motivated in a number of ways, for example the several frames of reference outlined in Engberg-Pedersen (1993) including semantic affinity, where several referents are represented in the same locus because of some association or semantic resemblance.[14] This may account especially for ideas and entities closely associated with the signer

---

12 This interpreter is a fluent L2 ASL signer with over 35 years of experience as a professional interpreter.
13 https://www.youtube.com/watch?v=pVQlJeESUgo
14 See Langacker, this volume, on categorization and iconic resemblance, and the notion of "family resemblances" (p. 113).

when positioned in a proximal space, such that the affinity, or conceptual closeness, is not between two entities indexed as near one another in a proximal space, but between the signer's body and the indexed entity. Our examples further demonstrate that items perceived as knowable and located in a central, proximal location may extend the notion of affinity to subjectively construed situations that are dynamic. This is seen especially where an item or event is first conceptualized as distant, but brought to a proximal space as the signer's relationship with it changes. In some of our examples, the change in spatial location coincides with a change of focus and perspective, e.g., distally located ONTARIO followed by the past event occupying a proximal space. In other examples, the change from distal to proximal location indexes the assimilation of new information (Lazard 2001), as with the signer not knowing if what she sees on the mountain distally is really snow, but having arrived at the top she confirms that it is. This new information is now indexed proximally, and elaborates the findings of P. Wilcox (2000), discussed in section 3.1 above.

Linguistic expressions in ASL and ISL that exemplify the CONCEPTUAL DISTANCE IS SPATIAL DISTANCE metaphor show a complicated relationship between the use of space and temporal referencing. In both ASL and ISL it is well recognized that the past is referenced as behind the signer and the future in front of the signer along a so-called time line, but the indexing of past events in a perceivable, proximal space directly in front of the signer suggests a complex conceptualization for signers, which is not unlike ways that past events have been reported for other languages in terms of speakers' gestures. For example Moroccan Arabic speakers, described as placing emphasis on past events and relationships (de la Fuente, Santiago, Román, Dumitrache, and Casasanto 2014), gesture about past events in a frontal, proximal location as a means of focus. Similarly, Ferreira-Brito (1984) reports that Urubu-Kaapor Sign Language signers position the past in front of them and the future behind them. Núñez and Sweetser (2006) propose that Aymara speakers position the past conceptually in front of them precisely because it is known and can be seen. The frontal, proximal positioning of past event scenes in some of our examples indicates that the relationship between time and spatial indexing in ASL and ISL is not straightforward. Spatial locational choices are influenced by the signer's construal of the event on a realis/irrealis cline, but also by the embodied expression of the relationship between time and space itself.[15]

---

[15] One of our reviewers commented that the central, proximal space is a kind of "default" space for signers—this is where the bulk of signed language articulation takes place. We contend, however, that signers almost always have locational choices. Our study shows that in these discourse examples, a central, proximal location is a motivated choice, not a default. Perhaps it is the case that the frequency with which signers engage in these types of discourse leads to the entrenchment and

Returning to the ideas of "neutral space" in 2.1 and arbitrary positioning in 2.2 above, we have seen more evidence from our examples that the central, proximal space the signer employs holds significance along the dimension of known/unknown information, where positioning elements outside this proximal space extends to something other than "what I know", for example to items difficult to conceptualize, the remote past as distinct from the present, and evidential sources construed as not germane to the present discourse situation. While not explored explicitly in this study, it would seem that such proximal/distal indexing is salient for the addressee along with the signer, who also has a view on the signer's space. The signer's spatial choices are thus intersubjective because they intend the addressee to understand the degree of construed knowability, and so to see the construed narrative world similarly. For this to take place, the pattern of usage must be conventionalized to the extent that both signer and addressee make similar inferences regarding the meaning of the use of space.

Notation key

ISL and ASL signs are in uppercase glosses. PRO.1/PRO.2/PRO.3 are first, second and third person pronouns. POSS.1/POSS.2/POSS.3 are possessive pronouns. Glosses of more than one word for a single sign have words separated by a period, e.g., WHATS.UP. Plus signs indicate repeated movement, e.g., DIFFERENT++. Fingerspelled words are indicated by letters separated by dashes, e.g., S-N-O-W. $_3$SIGN.TO$_1$ indicates that the sign moves from a 3s referent to a 1s referent. #WHAT is a "borrowed fingerspelling" that is not conventionally fingerspelled but is considered more sign-like. 'rt' means positioned or moving rightward; 'lt' means positioned or moving leftward. 'rh' is right hand; 'lh' is left hand. Following square brackets, –EMPH indicates that the content of the brackets is signed emphatically, -TOP indicates a topic-marked phrase, and –Y/N marks a yes/no question.

---

conventionalization of this use of space, thus it emerges as an (assumed) grammatical structure, but this needs to be investigated further.

References

Barberà Altimira, Gemma. 2015. *The Meaning of Space in Sign Language: Reference, Specificity and Structure in Catalan Sign Language Discourse*. Berlin: de Gruyter/Ishara Press.
Chafe, Wallace. 1994. *Discourse, Consciousness, and Time: The Flow and Displacement of Conscious Experience in Speaking and Writing*. Chicago and London: The University of Chicago Press.
Chafe, Wallace & Johanna Nichols. 1986. Introduction. In Wallace Chafe & Johanna Nichols (eds.), *Evidentiality: The Linguistic Coding of Epistemology*, vii-xi. Norwood, NJ: Ablex.
de Haan, Ferdinand. 2005. Encoding speaker perspective: Evidentials. In Zygmunt Frajzyngier, Adam Hodges & David S. Rood (eds.), *Linguistic Diversity and Language Theories*, 399–422. Amsterdam/Philadelphia: John Benjamins.
de Jorio, Andrea. 2000 [1832]. *Gesture in Naples and Gesture in Classical Antiquity: A Translation of La mimica degli antichi investigata nel gestire napoletano, Gestural Expression of the Ancients in the Light of Neapolitan Gesturing, and with an Introduction and Notes by Adam Kendon* (translated by Adam Kendon). Bloomington, IN: Indiana University Press.
de la Fuente, Juanma, Julio Santiago, Antonio Román, Cristina Dumitrache & Daniel Casasanto. 2014. When you think about it, your past is in front of you: How culture shapes spatial conceptions of time. *Psychological Science* 25(9). 1682–1690.
de Vos, Connie & Roland Pfau. 2015. Sign language typology: The contribution of rural sign languages. *Annual Review of Linguistics* 1. 265–288.
DeMatteo, Asa. 1977. Visual imagery and visual analogues in American Sign Language. In Lynn A. Friedman (ed.), *On the Other Hand: New Perspectives on American Sign Language*, 109–137. New York: Academic Press.
Dudis, Paul G. 2004. Body partitioning and real-space blends. *Cognitive Linguistics* 15(2). 223–238.
Emmorey, Karen, David Corina & Ursula Bellugi. 1995. Differential processing of topographic and referential functions of space. In Karen Emmorey & Judy Reilly (eds.), *Language, Gesture, and Space*, 43–62. Hillsdale NJ: Lawrence Erlbaum.
Emmorey, Karen, Edward Klima & Gregory Hickok. 1998. Mental rotation within linguistic and non-linguistic domains in users of American Sign Language. *Cognition* 68. 221–246.
Engberg-Pedersen, Elisabeth. 1993. *Space in Danish Sign Language: The Semantics and Morphosyntax of the Use of Space in a Visual Language*. Hamburg: SIGNUM-Press.
Fauconnier, Gilles. 1985. *Mental Spaces*. Cambridge, MA: MIT Press.
Fauconnier, Gilles & Mark Turner. 1996. Blending as a central process of grammar. In Adele Goldberg (ed.), *Conceptual Structure, Discourse, and Language*, 113–130. Stanford, CA: Center for the Study of Language and Information.
Fauconnier, Gilles & Mark Turner. 1998. Conceptual integration networks. *Cognitive Science* 22(2). 133–187.
Fauconnier, Gilles & Mark Turner. 2002. *The Way We Think: Conceptual Blending and the Mind's Hidden Complexities*. New York, NY: Basic Books.
Ferreira-Brito, Lucinda. 1984. Similarities and differences in two Brazilian sign languages. *Sign Language Studies* 42. 45–56.
Foran, Christopher. 1994. *Dictionary of the Methodic Irish Sign Language. A Transcript of the 1847 Manuscript*. Dublin: Dublin Deaf Association.
Francis, Tasheney. 2019. "I can't say if I didn't see"- Resident witness' avoidant strategies in the West Kingston Truth Commission. Presentation, Department of Linguistics, University of Manitoba, 28 November 2019.

Friedman, Lynn A. 1975. Space, time, and person reference in American Sign Language. *Language* 51(4). 940–961.
Givón, T. 1984. *Syntax: A Functional-Typological Introduction, Volume 1*. Amsterdam/ Philadelphia: John Benjamins.
Jacobowitz, E. Lynn & William C. Stokoe. 1988. Signs of tense in ASL verbs. *Sign Language Studies* 60. 331–340.
Janzen, Terry. 2004. Space rotation, perspective shift, and verb morphology in ASL. *Cognitive Linguistics* 15(2). 149–174.
Janzen, Terry. 2005. *Perspective Shift Reflected in the Signer's Use of Space*. CDS/CLCS Monograph Number 1, Centre for Deaf Studies, University of Dublin Trinity College, Dublin, Ireland.
Janzen, Terry. 2012. Two ways of conceptualizing space: Motivating the use of static and rotated vantage point space in ASL discourse. In Barbara Dancygier & Eve Sweetser (eds.), *Viewpoint in Language: A Multimodal Perspective*, 156–174. Cambridge: Cambridge University Press.
Janzen, Terry. 2019. Shared spaces, shared mind: Connecting past and present viewpoints in American Sign Language narratives. *Cognitive Linguistics* 30(2). 253–279.
Janzen, Terry, Barbara Shaffer & Lorraine Leeson. 2016. Do interpreters draw meaning from a speaker's multimodal text? Paper presented at the International Society for Gesture Studies (ISGS) 7, Sorbonne Paris 3, Paris, France, July 18–22, 2016.
Kendon, Adam. 2004. *Gesture: Visible Action as Utterance*. Cambridge: Cambridge University Press.
Kendon, Adam. 2014. Semiotic diversity in utterance production and the concept of 'language'. *Philosophical Transactions of the Royal Society B* 369: 201130293. 1–13.
Klima, Edward S. & Ursula Bellugi. 1979. *The Signs of Language*. Cambridge, MA: Harvard University Press.
Kuhn, Jeremy. 2016. ASL loci: Variables or features? *Journal of Semantics* 33(3), 449–491.
Lakoff, George & Mark Johnson. 1980. *Metaphors We Live By*. Chicago: The University of Chicago Press.
Lazard, Gilbert. 2001. On the grammaticalization of evidentiality. *Journal of Pragmatics* 33. 358–368.
Leeson, Lorraine, Terry Janzen & Barbara Shaffer. 2012. Motivations underlying pronoun location in two signed languages. Paper presented at Language, Culture and Mind V, Catholic University of Portugal, June 27–29, 2012.
Leeson, Lorraine, Terry Janzen & Barbara Shaffer. 2016. Leveraging visual conceptualization for interpreting practice: Visualization and gesture during message processing. Paper presented at Critical Link 8, Hariot Watt University, Edinburgh, Scotland, June 29 – July 1, 2016.
Leeson, Lorraine, Barbara Shaffer & Terry Janzen. 2018. Does signed language grammar include gesture? Cape Town, South Africa. Paper presented at International Society for Gesture Studies (ISGS) 8, July 4–8, 2018.
Leeson, Lorraine & John I. Saeed. 2012. *Irish Sign Language: A Cognitive Linguistic Account*. Edinburgh: Edinburgh University Press.
Liddell, Scott K. 1990. Four functions of a locus: Reexamining the structure of space in ASL. In Ceil Lucas (ed.), *Sign Language Research: Theoretical Issues*, 176–198. Washington, DC: Gallaudet University Press.
Liddell, Scott K. 1995. Real, surrogate, and token space: Grammatical consequences in ASL. In Karen Emmorey & Judy S. Reilly (eds.), *Language, Gesture, and Space*, 19–41. Hillsdale, NJ: Lawrence Erlbaum.
Liddell, Scott K. 2003. *Grammar, Gesture, and Meaning in American Sign Language*. Cambridge: Cambridge University Press.
Lillo-Martin, Diane. 1995. The point of view predicate in American Sign Language. In Karen Emmory & Judy S. Reilly (eds.), *Language, Gesture, and Space*, 155–170. Hillsdale NJ: Lawrence Erlbaum.

Lillo-Martin, Diane & Jon Gajewski. 2014. One grammar or two? Sign languages and the nature of human language. *WIREs Cognitive Science* 5. 387–401. doi: 10.1002/wcs.1297

Long, J. Schuyler. 1918. *The Sign Language: A Manual of Signs*, 2nd edn. Omaha, NB: Dorothy Long Thompson.

McNeill, David. 1992. *Hand and Mind: What Gestures Reveal About Thought*. Chicago: University of Chicago Press.

Meir, Irit, Carol A. Padden, Mark Aronoff & Wendy Sandler. 2007. Body as subject. *Journal of Linguistics* 43. 531–563.

Metzger, Melanie, 1995. Constructed dialogue and constructed action in American Sign Language. In Ceil Lucas (ed.), *Sociolinguistics in Deaf Communities*, 255–271. Washington, DC: Gallaudet University Press.

Núñez, Rafael E. & Eve Sweetser. 2006. With the future behind them: Convergent evidence from Aymara language and gesture in the crosslinguistic comparison of spatial construals of time. *Cognitive Science* 30. 401–450.

Oomen, Marloes & Vadim Kimmelman. 2019. Body-anchored verbs and argument omission in two sign languages. *Glossa* 4(1), 42. 1–36. DOI: https://doi.org/10.5334/gjgl.741

Parrill, Fey. 2012. Interactions between discourse status and viewpoint in co-speech gesture. In Barbara Dancygier & Eve Sweetser (eds.), *Viewpoint in Language: A Multimodal Perspective*, 97–112. Cambridge: Cambridge University Press.

Perniss, Pamela M. 2007a. Achieving spatial coherence in German Sign Language: The use of classifiers and perspective. *Lingua* 117(7). 1315–1338. doi.org/10.1016/j.lingua.2005.06.013

Perniss, Pamela M. 2007b. *Space and Iconicity in German Sign Language (DGS)*. MPI Series in Psycholinguistics.

Perniss, Pamela M. 2007c. Locative functions of simultaneous perspective constructions in German Sign Language narratives. In Myriam Vermeerbergen, Lorraine Leeson & Onno Crasborn (eds.), *Simultaneity in Signed Languages: Form and Function*, 27–54. Amsterdam/Philadelphia: John Benjamins.

Prince, Ellen. 1981. Toward a taxonomy of given-new information. In Peter Cole (ed.), *Radical Pragmatics*, 223–255. New York: Academic Press.

Sandler, Wendy & Diane Lillo-Martin. 2006. *Sign Languages and Linguistic Universals*. Cambridge: Cambridge University Press.

Schlichter, Alice. 1986. The origin and deictic nature of Winto evidentials. In Wallace Chafe & Johanna Nichols (eds.), *Evidentiality: The Linguistic Coding of Epistemology*, 46–59. Norwood, NJ: Ablex.

Shaffer, Barbara. 2012. Reported speech as an evidentiality strategy in American Sign Language. In Barbara Dancygier & Eve Sweetser (eds.), *Viewpoint in Language: A Multimodal Perspective*, 139–155. Cambridge: Cambridge University Press.

Shaffer, Barbara & Terry Janzen. 2016. Modality and mood in American Sign Language. In Jan Nuyts & Johan van der Auwera (eds.). *The Oxford Handbook of Mood and Modality*, 448–469. Oxford: Oxford University Press.

Shaffer, Barbara, Lorraine Leeson & Terry Janzen. 2017. What I know is here; what I don't know is somewhere else: Deixis and gesture spaces in American Sign Language and Irish Sign Language. Paper presented at the International Cognitive Linguistics Conference (ICLC) 14, Tartu, Estonia, July 10–14, 2017.

Stokoe, William C. Jr. 2005 [1960]. Sign language structure: An outline of the visual communication systems of the American deaf. *Journal of Deaf Studies and Deaf Education* 10(1). 3–37.

Stokoe, William C. Jr., Dorothy C. Casterline & Carl G. Croneberg. 1965. *A Dictionary of American Sign Language on Linguistic Principles*. Washington, DC: Gallaudet College Press.

Sutton-Spence, Rachel & Bencie Woll. 1998. *The Linguistics of British Sign Language: An Introduction*. Cambridge: Cambridge University Press.

Uyechi, Linda. 1996. *The Geometry of Visual Phonology*. Stanford, CA: CSLI Publications.

Wilcox, Phyllis Perrin. 2000. *Metaphor in American Sign Language*. Washington, DC: Gallaudet University Press.

Wilcox, Sherman & Corrine Occhino. 2016. Constructing signs: Place as a symbolic structure in signed languages. *Cognitive Linguistics* 27. 371–404.

Wilcox, Sherman & Phyllis Perrin Wilcox. 2015. In Bernd Heine & Heiko Narrog (eds.), *The Oxford Handbook of Linguistic Analysis*, 2nd edn., 843–863. Oxford: Oxford University Press.

Winston, Elizabeth A. 1995. Spatial mapping in comparative discourse frames. In Karen Emmorey & Judy S. Reilly (eds.), *Language, Gesture, and Space*, 88–114. Hillsdale NJ: Lawrence Erlbaum.

Darren Saunders and Anne-Marie Parisot

Insights on the use of narrative perspectives in signed and spoken discourse in Quebec Sign Language, American Sign Language, and Quebec French

1 Introduction

This chapter presents an overall analysis of the integration of enactment structures within signed and spoken discourse, and how theoretical perspectives on enactment (also known as constructed action *inter alia*) can be applied, including that of cognitive linguistics. In Section 3, we present an overall analysis of the presence and forms of enactment, as well as types of markers. In Section 4, based on the various forms of enactment, we discuss the use of gestures within these structures which are frequently integrated with lexicon as part of the process of producing two perspectives simultaneously; these are the perspective of the narrator, either signed or spoken, and that of the actant, whose role the narrator assumes during enactment. The languages described in this chapter are: 1) Quebec Sign Language (langue des signes québécoise, or LSQ), as produced by L1 signers and L2 signers with American Sign Language (ASL) or spoken French as their first language; 2) ASL (L1 signers); and 3) Quebec French (L1 speakers). We discuss the use of gestures in Section 5 and the challenges of including gestural aspects of enactment in linguistic models. In Section 6 we discuss formal linguistics as well as cognitive linguistics as theoretical approaches to the topic. We conclude with a proposal to base enactment analyses, which include both lexical and gestural elements, on the Langackerian complex symbol unit structure, as this allows both elements to be integrated into one complex unit.

2 Enactments

Enactments have been identified in signed language linguistics research as a phenomenon in signed languages where the signers *assume* the role of an actant in order to illustrate what the actant has done or said. This is comparable to the use of direct discourse or reported speech in spoken languages, where an utterance is

Darren Saunders, Université du Québec à Montréal, Canada, e-mail: saunders.daz@uqam.ca
Anne-Marie Parisot, Université du Québec à Montréal, Canada, e-mail: parisot.anne-marie@uqam.ca

reproduced by speakers to illustrate what has been said or thought. With the use of deictics within reported speech, the first person is understood to represent not the speaker who is reproducing an utterance, but the original person who produced the utterance (Engberg-Pedersen 1995; Lillo-Martin 2012).

We use the word "reconstruction" here as the utterances are not verbatim duplications but are instead *constructed dialogue* (Tannen 2007). This (re)construction of an utterance can be marked by a change in prosodic features in order to highlight that the original utterance is that of the actant and not the speaker (Couper-Kuhlen 1999). Furthermore, the (re)constructed utterance can be accompanied by gestures that may have accompanied the original utterance:

(1)   (gesture: "sticking a card into")
    But then they're like "Stick this card into this machine."

(Streeck 2002: 584)

In (1) we can see that, while reproducing the original utterance, the speaker attempts to simultaneously *emulate* the accompanying gestures. In signed language research, enactments have been analysed and identified under a number of nomenclatures with varying descriptions. Mandel (1977) identified enactment as an iconic device of *role switching*, highlighting the use of body and head position to mark the change of discursive roles when the signer switches from the role of narrator to that of actant. Loew (1984) identified it as *roleplay* where the signer "takes the role" of an actant, whereas Padden (1986) termed it *role shifting* where each actant is identified by a specific body position in a signed discourse to reconstruct an exchange of dialogue between the two actants. Padden asserts that *role shifting* is of a linguistic nature, refuting the theatral or mimical connotations associated with the phenomenon. However, Winston (1991) discusses the theatral value of it, qualifying it as *performative* where an event can be reported through the use of the characteristics of an actant and through the reproduction of his/her actions.

Furthermore, the notion of shifting as suggested by Padden (1986) is maintained by Poulin and Miller (1995) who address this as *referential shift*, spotlighting that the body of the signer is shifted to indicate that the actant, as a referent, is assumed. Different from Tannen's proposition of identifying constructed dialogue in speech, Metzger (1995) and Liddell and Metzger (1998) argue that it should be addressed as *constructed action* and that constructed dialogue is subsumed under this nomenclature. These authors stress that constructed action is where the utterances (signed or spoken), actions and attitudes of the actant are reconstructed to illustrate an event. In an example provided by Metzger (1995), an ASL signer assumes, or incarnates, the behaviours of the actant, Baker, in the first person, and presents Baker's actions, attitudes and utterances:

(2) to addressee   gaze forward to up left   lower lip extended/head tilt/gaze up left
MAN   CARD-IN-HAND   LOOK-UP,   "THAT (raise hand) THAT PRO.1"
'So one of the guys at the table says, "Yeah, I'm Baker, that's me".'
(Metzger 1995: 263)

The reconstitution of the signed utterance "Yeah, I'm Baker, that's me" includes other information such as the attitude, behaviour and actions of the actant, which is comparable to the prosodic effects as produced in reported speech in spoken languages (Couper-Kuhlen 1999).

Finally, this phenomenon has been identified by Ferrara and Johnston (2014) as *enactment*, proposing that gestural elements, which are frequently found in constructed action in Australian Sign Language (Auslan), are an integral part of the language. They argue that enactments "are considered partial demonstrations of behaviour – be it language (i.e., CD [constructed dialogue]) or non-linguistic action (i.e., CA [constructed action]). These demonstrations allow a speaker or signer to *show* rather than *tell* about an event" (Ferrara and Johnston 2014: 197; italics in original). This description of enactment corresponds to Clark's (1996) third way of signaling in communicating using linguistic and non-linguistic elements: *describe*, *indicate* and *demonstrate*. Enactment, or constructed action, is the signers (and speakers) demonstrating, or depicting, the actions of the others. For the sake of clarity and coherence, the term *enactment* will be used to discuss its nature and its theoretical implications in this chapter.

3 Presence of enactment and its markers

In this section, we present a portrait of the use of enactment in signed and spoken discourse. All the results presented here for LSQ (L1 and L2), ASL (L1), and French (L1) discourse are based on a dataset drawn from the *Projet Marqspat* corpus under the auspices of *Groupe de recherche sur la LSQ et le bilinguisme sourd*, at Université du Québec à Montréal (UQAM). *Projet Marqspat* is a corpus of spoken/signed data produced in four languages (LSQ, ASL, English and French) where all participants were exposed to the same elicitation conditions, including a four-hour test aimed at the production of specific morphosyntactic, semantic and discursive structures within an elicitation setting. All participants were exposed to forty-four video sketches without use of language, presenting different scenarios produced by actors. These were calibrated to elicit the linguistic expression of different concepts (quantity, point of view, etc.) and of different types of events such as descriptive or narrative events (Parisot et al. 2008; Parisot and Saunders 2019). The discourse data were collected from five groups of signers/speakers, with three participants in each group:

1) Deaf signers using LSQ as L1,
2) Deaf signers using LSQ as L2, who have ASL as L1,
3) Deaf signers using LSQ as L2, who have spoken French as L1,
4) Deaf signers using ASL as L1,
5) Non-deaf speakers having Quebec French as L1.[1]

In order to enable us to make comparisons between groups with varying discourse durations, our analysis of the presence of enactment structures is based on the ratio of enactment duration (total time when enactment was adopted and used) to discourse duration (the time to complete the narration after viewing the stimulus).

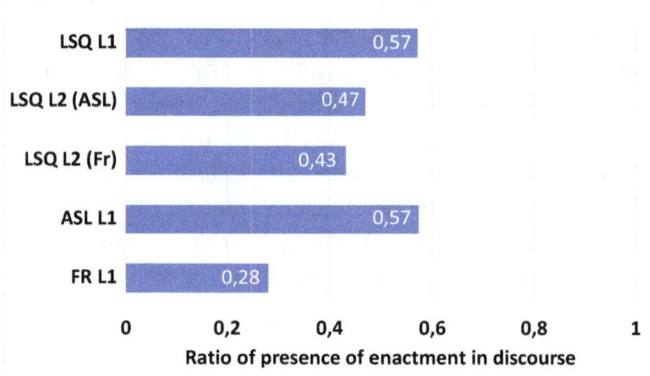

Figure 1: Ratio of duration enactment within discourse.

For the five groups analyzed regarding enactment, the comparison of the presence of enactment in Figure 1 shows that:
1) enactment is more present in signed than spoken discourse, and
2) enactment is more present in native signer discourse than in second language signer discourse, regardless of the first language of the signer producing the discourse.

Using the duration when enactment structures were present as well as the duration when enactments were not present, χ^2 tests were used to determine if there

---

1 For the first four groups, enactment was analyzed by Saunders (2016), Saunders and Parisot (2016), and Parisot and Saunders (2019). Enactments produced by the fifth group were analyzed by Parisot and Saunders (2022).

were any significant differences between the presence of enactment used in all five groups. Since there are no significant differences between LSQ-L1 (group 1) and ASL-L1 (group 4), where in both groups a similar proportion of time is occupied by enactment, the significant differences between LSQ-L1 and ASL-L1 are noted compared to the other three groups[2] (for more specific results, see Parisot and Saunders, 2022; Saunders and Parisot 2016).

Saunders (2016) proposes a description of the markers that are identified in the literature as being part of enactment structure as visual markers that enable the interlocutors to identify when the signer assumes a certain perspective, thus shifting away from the perspective of the narrator to that of the actant or vice versa (see also Thumann 2010 on the use of depiction by L2 ASL signers). The markers described by Saunders are head and body position, eye gaze, facial expression, hand and arm gestures, all of which are employed to represent the perspective of the actant. Not all markers are always manifested concomitantly. The following table is a summary suggested by Liddell and Metzger (1998) outlining the function of each enactment marker when used in a discourse:

Table 1: Summary of enactment markers (adapted from Liddell and Metzger 1998: 672).

Enactment markers	What they indicate
Articulation of words or signs or emblems	What the actant says or thinks
Direction of head and eye gaze	Direction actant is looking
Facial expressions of affect, effort, etc.	How the actant feels
Gestures of hands and arms	Gestures produced by the actant

3.1 Head and body position change

Mandel (1977) identifies head and body as two markers to highlight the presence of enactment in ASL, outlining the change of body or head position to indicate the distinction between the signer as narrator and that of actant. It was highlighted that head position change is more significant when the body is not used to mark enactments and that the head can be used to replace the body (Loew 1984). The rotational shift of the head and body is identified as a means to show that each person is saying something to the other in a constructed dialogue, and enables the interlocutors to recognize *who* is saying *what* (Padden 1986).

---

2 LSQ L1 vs. LSQ L2(ASL): χ^2=7.58, df=1, p=0.006; LSQ L1 vs. LSQ L2(Fr): χ^2=28.96, df=1, p<0.001; and LSQ L1 vs. Quebec French: χ^2=76.03, df=1, p<0.0001.

Working with the presence of markers (that is, working with the duration of enactments), head positions were used globally for all enactment structures in LSQ discourse, while body positions were used as enactment markers for 92% of enactments (Saunders 2016; Saunders and Parisot 2016). Similar results were found among ASL signers even though the use of the body occurred less (87%) than for LSQ signers (Parisot and Saunders 2019). Example (3) illustrates head and body positions used to indicate the action of being surprised in the enactment in the photo on the right. The photos in (3) show the modification of the head and body position from the non-enactment photo on the left, to the enactment in the photo on the right.

(3) LSQ (Projet Marqspat, 13LSQL1vidéo13, 01:21)[3,4]

 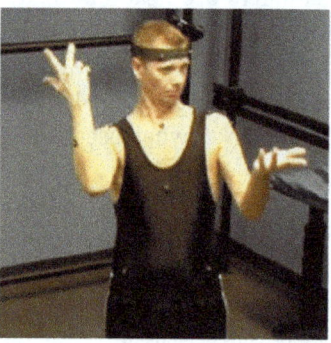

           MAN   SURPRISE

          Enactment$_j$ (with head and body shift)
MAN$_i$ BALD SURPRISE
'The bald man was taken by surprise.'

Example (4) illustrates a perspective change via enactment in the Quebec French group, where in 64% of cases we see a shift in head position and in 72% of cases, a shift in body position. This is less frequent than the LSQ and ASL L1 signers.[5] This

---

3 Examples 3, 4, 5, 8, 9, 11, 17, 18 and 19 are available in video format for viewing online: https://doi.org/10.5683/SP2/DSZXKL.
4 Glosses in capital letters denote lexical signs in both LSQ and ASL. Simultaneous information appears above the glosses, e.g., an enactment co-occurring with SURPRISE in this example.
5 The percentages given here differ from Parisot and Saunders (2022), where the comparison between Quebec French and LSQ L1 groups involved a different statistical process. The above is based on the presence of enactments (duration) whereas the results in Parisot and Saunders (2022) are based on tokens. In this study, based on tokens, the differences between LSQ and Quebec French speakers are presented differently: Head positions in the LSQ dataset were used for 47% of enactments whereas the body was used for 46%, and the French speakers used head position for 65%

reveals that enactments amongst Quebec French speakers can be produced without head and body position shifts as, for example, in (5).

(4) French (Projet Marqspat, 01FRblocA4, 57:34)

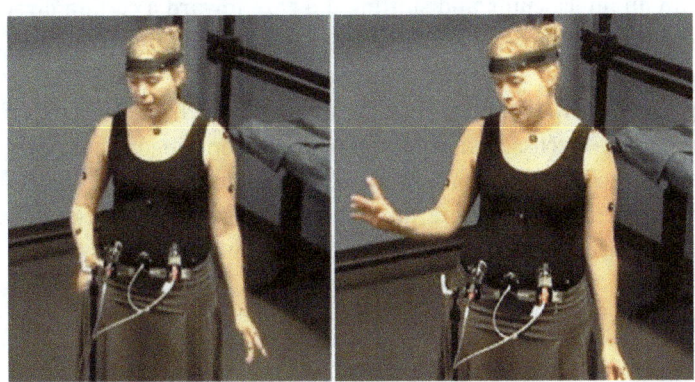

Enactment$_j$ (with body and head shift)
Il y a une première cliente$_i$ qui rentre, qui regarde un peu la table de chaussures...
'There is a first customer who enters, looking at the table with shoes...'

(5) French (Marqspat, 01FRblocA8a, 01:26)

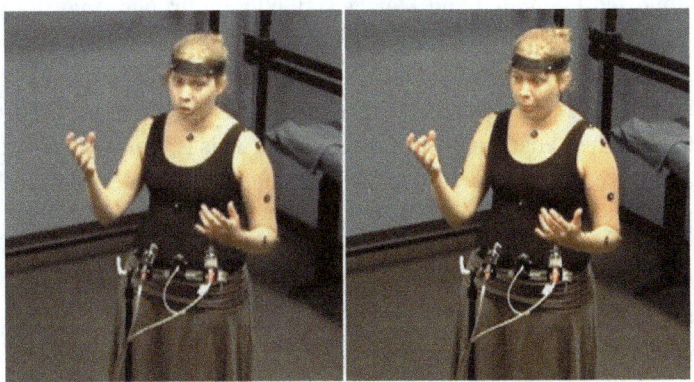

Enactment$_i$
Ah non, chus$_i$ en train de manger une de tes pommes
'Oh no, I$_i$'m eating one of your apples'

---

of enactments and body for 48%. We therefore distinguish the presence of a phenomenon (ratio of time in discourse) from its frequency (ratio of occurrence of enactment in discourse).

3.2 Eye gaze

Eye gaze and facial expressions are also identified as enactment markers (Loew 1984; Padden 1986, 1990). Eye gaze during enactments is described as discontinuing eye contact with an interlocutor, and shifting the gaze toward a certain direction, that is, what the actant is looking at (Meier 1990; Poulin and Miller 1995), be it an object, or another person in the constructed event.

Excluding partial non-dominant enactment forms, which are very rare in the data (this form will be discussed later in Section 3), discontinued eye contact with the interlocutor (based on duration), occurred throughout the enactment structures in LSQ (Saunders 2016; Saunders and Parisot 2016), with similar results found for the ASL group (Parisot and Saunders 2019). A frequency analysis (working with tokens) in Parisot and Saunders (2022) also shows that the regularity of discontinued eye contact with the interlocutor is found to be similar in L1 LSQ and L1 Quebec French.

3.3 Facial expressions

Facial expression is considered a means by which the signer can reveal the perspective, which may include the opinion, of the actant during enactments (Loew 1984). This idea is supported by Liddell and Metzger (1998) who propose that the facial expressions employed by the signer during enactment reflect the emotions felt by the actant. However, while Meier (1990) considers the use of facial expression as optional, Padden (1986) states that facial expressions ("face configuration") are not likely to be neutral when enactments are used in ASL. This is the case particularly when the facial expression is the only marker of enactment, and body and head shifts are not present as markers.

Ninety-eight percent of the enactment structures (excluding partial non-dominant forms) were supported by the use of facial expressions to recreate the reported events in LSQ (Saunders 2016; Saunders and Parisot 2016). ASL signers were reported to have 92% of enactment structures supported by facial expressions as a marker (Parisot and Saunders 2019). However, in comparing the LSQ and Quebec French groups, using a frequency approach (based on tokens), the use of facial expressions to represent the character is significantly more present in LSQ (47%) than in French (15%), which is significant using tokens with a factorial ANOVA analysis ($p<.0001$) (Parisot and Saunders 2022).

3.4 Hands and arms

Cormier, Smith and Sevcikova-Sehyr (2015) identify the use of hands and arms as a marker for enactments in enabling interlocutors to identify that expressed utterances and actions are those of the actant and not the signer. Loew (1984) states that it is precise prosodic changes of the hands that can be used to denote that the utterances and actions are those of the actant. Liddell and Metzger (1998) suggest that the hands can be used in different ways: to represent the hands of the actant as a linguistic medium to reconstruct utterances or to represent thoughts, and that the hands can be used as a gestural medium to reconstruct actions.

When comparing the use of hands and arms as markers for enactment, Parisot and Saunders (2022) find that Quebec French speakers (64% based on a frequency analysis) do this twice as much as the LSQ signers (33%). These authors hypothesize that the hands and arms are used more frequently in narration in LSQ, with partial dominant enactment forms most used by this group. Quebec French speakers, however, have the potential to use their hands and arms to reconstruct actants' gestures and actions while they provide narration in the auditory-oral modality.

4 Enactment forms

Enactment structures have been also described according to the various stages or "degrees" to which the perspective of the actant is embedded. Three levels of embedding can be distinguished:
1) when the event is reported completely through an enactment, which is in the perspective of the actant (complete enactment),
2) when an event is fully reported, but not completely through an enactment while narration is present simultaneously (partial dominant enactment),
3) when an event is reported partially in an enactment, but the perspective presented principally is that of the narrator (partial non-dominant enactment).

Various terms have been proposed as presented in Table 2 for comparison. For clarity, in this chapter, we use the terms proposed by Saunders (2016) and Saunders and Parisot (2016) highlighting the presence of enactment structure and the degree to which such phenomena occur as partial forms (dominant and non-dominant). This is discussed in sections 4.2 and 4.3.

Table 2: Terms proposed for different enactment forms.

	1	2	3
Saunders (2016)	Complete	Partial dominant	Partial non-dominant
Metzger (1995)	Direct action	Simultaneous direct and indirect action	Indirect constructed action
Cormier, Smith & Sevcikova-Sehyr (2015)	Complete	Reduced	Subtle

4.1 Complete enactment

This form is identified by Metzger (1995) as "direct action", highlighting that the actions depicted using the signer's body, head, facial expressions, and eye gaze represent those of the actant. Metzger acknowledges that this can often be seen as mime and can be difficult for L2 learners of ASL to use. Cormier, Smith and Sevcikova-Sehyr (2015) provide examples of this form where the signers express enactment wholly from the perspective of the actant, including the use of lexical material (signs), gestures (both manual and non-manual), and prosody (facial expressions and manner of movement) to represent the actant. Saunders (2016) highlights this form as sequential in nature, where the perspective of the narrator is shifted wholly to that of the actant for all enactment markers (without any comments or remarks from the narrator during the enactment) before reverting back to narrator at the end of the structure in LSQ. The sequential nature of this form is illustrated with examples in LSQ.

(6) LSQ (adapted from Poulin and Miller 1995: 121)

   <u>Enactment$_k$</u>
   INDEX$_{1k}$ HOLIDAY INDEX$_{1k}$ TRIP INDEX$_{1k}$ SON WITH
   'I'm on holiday, on a trip with my son.'

(7) <u>Enactment$_j$ (Action of taking cheese and putting it in the barrel)</u>
   TAKE CHEESE PUT-CHEESE-IN-BARREL
   '(She$_j$) took the cheese and put in the barrel.'

   (adapted from Poulin and Miller 1995: 122)

These two examples illustrate the use of complete enactment maintained during the utterance in (6) and the actions of an actant in (7). In (7) the signer wholly represents the actant putting the cheese in the barrel. More precisely, the movement of the hands (and arms) in these two examples is that of the actant where the actant's utterance is being expressed (6) and their actions are being reconstructed in (7).

Complete enactment is also found in Quebec French discourse, along with speech in (8) where the words, body, hands, face, and voice represent those of the actant, or with no speech in (9), where the voice (rattling sound), body, hands and face, are those of the actant.

(8) French (Projet Marqspat, 03FRblocB9, 04:18)

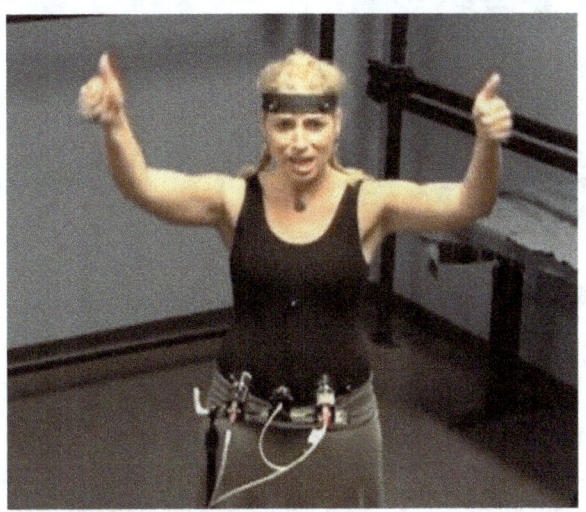

Pis lui$_i$ dans son kayac, le cabochon,
'And, in his kayak, the idiot,

              Enactment$_i$
il était là   « c'est beau Geneviève, t'as surfé sur la vague, c'est beau! »
he was like: "That's good Geneviève, you've surfed on the wave, that's good!"'

(9) French (Projet Marqspat, 03FRblocB9, 04:48)

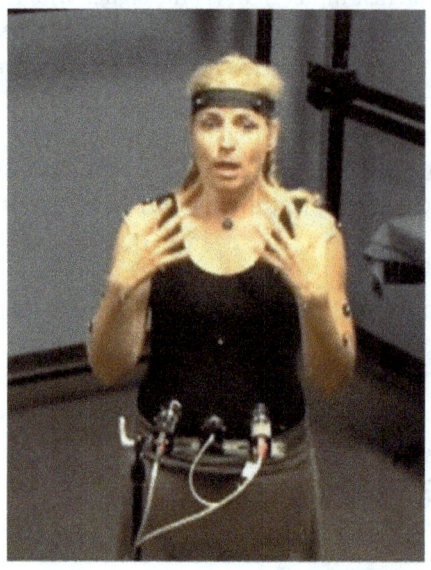

	Enactment$_i$	
J$_i$'étais dans le cinéma pis	(*râle*)	j'avais de la misère à respirer.
'I$_i$ was in the cinema and	(rattle)	I had trouble breathing.'

4.2 Partial dominant enactment

Partial dominant enactment enables the narrator to integrate both the narrator's and the actant's perspectives into signed discourse by simultaneously coordinating different enactment markers with signed narration. However, the actant's perspective is largely dominant since it is represented by physical markers as the signer adopts the attitude and actions of the actant during the signed narration, as in (10).

(10) Enactment: shifted head, body, eyes squinted, facial exp. showing the chill
WIND+++ [arms wrapping around body] WIND+++
'These winds were making me feel very cold!/I was very cold because of these winds!'

Example (10) demonstrates the use of partial dominant enactment, where the narration is placed within the reported event as presented by the enactment markers. The interlocutors know that the narrated information on the windy condition

(WIND+++) is not produced by the actant experiencing the event, but by the signer narrating this event, while principally assuming the role of the actant during the enactment structure.

This corresponds well with the theoretical notion proposed by Dudis (2004), who highlights that it is possible to "detach" a part of the body from depicting an event in order to add further information on the depiction itself. In following this line of thought, we consider that the LSQ sign WIND+++ is that of the signer narrating the event while the body, head, facial expression, and eye gaze are those of the actant. We propose that the enactment in (10) starts as "partial dominant" while the sign WIND is being produced and that it changes to complete enactment when the gesture of arms wrapping around the body shows how the actant behaved during the event. This then reverts back to partial dominant when the signer repeats the sign WIND. An element of simultaneity is noted by Metzger (1995), who labels it as "simultaneous direct and indirect action", highlighting that the narrator adds commentary on the event in lexical form within an enactment. For Cormier, Smith and Sevcikova-Sehyr (2015) it is a question of how the enactment markers (including the arms and hands) used in the complete form are *reduced*, enabling the signer to "withdraw" their arms/hands in order to use them to deliver a narrative commentary on the event being illustrated.

This kind of overlap of the actant's and speaker's perspectives was also found in the Quebec French dataset, as illustrated in example (11).

(11)   French (Projet Marqspat, 03FRblobB9, 04:00)

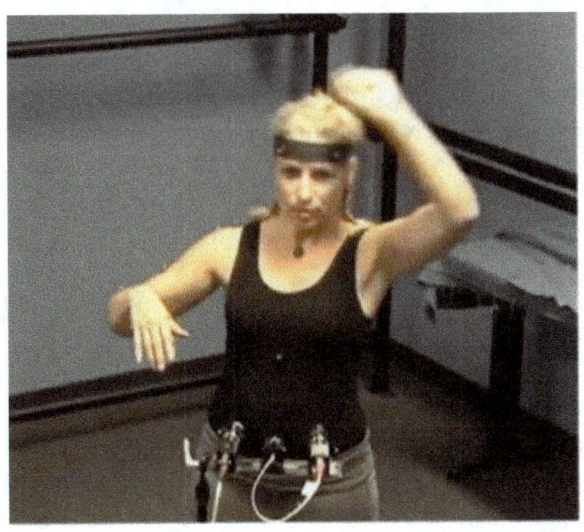

Enactment$_i$
J'avais le body$_i$ qui faisait *quequing quequing*, c't'une grosse affaire de plastic ça,
'I had the body$_i$ who was doing this: dong dong, it's a big plastic thing this,
Enactment$_k$
fac j$_k$'m'assommais au fur à mesure que j'essayais de m'sortir de d'là.
so I$_k$ was knocking myself out while I was trying to exit this.'

4.3 Partial non-dominant enactment

Partial non-dominant enactment is discussed as enactment used *subtly* in Cormier, Smith and Sevcikova-Sehyr (2015) in terms of the number of enactment markers within a narrated discourse produced principally from the perspective of the narrator. Similarly, Metzger (1995) discusses *indirect constructed action*, where the involvement of enactment markers is used minimally in a signed narration. Metzger gives an example where enactment is non-dominant through the use of the head and facial expression only:

(12)   gaze left/eye closed   gaze and head move right/head shakes
        PUNCH-NOSE (left hand) CL:V (fall-back) CL:5 (head-hit-wall)
        'and, **bam**, he's got a fist in his face. Knocked him right out of his chair and into the wall.'

(Metzger 1995: 265)

In this example the signer produces a partial enactment in a non-dominant way in ASL; his head and facial expression show the consequence of the blow to the face, resulting in him falling backwards and knocking his head on the wall.

The following example shows how the manner of reading a book is used in a subtle way in LSQ:

(13)   Enactment: bowed head, eyes on hands, facial exp: interested
        MAN IX$_{(z)}$ BOOK$_{(z)}$. READ+++$_{(z)}$

(Saunders 2016: 40)

Here, the signs BOOK and READ are located in a certain place, indicated by the subscript $_{(z)}$, which was established by pointing (IX). These two signs are produced at a small distance from the body of the signer, who demonstrates, using his head and facial expression, the interest shown by the actant while reading the book. This is a different form of enactment from, for example, the signer assuming the role of the actant in a complete way, which would require the signer to use not just his head and facial expression, as a form of body partitioning (Dudis 2004), but also his body, holding the book as if he were reading it.

4.4 Presence of enactment forms

While the enactment forms described above were identified from the signed examples in the *Projet Marqspat* data, there is also evidence of partial dominant enactment in Quebec French. However, although the literature has provided details on how the two different partial forms of enactment may be distinguished for signed discourse, none has been suggested for spoken language data. In the analysis above, we have mostly excluded Quebec French examples from our discussion except for the overlap of two different perspectives as observed for partial dominant enactment in example (11) above.

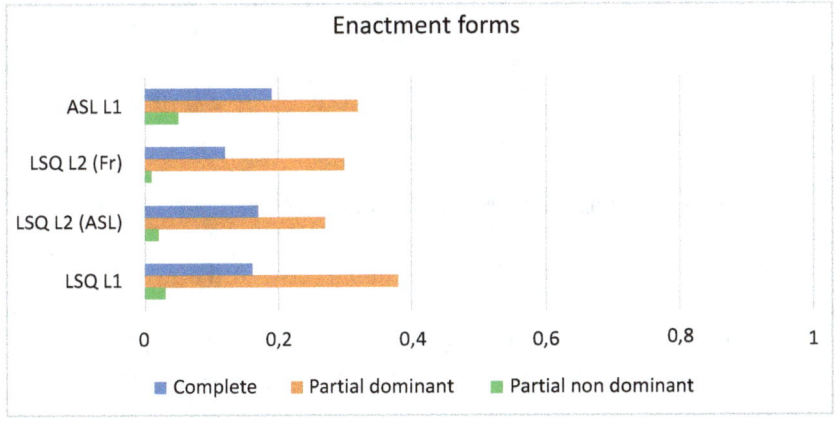

Figure 2: Presence of enactment forms in two languages, ASL and LSQ.

Figure 2 shows that the most frequently seen form of enactment for the two signed languages investigated, both for L1 and L2 users, is the partial dominant form. This form is most used when signers integrate two perspectives, their own and that of the actant's, with the body and head representing the actant while the narrator provides signed narration simultaneously.

We also note that complete enactment occupies a significant portion of the discourse, whereas partial non-dominant enactment is little used in comparison to the other forms; it is thus difficult to determine the nature and role of partial non-dominant enactment in the signed discourse. One study (Jantunen et al. 2019), based on a kinetic analysis of head and upper-torso movement for three enactment forms, using motion caption technology, identifies only complete and partial dominant enactment as significant from a kinetic point of view.

From the *Projet Marqspat* data we have identified partial dominant enactment as the most frequent form of enactment. This highlights the use of gestures to reconstruct actions from the perspective of an actant, where the signer can assume the actant's role when demonstrating or depicting the actions and the attitudinal behaviours of the actant. This leads our discussion to the involvement of elements seen as gestural in language production in the next section for both language modalities.

5 Gestural elements in enactments

There are a number of studies identifying gestures as recurring elements in enactments where the speaker or signer reconstructs the actions and attitudinal behaviours of the actant in reported speech or events (Ferrara and Johnston 2014; Kendon 2004; Quinto-Pozos 2007; Sidnell 2006). A number of gesture researchers refer to the continuum proposed by McNeill (1992: 37) which serves as a springboard for the discussion on types of gestures that are used.

(14)   Gesticulation > language-like gestures > pantomime > emblem > sign language

McNeill identifies three distinct traits which differ between the two ends of the continuum:
1) Speech, which is present in gesticulation and absent in signed languages;
2) Linguistic proprieties, which are present in signed languages but absent in gesticulation;
3) Degree of conventionality, which is high for signed languages and low for gesticulation where varying forms can differ between individuals, lacking uniformity among gesturers.

These three characteristics can help us to distinguish the two types of signalling: gestures, and signs of signed languages. However, the difference is not always clear. Kendon (2004), for example, discusses gestures which are widely used in southern Italy, and which could be argued to be more like emblems and thus more conventional. Kendon (1988) also describes gesticulations as gestures which accompany speech (co-speech gestures), and provides an example of a social worker who describes a psychiatric patient to other health and social professionals in a work-related discussion:

She says: ". . .and he just sits in his chair at night smokin' a big cigar. . ." As she says this, she changes her posture into a somewhat spread position and, concurrently with the words "smokin' a big cigar," she moves her hand back and forth in front of her mouth in a such a way as to suggest holding a long fat object and taking it in and out of the mouth. (Kendon 1988: 131–132)

This example shows that the person used her body and hands to produce gestures as part of a depiction of the smoker, similar to enactment discussed in this chapter.

Furthermore, Kendon (1988) describes language-like gestures as replacing speech for when the speaker cannot find a suitable word for the meaning they want to convey. Gullberg (1998) notes that such gestures are frequent for second language learners as well. Streeck (2002) provides an example in which gestures are not produced simultaneously with speech but in juxtaposition to it:

(15)   [. . .] *Brady goes like this* [gesture: hug, 3 kisses]

(Streeck 2002: 585)

As this example demonstrates, these gestures are produced without accompanying speech. They resemble a kind of pantomime which brings us to the question: can we distinguish between emblems and pantomime, which occupy the centre of the continuum? Kendon (1988) does not offer a definition for pantomime and McNeill (1992: 342) suggests that it consists of doing something resembling an action, for example hammering a nail. However, de Ruiter (2000) offers a definition which supports McNeill's example by stating that a pantomime consists of a series of gestures which imitate functional motor activities. This definition may be considered regarding enactments, as in examples (3) and (5), however we would question whether pantomime and enactment are the same thing; we argue that pantomime and enactment are different in their nature. Pantomime is used to amuse spectators by persuading them that the actions produced by the mime artist are realistic and may be believable – as if they were handling actual objects even though they are invisible. In other words, the actions produced in a pantomime are themselves an event in their own right. Enactments as produced by signers and speakers, on the other hand, are a reconstruction intended to transmit a specific meaning, perhaps with no intention of being realistic or even artistic. They exist in a referential framework in which the (reconstructed) acts are those of an actant. This idea of the signer or speaker assuming the role of the actant as a referent is put forward by Poulin and Miller (1995) who call it a *referential shift*.

Cassell and McNeill (1991) and McNeill (1992) offer us the insight that gestures can be organised from a narratology point of view, having three distinct levels where gestures can be produced: narrative, metanarrative and paranarrative. Gestures function differently at each level. First, iconic gestures are produced at the narrative level, enabling the speaker/signer to recreate or reconstruct actions that occurred in an event (the narration itself). Cassell and McNeill (1991) suggest that iconic gestures can be produced along with character perspective (as an actant) and observer perspective, where the observer "witnesses" the event from an outsider's point of view (Chafe 1976 and Meier 1990 further discuss the perspective of the thematic role of patient who is the recipient of some act that is expressed by the verb). Second, at the metanarrative level, metaphorical and deictic gestures occur, while the speaker/signer provides further details of the event itself which unfolds at the narrative level. Finally, the paranarrative level is identified as the level furthest away from the narration itself, allowing the speaker/signer to add and discuss their own experiences or opinions and to provide commentary on the event being narrated. This level can reveal the purpose of this narration, i.e., why this event is being reported to others (such as to illustrate something that has happened, to accentuate a humorous moment, to highlight a certain incident, etc.).

It is not difficult to see how narratology offers insights to the study of enactment. Complete enactment occurs when the speaker/signer assumes the role of the actant wholly, with all their physical articulators representing that character. This kind of gesture is comparable to iconic gestures which occur at the narrative level. When partial forms of enactment are employed (dominant or non-dominant), our examples show that the signer can operate at more than one level simultaneously: at the narrative level to illustrate the actions or attitude of the actant; at the metanarrative level to offer description of the event from the perspective of the narrator; and at the paranarrative level where the signer offers thoughts or opinions on what is being produced at other levels, be it a part of an action or part of a description of the event.

Based on the results of the data discussed in this chapter and following theoretical discussions of the role of gestures, we postulate that 1) we cannot put forward the idea that enactment is something exclusive to signed languages, since our data reveal that it can occur in both language modalities, signed and spoken; and 2) this discussion of gestures reinforces that gestures play a part in enactment in both language modalities. In other words, signers and speakers can integrate both lexical and gestural elements to produce enactment structures.

6 Theoretical application and discussion

In this section we discuss theoretical applications concerning enactment, underpinning the essential nature of how enactments integrate lexical and gestural material in either language modality. To do this, we address some theoretical proposals and consider their application to the *Projet Marqspat* empirical data.

From a formal point of view, both Lillo-Martin (1995) and Quer (2005) discuss how enactment (constructed action) is embedded in ASL sentences that incorporate the actant's point of view. Lillo-Martin discusses the use of the pronoun in the following ASL example:

(16)
           <u>   RS-i   </u>
           MOM_i $IX\text{-}1_i$ BUSY
           Mom's like, I'm busy!

                                                             (adapted from Lillo-Martin 1995: 162)

Lillo-Martin puts forward the idea that the first person pronoun produced during this enactment (indicated as RS here, an abbreviation for "role shift") refers to MOM and not to the signer, and compares this to the logophoric pronouns found in languages such as Ewe in Togo and Ghana (Clements 1975) and Gokana in Nigeria (Hyman and Comrie 1981). Logophoric pronouns enable the speakers of these languages to use a different set of pronoun forms in order to highlight a referent whose speech, thoughts, or feelings are being reported. Lillo-Martin (1995) argues that the logophoric pronoun in the above example arises when the ASL signer shifts the referential space to assume the role of the mother during enactment. Based on this reasoning, she proposes that this shift is governed by a Point of View predicate (POV) to introduce the logophoric context in which the enactment assumes the point of view of the mother.

On the other hand, Quer (2005) goes further, arguing that both the morphological non-manual features (NMF) and indexical shifts (including pronouns, temporal and locative indexicals) are triggered by a Point of View Operator (PVOp), which enables the signer to include morphological and interpretative properties during an enactment. However, neither of these propositions describes how enactment markers are employed at the onset of enactment, nor do they take into account differing gestural information that can be produced simultaneously during enactments, for example attitudinal facial expressions that the signer may use to express that of the actant. Quer's proposal does not account for signers' and speakers' ability to integrate two distinct perspectives simultaneously in an enactment (such as dominant and non-dominant partial forms), whereas more recent studies that discuss data for LSQ (L1 and L2), ASL (L1), and Quebec French, including the present study, highlight the different forms of complete and partial enactments and the possibility of simultaneity.

Rathmann and Mathur (2002) discuss gestural aspects in language processing related to the verbs in signed language which utilize space as part of verbal agreement. Rathmann and Mathur base their work on the idea that the space itself is gestural, as proposed by Liddell (1995), who argues that deictic pronoun forms cannot be considered linguistic since they are not listable, due to the infinite number of possibilities for how one could position these forms in a given space. For Liddell (2000), the loci—where referents are established in the signing space—are constructed mentally with the introduction of named entities, and verbs can use the representative space to highlight the thematic roles of the entities. In Liddell's model, the use of space, even though it has referential value, cannot be considered as part of the linguistic system since verbal agreement is established with gestural space. For this reason, Rathmann and Mathur (2002) propose a modification of Jackendoff's (1992; see also 2002) model of the architecture of language to include gestural space. This revised model highlights that language originates cognitively with conceptual structure (see Figure 3), then passes through syntactic structure, phonological structure, and the articulatory-perceptual interfaces, to its linguistic expression (output) or reception (input).

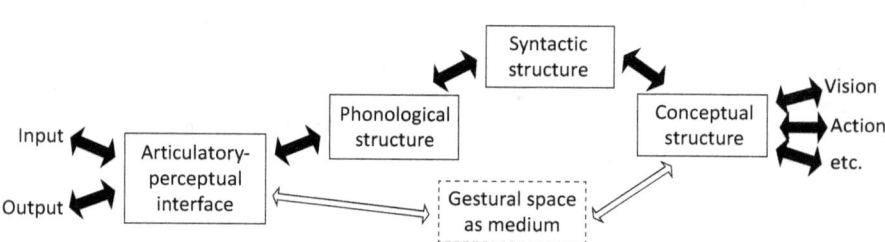

Figure 3: Rathmann and Mathur's proposed model including gesture space (adaped from Rathmann and Mathur 2002: 387).

Because the gestural space cannot pass through these structures as it is not linguistic, Rathmann and Mathur suggest that gestural information goes through its own distinct process, separate from the other structures where linguistic units are processed. They suggest that a separate channel links conceptual structure and articulatory-perceptual interfaces through the process "gestural space as medium" (see Figure 3). They argue that gestural information can be synchronized with the linguistic content by referring to two different proposals: McNeill's (2000) Growth Point Hypothesis and Kita's (2000) Information Packing Hypothesis. It is important to highlight that in Rathmann and Mathur's model, the linguistic content will have passed through syntactic and phonological structure before arriving at perceptual-articulatory interfaces where it integrates with gestural information. However, given that McNeill's and Kita's proposals highlight the synchronous nature of organizing gestures with linguistic units, we can now ask whether gestural information sometimes motivates the modification of the phonological structure in a coherent blend. There is a growing body of literature discussing the gradience of lexical units, and suggesting that a dichotomy between the two categories (phonological and gestural) is overly simplistic (Occhino and Wilcox 2017). In addition, Wilcox and Xavier (2013) discuss the relation between conventionality and symbolic complexity regarding the use of enactment (their term is "constructed action"). On one hand, they highlight that a simple enactment has the potential to lexicalize through repetition, e.g., brushing one's teeth. On the other hand, a complex enactment, involving detailed gestural information that may include precise actions and/or reactions in a reported event, "resist[s] lexicalization because the variation across usage events is too great to develop a low-level, lexical schema" (Wilcox & Xavier 2013: 100). Furthermore, there is a gradation between these two types of enactment in relation to the degree of symbolic complexity. This highlights another question we can ask regarding Rathmann and Mathur's (2002) proposal: whereas the model may be able to handle a simple enactment whereby the lexical material in the construction passes through syntactic and phonological structure and gestural material passes through the gestural space separately, at what point does the symbolic complexity of a complex enactment necessitate that interaction between the two take place before articulatory-perceptual interfaces?

As an example, the LSQ sign WALK is shown in its citation form in (17). By contrast, (18) shows a gestural example of walking hard against a strong wind, expressed solely by enactment via the upper torso, arms and hands, and facial expressions, but no lexical signs. But if an LSQ signer wishes to use this enactment as a partial form while simultaneously producing the lexical sign WALK as in (19), the movement of the lexical sign would be modified at the phonological level to include aspects of the enactment, demonstrating the difficult nature of walking against the wind.

(17)[6]

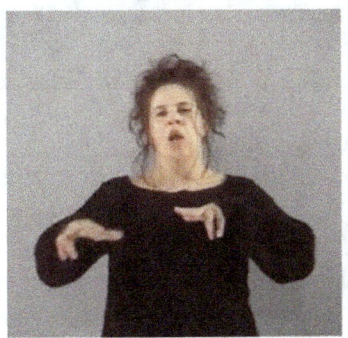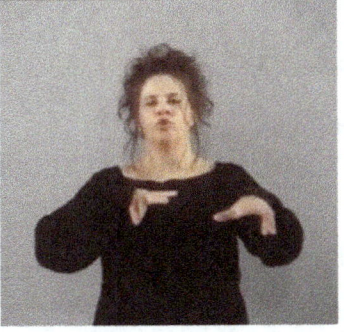

Citation form of sign in LSQ for WALK (adapted from Bourcier and Roy 1985: 42)

---

6 Examples (17), (18) and (19) can be viewed in video format online: https://doi.org/10.5683/SP2/DSZXKL

(18)

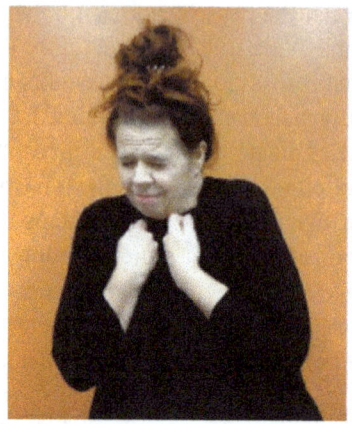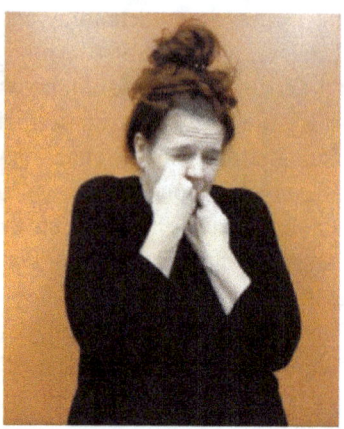

<u>Enactment</u>
gestures: arms and shoulders huddled and trying to hide the face against strong winds

(Parisot and Saunders 2019)

(19)

<u>Enactment (shoulders huddled, face struggling against the wind)</u>
WALK (slowly and with difficulty, synchronized with body movements)

(Parisot and Saunders 2019)

This integration is pertinent since the citation form of the sign in (17) cannot be produced unmodified if one also includes the body information indicated in (18), otherwise there would be a kind of cognitive dissonance for the signer/addressee. Another example of such dissonance is given in Glenberg and Kaschak (2002), who find that it takes speakers a longer time to say "open the drawer" while gesturing *closing* the drawer simultaneously, and it is produced more quickly when the gesture is the act of opening a drawer. This kind of cognitive coordination is found in WALK produced concomitant with partial enactment, in (19), thus the lexical word and the gesture are blended in terms of form at the phonological level, and not just at the output level as suggested by Rathmann and Mathur (2002).

Fauconnier and Turner (1996, 1998) discuss the conceptual blending of two distinct spaces which enables people to cognitively produce blended spaces that become the bases for thinking and expression. This model of blending spaces was adopted by Liddell and Metzger (1998) who discuss the use of constructed action. They argue that the surrogate space where the signer cognitively recalls the event is located in real space, where the articulators can be positioned to express something about the event using both language and gesture. Enactment occurs in a blended space when the signer assumes the role of the actant (found in surrogate space) with their articulators representing this person. It is from the blended space that the interlocutors can see the actions of the actant as represented by the signer in this blended space.

However, this blended space can be used in a more complex way if we consider the concept of body partitioning (Dudis 2004) where signers can partition the body, for example using one hand to represent the perspective of the narrator to add description to the event which is being embodied through enactment. Therefore, it is possible to portray the perspective of the narrator in a blended space as part of the real space (where the signer is found, narrating the event to others) and the embodied action of the actant as part of surrogate space, manifested by the signer's body in blended space. However, it is not just in signed languages that this kind of blending is found, as Parrill (2012) suggests that different viewpoints can be found in English, an example of which is (20).

(20)   *the man said, I ate a lobster*

(Parrill 2012: 101)

The concept of spaces is discussed by Parrill, who indicates that the speaker is found in the base space as encapsulated by the first proposition in (20) ("The man said...") and the speaker goes into story space to represent the man and what he has said ("I ate a lobster"). Blending happens in this example when the speaker "lends" their vocal cords to the actant to express the words from the perspective of the actant in the story space, resulting in a blended space.

Returning to Rathmann and Mathur's (2002) proposal, which includes a separate process for gestural information that is synchronously combined with linguistic material at the articulatory-perceptual interface, we propose instead that for at least complex enactments, gestural elements can affect phonological structure. Rathmann and Mathur's model does not allow this phenomenon to happen since in their view, gestural information is not passed through the phonological structure as this is reserved for linguistic units only. Langacker (1987, 2008) proposes a different angle for language analysis within his theory of Cognitive Grammar. He discusses the example of a gesture representing a sound, which would not be considered linguistic in a formal linguistics framework, such as in (21):

(21)   *The boy went* [NOISE].

(Langacker 1987: 80)

The unit [NOISE] is an iconic reconstitution of a sound that the boy made, which is similar to the rattle noise in (9) and *dong dong* in (11) above. According to Langacker, the meaning associated with this sound can be conceptualized and the unit is therefore meaningful and is also a self-symbolization. He argues that the "gesture, therefore, is both expressive and a facet of what is expressed. In effect, the gesture symbolizes itself" (Langacker 2008: 463). The concept of self-symbolization is further developed by Ferrara and Johnston (2014) who put forth the idea that an enactment is not encoded as a linguistic unit but as a unit which symbolizes itself, similar to [NOISE] in (21).

Cognitive Grammar does not distinguish between linguistic and gestural units since it is based on a global view of language and bypasses the well-known dichotomy that is found in formal linguistic analysis (Langacker 2008; Occhino and Wilcox 2017). With this in mind, Langacker (1991, 2008) proposes a language-based analysis using the symbolic unit Σ (sigma) which is *bipolar*, containing both a semantic pole (S) and a phonological pole (P), as diagrammed by Langacker (Figure 4).

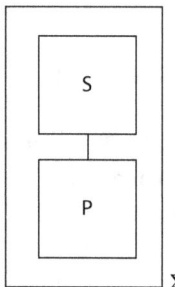

Figure 4: Symbolic unit Σ (Langacker 2008: 15, his Figure 1.2a; reproduced with permission from Oxford Publishing Limited through PLSclear).

This symbolic unit can represent any language-based unit, be it conventional (regular and entrenched units) or unconventional (non-regular and non-entrenched units such as most gestures). Furthermore, this symbolic unit can be combined with other symbolic units in a recursive manner to construct concepts in languages as complex symbolic units, as Figure 5 shows.

We can apply this analysis to the LSQ sign WALK, which is phonological, and which is modified by enactment in example (19) to depict the difficultness of

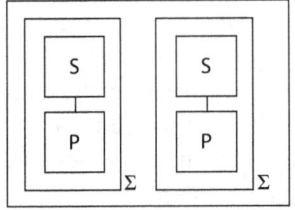

Figure 5: Complex symbolic unit (Langacker 2008: 15, his Figure 1.2b; reproduced with permission from Oxford Publishing Limited through PLSclear).

walking against the wind. WALK is modified phonologically in order to align with the enactment features. Since the symbolic unit for WALK is integrated with the symbolic unit representing the enactment – these two units become a complex symbolic unit where their phonological and gestural features can be modified and combined into one integrated complex signal.

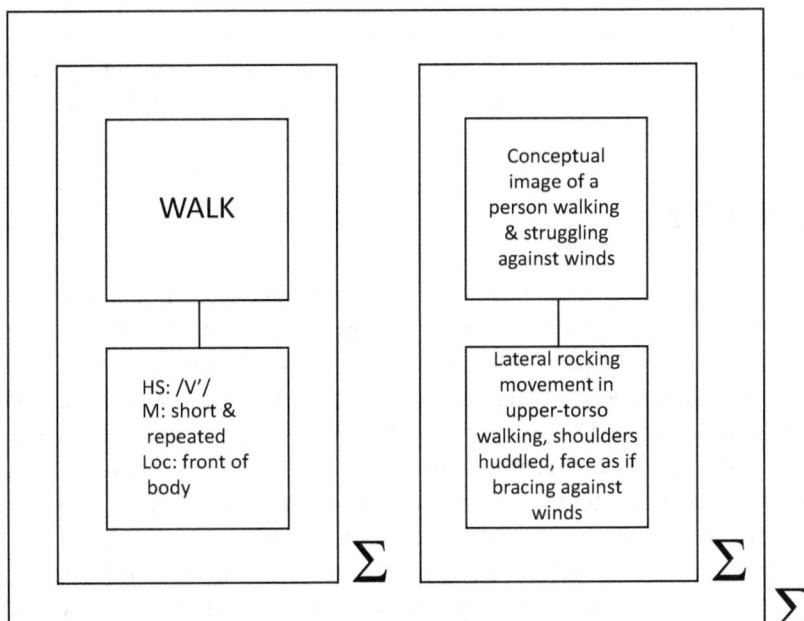

Figure 6: Example of a complex symbolic unit containing an enactment.

Wilcox (2018) points out that in a language it is possible to have lexical items which are conventionalized, or entrenched through repetition, and gestural items which are not conventionalized, but highly schematic. Figure 6 illustrates the possibility of including both simultaneously, that is the lexical element (WALK) and the highly schematic gestural use of the body through enactment, showing the struggle against the wind. The lexical element is tightly interwoven with the enactment as one complex symbolic unit. This addresses the problem of gradation, as discussed regarding Rathmann and Mathur's (2002) model in terms of degree of conventionality. One symbolic unit, regardless of its schematic complexity, can still integrate with another symbolic unit simultaneously, thereby becoming a highly schematic, complex symbolic unit as illustrated in Figure 6. Furthermore, this analysis can be applied to example (11), where in Quebec French, the speaker vocally produces *"quequing quequing"* ['dong dong'] while gesturally hitting her head with something, integrating both the perspectives of narrator and actant. This integration of gestural speech and embodied action is realized by combining both symbolic units into one complex symbolic unit, so that the movement and speech repetition are produced together without cognitive dissonance (Glenberg and Kaschak 2002).

The partial non-dominant enactment form is difficult to analyze since there were very few occurrences found in the Parisot and Saunders (2019) and Saunders (2016) datasets. It is also difficult to apply the analysis from signed languages to a spoken language such as Quebec French, since any decision about whether a partial form of enactment is dominant or non-dominant is very likely to be subjective.

7 Conclusion

In this chapter, we discussed a range of examples of enactment in LSQ (L1 and L2), ASL (L1), and Quebec French discourse, noting the presence and frequency of various enactment forms. Even though the frequency of enactment in general is lower for spoken language, enactment is found in both language modalities, signed and spoken (Quebec French in our case). Enactment, as we have shown, is mostly partial, where the gestural aspect of enactment from the perspective of the actant is integrated with lexicon, within the narration from the perspective of the narrator. Therefore, this allows two perspectives to be simultaneously portrayed. In the languages analyzed, complete and partial dominant forms are significantly present, with the proportion varying by language, but we noted that a few occurrences of partial non-dominant enactment were also identified. In other words, it appears that enactment, where the speaker/signer embodies the actant, is not a feature that belongs only to signed languages, but to languages in general, and reveals the role of cognition in creating signals—language and gestures—to (re)produce events from various perspectives: the actant's, whose actions are being (re)enacted, and the narrator's, who adds description of the event being reported. This highlights the gestures that play a part in enactments in both language modalities, which are produced along with lexical elements, particularly with partial dominant enactments.

In the data analyzed for this study, partial dominant enactment is established as the most frequent form of enactment, where lexical and gestural elements are produced simultaneously. We argue that elements of gestures can influence the lexical form, leading to a tightly interwoven unit, as Figure 6 shows above, basing our proposed model on a Langackerian analysis of complex symbolic units. In summary, we conclude that it is impossible to disregard the influence of gesture on the use of language because first, both can be produced concomitantly, and second, the inclusion of gesture can affect the phonological structure of the lexical unit. Future research could explore how various specific articulators are employed, e.g., use of the mouth, facial expressions, etc.; investigating these may reveal further nuances in the articulation of the perspective of both the actant and that of the signer/speaker as narrator.

References

Bourcier, Paul & Julie-Elaine Roy. 1985. La langue des signes LSQ. Montreal: L'Association des Sourds du Montreal Metropolitain.
Cassell, Justine & David McNeill. 1991. Gesture and the poetics of prose. *Poetics Today* 12(3). 375–404.
Chafe, Wallace L. 1976. Givenness, contrastiveness, definiteness, subjects, topics, and point of view in subject and topic. In Charles N. Li (ed.), *Subject and Topic*, 25–55. New York: Academic Press.
Clark, Herbert H. 1996. *Using Language*. Cambridge: Cambridge University Press.
Clements, George. 1975. The logophoric pronouns in Ewe: Its role in discourse. *Journal of West African Languages* 10(2). 141–171.
Cormier, Kearsy, Sandra Smith & Zed Sevcikova-Sehyr. 2015. Rethinking constructed action. *Sign Language & Linguistics* 18(2). 167–204.
Couper-Kuhlen, Elizabeth. 1999. Coherent voicing: On prosody in conversational reported speech. In Wolfram Bublitz & Uta Lenk (eds.), *Coherence in Spoken and Written Discourse: How to Create It and How to Describe It*, 11–32. Amsterdam/Philadelphia: John Benjamins.
de Ruiter, Jan Peter. 2000. The production of gesture and speech. In David McNeill (ed.), *Language and Gesture*, 284–311. Cambridge: Cambridge University Press.
Dudis, Paul G. 2004. Body partitioning and real-space blends. *Cognitive Linguistics* 15(2). 223–238.
Engberg-Pedersen, Elisabeth. 1995. Point of view expressed through shifters. In Karen Emmorey & Judy S. Reilly (eds.), *Language, Gesture, and Space*, 133–154. Hillsdale, NJ: Lawrence Erlbaum.
Fauconnier, Gilles & Mark Turner. 1996. Blending as a central process of grammar. In Adele E. Goldberg (ed.), *Conceptual Structure, Discourse and Language*, 113–130. Stanford, CA: CSLI Publications.
Fauconnier, Gilles & Mark Turner. 1998. Conceptual integration networks. *Cognitive Science* 22(2). 133–187.
Ferrara, Lindsay & Trevor Johnston. 2014. Elaborating who's what: A study of constructed action and clause structure in Auslan (Australian Sign Language). *Australian Journal of Linguistics* 34(2). 193–215.

Glenberg, Arthur M. & Michael P. Kaschak. 2002. Grounding language in action. *Psychonomic Bulletin & Review* 9(3). 558–565.

Gullberg, Marianne. 1998. *Gesture as a Communication Strategy in Second Language Discourse: A Study of Learners of French and Swedish.* Lund: Lund University Press.

Hyman, Larry M. & Bernard Comrie. 1981. Logophoric reference in Gokana. *Journal of African Languages and Linguistics* 3. 19–37.

Jackendoff, Ray. 1992. *Languages of the Mind: Essays on Mental Representation.* Cambridge. MA: MIT Press.

Jackendoff, Ray. 2002. *Foundations of Language: Brain, Meaning, Grammar, Evolution.* Oxford: Oxford University Press.

Jantunen, Tommi, Danny De Weerdt, Birgitta Burger & Anna Puupponen. 2019. The more you move, the more action you construct: A motion capture study on head and upper-torso movement in constructed action in Finnish Sign Language narratives. Paper presented at Theoretical Issues in Sign Languages Research 13, Hamburg, Germany, 26–28 September 2019.

Kendon, Adam. 1988. How gestures can become like words. In Fernando Poyatos (ed.), *Cross-cultural Perspectives in Nonverbal Communication*, 131–141. Toronto: C. J. Hogrefe.

Kendon, Adam. 2004. *Gesture: Visible Action as Utterance.* Cambridge: Cambridge University Press.

Kita, Sotaro. 2000. How representational gestures help speaking. In David McNeill (ed.), *Language and Gesture*, 162–185. Cambridge: Cambridge University Press.

Langacker, Ronald W. 1987. *Foundations of Cognitive Grammar: Volume 1, Theoretical Prerequisites.* Stanford: Stanford University Press.

Langacker, Ronald W. 1991. *Foundations of Cognitive Grammar: Volume 2, Descriptive Application.* Stanford: Stanford University Press.

Langacker, Ronald W. 2008. *Cognitive Grammar: A Basic Introduction.* Oxford: Oxford University Press.

Liddell, Scott K. 1995. Real, surrogate, and token space: Grammatical consequences in ASL. In Karen Emmorey & Judy S. Reilly (eds.), *Language, Gesture, and Space*, 19–41. Hillsdale, NJ: Lawrence Erlbaum.

Liddell, Scott K. 2000. Blended spaces and deixis in sign language discourse. In David McNeill (ed.), *Language and Gesture*, 331–357. Cambridge: Cambridge University Press.

Liddell, Scott K. & Melanie Metzger. 1998. Gesture in sign language discourse. *Journal of Pragmatics* 30(6). 657–697.

Lillo-Martin, Diane. 1995. The point of view predicate in American Sign Language. In Karen Emmorey & Judy S. Reilly (eds.), *Language, Gesture, and Space*, 155–170. Hillsdale, NJ: Lawrence Erlbaum.

Lillo-Martin, Diane. 2012. Utterance reports and constructed action. In Roland Pfau, Markus Steinbach & Bencie Woll (eds.), *Sign Language: An International Handbook*, 365–387. Berlin/Boston: De Gruyter Mouton.

Loew, Ruth Carolyn. 1984. *Roles and Reference in American Sign Language: A Developmental Perspective.* Minneapolis: University of Minnesota dissertation.

Mandel, Mark. 1977. Iconic devices in American Sign Language. In Lynn A. Friedman, (ed.), *On the Other Hand: New Perspectives on American Sign Language*, 57–107. New York: Academic Press.

McNeill, David. 1992. *Hand and Mind: What Gesture Reveals about Thought.* Chicago, IL: The University of Chicago Press.

McNeill, David. 2000. Catchments and contexts: Non-modular factors in speech and gesture production. In David McNeill (ed.), *Language and Gesture*, 312–328. Cambridge: Cambridge University Press.

Meier, Richard P. 1990. Person deixis in American Sign Language. In Susan D. Fischer & Patricia Siple (eds.), *Theoretical Issues in Sign Language Research, Volume 1: Linguistics*, 175–190. Chicago: The University of Chicago Press.

Metzger, Melanie. 1995. Constructed dialogue and constructed action in American Sign Language. In Ceil Lucas (ed.), *Sociolinguistics in Deaf Communities*, 255–271. Washington DC: Gallaudet University Press.

Occhino, Corrine & Sherman Wilcox. 2017. Gesture or sign? A categorization problem. *Behavioral and Brain Sciences* 40. 36–37.

Padden, Carol. 1986. Verbs and role-shifting in American Sign Language. In Carol Padden (ed.), *Proceedings of the Fourth National Symposium on Sign Language Research and Teaching*, 44–57. Silver Spring, MD: National Association of the Deaf.

Parisot, Anne-Marie, Alexandra Pilarski, Laurence Richer-Lemay, Julie Rinfret & Amélie Voghel. 2008. Description de la variation du marquage spatial en langue des signes québécoise (LSQ) [Description of variation of space markers in Quebec Sign Language (LSQ)]. Paper presented at the *Congrès de l'Acfas*, Quebec City, Canada, 5–9 May 2008.

Parisot, Anne-Marie & Darren Saunders. 2019. La représentation corporelle dans le discours signé [Enactment in signed discourse]. *LIDIL : Revue de linguistique et de didactique des langues* 60. https://doi.org/10.4000/lidil.6893

Parisot, Anne-Marie & Darren Saunders. 2022. Character perspective shift and embodiment markers in signed and spoken discourse. *Language in Constrast* 22(2), 259–289. https://doi.org/10.1075/lic.00022.par

Parrill, Fey. 2012. Interactions between discourse status and viewpoint in co-speech gesture. In Barbara Dancygier & Eve Sweetser (eds.), *Viewpoint in Language: A Multimodal Perspective*, 97–112. Cambridge: Cambridge University Press.

Poulin, Christine & Christopher Miller. 1995. On narrative discourse and point of view in Quebec Sign Language. In Karen Emmorey & Judy S. Reilly (eds.), *Language, Gesture, and Space*, 117–131. Hillsdale, NJ: Lawrence Erlbaum.

Quer, Josep. 2005. Context shift and indexical variables in sign languages. In Effi Georgala & Jonathan Howell (eds.), *Semantics and Linguistic Theory* 15, 152–168. Ithica, NY: CLC Publications.

Quinto-Pozos, David. 2007. Can constructed action be considered obligatory? *Lingua* 117(7). 1285–1314.

Rathmann, Christian & Gaurav Mathur. 2002. Is verb agreement the same crossmodally? In Richard P. Meier, Kearsy Cormier & David Quinto-Pozos (eds.), *Modality and Structure in Signed and Spoken Languages*, 370–404. Cambridge: Cambridge University Press.

Saunders, Darren. 2016. *Description des structures de représentation corporelle en langue des signes québécoise chez des locuteurs sourds langue première et langue seconde* [Description of enactment structures in Quebec Sign Language amongst Deaf first and second language users]. Montréal: University of Quebec at Montréal thesis.

Saunders, Darren & Anne-Marie Parisot. 2016. Constructed action in Quebec Sign Language (LSQ) amongst Deaf first language and second language users. Paper presented at the Theoretical Issues in Sign Language Research 12, Melbourne, Australia, 4–7 January 2016.

Sidnell, Jack. 2006. Coordinating gesture, talk, and gaze in reenactments. *Research on Language and Social Interaction* 39(4). 377–409.

Streeck, Jürgen. 2002. Grammars, words, and embodied meanings: On the uses and evolution of *so* and *like*. *Journal of Communication* 52(3). 581–596.

Tannen, Deborah. 2007. *Talking Voices: Repetition, Dialogue, and Imagery in Conversational Discourse*. Cambridge: Cambridge University Press.

Thumann, Mary Agnes. 2010. *Identifying Depiction in American Sign Language Presentations*. Washington: Gallaudet University dissertation.

Wilcox, Sherman. 2018. *Ten Lectures on Cognitive Linguistics and the Unification of Spoken and Signed Languages*. Leiden: Brill.
Wilcox, Sherman & André Nogueira Xavier. 2013. A framework for unifying spoken language, signed language and gesture. *Todas as Letras: revista de língua e literatura* [All letters: Language and Literature Magazine] 15(1). 88–110.
Winston, Elizabeth A. 1991. Spatial referencing and cohesion in an American Sign Language text. *Sign Language Studies* 73. 397–410.

IV Blending and metaphor

Anna-Lena Nilsson
Exploring Real Space blends as indicators of discourse complexity in Swedish Sign Language

1 Introduction

This explorative study[1] attempts to identify indicators of discourse complexity in Swedish Sign Language (svenskt teckenspråk or STS), by analyzing the Real Space blend structure of selected segments of such a discourse. Some crucial factors deemed to possibly contribute to the overall discourse complexity are discussed, such as: which perspective the signer uses and switching between such perspectives; the identity, type and location of blended entities; the number of blended entities; whether the entities are explicitly introduced and re-introduced or not; and which linguistic expressions (if any) are used about entities. Real Space blend tables are introduced as a tool for visualizing overall discourse complexity. The three discourse segments analyzed are of relatively equal length, but turn out to differ radically when it comes to the number and type of Real Space blends and blended entities they contain. It is suggested that the analyzed factors indicate overall degree of discourse complexity, and that Real Space blend tables can be a useful tool for operationalizing discourse complexity in signed languages. The more blends and blended entities a segment contains, the larger the table is.

Section 2 presents the theoretical background for the chapter, and in section 3 the study is introduced. Section 4 contains descriptions and analyses of the three discourse segments, which are then further discussed in section 5. Finally, in section 6 some conclusions and implications are presented.

---

[1] The chapter is based on parts of Study IV in my PhD-thesis (Nilsson 2010). At the time, Stockholm University did not require ethics approval for the project. The chapter has benefited from useful comments from three anonymous reviewers and the volume editors.

Anna-Lena Nilsson, Norwegian University of Science and Technology – NTNU, Norway,
e-mail: anna-lena.nilsson@ntnu.no

https://doi.org/10.1515/9783110703788-011

2 Theoretical background

The study is grounded in cognitive linguistics, in particular Mental Space Theory (Fauconnier 1985) and Conceptual Blending Theory (Fauconnier and Turner 1998, 2002, 2006). More specifically, a comprehensive, descriptive model for the use of space in signed language developed for American Sign Language (ASL) by Scott K. Liddell was applied. Central to the model is the fact that signers "frequently conceive of areas of the space around them, or even themselves, as if they were something else" (Liddell 2003: 141).

According to Mental Space Theory, all entities that we speak about are conceptual entities that exist within conceptual structures called *mental spaces*. Mental spaces are "small conceptual packets constructed as we think and talk, for purposes of local understanding and action" (Fauconnier and Turner 2006: 307). Linguistic structures also prompt the construction of mental spaces in the addressee, and in order for us to understand each other, the mental spaces constructed by speaker and addressee need to correspond.

Conceptual Blending Theory, or the Theory of Conceptual Integration, has its roots in Mental Space Theory and deals with a special type of relation between mental spaces called *blending* (Fauconnier and Turner 2002). Blending is a general cognitive process operating on two (or more) input spaces to yield a new mental space, *the blended space,* or *the blend*. When blending occurs, structure from the input spaces is projected onto the new blended space. Next we will look at a type of blend of specific interest for the analysis of signed languages – Real Space blends.

2.1 Real space blending

According to Liddell, a person's mental representation of the immediate surroundings constitutes a special type of mental space: Real Space.[2] Real Space is defined as "a person's current conceptualization of the immediate environment based on sensory input" (Liddell 2003: 82, see also Liddell 1995). This makes Real Space differ from other mental spaces in that it is *grounded*, i.e., "its elements are conceptualized as existing in the immediate environment" (Liddell 2003: 82).

Token blends are the type of Real Space blend that signers frequently construct using empty locations in the signing space ahead of them (Liddell 2003). Both the signer and the addressee make associations between the conceptual content the

---

[2] The convention used by Selvik (2006), with capital 'R' and 'S' as a reminder that Real Space does not refer to physical reality, is adopted here.

signer refers to with particular signs and an area in signing space. This prompts the construction of an invisible blended entity (a token) in that area. The signer can then direct signs toward that token, to refer to that particular conceptual content. To indicate their nature, Liddell transcribes blended entities using vertical brackets, a convention followed here too (see section 4).

Liddell also describes a category of signs that he refers to as *buoys*, which constitute a special kind of visible blended entity. These are signs produced with the signer's weak hand "held in a stationary configuration as the strong hand continues producing signs" (Liddell, 2003: 223). Buoys "maintain a physical presence that helps guide the discourse as it proceeds" (2003: 223). In the present study, only the *pointer buoy* is discussed. It is a pointing sign that can be directed towards (or, points at) blended entities but does not construct a blend of its own.

One of the buoy categories suggested by Liddell is the *fragment buoy*, where the signer's non-dominant hand remains in place from a previously produced two-handed sign (Liddell 2003: 248–250). It differs from all other buoys in not having a fixed form, and Nilsson (2007) suggests the term *sign fragments* instead, as this would differentiate these from buoys as signs with a fixed form. Sign fragments blend with the conceptual entity they refer to, and their function in STS is "[to tell] us who/what the topic of the discourse is" (Nilsson 2007: 183).

The signer's hand(s) and (parts of the) body can also form part of a Real Space blend (Liddell 2003: 151–157). This way of using the signer's body for reference in signed languages has also been termed, e.g., role play, role shift and body shift. To describe this, as well as a parallel process when describing co-speech gesturing, the concepts *representing* and *enactment* are also used (see e.g., Saunders and Parisot, this volume; Sweetser, this volume). According to Liddell, the signer becomes a visible blended entity, thus creating a "surrogate blend" (Liddell 2003: 152). In addition to the visible surrogate formed by (part of) the signer's body, a surrogate blend can also contain invisible surrogates. These can be blended with empty physical locations in signing space, and signs produced in other parts of the discourse provide evidence for their existence (Liddell 2003: 152). Since surrogates are blended entities, they too are indicated with vertical brackets.

Surrogate blends are frequently used for representing constructed dialogue (Tannen 1986) and constructed action (Winston 1991; Metzger 1995). According to Dudis (2004), when the signer is part of such a blend, the result is a visible |actor|. Dudis describes the partitionable zones of the body available to ASL signers, and how they can be partitioned off from the Real Space body, thus enabling the signer to increase the information accessible from surrogate blends by creating a multiple Real Space blend. In the analyzed discourse, the signer frequently partitions off her hands (and forearms) to produce lexical signs that tell the addressee more about what a surrogate in a particular surrogate blend is doing. Liddell and Metzger

(1998) also discuss this phenomenon, without using the term "partitionable zones", describing different types of constructed actions and their significance.

Since the original analysis of the data, there have been additions to the description of use of signing space. Following Wilcox and Occhino (2016), Martínez and Wilcox (2019) use the term *Place* for a meaningful spatial location and introduce the concept *placing* to refer to signs being produced at a specific meaningful location in space. They identify two different types: Placing-for-Creating, where a new meaningful space is created, and Placing-by-Recruiting, where an existing meaningful space is used. Though these concepts would unquestionably have been useful, a re-analysis of my data for this chapter based on them was not possible at this time.

2.2 Creating and understanding real space blends

Summing up their study of Real Space blends in Norwegian Sign Language (norsk tegnspråk, or NSL), Liddell and Vogt-Svendsen state: "Thus, contrary to the widely accepted (prescriptive) view that signers must identify every spatial element prior to making use of it, we find that this signer provides explicit identification of only some of the elements of her real space blends. The conceptual task of creating the remainder of each real space blends [sic] falls on the addressee" (Liddell and Vogt-Svendsen 2007: 193). They identify four sources of information that allow the addressee to create a Real Space blend that corresponds to the one created by the signer. These are: "shared knowledge of the world, shared knowledge of the current discourse, shared knowledge of NSL grammar, and the directional signs produced by the signer" (Liddell and Vogt-Svendsen 2007: 182).

To describe one type of knowledge an addressee needs to access in order to identify a discourse entity, I have used the concept *frame* (Fillmore 1982, 2006). A frame is a system of concepts "...related in such a way that to understand any one of them you have to understand the whole structure in which it fits; when one of the things in such a structure is introduced into a text, or into a conversation, all of the others are automatically made available" (Fillmore 2006: 373). Here, the concept is used to help explain that knowing that the context of an event is a hospital evokes what I have called a *hospital frame*, which makes it easier to identify an unspecified person as, e.g., a nurse, a doctor or a patient in some Real Space blends.

3 The study

In the present study, the Real Space blend structure of three segments of a STS discourse was analyzed, in order to explore ways to operationalize discourse complexity in a signed language. In addition, I introduce Real Space blend tables as a potential tool to make some of the suggested aspects of discourse complexity more easily observable.

3.1 Aims

One aim of the study was to identify factors that may contribute to a piece of signed discourse being perceived as complex. Here, I am using complexity in a very broad sense, as relating to morpho-syntactic complexity and semantic complexity, as well as more general discourse level complexity. The factors discussed as possible indicators of such complexity are: which perspective the signer uses, and switching between such perspectives; the identity, type and location of blended entities; the number of blended entities; whether entities are explicitly introduced and re-introduced or not; and which linguistic expressions (if any) are used in relation to them. The fact that the same entity can be talked about using blended entities such as tokens, visible surrogates, and invisible surrogates, or as not being part of a blend at all, is also discussed as something that might make a segment more or less complex.

Another aim was to try to construct a tool to operationalize such discourse complexity. To this end Real Space blend tables, where the structure and visual impression of a table reflect the general complexity in the segment it represents, are introduced. Such tables also provide a quick overview of, e.g., the number and type of blended entities used in a specific segment.

3.2 Data and method

The STS discourse used here consists of a nearly ten-minute long monologue, where the signer retells the contents of an autobiography she has read.[3] The title of the book is *Livets hjul: En självbiografi i dödens närhet* (1998; original title: *The Wheel*

---

[3] The whole discourse, recorded in 1998, with the original ELAN-transcriptions, can be viewed at: https://ntnu.cloud.panopto.eu/Panopto/Pages/Viewer.aspx?id=dd4690b7-1b5a-49a5-b935-abd-b00cc9b9a

of Life: A Memoir of Living and Dying), written by Elisabeth Kübler Ross. The signer retells the content freely, without any written notes. During the recording session, a native signer who had not read the book sat next to the camera as the addressee.

The recorded discourse was then transcribed using ELAN (see Crasborn and Sloetjes 2008).[4] As a part of that process, the source text had previously been divided into forty smaller chunks of varying length, based on content, but also prosody.[5] The division into chunks was completed in 2001, in order to make the transcription process more manageable. For this study, three segments of between 36 and 45 seconds in length, each consisting of two or three such chunks, were chosen (cf. Table 1). Segments were chosen for analysis due to an initial impression of being particularly simple or complex. Segments 1 and 3 are the longest, lasting 45 and 40 seconds respectively. As will become clear, there is no direct correlation between the duration of a segment and the number of Real Space blends it contains. Whereas Segment 1 only contains three blends and one sequence without blended entities, Segment 3 contains fifteen blends and four sequences with no blended entities. The analysis is presented both as text, describing the content and structure of each segment, and as tables.

Table 1: Analyzed segments.

Segment #	Duration	Time	Number of chunks	Number of Real Space Blends	Non-blended sequences
Segment 1	45 sec.	00:00–00:45	3	3	1
Segment 2	36 sec.	00:45–01:21	3	8	0
Segment 3	40 sec.	05:49–06:29	2	15	4

In the blend tables, glosses are used as described in more detail in section 4.1 when the first Real Space blend is presented. The choice of glosses to represent signs is always problematic (Rosenthal 2009; Antinoro Pizzuto and Garcia, this volume). Deciding on glosses for signs when the signer shifts to a perspective where she is representing one of many persons was particularly challenging. Though the signer herself is only one specific person, she sometimes represents one of many (non-specific) persons. If the English gloss has a specific singular form, this indicates that the signer represents one particular person of many, e.g., |doctor in audience|. But,

---

4 ELAN can be downloaded at https://archive.mpi.nl/tla/elan/download.
5 A translation of the whole discourse into English, divided into these chunks, is available at: https://osf.io/83kys?show=view&view_only=

when she represents any one of the many in the audience, this is indicated with additional words in the text, e.g., one of |many in audience|.

The signer's gaze and posture also play a vital part in creating Real Space blends, but for reasons of time and space were only taken into account when they seemed to be of particular relevance. Also, the fairly low technical quality of the recording made fine-grained gaze analysis difficult.

4 Description and analysis

4.1 Segment 1: content and structure

The first segment (Chunk 1–3) consists of the first 45 seconds, where the signer introduces the topic of her talk and gives some background information about the main character.[6] All translations of the signed discourse were made by me, and follow the original quite closely. They are therefore more of a transliteration than a translation into idiomatic English. The following is a translation of Segment 1 into English:

> Well, I have read a book by, written by, Elisabeth Kübler Ross. She was born in Switzerland, but moved to the US, because she married an American during WWII, well, right after, that's when she married. She studied to be a doctor, but digressed from that, began to study psychology and became a psychiatrist instead. She is a truly remarkable woman. She is known as "the lady of death", as she does a lot of research on death. What happens after death, what happens to a person before death, what happens in their minds? Well, maybe it's a bit difficult to tell what happens after death, but she at least seems to have found out some things.

Segment 1, despite being 45 seconds long, does not seem particularly complex. There are only three Real Space blends, which contain only three different blended entities: |EKR|,[7] |USA|, and |dying person|. When the signer talks about these she mainly uses token blends, and a majority of the meaningfully directed signs are directed towards |EKR|. There is, however, a very brief sequence that contains a surrogate blend. The signs produced in it, INDEX-C STUDY 'I study', could be regarded as redundant, as they constitute a repetition of something previously mentioned in the same chunk, NON-1ST-SING$^{>|EKR|}$ STUDY 'she studied'.

The Real Space blend structure of Segment 1 is illustrated in Table 2 below, where signs are transcribed from top to bottom in the order they occur in the

---

6 Segment 1, with translations, can be viewed at: https://ntnu.cloud.panopto.eu/Panopto/Pages/Viewer.aspx?id=80aa3298-d288-4e7f-81c2-ad4f00b723a7
7 Elisabeth Kübler Ross.

segment. To illustrate the chunk structure within a segment, the second chunk of a segment is shaded, and if there is a third chunk, that part of the table is not shaded. Thus, in Table 2, Chunks 1 and 3 are not shaded, but Chunk 2 is. Each Real Space blend is given a unique number, in Column 1 of Table 2, consisting of the number of the segment where it occurs and a running number for when it occurs. Thus, 1:1 is the first Real Space blend in Segment 1, 1:2 the second blend in Segment 1, etc.

In this introductory sequence, the signer first states that she has read a book by Elizabeth Kübler Ross. She introduces the main character and author of the book by fingerspelling the full name. In Column 6 in Table 2, the expressions used about discourse entities in Real Space blends are glossed. These glosses mainly represent noun phrases (including pronouns). When signs are directionally modified, information regarding that is also provided, e.g., NON-1ST-SING$^{>|EKR|}$.[8] Two signs being produced simultaneously are indicated with a + after the first gloss. In addition to pronouns, other pointing signs, and the noun classifier cl-PERSON, verbs are also meaningfully directed in signing space. They are not listed in Column 6 since the addressee is assumed to have already correctly identified the entities in the blend.

Returning now to the analysis, as no signs have been meaningfully directed yet, no Real Space blend has been created during this first sequence. Therefore, no Real Space blend number is assigned yet in Column 1 in Table 2.

Column 2 provides information regarding the perspective from which the signer produces signs. The discourse is not strictly a narrative, but several discourse strategies previously described as typical of narratives are used in it. To avoid erroneous associations with narrative discourse, the label 'signer's perspective' was chosen, not 'narrator's perspective'. Signs are either produced from the signer's perspective, or information is provided regarding from which discourse character's perspective the signs are produced.

The introduction of the main character is followed by the signs SELF cl-PERSON$^{>|EKR|}$, with the second sign located to the signer's left, thus associating that area in signing space with Kübler Ross. When the signer makes an association between the conceptual content she refers to with particular signs and an area in signing space, like this, it prompts the construction of a blended entity in that area, constructing a Real Space blend. So far, it contains one blended entity, the token |EKR|, to the left of the signer. This first Real Space blend in Section 1 is numbered 1:1 in Column 1, which also contains information regarding whether it is a token blend (token) or a surrogate blend (surr.).

---

[8] Transcription notes for the glossing, and the analyzed segments fully glossed and translated can be downloaded, see links on p. 300.

The identity of a blended entity is given in Column 3, and for this first token it is |EKR|. Column 4 contains information regarding whether each blended entity is a token or a surrogate. For surrogates there is also information regarding whether they are visible surrogates, i.e., consisting of (part of) the signer's body, or invisible surrogates, i.e., consisting of areas in signing space. More detailed information regarding the location of the blended entity is provided in Column 5. The token |EKR| is located to the left of the signer, at mid height, i.e., approximately at chest height. This token |EKR| will frequently be used when the signer talks about Kübler Ross. Both the pronominal pointing sign NON-1ST-SING$^{>x}$ and other signs are directed towards |EKR| during the rest of the segment.

Table 2: Real Space blend table for Segment 1, Chunk 1–3.

1 Real Space Blend	2 Perspective	3 Blended entity	4 Type of blended entity	5 Location of blended entity	6 Expressions used about the entities
---	signer	---	---	---	INDEX-C #ELISABETH #KUBLER #ROSS
1:1 token	signer	|EKR| |USA| |EKR|	token token token	left of signer/mid in front of signer/high left of signer/mid	SELF Cl-PERSON$^{>\|EKR\|}$ INDEX$^{>forward/high}$ USA NON-1ST-SING$^{>\|EKR\|}$, NON-1ST-SING$^{>\|EKR\|}$ SELF, NON-1ST-SING$^{>\|EKR\|}$
1:2 surr.	|EKR|	|EKR|	visible surrogate	signer, excl. hands producing INDEX-C STUDY	INDEX-C
1:3 token	signer	|EKR|	token	left of signer/mid	NON-1ST-SING$^{>\|EKR\|}$, PSYCHOLOGY/DOCTOR NON-1ST-SING$^{>\|EKR\|}$, NON-1ST-SING$^{>\|EKR\|}$, Cl-PERSON$^{>\|EKR\|}$ WOMAN, NON-1ST-SING$^{>\|EKR\|}$, NON-1ST-SING$^{>\|EKR\|}$, DEATH/LADY NON-1ST-SING$^{>\|EKR\|}$, NON-1ST-SING$^{>\|EKR\|}$, HUMAN-BEING
		|dying person|	token	left of signer/low	Cl-PERSON$^{>\|dying person\|}$ NON-1ST-SING$^{>\|EKR\|}$,
		|EKR|	token	left of signer/mid	NON-1ST-SING$^{>\|EKR\|}$

Several tokens can be created as part of the same token blend, and the next entity introduced is inanimate, USA, and also becomes part of blend 1:1. The location in signing space used for the blended entity |USA| is visible from the verb: MOVE-

FROM-TO$^{>|\text{EKR}|\text{-forward/high}}$, as it ends at a location in front of the signer approximately the height of her forehead. It is not until the following signs (INDEX$^{>\text{forward/high}}$ USA) are produced, however, we know the identity of the place to which Kübler Ross moved. The signer continues to talk about Kübler Ross, using three instances of NON-1ST-SING$^{>|\text{EKR}|}$, one in combination with the sign SELF, and these signs are also listed in Column 6. When several different expressions are used about an entity, also when one expression is repeated, the glosses are separated with a comma (,).

The signer's gaze also plays a vital part in creating Real Space blends, and here it seems to be of particular relevance. The signer has mainly held her gaze directed at the addressee, but now she breaks eye contact and rapidly produces two signs from the perspective of a discourse entity: INDEX-C STUDY ("I study"). When the signer herself, or parts of her, becomes part of a blend, this creates a surrogate blend. As no other animate discourse entity has been introduced, and the signer has said that Kübler Ross was studying to become a doctor, INDEX-C refers to her, and the signer's body as a visible surrogate |EKR| represents her. Surrogate blends are also Real Space blends, here they are given running numbers as part of the same system as token blends, making this blend 1:2. When the perspective is that of a discourse character, as in surrogate blends, the identity of that blended entity is stated in vertical brackets in Column 2. In 1:2 the perspective is that of |EKR|. There are no invisible surrogates, so only |EKR| is listed in Column 3, and it is the only visible surrogate listed in Column 4.

To study, you do not actually stretch out your hands, palms facing up, with repeated ulnar contact, as the signer does to produce the sign STUDY. Therefore, the hands that produce this sign are not part of the surrogate, and in Column 5 the blended entity is described as 'signer', excluding the hands producing INDEX-C STUDY. This constitutes use of a partitionable zone, where the signer's hands and forearms are partitioned, producing lexical items telling the addressee what the surrogate is doing. The signer's hands and forearms sometimes are, and sometimes are not, part of a surrogate blend. Therefore Column 5 contains specific mention of which signs the hands/forearms are producing during a surrogate blend and whether or not these signs are considered part of the surrogate. Only INDEX-C is listed in Column 6, as that is the sign that is used about the discourse entity.

The signer then returns to the signer's perspective, and uses several different signs directed towards the token |EKR| to her left to talk about Kübler Ross. Using tokens from the signer's perspective makes this a token blend. To avoid highly complex analyses regarding whether the signer returns to a previous token blend or creates a new one, whenever the signer switches from one Real Space blend to another a new blend number is assigned, making this blend 1:3. Now, the signer begins to talk about another entity, which will occur frequently during the whole discourse, namely the group of people that Kübler Ross interviews and/or works with. Exactly who they are varies. First the signer talks about how Kübler Ross does research on death, and what happens to people before and after death. The first mention of these persons is glossed dying person, but she later also talks about a dying patient, cancer patients, etc. What several of the different constellations of people referred to have in common is that they are people who are dying, and they meet Kübler Ross. Her research on death is mentioned before this dying person is introduced, and it is this contextual information alone that tells an addressee the sign HUMAN-BEING here refers to a dying person, and not just any person. The sign HUMAN-BEING is followed by cl-PERSON$^{>|\text{dying person}|}$, directionally modified to indicate the location of that token to the signer's left. The location of this token is listed as left of signer/low, as |dying person| seems to be located lower than |EKR|. This impression, however, is largely based on the signer's use of gaze direction and directionally modified verbs, and not related to any measurable difference regarding exact location in signing space (Nilsson 2008).

Finally, after introducing the dying person, the signer returns to talking about Kübler Ross, using two more instances of NON-1ST-SING$^{>|\text{EKR}|}$ and one instance of SEEMS$^{>|\text{EKR}|}$, which is a verb and therefore not glossed in the table. As the token |EKR| remains in the same location as before the dying person was introduced, this is analyzed as still taking place within blend 1:3. A Real Space blend is regarded as the same one as long as the token(s) remain the same, even though they may not be explicitly mentioned again, and as long as the signer's perspective is the same.[9] If a referent is qualified, i.e., if the signer first talks about, for example, a dying patient in general, then talks about a more specific *cancer* patient, this is regarded as use of the same Real Space blend if nothing else has changed. If the signer changes the subject and uses new tokens, that makes it a new Real Space blend.

4.2 Segment 2: Content and structure

The next segment consists of Chunks 4–6, directly after Segment 1, and is of similar length (36 seconds).[10] The signer now presents more details about Kübler Ross and her ideas:

> Moreover, she enjoys talking to patients, patients who are going to die soon. She thinks that today's health care is too focused on life and living. Even though some people may need

---

[9] Fridman-Mintz and Liddell (1998: 262), on the other hand, describing the same kind of phenomenon as *Grounded Mental Spaces*, consider "[a]ddition or erasure of elements from a previous mental space" to be "[m]otivating factors in the creation of new spaces".

[10] Segment 2, with translations, can be viewed at: https://ntnu.cloud.panopto.eu/Panopto/Pages/Viewer.aspx?id=935dbb8c-5cb7-4be6-b12b-ad4f00b9590c

someone to talk to, some people also need to die. According to her, there are certain rules; she calls it lessons, the lessons of life. And once you have done all your lessons, gone through all of them piece by piece, then somebody above will allow that you die.

There are eight Real Space blends in Segment 2, compared to three in Segment 1, and there are also more tokens. The |dying person EKR talks to| becomes a |dying patient|, then the signer talks about only |some of the dying patients|, and finally the more general |dying patient| reappears. In addition to these blended entities, there are the tokens |EKR|, and |somebody above|. There are three surrogate blends, each containing a different visible surrogate, and each with its accompanying invisible surrogate.

The first Real Space blend (2:1, Table 3) contains the same token |EKR| as in blend 1:3 (in Table 2). A segment boundary was inserted here as a consequence of the somewhat artificial, previously made, division of the discourse into chunks and segments. As 2:1 is part of Segment 2, it is considered a new token blend, with a new number. The signer continues to talk about Kübler Ross with an instance of NON-1ST-SING$^{>x}$ directed towards |EKR| to her left. This mention of Kübler Ross also serves as information regarding whom the signer will represent in the coming surrogate blend, created by using the verb DISCUSS-WITH$^{>|dying person|}$ in 2:2. Through blending, the signer's body is now perceived as the blended entity |EKR|. Again, hands and forearms are not part of the surrogate, but partitioned, producing a verb telling the addressee what the surrogate is doing. This surrogate blend is therefore not analyzed as an instance of constructed action. In addition to this visible surrogate there is an invisible surrogate |dying person EKR talks to|, located to the left of the signer. Both the visible and the invisible surrogates are glossed in Columns 3 and 4 in the table. When a visible surrogate is accompanied by an invisible surrogate, this is indicated with a + before the invisible surrogate in Column 4.

As the signer produces the verb DISCUSS-WITH$^{>|dying person|}$, her gaze and hands indicate where the entity that |EKR| interacts with is located. Using such verbs, it can be more or less clear whether a surrogate blend is created or not. Table 3 indicates the analytical choice that suggests a surrogate blend was created.

To specify the dying persons Kübler Ross enjoys talking to, the signer returns to the signer's perspective, creating blend 2:3. In this token blend, she directs an instance of NON-1ST-SING towards the token |EKR| again. Before creating the next blend, which is a surrogate blend, the signer first produces the signs MEDICAL-SERVICE TODAY 'today's health care', followed by the signs TOO MUCH. The production of these signs tells us the identity of the next visible surrogate, but does not in itself create a surrogate blend. The signs are therefore glossed in Column 6, for blend 2:3, where they are included since they help the addressee identify the surrogates in blend 2:4.

The signer then produces the verb FOCUS>|dying patient| as a surrogate representative of today's health care, focusing on the invisible surrogate |dying patient| to her left, and we have a new surrogate blend (2:4). The hands are not part of the surrogate, since they do not illustrate what doctors or nurses do with their hands when they focus on a dying patient. They are partitioned, and produce the lexical item FOCUS, a verb telling the addressee what the surrogate is doing, therefore not analyzed as constructed action. The sign LIVE, which is repeated three times from the same perspective in 2:4, is a different matter, however. This is analyzed as the signer representing one of the large group of people that today's health care consist of, i.e., the visible surrogate |today's health care|, animatedly telling an invisible surrogate |dying person| that they must live: LIVE! LIVE! LIVE! Therefore, the signer's hands and forearms are considered part of the surrogate, making this constructed dialogue.

Table 3: Real space blend table for Segment, Chunk 4–6.

1 Real Space Blend	2 Perspective	3 Blended entity	4 Type of blended entity	5 Location of blended entity	6 Expressions used about the entities
2:1 token	signer	|EKR|	token	left of signer/mid	NON-1st-SING>|EKR|
2:2 surr.	|EKR|	|EKR|	visible surrogate	signer, excl. hands producing DISCUSS-WITH>|dying person|	
		|dying person EKR talks to|	+ invisible surrogate	left of signer/low	
2:3 token	signer	|dying patient|	token	left of signer/low	cl-PERSONx2 PATIENT cl-PERSON-plur DIE PATIENT WILL ON WAY DIE, NON-1st-PLUR>|dying patients|
		|EKR|	token	left of signer/mid	NON-1st-SING>|EKR| MEDICAL-SERVICE TODAY
2:4 surr.	|today's health care|	|today's health care|	visible surrogate	signer, excl. hands producing FOCUS>|dying patients| but incl. hands producing LIVE!x3>|dying patients|	
		|dying patient EKR talks to|	+ invisible surrogate	left of signer/low	

Table 3 (continued)

1 Real Space Blend	2 Perspective	3 Blended entity	4 Type of blended entity	5 Location of blended entity	6 Expressions used about the entities
2:5 token	signer	|some of the dying patients|	token	left of signer/low	ONE PART
2:6 token	signer	|EKR|	token	left of signer	NON-1st-SING$^{>\|EKR\|}$ ONE #LESSON IN LIFE
		|EKR|	token	left of signer	NON-1st-SING$^{>\|EKR\|}$ #LESSON IN LIFE, ALL #LESSONS, ONE LESSON
2:7 surr.	|person doing lessons|	|person doing lessons|	visible surrogate	signer, incl. hands producing LEAF-THROUGH$^{>\|lessons\ of\ life\|}$	
		|lessons of life|	+ invisible surrogate	left of signer/low	
2:8 token	signer	|somebody above|	token	above signer	UP$^{>up}$ HEAVEN SOMEONE
		|dying patient|	token	left of signer/low	NON-1st-SING$^{>\|dying\ patient\|}$

The signer also describes Kübler Ross's idea that there are two kinds of dying patients: some who may need somebody to talk to, and some who need to die. Both groups are introduced with the phrase ONE PART 'some' from the signer's perspective. As the signer's gaze is not directed down to her left until she produces the second instance of the two signs, it is not until this mention of the second group of dying patients that a token blend (2:5) is created. Therefore, the glosses ONE PART occur only once in Column 6 in the table.

Though the signer continues to produce signs from the signer's perspective, the next sequence has been analyzed as a new blend (2:6), since she now introduces a completely new topic which is then described in more detail. Using four different expressions, she introduces an inanimate entity that is a central idea in the world view of Kübler Ross: lessons of life. No blended entity is created yet, but these signed expressions are necessary for the addressee's understanding of the next surrogate blend and are therefore listed in Column 6.

Following this introduction, these lessons of life constitute an invisible surrogate in the next surrogate blend (2:7). This third surrogate blend in the segment consists of the verb LEAF-THROUGH$^{>\|lessons\ of\ life\|}$. Here, the signer is a visible surrogate, and the addressee must infer from the context that she is a |person doing lessons|. Again, the signer represents one out of a group of people. From the previous context, the addressee can infer that the objects being leafed through are the lessons of life that a person has to go through. Interestingly, these lessons, which do not consist of any concrete matter, are described as if they are things that can be leafed through with your hands, and leafing through these invisible entities equals doing your lessons.[11] The sign is analyzed as an instance of constructed action, where hands and forearms are part of the surrogate. This verb is similar to DISCUSS-WITH$^>$ |dying person| in that it is directed toward something invisible that is acted on, but here the hands and forearms are considered part of the surrogate and not partitioned.

The signer then returns to producing signs from the signer's perspective, and in the final token blend of Segment 2 (2:8), one more token is introduced: |somebody above|, which is an entity that decides whether a person is allowed to die or not.

4.3 Segment 3: Content and structure

Segment 3 consists of Chunks 25–26. These two chunks were chosen due to an initial impression of their being particularly complex.[12] The signer describes how Kübler Ross invites dying patients to accompany her to lectures she gives, and how various parts of audiences react to this.

> Then, she will say that these people are patients who are about to die. After that one-hour lecture, she will invite the audience to ask questions. She will say 'Go ahead, ask questions, they are about to die any time now, maybe tomorrow, the day after tomorrow, or today – maybe during this lecture. . . Feel free to ask them questions.' But the audience is usually completely nonplussed, not wanting to ask anything. Then, gradually, they start, and more and more questions will be asked. And a lot of people have also been helped during her lectures, thinking 'So, this is me, these are my feelings. . .' And many doctors are afraid to face the fact that even though they try to save the life of a patient, that patient may still die, this may happen quite often. . . However, her lectures will introduce them to a different way of thinking. If somebody dies, it's not such a big deal, it's because it was time for him or her to die.

Judging by the exceptionally large Real Space blend table, Segment 3 is indeed highly complex. The segment contains a number of sequences that can be analyzed

---

[11] Similarly, it has been noted for interpreted ASL discourse that the interpreter "actually places 'fear' to his right and interacts with it, as if this abstract concept were an interlocutor in a conversation" (Winston and Monikowski, 2003: 217).
[12] Segment 3, with translations, can be viewed at: https://ntnu.cloud.panopto.eu/Panopto/Pages/Viewer.aspx?id=9499cc08-f709-4c32-82e1-ad4f00ba9d36

in more than one way, but I have chosen one analysis for Table 4 and the description below. There are two sequences where it seems as if there is a false start, possibly the signer changes her mind regarding how to express something. Table 4 contains an analysis of the whole segment, but only the first part (blends 3:1–3:9) is described in detail.

Segment 3 is approximately 40 seconds long, which makes it fairly equal in length to Segment 1. But whereas Segment 1 contains only three Real Space blends and one non-blended sequence, Segment 3 contains fifteen blends and four non-blended sequences. The segment contains three different visible surrogates: |EKR|, |many in audience|, and |doctor in audience|. As in Segment 2, the surrogate sometimes represents a whole group. These visible surrogates occur more than once, and when they occur there is usually at least one (sometimes two) additional invisible surrogate(s), e.g., |dying patients|, a never explicitly mentioned |audience|, and |doctor's patient who dies|. The signer frequently and rapidly switches between these surrogates, sometimes without much previous indication to help the addressee identify which discourse entity she currently represents. In all, there are six different blended entities to keep track of: |EKR|, |patients|, the |audience|, |many in audience|, |doctor in audience|, and |doctor's patient who dies|. The |patients| are later qualified as |dying patients| but still counted as one discourse entity. Except for |EKR|, these entities are all non-specific.

The beginning of Segment 3 can be analyzed in at least two different ways. Table 4 is based on the analysis that the signer first produces a sign that has been glossed NON-1ST-SING$^{>|EKR-f|}$, followed by the verb SAY. She then seems to decide that she needs to clarify the identity of the token towards which the pointing sign NON-1ST-SING was directed, and adds a combination of two simultaneous signs. While her non-dominant hand produces a POINTER buoy, directed towards |EKR-f|, the dominant hand produces the fingerspelled pronoun #SHE$^{>|EKR-f|}$. As both signs are directed towards a token, this is a token blend. With only one person in the discourse that can be uniquely identified with *she*, the identity of the token is clear.

Next, in 3:2, the signer represents Kübler Ross. As the surrogate |EKR|, she begins to set the scene for the rest of the segment, introducing a group of dying patients that have accompanied Kübler Ross to the lecture she is giving (introduced in Chunk 24). The introduction of the dying patients is directed spatially towards an invisible surrogate, the |audience|. Though the audience is not explicitly mentioned, a lecture frame (Fillmore 1982) entails there being an audience present, and this audience will be part of several of the following surrogate blends. There is one more invisible surrogate, the group of |dying patients| that |EKR| introduces to the |audience|, which the signer points at twice with her left hand in 3:2. This POINTER buoy is produced by the signer representing |EKR| and points at an "important element in the discourse" (Liddell 2003: 250), namely the invisible surrogate that it will gradually be possible to identify as |dying patients|. At the same time, the signer produces another referring sign with her dominant hand towards the same direction, THAT-IS. To help the addressee identify this invisible surrogate, the following phrase is added: SICK Cl-PERSON-PLUR$^>$|patients| INDEX$^>$|patients| WILL ON WAY DIE. During the last four of those signs the POINTER buoy reappears on her non-dominant hand.

Next comes blend 3:3, and the sign combination LECTURE FINISH ONE-HOUR is analyzed as additional information from the signer's perspective, since the signer directs her gaze at the addressee. The POINTER buoy produced with the non-dominant hand of the signer as |EKR| in 3:2 is still held while those signs are produced, and analyzed as still directed towards the invisible surrogate |dying patients|. In Table 4, the surrogate blend is represented as *backgrounded* during this comment from the signer's perspective, marked as BG in Columns 1, 3, and 4 respectively for blend 3:3.

After this additional information from the signer's perspective, the signer returns to the perspective of Kübler Ross directing her gaze at |dying patients|. While she thus creates blend 3:4, the POINTER buoy produced with her non-dominant hand in 3:3 (and 3:2) is still held for a short while, but disappears when the first verb is produced. In this new surrogate blend, the signer as |EKR| invites the invisible surrogate |dying patients| onto the stage, between herself and the |audience|, using the directionally modified verb INVITE$^>$|dying patients|forward/right-new location in front of |EKR|. This instance of INVITE moves the surrogate |dying patients| from the previous location forward/right to a location in front of the signer as |EKR|. This movement also indicates that an |audience|, whose presence can be inferred through the lecture frame, would be located in front of the signer/remote. Having thus moved the invisible surrogate |dying patients| to a place on a |stage| between |EKR| and an |audience|, in 3:4 the signer as |EKR| tells the |audience| that they should ask the |dying patients| questions. Again, she uses a directionally modified verb: ASK-QUESTIONS$^>$|audience|-|dying patients|.

Towards the end of 3:4, a pointing sign combined with LECTURE creates analytical problems because it is hardly visible. In Table 4, the analysis chosen is that it is an instance of THERE$^>$|the place of the lecture| followed by the noun LECTURE.[13] Regardless of what kind of pointing sign it actually is, the signer then directs her gaze at the addressee and produces a gesture which indicates an uncertainty as to what might happen with the dying patients who are present during the lecture. This, too, can be analyzed in different ways. For the analysis in Table 4, since the signer produces a

---

13 An alternate analysis could be NON-1st-SING$^>$|the place of the lecture| LECTURE.

meaningful gesture, it was analyzed as a return to the signer's perspective, making it a non-blended sequence.

The signer then creates another surrogate blend, where she represents |EKR|, blend 3:5. She does so by repeating the verb INVITE$^{>|\text{dying patients}|\text{forward/right-new location in front of }|\text{EKR}|}$, directionally modified in the way it was at the beginning of 3:4. Immediately after this, she resumes eye contact with the addressee and produces another meaningfully directed verb, namely a repetition of the verb ASK-QUESTIONS$^{>|\text{audience}|-|\text{dying patients}|}$, as produced in 3:4. Since the sign is produced with the signer's gaze directed at the addressee, this is analyzed as constructing the new token blend 3:6.

Before 3:6 ends, the signer produces a brief instance of the noun MANY, lasting approximately 5 frames (approx. 0.2 sec.). This is the same strategy that was used, e.g., at the end of 2:3, where the signer identifies the kind of entity she will blend with in the next (surrogate) blend. The entity she will blend with in 3:7 is thus introduced in 3:6, with the sign MANY, while she moves her gaze and head away from the addressee. She assumes a new position of her head (and body), thus creating the new surrogate blend 3:7. The last group of people requested to do something was the invisible surrogate |audience|, which |EKR| told to ask the |dying patients| questions. The recently produced instance of MANY thus serves to delimit the group *many in the audience* from the whole of the audience. The signer's facial expression is that of a person who does not know what to do, and her gaze is directed far up and away to the right. In this surrogate blend, the signer represents one of the |many in audience|. She produces a two-handed sign glossed NONPLUSSED, and her hands are not part of the surrogate blend but partitioned to produce a sign telling the addressee that the surrogate is nonplussed and not doing anything. NONPLUSSED is first held with both hands for 33 frames (approx. 1.3 sec.), which is a long time for a single sign to last.

In order to tell the addressee what the audience is not doing, the signer must insert a comment from the signer's perspective: DON'T-WANT ASK. These two signs are produced with her dominant hand, while the non-dominant hand remains in the position of NONPLUSSED for another 12 frames (approx. 0.5 sec.) as a sign fragment. This sign fragment backgrounds the visible surrogate |many in audience|. Part of the signer's posture also keeps the surrogate active, as does the signer's facial expression. However, since the signer resumes eye contact with the addressee and produces additional lexical information (DON'T-WANT ASK), the sequence is analyzed as mainly told from the signer's perspective, creating blend 3:8.

The signer returns to producing the two-handed version of NONPLUSSED, now held for 20 frames (approx. 0.8 sec.). She is once again a visible surrogate representing one of the |many in audience|, thus creating blend 3:9 with her hands partitioned to produce a sign telling us something about that surrogate. Next she produces the phrase GRADUALLY BEGIN, followed by the verb ASK-QUESTIONSx6$^{>|\text{dying patients}|}$. The

Table 4: Real Space blend table for Segment 3, Chunk 25–26.

1 RSB	2 Perspective	3 Blended entity	4 Type of blended entity	5 Location of blended entity	6 Expressions used about the entities
3:1 token	signer	|EKR|	token	in front of signer	NON-1st-SING$^{>\|EKR\text{-}f\|}$, #SHE$^{>\|EKR\text{-}f\|}$ + POINTER$^{>\|EKR\text{-}f\|}$
3:2 surr.	|EKR|	|EKR|	visible surrogate + invisible surrogate	signer, incl. hands producing THAT-IS + POINTER$^{>?}$ forward/right	THAT-IS + POINTER$^{>?}$
	not yet stated				
		|EKR|	visible surrogate + invisible surrogate	signer, incl. hands producing SICK CL-PERSON-PLUR$^{>\|patients\|}$ INDEX$^{>\|patients\|}$, forward/right	SICK CL-PERSON-PLUR$^{>\|patients\|}$ INDEX$^{>\|patients\|}$,
		|patients|			
		|EKR|	visible surrogate + invisible surrogate	signer, incl. hands producing WILL ON WAY DIE + POINTER$^{>\|dying\ patients\|}$ forward/right	WILL ON WAY DIE + POINTER$^{>\|dying\ patients\|}$
		|dying patients|			
3:3 BG surr.	signer	BG |EKR|	BG visible surrogate +	signer, incl. hands producing POINTER$^{>\|dying\ patients\|}$	
		BG |dying patients|	BG invisible surrogate	forward/right	POINTER$^{>\|dying\ patients\|}$
3:4 surr.	|EKR|	|EKR|	visible surrogate +	signer, incl. hands producing POINTER$^{>\|dying\ patients\|}$	
		|dying patients|	invisible surrogate	forward/right	POINTER$^{>\|dying\ patients\|}$

Table 4 (continued)

1 RSB	2 Perspective	3 Blended entity	4 Type of blended entity	5 Location of blended entity	6 Expressions used about the entities
		|EKR|	visible surrogate + invisible surrogate	signer, incl. hands producing the verb INVITE[>|dying patients|forward/right-new location in front of |EKR|]	
		|dying patients|			
		|EKR|	visible surrogate + invisible surrogate	moved from forward/right to in front of signer-/close with the modified verb INVITE	
		|audience|	+ invisible surrogate	signer, incl. hands producing ASK-QUESTIONS[>|audience|-|dying patients|]	NON-1st-SING[>|dying patients|]
		|dying patients|	+ invisible surrogate	in front of signer/remote	THERE[>|the lecture|] LECTURE
		|EKR|	visible surrogate + invisible surrogate	in front of signer/close signer, incl. hands producing THERE[>|the lecture|] LECTURE	
		|dying patients|		in front of signer/close	
---	signer	---	---	---	---

Table 4 (continued)

1 RSB	2 Perspective	3 Blended entity	4 Type of blended entity	5 Location of blended entity	6 Expressions used about the entities
3:5 surr.	|EKR|	|EKR|	visible surrogate	signer, incl. hands producing the verb INVITE$^{>\|dying\ patients\|}$ forward/right-new location in front of |EKR|	
		|dying patients|	+ invisible surrogate	moved from forward/right to in front of signer-/close	
3:6 token	signer	|audience|	token	in front of signer/ remote	
		|dying patients|	token	in front of signer/ close	
					MANY
3:7 surr.	|one member of the audience|	|many in audience|	visible surrogate	signer, excl. hands producing NONPLUSSED	
3:8 BG surr.	signer	BG |many in audience|	BG visible surrogate	sign fragment on left hand; NONPLUSSED	
3:9 surr.	|many in audience|	|many in audience|	visible surrogate	signer excl. hands; first sign fragment, then both hands; NONPLUSSED	
		|many in audience|	visible surrogate	signer excl. hands producing ASK-QUESTIONSx6$^{\|dying\ patients\|}$	
		|dying patients|	+ invisible surrogate	in front of signer/ close	
---	signer	---	---	---	MANY

Table 4 (continued)

1 RSB	2 Perspective	3 Blended entity	4 Type of blended entity	5 Location of blended entity	6 Expressions used about the entities
3:10 surr.	|many in audience|	|many in audience|	visible surrogate	signer excl. hands producing HAVE-A-FEELING	
					INDEX-C
				signer incl. hands producing AHA INDEX-C, HOW FEEL-INSIDE	
---	signer	---	---	---	MANY DOCTOR
3:11 surr.	|doctor in audience|	|doctor in audience|	visible surrogate	signer, incl. hands producing POSS-C PATIENT INDEX-C TRY SAVE LIFE OF INDEX-C. gesture DIE.	POSS-C, INDEX-C, INDEX-C
		+ |doctor's patient who dies|	invisible surrogate	in front of signer	
---	signer	---	---	---	---
3:12 surr.	|doctor in audience|	|doctor in audience|	visible surrogate	signer, incl. hands producing INDEX$^{>forward/high}$	INDEX$^{>forward/high}$
		+ |the lecture|	invisible surrogate	in front of signer/remote	
3:13 token	signer	|the lecture|	token	in front of signer/remote	ARRIVE-AT$^{>\|the\ lecture\|}$
3:14 surr.	|doctor in audience|	|doctor in audience|	visible surrogate	signer, incl. hands producing FAIL LEAVE-IT.	
3:15 token	signer	|doctor's patient who dies|	token	in front of signer	NON-1st-SING$^{>\|doctor's\ patient\ who\ dies\|}$

signer's gaze alternates between the gaze direction of the surrogate and having eye contact with the addressee, but the sequence has still been analyzed as belonging to 3:9. The verb ASK-QUESTIONSx6$^{>\|dying\ patients\|}$ moves from the signer as a visible instance of |many in audience| towards |dying patients|.

5 Discussion

This explorative study was conducted using limited data from only one signed discourse, in order to develop ideas and tools to operationalize discourse complexity in STS. For more generalized conclusions to be made, much more data will have to be analyzed. There are, however, still things we can learn from this study.

Comparing Tables 2, 3 and 4, their sizes alone indicate that Segment 3 is more complex than the other two. Additionally, Segment 3 has long sequences where Column 6, for expressions used about discourse entities, is completely empty, which means an addressee gets little help identifying referents. To understand what the signer is expressing, it is crucial that the addressee conceptualizes the discourse content in a similar way. In the segments analyzed here, many of the spatial conceptualizations in front of the signer are invisible. The identities of both visible and invisible Real Space blends are not always explicitly expressed by the signer, making the addressee's task of identifying them more difficult. Producing Segment 3, the signer frequently resumes eye contact with the addressee, checking for feedback and possible indications that clarification is needed, suggesting she might be aware that what she is producing can be difficult to follow. This is especially visible from blend 3:8 and onwards, perhaps indicating she knows that is a particularly complex piece of discourse.

The signer introduces, describes the actions of, and reintroduces discourse entities in different ways. Sometimes, she uses several different noun phrases (including pronominal pointing signs) about one single entity, repeatedly mentioning it mainly from the signer's perspective using token blends (cf. Segment 1 about Kübler Ross). The result is comparatively few Real Space blends, and arguably a relatively simple discourse structure. There are, however, also sequences where the signer uses comparatively few noun phrases, producing several directionally modified verbs and surrogate blends instead (cf. Segment 3). She then frequently switches between different discourse entities' perspectives, as well as the signer's perspective, visible from how few glosses there are in Column 6 in the tables. As it can thus be harder to identify who the signer is talking about, as well as who is doing what to whom, this kind of discourse may be more inferentially complex, creating an additional processing load for the addressee.

To indicate the identity of the visible surrogate in an upcoming surrogate blend the signer often uses a noun phrase, either produced towards the end of a sequence produced from the signer's perspective, or in a non-blended sequence.[14] Such indi-

---

[14] For a discussion of framing constructed action (i.e., identification of the referent) in British Sign Language, cf. Cormier, Smith and Zwets (2013).

cations of whose perspective she will shift to can consist of an explicit mention of that entity, like the noun phrase MANY DOCTOR in the non-blended sequence before 3:10. But they also consist of one or several signs that only indicate the frame necessary to identify the surrogate, like the signs MEDICAL-SERVICE TODAY, in 2:3. In 2:4, the signer shifts to the perspective of (somebody working in) today's health care. The invisible surrogate |dying patient|, in the same Real Space blend, is never explicitly referred to with any sign. The identity of that entity has to be inferred from the current frame, and from other signals such as the fact that it is addressed by the visible surrogate |today's health care|. The invisible surrogate being located in front of and slightly lower than |today's health care|, possibly in an equally invisible |hospital bed|, can also be regarded as a clue. Thus, despite what has been widely accepted, and as stated by Liddell and Vogt-Svendsen, signers do not have to "identify every spatial element prior to making use of it" (Liddell and Vogt-Svendsen 2007: 193). In 2:2–2:3, the addressee has to identify the invisible surrogate |dying patient| with the aid of several signs, e.g., cl-PERSONX2 PATIENT, which are produced after the surrogate blend where the verb DISCUSS-WITH$^{>|\text{dying person}|}$ is used. (The visible surrogate in this blend is |EKR|, who was identified prior to the blend, with the sign NON-1ST-SING$^{>|\text{EKR}|}$.)

Verbs are produced both from the signer's perspective and from that of a discourse entity. Regardless of which, the addressee must identify all the discourse entities correctly to be able to construct mental spaces corresponding to those of the signer. We see one particularly clear example of this when the signer uses a verb to change the spatial location of an invisible surrogate: INVITE$^{>|\text{dying patients|forward/right-new location in front of |EKR|}}$. To understand which discourse entity is located where in signing space after this verb, the addressee must have identified the invisible surrogates correctly already when they were first introduced.

Though gaze direction and the position of the signer's head and body have not been the focus of this analysis, they have been mentioned. There are instances where they are instrumental in indicating whether signs are produced from the signer's perspective or from that of a discourse entity, and in the latter case, from whose perspective they are produced. In 3:7 and 3:9, for example, changed posture and gaze direction indicate that the signer has shifted to the perspective of one of |many in audience|. Resuming eye contact with the addressee is often a signal that the signer is resuming her role as signer/narrator.

Analyzing American Sign Language discourse, Thumann (2013) describes how to identify surrogates in what she calls *depiction*, as well as switches between instances of depiction. Like the work of Wilcox & Occhino (2016) and Martínez & Wilcox (2019), Thumann's work was published after my original analysis (Nilsson 2010), but they all contribute in valuable ways to our knowledge about identifying who does what to whom in a signed discourse. Nilsson (2010) also contains an analysis of simultaneous interpretations of the three segments in this study, showing that especially interpreters who are L2-users of STS had more problems correctly identifying discourse entities in Segment 3.

6 Conclusions and implications

The three analyzed segments are all of similar length, but differ radically when it comes to the number of Real Space blends and blended entities they contain. Token blends and non-blended sequences, where the discourse is presented from the signer's perspective, tend to create a simpler discourse structure with comparatively few Real Space blends and relatively few entities. Surrogate blends, on the other hand, where signs are produced from the perspective of different discourse entities, create a more complex discourse structure with more Real Space blends, and more discourse entities. Presenting signed discourse in Real Space blend tables makes this difference in discourse complexity visible.

Surrogate blends can contain both visible and invisible surrogates that can be specific like |EKR|, or non-specific like, e.g., |dying patient| and |person doing lessons|. Even non-concrete entities such as ideas can be part of surrogate blends as, e.g., |lessons of life|. Sometimes a visible surrogate represents one person out of a group of people, like one of |many in audience|. That group may have been introduced with several signs, e.g., SICK cl-PERSON-PLUR$^>$|patients| INDEX$^>$|patients|, but may also never have been explicitly mentioned. The identity must then be inferred from the context and the current frame, as an |audience| is identified via the lecture frame.

Towards the end of a token blend or a non-blended sequence, the signer often produces signs that indicate whom she will represent in the coming surrogate blend. Having blended with one of the discourse entities, as part of a surrogate blend, her hands and arms can either be part of that visible surrogate or be partitioned. When they are part of the surrogate, this constitutes constructed dialogue or constructed action. When they are partitioned, however, they produce signs that add information regarding what the surrogates are doing.

Throughout the discourse, there is constant variation between types of blended entities, and whether they are explicitly or implicitly introduced, as well as in the numerical density of Real Space blends. This seems to contribute to the complexity of the discourse and how cognitively demanding it is to process, something that could be further investigated in future psycholinguistic studies. It is hoped that this detailed analysis, as well as the suggested Real Space blend tables, can be of use in further studies of signed discourse, and help operationalize discourse complexity in signed languages.

Transcription notes

In the text, and in Columns 5 (Location of blended entity) and 6 (Expressions used about the entities) in the Real Space blend tables, signs are represented with glosses. A full Transcription key can be found at: https://osf.io/qc69d?show=view&view_only=

The three analyzed segments have also been glossed in full, with the text divided into numbered chunks, and this document can be found at: https://osf.io/kvrtc?show=view&view_only=

References

Cormier, Kearsy, Sandra Smith & Martien Zwets. 2013. Framing constructed action in British Sign Language narratives. *Journal of Pragmatics* (55). 119–139.

Crasborn, Onno & Han Sloetjes. 2008. Enhanced ELAN functionality for sign language corpora. In Onno Crasborn, Eleni Efthimiou, Thomas Hanke, Ernst D. Thoutenhoofd & Inge Zwitserlood (eds.), *The third workshop on the representation and processing of sign languages: Construction and exploitation of sign language corpora [a workshop given at the Sixth International Conference on Language Resources and Evaluation, 26 May – 1 June 2008, Marrakech, Morocco*, 39–43. Paris: European Language Resources Association.

Dudis, Paul G. 2004. Body partitioning and real-space blends. *Cognitive Linguistics* 15(2). 223–238.

Fauconnier, Gilles. 1985. *Mental Spaces*. Cambridge, MA: MIT Press.

Fauconnier, Gilles & Mark Turner. 1998. Conceptual integration networks. *Cognitive Science* 22(2). 133–187.

Fauconnier, Gilles & Mark Turner. 2002. *The Way We Think: Conceptual Blending And The Mind's Hidden Complexities*. New York: Basic Books.

Fauconnier, Gilles & Mark Turner. 2006. Conceptual Integration Networks. In Dirk Geeraerts (ed.), *Cognitive Linguistics: Basic Readings*, 303–371. Berlin/New York: Mouton de Gruyter.

Fillmore, Charles J. 1982. Frame semantics. In Linguistic Society of Korea (ed.), *Linguistics in the Morning Calm*, 111–137. Seoul: Hanshin Publishing Company.

Fillmore, Charles J. 2006. Frame semantics. In Dirk Geeraerts (ed.), *Cognitive Linguistics: Basic Readings*, 373–400. Berlin/New York: Mouton de Gruyter.

Fridman-Mintz, Boris & Scott K. Liddell. 1998. Sequencing mental spaces in an ASL narrative. In Jean-Pierre Koenig (ed.), *Discourse and Cognition: Bridging the Gap*, 255–268. Stanford: Center for the Study of Language and Information, Leland Stanford Junior University.

Kübler Ross, Elisabeth. 1998. *Livets hjul: En självbiografi i dödens närhet* [The Wheel of Life: A Memoir of Living and Dying, translated by Göran Grip]. Stockholm: Natur & Kultur.

Liddell, Scott K. 1995. Real, surrogate, and token space: grammatical consequences in ASL. In Karen Emmorey & Judy S Reilly (eds.), *Language, Gesture, and Space*, 19–41. Hillsdale, NJ: Lawrence Erlbaum.

Liddell, Scott K. 2003. *Grammar, Gesture, and Meaning in American Sign Language*. Cambridge: Cambridge University Press.

Liddell, Scott K. & Melanie Metzger. 1998. Gesture in sign language discourse. *Journal of Pragmatics* 30. 657–697.

Liddell, Scott K. & Marit Vogt-Svendsen. 2007. Constructing spatial conceptualizations from limited input: Evidence from Norwegian Sign Language. In Susan D. Duncan, Justine Cassell & Elena T. Levy (eds.), *Gesture and the Dynamic Dimension of Language. Essays in Honor of David McNeill*, 173–194. Amsterdam/Philadelphia: John Benjamins.

Martínez, Rocío, & Sherman Wilcox. 2019. Pointing and placing: Nominal grounding in Argentine Sign Language. *Cognitive Linguistics* 30(1), 85–121.

Metzger, Melanie. 1995. Constructed dialogue and constructed action in American Sign Language. In Ceil Lucas (ed.), *Sociolinguistics in Deaf Communities*, 255–271. Washington, DC: Gallaudet University Press.

Nilsson, Anna-Lena. 2007. The non-dominant hand in a Swedish Sign Language discourse. In Myriam Vermeerbergen, Lorraine Leeson & Onno Crasborn (eds.), *Simultaneity in Signed Languages: Form and Function*, 163–185. Amsterdam/Philadelphia: John Benjamins.

Nilsson, Anna-Lena. 2008. *Spatial Strategies in Descriptive Discourse: Use of Signing Space in Swedish Sign Language. CDS/CLCS Monograph Number 2*. Drumcondra, Ireland: Centre for Deaf Studies, University of Dublin, Trinity College. http://urn.kb.se/resolve?urn=urn:nbn:se:su:diva-26065

Nilsson, Anna-Lena. 2010. Real Space blends in Swedish Sign Language as an indicator of discourse complexity in relation to interpreting. In Anna-Lena Nilsson *Studies in Swedish Sign Language: Reference, Real Space Blending, and Interpretation*. Stockholm: Stockholm University. Department of Linguistics dissertation. http://urn.kb.se/resolve?urn=urn:nbn:se:su:diva-37142

Rosenthal, Abigail. 2009. Lost in transcription: The problematics of commensurability in academic representations of American Sign Language. *Text & Talk* 29(5). 595–614.

Selvik, Kari-Anne. 2006. *Spatial Paths Representing Time. A Cognitive Analysis of Temporal Expressions in Norwegian Sign Language. Acta Humaniora no. 247*. Oslo: Faculty of Humanities, University of Oslo dissertation.

Tannen, Deborah. 1986. Introducing constructed dialogue in Greek and American conversational and literary narrative. In Florian Coulmas (ed.), *Direct and Indirect Speech*, 311–332. Berlin/New York: Mouton de Gruyter.

Thumann, Mary. 2013. Identifying recurring depiction in ASL presentations. *Sign Language Studies* 13(3). 316–349.

Wilcox, Sherman, & Corrine Occhino. 2016. Constructing signs: *Place* as a symbolic structure in signed languages. *Cognitive Linguistics* 27(3). 371–404.

Winston, Elizabeth A. 1991. Spatial referencing and cohesion in an American Sign Language text. *Sign Language Studies* 73. 397–410.

Winston, Elizabeth A. & Christine Monikowski. 2003. Marking topic boundaries in signed interpretation and transliteration. In Melanie Metzger, Steven Collins, Valerie Dively & Risa Shaw (eds.), *From Topic Boundaries to Omission: New Research on Interpretation, Volume 1*, 187–226. Washington, DC: Gallaudet University Press.

Tommaso Russo and Paola Pietrandrea
Metaphors and blending in Italian Sign Language discourse: A window on the interaction of language and thought

1 Signed Language metaphors and Blending Theory

According to Peirce (1931–1958), iconicity is a semiological property of linguistic and nonlinguistic signs occurring when the form of a sign is highly reminiscent of its meaning, and in this chapter we deal with the role of iconicity in signed language metaphors.[1] In spite of being one of the most studied properties of natural languages, metaphor is still a hotly debated issue. We define metaphor as the semantic process that allows talking about a given domain by using terms usually referring to another domain. For example, if a speaker says that a particular moment in her life was "like a clearing in an intriguing forest", she is talking about life by employing terms describing journeys. The addressees understand that the speaker is giving an account of her experience from a particular point of view: she is looking at the topic of her discourse, LIFE, the *target domain*, from the point of view of another kind of experience, JOURNEYS, the *source domain* (see Kövecses [2002] 2010).

Signed language metaphors are frequently characterized by the presence of iconic features. In this chapter, we describe the mechanisms that allow signed languages to integrate highly iconic features in metaphors while respecting the structural semantic restrictions of the linguistic system. We also study the relation between iconicity and more general cognitive and semantic abilites, which play a role in the production and comprehension of metaphor, as in many other domains of language, e.g., analogic image-schemas.

---

[1] (From Paola Pietrandrea) My friend and colleague Tommaso Russo drafted this chapter before his death in 2007. I located and added missing figures with the invaluable assistance of Barbara Pennacchi (IST CNRS, Rome, Italy) and updated the bibliography. I also tried to make more explicit some parts of the text, based on the countless discussions Tommaso and I had regarding iconicity in signed language in the early years of our respective scientific work. Some of what follows is an elaborated version of Russo (2005).

Tommaso Russo, Università della Calabria, Italy
Paola Pietrandrea, Université de Lille & CNRS UMR STL 8163, France,
e-mail: paolapietrandrea@gmail.com

https://doi.org/10.1515/9783110703788-012

One productive way to deal with such phenomena is to address them through the theoretical instruments provided by a collection of theories that go by various names, but altogether here we will refer to as "Blending Theory" (Turner and Fauconnier 1995; Fauconnier and Turner 2002). Blending Theory studies the role played by analogic-imagistic mental constructs (what Fauconnier 1994 called "mental spaces") in human comprehension and conceptualization processes. Blending Theory thus focuses on both the linguistic and cognitive processes that enable the integration of different inputs in a single mental representation. Blending Theory has been applied to the study of signed languages mainly at two levels: 1) the explanation of indexical features in signed languages grammars (e.g., Liddell 2003); and 2) the analysis of body partitioning (Dudis 2004; Wulf and Dudis 2005) in both literal and metaphorical utterances.

Less attention has been devoted in the literature to Blending Theory as a theoretical instrument useful to model the interaction (Black [1979] 1993) and cross-mapping (Lakoff and Johnson 1999) of target and source semantic domains in signed language metaphors. In this chapter, we argue that Blending Theory can be productively applied to the study of signed metaphors in discourse and that it can also be useful in establishing comparisons between spoken and signed language metaphors.

This chapter is organized as follows: We introduce the notion of discursive iconicity in Section 2. In Section 3 we present previous models of the interaction between iconicity and metaphors (in particular, Taub 2001). In Sections 4.1 through 4.3 we present Russo's (2000, 2004a, 2004b) model and examine blending processes both in spoken and signed language metaphors; the examples are extracted from a corpus of Italian Sign Language (Lingua dei Segni Italiana, or LIS) metaphors collected in Rome (see Russo 2000, 2004a, 2004b). In Section 5, we frame Russo's analysis of the semantic and conceptual processes at play in signed metaphors against the background of a much wider question: how and to what extent are the conceptualization processes involved in blending influenced by language-specific constraints and constructs? Or, in other terms, do linguistic constructs partially shape or influence our thought processes?[2] We suggest that signed languages provide an interesting standpoint to reframe this traditional cognitive and philosophical problem.

---

2 See Slobin's (1987, 2003) thinking for speaking hypothesis.

2 Iconicity in signed and spoken languages

A key feature of the linguistic structure of signed languages (and an important feature for spoken languages) is iconicity. By "iconicity" we mean a mapping between certain features of the form of a signed unit and certain aspects of its meaning. This mapping, which is generally inherent in the language system, can be productive in discourse. It is now recognized that both diagrammatic and image-like iconic forms, to use Charles Sanders Peirce's (1931–1958) widely-used terminology, are present in spoken languages to a degree much higher than has been acknowledged in the past (e.g., see Givón 1989, 2002; Haiman 1980, 1983, 1985; Waugh 1993; Dressler 1995; Langacker, this volume; also see Pietrandrea and Russo 2007 for a review). Nevertheless, these structures seem much more pervasive in signed languages. This characteristic of signed languages is likely due to their visual-gestural modality, but also to the fact that signs are used predominantly in face-to-face interactions and that they have very limited written forms.

In previous work (Russo 2004b; Pietrandrea and Russo 2007; Antinoro Pizzuto and Pietrandrea 2001; Pietrandrea 2002) we argued that the standardization processes imposed by the written tradition of spoken languages play a major role in the decrease of iconicity in some spoken language structures. As well, the linear temporal dimension of the phono-acoustic channel seems to downplay certain kinds of iconic devices in spoken languages (Pietrandrea 2002; see Pietrandrea and Russo 2007 for extensive discussion). Signed language structures are, thus, better compared to spoken rather than to written language. The multimodal, simultaneous and iconic layering in signed language usage may find a counterpart in the layering of oral production and nonverbal signals, which includes co-speech gesturing (McNeill 1992; Cuxac 2000; Pizzuto 2001; Liddell 2003; Kendon 2004; Brennan 2005). Our analysis of signed language iconic phenomena stems from the hypothesis that iconic devices are "linguistic traces" of the nondiscrete, analogic conceptualization processes that take place during language production and understanding, both in spoken and signed language.

Russo, Giuranna, and Pizzuto (2001) and Russo (2004a) distinguish between two kinds of iconicity: *frozen* or *dormant iconicity* and *productive* or *dynamic iconicity*. Frozen iconicity concerns the relations between form and meaning that can be identified in sublexical, lexical and morphological structures of isolated signs. This type of iconicity has been widely studied in the signed language literature (e.g., Klima and Bellugi 1979; Boyes Braem 1981; Pizzuto and Volterra 2000; P. Wilcox 2000; Taub 2000, 2001; Pietrandrea 2002; S. Wilcox 2004). It has been extensively argued that the iconic features of signs do not contrast with the inherent linguistic character of signed languages; indeed, this type of iconicity varies across signed languages and cultures as shown by many authors (Pizzuto and Volterra 2000;

Taub 2001; Pietrandrea 2002; Russo 2004a; among others). Dynamic iconicity is the form-meaning correspondence that can be established in discursive contexts. This type of iconicity is variously labelled in the signed language literature as the iconicity of productive forms (Johnston and Schembri 1999; Brennan 1992, 2005), *iconicité discursive* (Jouison 1995), *Grande Iconicité* (Cuxac 2000) or dynamic iconicity (Russo, Giuranna, and Pizzuto 2001; Russo 2004a). These authors have different labels for the iconic features (of signs) that become evident in discourse usage, which are not clearly identifiable when individual signs are isolated.

This type of iconicity is often evoked in the analyses of so-called "classifier forms",[3] or "polymorphemic productive forms" (Brennan 1992, among others). Polymorphemic forms encode ad hoc categories (Barsalou 1983; Mauri 2017), that is, forms expressing linguistic meanings constructed spontaneously to achieve goals relevant to the current situation, which usually are not listed in a dictionary despite the fact that they can occur very frequently in signed texts. As noted by Brennan (1992), one prominent feature of productive forms is that they are visually motivated, hence iconic. Building on Brennan (1990), who observes that for BSL "what may appear to be 'dormant' iconicity may be 'revitalized' by the signer to create novel forms" (1990: 130), Johnson and Schembri (1999), also accepting the distinction between frozen and productive lexicon, observe that this revitalization of the frozen lexicon takes place in discourse. In Russo's terms (Russo, Giuranna, and Pizzuto 2001; Russo 2004a), dynamic iconicity includes iconic uses of polymorphemic productive forms constructed in discourse while the signer is describing a character or a scene. Classifier handshapes, which are particular types of polymorphemic productive forms,[4] constitute a closed class of handshapes (Emmorey 2003; Brennan 2001; Cuxac 2000). These forms have various lexical and grammatical functions: they can have verbal functions as well as locative-adverbial meanings, and are very often used as proforms. Most importantly, these forms have dynamic iconic qualities that are related to the visual-gestural modality of signed languages. When classifier handshapes are employed in a narrative or in a visual description of a scene, the signer can choose, according to her personal style, to render a scene iconically. For example, if a signer, in a narrative context, is describing the movement of a particular animal, she can choose among several polymorphemic productive forms to stress a given feature of the scene. When a LIS signer describes

---

[3] The term "classifier" is used throughout this paper following the literature on the topic. Nevertheless, we use it with some caution since we do not think that the productive forms used in signed languages can be easily compared to spoken language classifiers (cf. Schembri 2003; Slobin et al. 2003).

[4] We assume that these would also include the sets of locations and movements that can be added to the classifier handshapes when they are employed.

a squirrel climbing on a tree, she may decide to use the bent V handshape with moving fingers to iconically represent the movements of the squirrel's paws, or she can choose the S handshape that iconically represents the body and tail of the squirrel.

Very often, dynamic iconicity involves a shift within the semantic spectrum of classifier handshapes (Russo 2004a) in a discourse context. In discourse, indeed, various features of these forms can be related to different features of a *denotatum*. Also, iconic visual features of one handshape can be mapped onto different *denotata* according to the discursive context. As shown in previous work (Russo 2004a) the same handshape can be employed by the same signer in two different moments of the same narrative to address two very different meanings. For example, in LIS the open, spread form of a 5-classifier handshape can be used to represent any flat surface. Thus a signer can use it to indicate the form of a leaf as in Figure 1a, the form of a newspaper sheet as in Figure 1b, and the form of a flag as in Figure 1c:

(a) LEAF (b) NEWSPAPER (c) FLAG

Figure 1: LEAF in (a) and NEWSPAPER in (b) from Russo (2000); FLAG in (c) from Radutzky (ed., 1992), number 120.2, used with permission.

In contrast to their frozen lexical counterparts, classifier handshapes allow the signer to represent objects via a metonymic process, that is, by referring to something using something else that is salient and associated with it. In the case of signs employing iconic classifier handshapes, as seen in LIS in Figure 1, the form of the handshape can indeed metonymically evoke an associated meaning; for example in Figure 1(a), the open, spread, and flatness of the 5-classifier handshape can profile the spread form of a leaf and therefore stand for it metonymically.

Signers know the conditions that allow for an unambiguous interpretation of classifier handshapes, and they seem to respect linguistic and pragmatic constraints in producing these forms. For example, if a signer already introduced in the narrative the *topic* of a leaf moving with the wind and there are no other candidates that can be addressed through the same form, it is probable that a 5-classifier handshape, slowly weaving down in front of the signer would be interpreted as a falling leaf. The polysemic, potential semantic value of the handshape is, thus, semantically clarified in and through the context.

In previous work on iconicity, Russo analyzed this peculiar use of polymorphemic productive forms and called them *iconicity recast in discourse,* or *semantic redetermination of iconic polymorphemic forms* (Russo, Giuranna, and Pizzuto 2001; Russo 2004a, 2004b).

This semantic redetermination, as also suggested in other descriptions of polymorphemic forms (Brennan 1994; Cuxac 2000), respects modality-specific and language-specific constraints. Across signed languages, for example, every classifier handshape can be used to address a limited number of semantic domains. In addition, in most cases, although not in every case, this dynamic iconic use of polymorphemic forms to convey a particular meaning is preceded by the use of a frozen form that introduces the discourse topic (see also Cuxac 2000; Fusellier-Souza 2004). Cuxac and collaborators call these forms *transfert de formes*. Dynamic iconic forms often act as an elaboration or a specification of the previously introduced topic. We suggest below that the semantic redetermination of iconic polymorphemic forms also plays an important role in metaphor production and comprehension. Metaphors produced in discourse, as we will see below, often involve polymorphemic forms, and make use of iconic recasting devices of the sort mentioned above.

3 Iconicity and metaphor

The interaction of metaphor and iconicity in signed languages has been characterized by Taub (2001) in terms of a double mapping: "a metaphorical mapping from concrete to abstract conceptual domains and an iconic mapping from the concrete source domain and the linguistic forms that represent it" (Taub 2001: 97). An important advantage of Taub's analysis is that it clearly distinguishes iconic and metaphoric constructions in signed languages.

In the LIS lexicon we identified many cases of signs displaying both iconic-metonymic and iconic-metaphorical mappings. Thus metaphors seem to be built within the lexicon and can be identified in many different lexical families that share a particular handshape or location. This is the case for the LIS family of signs, UNDERSTAND, KNOW, FORGET, and THINK, all sharing the forehead location.

According to Taub's model we can regard a frozen signed metaphor, as in the LIS sign UNDERSTAND, shown in Figure 2, as featuring both an iconic and a metaphorical mapping. The iconic mapping establishes a relation between the linguistic form (the forehead location) and a source domain, while the metaphorical mapping establishes a relation between the source domain and some target domain features.

Figure 2: The LIS sign UNDERSTAND (from Russo 2000).

All metaphors, indeed, can be characterized as a mapping between a source domain and target domain. In the Italian expression *ho afferrato l'idea* (roughly 'I got the idea') the source domain of GRASPING is mapped onto the target domain of UNDERSTANDING. This mapping also applies to the LIS sign UNDERSTAND, although the latter displays an additional iconic mapping as outlined in Table 1.

Table 1: The metaphorical double mapping in the LIS sign UNDERSTANDING.

Iconic Mappings	Metaphorical Mappings	
Articulators:	Source Domain Elements:	Target Domain Elements:
Empty air space	OBJECT	IDEA
Forehead	HEAD	MIND
Flat-5 HS at FH	HAND AS AN INSTRUMENT USEFUL TO GRASP AN OBJECT	CAPACITY TO UNDERSTAND
Movement toward the signer while hand closes	GRASPING AN OBJECT	EXPRESSION OF THE ACT OF UNDERSTANDING
Signer	RECEIVER	PERSON WHO UNDERSTANDS

Wilcox (2000) and Taub (2001) show that previous work on signed language metaphors (e.g., Boyes Braem 1981; Wilbur 1987; Brennan 1992, 1994) failed to distinguish iconicity and metaphor in a clear-cut way. Taub's model, however, treats iconic and metaphorical mappings separately. Nevertheless we claim that Taub's model still leaves many questions open, for example: how can metaphor and iconicity interact? Does the mapping between the source and target domains influence the iconic linguistic devices involved in the production of the metaphor?[5] For a concrete example, why is the location parameter of the LIS sign UNDERSTAND articulated at the forehead if the target domain has no influence on the iconic mapping? Indeed, another part of the signer's body could have functioned equally well to represent a CONTAINER source, but the forehead location is chosen because it is a metonym for MENTAL ACTIVITY. Thus even in the frozen lexicon there is evidence that the target domain has an influence over the choice of iconic forms used to convey the metaphor. In the frozen lexicon of a signed language it is possible to find many instances of the same source-to-target mappings as, for example, UNDERSTANDING IS GRASPING or COMMUNICATING IS SENDING. These are very often entrenched metaphors, which, as suggested by Wilcox (2005), can be highly productive and can generate different metaphorical expressions grounded in the same mappings.

Nevertheless, in discourse, it is possible to find metaphors that, in spite of being related to some entrenched source-to-target mapping, are fully interpretable only with reference to the context and to previous topics. We suggest that the analysis of these types of metaphors is crucial to fully understand how metaphorical and iconic mappings interact.

We showed above that iconic devices in signed languages are at the same time highly dependent on contextual and pragmatic constraints while being fully integrated within the linguistic system. Consequently, we hypothesize that the iconic devices occurring in metaphors interact with the semantic mappings between a source and target domain established in a particular discourse context. Further, we suggest that the same mechanism of discursive semantic redetermination at play in dynamic iconic structures also applies to classifier handshapes used in signed metaphors. In this case, it is the mapping between the source and target domains established in discourse that recasts the language-specific semantic spectrum of iconic polymorphemic forms. Iconic signed units do not map onto any feature of the source independent from the target; they are semantically redetermined so as to represent features shared by both the target and the source. This process entails a reference to an intermediate mapping-space onto which semantic features of both the source and the target are projected. Since the *dynamic iconic recasting* mechanism is more clearly identifiable in discourse (where the cues for the semantic reinterpretation are explicit), we will focus on metaphors produced in discourse rather than lexicalized frozen metaphors.

---

5 Wilcox (2005) addresses a similar question.

4 An interpretation of the schematization processes involved by iconic metaphors

We claim that in signed language metaphors, the iconic mapping concerns semantic features that are shared by both the source and the target domains. The iconic mapping at play draws together features related to both domains analogically. This process is realized by making reference to an intermediate mapping space onto which are projected semantic features of both the source and the target, profiling certain similarities between the two domains. As Taub (2001) noticed, iconicity in spoken and signed languages always involves a process of schematization of the concept that is represented by the iconic linguistic forms. Such a process is called an *analogue building model* of spoken and signed iconicity (Taub 2001; for a similar treatment see also Russo 2000, 2004b). While we agree with this part of Taub's proposal, we argue that these schematization processes in iconic signed language metaphors also involve a reference to an intermediate mapping between the source and the target domains. Thus, iconicity mirrors one key feature of metaphor: the creative process of highlighting a strong similarity between two domains that are generally conceived as separate. Here we rely on Fauconnier and Turner's (2002) Blending Theory to support this hypothesis.

4.1 Spoken language metaphors and Blending Theory

As we mentioned above, a defining feature of metaphors is the potential to talk about something using terms typically related to something very different. For example, if someone says *Jerry's mental wheels are oiled*,[6] we understand that the speaker is talking about the MIND of a person using terms related to MACHINES. Examples like this are the result of a cross-domain mapping between two different conceptual domains (Lakoff and Johnson 1999; Fauconnier and Turner 2002). From this point of view, in processing the metaphor *Jerry's mental wheels are oiled*, an understanding of key properties of the target domain THE MIND comes about through the experience of the source domain MACHINES. As researchers have noted (Ricoeur 1975; Ortony 1979; Glucksberg and Keysar 1990), when a metaphor is used, the cross-domain mapping has the effect of presenting two domains considered

---

[6] For English metaphors we draw on the Metaphors of Mind online databank (http://www.cs.bham.ac.uk/~jab/ATT-Meta/Databank/index.html).

unrelated as though they *were* related. As another example, the metaphor in (1) illustrates the metaphor IDEAS ARE CREEPING ANIMALS. In (1) we are led to conceive of similarities between an idea slowly entering our consciousness and how certain animals move by creeping:

(1) *An unexpected idea was slowly creeping into my consciousness.*

Lakoff and Turner (1989: 123) explain this relevant property of conceptual metaphor by saying that "when a target domain is understood metaphorically, it will share some image-schematic structure with the source domain, structure that may have been in part introduced by the metaphor. In short, on our view, metaphor always results in a similarity of image-schema structure between the source and the target domains". This cross-domain metaphorical mapping in part builds on a pre-existing image-schematic structure which the two domains share (see also Lakoff 1987; Lakoff and Johnson 1999). Metaphors frequently introduce source domain properties into the target domain, and the metaphoric process creatively reshapes the target domain.

Although some shared properties must be required, similarity between the source and the target is indeed construed, at least to an extent, by introducing attributes of the target into the source domain and selecting and stressing certain properties of the source. However, it is easy to find metaphorical examples in which the similarity between the two domains does not seem to exist: for example English expressions linking a human (the target domain) and a non-human source domain as in (2), or expressions linking a human activity and a natural-world phenomenon as in (3).

(2) *He gloomed.*

(3) *His career is on the rocks.*

In other terms, metaphors are able to point out similarities between domains that we have not yet considered, giving us new ways of looking at a particular domain. As outlined in Russo (2005), while Lakoff and Johnson do not explicate this creative process, other researchers (e.g., Turner and Fauconnier 1995; Fauconnier and Turner 2002) give a detailed account of this component of this process. Taking both signed and spoken languages into account, theories of metaphor must consider the process of selecting and profiling features that introduce an unexpected similarity between the source and the target. Fauconnier and Turner explain metaphors as interactions between mental spaces. A mental space (Fauconnier 1994) is "an online analogic representation of the semantic structures involved in a particular utterance" (Russo 2005: 338). A *blended space* is a mental space in which "structure from two input mental spaces is projected" (Fauconnier and Turner 2002: 47). The blended space is an independent structure derived from some elements in two (or more) input mental spaces along with a "generic space", which is a structure containing elements common to the source and target, but it is more than just the sum of such elements (Fauconnier and Turner 1995). Some blends seem to become entrenched over time, but others can be quite novel (see Grady, Oakley, and Coulson 1999). Applied to metaphor, the blended space is a new space unifying features unique to the two domains involved in the metaphor.

Under this framework, the metaphor of the creeping idea in (1) would be explained by the activation of a blended space: in the blend, ideas are conceptualized as moving entities that can hide, creep in the darkness, suddenly appear, and perhaps also suddenly attack humans. This process can be represented schematically with reference to the four different mental spaces represented in Figure 3:

(i) **A target input space:** BECOMING AWARE OF A CERTAIN IDEA.
(ii) **A source input space:** ANIMALS MOVING FROM DARKNESS TO LIGHT.
(iii) **A generic space:** CHANGE OF CONDITION FROM AN OLD CONDITION TO A NEW CONDITION.
(iv) **A blended space:** IDEAS CHANGING FROM HIDING AND CREEPING TO BEING VISIBLE IN FULL LIGHT

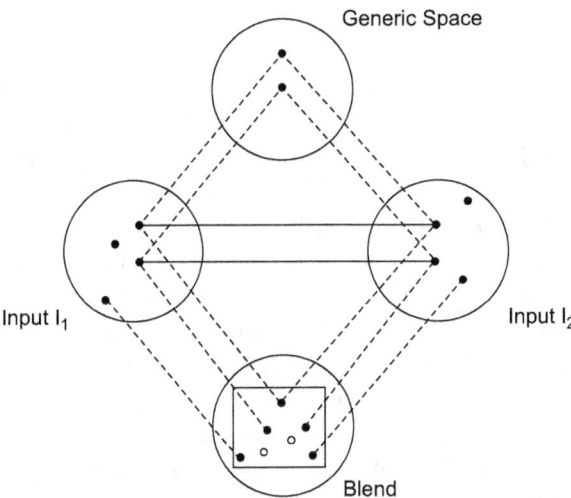

Figure 3: Mental spaces interacting in a blend (from Fauconnier and Turner 1998: 143).

Russo (2005) notes that the same blending process can result in multiple related metaphors, for example (4), and the more complex case in (5).

(4) *The idea finally appeared to me in full light.*

(5) *The elusive memory I'd been trying to force swam across the surface of my mind again and disappeared.*

With respect to signed language metaphors, iconicity does not generally map features of just the source domain onto the signed form, but rather it maps features from both the source and the target domains, emphasizing the similarity between the two domains. As a result, the role of iconicity in signed language metaphors seems to us more compatible with Turner and Fauconnier's (1995) and Fauconnier and Turner's (2002) account of the role of blending. This leads us to claim that the iconic features of signed language metaphors are the expressive manifestation of a blending process active in the minds of both the signer and the recipient during a successful communication involving metaphor (Russo 2005).

As we will show in the next section, the iconic features of productive signs show how a creative "fit" between the source and target domains can be achieved through a metaphorical cross-domain mapping. In addition, a metonymical mapping is activated to ease the schematization process occurring between the features of the blend and its iconic manifestation.

4.2 LIS metaphors and Blending Theory

Here we examine some examples from a corpus gathered for Tommaso Russo's dissertation research, comprising 5 LIS poems, 3 dramatized narrative monologues, and 3 lectures (see Russo 2000, 2005). The excerpt in (6) is from a signer giving a talk on teaching written Italian to deaf children during a conference on bilingual education in Italy (Russo 2005; see also Chiri and Lerda 1997). The signer says that hearing children can easily learn written words through an association between the form of the letters and the mental images of the articulatory movements made when they are speaking. He then describes the process of learning written Italian by deaf people wherein they memorize the letters of written words, associate them to particular meanings, and eventually learn to understand full written sentences. The signer explains that this is essentially a visual process and he introduces the following broad metaphorical comparison in his talk: READING/UNDERSTANDING WRITTEN WORDS IS TAKING PICTURES.

(6) (a)

LOOK   WORD   SAME.AS   TAKE.PICTURE   WORD.INTO.HEAD
(Loc: head)[7]

'When I see a word written on a paper, it's like I'm taking a picture of that word which allows me to remember it.'

(b)

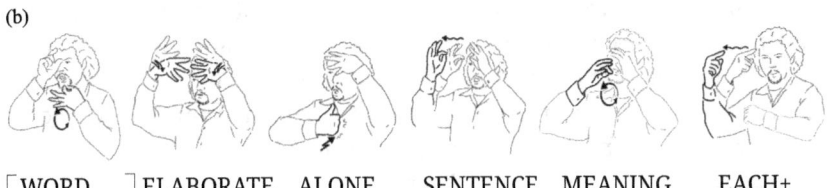

[WORD   ]ELABORATE   ALONE   SENTENCE   MEANING   EACH+
[MEANING]

'I figure out the meaning of the words in my mind and then I can understand the meaning of the sentence word by word.'

Although the sign SAME.AS in (6a) explicitly introduces the analogy, the utterances contain a metaphor where the target domain of ASSOCIATING WRITTEN WORDS WITH MEANINGS is mapped onto the source domain of TAKING A PICTURE (AND DEVELOPING THE FILM).

It can be noted that the iconic constructions used in (6a and b) do not simply map the source onto the signed form, rather the iconic signs recruit features from each semantic domain. TAKE.PICTURE reflects the source domain of PHOTOGRAPHY, but the sign WORD, articulated novelly at the head of the signer, reflects the target domain of UNDERSTAND AND MEMORIZE WORDS. The sign MEANING is also from within the target domain. Other signs, such as ELABORATE and EACH, index both the source and the target. These iconic signs together "reflect an independent analogic mental representation, a blended space" (Russo 2005: 343), in which WORDS ARE PHOTOGRAPHS and SENTENCE MEANINGS ARE PHOTOGRAPHIC FILM BEING DEVELOPED.

---

7 LIS signs are glossed as English words. Two or more words separated by periods (e.g., TAKE. PICTURE) indicate that more than one English word is needed to express the meaning of the sign. "Loc" identifies a novel location in the articulation of the sign. Two signs enclosed in square brackets indicates two signs simultaneously articulated, one on each hand (see 6b). The gloss followed by plus signs (e.g., EACH+) means that the movement of the sign is repeated. Bent-5 CL is a classifier sign with an open '5' handshape, fingers bent.

It should be noted that in this blend the concrete features of the source, for example in this case of the frame (following Fillmore 1985) of HANDLING A CAMERA, coexist with certain abstract features of the target. WORDS and MEANINGS, as concepts in the target domain, are not represented in terms of the source domain frame element PICTURES, but are introduced through their frozen lexical forms, i.e., the signs WORD and MEANING respectively. These forms are articulated in locations related to the features they acquire in the blend: the sign WORD is first produced in front of the signer to indicate a word written on a sheet of paper, and then the same bent-L handshape moves to the forehead and a stamping motion is added to indicate that the word is being *impressed* into the signer's head. Thus the iconic features of the signs are also related to some features of the target being projected in the blend: this is evident because the FOREHEAD location is chosen. This location obviously refers metonymically to mental activity rather than to the (concrete) activity within the frame of TAKING PICTURES as the source domain. The metaphorical and iconic mappings of the construction TAKE.PICTURE in (6a) is elaborated in (7) which can be represented as in Figure 4.

(7) TAKE.PICTURE (of a word) (location: forehead)

The signed utterances in (6a and b) rely on a blended mental space in which features of both the source and target are projected. Thus the iconic properties that map onto the lexical forms do not come from the source domain but emerge in the blended space. Additionally, the word being stamped on the signer's forehead metonymically represents the mental process of learning words in his mind, which is apparent in this novel blend. Indeed, iconicity provides an interesting window on the creative processes taking place when features of two different domains are projected in a unique mental representation. The iconic features of signs show how a creative "fit" between the source and the target domains can be achieved through conceptual blending. Dynamic iconicity highlights the common ground of the source and target domains and projects the blended structure onto the expressed signed forms. Finally, the novel metaphorical expressions reflect at least two different conceptual metaphors: MEMORIZING IS TAKING PICTURES and UNDERSTANDING IS DEVELOPING PHOTOGRAPHIC FILM.

In the signed discourse we analyzed, the two metaphors are bound together in a coherent analogic representation that is iconically mapped onto the signed forms. Many other instances of multiple metaphors were found in our corpus. The presence of these metaphors are evident in the creation of the blended space.

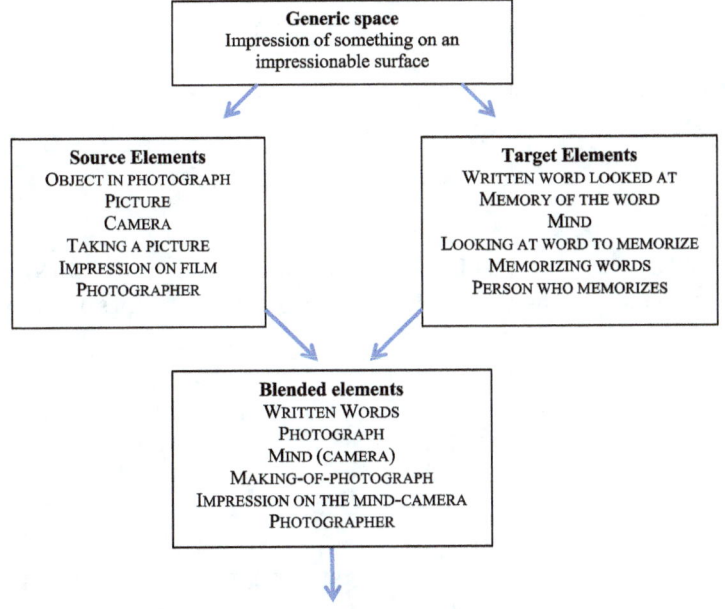

Figure 4: The metaphorical and iconic mappings of the construction TAKE.PICTURE (of a word) (location: forehead).

Our second example in (8a and b) was produced in the same context as example (6). The signer now explains that deaf children are very often incapable of memorizing the form of a word if it is not related to a specific image. In addition, he notes that if the child cannot remember an image associated with a word, he also cannot remember the word. In making this latter point the signer evokes the metaphor REMEMBERING WORDS IS LINKING OBJECTS.

(8) (a)

WORD.INTO.HEAD   bent-5 CL   HOOK   CHAIN
'The words in the mind became hooked to an image, like two rings on a chain.'

(b)

TAKE.AWAY,   WRITING   SENTENCE   DISAPPEAR
'When the image is taken away (forgotten), the words also disappear from the mind.'

In (8) the iconic features in the signs HOOK, CHAIN, and TAKE.AWAY from the source domain are mapped onto the articulation of the signs WRITING, WORD, and DISAPPEAR in the target domain, projected onto the blend. In addition, the bent-5 classifier handshape relates to a MENTAL IMAGE. This classifier form is not usually used for solid objects nor would it be apt for something that can be hooked, instead it is typically reserved for visual, non-compact things and, thus, it iconically represents features of the target projected in the blend rather than features of the source. These iconic features in the novel metaphorical utterance are a result of the blended mental space. By extension then, they could be elaborated as, for example, memories of images and words being hooked up, chained one onto the other, and either gaining stability or crashing together.

Importantly, the non-manual markers are noteworthy in this case. Here the signer's downward gaze and squinted eyes highlight the fact that a non-visible mental process is in play as the signs HOOK and CHAIN are articulated. Mouthing components are also produced, emphasizing the metaphorical actions, co-occurring with HOOK, CHAIN and DISAPPEAR. The complex mappings involving HOOK are represented in Figure 5.

Finally, classifier handshapes in both (6) and (8) play a role in encoding the main elements of the blend. Within the semantic spectrum of these classifier handshapes, this usage is thus semantically redetermined through reference to the

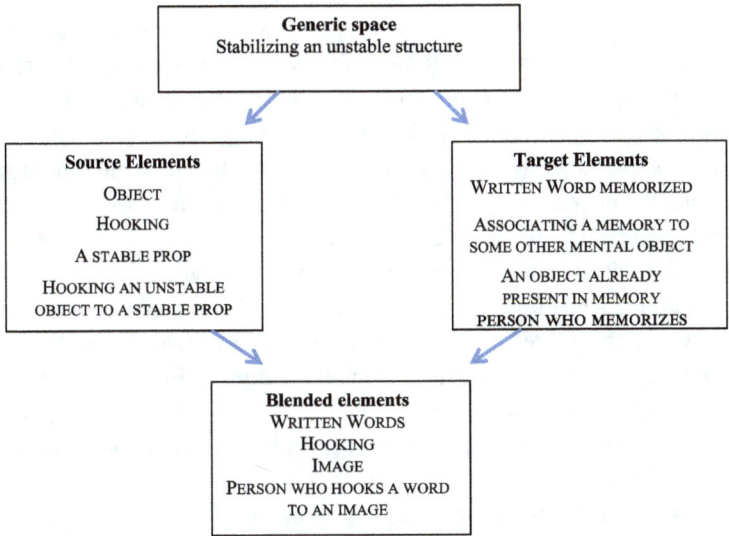

Metonymic mappings between the non-concrete features of the blend and concrete objects (e.g., WORD → SPATIAL ENTITY, IMAGE → SPATIAL ENTITY)

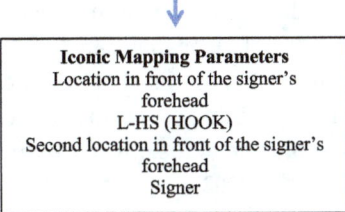

Figure 5: Complex mappings at play in the sign HOOK.

blend – this frequently occurs via a conventional metonym, as in the case of the bent-5 handshape whose form metonymically recalls an IMAGE and whose location in front of the signer's forehead indexes his role in the blended space. The IMAGE is metaphorically HOOKED TO A WORD INSIDE THE MIND of a person.

5 Interaction of the visual-gestural modality, the linguistic system, and cultural background

Taub (2001; and others) correctly highlights that the abstract character of targets cannot be represented through iconic devices and that iconicity can only play a role in the representation of the source domain. In this chapter we have argued that iconicity plays a role in the encoding of blends. Blends, unlike target domains, always provide some concrete representation of the properties shared by the target and source. In addition, the metonymic mappings between non-concrete features of the blend and concrete entities scaffold the iconic mapping between the blend and the linguistic expression. Thus, blends are always sufficiently concrete to generate some analogic image-like representation, which allows them to be iconically represented through the visual-gestural modality.

As shown above, dynamic iconic structures very often involve a semantic shift that affects classifier forms. In the case of metaphors this semantic shift involves a mapping between the target and the source, mediated through the blending process. Dynamic iconic metaphors thus provide a unique linguistic manifestation of the properties of a blend. In discourse, properties of both the target and the source domains are frequently projected onto an intermediate blend, which is subsequently addressed by the dynamic iconic structures.

An additional argument to support this hypothesis is the fact that signed metaphoric utterances often show iconic features which seem to be contradictory or incoherent. As we have seen in the LIS metaphors in the examples above, it is possible to take mental pictures of words, and to hook up words and images. The literature attests that a signer can take their brain out of their head and wash it (to get rid of impure thoughts) (Wilcox 2005: 269), or they can turn a dial on their chest "as if adjusting the heat dial of an iron" (Brennan 1994: 387) or drink some more knowledge (Jarque 2005). One of the defining properties of blends is that features of very distant domains, incompatible one to the other, are condensed in a unified representation (Fauconnier and Turner 2002). Iconic features of signs can simultaneously represent semantic features that would be incompatible if taken literally, but because they are projected in a blended mental space, are compatible as a metaphor. We reject, however, the hypothesis that blending processes bind together different input domains in a totally unconstrained manner. Our analysis shows that three distinct types of constraints apply to blending processes:

(i) modality-specific features of signed languages;
(ii) language-specific features of semantic domains;
(iii) the cultural background of a particular deaf community.

Blending processes are activated in ways that are peculiar to the visual-gestural modality (Kendon 2004; Liddell 2003). In spoken languages, blending processes involve imagery and build a bridge between multimodal layers of speech, including co-occurring gestures (McNeill 1992; Kendon 2004). In signed languages, productive polymorphemic forms and non-manual markers take the role that would be played in speech by gestures and other non-verbal elements of language. Nevertheless, in signed languages these processes are integrated within a linguistic system that is entirely expressed in the visual-gestural modality. Blending interacts with both semantic and grammatical features specific to a given signed language framed within the cultural background of a given deaf community.

LIS semantic organization drives and constrains the blending processes of LIS metaphors: the semantic extensions of polymorphemic forms are metonymically related to concrete and abstract entities in ways consistent with many other linguistic uses. In addition, cultural background influences the semantic domains involved in metaphor usage, including the cultural frames (Fauconnier and Turner 2002; Wilcox 2005) shared by deaf communities and the semantics of signed metaphors and thus specific blending processes.[8]

Cross-linguistic studies of metaphor in signed languages show that interesting cultural and linguistic variability is at play in the sources mapped onto the domains of MIND and COMMUNICATION. For example, as shown by Wilcox (2000, 2005), the UNDERSTANDING IS GRASPING metaphor is found in a number of signed languages including LIS, however the sign UNDERSTAND in ASL is not an UNDERSTANDING IS GRASPING metaphor. Jarque (2005) shows that the domain of CONSUMING FOODS AND LIQUIDS is frequently mapped onto mind activities such as KNOWING and LEARNING in Catalan Sign Language (Llengua de signes catalana). In sum, the iconic devices that create a relation between a conceptual blend and its linguistic metaphoric expressions seem to offer a window on how conceptual integration processes, linguistic constraints, and cultural regularities interact.

Our analysis provides evidence for Slobin's thinking-for-speaking hypothesis (1987, 2003). According to Slobin, language can either constrain or facilitate the thought processes that occur during linguistic activity. On-line discursive processes often shape the way we think and influence our profiling of the elements of a concept that we deem as salient. For example, the typological properties of a language seem to drive our thought processes when speaking, and they may even influence our thought processes in general: languages that obligatorily mark gender on nouns highlight gender distinctions in narratives; languages that express topological distinctions through references to cardinal points (north, south, etc.) orient their speakers to these reference points (Slobin 2003: 176). This holds true for signed language metaphor, where iconicity during blending promotes the central role of visual imagery in metaphoric cross-domain mapping.[9]

---

[8] "Frame" here refers to the socially shared and culturally defined cognitive structures that guide the perception and representation of reality (see Goffman 1974). The term is also used in AI with reference to complex data structures that provide information about the concepts and relations of concepts (see Minsky 1974).

[9] See Russo (2005) for evidence of the importance of visual imagery in LIS metaphors.

6 Conclusion

Applying a Blending Theory analysis to signed language discourse allows us to better characterize the interplay between iconicity and metaphor. We argue that, rather than generically mapping some features of the source domain onto the signed form, iconicity provides a mapping between the signed form and semantic features of both the source and target domains that are projected in the blend. In this sense, these metaphors are an interesting window into conceptualization processes at play in signers' creative use of language.

We may wonder to what extent these findings can be extended beyond LIS to shed light on the interaction between metaphor and iconicity in general. As we have shown, it is true that blending processes are constrained by linguistic properties, cultural attributes, and modality; nevertheless, we think that studying linguistic metaphors in signed languages contributes significantly to our knowledge of conceptual metaphor as a whole. In comparing spoken and signed language, we must always take into account that signed languages are visual languages used in face-to-face interactions. Thus the comparison must be between interactive face-to-face activities in both speech and signing. The multimodal layering of iconic devices in signed language articulation that we have investigated in this chapter must be compared with the multimodal nature of speech activities, taking into account the cultural frameworks within which these take place. Our analysis of metaphors and iconic devices in LIS provides a relevant contribution to the study of interactions between language-independent conceptual processes and language-specific structures.

References

Antinoro Pizzuto, Elena & Paola Pietrandrea. 2001. The notation of signed texts: Open questions and indications for further research. *Sign Language & Linguistics* 4(1/2). 29–45.
Barsalou, Laurence W. 1983. Ad hoc categories. *Memory & Cognition* 11(3). 211–227.
Bellugi, Ursula & Edward Klima 1976. Two faces of sign: Iconic and abstract. In Steven Harnad, Horst Steklis & Jane Lancaster (eds.), *Origins and Evolution of Language and Speech*, 514–538. New York: New York Academy of Science.
Black, Max. 1993 [1979]. More about metaphor. In Andrew Ortony (ed.), *Metaphor and Thought*, 19–41. Cambridge: Cambridge University Press.
Boyes Braem, Penny. 1981. *Significant Features of the Handshape in American Sign Language*. Berkeley: University of California, Berkeley dissertation.
Brennan, Mary. 1990. *Word formation in British Sign Language*. Stockholm: University of Stockholm dissertation.

Brennan, Mary. 1992. The visual world of British Sign Language: An Introduction. In David Brien (ed.), *Dictionary of British Sign Language/English*, 1–118. London: Faber and Faber.
Brennan, Mary. 1994. Pragmatics and productivity. In Inger Ahlgren, Brita Bergman & Mary Brennan (eds.), *Perspectives on Sign Language Structure: Papers from the Fifth International Symposium on Sign Language Research. Vol. 1; Salamanca, Spain, 25–30 May 1992*, 372–390. Durham: ISLA.
Brennan, Mary. 2001. Encoding and capturing productive morphology. *Sign Language & Linguistics* 4(1/2). 47–62.
Brennan, Mary. 2005. Conjoining word and image in British Sign language (BSL): An exploration of metaphorical signs in BSL. *Sign Language Studies* 5(3). 360–382.
Chiri, Daniele & Maria Teresa Lerda. 1997. Un'esperienza di bilinguismo in scuola materna: rapporti fra rieducazione ed educazione [An experience of bilingualism in kindergarten: relationships between re-education and education]. Paper presented at the 1996–1997 Seminars, Institute of Psychology (Division of Neuropsychology of Language and Deafness), National Research Council (CNR), Rome, 30 January 1997.
Cuxac, Christian. 2000. *La Langue des Signes Française (LSF). Les voies de l'iconicité* [French Sign Language (LSF): Pathways to iconicity]. *Faits de Langues* [Language Facts] 15/16. Paris: Ophrys.
Dressler, Wolfgang U. 1995. Interactions between iconicity and other semiotic parameters in language. In Raffaele Simone (ed.), *Iconicity in Language*, 21–38. Amsterdam/Philadelphia: John Benjamins.
Dudis, Paul G. 2004. Body partitioning and real-space blends. *Cognitive Linguistics* 15(2). 223–238.
Emmorey, Karen (ed.). 2003. *Perspectives on Classifier Constructions in Sign Languages*. Mahwah, NJ: Lawrence Erlbaum.
Fauconnier, Gilles. 1994 [1985]. *Mental Spaces: Aspects of Meaning Construction in Natural Languages*. Cambridge: Cambridge University Press.
Fauconnier, Gilles & Mark B. Turner. 1998. Conceptual Integration Networks, *Cognitive Science* 22(2). 133–187.
Fauconnier, Gilles & Mark Turner. 2002. *The Way We Think: Conceptual Blending and the Mind's Hidden Complexities*. New York: Basic Books.
Fillmore, Charles J. 1985. Frames and the semantics of understanding. *Quaderni di Semantica* 6(2). 222–254.
Fusellier-Souza, Ivani. 2004. *Sémiogenèse des langues des signes. Étude de langues des signes primaires (LSP) pratiquées par des sourds brésiliens* [Semiogenesis of Sign Languages: Study of Primary Sign Languages (PSL) Practiced by Deaf Brazilians]. Paris: University of Paris VIII dissertation.
Givón, T. 1989. *Mind, Code, and Context: Essays in Pragmatics*. Hillsdale, NJ: Lawrence Erlbaum.
Givón, T. 2002. *Bio-Linguistics: The Santa Barbara Lectures*. Amsterdam/Philadelphia: John Benjamins.
Glucksberg, Sam & Boaz Keysar. 1990. Understanding metaphorical comparisons: Beyond similarity. *Psychological Review* 97(1). 3–18.
Goffman, Erving. 1974. *Frame Analysis: An Essay on the Organization of Experience*. New York: Harper & Row.
Grady, Joseph E., Todd Oakley & Seana Coulson. 1999. Conceptual blending and metaphor. In Raymond W. Gibbs, Jr. & Gerard J. Steen (eds.), *Metaphors in Cognitive Linguistics: Selected papers from the 5th International Cognitive Linguistics Conference, Amsterdam, 1997*, 101–124. Amsterdam/Philadelphia: John Benjamins.
Haiman, John. 1980. The iconicity of grammar: Isomorphism and motivation. *Language* 56(3). 515–540.
Haiman, John. 1983. Iconic and economic motivation. *Language* 59(4). 781–819.
Haiman, John (ed.). 1985. *Iconicity in Syntax: Proceedinghs of a Symposium on Iconicity in Syntax, June 24–6, 1983*. Amsterdam/Philadelphia: John Benjamins.

Jarque, Marie-Josep. 2005. Double mapping in metaphorical expressions of thought and communication in Catalan Sign Language (LSC). *Sign Language Studies* 5(3). 292–316.
Johnston, Trevor & Adam Schembri. 1999. On defining lexeme in a signed language. *Sign Language & Linguistics* 2(2). 115–185.
Jouison, Paul. 1995. *Écrits sur la Langue des Signes Française* [Writings on French Sign Language]. (Edition prepared by Brigitte Garcia). Paris: L'Harmattan.
Kendon, Adam. 2004. *Gesture: Visible Action as Utterance*. Cambridge: Cambridge University Press.
Klima, Edward & Ursula Bellugi. 1979. *The Signs of Language*. Cambridge, MA: Harvard University Press.
Kövecses, Zoltán. 2010 [2002]. *Metaphor: A Practical Introduction*. New York: Oxford University Press.
Lakoff, George. 1987. *Women, Fire, and Dangerous Things: What Categories Reveal about the Mind*. Chicago: University of Chicago Press.
Lakoff, George & Mark Johnson 1980. *Metaphors We Live By*. Chicago: University of Chicago Press.
Lakoff, George & Mark Johnson 1999. *Philosophy in the Flesh*. New York: Basic Books.
Lakoff, George & Mark Turner. 1989. *More Than Cool Reason: A Field Guide to Poetic Metaphor*. Chicago: University of Chicago Press.
Liddell, Scott K. 2003. *Grammar, Gesture, and Meaning in American Sign Language*. Cambridge: Cambridge University Press.
Mauri, Caterina. 2017. Building and interpreting ad hoc categories: A linguistic analysis. In Joanna Blochowiak, Cristina Grisot, Stephanie Durrleman-Tame & Christopher Laenzlinger (eds.), *Formal Models in the Study of Language: Applications in Interdisciplinary Contexts*, 297–326. Cham: Springer.
McNeill, David. 1992. *Hand and Mind: What Gestures Reveal About Thought*. Chicago: University of Chicago Press.
Minsky, Marvin. 1974. *A Framework for Representing Knowledge*. MIT-AI Laboratory Memo 306, June, 1974.
Ortony, Andrew. 1993 [1979]. The role of similarity in similes and metaphors. In Andrew Ortony (ed.), *Metaphor and Thought*, 342–356. New York: Cambridge University Press.
Peirce, Charles Sanders. 1931–1958. *Collected Papers of Charles Sanders Peirce*. Cambridge, MA: Harvard University Press.
Pietrandrea, Paola. 2002. Iconicity and arbitrariness in Italian Sign Language. *Sign Language Studies* 2(3). 296–321.
Pietrandrea, Paola & Tommaso Russo. 2007. Diagrammatic and imagic hypoicons in signed and verbal languages. In Elena Pizzuto, Paola Pietrandrea, and Raffaele Simone (eds.), *Verbal and Signed Languages: Comparing Structures, Constructs and Methodologies*, 35–56. Berlin/New York: Mouton de Gruyter.
Pizzuto, Elena, Emanuela Cameracanna, Serena Corazza & Virgina Volterra. 1995. Terms for spatio-temporal relations in Italian Sign Language (LIS). In Raffaele Simone (ed.), *Iconicity in Language*, 237–256. Amsterdam/Philadelphia: John Benjamins.
Pizzuto, Elena & Virginia Volterra. 2000. Iconicity and transparency in sign languages: A cross-linguistic, cross-cultural view. In Karen Emmorey & Harlan Lane (eds.), *The Signs of Language Revisited: An Anthology to Honor Ursula Bellugi and Edward Klima*, 261–286. Mahwah, NJ: Lawrence Erlbaum.
Radutzky, Elena (ed.). 1992. *Dizionario bilingue elementare della lingua italiana dei segni* [Elementary Bilingual Dictionary of Italian Sign Language]. Roma: Edizioni Kappa.
Ricoeur, Paul. 1975. *La métaphore vive* [The living metaphor]. Paris: Éditions du Seuil.
Russo, Tommaso. 2000. *Immagini e metafore nelle lingue parlate e segnate: modelli semiotici e applicazioni alla LIS* [Images and Metaphors in Spoken and Signed Languages: Semiotic Models

and Applications to LIS]. Rome/Calabria/Palermo: University of Rome, University of Calabria, and University of Palermo dissertation.

Russo, Tommaso. 2004a. Iconicity and productivity in sign language discourse: An analysis of three LIS discourse registers. *Sign Language Studies* 4(2). 164–197.

Russo, Tommaso. 2004b. *La mappa poggiata sull'isola. Iconicità e metafora nelle lingue dei segni e nelle lingue vocali* [The Map Laid Down Upon the Island: Iconicity and Metaphor in Signed and Spoken Languages]. Rende: Centro Editoriale e Librario, Università della Calabria.

Russo, Tommaso. 2005. A Crosslinguistic, cross-cultural analysis of metaphors in two Italian Sign Language (LIS) registers. *Sign Language Studies* 5(3). 333–359.

Russo, Tommaso, Rosaria Giuranna & Elena Pizzuto. 2001. Italian Sign Language (LIS) poetry: Iconic properties and structural regularities. *Sign Language Studies* 2(1). 84–112.

Sallandre, Marie Anne. 2001. Va-et-vient de l'iconicité en Langue des Signes Française [Alternating iconicity in French Sign Language]. *Acquisition et Interaction en Langue Etrangère* [Foreign Language Acquisition and Interaction] (15): 37–59.

Schembri, Adam. 2003. Rethinking 'classifiers' in signed languages. In Karen Emmorey (ed.), *Perspectives on Classifier Constructions*, 3–34. Mahwah, NJ: Lawrence Erlbaum.

Slobin, Dan. I. 1987. Thinking for speaking. *Proceedings of the Thirteenth Annual Meeting of the Berkeley Linguistics Society*, 435–445. Berkeley: Berkeley Linguistics Society.

Slobin, Dan. I. 2003. Language and thought online: Cognitive consequences of linguistic relativity. In Dedre Gentner & Susan Goldin-Meadow (eds.), *Language in Mind: Advances in the Study of Language and Thought*, 157–191. Cambridge, MA: MIT Press.

Slobin, Dan I., Nini Hoiting, Marlon Kuntze, Reyna Lindert, Amy Weinberg, Jennie Pyers, Michelle Anthony, Yael Biederman & Helen Thumann. 2003. A cognitive/functional perspective on the acquisition of "classifiers". In Karen Emmorey (ed.), *Perspectives on Classifier Constructions*, 271–296. Mahwah, NJ: Lawrence Erlbaum.

Taub, Sarah F. 2000. Iconicity in American Sign Language: Concrete and metaphorical applications. *Spatial Cognition and Computation* 2(1). 31–50.

Taub, Sarah F. 2001. *Language from the Body: Iconicity and Metaphor in American Sign Language*. Cambridge/New York: Cambridge University Press.

Turner, Mark & Gilles Fauconnier. 1995. Conceptual integration and formal expression. *Metaphor and Symbolic Activity* 10(3). 183–204.

Waugh, Linda R. 1993. Les degrés d'iconicité diagrammatique dans le lexique [Degrees of diagrammatic iconicity in the lexicon]. *Faits de Langues* [Language Facts] 1: *Motivation et Iconicité*, 227–234. Paris: Ophrys.

Wilbur, Ronnie B. 1987. *American Sign Language: Linguistic and Applied Dimensions.* Boston, MA: College Hill Press.

Wilcox, Phyllis Perrin. 2000. *Metaphor in American Sign Language.* Washington, DC: Gallaudet University Press.

Wilcox, Phyllis Perrin. 2005. What do you *think?* Metaphor in thought and communication domains in American Sign Language. *Sign Language Studies* 5(3). 267–291.

Wilcox, Sherman. 2004. Cognitive iconicity: Conceptual spaces, meaning, and gesture in signed languages. *Cognitive Linguistics* 15(2). 119–147.

Wulf, Alyssa & Paul Dudis. 2005. Body partitioning in ASL metaphorical blends. *Sign Language Studies* 5(3). 317–332.

V Grammatical constructions

Elisabeth Engberg-Pedersen
The mouth shrug and facial consent in Danish Sign Language

1 Introduction

The topic of this chapter is two facial expressions which recur regularly in Danish Sign Language (dansk tegnsprog, or DTS) discourse: one is the mouth shrug, which appears to originate in an emblem in common use in society at large, the other is facial consent, which consists of a raised upper lip and possibly wrinkling of the nose. The origin of the latter is not known.

Wilcox (2004) suggests two routes for the incorporation of gesture into signed languages. Along the first route, a gesture becomes a lexical item in a signed language and may then grammaticalize in the same way as lexical items may become grammatical morphemes in spoken languages. Wilcox mentions two possible sub-routes, one from "a quotable gesture" (2004: 49), i.e., an emblem, the other one from an improvised gesture. The sub-routes are distinguished by the degree of conventionalization of the source gesture, but share the feature that the source gesture has a specific form and meaning.

By contrast, gestures of the second route are both phonologically and semantically schematic. They are non-conventional and move via intonation to bound morphemes. Their schematic nature makes them fit for becoming dependent elements. The examples discussed by Wilcox involve the manner of movement and the location of manual signs. Changes in location and manner of movement often have a gradient quality analogous to intonation in spoken languages. Manner of movement begins as "a paralinguistic gestural element" (Wilcox 2004: 65) and becomes less gradient in its meaning and form and more restricted in its grammatical function, ending as an obligatory inflectional or derivational morpheme like the "soft" movement of the ASL sign MUST in sentence final position where the sign has an epistemic modal meaning. Wilcox mentions "various facial, mouth, and eye gestures" (2004: 48) in relation to the second route. Thus, like manner of movement such gestures may enter the linguistic system by becoming part of the intonation and end up as grammatical markers. In a later paper, Wilcox (2009) lists the facial markers

---

Acknowledgements: I would like to thank the signers, the instructor Eva Abildgaard, three anonymous reviewers for their comments, and the Oticon Foundation. All shortcomings are of course mine.

Elisabeth Engberg-Pedersen, University of Copenhagen, Denmark, e-mail: eep@hum.ku.dk

https://doi.org/10.1515/9783110703788-013

of interrogatives, topics, adverbials, conditionals, and imperatives in ASL and the widespread use of, among other signals, an eyebrow raise to mark polar questions in many signed languages. He sees them as originating in facial gestures of emotional expression.

This study is part of a larger study of the ways epistemic modality is expressed in DTS (Engberg-Pedersen 2021). The two facial expressions were picked out for treatment here because they deserve discussion in relation to Wilcox's two routes of grammaticalization. Being expressed on the face, they qualify for inclusion in Wilcox's second route from gesture to grammatical marker in a signed language. They are both made with muscles around the mouth and exclude all other mouth actions, but their origins differ. As a signal of speaker uncertainty and a signal of consent, they do indeed have semantic scope over propositions like the facial markers in ASL listed by Wilcox, but they are not produced simultaneously with manual signs expressing the proposition, rather with anaphors of the propositions, with interjections, or by themselves, i.e., they are not dependent.

Moreover, although the mouth shrug is claimed to originate in emotions, i.e., emotions of meekness and submissiveness, its immediate origin is an emblem, albeit a non-manual one. This qualifies it for the first route described by Wilcox, and especially the first sub-route of the first route. But the mouth shrug does not have a lexical counterpart.

The mouth shrug and facial consent do not fit easily into Wilcox's analysis of routes of grammaticalization in signed languages. Neither do they fit into other analyses of the role of the mouth in signed languages (especially Crasborn et al. 2008). In Section 5, I shall discuss their status in relation to Wilcox's (2004) classifications and other classifications of mouth actions and the relationship between facial and manual signals in the signed language linguistics literature (Crasborn et al. 2008; Fontana 2008; Sandler 2009). Until then, I shall call the mouth shrug and facial consent *signals* to forestall any presumptions about their linguistic status.

The chapter is structured as follows: I will present the data in Section 2. Section 3 first presents the treatment of the mouth shrug in the gesture and signed language linguistics literature, and then the analysis of its distribution and uses in DTS. Section 4 follows the same pattern for facial consent. Finally, Section 5 discusses the results in light of Wilcox's (2004) claims about grammaticalization routes from gesture to linguistic elements in signed languages, earlier classifications of mouth actions, and the relationship between manual and non-manual signals.

2 The data

The data consist of video recordings of dialogues based on a task that was meant to elicit expressions of doubt (Engberg-Pedersen 2021).[1] The participants saw a video-recorded instruction by a native signer describing an imaginary situation where participants were aboard a decrepit lifeboat in the middle of the Pacific. The lifeboat held fifteen objects (represented on cards), and the participants' task was to order the objects in terms of their possible contributions to the chances of survival since they might have to throw the objects overboard one by one to avoid sinking.

Four pairs of native signers (deaf signers of deaf parents) are included in the study. They were between 26 and 69 years of age, six of them between 26 and 40. Among the participants were two mothers and their adult sons (AN is the mother of JE, and AG the mother of MA in Table 1). Family members were not paired in the task situation. An examination of their signing with respect to the signals under study showed that the frequency patterns in the family members' use of the signals did not differ from the patterns of the other signers (see Table 1). There does not appear to be any mutual influence in the use of the signals between the members of each pair of signers either (see Table 1).

The dialogues were recorded in 2016 in a studio at the University of Copenhagen, where the signers were instructed in the procedure by a native-signer assistant on video; the assistant was also present in the beginning of the sessions so that the signers could ask her to clarify unclear points. The recordings were made by means of three cameras, one on each signer and one on them as a pair. The signers were placed facing each other with a long, narrow, low table between them. They used the table to sort the fifteen cards, each with a picture and a brief description of the object in Danish. The recordings were annotated by the native-signer assistant in collaboration with me.

---

[1] The Faculty of Humanities, University of Copenhagen does not currently require research projects involving human participants to be approved by the Research Ethics Committee at the Faculty. The data collection pertaining to this article has been reported to the University of Copenhagen registry of projects and has received the approval based on GDPR compliance. Project registration file number: 504-0052/18-4000. All data/recordings were made with the informed consent of the participants. The project was supported by the Oticon Foundation.

Table 1: Amount of data in minutes and seconds and number of tokens of the mouth shrug and facial consent in the four dialogues.

ID	Minutes:seconds of conversation	Number of tokens of the mouth shrug	Number of tokens of facial consent
JE with KE	9:02	20	13
KE with JE	9:02	1	18
CH with NI	12:30	24	3
NI with CH	12:30	9	2
AN with AG	7:31	15	0
AG with AN	7:31	5	9
MA with MO	13:00	7	11
MO with MA	13:00	7	4
Total	42:03	88	60

3 The mouth shrug

3.1 The mouth shrug in gesture studies and signed language linguistics

The most persistent facial activity in the mouth shrug in my data is the chin raiser (AU17), often combined with lip corner depressor (AU15), cf. Ekman and Friesen's (1978) *Facial Action Coding System*.[2] The mouth shrug is described in the literature on gestures as "the mouth shrug" (Debras 2017) or "the horseshoe-shaped mouth" (Ekman 2009: 102) and is often included in the form features of "the shoulder shrug" or simply "the shrug". In what follows, I shall summarize the gesture literature on shrug signals. The literature is somewhat marred by the use of words, e.g., "pout" for signals whose form features are not described very precisely.

3.1.1 The (shoulder) shrug

In *The Expression of the Emotions in Man and Animals*, Darwin (1890) described what he calls "the shoulder shrug" as a gesture of impotence, resignation and unwillingness. The form features that he mentions include an open mouth, but as

---

[2] AU stands for Action Unit. The Action Units can be seen here: https://imotions.com/blog/learning/research-fundamentals/facial-action-coding-system/ (Farnsworth 2019).

pointed out by Givens (1977), the gentleman in the photos meant to demonstrate the shoulder shrug clearly shows a closed mouth (Darwin 1890: Tab VI, between pages 276 and 277). Darwin finds the motivation for the shoulder shrug in its being the antithesis of a threatening position: raised brows and raised shoulders are signals of lack of aggression and threat in contrast to a frown, the head held erect and squaring of the shoulders as signals of aggression.

In contrast to Darwin, Streeck (2009) interprets the raising of the articulators of the shrug—the shoulders, the eyebrows, the hands and forearms—as "displays of distancing and disengagement" (2009: 191). He only mentions the mouth once, namely as "spread lips" (Streeck 2009: 190).

Debras (2017) studied a cluster of forms under the heading "the shrug" in dialogues in English to show that "the shrug is not just an emblem, i.e., a fixed form with a stable meaning across contexts, but constitutes a more complex and dynamic network of related forms and functions" (2017: 5). In her data the most frequent shrug component was lifted shoulders, followed by a lateral head tilt and forearm(s) supine (what I annotate as PALM-UP). Debras found that a mouth shrug and what she calls "pout" are fairly infrequent in her data, but like Morris (1994), she claims that a mouth shrug can be used by itself with the function of a shrug. Debras also found that the mouth shrug can occur with other facial actions: squinted eyes or furrowed brows, smiles, head nod or headshake.

Based on an analysis of the context of each occurrence, Debras (2017) found the following three main uses of the shrug: 1) *attitudinal shrugs*: incapacity, inaction, submissiveness; 2) *shrugs expressing affect*: indifference, rejection; 3) *epistemic shrugs*: indetermination, common ground.

Like Darwin, Givens sees submissiveness—"a non-dominant or non-assertive social position" (Givens 1977: 13)—as the primary function of the shoulder shrug, including what he describes as "shoulder supination" (e.g., 1977: 23), head tilt, rotated-upward palm gestures, pouting and brow raise. He describes shoulder shrugs, including pouts, as parts of a behavior displaying meekness and uncertainty about social relations in interactions with an assertive interlocutor. In his data, the behavior had the effect of reducing dominant-like behavior in the other person. Givens claims that "[p]outing, like shoulder shrugging, can communicate a submissive, a disarmingly childlike, social attitude" (1977: 21) and mentions similar behavior among nonhuman primates who feel threatened, children who find themselves in a threatening situation or wish to obtain something from an adult, and flirting women. While many of the signals, including raised shoulder, may be motivated by a cowering posture designed to protect the body in the case of threat, Givens suggests that lip-pouting may derive from "an infantile pattern, pan-human and general among higher primates, of protruding the lips while whimpering or while reacting negatively to circumstances over which one has little or no control" (1977: 24).

3.1.2 The pout

As seen above, several gesture researchers talk about the pout as part of the shrug. In literature on chimpanzees (Parr et al. 2007), the pout is described as a combination of chin raiser (AU17), lip funneler (AU22) and lips part (AU25), i.e., the action of separating the lips slightly. This particular signal typically occurs in "contexts of embraces, invitations, play, approaches, and in response to aggression. . . Therefore, pouts may represent a need for contact, or reassurance, and physical affinity" (Parr et al. 2007: 177). This is a different form from the one studied here. In the signal under study, the lips may be slightly pushed forward (lip funneler AU22), but they are always closed. Although both the pout and the mouth shrug include chin raiser, there appears to be different motivations for the two. The pout may have an appealing function, whereas the mouth shrug with chin raiser and with or without lip corner depressor (AU15) has its origin in the individual's cowering in the face of threat. What unites the two may be submissiveness.

3.1.3 The facial shrug or the mouth shrug

Chovil describes "a retraction of one mouth corner" (1991/1992: 183) in human beings as part of what she calls "the facial shrug", or as a signal of thinking about what to say; a full facial shrug includes: "the corners of the mouth pulled down into a horseshoe shape as well as brow flashes and retraction of mouth corners" (Chovil 1991/1992: 186). In her study, the facial shrug occurred with phrases like *I don't know*, *Oh well*, *Okay*, or "when the person conceded something in the discussion, was reacting with resignation, or decided when they had done something well enough" (Chovil 1991/1992: 183). One more function was as backchannel responses, i.e., signals that the listener was paying attention without displaying a personal reaction. The signal was not always redundant.

Morris (1994) lists "mouth shrug" as a disclaimer gesture in the western world. He describes its formal characteristics as the mouth corners pulled down "briefly, as far as possible" (Morris 1994: 165) and sees it as part of the "shrug complex" (1994: 165), which also includes raised eyebrows, raised shoulders and spread palms. Morris claims that the mouth shrug can be used by itself with the same meaning as the full shrug, i.e., "'I don't know', 'It's nothing to do with me', or 'I don't understand'" (1994: 165).

To test whether more shrug components are used to express more emphasis, or whether each formal component contributes a separate meaning, Debras (2017) examined form-meaning correspondences statistically and found that the mouth shrug clustered with epistemic indetermination and is far removed from the expression of affect, attitudes and common ground in her data. She saw the mouth shrug as "a visual modal marker of subjective disengagement" (2017: 23; cf. Streeck's "displays of distancing and disengagement" (2009: 191)) and concluded: "A seemingly peripheral component like the mouth shrug can be used as a shrug variant on its own, but only to express one specific meaning, in this case epistemic indetermination" (Debras 2017: 27). The motivation for the closed mouth can be found in the speaker's uncertainty, she claims: "When the speaker has nothing to say, his or her mouth is literally disposed in a way that makes it impossible to speak" (Debras 2017: 19).

Ricci Bitti et al. (2014) developed a test of facial expressions corresponding to different types of lack of knowledge. Through role play they obtained 36 photos of facial expressions produced in circumstances where the participants expressed doubt. Then decoders evaluated the facial expressions on the photos in free verbal answers, and the answers were subsequently classified in three categories: denial of knowledge but no uncertainty, doubt: "I am not sure", and uncertainty but with an additional element: "I am not sure but thinking about it". When the decoders evaluated each expression in the photos on a likert scale in relation to the semantic types, it turned out that chin raiser (AU17) and lip corner depressor (AU15) were present in all three types of facial expression, but doubt involved also inner and outer brow raiser (AU1, AU2), whereas "I am not sure but thinking about it" involved brow lowerer (AU4), lid tightener (AU7) and averted gaze.

3.1.4 Signals similar to the mouth shrug in the signed language linguistics literature

In the signed language linguistics literature, Liddell (1980: 39) mentions "pushing up the lower lip" as part of the facial expression accompanying headshake in negation of a sentence in ASL, but does not describe the signal as expressing the signer's doubt. However, such an interpretation is found in descriptions of a number of signed languages.

Like Ekman (2009) Siyavoshi (2019; see also Martínez, Siyavoshi, and Wilcox 2019) uses the term "horseshoe mouth" about a marker of subjective assessment and epistemic modality in Iranian Sign Language (Zaban Eshareh Irani, or ZEI). In Spanish Sign Language (Lengua de Signos Española, or LSE) epistemic necessity may be expressed by means of a facial expression consisting of a frown and pursed lips or downward movement of the mouth corners and upward movement of the lower lip (Cabeza-Pereiro 2013; Cabeza-Pereiro and Iglesias-Lago 2015). According to Martínez, Siyavoshi, and Wilcox (2019), Iglesias-Lago in an unpublished dissertation from 2006 states that epistemic possibility may be expressed by the horseshoe mouth by itself in LSE. Gianfreda, Volterra, and Zuczkowski (2014) mention that in

Italian Sign Language (Lingua dei Segni Italiana, or LIS) the mouth shrug occurs with a number of signs indicating uncertainty or lack of knowledge, including the sign SAPERE-NO ('don't know'); it may also occur before a sequence of signs to signal uncertainty. That is, the signal that is the object of study here is identical to signals of doubt or epistemic modality in ZEI, LSE, and LIS (see also Engberg-Pedersen 2021).

In sum, the mouth shrug has been described in the gesture literature as part of a more comprehensive behavior indicating submissiveness, distancing, but also more specifically lack of knowledge or doubt. Unfortunately, it is not always clearly distinguished from the pout. In ZEI, LSE, and LIS, the mouth shrug has been described as a signal of subjective assessment, epistemic modality, epistemic necessity or possibility, and doubt.

3.2 The mouth shrug in DTS

3.2.1 The mouth shrug's cooccurrence with other non-manual signals

In the data there are 88 tokens of the chin raiser (AU17) (see Table 1). In many cases, it combines with the lip corner depressor (AU15) as in Figure 1. The token in Figure 1 is used with headshake, raised shoulders, brow lowerer (AU4), head tilt and with PALM-UP.[3] The totality is a reaction ("we really can't use it") to the signer's own incredulous question "but the map?!", which was suggested by her interlocutor as an important object. In Ricci Bitti et al.'s (2014) data brow lowerer occurred with the mouth shrug when the signal was interpreted as "I am not sure but thinking about it". In Figure 1 the signer is not in doubt; towards the end of this section, I shall get back to why the signer uses the mouth shrug here.

Figure 2 is an example of chin raiser (AU17) with lip funneler (AU22) and no lip corner depressor. The signer here points to one of the cards and looks questioningly at the interlocutor, i.e., she tries to elicit an answer as to the usefulness of the object on the card. As mentioned in Section 3.1, lip funneler can be used for appeals (Parr et al. 2007).

Chin raiser with or without lip corner depressor occurs with other signals of the shoulder shrug (see Section 3.1), especially lateral head tilt (a sideways "nod")

---

[3] Many gesture researchers (e.g., Ekman 2009; Debras 2017) analyze one or two palm-up open hands (Müller 2004) as part of the shrug. As palm-up open hands has many other functions in DTS (Engberg-Pedersen 2002) and the mouth shrug cooccurs with other manual signs, the combinations of the mouth shrug and manual signs is a special focus point in this analysis. As PALM-UP (or PU) has recently spread as a way of annotating one or two palm-up open hands, I have adopted this way of annotating it here without any claim as to whether it should be analyzed as a sign or a gesture.

Figure 1: Chin raiser with lip corner depressor, brow lowerer, headshake, head tilt and raised shoulders. The hands show the PALM-UP gesture.

Figure 2: Chin raiser and lip funneler. One hand is pointing to a card.

and raised shoulders, but also with movements of the body from side to side or head tilts to both sides, which are other signals of uncertainty in DTS (Engberg-Pedersen 2021). In Figure 3 chin raiser (with slight lip funneler) occurs with inner and outer brow raiser, head nodding and PALM-UP followed by a point to one of the cards. The sequence occurs after a suggestion made by the other signer that they should keep a bottle of alcohol, and the signer indicates approval of the suggestion. The use of brow raiser here goes against Ricci Bitti et al.'s (2014) claim that brow raiser occurs when the mouth shrug signals doubt.

The same signer also uses chin raiser with lip corner depressor and a brief head tilt (Figure 4). In Figure 4, she is looking away, a signal indicating Ricci Bitti et al.'s (2014) third type of lack of knowledge, i.e., "I am not sure but thinking about it". The

Figure 3: Chin raiser and slight lip funneler, inner and outer brow raiser and head nodding. The hands make PALM-UP.

signal is used with a combination of PALM-UP and a raised index finger as a response to a suggestion made by the other signer.

Figure 4: Chin raiser, lip corner depressor, head tilt and averted eyes. The hand is PALM-UP with a raised index finger.

3.2.2 The chin raiser's semantic scope and functions

The chin raiser occurs with PALM-UP (31 tokens), POINT (4 tokens), YES (8 tokens), and "others" (other signs; 10 tokens); moreover, there are 35 tokens of the chin raiser with no signs. In the "others" group we find NO-IDEA and DOUBT as expressions of epistemic uncertainty, the first person pronoun used to express epistemic modal evaluation (Engberg-Pedersen 2021), HARDLY also in an epistemic modal evaluation, APPROXIMATELY when the signer is making an estimate, PUSH-ASIDE and THROW-AWAY about the cards, and MEAN (in the sense of 'signify'). The last three signs occur once each and by the same signer. Except for MEAN, the signs in "others" express uncertainty or negativity.

PALM-UP and POINT can be grouped together since they both index propositions. POINT is used to refer to the cards and stands metonymically for a full proposition, namely whether to include the object on the card among the useful objects or not. YES, NO-IDEA, DOUBT, the first person pronoun used to express epistemic modal evaluation, HARDLY, and APPROXIMATELY all have scope over a proposition. That is, when the mouth shrug occurs with a manual sign, it is a sign that either indexes or has scope over a proposition, and the mouth shrug contributes to the modification of that proposition.

In most instances of the mouth shrug occurring by itself without a manual sign (35 tokens), it is used as a backchannel signal (cf. Chovil 1991/1992). As a backchannel signal, the mouth shrug is often accompanied by a head nod and in some cases by the lifting of one index finger from the hands' rest position. The signal without any manual sign is also used in a separate turn to respond to a comment made by the other signer, and it may be a reaction to something the signers see (especially an object on a card) in situations where they do not have eye contact with their interlocutor.

With PALM-UP and YES the signal can be used to respond to a question or a statement made by the other signers in the dialogues (the first use of chin raiser in (1); the annotation key follows Section 5 Discussion below).

(1) Signer 1 (S1) suggests that they should keep the bottle of alcohol since it may give warmth.

    Signer 2 (S2) (during the first part of S1's suggestion):   br-------
    wide eyes
    nodding
    PALM-UP
    cr--------
    'Yes.'

    S1:   BUT EVEN-SO DRINK / AFTERWARDS FAST COLD /
           'But even if we drink it, we may quickly be cold.'

    S2:   hn--------
           PALM-UP
           yes
           'Yes indeed!'

S1: DOUBT
'I don't know.'

S2: head tilt
looks away
PALM-UP
cr--------
'Hmm! Well...'

Interestingly, S2 first agrees with S1 (S2's first utterance in (1); see Figure 3), but when S1 expresses doubts, she responds by using non-manual signals of doubt demonstrating Ricci Bitti et al.'s (2014) third type ("I don't know, but I am thinking about it") (S2's final utterance in (1); see Figure 4), thereby acknowledging S1's doubts, but nevertheless giving supporting evidence for the usefulness of the alcohol in what follows after her last line in (1). She uses chin raiser both when she approves of S1's suggestion, and when she mirrors S1's doubts. In the first case, chin raiser is accompanied by eye contact, eye widening, nodding, and brow raiser: "You are right, and I didn't think of that myself". In the second instance, besides raising her chin, she averts her eyes as if she is speculating, and she makes a brief head tilt ("I don't know, but I am thinking about it"). That is, chin raiser can be used with other signals in configurations with almost opposite meanings. Even though it is a signal of doubt (Chovil 1991/1992; Ricci Bitti et al. 2014), indetermination (Debras 2017), or disengagement (Streeck 2009), it can be used in expressions of agreement in cases where it combines with raised brows and, in this case, nodding, and it can be used to align with the interlocutor's doubt. But it retains its basic meaning in both cases: in the former case, it shows that the signer had not thought about the suggestion herself thereby signaling being impressed by the interlocutor; in the latter case, it indicates lack of knowledge, but in combination with the other signals, also a willingness to consider the proposal.

When the signers use chin raiser with PALM-UP after their own statement, they may use it to reduce the force of their statement by seemingly expressing doubt or appealing to their interlocutor for approval as a tag (Engberg-Pedersen 2021). One signer makes a suggestion, and while he is holding his hands in the final position of a sign, his interlocutor is nodding, but does not initiate a turn, so after a pause the first signer changes to PALM-UP with chin raiser and head tilt, and his interlocutor makes a slightly deeper nod, but still does not take the turn.

Example (2) exemplifies a signer's use of chin raiser with other signals to express his doubt about an object on a card (see Figure 5).

(2)   head tilt
    card----------------------
    POINT+card   PALM-UP
                          cr--------
                          lcd------
    'This thing, I don't really know.'

The signer keeps looking down at the cards all through the utterance, which suggests that the sequence is rather used to express doubt than to ask a question. The shrug with PALM-UP in (2) has a predicational function in relation to the point to the card, which constitutes the topic of the utterance.

Figure 5: Chin raiser with lip corner depressor and head tilt.

Example (3) is a parallel example except that the signer clearly addresses her interlocutor. She asks what to do with an object by presenting it in a nominal and then uses the mouth shrug with PALM-UP (see Figure 6) in a question to her interlocutor.

(3)   S1:   sideways
           POINT+addressee ROPE attention NYLON ROPE THREE [METER   PALM-UP
                                                                          cr--------
                                                                           lcd-------
    'Listen, the rope hey the nylon rope of three meters, what about that?'

S2:   hn---------
                                                  [PALM-UP
                                                  cr-------
                                                  lcd------
                                                  'I think so, yes!'

Figure 6: Chin raiser with lip corner depressor and sideways movements of the body.

Example (3) also demonstrates the use of the mouth shrug with PALM-UP in a response, here even before S1 has reached the point where she uses the mouth shrug and PALM-UP to ask the question.

The mouth shrug is used with both headshake and head nodding (see example (3)). There are 27 tokens with head nodding out of the total of 88 occurrences of chin raiser. Twelve tokens are accompanied by headshake, 13 by head tilt, and 6 by movements to both sides of either the head or the body. Movements to both sides suggest alternatives, and this may also be the origin of the head tilt as part of the shrug. The mouth shrug with headshake is used in responses to negative questions from the interlocutor, and by one signer, with PALM-UP in a response to her own question ("How many? <u>I don't know</u>") and in an attachment to her own negative statement ("No, to be honest no. There aren't mosquitoes at sea above the water, <u>no</u>."). In some cases this signer uses the mouth shrug in rejections of her interlocutor's suggestions even when she is not in doubt. So why does she use the facial shrug? The answer may be found in another instance of the mouth shrug with headshake. The signer feels that her interlocutor wants to keep everything in the boat, but that is not possible:

(4)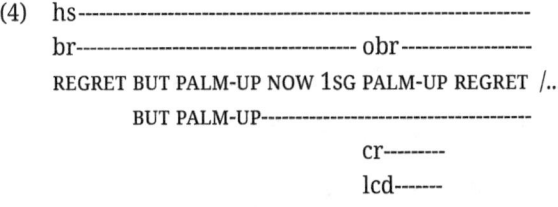
'I am sorry, but really now I am sorry...'

All through this example the signer is shaking her head, i.e., she is rejecting her interlocutor's suggestions, but at the same time, she mitigates the aggression implied by the rejection by expressing her regrets. That is, the mouth shrug can be used not only to signal uncertainty but also to mitigate aggression (cf. Darwin 1890; Givens 1977; and see Section 3.1 above) where there is only a pretense of uncertainty.

In sum, chin raiser with or without lip corner depressor may combine with manual signs to express epistemic modal evaluations of propositions expressed by statements, questions, or topical nominals (especially POINT) representing a proposition ("What should we do with this object?"). The proposition is then indexed by a simultaneous PALM-UP (cf. Müller 2004) or point to a card. When there is no manual sign with the mouth shrug, the proposition is implied by the context. This means that the mouth shrug, or the entirety of the non-manual signals, has a modifying function in combinations with PALM-UP, POINT, no sign or YES: it expresses the signer's epistemic modal evaluation as a modification of a proposition. When it is used with other manual signs, it reinforces the semantic element of uncertainty (NO-IDEA, DOUBT, APPROXIMATELY). With HARDLY the chin raiser is used to reject a suggestion made by the interlocutor. Here the mouth shrug can be analyzed either as a reinforcement of the epistemic modal evaluation of HARDLY or as a mitigator of the aggression implied by the negative response.

The mouth shrug is used as a backchannel signal in tags with manual signs of doubt or lack of knowledge, in affirmative, negative and thoughtful responses to suggestions made by the other signer, after a topic to raise the question about what to do with the thing mentioned in the topic, or in a remark to oneself about one's doubts about something. As a signal with epistemic modal meaning, the mouth shrug may combine with both head nodding and headshake. With head nodding the signal can be interpreted as "You are right, I hadn't thought about that", and with head shake, the mouth shrug is used as a signal of uncertainty, in responses to negative statements made by the other signer, or as a way of mitigating a rejection.

4 Facial consent

4.1 Upper lip raiser and nose wrinkler in gesture studies and signed language linguistics

The other signal under study here consists of raising one or both sides of the upper lip (AU10), see Figure 7. The signal may involve lid tightener (AU7) or squint (AU44), nasolabial deepener (AU11) or nose wrinkler (AU9) (see Figures 7 and 8).

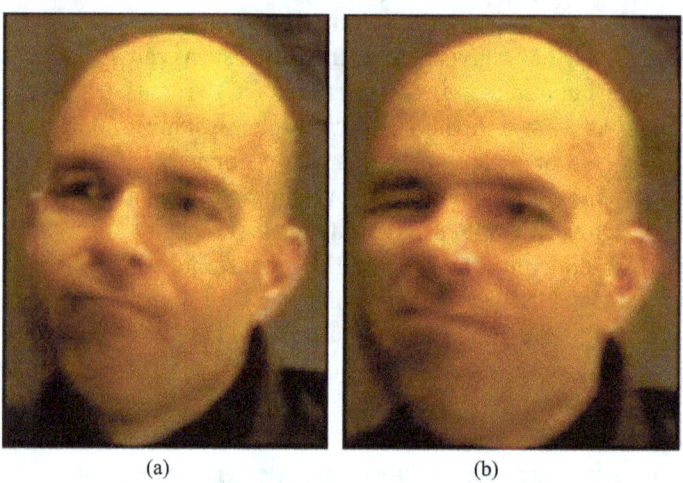

(a)   (b)

Figure 7: Facial consent with smiling: in (a) before the expression of facial consent (with the final stage of the mouthing of the Danish word meaning 'deaf'), and in (b) the expression of facial consent with one-sided upper lip raiser (AU10) and one-sided squint (AU44).

In the gesture literature, Ekman and Friesen (2003; see also Chovil 1991/92) show that upper lip raiser may be part of the facial expression of disgust or part of the emblem of disgust. Chovil (1991/92) mentions that nose wrinkling may be used with rejection of a suggestion, and Ricci Bitti writes that "[t]he expression of interpersonal refusal is generated through a facial configuration that includes partial reduction of the eyelid opening and, in certain cases, lifting of the upper lip" (2014: 1343).[4]

In the signed language linguistics literature, nose wrinkle and raised upper lip are mentioned as parts of the non-manual marking of relative clauses in ASL (Coulter 1978; Liddell 1980). The photos in Liddell (1980: 48) show that raised upper lip is also

---

[4] According to Marianne Gullberg (p.c.), upper lip raiser and/or nose wrinkler are not known to be used to express consent in studies on gestures.

Figure 8: Facial consent with one-sided upper lip raiser (AU10), one-sided squint (AU44) and nose wrinkler (AU9).

part of the non-manual signal "cs" which modifies certain signs for proximity in time or space. Wilbur refers to an unpublished study by Wood that "documents the existence of a repeated nose wrinkle for referential and pragmatic purposes that has no obvious non-signing gestural origin" (Wilbur 2009: 251), but she does not specify the pragmatic purposes. A possible origin is also at stake in Ottenheimer's claim that Nicaraguan Sign Language (Idioma de Señas de Nicaragua) (requires a nose wrinkle when a question is signed, but contrary to what is the case in ASL, Ottenheimer sees its use in Nicaraguan Sign Language questions as an example of the fact that "a gesture that is commonly (but unconsciously) used by hearing speakers" (2012: 124) has been incorporated into the country's signed language since "a nose wrinkle is a common accompaniment to spoken Spanish questions in Nicaragua" (2012: 124). Roush finds that nose wrinkle is one of several "nonmanual politeness markers" (2011: 345) in ASL. De Vos, van der Kooij, and Crasborn (2009) write that nose wrinkle may occur with eyebrow furrow in wh-questions in Sign Language of the Netherlands (Nederlandse Gebarentaal, or NGT), and they give an example where nose wrinkle by itself substitutes for other markings of a wh-question. In a study of Sivia Sign Language (LSSiv), a village sign language of Peru, Clark (2017: 145) shows that "wrinkled nose" is part of two facial configurations that distinguish the two lexical signs DIRTY/GROSS and DANGEROUS(ANIMAL), but these signs seem to be used also by themselves as adjectives meaning 'dirty' and 'dangerous(animal)'. These uses accord with the negative function of nose wrinkle in gestures of disgust. In LSSiv nose wrinkle is also used with an open mouth to indicate high numbers.

In some northern European signed languages, nose wrinkle is mentioned as a backchannel signal or a signal of consent. Mesch (2016) mentions nose wrinkle as one of the non-manual signals that turned up in her study of backchannel responses in Swedish Sign Language (svenskt teckenspråk, or STS), but she does not describe its specific function(s). Brennan (1992: 32) mentions that "nose puckering and a backward head nod" are among the non-manual features used in British Sign Language (BSL) for expressing consent (glossed in Brennan as **that's right**), and Papaspyrou et al. (2008: 181) describe a facial gesture of one-sided raising of a wing of the nose and depict it as *mimische Zustimmung* ('mimical consent') in German Sign Language (Deutsche Gebärdensprache, or DGS).[5]

In sum, the gesture literature mentions nose wrinkle and raising of the upper lip as part of a facial expression of disgust or rejection, and in signed languages they have been identified as non-manual markers of relative clauses, reference, politeness (all in ASL), questions (Nicaraguan Sign Language), and wh-questions (NGT). For three signed languages in northern Europe a similar signal is mentioned as a backchannel signal (STS) or a signal of consent (BSL and DGS). The functions span affect (especially spoken languages and LSSiv), grammar, and interaction. Nose wrinkling is mentioned in one context (Wood in Wilbur 2009) as a signal that does not originate in facial gestures in the hearing community (ASL), and in another (Ottenheimer 2013) as an example of the exact opposite: a signal taken over from the hearing community (Nicaraguan Sign Language). However, the particular function of upper lip raiser and nose wrinkle as expressions of consent is only attested for two signed languages, or possibly three, including STS. Paul Dudis and Terra Edwards (p.c. 2022) note that facial consent is also used in ASL.

4.2 Facial consent in DTS

It appears from Table 1 that there were 60 tokens of the signal in the data, and that it was used by all signers except one. As mentioned in Section 4.1, there is some variation in how the signal is made, but one-sided or two-sided upper lip raiser (AU10) is the most persistent signal. In most of the occurrences the signal is very short, but it may be repeated a couple of times (counted as one token in Table 1), and it may be prolonged. In this section, I describe the signal's distribution in relation to the manual signs and its functions.

---

5 I wish to thank Cornelia Loos for bringing the points about BSL and DGS to my attention.

Out of the sixty tokens of the signal in the data, 35 occurred with no manual sign, 13 with YES, 8 with PALM-UP, 2 with a point to the addressee, and 2 with other signs, i.e., PLASTIC and SORT. In the examples with PLASTIC and SORT, the signal is used in responses to the other signer, not to modify PLASTIC and SORT. Nineteen of the sixty tokens are made with simultaneous head nodding, and fifteen are made with other types of consent, i.e., YES, RIGHT, head nodding, either just before or just after the expression of facial consent.

Six tokens are made with headshake, but express agreement with a negative statement. Example (5) precedes a use of the signal with headshake.

(5) S1:   ?____   neg___
        WAIT BOAT-SAIL / PALM-UP /
        'Do we expect to be able to steer the boat? No!'

Just after S1 has started PALM-UP with the negative facial expression, S2 signs PALM-UP, starts shaking his head and makes the facial consent signal, that is, the signal is used with headshake as a signal of agreement with S1's negative statement that they cannot steer the boat.

To find out whether facial consent can be used to answer a question for information by itself, we should look at examples where it is not supported by manual signs such as YES or by head nodding or headshake, but is used either with PALM-UP, a point to the person asking the question or with no manual sign. There are eight such examples in the data. Three of these are backchannel signals, three are reactions to statements, not to questions, made by the interlocutor, one can't be classified, and one comes at the end of a suggestion that goes against a preceding argument made by the interlocutor himself: after he has made the suggestion, the signer looks down, makes the facial consent signal and then looks up and says "It's probably crazy, so drop it!" His raising his upper lip expresses agreement with what he expects his interlocutor to say. There are no uses of facial consent to answer a question for information in the data. This is by far not conclusive evidence against the possibility of using the signal for this purpose, however. First, there are not enough examples in the data, and second, the data type does not encourage questions for information, but arguments and suggestions. When asked whether it is possible to use facial consent to answer an information question in the affirmative, one signer gave an example where he felt that facial consent would be okay, namely when asked "Don't you think he looks obese?". However, this is obviously not a question for information, but an expression of agreement with the person asking the question. The signer was in doubt whether the signal could be used to answer invitations such as "Would you like to come with us to the beach?" or "Would you like a piece of cake?".

In sum, the signal facial consent made by especially upper lip raiser is used as a backchannel signal and, in responses, by itself or with other signals and manual signs of consent to express agreement with one's interlocutor. With a headshake it expresses agreement with a negative statement. Facial consent does not share meaning with what has been written about nose wrinkle and raised upper lip in the gesture literature (see Section 4.1). It appears that there is a unique use of this facial signal to express consent in at least BSL, DGS, DTS, and possibly also STS and ASL, i.e., it may be an areal or inherited phenomenon, without any established influence from gestures.[6]

5 Discussion

In the introduction, I raised the question of how the mouth shrug and facial consent fit into Wilcox's (2004) framework of two diachronic pathways of gestures into signed languages. His criteria for the classifications are whether the gesture has a full form and meaning (route 1) or is merely schematic and thus dependent on something else (route 2) and, within the cases of route 1, whether it has a conventional status as an emblem before it is integrated into a signed language (route 1a) or not (route 1b). It should be added here that Wilcox's main concern is not non-manual signals, but manual signs or modifications of manual signs. He mentions briefly a number of facial signals that appear to have their origins in emotional gestural expressions and end up as proposition modifiers in signed languages after a transition state as paralinguistic intonation.

Since Wilcox's two routes are routes for the integration of gestures into signed languages, they are only relevant in relation to markers that have indeed acquired linguistic status in a signed language. But if the routes are seen as criterial for establishing what is linguistic and what not, examining how the mouth shrug and facial consent fit into Wilcox's framework may contribute to throwing light on their status.

According to the gesture literature, the mouth shrug has its origin in an emotional facial gesture of meekness and submissiveness, but has acquired an emblematic status as a signal of doubt in society at large. In DTS, it has semantic scope over propositions. These may be indexed by PALM-UP or POINT made simultaneously with the mouth shrug, or the proposition may be inferable from the immediate context.

---

[6] A native signer, Mads Jonathan Pedersen (p.c.), gave the anecdotal evidence that a signer from Argentina visiting Denmark spontaneously asked what "that nose activity" was about. On a speculative note, I would like to suggest that facial consent may originate in the wink as a signal of shared knowledge.

In that sense the mouth shrug is dependent relative to the manual signs, cf. Wilcox's claim that "when manual and facial gestures combine, the facial gesture often modulates the meaning of the manual gesture in some way, an indication that it is dependent relative to the more autonomous manual gesture" (2004: 59). But the mouth shrug does not play a subsidiary role in relation to the manual signs: it is the focus of the utterance when it is used with PALM-UP or POINT and expresses the signer's epistemic modal evaluation of the proposition (see, for instance, example (2) in Section 3.2.2). Thus, at least in these contexts, it is not grammatical according to the grammaticalization theory of Boye and Harder (2012), which suggests a definition of grammatical status as the status of those items that cannot be focused in a sentence.

Is it then a lexeme that has not reached the end of Wilcox's first route? Although it has a consistent meaning of speaker uncertainty, its meaning must often be interpreted in relation to other facial signals; it can, for instance, be used to mitigate aggression in rejections of suggestions made by others (cf. Darwin 1890; Givens 1977; also see Section 3.1 above). Its functions in signing appear to be identical to its functions as an emblematic non-manual gesture (see, especially, Debras (2017); and Section 3.1). Thus there is no reason to see it as a specifically linguistic, "non-gestural" part of DTS. It might be speculated that what detains it from becoming fully integrated as a linguistic element is its continued use as a gesture in society at large and the fact that it is not obligatory in contrast to, for instance, signals of sentence types (cf. Wilcox 2004).

Facial consent resembles the mouth shrug in expressing an evaluation of a proposition without being subsidiary to it. However, it is more clearly an interjection than the mouth shrug. In contrast to the latter, it is not used in tag position, but only to respond to suggestions by an interlocutor or, in rare cases, oneself. Moreover, it does not appear to have started its life as a gesture (but see footnote 6), but has a conventional meaning in DTS and some other northern European signed languages and possibly ASL. Thus, it appears to be an instance of an arbitrary, conventional non-manual sign with a lexical status. That is, neither the mouth shrug nor facial consent exemplify Wilcox's (2004) pathways from gesture to grammatical marker in signed languages, but they throw light on the general discussion of what is gestural and what is linguistic in signed languages.

In what follows, I will discuss the mouth shrug and facial consent in relation to other classifications of mouth actions in the signed language linguistics literature. It may be claimed that especially facial consent is not a mouth action since it is generally perceived and described as "nose wrinkle" by signers, but its most persistent form feature is raised upper lip, and like the mouth shrug, it excludes any other mouth action.

Building on earlier research into a number of signed languages, Crasborn et al. (2008) use *mouth actions* about all mouth activities and distinguish *mouthings*, derived from a spoken language, from *mouth gestures* formed within a signed language.[7] They classify mouth actions in three signed languages as: 1) *mouthings*, i.e., the mouth action borrowed from a spoken language; 2) adverbial or adjectival *mouth gestures* that modify the meaning of a simultaneous manual sign; 3) semantically empty mouth gestures that are motoric *echoes* of the manual component of simultaneous signs; 4) *enacting mouth gestures* where the mouth performs an action like chewing; and 5) *mouth activity in the context of whole-face activity* where the mouth action is seen in the context of other actions of the face, especially in expressions of affect. Mouth actions of the last type do not have independent form and meaning, they are not bound to individual lexemes made simultaneously, and they are not borrowed from a spoken language.

The DTS mouth shrug and facial consent are not mouthings of a word in any spoken language. Neither are they modifications of clause constituents expressed manually as Crasborn et al.'s (2008) type 2 since they may occur by themselves, and to the extent they modify the manual signs, they modify full propositions. Neither signal is semantically empty or "echos" the movements of the hands in contrast to mouth actions of type 3. That leaves us with two possibilities, type 4, enacting mouth gestures, and type 5, whole-face mouth actions.

The enacting mouth gestures have an independent meaning and are not borrowed from a spoken language, they imitate general human or animal behavior. Crasborn et al. (2008) mention examples such as biting, chewing and shouting. The meaning of the mouth shrug differs radically from the meaning of the examples of enacting mouth gestures given by Crasborn et al. (2008); it does not describe the manner of an action but has a proposition-modifying function. Moreover, Crasborn et al. do not mention any use of enacting mouth gestures without simultaneous manual signs, but the mouth shrug occurs by itself in almost 40% percent of its occurrences in the DTS data (35 out of 88 tokens). The mouth shrug might be seen as an enactment of the disclaimer gesture known from the western world (Morris 1994), but the mouth shrug is not an enactment or imitation of a gesture, it is the gesture in common use in society at large.

Is the mouth shrug then a mouth action of the fifth type, i.e., part of a whole-face action? As we have seen, the mouth shrug often occurs with other non-manual signals such as raised brow, brow furrow, squint, head tilt, head nod, and sideways head or body movements. Some of these are described in the gesture literature as parts of the shrug, others have distinct meanings (e.g., head nod and headshake). In all the combinations, the mouth shrug keeps its basic meaning of lack of knowledge or indetermination (cf. Debras 2017). It may occur with apparently opposed

---

[7] Crasborn et al. (2008) do not see any conflict between the term *mouth gesture* and the claim that such gestures are linguistic.

non-manual signals such as head nod and headshake and with raised brows and brow furrow and still keep its basic meaning. Even in cases where the signers are not in doubt, the use of the mouth shrug may be seen as a way of mitigating the aggression of an otherwise forceful statement by seemingly expressing uncertainty. As pointed out by Langacker (2013), there is a tight link between knowledge and power or control. Langacker describes epistemic modality as a striving for control of a process that the conceptualizer does not see as part of reality. Seemingly expressing uncertainty when exercising the power of knowledge is a way of mitigating the aggression. Thus the mouth shrug enters into "whole-face actions" with its own meaning, which refutes the classification of the mouth shrug as a whole-face action.

Facial consent does not resemble any known mouth action or mouth gesture with a similar meaning. Neither is it part of a whole-face activity. The whole-face gesture that involves raised upper lip is disgust, but facial consent has nothing to do with disgust. Facial consent may occur with other signals of the face, but either these other signals contribute to the flash-like tension of the face, e.g., squint, which make them form variants, or they reinforce the signal's meaning of consent, e.g., head nod or headshake.

In sum, neither the mouth shrug nor facial consent fits into the classification of mouth actions suggested by Crasborn et al. (2008). A reason may of course be that the classification was never meant to include mouth actions like the mouth shrug or facial consent. Crasborn et al. see mouth actions of all five types as having "an undisputed linguistic status within sign languages" (2008: 46). The mouth shrug might then be dismissed because of its gestural status, but facial consent appears to be an exception to their classification system.

In contrast to Crasborn et al. (2008), some signed language linguists see all mouth actions as gestural. Fontana (2008) compares mouth gestures and mouthings to co-verbal gestures and manual signs to spoken language words. She analyzes mouth actions of both types as global and synthetic entities that "are not independent units because they have a general meaning which is specified by the corresponding manual level" (Fontana 2008: 117). This is only true of the mouth shrug and facial consent in that they evaluate propositions, but their meanings are as precise as many words with an epistemic modal or interaction-oriented meaning.

Sandler (2009) also argues for analyzing the mouth actions as gestures in signed languages. With reference to Kendon's (2004) work on gesture, she claims that "most researchers agree that some kinds of expression are prototypically linguistic and others prototypically gestural, while acknowledging that there may be grey areas in between" (Sandler 2009: 242). Her main claim is that the hand and the mouth combine "in a simultaneous and complementary fashion linguistically organized material with holistic and iconic expressions" (Sandler 2009: 242). In spoken languages the mouth expresses the linguistically organized material, and the hands the holistic expressions; in signed languages the roles of the hand and the mouth are reversed, Sandler claims (see Ruth-Hirrel, this volume, and Sweetser, this volume, for discussions of "holistic" and "compositional" in relation to gestures).

Decomposability is one possible criterion of being linguistic. Another is combinability. It has been shown that the oral modality of spoken language communication and the manual modality of signed language communication show duality of patterning involving both decomposability and combinability (but see the discussion of duality of patterning in Kendon, this volume).

The mouth shrug and facial consent are indeed holistic, but both may combine with other non-manual signals simultaneously, and some of these may occur by themselves with their own meanings (head nod, headshake and, for the mouth shrug, sideways movements of the head or body). Moreover, they combine with the manually expressed sequence in non-accidental ways in DTS.

Kendon (this volume) argues against using "gestural" in relation to signing as "it leads to the idea that there is a separate 'gesture system', categorically distinct from 'language'", which he sees as a mistake. Rather, Kendon claims, in signing, "the signer uses a diverse repertoire of elements" (this volume, 454). What we can talk about is conventionalization. I see the analysis of the mouth shrug and facial consent presented here as a contribution to analyses of how the various signals are integrated in signed communication. With their persistent form-meaning pairing, the mouth shrug and facial consent are conventional signals in DTS, signals that appear to defy current suggestions of how mouth and facial activity and manual signs are integrated in signed languages.

Annotation key

The annotations follow the conventions developed for signed languages. Only what is deemed relevant to understanding the examples in context is annotated. Manual signs are written as glosses in small caps. When the use of one or two hands is irrelevant, the manual signs are annotated by one gloss. When the use of two hands is relevant, the signs are annotated by identical glosses one above the other. If one hand lingers in the position of a sign while the other hand articulates additional signs, the gloss for the first sign is followed by a broken line. Mouth actions are annotated below, and actions of the upper part of the face above, the glosses for manual signs. If the actions are described by form, annotation of the forms are followed by a broken line. If the actions are interpreted (*neg* for negation and ? for a question), they are written on a solid line. The length of the lines indicate the duration of the signals in relation to the manual signs.

POINT+card	A plus sign followed by a word in small letters indicates how the sign is modified; in this case, the point is directed at a card.
1SG	A pronoun with first-person reference.
attention	*Attention* indicates that the signer tries to get the interlocutor's attention, especially by waving their hand.
yes	A word below the gloss for a sign indicates silent (partial) mouthing of the word.
hs----	Headshake
hn----	Head nod
br----	Brow raiser
obr---	Outer brow raiser
cr---	Chin raiser
lcd---	Lip corner depressor
card---	Eye gaze towards cards with pictures of objects on the table
[	A bracket is used to indicate the start of simultaneous signing in two signers' utterances.

References

Boye, Kasper & Peter Harder. 2012. A usage-based theory of grammatical status and grammaticalization. *Language* 88(1). 1–44.

Brennan, Mary. 1992. The visual world of British Sign Language: An introduction. In David Brien (ed.), *Dictionary of British Sign Language/English*, 1–133. London: Faber and Faber.

Cabeza-Pereiro, Carmen. 2013. Modality and linguistic change in Spanish Sign Language (LSE): Obligation and epistemic necessity from the Fernández Villabrille dictionary (1851) to the DNLSE (2008). *CogniTextes* 10. 1–16.

Cabeza-Pereiro, Carmen & Silvia Iglesias-Lago. 2015. Spanish Sign Language. In Julie Bakken Jepsen, Goedele De Clerck, Sam Lutalo-Kiingi & William B. McGregor (eds.), *Sign Languages of the World: A Comparative Handbook*, 729–769. Berlin/Boston: De Gruyter Mouton and Preston, UK: Ishara Press.

Chovil, Nicole. 1991/1992. Discourse-oriented facial displays in conversation. *Research on Language and Social Interaction* 25. 163–194.

Clark, Brenda R. 2017. *A Grammatical Sketch of Sivia Sign Language*. Manoa, HI: University of Hawai'i at Manoa dissertation.

Coulter, Geoffrey R. 1978. Raised eyebrows and wrinkled noses: The grammatical function of facial expression in relative clauses and related constructions. In Frank Caccamise & Doin Hicks (eds.), *American Sign Language in a Bilingual, Bicultural Context: Proceedings of the Second National Symposium on Sign Language Research and Teaching*, 65–74. Silver Spring, MD: National Association of the Deaf.

Crasborn, Onno A., Els van der Kooij, Dafydd Waters, Bencie Woll & Johanna Mesch. 2008. Frequency distribution and spreading behavior of different types of mouth actions in three sign languages. *Sign Language & Linguistics* 11(1). 45–67.

Darwin, Charles. 1890 [1872]. *The Expression of the Emotions in Man and Animals*, 2nd edn. London: John Murray.

de Vos, Connie, Els van der Kooij & Onno Crasborn. 2009. Mixed signals: Combining linguistic and affective functions of eyebrows in questions in Sign Language of the Netherlands. *Language and Speech* 52(2/3). 315–339.

Debras, Camille. 2017. The shrug: Forms and meanings of a compound enactment. *Gesture* 16(1). 1–34.

Ekman, Paul. 2009 [1985]. *Telling Lies: Clues to Deceit in the Marketplace, Politics, and Marriage*, 4th edn. New York: W. W. Norton and Company.

Ekman, Paul & Wallace V. Friesen. 1978. *Facial Action Coding System*. Palo Alto, CA: Consulting Psychologists Press.

Ekman, Paul & Wallace V. Friesen. 2003. *Unmasking the Face: A Guide to Recognizing Emotions from Facial Clues*. Los Altos, CA: Malor Books.

Engberg-Pedersen, Elisabeth. 2002. Gestures in signing: The presentation.gesture in Danish Sign Language. In Rolf Schulmeister & Heimo Reinitzer (eds.), *Progress in Sign Language Research: In Honor of Siegmund Prillwitz/Fortschritte in der Gebärdensprachforschung: Festschrift für Siegmund Prillwitz* (40), 143–162. Hamburg: Signum Verlag.

Engberg-Pedersen, Elisabeth. 2021. Markers of epistemic modality and their origins: Evidence from two unrelated sign languages. *Studies in Language* 45(2). 277–330. https://doi.org/10.1075/sl.19065.eng

Farnsworth, Bryan. 2019. *Facial Action Coding System (FACS): A Visual Guidebook*. https://imotions.com/blog/learning/research-fundamentals/facial-action-coding-system/

Fontana, Sabina. 2008. Mouth actions as gesture in sign language. *Gesture* 8(1). 104–123.

Gianfreda, Gabriele, Virginia Volterra & Andrzej Zuczkowski. 2014. L'espressione dell'incertezza nella Lingua dei Segni Italiana (LIS). *Ricerche di Pedagogia e Didattica – Journal of Theories and Research in Education* 9(1). 199–234.

Givens, David B. 1977. Shoulder shrugging: A densely communicative expressive behavior. *Semiotica* 19(1/2). 13–28.

Kendon, Adam. 2004. *Gesture: Visible Action as Utterance*. Cambridge: Cambridge University Press.

Langacker, Ronald W. 2013. Modals: Striving for control. In Juana I. Marín-Arrese, Marta Carretero, Jorge A. Hita, & Johan van der Auwera (eds.), *English Modality: Core, Periphery and Evidentiality*, 3–55. Berlin/Boston: De Gruyter Mouton.

Liddell, Scott K. 1980. *American Sign Language Syntax*. The Hague: Mouton.

Martínez, Rocío, Sara Siyavoshi & Sherman Wilcox. 2019. Advances in the study of signed languages within a cognitive perspective. *Hesperia. Anuario de Filología Hispánica* XXII(2). 29–56.

Mesch, Johanna. 2016. Manual backchannel responses in signers' conversation in Swedish Sign Language. *Language and Communication* 50. 22–41.

Morris, Desmond. 1994. *Bodytalk: A World Guide to Gestures*. London: Jonathan Cape.

Müller, Cornelia. 2004. Forms and uses of the Palm Up Open Hand: A case of a gesture family? In Cornelia Müller & Roland Posner (eds.), *The Semantics and Pragmatics of Everyday Gestures: Proceedings of the Berlin Conference, April 1998*, 233–256. Berlin: Weidler Buchverlag.

Ottenheimer, Harriet J. 2012. *The Anthropology of Language: An Introduction to Linguistic Anthropology*, 3rd edn. Belmont, CA: Wadsworth Cengage Learning.

Papaspyrou, Chrissostomos, Alexander von Meyenn, Bettina Herrmann & Michaela Matthaei (eds.). 2008. *Grammatik der Deutschen Gebärdensprache aus der Sicht Gehörloser Fachleute* [A Grammar of German Sign Language from the Perspective of Deaf Professionals]. Hamburg: Signum Verlag.

Parr, Lisa A., Bridget M. Waller, Sarah J. Vick & Kim A. Bard. 2007. Classifying chimpanzee facial expressions using muscle action. *Emotion* 7(1). 172–181.

Ricci Bitti, Pio E. 2014. Facial expression and social interaction. In Cornelia Müller, Allan Cienki, Ellen Fricke, Silva H. Ladewig, David McNeill & Jana Bressen (eds.): *Body – Language – Communication: An International Handbook on Multimodality in Human Interaction, Vol. 2*,1342–1349. Berlin/München/Boston: De Gruyter Mouton.

Ricci Bitti, Pio E., Luisa Bonfiglioli, Paolo Melani, Roberto Caterina & Pierluigi Garotti. 2014. Expression and communication of doubt/uncertainty through facial expression. *Ricerche di Pedagogia e Didattica – Journal of Theories and Research in Education* 9(1). 159–177.

Roush, Daniel R. 2011. Language between bodies: A cognitive approach to understanding linguistic politeness in American Sign Language. *Sign Language Studies* 11(3). 329–374.

Sandler, Wendy. 2009. Symbiotic symbolization by hand and mouth in sign language. *Semiotica* 174. 241–275.

Siyavoshi, Sara. 2019. Hands and faces: The expression of modality in ZEI, Iranian Sign Language. *Cognitive Linguistics* 30(4). 655–686.

Streeck, Jürgen. 2009. *Gesturecraft: The Manu-facture of Meaning*. Amsterdam/Philadelphia: John Benjamins.

Wilbur, Ronnie B. 2009. Effects of varying rate of signing on ASL manual signs and nonmanual markers. *Language and Speech* 52(2/3). 245–285.

Wilcox, Sherman. 2004. Gesture and language: Cross-linguistic and historical data from signed languages. *Gesture* 4(1). 43–73.

Wilcox, Sherman. 2009. Symbol and symptom: Routes from gesture to signed languages. *Annual Review of Cognitive Linguistics* 7. 89–110.

Erin Wilkinson, Ryan Lepic, and Lynn Hou
Usage-based grammar: Multi-word expressions in American Sign Language

1 Introduction

In this chapter, we argue that the usage-based notion of *recycling* of sequential units, as it has been articulated in the study of multi-word expressions in spoken languages, provides a useful template for analyzing signed language data. We discuss four case studies of sequential constructions in American Sign Language (ASL) that rest on a continuum from more flexible to more highly fixed. These examples demonstrate that ASL users frequently produce and re-use analyzable units, whether individual signs or larger multi-word expressions. We find that ASL constructions are recycled as structured units that display different levels of fixedness and complexity, and at multiple levels of schematization. We analyze these constructions as participating in emergent networks of relatively fixed, conventionalized constructions. These constructions become repurposed with more specialized grammatical functions in wider contexts and repackaged as increasingly holistic units.

In the study of spoken languages, particularly English, recurring multi-word expressions (also referred to as *prefabs* or *collocations*) have been instrumental in guiding linguists to recognize the domain-general processes involved in language processing and use (e.g., Erman and Warren 2000; Dąbrowska 2014; Ambridge 2020). Of these, one key process is the automation of frequent routines (Bybee 2001, 2006). The interplay between language structure and language use has also been explored in signed languages, but to a lesser extent (Wilkinson 2016; Janzen 2018; Lepic 2019). This difference is due, in part, to the fact that studies of signed languages have largely focused on the domains of phonology and syntax as they were defined under American Structuralism and Generative Grammar.

Over the past several decades, linguists have also been concerned with describing structures that seem to be unique to signed languages, especially visual and bodily aspects of signing, and comparisons with non-signers' co-speech gestures. These discussions have focused on units of signing that can be labeled as morphologically complex versus morphologically simple, in the case of classifier constructions, or as linguistic versus gestural, in the case of constructed action (see Lepic

---

Erin Wilkinson, University of New Mexico, USA, e-mail: ewilkins@unm.edu
Ryan Lepic, Gallaudet University, USA, e-mail: ryan.lepic@gallaudet.edu
Lynn Hou, University of California, Santa Barbara, USA, e-mail: lhou@linguistics.ucsb.edu

https://doi.org/10.1515/9783110703788-014

and Occhino 2018). These categories are often assumed as objective realities, but they are constructs that are imposed by linguists, and may or may not align with the category judgments that individual language users may make (Wilcox and Occhino 2016; Kusters and Sahasrabudhe 2018; see also Antinoro Pizzuto and Garcia, this volume).

Our view of grammatical structures as emergent, rather than deriving from pre-determined categories such as phonology, syntax, or gesture, is inspired in part by Sherman Wilcox's (2014) paper, "Moving beyond structuralism: Usage-based signed language linguistics". As Wilcox explains, while structuralist analyses take formal features and categories as given *a priori*, usage-based analyses consider the units of grammar to emerge from linguistic experience, with differing sizes and levels of complexity. In other words, structuralist analyses focus on how discrete building blocks combine to derive complex utterances. In contrast, usage-based analyses recognize that all linguistic units blur at the edges, as a function of how often they are encountered, and in what contexts.

In this chapter, we define a multi-word expression as a sequence of identifiable words that also functions as a holistic unit. In Section 2, moving beyond an atomistic view of words, we explore holism in terms of the degree of fixedness in structure and conventionalization of meaning in multi-word expressions. In Section 3, we examine evidence for the repackaging and schematization of multi-word expressions that leads to fixed, conventionalized constructions as well as novel constructions. In Section 4, we identify recycled, loosely conventionalized units in an ASL monologue. From this, we conclude that language use, in the form of recycling of formulaic phrases, drives the conventionalization and schematization of multi-word expressions in ASL.

2 Identifying multi-word expressions

2.1 Chunks of recurring structure

The usage-based approach that Wilcox (2014) champions is founded on data from spoken (and written) languages (see Langacker 1987; Barlow and Kemmer 2000; Croft 2000; Goldberg 2019). The term *usage-based* was introduced by Langacker (1988), and usage-based theory has been further developed and expanded primarily by Bybee (2001, 2007, 2010). Here, we also adopt Dąbrowska's (2014) conceptualization of usage-based grammar, specifically. As we discuss, Dąbrowska's useful notion of "recycling utterances" has not yet been applied to signed language data, even among studies taking a cognitive, usage-based approach.

The central premise of usage-based theory is that a language user's mental representation of their language is emergent from their experience using that language. From this perspective, grammar is viewed as "the cognitive organization of one's experience with language" (Bybee 2006: 774). Cognitive representations are built up as language users encounter perceptible signals in meaningful contexts such as face-to-face interaction. Across instances of language use, learners extract recurring form-meaning pairings as symbolic units (Langacker 1988). As similar form-meaning units are encountered across usage events, language users construct and strengthen mental categories that guide future language use and processing. Units that are encountered more often, in a variety of contexts, are more strongly represented in a language user's mind than units that are encountered infrequently. These emergent units also vary in size and complexity, yielding a diversity of holistic "chunks" of learned symbolic structures.

As Dąbrowska (2014) shows, it is useful to conceptualize a language user's capacity for productive language use as the continual recycling of learned chunks of varying sizes. These learned language chunks include phrases containing specific words alongside variable, more schematic slots. An example is given in Figure 1, which models the *superimposition* (Dąbrowska 2014: 623) of two chunks of structure to yield new units: the usage-based operation of superimposition combines stored chunks of language structure, such that their corresponding elements are fused together. The other usage-based operation of *juxtaposition* (not illustrated here) places stored chunks of language structure next to each other in a temporal sequence.

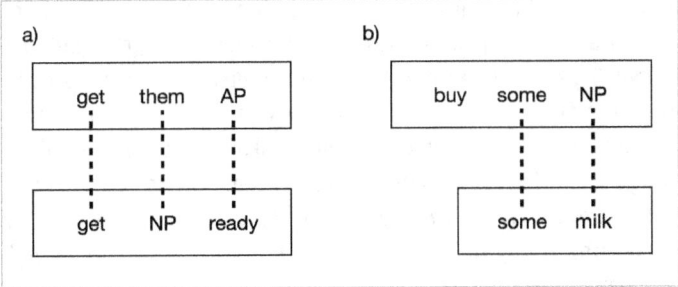

Figure 1: Superimposition of chunks with corresponding elements to form the units (a) *get them ready* and (b) *buy some milk* (after Dąbrowska 2014: 623–624).

In this analysis, a frequent form-meaning combination such as [*some milk*] is analyzed as a fixed phrase, while a recurrent form-meaning combination with an open slot such as [*buy some NP*] is analyzed as a constructional frame. Dąbrowska (2014) and Dąbrowska and Lieven (2005), studying child and adult language, demonstrate that it is possible to analyze the majority of a speaker's utterances as recycling previous chunks of structure. Dąbrowska's findings support the usage-based hypothesis that chunks of language structure emerge from and accumulate across instances of language use (Dąbrowska 2014).

For example, Dąbrowska argues that a complex utterance attested in her adult corpus, *You're not going to tell me what happened when you went to Luke's house*, can be assembled from four chunks of structure that recur often in the corpus of utterances from the same speaker. Figure 2 shows the superimposition of four chunks to yield the target complex utterance; the numbers in the top corner of each chunk indicate the token frequency for a particular chunk in the corpus (see Dąbrowska 2014, Section 4):

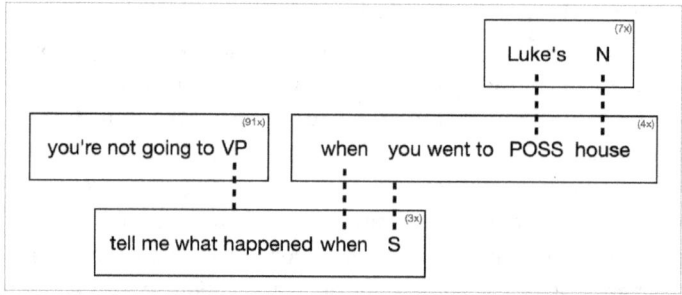

Figure 2: Superimposition of corresponding chunks to form the complex utterance *You're not going to tell me what happened when you went to Luke's house* (after Dąbrowska 2014: 636).

Dąbrowska shows that chunks of language structure are not wholly discrete units, but rather partially-overlapping representations that cohere into mutually-reinforcing families (2014: 643). For example, the chunk [*when you went to POSS house*] is attested only four times in Dąbrowska's corpus, but the target utterance in Figure 2 can be formed from other chunks as well. Dąbrowska gives the following possibilities, among others, for chunks in the corpus that can be recycled and superimposed to yield the target clause *when you went to Luke's house* (2014: 637). In (1), the superscripted numbers again indicate token frequencies in Dąbrowska's corpus of the speaker's earlier output:

(1) [*when S*]$^{(50+)}$ + [*you went to POSS house*]$^{(7x)}$ + [*Luke's N*]$^{(7x)}$
[*when S*]$^{(50+)}$ + [*you VP*]$^{(50+)}$ + [*NP went to POSS house*]$^{(45x)}$ + [*Luke's N*]$^{(7x)}$
[*when S*]$^{(50+)}$ + [*you went to NP*]$^{(50+)}$ + [*POSS house*]$^{(50+)}$ + [*Luke's N*]$^{(7x)}$
[*when you went DIR*]$^{(41x)}$ + [*to NP's house*]$^{(50+)}$ + [*Luke*]$^{(50+)}$
[*when NP went to NP's house*]$^{(16x)}$ + [*you VP*]$^{(50+)}$ + [*Luke*]$^{(50+)}$

This approach, which acknowledges that any particular complex unit may be created in a number of mutually compatible ways, also naturally accounts for individual variation between language users (for example, see Dąbrowska and Street 2006 concerning variation among English speakers' comprehension of passive sentences and Dąbrowska 2018 for the implications of individual differences among English speakers for usage-based linguistic theories). Analysts may not wish to assume that all speakers necessarily share a particular constructional frame such as [*when you went to POSS house*]. Instead, a usage-based theory acknowledges that language users can follow a variety of mutually compatible routes to the same end, based on their own inventory of language chunks extracted from their own language experiences.

A complementary view of recycling has also been proposed in Stefanowitsch and Gries (2003) and Gries and Stefanowitsch (2004) from a corpus-based perspective. In what they term a *collostructional analysis*, Stefanowitsch and Gries show that particular lexical items can become affiliated with one another, or often recur in identifiable slots of grammatical schemas. They examine a range of schematic construction types in English, showing, for example, that the noun slot in the frame [*N waiting to happen*] is not a completely open slot, in which any noun might freely appear, but rather is most often filled by particular nouns such as *accident* or *disaster* (Figure 3). Their analysis takes sequences of frequently co-occurring items as a foundation for further analysis, showing that words are not interchangeable beads on a linear string. Instead, individual words and larger phrasal structures preferentially combine as affiliates, and are recycled often across utterances.

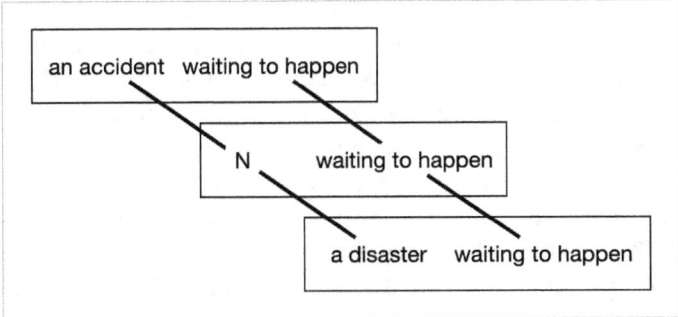

Figure 3: Overlap between fixed phrases and related constructional frames: [*N waiting to happen*] (after Stefanowitsch and Gries 2003: 217; Bybee 2006: 713).

The relationships between the chunks in these figures differ in that Figures 1 and 2 show superimposition, where multiple chunks, whether fully fixed or partially schematic, combine to yield a new unit. In Figure 3, the links between fixed phrases and the constructional frame show the structure of a constructional network as an aspect of linguistic knowledge. We view the constructional frame [*N waiting to happen*] as emergent from the fixed phrases [*an accident waiting to happen*] and [*a disaster waiting to happen*], codifying the relationship between them without replacing them in linguistic knowledge. In both cases, frequently-recycled chunks of structure are the basis for grammatical productivity and the identification of larger grammatical patterns.

2.2 Looking for multi-word expressions in signed languages

In the cognitive literature on signed languages, previous studies have dealt primarily with different types of symbolic structure and motivation observed among signs and grammatical constructions. Fewer studies have pursued the usage-based hypothesis specifically (examples include Wilkinson 2016; Janzen 2018; Lepic 2019; Hou 2022). In part, this gap reflects a lack of adequate data: frequency of use, as quantified by corpus data, is essential for testing usage-based hypotheses, and even the largest corpora of signed languages are still quite small. However, even among specifically usage-based studies, the notion of recycling learned chunks of structure has not yet been explored in much detail.

There is, however, a strong tradition in the cognitive linguistic analysis of signed languages that documents degrees of holism and analyzability that characterize iconic signs. A number of studies have explored the systematic motivations that shape how signs are used in context, in ASL and other signed languages (French Sign Language (langue des signes du française): Cuxac and Sallandre 2007; Garcia and Sallandre 2014; Danish Sign Language (dansk tegnsprog): Engberg-Pedersen 2003; ASL: S. Wilcox 2004; P. Wilcox 2004; Dudis 2004; Occhino 2017; Finnish Sign Language (suomalainen viittomakieli): Jantunen 2017). Additional cognitive studies of signed language structure have shown that signs participate in larger symbolic constructions beyond the level of individual signs (Irish Sign Language: Leeson and Saeed 2012; Swedish Sign Language (svenskt teckenspråk): Nilsson 2008; Argentine Sign Language (Lengua de señas argentina): Wilcox and Martinez 2020; ASL: Janzen 2004, 2017; Australian Sign Language (Auslan): Ferrara and Hodge 2018).

Although (spoken language) multi-word expressions are common in corpus linguistic research (as discussed in Section 2.1), few multi-*sign* expressions have been identified and analyzed. Idioms are a well-known class of multi-word expressions (Fillmore, Kay and O'Connor 1988; Croft and Cruse 2004). However, ASL has been commonly said to have very few idioms. One ASL idiom can be represented in a glossed form as TRAIN GONE, (SORRY) (e.g., Cohen 1994).[1] Like the English idiom *missed the boat*, this ASL idiom means that a window of opportunity has closed. Lists of purported ASL idioms can often be found in instructional materials shared by ASL teachers (e.g., Ganezer and Posner's 2017 DVD[2]). However, many of these items are single signs that require a full phrase to be translated into English, such as the single sign glossed BARELY.GETTING.BY,[3] or signs that are difficult to render concisely in English, such as the single sign glossed KISS.FIST,[4] which overlaps partially with the meanings of the English words *love* and *appreciate*. It is not clear to us that these single signs are actually "idioms" in the same sense that a multi-word expression might be (Fillmore, Kay, and O'Connor 1988). In any case, these single signs are certainly not multi-word expressions in ASL. To these examples we could add phrases that some signers identify as ASL idioms, such as (FISH) SWALLOW[5] 'to be gullible', DISCUSS DRY 'end of discussion!', and FINISH TOUCH 'have visited before'. These phrases have not been thoroughly researched as far as we are aware; we are unsure about the range of variation in structure or meaning that these phrases exhibit in actual use.

Here we view idiomaticity as only one diagnostic for assessing the conventionality of a holistic unit, rather than a necessary or sufficient condition for identifying a multi-word expression. The next section further discusses how we evaluate and represent conventionality in multi-word expressions, regardless of whether they have achieved semantically "idiomatic" status.

---

1 ASL researchers typically use English glosses in upper case to represent (manual) signs. Glosses approximate sign meanings. However, glossing is highly idiosyncratic and is fundamentally shaped by the researcher's analysis of the phenomenon at hand. Glossing also conceals the form of the intended signs. We try to work around this problem by also providing stills from movies and/or links to the original data when possible. Here, glosses separated by a hyphen represent two-sign units. Words separated by a hyphen in parentheses (-) indicate that the two elements have become (partially) fused together. Words separated by a period within a gloss (e.g., BRING.IN) denote that more than one English word is used to represent a single ASL sign. Lower case 'fs-' refers to fingerspelling (e.g., fs-HOLE). The slash in LOOK/'reaction' specifies the function expressed by the sign. ASL pronouns are glossed as PRO.1, PRO.2, and PRO.3. In some examples, the hands are identified as either dominant (dh) or non-dominant (ndh).
2 https://everydayasl.com/products/aslidioms5
3 This sign also can be glossed as FRUGAL (https://www.lifeprint.com/asl101/pages-signs/f/frugal.htm) or SCARCE (https://www.handspeak.com/word/search/index.php?id=1887)
4 https://aslsignbank.haskins.yale.edu/dictionary/gloss/166.html
5 https://www.handspeak.com/word/search/index.php?id=5607

2.3 Flexible use of INTERPRETER BRING.IN in ASL

As described in Section 2.1, the usage-based definition of grammar is "the cognitive organization of one's experience with language" (Bybee 2006: 774), and this cognitive organization can be characterized as the recycling of mutually overlapping formulaic utterances (Dąbrowska 2014). Beyond compositionality or idiomaticity alone, conventionality plays a large role in the analysis of grammatical patterns.

Lepic (2019: 9) identifies two two-sign units that have not reached a fully fixed, semantically idiomatic status, but at the same time, seem to be recurring conventional multi-word expressions in ASL. These units are glossed INTERPRETER BRING.IN 'to get an interpreter' (Figure 4) and TAKE.TO HOSPITAL 'to be taken to the hospital'. As Lepic demonstrates, these units are not fixed in form, but rather co-occur often, in varied configurations. However, the fact that these signs preferentially appear together must make up part of a signer's grammatical knowledge of ASL.

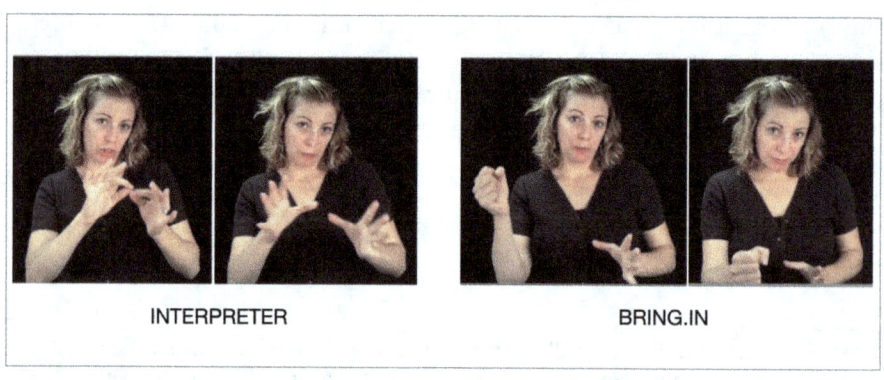

Figure 4: INTERPRETER BRING.IN (Lepic 2019, Figure 2a; https://youtu.be/uXdL5njDiBU?t=107).

The ASL sign BRING.IN denotes that some external force directs the placement of a human entity. The act of 'bringing in' is intentional, in response to the demands of a particular situation. We might assume that the sign BRING.IN combines freely with any pair of human agent and theme arguments. However, the sign BRING.IN appears, based on our observations, to be reserved for certain types of events; BRING.IN is commonly used in reference to events like 'dispatching interpreters', 'imprisoning criminals', and 'assigning interns'. BRING.IN also seems to be avoided in other contexts, such as 'hospitalizing a patient' (where

TAKE.TO seems preferred, instead) or 'calling a doctor' (where SUMMON seems preferred).[6]

Following Dąbrowska's (2014) notions of superimposition and juxtaposition as the two routes through which conventional chunks of language structure are recycled to create new utterances, we represent the affiliation between the signs INTERPRETER and BRING.IN as in Figure 5. This representation shows these signs as the analyzable parts of a larger holistic unit,[7] and contrasts with purely "item-based" representations, in which each sign is an equal element in a sequence, with no additional affinities between them.

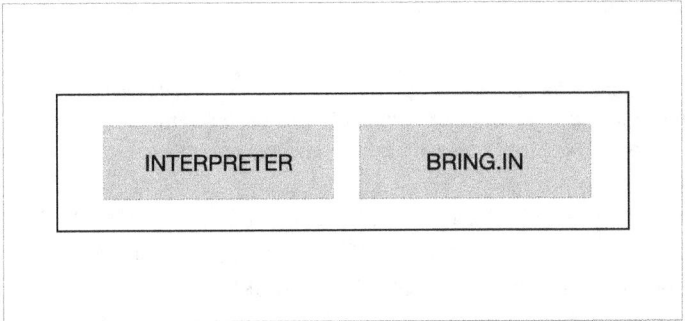

Figure 5: The [INTERPRETER BRING.IN] schema.

The signs INTERPRETER and BRING.IN not only appear adjacent to one another, but they also form a conventional unit unto themselves, which may be combined with other sign constructions, and even appear in variable orders (cf. Dąbrowska's 2014: 645 proposal about "packets"). So, we wish to model some cohesion between signs in a sequence to account for how this multi-word unit is used. These alternative representations are shown in Figure 6.

The signs BRING.IN and INTERPRETER need not occur in a fixed sequence, or one immediately following the other. Another example is a complex structure involving reported speech and a topic-marked direct object: ASK, LAST NIGHT INTERPRETER, WHICH AGENCY BRING.IN ('I asked them, which agency assigned

---

[6] We thank one reviewer for pointing out that the use of BRING.TO in contexts of mental health inpatient care may profile the involuntary nature of BRING.TO.
[7] Our representations unfortunately seem to suggest that signs are "building block"-like elements with well-defined boundaries. For practical reasons, our Figure representations involve straight edges, but we view schemas as exemplar clouds that may change in shape and density due to frequency/robustness of individual instances of language use. In such a representation, every experienced exemplar contributes to the dynamic strength and structure of a schema.

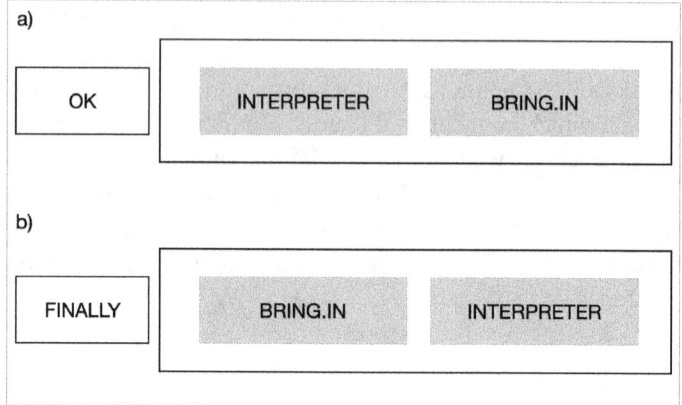

Figure 6: Schematic representations for ASL utterances meaning (a) '...they agreed to get an interpreter...' (Lepic 2019, ex.1a; https://youtu.be/uXdL5njDiBU?t=107) and (b) '...they finally gave me an interpreter...' (Lepic 2019, ex.1b; https://youtu.be/VTE-KpB109E?t=64s).

you the interpreter from last night?'). In this utterance, the signs INTERPRETER and BRING.IN are separated by the phrase WHICH AGENCY. The superimposition of WHICH AGENCY between the signs INTERPRETER and BRING.IN, as elements of a larger holistic schema, can be shown as in Figure 7.

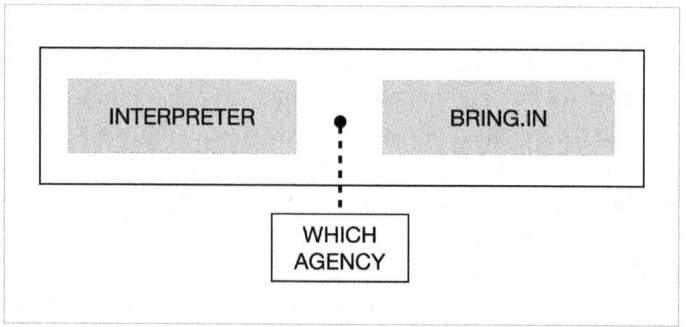

Figure 7: Schematic representation for an ASL utterance meaning 'which agency assigned you the interpreter?' (Lepic 2019, ex.1c; https://youtu.be/PhVxvTsIsrw?t=509s).

Rejecting a view of ASL utterances as strings of individual, equally interchangeable atoms that are ordered according to purely structural rules, we instead see multi-word expressions as holistic units, chunks of structure that vary in size, length, and degree of conventionalization and schematization. It is through recycling and repeated use that sequences of signs cohere together, ultimately causing languages to gradually and dynamically shift over time. This leads us to consider the repackaging of increasingly fixed multi-word expressions.

3 Repackaging of fixed multi-word expressions

3.1 Fusion in fixed NOT-collocations in ASL

Having just discussed a two-sign unit in ASL whose elements can occur in either order, or be separated by other signs, we now consider what happens when two signs occur together so regularly that the boundary between them has become blurred to some degree.

The gradual repackaging of multi-word expressions into a single unit has been described in Wilkinson's (2016) study of NOT. Arguing for frequency effects in ASL, Wilkinson presents examples in frequent sequences of signs of what Bybee (2001: 60) calls special (i.e., extreme) phonetic reduction, such that sequential multi-word strings have become fixed in form, and increasingly repackaged into a semantically and phonologically holistic unit.

Looking at 22 hours of naturalistic ASL signing supplemented with data from Morford and MacFarlane (2003), Wilkinson (2016) identifies 956 tokens of the manual negator NOT occurring in sequence with another sign.[8] Because the 956 NOT tokens are distributed across 308 unique collocation types, Wilkinson calculates the frequency of co-occurrence between NOT and each of the other signs that it appears with, finding a range of usage patterns: NOT frequently occurs in the two-sign sequence NOT UNDERSTAND (33 tokens), in the two-sign sequence WILL NOT (10 tokens), and less frequently, in sequences such as NOT INVITE (1 token). Overall, these least-frequent types accounted for 27% of NOT-collocation tokens (Wilkinson 2016, Appendix 1). Infrequent constructions like NOT INVITE are nevertheless stored as exemplars, as frequency alone does not determine storage; this has been similarly proposed for low-frequency collocations (e.g., idioms) by Dąbrowska (2014: 627). While high frequency is an indicator of a highly used and therefore well-entrenched construction, the reverse interpretation, that infrequent constructions are not well-entrenched, is not necessarily true. On the basis of this range of frequency counts for NOT-collocations, Wilkinson demonstrates that there are many degrees of fusion between the elements of a(n analyzable) two-sign sequence, based on frequency of occurrence.

---

[8] Some of the NOT examples here fall under Wilkinson's University of Manitoba Research Ethics Board approved study "Sociolinguistic variation in Canadian ASL discourse" in 2010.

For example, Wilkinson reports some variation in the formation of the sequence NOT UNDERSTAND, with the sign UNDERSTAND being variously articulated at the forehead (11 tokens), eyes/nose (4 tokens), cheek/chin (17 tokens), or torso (1 token) (Wilkinson 2016: 96, Table 2). These different places of articulation result from blurring between the boundaries of NOT, which is canonically articulated at the signer's chin, and the following sign UNDERSTAND, which is canonically articulated at the signer's forehead. As these two signs are frequently recycled as a single structured unit, their individual articulations begin to blur. In particular, UNDERSTAND is often seen to change its place of articulation to be nearer to the place of articulation for NOT, as a function of their frequent co-occurrence (Figure 8).

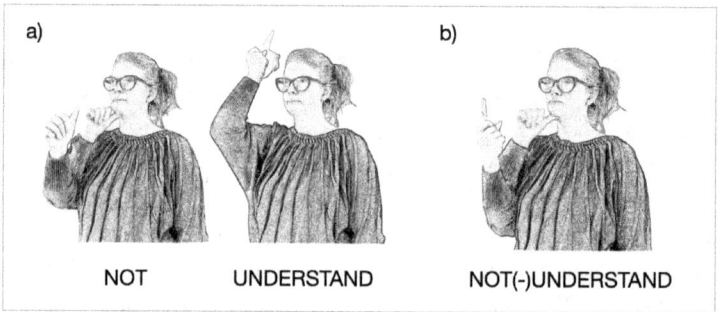

Figure 8: (a) two-sign NOT UNDERSTAND and (b) fused NOT(-)UNDERSTAND.

We conceptualize this repackaging of signs within a collocation in the following way. In some instances, both signs are more transparent in meaning and form. For example, Wilkinson (2016) reports that instances where NOT and UNDERSTAND are clearly and fully articulated tend to be instances that code a literal 'lack of comprehension' on the part of some animate experiencer. These signs as units in a fixed sequence are represented in Figure 9.

In other cases, the components of this collocation have become somewhat less transparent, both in meaning and in form. Wilkinson (2016) shows that utterances in which the articulation of UNDERSTAND has been lowered from its canonical place of articulation near the forehead tend to code concepts like 'indifference', beyond true lack of comprehension (see also Janzen 2018 on additional functions of UNDERSTAND). This shift in both the meaning and form of UNDERSTAND reflects that the individual signs NOT and UNDERSTAND have receded into the background to some degree, and that the construction as a whole, which we gloss as NOT(-)UNDERSTAND, has emerged as a predominant construction in place of its parts. This gradual shift and blurring between the component signs of this two-sign unit is represented in Figure 10.

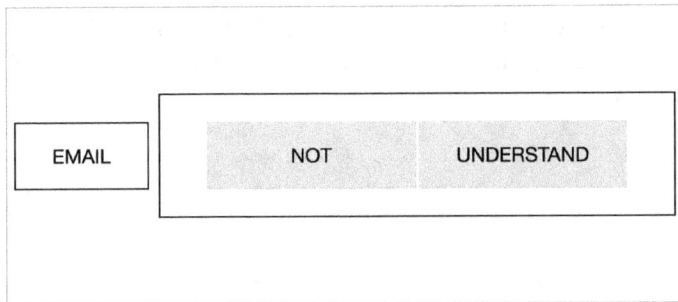

Figure 9: Schematic representation for NOT UNDERSTAND in an ASL utterance meaning 'if you do not understand what is meant over email, or by phone, then meet in person' (Wilkinson 2016, ex. 5; https://youtu.be/4yPu-mL5HgY?t=257).

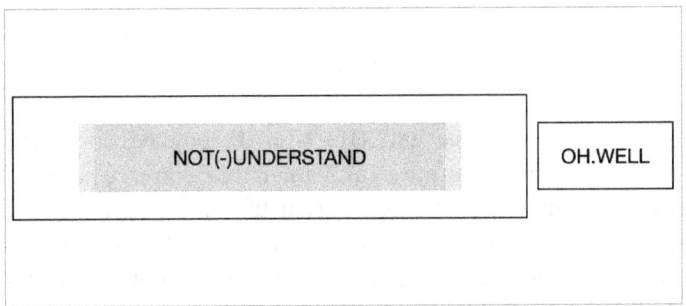

Figure 10: Schematic representation for NOT(-)UNDERSTAND in an ASL utterance meaning 'I see hearing employees talking to each other, but I don't get it, oh well' (Wilkinson 2016, ex. 7; *An Introduction to American Deaf Culture: Rules of social interaction* [26:44]).

A more extreme case of phonological restructuring is the case of NOT(-)HAVE. TO 'don't have to', the most frequent NOT-collocation in Wilkinson's (2016) data (39 tokens). In the data, there was only one instance of NOT and HAVE.TO being articulated as two distinct forms in a sequence (Figure 11a).[9] The remaining 38 forms

---

9 In this case, NOT and HAVE.TO were articulated with different hands. The signer produced the following sequence, alternating between their dominant (dh) and non-dominant (ndh) hands:

TAP.ON.ARM(dh) LOOK.PRO.1(dh) PRO.1(dh) NOT(ndh) HAVE.TO(dh)
'You don't need to tap a person on the arm to get their attention'

Here, the sign HAVE.TO is referring to 'obligation', and it is easy to see that these two sign tokens are separate signs, rather than a fused construction, given that they are made with different articulators (from *An Introduction to American Deaf Culture: Rules of social interaction* [14:58]; Wilkinson 2016, ex.1).

were articulated as the fused construction NOT.HAVE.TO (Figure 11b), which combines both the handshapes and the movements of the former signs NOT and HAVE.TO into a single sign form.

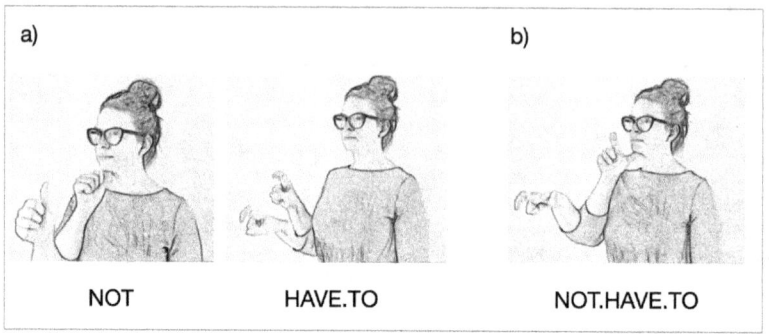

Figure 11: (a) two-sign NOT HAVE.TO and (b) fused NOT.HAVE.TO.

In Wilkinson's data, there is little evidence that NOT.HAVE.TO should be conceptualized primarily as a sequence of two separate signs. Rather, this sequence has been repackaged as a holistic unit, largely obscuring the structure of its original parts. Wilkinson (2013) demonstrates a similar repackaging of the sign UP.TO.YOU, which is a fusion of the former two-sign sequence THINK and SELF. For units like UP.TO.YOU and NOT.HAVE.TO, an articulation that could be analyzed as a multi-word expression has become heavily restructured to yield a single sign, the result of which is represented in Figure 12:

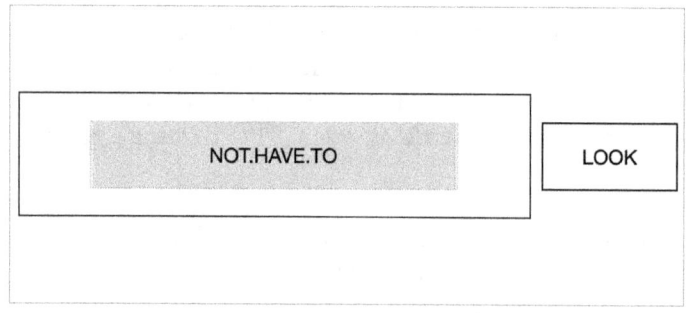

Figure 12: Schematic representation for NOT.HAVE.TO in an ASL utterance meaning 'so you don't have to keep checking' (https://youtu.be/RZJ9P0-NbUQ?t=46).

As Wilkinson (2016) notes, an additional clue about the degree to which NOT.HAVE.TO has been entrenched as an autonomous representation, rather than a primarily two-sign unit, comes from how this unit's meaning has drifted from the literal meaning of 'not being obligated'. In many cases, the unit NOT.HAVE.TO instead functions to code (a lack of) social obligation or a possible course of action. As its meaning has become less transparent, the fixed sequence NOT.HAVE.TO has been reanalyzed as a single unit.

We see this pattern of becoming less transparent as a gradual blurring of boundaries between elements in an analyzable, holistic unit. However, this is also an extreme outcome, as many multi-word expressions may retain their internal structure even as they become increasingly specialized. Accordingly, the following section explores how a high-frequency sign is reused in multiple overlapping schemas.

3.2 Multiple schematization of LOOK in ASL

As schemas containing analyzable internal structure, grammatical constructions also exist at different levels of schematization, and with different degrees of fixedness. This is evident with the ASL sign LOOK, which participates in overlapping multi-word expressions, forming a network of conventionalized constructions. Hou (2022) investigates the co-occurrence of LOOK with other ASL signs and proposes that LOOK codes physical or metaphorical 'vision', or introduces a psychological 'reaction'. Figure 13 shows LOOK coding each of these functions. The context for Figure 13a is PRO.2 LOOK fs-VIDEO 'have a look at the video', and the context for Figure 13b is LOOK MIND.PUZZLED. Though LOOK MIND.PUZZLED may be rendered literally in English as 'I look at it and am puzzled', a more precise English rendering is 'it's baffling to me' or 'I just don't get it'; i.e., the physical act of 'looking' has been backgrounded to some degree.

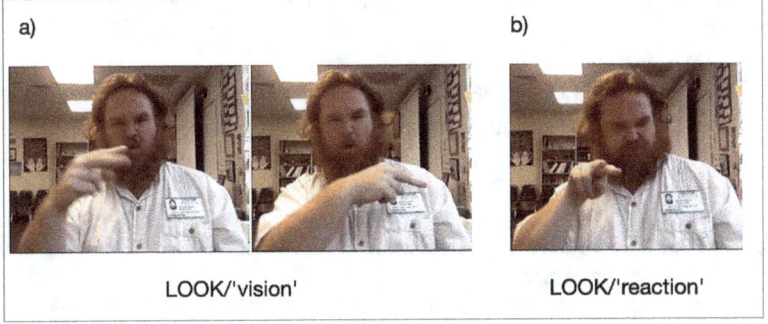

Figure 13: (a) LOOK/'vision' and (b) LOOK/'reaction' (Hou 2022, Figure 2; https://www.facebook.com/groups/ASLTHAT/permalink/2024014911163339/).

Hou analyzes 174 tokens of LOOK exhibiting this reaction function, abbreviated as LOOK/'reaction',[10] collected from over 8 hours of ASL signing.[11] Among these, Hou identifies several recurring multi-word sequences formed with LOOK. As Table 1 shows, 10% of LOOK/'reaction' tokens occur in the three-sign sequence PRO.1 LOOK OH.I.SEE. The ASL sign OH.I.SEE is commonly used for backchanneling or signaling awareness. Figure 14 shows an example of the recurring multi-word sequence PRO.3 LOOK OH.I.SEE in context.

Table 1: Frequent (n>3) LOOK trigrams in 174 tokens of LOOK/'reaction' (Hou 2022).

Trigram			Count	
PRO.1	LOOK	OH.I.SEE	17	10%
PRO.1	LOOK	PRO.1	12	7%
PRO.3	LOOK	OH.I.SEE	7	4%

| PRO.3 | LOOK | OH.I.SEE | DEAF | FINE |

Figure 14: '. . .he was like, oh, you're deaf, got it. . .' (Hou 2022, Figure 13; https://youtu.be/zlR2EGi6_wA?t=160).

Table 1 also shows that 7% of LOOK/'reaction' tokens occur in the three-sign sequence PRO.1 LOOK PRO.1. Here, the repetition of the first-person pronoun signals a pivot

---

10 The multiple schematization of LOOK/'reaction' also seems to involve constructed action. While beyond the scope of this chapter, it would be interesting to explore the range of schematicity in LOOK/'reaction' constructions in a variety of contexts.

11 Because they tend to exhibit different formal properties (Hou 2022), we might be tempted to consider the tokens of LOOK in Figure 13 as "separate" signs. However, Hou demonstrates the 'vision' and 'reaction' functions that are coded by LOOK do not derive solely from the form of the sign in isolation. Rather, the meaning that can be attributed to an instance of LOOK emerges from the sequence of signs that it participates in.

to a statement of the signer's reaction. The four-sign sequence PRO.1 LOOK PRO.1 WAVE.NO 'I was like, no way', attested three times in Hou's data, is one example of such a pivot construction.

In Hou's data, the first person pronoun PRO.1 and the interaction-oriented sign OH.I.SEE are the most frequent collocates of LOOK/'reaction'. As Table 2 shows, in addition to 7% of tokens following PRO.1, a further 11% occur after third person experiencers (PRO.3 and PEOPLE). Similarly, beyond the 21% of tokens occurring before OH.I.SEE, several 'reaction' signs, that is WELL[12], GET.INSPIRED, HOLD.ON, MIND.PUZZLED, WOW, and FINE account for an additional 20% of LOOK/'reaction' tokens. This distribution suggests that certain types of signs frequently participate in the LOOK/'reaction' construction in ASL.

Table 2: Frequent (n>3) LOOK bigrams in 174 tokens of LOOK/'reaction' (Hou 2022). Note that the percentages do not = 100, as tokens in frequent trigrams (from Table 1 above) are counted for both of their bigrams.

	Bigram		Count	
PRO.1	LOOK		95	55%
	LOOK	OH.I.SEE	36	21%
	LOOK	PRO.1	13	7%
PRO.3	LOOK		11	6%
	LOOK	WELL	10	6%
PEOPLE	LOOK		8	5%
WELL	LOOK		5	3%
	LOOK	WOW	5	3%
	LOOK	YES	5	3%
	LOOK	GET.INSPIRED	4	2%
	LOOK	HOLD.ON	4	2%
	LOOK	MIND.PUZZLED	4	2%
	LOOK	FINE	4	2%

Hou (2022) proposes that the frequently-recycled sequences of [PRO.1 LOOK] and [LOOK OH.I.SEE] are prefabs (Bybee and Cacoullos 2009; Bybee 2010) that are already assembled and ready to use "off the shelf", functioning as subjective stance markers in ASL. These prefabs are highly fixed as multi-word expressions. At the same time, these fixed sequences also instantiate a more schematic multi-word template, yielding low-level schemas with slots that can be filled with other signs. The template for one such schema, [(experiencer) LOOK reaction], is shown in Figure 15.

---

12 WELL is glossed as PALM.UP in Hou (2022).

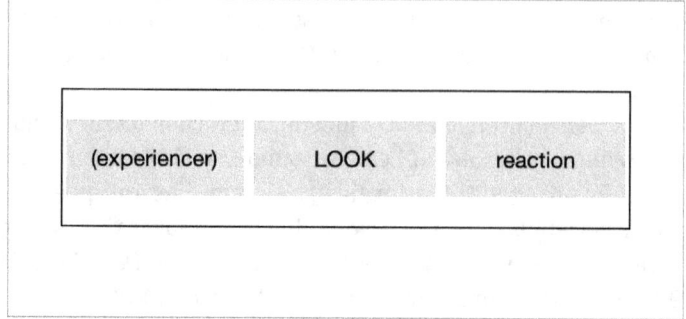

Figure 15: A schematic representation for the LOOK/'reaction' construction.

An example of how this schema is involved in the recycling of utterances is given in Figure 16. Here, a chunk of structure representing the recurring unit [PRO.3 LOOK] and another chunk of structure representing the recurring unit [LOOK OH.I. SEE] are superimposed onto the schematic [(experiencer) LOOK reaction] template.

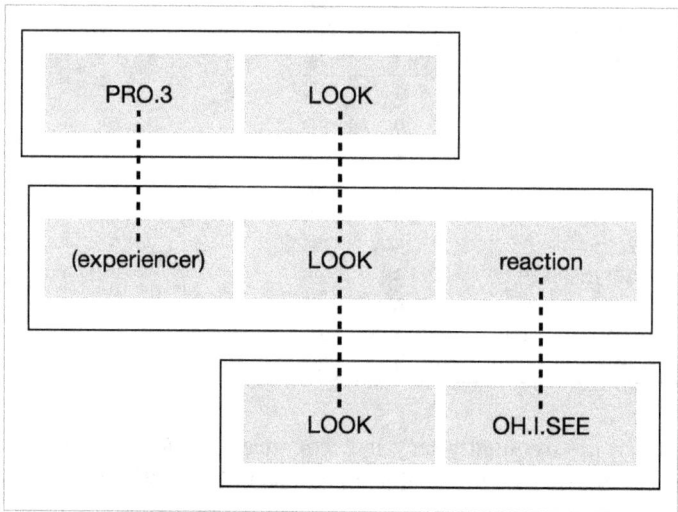

Figure 16: Superimposition of corresponding chunks to form the complex utterance PRO.3 LOOK OH.I.SEE 'they're like, oh!'

In Hou's data, 21% of tokens have the [reaction] slot filled by the interactive sign OH.I.SEE while 27% of tokens have that slot filled with signs occurring only once, including WHAT'S.UP, STOMACH.TURN, and CONCERNED. These low-frequency collocations reflect the productive use of this template. Similarly, though 61% of tokens have the optional [experiencer] slot filled by first- or third-person pronouns, the slot is often filled by other experiencers, such as JUDGE, STUDENT, and DEAF ('deaf people') and sometimes the experiencer is not explicitly mentioned at all.

As Hou demonstrates, among these chunks of linguistic structure involving LOOK/'reaction', there are units of varying sizes and levels of schematicity. A unit like [(experiencer) LOOK reaction] has two schematic elements which can be aligned with and superimposed onto a fully fixed unit like the recurring collocation [LOOK OH.I.SEE] in the course of language use. The result is that a network of fixed, conventionalized units emerges, opening an opportunity for more units to be further recycled into newer structures. We discuss additional examples of recycling of fixed and schematic structures in the next section.

4 Recycling schematic constructions in an ASL narrative

4.1 NOT and OH.I.SEE revisited

Having discussed multi-word units in terms of their fixedness and schematicity, as well as the network of constructions they instantiate, we turn to discuss how complex, analyzable units are used and recycled in a short ASL monologue. The "Firefighters" video that we analyze features one signer sharing some prepared trivia about firefighters, and appears to be intended for a younger ASL-signing audience.[13]

An ASL-fluent coder identified each manual sign produced in the video, a total of 474 sign tokens, and labeled each token with an English gloss based on the meaning and/or form of the sign. Tokens were spot-checked for consistency among glosses and grouped together according to primarily morphological criteria. Table 3 provides a summary of the most frequent signs in this dataset, as a first look at the data.

As shown in Table 3, many pointing signs were produced, with a variety of movement patterns. These were collapsed into a broad "pointing" type, and into more specific subtypes, such as POINT.SG.RIGHT, a single point to the signer's right. This dual-layer coding allows us to calculate token-frequencies at different grains of specificity (cf. Konrad et al. 2012). Due to the short length of the monologue, the topic

---

[13] We follow Hou, Lepic, and Wilkinson's (2020) procedure for using public internet data. The video and English transcript are found at https://www.youtube.com/watch?v=N7bQ1gkCTzU ("Did You Know That?! Fire Poles and Dalmatians").

Table 3: Sign types occurring with token frequency of >10 in the "Firefighters" monologue.

Rank	Type	Tokens	Subtype	Tokens	Notes
1	POINT	59	POINT.SG.RIGHT	21	
			POINT.SG.AHEAD	14	https://aslsignbank.haskins.yale.edu/dictionary/gloss/1712.html
			POINT.SG.OTHER	10	incl. 6 types w/ ≤3 tokens each: POINT.YOU, POINT.LEFT, POINT.DOWN, POINT.DOWN/LEFT, POINT.DOWN/RIGHT, POINT.AHEAD/RIGHT
			POINT.DIRECTION	7	incl. 4 types w/ ≤3 tokens each: POINT.MOVE.UP, POINT.UP, POINT.MOVE.DOWN, POINT.MOVE.DOWN.INTO
			POINT.PL	7	incl. 4 types w/ ≤3 tokens each: POINT.CIRCLE.RIGHT, POINT.CIRCLE.DOWN, POINT.ARC.LEFT, POINT.RIGHT+POINT.LEFT
2	bent-V*	28			*see Table 4
3	THAT	13	THAT.AHEAD	7	https://aslsignbank.haskins.yale.edu/dictionary/gloss/1199.html
			THAT.OTHER	6	incl. 3 types with ≤3 tokens each: THAT.RIGHT, THAT+POINT.RIGHT, THAT.NDH
4	FIRE	13			https://aslsignbank.haskins.yale.edu/dictionary/gloss/457.html
5	POLE	11			https://aslsignbank.haskins.yale.edu/dictionary/gloss/911.html
6	FIREFIGHTER	10			https://aslsignbank.haskins.yale.edu/dictionary/gloss/133.html
7	HORSE	10			https://aslsignbank.haskins.yale.edu/dictionary/gloss/391.html

skews the counts quite a bit; we do not expect that FIRE, POLE, or FIREFIGHTER should be especially frequent signs in ASL in general, but it is not surprising that they are among the most frequent signs here.

What particularly interests us is the second-most frequent sign type, the bent-V. The data yielded 28 bent-V tokens, which are discussed further in Section 4.2. A glossed ASL dataset can also be used to examine how signs are used in context. Here we use "Firefighters" to assess whether individual signs are an appropriate unit of analysis for discussing grammatical patterns in ASL, or if signs instead cohere in larger units, as loosely conventionalized structures which are frequently recycled and recombined.

Our data generated other types of recycled units like NOT and LOOK constructions, allowing us to continue the discussion of these signs from Section 3. "Firefighters" contains four tokens of NOT and two tokens of OH.I.SEE. Three of the NOT tokens transparently negate the following sign. In (2) to (4), parallel to the NOT UNDERSTAND schema proposed in Figure 9 above, we conceptualize these signs as more-or-less independent elements. They are not only transparent in meaning, but the two signs are also identifiable as separate articulations, each with their own movements.

(2) HAVE THAT SPIRAL.STAIRCASE, **NOT** STRAIGHT.STAIRCASE, WAVE.NO, SPIRAL. STAIRCASE
'Have a spiral staircase, rather than a straight one.'
(https://youtu.be/N7bQ1gkCTzU?t=21)

(3) WOOD POLE **NOT** SAFE WHY
'A wooden pole isn't safe because. . .'
(https://youtu.be/N7bQ1gkCTzU?t=144)

(4) WELL, **NOT** fs-ALL USE POLE WHY
'Well, not all (fire stations) have a pole installed, due to. . .'
(https://youtu.be/N7bQ1gkCTzU?t=163)

The fourth NOT token co-occurs with the sign WHY, in the repackaged unit WHY(-) NOT, in (5). As Wilkinson (2016: 92–95) describes, the frequent combination of WHY and NOT often functions to elicit permission or agreement from an interlocutor. Here, a firefighter makes a suggestion to his superior, and we observe that the articulation of WHY is affected by the following sign NOT. Rather than beside the head, WHY is articulated near the center of the forehead, and is re-timed to anticipate the following NOT. We conceptualize the relationship between WHY and NOT to be analogous to NOT(-)UNDERSTAND, as represented in Figure 10: the fixed sequence WHY(-)NOT is emerging as a predominant construction over the two signs as individual, independent units.

(5) POINT TAP HIS BOSS SUPERIOR, HEY **WHY(-)NOT** GO.AHEAD MAKE fs-HOLE
'He suggested to his boss, why don't we put in a hole.'
(https://youtu.be/N7bQ1gkCTzU?t=106)

Similarly, consistent with Hou's (2022) discussion of LOOK and OH.I.SEE, both tokens of OH.I.SEE in "Firefighters" co-occur with a sign belonging to the LOOK family of signs in ASL, which introduces an experiencer's reaction:

(6) AFTER THAT, PEOPLE **MANY.LOOK.IN.DISBELIEF** OH.I.SEE
'And people were amazed (that the method worked).'
(https://youtu.be/N7bQ1gkCTzU?t=134)

(7) BARK, HELP PEOPLE HEAR **MULTIPLE.LOOK.LEFT OH.I.SEE** POINT HURRY
'Their barking would help alert people to the rushing (firefighters).'
(https://youtu.be/N7bQ1gkCTzU?t=214)

MULTIPLE.LOOK.LEFT in (7) is a two-handed sign, with each hand configured in the 2 handshape that is used in LOOK (Figure 17b). The sign MANY.LOOK.IN.DISBELIEF in (6) is also a two-handed sign, with each hand in a 4 handshape (Figure 17a). The use of both hands codes multiple experiencers participating in the same 'looking' event (Lepic et al. 2016). Like LOOK, these signs are formed with the fingertips directed to a region of signing space associated with a stimulus that is seen and provokes a reaction from the experiencers (Wilcox and Occhino 2016). Both signs are used here in ways that recycle aspects of the recurring [LOOK OH.I.SEE] schema (Figure 16), as described by Hou (2022).

Figure 17: (a) '(the people were) amazed (it worked)' (https://youtu.be/N7bQ1gkCTzU?t=134) and (b) '(it) would alert (the people)' (https://youtu.be/N7bQ1gkCTzU?t=214).

Once we conceptualize ASL signing as made up of overlapping configurations of units that have been schematized at multiple levels, we not only see recurring sequential units, but also find that units are recycled into a variety of fixed and flexible constructions. We observe a similar pattern of recycling with loosely conventionalized, depictive signs, which we discuss next.

4.2 Loosely conventionalized units: The bent-V/'legs' schema

In ASL linguistics, the bent-V handshape is sometimes considered a "classifier" or "depicting" sign, used to represent legs. While classifier handshapes and classifier constructions are relatively well investigated compared to other types of constructional units in signed languages, classifier handshapes have been viewed mostly as semantically heavy units that participate in complex simultaneous constructions (Supalla 1986; Emmorey 2003). Instead, we propose here that the bent-V handshape (and other similar items) can be reanalyzed as participating in recycled constructions exhibiting a greater or lesser degree of schematicity. In "Firefighters", signs formed with the bent-V handshape were annotated like any other sign, without assuming a separate category of "classifier" signs (Lepic and Occhino 2018). We indeed find that many signs that are formed with the bent-V handshape refer to 'leg-related' concepts (see also Anible's 2016, 2020 related analysis of the V handshape to represent 'legs').

Among the bent-V signs, we see re-use of particular forms, such as the single signs SLIDE.DOWN.POLE (6 times) and ANIMAL.GALLOPING (4 times), and recurring mappings of meaning to form. As Table 4 shows, half (14 tokens) of the identified bent-V signs refer to the movement of an individual walking, jumping, or sliding. A smaller number (9) are two-handed forms in which the two hands represent multiple sets of legs, whether the four legs of a horse or dog, or the legs of multiple moving humans or animals. Finally, some signs (5) refer not to legs directly, but rather to architectural installations like staircases, with salient shapes that people and animals move along.

Table 4: Subtype analysis of 28 bent-V/'legs' tokens in the "Firefighters" monologue.

Type	Tokens	Subtype	Tokens
one hand, one pair of legs	14	SLIDE.DOWN.POLE	6
		WANDER.UP	3
		JUMP.ON.POLE	2
		HOP.IN.CAR	1
		DESCEND.INTO.HOLE	1
		WALK.DOWN	1
two hands, multiple pairs of legs	9	ANIMAL.GALLOPING	4
		MOVE.AROUND	3
		ANIMAL.STANDING	2
architectural shape	5	SPIRAL.STAIRCASE	3
		STRAIGHT.CHUTE	1
		STRAIGHT.STAIRCASE	1

From this distribution, we analyze the bent-V handshape as participating in a productive morphological schema: bent-V/'legs'.[14] This is an initial analysis on the basis of a small dataset, however, this general pattern of relative frequency of types and subtypes is correlated with flexibility and productivity of grammatical constructions (Bybee 1995; Hay and Baayen 2005). Considering related individual signs as instantiating more abstract morphological schemas is also in line with recent cognitive analyses of sub-sign structure in ASL (Lepic 2016; Lepic and Padden 2017; Occhino 2017; Lepic and Occhino 2018).

Relevant to our argument for recognizing recycling of multi-word units in ASL, we observe that the two tokens of bent-V JUMP.ON.POLE, glossed in (8) and (9), occur before bent-V SLIDE.DOWN.POLE, and co-occur with the independent sign POLE. Although we observe some variation with the ordering of these three signs, they also seem to form a chunk of recurring structure that is recycled within the data. This is parallel to our analysis of the flexible unit INTERPRETER BRING.IN in Section 2.3.

As (8) shows, JUMP.ON.POLE and SLIDE.DOWN.POLE are formed with overlapping articulation: JUMP.ON.POLE leaves both hands ready to immediately articulate SLIDE.DOWN.POLE without any additional transitional movements. In (9), however, these two signs are separated by three intervening signs, WOOD POLE GRAB.POLE ('grab the wooden pole'). JUMP.ON.POLE and SLIDE.DOWN.POLE appear to behave as a holistic unit on the one hand, and as a structured phrase, on the other, leading us to schematize these signs as a structured, recurring whole (Figure 18).

(8) KNOW.THAT FIRE fs-STATION POINT TEND.TO HAVE POLE FOR FIRE FIGHTER, SIGN FIREFIGHTER, **JUMP.ON.POLE(-)SLIDE.DOWN.POLE** ARRIVE FIRST FLOOR
'You may know that fire stations usually have poles for firefighters to be able to slide down to the first floor.'
(https://youtu.be/N7bQ1gkCTzU?t=1)

(9) HAPPEN HURRY SOMEONE SUMMON COME.ON, POINT fs-DAVID **JUMP.ON.POLE** WOOD POLE GRAB.POLE **SLIDE.DOWN.POLE**
'. . . as (he was working), somebody called for David to hurry over, so he grabbed onto the wooden pole and slid down.'
(https://youtu.be/N7bQ1gkCTzU?t=89)

---

[14] Here the function label 'legs' is chosen as the label for the general schema. However, related sub-schemas may refer to the more specific functions 'pair-of-legs', 'multiple-legs', and 'shape'.

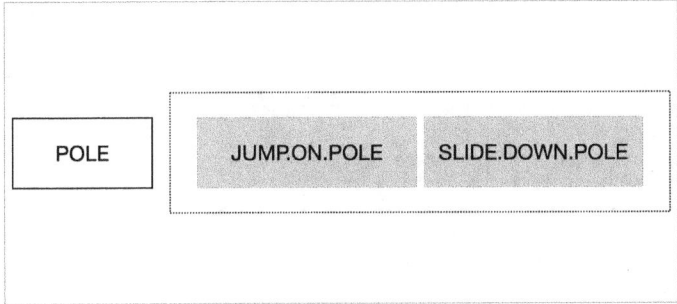

Figure 18: The [(POLE) JUMP.ON.POLE SLIDE.DOWN.POLE] schema.

Looking at other bent-V signs in "Firefighters", we observe that four of the five bent-V/'shape' tokens also occur together in one utterance. The signer depicts the shape of a spiral staircase, contrasts it with a straight staircase, repeats the depiction of the spiral staircase, and then mentions a third type of installation, an "incline chute". Each of these three installation types is referred to with the bent-V handshape moving in a trajectory motivated by the shape of the referent:

(10) REALLY LONG.AGO, OFTEN fs-COMMON POINT FIRE fs-STATION POINT HAVE THAT **SPIRAL.STAIRCASE**, NOT **STRAIGHT.STAIRCASE**, WAVE.NO, **SPIRAL.STAIRCASE**, fs-OR POINT **STRAIGHT.CHUTE** SLIDE.DOWN
'It used to be very common for fire stations to have a spiral staircase, not a straight staircase but rather a spiral one, or to have a chute to slide down.'
(https://youtu.be/N7bQ1gkCTzU?t=16)

We consider these tokens to be linked together, not strictly by virtue of their frequent or conventional co-occurrence, but rather by the fact that they are repeated instances of the same grammatical schema. This schema has been recycled to yield related signs in succession. Treating each of these signs as an individual atom of structure would lead analysts to miss the fact that they occur together in a sequence of interdependent signs, each motivated by the one before it. We represent the interdependent nature of these successive instances of a grammatical schema in Figure 19, with a solid black arrow linking the recycled instances.

These instances of the bent-V/'shape' schema in "Firefighters" suggest that multi-word expressions need not be fully conventionalized structures, but rather, they may include more loosely conventionalized signs. These examples show that recycled utterances encompass many unit types, including fused, fixed, and flexible constructions. These constructions emerge from each signer's experience with ASL,

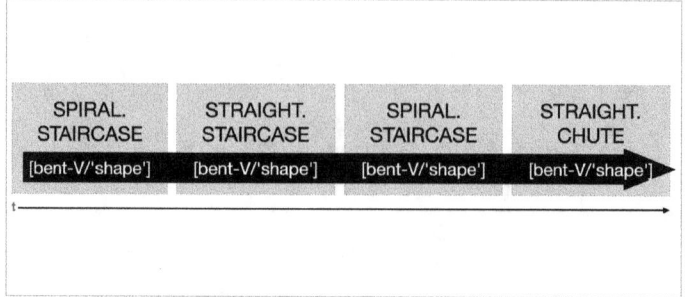

Figure 19: Recycled [bent-V/'shape'] schema in a sequence of signs over time (t).

as the sum of their exposure to recurring multi-sign expressions. From this perspective, it indeed seems that recycling of utterances is pervasive in ASL.

5 Conclusion

The point of departure for this paper has been Sherman Wilcox's (2014) call for signed language linguists to move "beyond structuralism". Heeding this call requires us to see linguistic patterns as continually shaped by language experience, such that the structures that are frequently encountered and used serve as the foundation for our dynamic knowledge of a language. Language use, including individual variability, is not separable from the structure of language. Indeed, structure emerges from use (Bybee 2010; Christiansen and Chater 2016). Adopting a construction-theoretic, usage-based approach to the analysis of signed languages lays the ground for a fresh perspective on the roles that language use and experience play in these grammars.

From this usage-based perspective, linguistic knowledge can be viewed through two related lenses (Bybee 2010; Langacker 2008). For individuals, recurring structures become progressively *entrenched* as established units requiring less monitoring or processing. For language communities, recurring structures that are well-known and commonly shared become highly *conventionalized*, and seed the dynamic development of newer structures. Conventionalization, like individual entrenchment, is a continual dynamic process rather than a progression with a defined endpoint. Both processes lead to repurposing structural units, with language use and experience over time among signers causing the structure and functions of the constructions to change.

As we have argued here, this usage-based conceptualization of grammar leads us to see that recurring structures are also *recycled* structures. Utterances that are often repeated by individuals and within a language community may be flexibly repurposed, or take on additional, specialized functions, according to the contexts in which they are (re)used. Extending this view to ASL grammar, we have discussed examples of units that seem to be frequently recycled in ASL. Larger, looser units such as [INTERPRETER BRING.IN] and the bent-V/'legs' schema can be flexibly repurposed and combined with other complex units to yield new structured utterances. Tighter, fixed units such as NOT.HAVE.TO have had aspects of their internal structure eroded, yielding smaller, more compact units. Examples like these lead us to see that ASL signers, too, likely experience constructions as units that are continually accessed and repackaged through the processes of perception, processing, storage, retrieval, and production. For individual language users and collectively, across signers, these processes cause language structure to shift continuously and dynamically over time.

A traditional structuralist view, in which "words and rules" derive well-formed sentences, has often been applied to signed language analysis. In contrast to this, we have argued that the building blocks of a signed language like ASL are not limited to individual signs as beads on a linear string. Instead, signed units vary in length, complexity, and schematicity. Signed units also extend to include larger, recurring sequences of signs, and those larger units have not been traditionally analyzed as such in signed language linguistics. Some of these sequential units are wholly fixed constructions, while others are looser, more schematic units. Both types are recycled in the course of language use, overlapping with one another as language users combine them to create new utterances. As we have used it here, a unit is not just the most simple atom of a construction; instead, it is a more "holistic" unit that can be identified based on its fixedness, complexity, schematicity, and function.

In proposing that signed language structures are recycled structures, and that recurring utterances have a holistic character, we are arguing against some foundational ideas in our field: signed language linguists routinely highlight the creativity and productivity of signed utterances as the hallmarks of language. However, these foundational ideas derive from structuralist conceptions of language. As suggested above, in the discussion of the bent-V family of signs, many signed language linguists assume a separate category of signs, referred to as "classifier" or "depicting" signs, which contrast with conventionalized "lexical" signs. As Lepic and Occhino (2018) argue, the assumed difference is that depicting signs have compositionally meaningful structure, while lexical signs lack such structure. This is a false dichotomy. As we have shown, signed units are holistic units that exhibit degrees of analyzable internal structure. This holds true for single signs and fixed sequences of signs alike. Given how robustly signers use depicting signs in ASL, we propose that putting them into a separate category prevents us from understanding how sign schemas, through recycling, progressively structure ASL utterances. By looking beyond the false structural dichotomy of atomistic vs. compositional, we can better understand how more fixed and more flexible units are deployed in ASL use.

Moving beyond structuralism, here we have seen that as structures are used and reused, their functions shift, and their internal boundaries blur. Our case studies here suggest that there are surely additional multi-word expressions in ASL that have yet to be identified and analyzed. Rather than simply identifying sequences of signs, it is important to attend to the functions that these recurring sequences of signs may perform, regardless of the meaning of any particular sign in isolation. It is through patterns of fixedness and schematicity in multi-word expressions that language experiences cohere into a network of linguistic knowledge. This shift within signed language linguistics also aligns with research on spoken language structure, suggesting that recycling utterances is a regular cognitive mechanism regardless of the modality of language. Since schematicity is viewed to be the default, some recycled constructions are schematic and simple, while others are schematic and more complex, in signed and spoken languages alike.

This observation points toward additional avenues for understanding the nature of recycling from a cognitive perspective. Humans are creatures of habit, and we rely on our past and current experiences to plan and predict upcoming experiences. The resources that we use to construct utterances, then, are derived from the memories of utterances we have experienced. To date, research on how exemplars of language experience are recycled to form new utterances has been carried out for spoken languages only (e.g., Dąbrowska 2014; Ambridge 2020). However, several factors concerning sign usage can shed additional light on the nature of recycling. First, it has been argued that the structure of ASL and other signed languages is less linear and sequential compared to spoken languages (Leeson and Saeed 2012). This raises questions, which we have explored, about the nature of the units that are recycled, and the degree of flexibility, complexity or schematicity they may exhibit. Second, it has been shown that deaf signing communities are characterized by heterogeneity in language acquisition and language transmission (Singleton and Meier 2021). In other words, many deaf signers' language experiences are shaped by interaction with others who have highly variable signing experience, and there are concomitant individual differences in language experience across signers' lifespans. This raises questions about how and which multi-word expressions may be acquired or processed by young deaf signers. Do processes of visual chunking in deaf signers compare to auditory chunks for hearing speakers (Hou and Morford 2020; Villwock et al. 2021; Christiansen and Chater 2016)? Do signers store abstractions or exemplars of signed language usage in their mental representation of their grammars (Ambridge 2020)? Unfortunately, there is not yet a rich enough body of ASL data that can be used to identify constructions and frequency effects among deaf signers (Hou and Morford 2020). Nevertheless, the idea that sequential structures may be chunked and recycled opens up new lines of inquiry about signed language acquisition, development, and processing (Hou 2022). These questions merit further investigation, and there is much that we do not know about the role that modality and heterogeneity play in how utterances are recycled.

We agree with Wilcox (2014) that it is by moving beyond structuralism in signed language linguistics that the answers to these questions can be better understood. It is crucial that we state and interrogate our assumptions about how language works, if we wish to better understand how signed languages are structured and used. Adopting a usage-based conceptualization of language allows us to sidestep lingering structuralist pitfalls, while also moving toward ever more cognitively plausible models of linguistic knowledge.

References

Ambridge, Ben. 2020. Against stored abstractions: A radical exemplar model of language acquisition. *First Language* 40(5–6). 509–559. https://doi.org/10.1177/0142723719869731

Anible, Benjamin. 2016. *Iconicity Effects in Translation Direction: Bimodal Bilingual Lexical Processing*. Albuquerque: University of New Mexico dissertation.

Anible, Benjamin. 2020. Iconicity in American Sign Language–English translation recognition. *Language and Cognition* 12(1). 138–163. doi:10.1017/langcog.2019.51

Barlow, Michael & Suzanne Kemmer (eds.). 2000. *Usage-Based Models of Language*. Stanford, CA: CSLI Publications.

Bienvenu, MJ & Betty Colonomos. 1985. *An Introduction to American Deaf Culture: Rules of Social Interaction* (#1, 5-DVD set). Burtonsville, MD: Sign Media, Inc.

Bybee, Joan. 1995. Regular morphology and the lexicon. *Language and Cognitive Processes* 10: 425–455.

Bybee, Joan. 2001. *Phonology and Language Use*. Cambridge: Cambridge University Press. doi:10.1017/CBO9780511612886

Bybee, Joan. 2006. From usage to grammar: The mind's response to repetition. *Language* 82(4). 711–733.

Bybee, Joan. 2007. *Frequency of Use and the Organization of Language*. Oxford: Oxford University Press.

Bybee, Joan. 2010. *Language, Usage and Cognition*. Cambridge: Cambridge University Press. doi:10.1017/CBO9780511750526

Bybee, Joan L. & Rena Torres Cacoullos. 2009. The role of prefabs in grammaticization: How the particular and the general interact in language change. In Roberta Corrigan, Edith A. Moravcsik, Hamid Ouali & Kathleen M. Wheatley (eds.), *Formulaic Language, Vol. 1. Distribution and Historical Change*, 187–218. Amsterdam/Philadelphia: John Benjamins.

Christiansen, Morten H. & Nick Chater. 2016. *Creating Language: Integrating Evolution, Acquisition, and Processing*. Cambridge, MA: MIT Press.

Cohen, Leah Hager. 1994. *Train Go Sorry: Inside a Deaf World*. Boston/New York: Houghton Mifflin.

Croft, William. 2000. *Explaining Language Change: An Evolutionary Approach*. London: Longman.

Croft, William & D. Alan Cruse. 2004. *Cognitive Linguistics*. Cambridge: Cambridge University Press.

Cuxac, Christian & Marie-Anne Sallandre. 2007. Iconicity and arbitrariness in French Sign Language: Highly iconic structures, degenerated iconicity and diagrammatic iconicity. In Elena Pizzuto, Paola Pietrandrea & Raffaele Simone (eds.), *Verbal and Signed Languages: Comparing Structure, Constructs and Methodologies*, 13–33. Berlin/New York: Mouton de Gruyter.

Dąbrowska, Ewa. 2014. Recycling utterances: A speaker's guide to sentence processing. *Cognitive Linguistics* 25(4). 617–653. https://doi:10.1515/cog-2014-0057.

Dąbrowska, Ewa. 2018. Experience, aptitude and individual differences in native language ultimate attainment. *Cognition* 178. 222–235. https://doi.org/10.1016/j.cognition.2018.05.018

Dąbrowska, Ewa & Elena Lieven. 2005. Towards a lexically specific grammar of children's question constructions. *Cognitive Linguistics* 16(3). 437–474. https://doi.org/10.1515/cogl.2005.16.3.437.

Dąbrowska, Ewa & James Street. 2006. Individual differences in language attainment: Comprehension of passive sentences by native and non-native English speakers. *Language Sciences* 28(6). 604–615. https://doi.org/10.1016/j.langsci.2005.11.014.

Dudis, Paul G. 2004. Body partitioning and real-space blends. *Cognitive Linguistics* 15(2): 223–238.

Emmorey, Karen (ed.) 2003. *Perspectives on Classifier Constructions in Sign Languages*. Mahwah, NJ: Lawrence Erlbaum.

Engberg-Pedersen, Elisabeth. 2003. How composite is a fall? Adults' and children's descriptions of different types of falls in Danish Sign Language. In Karen Emmorey (ed.), *Perspectives on Classifier Constructions in Sign Languages*, 311–332. Mahwah, NJ: Lawrence Erlbaum.

Erman, Britt & Beatrice Warren. 2000. The idiom principle and the open choice principle. *Text & Talk* 20(1). 29–62.

Ferrara, Lindsay & Gabrielle Hodge. 2018. Language as description, indication, and depiction. *Frontiers in Psychology* 9(716). https://doi.org/10.3389/fpsyg.2018.00716.

Fillmore, Charles J., Paul Kay & Mary Catherine O'Connor. 1988. Regularity and idiomaticity in grammatical constructions: The case of *let alone*. *Language* 64(3). 501–538. https://doi.org/10.2307/414531.

Garcia, Brigitte & Marie-Anne Sallandre. 2014. Reference resolution in French Sign Language (LSF). In Patricia Cabredo Hofherr & Anne Zribi-Hertz (eds.), *Crosslinguistic Studies on Noun Phrase Structure and Reference*, 316–364. Leiden: Brill. doi: https://doi.org/10.1163/9789004261440_012.

Ganezer, Gilda & Avery Posner. 2017. *Idioms and Phrases in American Sign Language, Volume 1–5* (5-DVD set). Commack, NY: Everyday ASL Productions, Ltd.

Goldberg, Adele E. 2019. *Explain Me This: Creativity, Competition, and the Partial Productivity of Constructions*. Princeton, NJ: Princeton University Press. https://doi.org/10.2307/j.ctvc772nn.

Gries, Stefan Th. & Anatol Stefanowitsch. 2004. Extending collostructional analysis: A corpus-based perspective on 'alternations'. *International Journal of Corpus Linguistics* 9(1). 97–129. https://doi.org/10.1075/ijcl.9.1.06gri.

Hay, Jennifer B. & Harald Baayen. 2005. Shifting paradigms: Gradient structure in morphology. *Trends in Cognitive Sciences* 9(7). 342–348. https://doi.org/10.1016/j.tics.2005.04.002.

Hou, Lynn. 2022. Looking for multi-word expressions in American Sign Language. *Cognitive Linguistics* 33(2). 291–337. https://doi.org/10.1515/cog-2020-0086.

Hou, Lynn, Ryan Lepic & Erin Wilkinson. 2020. Working with ASL internet data. *Sign Language Studies* 21(1). 32–67. https://doi.org/10.1353/sls.2020.0028.

Hou, Lynn & Jill P. Morford. 2020. Using signed language collocations to investigate acquisition: A commentary on Ambridge (2020). *First Language* 40(5–6). 585–591. https://doi.org/10.1177/0142723720908075.

Janzen, Terry. 2004. Space rotation, perspective shift, and verb morphology in ASL. *Cognitive Linguistics* 15(2). 149-174.

Janzen, Terry. 2017. Composite utterances in a signed language: Topic Constructions and Perspective-taking in ASL. *Cognitive Linguistics* 28(3). 511–538.
Janzen, Terry. 2018. KNOW and UNDERSTAND in ASL: A usage-based study of grammaticalized topic constructions. In K. Aaron Smith & Dawn Nordquist (eds.), *Functionalist and Usage-based Approaches to the Study of Language: In Honor of Joan L. Bybee*, 59–87. Amsterdam/Philadelphia: John Benjamins.
Jantunen, Tommi. 2017. Constructed action, the clause and the nature of syntax in Finnish Sign Language. *Open Linguistics* 3(1). 65–85.
Konrad, Reiner, Thomas Hanke, Susanne König, Gabriele Langer, Silke Matthes, Rie Nishio & Anja Regen. 2012. From form to function. A database approach to handle lexicon building and spotting token forms in sign languages. In Onno Crasborn, Eleni Efthimiou, Evita Fotinea, Thomas Hanke, Jette Kristoffersen & Johanna Mesch (eds.), *Workshop Proceedings, 5th Workshop on the Representation and Processing of Sign Languages: Interactions between Corpus and Lexicon Language Resources and Evaluation Conference (LREC), Istanbul, May 2012.* 87–94.
Kusters, Annelies & Sujit Sahasrabudhe. 2018. Language ideologies on the difference between gesture and sign, *Language and Communication* 60. 44–63.
Langacker, Ronald W. 1987. *Foundations of Cognitive Grammar, Volume 1: Theoretical Prerequisites*. Stanford, CA: Stanford University Press.
Langacker, Ronald W. 1988. A usage-based model. In Brygida Rudzka-Ostyn (ed.), *Topics in Cognitive Linguistics*, 127–161. Amsterdam/Philadelphia: John Benjamins.
Langacker, Ronald W. 2008. *Cognitive Grammar: A Basic Introduction*. Oxford/New York: Oxford University Press.
Leeson, Lorraine & John Saeed. 2012. Word order. In Roland Pfau, Markus Steinbach & Bencie Woll (eds.), *Sign Language: An International Handbook*, 245–265. Berlin/Boston: De Gruyter Mouton.
Lepic, Ryan. 2016. The great ASL compound hoax. In Aubre Healey, Ricardo Napoleão de Souza, Pavlina Pešková & Moses Allen (eds.), *Proceedings of the High Desert Linguistics Society Conference, Volume 11*, 227–250. Albuquerque, NM: University of New Mexico.
Lepic, Ryan. 2019. A usage-based alternative to "lexicalization" in sign language linguistics. *Glossa* 4(1). https://doi.org/10.5334/gjgl.840.
Lepic, Ryan, Carl Börstell, Gal Belsitzman & Wendy Sandler. 2016. Taking meaning in hand: Iconic motivations in two-handed signs. *Sign Language & Linguistics* 19(1). 37–81. http://dx.doi.org/10.1075/sll.19.1.02lep.
Lepic, Ryan & Corrine Occhino. 2018. A Construction Morphology approach to sign language analysis. In Geert Booij (ed.), *The Construction of Words: Advances in Construction Morphology*, 141–172. Cham, Switzerland: Springer. https://doi.org/10.1007/978-3-319-74394-3_6.
Lepic, Ryan & Carol Padden. 2017. A-morphous iconicity. In Claire Bowern, Laurence Horn, & Raffaella Zanuttini (eds.), *On Looking into Words (and Beyond): Structures, Relations, Analyses*, 489–516. Berlin: Language Science Press. https://doi.org/10.5281/zenodo.495463.
Morford, Jill P. & James MacFarlane. 2003. Frequency characteristics of American Sign Language. *Sign Language Studies* 3(2). 213–225.
Nilsson, Anna-Lena. 2008. Spatial strategies in descriptive discourse: Use of signing space in Swedish Sign Language. *CDS/CLCS Monograph Number 2*. Drumcondra, Ireland: Centre for Deaf Studies, University of Dublin, Trinity College.
Occhino, Corrine. 2017. An introduction to embodied cognitive phonology: Claw-5 handshape distribution in ASL and Libras. *Complutense Journal of English Studies* 25. 69–103.

Singleton, Jenny & Richard Meier. 2021. Sign language acquisition in context. In Charlotte Enns, Jonathan Henner & Lynn McQuarrie (eds.), *Discussing Bilingualism in Deaf Children: Essays in Honor of Robert Hoffmeister*, 17–24. New York: Routledge.

Stefanowitsch, Anatol & Stefan Th. Gries. 2003. Collostructions: Investigating the interaction of words and constructions. *International Journal of Corpus Linguistics* 8(2). 209–243. https://doi.org/10.1075/ijcl.8.2.03ste.

Supalla, Ted. 1986. The classifier system in American Sign Language. In Colette Craig (ed.), *Noun Classes and Categorization: Proceedings of a Symposium on Categorization and Noun Classification, Eugene, Oregon, October 1983*. 181–214. Amsterdam/Philadelphia: John Benjamins.

Villwock, Agnes, Erin Wilkinson, Pilar Piñar & Jill P. Morford. 2021. Language development in deaf bilinguals: Deaf middle school students co-activate written English and American Sign Language during lexical processing. *Cognition* 211, June 2021. 104642. https://doi.org/10.1016/j.cognition.2021.104642.

Wilcox, Phyllis Perrin. 2004. A cognitive key: Metonymic and metaphorical mappings in ASL. *Cognitive Linguistics* 15(2). 197–222. https://doi.org/10.1515/cogl.2004.008.

Wilcox, Sherman. 2004. Cognitive iconicity: Conceptual spaces, meaning, and gesture in signed languages. *Cognitive Linguistics* 15(2). 119–147.

Wilcox, Sherman. 2014. Moving beyond structuralism: Usage-based signed language linguistics. *Linguas de Señas e Interpretación* 5. 97–126.

Wilcox, Sherman & Rocío Martínez. 2020. The conceptualization of space: *Places* in signed language discourse. *Frontiers in Psychology* 11:1406. 1–16. https://doi.org/10.3389/fpsyg.2020.01406.

Wilcox, Sherman & Corrine Occhino. 2016. Constructing signs: Place as a symbolic structure in signed languages. *Cognitive Linguistics* 27(3). 371–404.

Wilkinson, Erin. 2013. A functional description of SELF in American Sign Language. *Sign Language Studies* 13(4). 462–490.

Wilkinson, Erin. 2016. Finding frequency effects in the usage of NOT collocations in American Sign Language. *Sign Language & Linguistics* 19(1). 82–123. https://doi.org/doi 10.1075/sll.19.1.03wil.

André Nogueira Xavier and Rocío Anabel Martínez
Possibility modals in Brazilian Sign Language and Argentine Sign Language: A contrastive study

1 Introduction

This chapter is a tribute to our mentor, colleague, and friend, Dr. Sherman Wilcox, with whom we have analyzed several aspects of the grammars of Brazilian Sign Language (Língua Brasileira de Sinais, or Libras), and Argentine Sign Language (Lengua de Señas Argentina, LSA). In particular, his research on modality in ASL (Wilcox and Wilcox 1995; Wilcox and Shaffer 2006; Wilcox, Rossini and Antinoro Pizzuto 2010; Xavier and Wilcox 2014) is the inspiration and basis for the present study.

In this chapter, we analyze possibility modals in Libras and LSA contrastively. Libras and LSA are two unrelated Latin American signed languages. Libras is the national signed language used all over Brazil, although Indigenous signed languages and village signed languages do exist (Ferreira Brito 1990; Almeida-Silva and Nevins 2020). Its origins are believed to date back to the foundation of the first residential school, currently called INES (National Institute for Deaf Education), in the city of Rio de Janeiro in 1855 and the emergence of a deaf community around it (Berenz 2003). As INES was founded with the help of the French deaf priest Huet, who directed the institute and taught there in its first years, Libras is claimed to be descended from French Sign Language (langue des signes française, or LSF). LSA is the national signed language used throughout Argentina (Massone and Machado 1994). Its history is closely tied to the first two residential schools founded by the end of the 19th century in Buenos Aires: the school for deaf boys (now Bartolomé Ayrolo School) and the school for deaf girls (now Osvaldo Magnasco School). Given that the school for deaf boys was founded by Italian priests, and that there were

---

Acknowledgements: We are indebted to Dr. Sherman Wilcox for his friendship and his constant support. We also want to express our gratitude to Daiane Ferreira, Elisane Alecrim, Diego Morales, Verónica Armand, Monica Curiel, Maria Josep Jarque, João Paulo da Silva, Rita Stein, and the anonymous reviewers for their contributions, comments and questions. Lastly, we would like to thank Dr. Terry Janzen and Dr. Barbara Shaffer for their devoted work in editing this chapter. Any remaining flaws are our own.

André Nogueira Xavier, Federal University of Parana (UFPR), Brazil, e-mail: andrexavier@ufpr.br
Rocío Anabel Martínez, Universidad de Buenos Aires & Consejo Nacional de Investigaciones Científicas y Técnicas, Argentina, e-mail: rociomartinez@conicet.gov.ar

https://doi.org/10.1515/9783110703788-015

a considerable number of Italians among the staff and students, Italian Sign Language (Lingua dei Segni Italiana, or LIS) is considered an important influence on the emergence of LSA.

Although Libras and LSA can be considered two of the most studied South American signed languages (McBurney 2012), research on them is scarce especially in domains such as modality. Our main goal is to contribute to advancing the understanding of Libras and LSA possibility modals by replicating Xavier and Wilcox's (2014) pilot study. To accomplish this goal, we have organized this chapter as follows. In Section 2 we briefly summarize van der Auwera and Plungian's (1998) framework within which our analysis is conducted. In Section 3 we report on the application of this framework to ASL and briefly summarize what is known about Libras and LSA possibility modals. In Section 4 we describe the method we employed to collect and analyze Libras and LSA possibility modals. In Section 5 we report our findings for each language and in Section 6 we compare them, highlighting similarities and differences between Libras and LSA. Finally, Section 7 is an overall conclusion.

2 Modality in spoken languages

Although some authors conceive of the semantic domain of modality in a broader way so as to include volition and/or evidentiality (Givón 1984; Palmer 1986; Bybee, Perkins and Pagliuca 1994), others such as Anderson (1982) and van der Auwera and Plungian (1998) have restricted it to necessity and possibility. For their analysis the latter have developed semantic maps, which represent these notions in terms of domains and subdomains. Specifically, in van der Auwera and Plungian's framework both necessity and possibility modalities are divided into two domains, epistemic and non-epistemic.

In Table 1 we illustrate, based on van der Auwera and Plungian (1998), the possibility modality domain and subdomains with examples from English. Epistemic modality refers to a judgement by the speaker. That is to say, it is a speaker's evaluation concerning the degree of certainty or probability of the truth of a proposition, such as example (e). Non-epistemic modality includes two subdomains: participant-internal and participant-external. The participant-internal subdomain encompasses the kind of possibility internal to a participant engaged in the state of affairs, such as physical ability, as in example (a), and mental capacity, as in (b). The participant-external subdomain refers to circumstances that are external to any participant engaged in some state of affairs, and that make this situation possible. This subdomain is, in turn, divided into two others, non-deontic and deontic, as in

(c) and (d). The difference between them is that in the non-deontic modality, the source of enabling or compelling circumstances external to the participant is more diffuse, whereas in the deontic modality the source is a social or ethical norm.

Table 1: The expression of possibility modality in English.

Possibility			English
	Participant-internal	Physical ability	(a) I **can** slide a heavy table.
		Mental capacity	(b) I **can** do math in my mind.
	Participant-external	Non-deontic	(c) I **can** reach the roof with a ladder.
		Deontic	(d) You **can** smoke in here.
		Epistemic	(e) He **must** have arrived.

As our examples in Table 1 suggest, English *can* is polysemous, since it can be used to express at least four different meanings within the possibility domain. Other languages, however, may exhibit separate lexical items or different linguistic resources to express these meanings (see Narrog 2009 on the expression of modality in Japanese).

Based on Bybee, Perkins, and Pagliuca's (1994) work, van der Auwera and Plungian (1998) propose semantic maps for modality and hypothesize that the semantic domains these maps describe are the result of grammaticization, that is, of a process through which lexical sources with more concrete meaning develop grammatical, and consequently more abstract, meanings. For the possibility domain, as shown in the semantic map in Figure 1, the authors assume that the grammaticization pathway starts with the development of participant-internal meanings, since their lexical sources usually relate to physical strength, as is the case of English *may*, which meant in Old English 'be strong', or intellectual/cognitive capacity, as in English *can*, which originally meant 'know' (van der Auwera and Plungian 1998: 92, citing Bybee, Perkins, and Pagliuca 1994). From the participant-internal meanings, possibility modals may develop a participant-external meaning which, in turn, can be the source for the development of an epistemic meaning. In Bybee, Perkins, and Pagliuca's view, the development of these two meanings occurs through a semantic generalization process, which contrasts with the process that gives rise to the deontic possibility meaning. In van der Auwera and Plungian's view, such meaning evolves from a general participant-external possibility meaning through a "semantic shrinking or specialization" (van der Auwera and Plungian 1998: 88) process. In Figure 1, a further stage in grammaticization is represented by the meanings to the right of the center box. This stage is referred to by van der Auwera and Plungian (1998: 104) as "demodalization", since, as the meanings themselves suggest, future, condition, concession and complementation acquire new grammatical functions.

This has happened, for example, with the English modal *should* which can be used as a conditional marker, as in *Should you need anything, please call this number*.

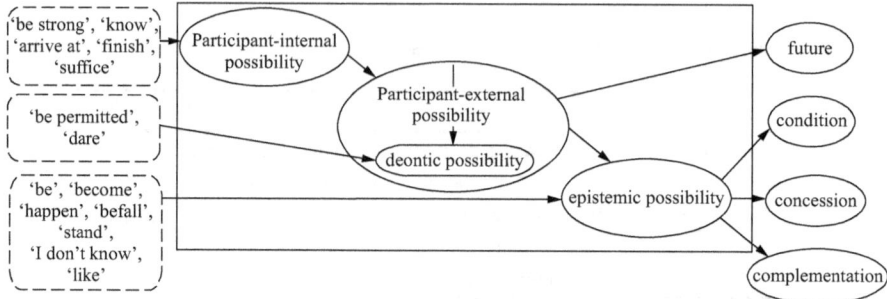

Figure 1: Possibility grammaticization pathway (from p. 94, van der Auwera, Johan & Vladimir A. Plungian. 1998. Modality's semantic map. *Linguistic Typology* 2(1). 79–124).

Given this, synchronic polysemy, as observed in modals such as English *may* and *can*, is expected because it results from a cumulative process of semantic change. Consequently, synchronic polysemy can give us insights into the grammaticization path of a given modal, especially when diachronic data are not available.

3 Modality in signed languages

The first known publication on modality in a signed language was authored by Ferreira Brito (1990), who analyzed Libras (see Section 3.1 below). In ASL the first study was undertaken by Wilcox and Wilcox (1995). In addition to documenting ASL lexical modal signs such as SHOULD, MUST, CAN, POSSIBLE, CAN'T, among others, the authors report the systematic use of different manners of hand movement in distinguishing modal meanings. They report that modals expressing strong obligation (e.g., MUST) or strong possibility/probability (e.g., CAN) are produced with stressed and non-reduplicated movement, as opposed to modals expressing weak obligation (e.g., SHOULD) or weak possibility/probability (e.g., POSSIBLE), which are articulated with unstressed and reduplicated movement. Wilcox and Wilcox also attest the use of non-manuals in the expression of modality in ASL. According to them, in addition to the fact that the non-manuals are quite similar to the ones employed with imperatives and requests for information, their use may be simultaneous with the production of a lexical modal sign or, similarly to intonation, with a string of lexical items in an utterance.

Shaffer (2000, 2002) and Wilcox and Shaffer (2006) published the first known modality studies that applied van der Auwera and Plungian's framework to the analysis of a signed language. These authors adopted van der Auwera and Plungian's framework due to its capacity to explain the polysemy they observed in ASL necessity and possibility as a result of grammaticization. Drawing on diachronic and synchronic data, these studies showed not only that ASL MUST/SHOULD and CAN/POSSIBLE are used across the traditional semantic domains and subdomains that van der Auwera and Plungian proposed, but that they also have lexical sources with more concrete meanings, namely OWE, REQUIRE, and STRONG. Thus, Shaffer (2000, 2002), and Wilcox and Shaffer (2006) demonstrate that ASL follows the same grammaticization patterns proposed for spoken languages, which, according to Bybee, Perkins, and Pagliuca (1994), typically involve both semantic and phonological changes. In comparison to their lexical sources, MUST/SHOULD and CAN/POSSIBLE have developed more general meanings and, consequently, are not restricted to their original ones—financial debt and physical strength—respectively. In addition, the forms have undergone phonological change. For example, while OWE and REQUIRE are two-handed signs, MUST and SHOULD have become one-handed. The lexical source STRONG has a more proximal joint flexion, specifically at the elbow, CAN and POSSIBLE now exhibit a more distal joint flexion at the wrist.

Shaffer (2000, 2002) also investigated the ASL negative modal CAN'T. When describing this sign, she draws attention to the fact that it does not share any formational similarities with its positive counterpart CAN and, thus, conforms to a tendency according to which suppletive negative modals are prevalent cross-linguistically (van der Auwera 2001). She further says that in LSF, the formationally similar sign INTERDIT means 'must not', and as such is only used as a negative necessity modal. This contrasts with ASL CAN'T, which also expresses negative possibility meanings including physical inability, mental inability, deontic prohibition, and non-deontic impossibility. These meanings are referenced in Figure 2 in the grammaticization pathway proposed by Shaffer for ASL CAN'T.

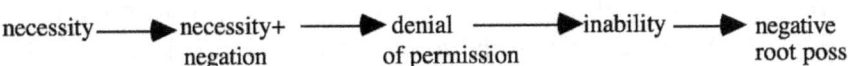

Figure 2: Grammaticization pathway for ASL CAN'T, with permission from Shaffer (2000: 203).

Despite the similarities in grammaticization pathways for markers of modality in signed and spoken languages, at least two aspects of signed languages have been noted. First, gestural origins of modals have been documented (Shaffer 2000, 2002; Wilcox and Shaffer 2006; Janzen and Shaffer 2002; Shaffer and Janzen 2016; Siyavoshi 2019; Jarque 2019) and second, two linguistic channels—facial and manual—together convey modal meanings. Wilcox (2009) proposes that gestures enter the linguistic system via two distinct grammaticization pathways (Figure 3).

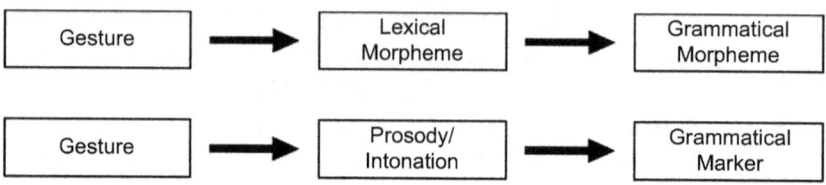

Figure 3: Signed language grammaticization pathways proposed by Sherman Wilcox and adapted from figures in, for example, Wilcox (2009).

In the first pathway, gestures are sources of lexical and grammatical morphemes in signed languages. For example, ASL CAN has its origins in old LSF POUVOIR 'can', which grammaticized out of the lexical sign FORT 'strong', which in turn results from the lexicalization of a gesture indicating physical strength (Wilcox and Shaffer 2006). In the second pathway, elements become directly incorporated into signed language morphology, bypassing a lexical stage. For instance, Wilcox, Rossini and Antinoro Pizzuto (2010) analyze a prosodic gestural manner of movement indicating degrees of impossibility seen in one LIS negative modal sign (glossed as IMPOSSIBLE-H-fff) with no lexical stage intervening. More recently, in the analysis of Catalan Sign Language (lengua de signes catalana or LSC), Jarque (2019) analyzed a third pathway where gestural elements enter the language directly as discourse markers, again without passing through a lexical stage. These discourse markers acquire a grammatical function and are a product of pragmaticalization. For instance, Jarque describes the way the palm-up gesture, accompanied by non-manuals, incorporates specific modal functions in LSC discourse, such as certainty, uncertainty, and permission, among others.

Regarding the importance of the two linguistic channels, many of the abovementioned researchers have pointed out that modal meanings in signed languages are produced not only with manual signs but also with non-manuals. For instance, Siyavoshi (2019) presents a study of the interaction between manual and non-manual markers in Iranian Sign Language (Zaban Esharey Irani, or ZEI), focusing on squinted eyes, brow furrow, and downturned lip corners (see Siyavoshi, this volume, for a similar discussion of these features in ZEI relative clauses). Following Langacker's (2013) model of modality, which classifies modals into two kinds, effective and epistemic, she suggests that effective control, including effective modality, tends to be expressed on the hands, while facial markers play an important role in marking epistemic assessment, one manifestation of which is epistemic modality. ZEI, like other signed languages, exhibits an asymmetry between the number of manual signs and facial markers expressing epistemic modality. While the face can be active in the expression of effective modality, it is commonly the only means of expressing epistemic modality.

This chapter aims to contribute to our understanding of signed language modality by offering a contrastive study of possibility modals in two historically unrelated South American signed languages using van der Auwera and Plungian's (1998) framework, and following the research done on ASL (Shaffer 2000, 2002; Wilcox and Shaffer 2006), Libras (Xavier and Wilcox 2014), ZEI (Siyavoshi 2019) and LSC (Jarque 2019). Here we extend Xavier and Wilcox's (2014) pilot study of the expression of modality in Libras by collecting data from two additional fluent Libras signers and two fluent LSA signers. We also explore whether LSA data support the claim that negative modal signs tend to be suppletive, as has been demonstrated for ASL and Libras. Here, we focus primarily on non-epistemic modals, which are believed to be primarily articulated with the hands, and leave the analysis of epistemic modals for a future study.

3.1 Libras

As mentioned earlier, Ferreira Brito (1990) carried out the first known analysis of modality in a signed language. In her study, which documented Libras lexical modal signs such as NEED, PROHIBITED, CAN, and IMPOSSIBLE, among others, the author attests to a difference between deontic modals related to obligation, and epistemic modals related to possibility and probability. According to Ferreira Brito, deontic modals are expressed with simple and energetic movements, whereas epistemic modals are expressed with nonenergetic movement of the hands.

Xavier and Wilcox (2014) documented three Libras positive possibility modals, which we illustrate here as POSSIBLE-A (Figure 4a), POSSIBLE-S (Figure 4b) and POSSIBLE-L[1] (Figure 4c). In Figure 5, five Libras negative possibility modals, namely, IMPOSSIBLE-U (Figure 5a), IMPOSSIBLE-V (Figure 5b), IMPOSSIBLE-S (Figure 5c), IMPOSSIBLE-L (Figure 5d), and PROHIBITED (Figure 5e) are shown. Among the negative modals, only one clearly derives from its positive counterpart, IMPOSSIBLE-L. This sign is formed by combining POSSIBLE-L and the non-manual markers of headshake and compressed lips. The others are suppletive forms, as is often the case for negative modals (van der Auwera 2001).

---

[1] In Xavier and Wilcox's (2014) glossing conventions, possibility modals are generally represented with the gloss POSSIBLE, if positive, or IMPOSSIBLE, if negative, plus a letter that refers, in the Libras manual alphabet, to their handshape, which is adopted here. Thus, POSSIBLE-A refers to a possibility modal sign produced with the handshape A. An exception to this convention is PROHIBITED.

(a) POSSIBLE-A (b) POSSIBLE-S (c) POSSIBLE-L

Figure 4: Libras positive possibility modals.

(a) IMPOSSIBLE-U (b) IMPOSSIBLE-V

(c) IMPOSSIBLE-S (d) IMPOSSIBLE-L

(e) PROHIBITED

Figure 5: Libras negative possibility modals.

Xavier and Wilcox (2014) report that among the possibility modals, POSSIBLE-A, IMPOSSIBLE-U, and IMPOSSIBLE-V were the most frequently used in their dataset, and that they were the most polysemous. POSSIBLE-A was not attested in the deontic context (permission), in which case POSSIBLE-S was used. IMPOSSIBLE-U and IMPOSSIBLE-V, on the other hand, were used in all contexts. However, based on one of their informant's intuitions, the authors concluded that although all four signs expressed a broad range of possibility types they were not interchangeable. IMPOSSIBLE-U seems to express a stronger degree of judgement regarding impossibility in comparison with IMPOSSIBLE-V. Xavier and Wilcox also report that in their study PROHIBITED had more restricted uses, since it only occurred in a negative deontic context.

Based on their analysis of synchronic polysemy, Xavier and Wilcox (2014) claim that POSSIBLE-A, IMPOSSIBLE-U and IMPOSSIBLE-V appear to have undergone significant grammaticization. Their claim is based on the observation that these modals were attested in all possibility semantic domains, from participant-internal through epistemic. The authors also suggest potential lexical sources with more concrete meanings for three of the documented possibility modals: GIVE for POSSIBLE-A, WIN for POSSIBLE-L and BUSY for IMPOSSIBLE-V. As for IMPOSSIBLE-U, Xavier and Wilcox believe that it is a borrowing from LIS IMPOSSIBLE which, according to Wilcox (2009), results from the grammaticization of LIS DEAD, which, in turn, might have originated from the Roman Catholic benediction gesture used in the blessing of the dead. Thus, LIS IMPOSSIBLE offers further evidence that signed language modals often have gestural origins.

3.2 LSA

There is little research on modality in LSA. Curiel and Massone (1995) were the first known authors to carry out research on this topic. They explore two modality types, deontic and epistemic, paying attention to not only manual signs but also to non-manual markers. Concerning epistemic modality, they analyze lexical signs for: 1) degree of necessity; 2) degree of possibility; and 3) degree of commitment. Necessity in an affirmative sense is usually manifested with the sign NECESSARY, whereas the negative is articulated with the same sign plus non-manual markers of negation and the sign NO after the modal sign (meaning 'not necessary'). Possibility is usually marked with the affirmative signs POSSIBLE (Figure 6a), MAY-BE-POSSIBLE (Figure 6b), and the negative sign IMPOSSIBLE (Figure 6c). Curiel and Massone (1995) claim that these signs are usually accompanied by non-manual markers, which simultaneously convey semantic information regarding possibility and the commitment of the signer towards the content of the proposition. Lastly, there are several lexical signs that mark the degree of commitment to the truth of the proposition, such as TRUE, CORRECT, SURE, FALSE, THINK, KNOW, and SEEM. These lexical signs are usually accompanied by non-manuals expressing degree of commitment.

Regarding speaker commitment, Curiel and Massone (1995) also report that general tension of the face usually marks a high degree of commitment; downturned mouth corners convey hypotheticality, mouth corners stretched and lips slightly pressed together express doubt, and half-smiling lips, desire.

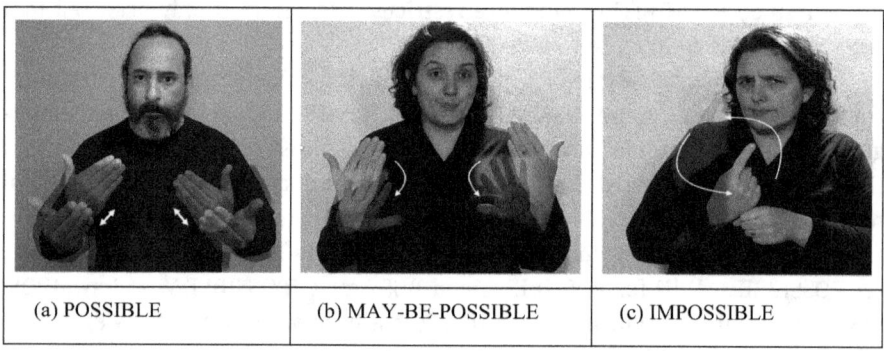

Figure 6: Selection of LSA possibility signs.

Regarding deontic modality, permission is expressed with POSSIBLE (Figure 6a), PERMIT (Figure 7a), and LET (Figure 7b). PERMIT is used in more formal situations and, especially, to express norms. It is often used as a directional verb, meaning to request permission. POSSIBLE has been more frequently observed to express norms in more informal situations. The sign LET is often related to permission concerning decisions that other people make, and not imposed norms. Prohibition is expressed mainly through the sign PROHIBIT (Figure 7c). It is especially used to refer to strong prohibitions, either related to institutions (laws, rules, etc.) or to social norms.

To date, no studies of LSA using van der Auwera and Plungian's framework have been published. Thus, the present contribution offers an alternative approach to the analysis of the expression of modality in LSA and adds to our understanding not only of how this language works, but in addition, it allows for comparison between LSA and other languages using van der Auwera and Plungian's framework.

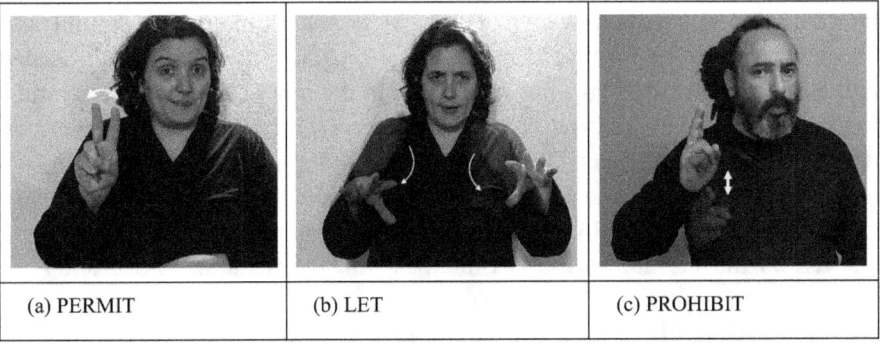

| (a) PERMIT | (b) LET | (c) PROHIBIT |

Figure 7: Selection of LSA signs within the deontic modality (permission and prohibition).

4 Method

Data from Libras and LSA were collected via interviews by the authors, with deaf consultants.[2] The interviews were conducted in each author's national signed language (Xavier in Libras, Martínez in LSA). Portuguese and Spanish played no part in the interviews. Due to the COVID-19 pandemic, the interviews were conducted on Zoom. Written informed consent was obtained from the interviewees for the publication of limited demographic information as well as images to illustrate the data in this chapter.

The interviews were designed as adaptations of the method used in Xavier and Wilcox (2014), which was adapted from Shaffer (2000) and Shaffer and Wilcox (2006), using van der Auwera and Plungian's (1998) framework. The Xavier and Wilcox (2014) study drew on semi-structured interview data from a fluent female deaf signer from the city of Sao Paulo, Brazil. The interview consisted of two parts. In the first part, the interviewer asked questions designed to elicit necessity and possibility modals expressing a wide range of positive and negative modal func-

---

2 The two Brazilian signers are Daiane Ferreira (DF) and Elisane Alecrim (EA). DF was born and lives in Curitiba, Paraná state. EA was born in Foz do Iguaçu, in the west of Paraná state, and has lived in Curitiba for the last 8 years. Both DF and EA learned Libras at a school for the deaf (DF from 2 years old and EA from 4 years old). DF holds a BA in education and an MA in signed language translation. Currently she works as a professor training prospective Libras teachers. EA holds a degree in Libras teaching and is currently pursuing her MA in linguistics.

The two deaf Argentine signers are Diego Morales (DM) and Verónica Armand (VA). Both have deaf parents and have used LSA since birth. DM has always lived in Buenos Aires, whereas VA was born in Córdoba and moved to Buenos Aires when she was 30 years old. Both have been actively involved in the struggle for the recognition of LSA and the advancement of deaf people's human rights in Argentina. They both hold degrees in LSA education and have many years of experience teaching LSA.

tions included in van der Auwera and Plungian's semantic map. In the second part, the interviewer asked for examples and usage explanations of the modals elicited in the first part. At times, the questions used in the first part did not successfully elicit the necessity and possibility modals. Excerpt (1) is reproduced (but reformatted) from Xavier and Wilcox (2014: 464–465). In order to elicit a possibility modal in an epistemic context, the interviewer asked the interviewee the question below in which no modal possibility sign was used. In spite of that, as expected by Xavier and Wilcox, the question was successful in eliciting the modal sign POSSIBLE-A.

(1) Interviewer: [PT-rt DRIVE FOR-THREE-HOURS]-y/n
 'Can you get (there) by car in three hours?'
 Interviewee: FOR-THREE-HOURS CALM POSSIBLE-A
 'In three hours, I can. With no rush.'

Following the interview format used for Libras in Xavier and Wilcox (2014), our Libras and LSA interviews also comprised two parts. In the first part, the four interviewees were asked questions based on the scenarios described in Table 2. However, if the interviewee did not use any possibility modals when answering a given question, we presented an alternate scenario. In the second part, after letting the interviewees know the purpose of the interview, we discussed the modals used in their responses to each scenario with them. Some interviewees then offered additional examples. We then verified whether other modals could also be employed in the same context, and discussed differences in non-manual markers and manner of movement.

Table 2: Scenarios used to obtain Libras and LSA possibility modals.

Possibility	Affirmative	Negative
Non-epistemic, participant-internal, physical ability	Sliding a small and light table.	Sliding a large and heavy table.
Non-epistemic, participant-internal, mental capacity	Doing simple mathematical computations in their mind. Being approved in a signed language test.	Doing complex mathematical computations in their mind. Being approved in an English test.
Non-epistemic, participant-external, non-deontic	Leaving their house and arriving at the university within 1 hour and 30 min. Arriving at the university from different places (the bus station, another city) within 1 hour and 30 minutes or 1 hour.	Leaving their house and arriving at the university within 30 minutes or 15 minutes. Arriving at the university from different places (the bus station, another city) within 30 minutes or 15 minutes.

Table 2 (continued)

Possibility	Affirmative	Negative
Non-epistemic, participant-external, deontic	Smoking at a place without any no-smoking sign. Students bringing their own food to school.	Smoking at a nonsmoking place. Students bringing toys to school.

Eudico Language Annotator (Elan) was used to gloss and annotate the data. We focused our annotation primarily on the manual signs, and non-manuals were annotated only when they seemed relevant for the non-epistemic modality analysis. In the following section, we provide examples of Libras and LSA modal signs in context.³

5 Data analysis

5.1 Libras

In addition to the modals documented by Xavier and Wilcox (2014), illustrated in our Figures 4 and 5, DF also signed a negative modal glossed here as IMPOSSIBLE-1, elicited when answering a question regarding mental capacity. See Figure 8.

Figure 8: IMPOSSIBLE-1.

---

3 Sign glosses are written in capital letters. Square brackets indicate a phrase accompanied by one or more non-manual: [. . .]-HS refers to an accompanying headshake; -CL means compressed lips; -Y/N is a yes/no question; and -WH is a 'wh' question; -EMPH means with emphasis. Glosses for directional signs such as LSA HELP include a number before and/or after to mark their initial/final references to discourse persons: 1 for first person (HELP-1), 2 for second person (HELP-2); and 3 for third person (HELP-3). PRO-1 is a first person pronoun.

DF used IMPOSSIBLE-1 (roughly translated as 'I doubt it') twice when she explained she could not do a sequence of mathematical operations mentally. Example (2) illustrates one instance of use, with the sign accompanied by a headshake (HS) and retracted lips (RL).

(2) IF ADDITION SUBTRACTION DIVISION MIX SAME TIME CALCULATE [**IMPOSSIBLE-1**]-HS/RL NOT
'If (there is) addition, subtraction and division (all) mixed at the same time, I can't calculate (it).'

In the following subsections, examples of usage are extracted from EA's and DF's interviews. These are listed in Table 2 above. Although we were able to elicit most of the expected modal meanings through our interview, there were some gaps.

5.1.1 Physical ability

When answering a question about sliding a table, both EA and DF used POSSIBLE-A to express that they could do it if the table was light and used IMPOSSIBLE-U to say that they would not be able to if the table was heavy. Example (3) shows EA's elicited utterance.

(3) DEPEND TABLE. HAVE NORMAL LIGHT **POSSIBLE-A** SLIDE-TABLE. HAVE OTHER HARD **IMPOSSIBLE-U** SLIDE-TABLE
'It depends on the table. There are normal light ones, I can slide them. There are others (that are) hard, I can't slide them.'

In another context, EA used IMPOSSIBLE-V to convey that, as a smoker, she is sometimes physically incapable of staying at non-smoking facilities due to anxiety. This is shown in (4).

(4) SOMETIMES ANXIOUS ALSO ANXIOUS NERVOUS PRO-1 NEED LEAVE BEFORE LEAVE. **IMPOSSIBLE-V** STAY
'Sometimes I (get) anxious and nervous, (so) I need to go out. I can't stay.'

5.1.2 Mental capacity

Examples (5) and (6) show that EA used POSSIBLE-A to express her capacity to do simple mathematical computations mentally, without pencil and paper, or a calculator. André Xavier (AX) was the interviewer.

(5) AX: FOUR MULTIPLIED-BY FIVE. . .
'Four multiplied by five. . .'
EA: TWENTY
'Twenty.'
AX: PAPER NOTHING
'not using any paper.'
EA: TWENTY
'Twenty.'
AX: BRAIN
'just your mind.'
EA: YES
'Yes.'
AX: [ANSWER]-y/n
'(Can you) answer?'
EA: **POSSIBLE-A**(repeated short movements)
'I can.'

(6) ONLY SHORT **POSSIBLE-A**(single stroke) ONLY NUMBER FOR-EXAMPLE FIVE NO FOUR MULTIPLIED-BY FIVE PLUS THREE **POSSIBLE-A**(single stroke)
'I can (calculate) only short (sequences of mathematical operations). For example, five, sorry, four multiplied by five, plus three, I can.'

A difference in the production of POSSIBLE-A in (5) and (6) has to do with manner of movement. In (5) POSSIBLE-A is produced with short, repeated movement, whereas in (6), it is produced with a single stroke. EA explained that the movement repetition indicates that the activity can be performed more easily.

In contrast, shown in (7), DF used POSSIBLE-L to indicate that she could do simple mathematical operations mentally.

(7) ADDITION ADDITION SAME **POSSIBLE-L** SUBTRACTION SUBTRACTION **POSSIBLE-L**
'If it's only addition or only subtraction, I can do it.'

In an example of another way to express mental inability, DF used POSSIBLE-L plus a negative headshake and the sign NO, as in (8). Here the headshake (hs) and compressed lips (cl) had scope over MIND-CRASH FINISH POSSIBLE-L LONG-STRING.

(8) SORRY [MIND-CRASH, FINISH. **POSSIBLE-L** LONG-STRING]-hs/cl NO
'Sorry, my mind would crash. Done. I couldn't (calculate) a long sequence.'

5.1.3 Non-deontic

When asked if she could travel from her house to the university, EA used POSSIBLE-A to say she could get to the university in one hour by Uber, provided that the driver used Google Maps to find the shortest way, shown in (9). By contrast, she said that it would not be possible to get to the university in one hour and thirty minutes by bus, because buses stop along the way. EA expressed this impossibility with the modal IMPOSSIBLE-S, in (10).

(9)   FOR-EXAMPLE CATCH TWO-HOUR GET-THERE THREE-HOUR TIME-INTERVAL HOW STRATEGY SEE M-A-P-S GOOGLE-MAPS SHORT SHORT DISTANT DISTANT SEE **POSSIBLE-A** GO NEAR OR GO DISTANT TIME THIS-WAY **POSSIBLE-A** GO ONE-HOUR **POSSIBLE-A**
'For example, I could catch (an Uber) at two to get there at three, within this one-hour interval. What would my strategy be? I would see Google Maps for short ways and see if I can go a short way or a long way. Thus, I can make it in one hour. I can.'

(10)   IF PRO-1 CATCH BUS **IMPOSSIBLE-S** BECAUSE BUS MORE FAR BECAUSE TIME ARRIVE ARRIVE ARRIVE **IMPOSSIBLE-S**
'If I catch a bus, I can't (make it to the University), because by bus it takes longer, because it makes stops all the way down. I can't make it (in one hour and a half).'

According to DF's intuition, POSSIBLE-S would not be appropriate in a context such as (9). In her view, such usage would represent an influence of Portuguese onto Libras, since the corresponding spoken word that is usually partially or completely mouthed along with it, *pode/po*, would be used in a deontic or positive epistemic sense.[4] Interestingly, the negative counterpart of POSSIBLE-S can be used in the context of (9).

In (11), EA used IMPOSSIBLE-U to assert that she could not arrive at the university in one hour, and certainly not in less. Considering distance and traffic, she also conveyed different degrees of impossibility for various short time intervals by modulating the sign. EA produced IMPOSSIBLE-U, canonically one-handed, with two hands to express that going from her house to the university in thirty minutes would be quite impossible. To say that the same journey would be even harder

---

[4] Of note, it is common to see signers producing POSSIBLE-A accompanied by mouthing the Portuguese word *dá* ('gives'), which is also used in Brazilian Portuguese to express possibility.

with less time, just fifteen minutes, she produced IMPOSSIBLE-U with the movement lengthened, and with non-manuals such as furrowed eyebrows. These sign modulations are illustrated in Figure 9, and support dos Santos and Xavier's (2019) description of similar cases as ways to express degrees of intensity in Libras.

(11) AX: [BUS OK]-Y/N
'By bus, ok?'
EA: [ONE-HOUR]-Y/N+HS NO BECAUSE TIME AFTERNOON **IMPOSSIBLE-U** NO-WAY CAR POSSIBLE-A
'Within one hour (only)? No! Because (of the traffic) in the afternoon I can't (make it). No way! By car, I can.'

(...)

AX: [THIRTY MINUTE]-Y/N
'In thirty minutes?'
EA: THIRTY MINUTE NO-WAY **IMPOSSIBLE-U**(two hands) NO-WAY CANCEL
'Thirty minutes, no way! Impossible! No way! I would cancel it.'
AX: [FIFTEEN MINUTE]-Y/N
'In fifteen minutes?'
EA: **IMPOSSIBLE-U**(movement lengthening) FIFTEEN MINUTE **IMPOSSIBLE-U**(movement lengthening)
'Impossible! It is impossible in fifteen minutes!'

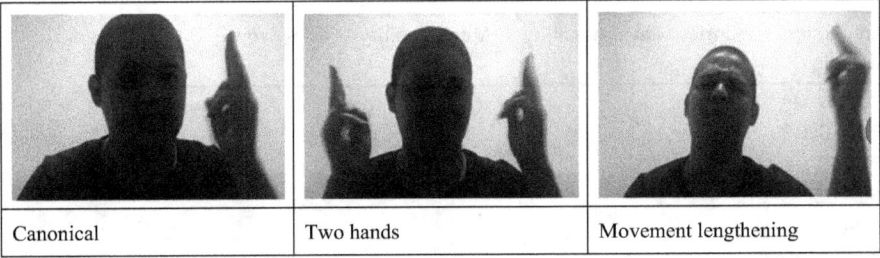

| Canonical | Two hands | Movement lengthening |

Figure 9: Neutral and intensified forms of IMPOSSIBLE-U.

5.1.4 Deontic

Both DF and EA used POSSIBLE-S to express permission. For DF, POSSIBLE-S indicates that one can smoke freely if there is no sign prohibiting smoking, as in (12).

(12) IF EMPTY MEAN **POSSIBLE-S** SMOKE FREE EMPTY NOTHING
'If there is no no-smoking prohibition sign, that means one can smoke freely since there is no sign.'

DF signed PROHIBITED in answer to a question about where there was a visible no-smoking sign (13). EA noted that like DF, prohibition can also be expressed by IMPOSSIBLE-V as in (14).

(13) IF NO-SMOKING-SIGN, **PROHIBITED** SMOKE **PROHIBITED**
'If there is a no-smoking prohibition sign, (you) can't smoke.'

(14) HERE SMOKE **IMPOSSIBLE-V** OR PROHIBITED
'(You) can't or are not allowed to smoke here.'

5.1.5 Summary of Libras findings

Table 3 summarizes our findings for the Libras dataset, by indicating the contexts in which each modal was attested. This table does not represent a complete map of Libras possibility modal meanings, because it is based on elicited data from only two participants.

Table 3: Summary of the Libras findings.

Libras sign/semantic domains	Physical ability	Mental ability	Non-deontic	Deontic
POSSIBLE-A	✓	✓	✓	
POSSIBLE-S			✓	✓
POSSIBLE-L		✓		
IMPOSSIBLE-U	✓		✓	
IMPOSSIBLE-V	✓			✓
IMPOSSIBLE-S			✓	
IMPOSSIBLE-L		✓		
PROHIBITED				✓
IMPOSSIBLE-1		✓		

As can be seen in Table 3, POSSIBLE-A is highly polysemous, occurring in almost all contexts. The only meaning we didn't find was permission, which was instead conveyed by POSSIBLE-S. This supports Xavier and Wilcox's (2014) findings, but also advances their work. Note that they offer evidence that POSSIBLE-A can express non-deontic possibility, that is, it refers to participant-external enabling circumstances.

As for the negative possibility modals, Table 3 also reinforces Xavier and Wilcox's results in showing that IMPOSSIBLE-U and IMPOSSIBLE-V are the most polysemous and that these signs can overlap, since both can convey physical inability. It is noteworthy, however, that PROHIBITED only expresses prohibition, as found in both Xavier and Wilcox's study and in the present study.

Finally, Table 3 shows that POSSIBLE-L, IMPOSSIBLE-L,[5] and IMPOSSIBLE-1 were attested in our data to only express mental capacity, while IMPOSSIBLE-S expressed non-deontic modality. Both DF and EA suggested that, among the negative possibility modals, IMPOSSIBLE-S is the least frequent.

5.2 LSA

In the two LSA interviews (DM: 36 minutes; VA: 32 minutes) most of the possibility modals described in Curiel and Massone's (1995) original exploratory work are attested. These are illustrated in Figures 6 and 7 in Section 3.2 above.

It is relevant to note that the signs POSSIBLE (Figure 6a) and MAY-BE-POSSIBLE (Figure 6b) are related. Both are symmetrical two-handed signs, with the same B handshape, initial location, and initial palm orientation. The difference between them is that POSSIBLE has a linear, oscillating movement with the palms of the hands always directed toward the signer's body, whereas MAY-BE-POSSIBLE is produced with an arc movement that starts with the palms toward the signer and ends with the palms oriented away from the signer. IMPOSSIBLE (Figure 6c) is an unrelated, asymmetrical two-handed sign with a 1 handshape on the dominant hand, moving in a circular path. The end of the circular path corresponds to a contact with the non-dominant hand, which has a closed-fist handshape (similar to ASL 'S') with no movement. More research is needed to understand the possible origins of these signs.

It appears that the signs PERMIT, PROHIBIT and LET are unrelated (See Figure 7). PERMIT is a one-handed sign that is produced with an oscillating 2 handshape with the palms directed away from the signer. Although a more thorough study is needed, DM believes the origin of this sign is the gesture of calling the attention of the teacher to ask for permission to do something. The sign PROHIBIT is a one-handed sign produced with an oscillating up and down movement with an H handshape. DM claims

---

5 João Paulo da Silva (personal communication) observed that in his corpus, the use of IMPOSSIBLE-L related to physical capability.

the origin of this sign comes from the action of a teacher or supervisor using a ruler to hit the hand of a student. Lastly, the sign LET is a symmetrical two-handed sign that starts with a closed B handshape and finishes with a 5 handshape with an arc movement. The final location usually changes to indicate the beneficiary, the entity that is allowed to do something.

In the following subsections, we present examples of usage extracted from DM's and VA's interviews, and as with Libras above, we adopt the possibility meanings proposed by van der Auwera and Plungian (1998).

5.2.1 Physical ability

In answering the questions about sliding a table, both DM and VA used POSSIBLE to express that they could do it, and IMPOSSIBLE to say that they would not be able to do it. When they were uncertain about the possibility of sliding the table, they used MAY-BE-POSSIBLE. Example (15) shows the three signs, as used by VA.

(15)   DEPEND. PRO-1 **POSSIBLE** SLIDE-HEAVY-TABLE-WITH-EFFORT, **MAY-BE-POSSIBLE.** IF **IMPOSSIBLE** CALL-3 ANOTHER PERSON. PERSON-COME, 3-HELP-1 SLIDE-TABLE
'It depends. I could slide a heavy table with effort, maybe. If I found it impossible, I would call another person to help me slide it.'

5.2.2 Mental capacity

Examples (16) and (17) show that the signers used POSSIBLE, MAY-BE-POSSIBLE and IMPOSSIBLE to express both physical ability and mental capacity.

(16)   YES **POSSIBLE** AUTOMATIC TWO PLUS TWO FOUR CERTAINTY AUTOMATIC
'Yes, I definitely can do simple mathematical computations.'

(17)   NO **IMPOSSIBLE.** PRO-1 IF PRO-1 STUDY NOTHING NO ACHIEVE ENGLISH IF. PRO-1 MUST LEARN STUDY ENGLISH IMPROVE **MAY-BE-POSSIBLE** TO-SEE. ADVANCE PASS NOT-PASS HAVE-NO-IDEA.
'No, it is impossible. If I do not study anything I would not pass the English (test). I have to learn the language, and then it may be possible to see some improvement. Whether I would pass the test or not, I have no idea.'

5.2.3 Non-deontic

As with the Libras examples in Section 5.1.3 above, the questions intended to elicit non-deontic possibility modals concerned the amount of time needed to arrive at the university in Paraná (Entre Ríos province) from different places (the bus station, another city, their home). The possibility modals produced were POSSIBLE, MAY-BE-POSSIBLE and IMPOSSIBLE. The signers were asked to evaluate various external enabling conditions, such as the mode of conveyance (bus, car, helicopter, walking) and possible setbacks (traffic jams, accidents, among others). They also speculated about the amount of time that it would take to go from one place to the other. Examples are shown in (18), (19), and (20).

(18) BUS-STATION THREE-BLOCKS-AWAY, 15 MINUTE ARRIVE **POSSIBLE** YES WALK YES
'It is three blocks away from the bus station, so it is possible to arrive in 15 minutes. It is within walking distance.'

(19) BUENOS-AIRES ARRIVE PARANA ONE-HOUR NO **IMPOSSIBLE**.
[FORGET]-ᴇᴍᴘʜ. ONLY TRAVEL-BY-HELICOPTER
'It is impossible to travel from Buenos Aires to Paraná in one hour. Forget it! It could only be done by helicopter.'

(20) YES SANTA-FE CITY TRAVEL ARRIVE PARANA ONE-HOUR ENOUGH **MAY-BE-POSSIBLE**
'It may be possible to travel from Santa Fe to Paraná in one hour.'

5.2.4 Deontic

To elicit the deontic meanings of permission and prohibition, two scenarios were given: 1) smoking in various settings and 2) students bringing things to school. The interviewees used five signs conveying permission: POSSIBLE (Figure 6a), PERMIT (Figure 10a), ASK-FOR-PERMISSION (Figure 10b), MAY-BE-POSSIBLE (Figure 6b), and LET (Figure 7b). The interviewees suggested that the LSA sign PERMIT carried more force than POSSIBLE and MAY-BE-POSSIBLE.

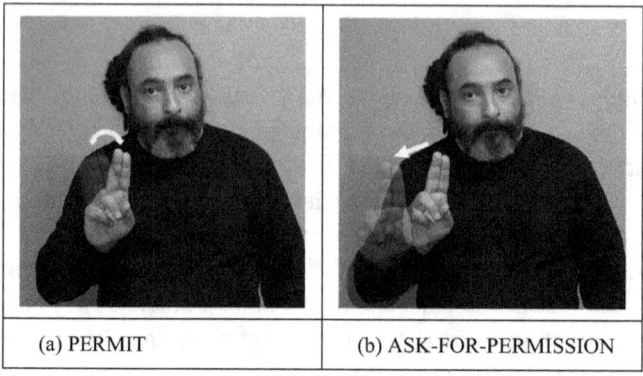

| (a) PERMIT | (b) ASK-FOR-PERMISSION |

Figure 10: LSA modals of permission.[6]

Examples (21) and (22) illustrate the use of POSSIBLE, PERMIT and ASK-FOR-PERMISSION to express that someone is allowed by a norm (e.g., the school's rules regarding food, as in (21)) or by an authority (e.g., the teacher in (22)) to perform an action.

The signs PERMIT and ASK-FOR-PERMISSION are related. PERMIT has either an H or a 2 handshape that has as oscillating movement (seen in Figures 7a and 10a), whereas ASK-FOR-PERMISSION has the same handshape (H or 2) but has a linear movement and can change the initial and final location to include arguments, because it is a directional verb.

(21) DEPEND. PROBLEM HEALTH CELIAC-DISEASE C-E-L-I-A-C CELIAC-DISEASE FOOD IMPOSSIBLE(two hands) OH SPECIAL BRING YES **POSSIBLE**.
'It depends. If somebody has a condition, such as celiac disease, where you cannot eat the (school's) food; it is possible to bring your own special food.'

(22) PRO-1 SEEM NO. SOME WRITE-NOTE NOTEBOOK **PERMIT POSSIBLE** BRING **PERMIT** DEPEND TEACHER WRITE-NOTE ASK-FOR BRING ACCEPT **ASK-FOR-PERMISSION** MUST **ASK-FOR-PERMISSION** FIRST.
'I do not think so. Some (teachers) write notes saying it is allowed to bring (toys). The permission depends on the teacher. If the teacher accepts, it is possible. But first you have to ask for permission.'

---

[6] Note that both PERMIT and ASK-FOR-PERMISSION can be articulated with either the 2 handshape as in Figure 7a, or the H handshape as in Figure 10a. Why there are two phonetic variants for these signs is not clear, and more research is needed in this area.

An example of LET is given in (23). LET is a directional verb, and includes the target entity in the final location, in this case, the (first person) signer. This example indicates politeness in that the signer requests permission to check the school rules about something.

(23) **LET-1** SEE **LET-1** SEE POINT SCHOOL RULES FIRST.
'Let me see. Let me see the school rules first.'

Example (24) shows MAY-BE-POSSIBLE expressing deontic modality. While deontic modals commonly refer to social norms, in (24) the signer comments on her own situation that contrasts the possibility of smoking outdoors but prohibits smoking inside the house for the sake of the family's health.

(24) OUTSIDE PARK AIR SMOKE **MAY-BE-POSSIBLE**, INSIDE SMOKE NO. TAKE-CARE HEALTH FAMILY PRO-1, NO HOUSE INSIDE NO CERTAINTY TO-MEAN **PROHIBIT**(2 hands) CERTAINTY
'It may be possible to smoke outside, at a park. Inside the house it is not. I care about my family's health, so smoking inside is absolutely prohibited.'

When expressing that one cannot smoke inside their house as in (24), VA used the sign PROHIBIT. However, when saying that students are not allowed to bring food to school, DM used both PROHIBIT and IMPOSSIBLE in (25). The interviewees said that just as PERMIT carries more force than POSSIBLE and MAY-BE-POSSIBLE, there is a similar difference in degree of force between PROHIBIT and IMPOSSIBLE.

(25) STUDENTS POINT BRING FOOD NO **PROHIBIT IMPOSSIBLE** WHY INSTITUTION SCHOOL TO-BE-RESPONSIBLE IF COOK FOOD BAD
[WHERE IT-COMES-FROM WHERE]-WH [SCHOOL OR BROUGHT-FOOD]-WH POINT RULES **PROHIBIT**
'Students can't bring food (to the school), because the institution is responsible. If there is a problem with the food, the school does not know whether the problem comes from the school (kitchen) or from the food brought (by the students), so it is prohibited.'

5.2.5 Degrees of intensification and force

Of note, intensification of these signs was attested in the LSA dataset. In (24), for example, PROHIBIT, typically a one-handed sign (Figure 11a), was produced with two hands to express absolute prohibition (Figure 11b). Other typically one-handed modal signs can also have intensified meaning with the addition of a second hand.

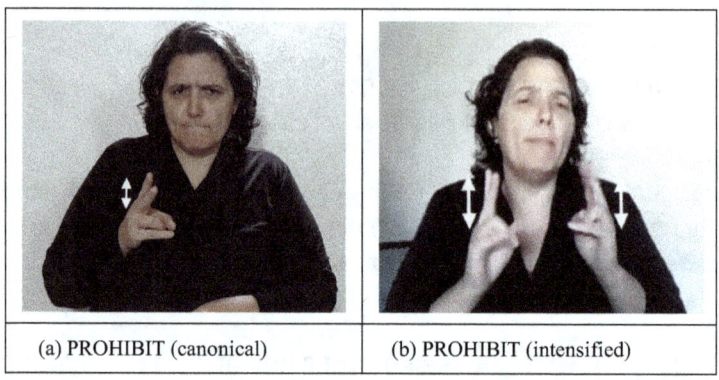

| (a) PROHIBIT (canonical) | (b) PROHIBIT (intensified) |

Figure 11: Canonical and intensified forms of LSA PROHIBIT.

The interviewees mentioned that certain non-manuals along with changes in the articulation of the signs themselves can further indicate various degrees of possibility, whether positive or negative. For instance, DM mentions that POSSIBLE can be signed with the head tilting backward and with a larger movement of the sign, showing the highest degree of possibility. Another example is IMPOSSIBLE, which can be signed with head tilting forward, furrowed eyebrows, and modification of the movement, indicating intensification (cf. Shaffer and Janzen 2016; Wilcox and Shaffer 2006 for related discussion on ASL).

5.2.6 Summary of LSA findings

According to our data, the LSA signs POSSIBLE, MAY-BE-POSSIBLE and IMPOSSIBLE are highly polysemous. Table 4 shows that our interviewees used these signs for all the semantic domains of non-epistemic possibility. On the contrary, PERMIT, PROHIBIT and LET have more limited function, since they were found only in contexts with deontic meaning. Because this table is based on the data collected from just two participants, it is important to understand that we do not intend it to represent a complete map of LSA possibility modal meanings.

Table 4: Summary of LSA findings

LSA sign/ semantic domain	Physical ability	Mental ability	Non-deontic	Deontic
POSSIBLE	✓	✓	✓	✓
MAY-BE-POSSIBLE	✓	✓	✓	✓
IMPOSSIBLE	✓	✓	✓	✓
PERMIT				✓
PROHIBIT				✓
LET				✓

6 A comparison of Libras and LSA non-epistemic possibility modals

Despite the limitations of our data, we can state that the possibility modal systems of Libras and LSA cover all the non-epistemic meanings of the semantic map proposed by van der Auwera and Plungian (1998). We also show that in both languages there are polysemous possibility modals and other modals with more limited meanings. Among the Libras modals, our data suggest that possibility modals vary in terms of how polysemous they are. POSSIBLE-A, for instance, is the most polysemous modal in the Libras dataset, occurring in all contexts examined except in the deontic sub-domain. The negative possibility modals IMPOSSIBLE-U and IMPOSSIBLE-V are also polysemous, but they were not attested in as many contexts. For the modals with more limited meaning, our data suggest that PROHIBITED is one such case, as it was only attested expressing prohibition, similar to what Xavier and Wilcox (2014) found. In LSA there are three possibility modals, POSSIBLE, MAY-BE-POSSIBLE, and IMPOSSIBLE, that are highly polysemous, since they were employed in all the possibility domains and subdomains, whereas the remaining modals were produced only in deontic contexts (PERMIT, LET, PROHIBIT).

Regarding the polarity of the modals, our data suggest that, in comparison to LSA, Libras has more positive and negative possibility modals. In Libras, mental ability was expressed by the positive modals POSSIBLE-A and POSSIBLE-L and the negative modals IMPOSSIBLE-V and IMPOSSIBLE-U. Although it is not yet clear whether the positive modals are synonymous, based on Xavier and Wilcox's work and DF's intuitions, we can state that the negative modals are not. IMPOSSIBLE-U expresses a stronger sense of impossibility in comparison with IMPOSSIBLE-V. Similarly, in LSA, the two positive signs produced within the physical ability subdomain are not synonymous, given that POSSIBLE expresses a higher degree of capacity than MAY-BE-POSSIBLE. This difference in the degree of strength (e.g., of force or certainty) is also observed among LSA deontic modals. PERMIT and PROHIBIT seem to be a stronger expression of permission and prohibition than POSSIBLE, MAY-BE-POSSIBLE, or IMPOSSIBLE.

Regarding suppletion in LSA, the present study shows that the LSA negative modals IMPOSSIBLE and PROHIBIT are not related to their positive counterparts lexically or in form. This supports the crosslinguistic tendency of languages having suppletive negative modals, as has been demonstrated for Libras and also for other signed and spoken languages (Shaffer 2002; van der Auwera 2001).

Despite these differences, the Libras and LSA signers exhibited similar strategies to express intensification, by modulating the manner of movement of the signs, and by adding the other hand. Regarding an increase in intensification, both Libras and LSA signers lengthened the movement of possibility signs. In Libras a reduplicated movement of POSSIBLE-A was also observed to signal that accomplishing a task could be done with ease, for example, sliding a table. Using two hands for typically one-handed signs to increase intensity was observed in Libras IMPOSSIBLE-U and LSA PROHIBIT.

7 Final remarks

In the present chapter, we offer a comparative study of possibility modals in two historically unrelated South American signed languages, Libras and LSA. In order to collect comparable data from these languages, we replicated part of Xavier and Wilcox's (2014) study on the expression of modality with two fluent deaf Libras signers and two fluent deaf LSA signers. We conducted a semi-structured interview with each signer, based on van der Auwera and Plungian's (1998) framework, where we presented the scenarios created by Xavier and Wilcox. By doing so, we were able to elicit positive and negative possibility modals expressing all the non-epistemic meanings predicted by that framework.

Despite its limitations, this chapter advances our knowledge of the expression of modality in Libras and LSA. In addition, it offers further evidence of polysemy in modals, which we believe is a byproduct of their grammaticization process, and of the crosslinguistic tendency for negative modals to be historically unrelated to their positive counterparts. However, there are still many issues that we have been unable to address: 1) the description of Libras and LSA necessity modals as well as other potential manual and non-manual modals; 2) the interaction between signs and facial markers to convey modal meaning; 3) the syntactic distribution of modals including "doubling" constructions; 4) the grammaticization pathways of manual plus non-manual modal constructions; and 5) the interaction between modality and other semantic domains, such as tense, aspect, evidentiality, and negation.

In future work, we would like to more carefully evaluate the strengths and weaknesses of our framework and the method we employed. On the one hand, this framework and method allowed us to compare similarities and differences between two different signed languages. On the other hand, our methodology may have led us to make undue assumptions about category membership. This proved to be a challenge in certain cases of our analysis where more than one interpretation seemed possible, and could become problematic because we wish to take into account Langacker's (2013) proposal that epistemic meaning seems to be present much of the time when modals are used. In Langacker's framework, all non-epistemic modals have an epistemic embedded core. This can be illustrated with our elicitations within the non-epistemic domain (leaving from one place and arriving at another within a certain amount of time). Clearly, besides triggering the signers' knowledge of external circumstances for the trip (distance, traffic, etc.), it also triggered their subjective assessment of whether the trip could or could not happen in a given period of time.

References

Almeida-Silva, Anderson & Andrew Ira Nevins. 2020. Observações sobre a estrutura linguística da Cena: a língua de sinais emergente da Várzea Queimada (Piauí, Brasil) [Observations on the linguistic structure of Cena: The emerging signed language of Várzea Queimada (Piauí, Brazil)]. *Revista Linguagem e Ensino* [Journal of Language and Teaching], 23(4). 1029–1053.

Anderson, Lloyd B. 1982. The "perfect" as a universal and as a language-particular category. In Paul J. Hopper (ed.), *Tense-Aspect: Between Semantics & Pragmatics*, 227–274. Amsterdam/Philadelphia: John Benjamins.

Berenz, Norine. 2003. Surdos Venceremos: The rise of the Brazilian Deaf Community. In Leila Monaghan, Constanze Schmaling, Karen Nakamura & Graham H. Turner (eds.), *Many Ways to Be Deaf: International Variation in Deaf Communities*, 173–193. Washington, DC: Gallaudet University Press.

Bybee, Joan, Revere Perkins & William Pagliuca. 1994. *The Evolution of Grammar: Tense, Aspect and Modality in the Languages of the World*. Chicago: University of Chicago Press.

Curiel, Mónica & María I. Massone. 1995. Verbos modales en la Lengua de Señas Argentina [Modal verbs in Argentine Sign Language]. Paper presented at *Segundas Jornadas de Lexicografía* [Second Conference on Lexicography]. Universidad de Buenos Aires, Buenos Aires, Argentina.

dos Santos, Thiago Steven & André Nogueira Xavier. 2019. Recursos manuais e não-manuais na expressão de intensidade em libras [Manual and non-manual resources in the expression of intensity in Libras]. *Leitura* 63. 120–137.

Ferreira Brito, Lucinda. 1990. Epistemic, alethic, and deontic modalities in a Brazilian Sign Language. In Susan D. Fischer & Patricia Siple (eds.), *Theoretical Issues in Sign Language Research. Volume 1: Linguistics*, 229–260. Chicago: University of Chicago Press.

Givón, T. 1984. *Syntax: A Functional-Typological Introduction. Volume 1*. Amsterdam/Philadelphia: John Benjamins.

Jarque, Maria J. 2019. *Grounding, Subjectification and Deixis: Modal Constructions in Catalan Sign Language and Their Interaction with Other Semantic Domains*. Barcelona: Universitat de Barcelona dissertation.

Janzen, Terry & Barbara Shaffer. 2002. Gesture as the substrate in the process of ASL grammaticization. In Richard P. Meier, Kearsy Cormier & David Quinto-Pozos (eds.), *Modality and Structure in Signed and Spoken Languages*, 199–223. Cambridge: Cambridge University Press.

Langacker, Ronald W. 2013. Modals: Striving for control. In Juana I. Marín-Arrese, Marta Carretero, Jorge Arús Hita & Johan van der Auwera (eds.), *English Modality: Core, Periphery and Evidentiality*, 3–55. Berlin/Boston: de Gruyter Mouton.

Massone, María I. & Emilia Machado. 1994. *Lengua de Señas Argentina: Análisis y Vocabulario Bilingüe* [Argentine Sign Language: Analysis and Bilingual Vocabulary]. Buenos Aires: Edicial.

McBurney, Susan. 2012. History of sign languages and sign language linguistics. In: Roland Pfau, Markus Steinbach & Bencie Woll (eds.), *Sign Language: An International Handbook*, 909–948. Berlin/Boston: de Gruyter Mouton.

Narrog, Heiko. 2009. *Modality in Japanese: The Layered Structure of the Clause and Hierarchies of Functional Categories*. Amsterdam/Philadelphia: John Benjamins.

Palmer, Frank. 1986. *Mood and Modality*. Cambridge: Cambridge University Press.

Shaffer, Barbara. 2000. *A Syntactic, Pragmatic Analysis of the Expression of Necessity and Possibility in American Sign Language*. Albuquerque, NM: University of New Mexico dissertation.

Shaffer, Barbara. 2002. CAN'T: The negation of modal notions in ASL. *Sign Language Studies* 3(1). 34–53.

Shaffer, Barbara & Terry Janzen. 2016. Modality and mood in American Sign Language. In Jan Nuyts & Johan van der Auwera (eds). *The Oxford Handbook of Modality and Mood*, 448–469. Oxford: Oxford University Press.

Siyavoshi, Sara. 2019. Hands and faces: The expression of modality in ZEI, Iranian Sign Language. *Cognitive Linguistics* 30(4). 655–686.

van der Auwera, Johan. 2001. On the typology of negative modals. In Jack Hoeksema, Hotze Rullmann, Víctor Sánchez-Valencia & Ton van der Wouden (eds.), *Perspectives on Negation and Polarity Items*, 23–48. Amsterdam/Philadelphia: John Benjamins.

van der Auwera, Johan & Vladimir A. Plungian. 1998. Modality's semantic map. *Linguistic Typology* 2(1). 79–124.

Wilcox, Sherman. 2009. Symbol and symptom: Routes from gesture to signed language. In Francisco José Ruiz de Mendoza Ibáñez (ed.), *Annual Review of Cognitive Linguistics, Volume 7*, 89–110. Amsterdam/Philadelphia: John Benjamins.

Wilcox, Sherman, Paolo Rossini & Elena Antinoro Pizzuto. 2010. Grammaticalization in sign languages. In Diane Brentari (ed.), *Sign Languages*, 332–354. Cambridge: Cambridge University Press.

Wilcox, Sherman & Barbara Shaffer. 2006. Modality in American Sign Language. In William Frawley (ed.), *The Expression of Modality*, 207–238. Berlin/New York: Mouton de Gruyter.

Wilcox, Sherman & Phyllis Wilcox. 1995. The gestural expression of modality in ASL. In Joan Bybee & Suzanne Fleischman (eds.), *Modality in Grammar and Discourse*, 135–162. Amsterdam/Philadelphia: John Benjamins.

Xavier, André Nogueira & Sherman Wilcox. 2014. Necessity and possibility modals in Brazilian Sign Language (Libras). *Linguistic Typology* 18(3). 449–488.

Sara Siyavoshi
The semantics of relative clause constructions in Iranian Sign Language

1 Introduction

Relative clauses are a type of subordinate clause that specify the reference of a noun phrase (Andrews 2007: 206). In fact, they are finite-clause noun modifiers. The nominal expression in relative clause constructions specifies a basic type and the clause as a whole identifies a particular instance of that type.[1] The nominal and the clause "are integrated to form a higher-level nominal through a correspondence between the nominal profile and a schematic clausal participant" (Langacker 2008: 426). The semantic foundation in forming a relative clause is the fact that a clausal participant in the relative clause also functions as a clausal participant of the main clause. For instance, an entity that functions as the trajector in the main clause is either the trajector or landmark of the relative clause. In Langacker's Cognitive Grammar account (2008: 70–73, 518), the trajector is the primary semantic focus of a linguistic expression and the landmark is the secondary semantic focus of that expression, i.e., it is a profiled relation. The trajector and landmark are two salient entities that are characterized as the first and second semantic focus evoked in building up to the full conception of a profiled relationship. For example, in (1), 'the kid' is the trajector of the relative clause (here the clausal subject), which profiles the process of *winning*. This entity is also the landmark of another process, *talking to*, profiled by the main clause.

(1)   *I talked to the kid who won the prize.*

A relative clause is a finite clause profiling a specific event, here *winning*, that is meant to restrict the category 'kid'. Definiteness of the head noun and the finiteness of the clause are important grammatical features of relative clauses. Syntactically, a relative clause is a complete clause that modifies a nominal expression and functions as a path to assist the interlocutor to single out an individual or a member from a group of referents.

---

1 "Types" are addressed further below.

Sara Siyavoshi, Islamic Azad University, Fereshtegaan International Branch, Iran,
e-mail: sara.siyavoshi@gmail.com

Almost all languages use relative clause in one way or another. Different strategies of relativization in different languages relate to the specific features of languages, such as word order patterns and the availability of certain pronouns. Relative clauses can follow or precede the head, or even include the head. Some languages use relative pronouns (de Vries 2018).

By looking at the body of research in signed language linguistics, we see that relativization strategies in signed languages are very dependent on non-manual markers (e.g., Liddell 1978, 1980; Perniss, Pfau, and Steinbach 2007; Branchini and Donati 2009; Dachovsky and Sandler 2009; Tang and Lau 2012; Kubus and Nuhbalaoğlu 2018). Simultaneous syntax and the multi-channel expression of linguistic messages as characteristics of the grammars of signed languages provide less dependency on word order and more on non-manual markers (NMMs) in grammatical strategies, including relativization. Deeper investigation in signed language grammars requires better understanding of non-manual markers in general, and facial displays in particular. As Tang and Lau (2012: 350) note, the spreading domain of the NMMs offers a clue to understand syntactic dependencies and allows us to analyze relativization strategies in signed languages.

Similar to other signed languages, Iranian Sign Language (Zaban Eshareh Irani, or ZEI) makes use of space and simultaneous manual and non-manual markings to build syntactic structures. The present study focuses on relative clause constructions in ZEI by introducing their associated manual and facial markers and analyzing the different functions of them. The purpose is to explain the conceptualization of relative structures and to study relative clause structures in ZEI from a Cognitive Grammar point of view, and by focusing on three prominent relative clause markers: pointing, raised brow and squinted eyes. The data for this study come from storytelling videos on social media by Iranian signers, although example (5) is from an elicitation data session in which the signer is asked to tell the 'pear story' (Chafe 1980) to another person. The purpose of the original study was to document ZEI in a documentation project.[2]

Section 2 summarizes the Cognitive Grammar account in analyzing relative clause structures by focusing on a broader concept in grammar, that of refer-

---

[2] Examples (2, 3, and 5) are taken from videos that first appeared on the public Telegram Channel, but only available up to 2016. These videos were downloaded prior to the Telegram Channel becoming unavailable, and permission to use them in the current study was obtained from the ZEI signers themselves. Permission to use video for example (4) was obtained from a signer in a ZEI documentation project. Dr. Yasaman Choobsaz of Razi University of Kermanshah conducted the documentation project in 2020 in collaboration with The Endangered Languages Archive (ELAR). Example (6) is taken from my dissertation project (Siyavoshi 2019a), which received approval from the Institutional Review Board (IRB) at the University of New Mexico.

ence point. Section 3 reviews findings on relative clause structures and the role of non-manual markers in the literature on signed language linguistics. In Section 4, relative clause constructions in ZEI are examined by identifying three prominent relative clause markers: pointing, raised eyebrows, and squinted eyes, and in section 5, a discussion on analyzing relative clause markers and the semantics of relative clauses within a cognitive linguistic perspective is presented. Conclusions are in section 6.

2 Relative clauses in Cognitive Grammar

Whereas an adverbial clause modifies another clause, a relative clause modifies a nominal expression (Langacker 2008). Relative clauses *restrict* the selection of instances from a set denoted by a concept and elaborate a conceptual substructure of the intended nominal conceptualization. As Schilperoord and Verhagen (1998: 156) state, "restrictive relative clauses can be treated as a way for the speaker to signal the level of accessibility of a nominal referent". They argue that relative clause constructions are about conceptual dependency more than anything. The conceptualization of the intended referent of the nominal is dependent on the conceptualization of the relative clause. This is what makes a relative clause restrictive.[3] Without the presented content in the relative clause, the conceptualization of one of the participants profiled in the matrix clause is incomplete. Thus, a relative clause is one that the nominal head is conceptually dependent on. The conceptual dependency can be explained by the dual function of the head noun.

2.1 Dual function of the head noun

A relative construction has two constituents: a nominal expression that defines a basic type, and a clause that singles out a particular instance of that type. The nominal referent, which is a participant in the process profiled by the relative clause, also has a semantic role in the matrix clause (Langacker 2009: 30). A construction with a relative clause consists of two processes or events: the matrix event that profiles a relation between its participants, and the relative clause event

---

3 A nonrestrictive relative clause is a kind of relative clause that, unlike restrictive relative clauses, does not identify a participant but rather, provides additional information about it. A nonrestrictive relative clause "serves merely to give the hearer an added piece of information about an already identified entity, but not to identify that entity" (Comrie 1989: 138).

that profiles another relation. A single entity plays a role as a participant both in the matrix event and in the relative clause event. To conceptualize the main clause, one needs to understand the correspondence between the participants of the relative and the main clause through conceptual integration. The dual function of the nominal makes the conceptualization of the relative clause and the matrix clause interdependent.

In his analysis of different structures comprising English relative constructions, Langacker (2008) shows that these constructions are structurally quite diverse, and that the nominal and clausal components do not always combine directly to form a grammatical constituent. He concludes then that the essence of relative clause constructions does not consist in any specific structural configuration. "Their essential feature is semantic: a relative clause is one invoked to characterize a nominal referent identified as a participant in the clausal process (2008: 426).

In the coming sections of this paper, I argue that relative clause constructions are cases of *reference-point relationships* (Langacker 2013) conceptually. In fact, the participant with a semantic role in both the relative clause and the matrix clause (sometimes called the "pivot", Langacker 2008) gains this role over two processes sequentially: first, its role as a participant in the relative clause is activated by the relative clause itself. Then this role functions as a reference point for accessing the event profiled in the matrix clause. The reference point relationship is a type of mental scanning (Langacker 2008: 83) that has various manifestations in language and grammar. There are conceptual, and consequently semantic, similarities between relative clause constructions and other types of reference-point relationships in grammar, which might explain constructional similarities between them. The reference-point relationship as a Cognitive Grammar concept is described in the following section.

2.2 Reference point

Reference-point relationships are part of our mental experience, with various manifestations in grammar. Conceptualizing a reference point is described as the ability to invoke the conception of one entity for purposes of establishing mental contact with another, i.e., to single it out for individual conscious awareness (Langacker 2013: 417).

As illustrated in Figure 1, the conceptualizer (C) uses a reference point (R) to make a mental contact with the target (T). For an entity to function as a reference point, it must first be activated in the conceptual "dominion" (Langacker 2008: 84) and thus be established as an entity currently capable of serving in that capacity (Langacker 2013: 418).

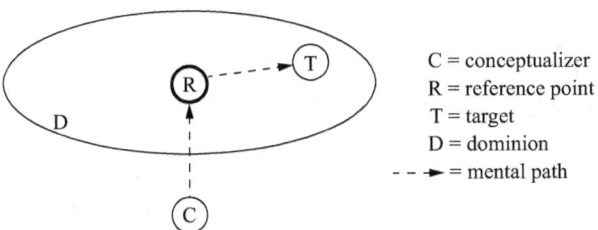

Figure 1: Reference point (Ronald W. Langacker, "Reference-point constructions"; in *Mouton Classics: From Syntax to Cognition. From Phonology to Text*, Berlin/Boston: de Gruyter Mouton, 2013, p. 418, fig. 2).

Mental scanning means that a discrete mental path is taken, starting from a salient entity for the conceptualizer and scanning along the path in order to find or identify another entity. "We can best appreciate this from a perceptual example. We often direct attention to a perceptually salient entity as a point of reference to help find some other entity, which would otherwise be hard to locate" (Langacker 2008: 83). In one of Langacker's examples, for instance, a speaker wants to draw the listener's attention to a duck on a lake. However, a boat is easier to locate from a distance. Once the listener finds the boat from afar, the duck can be seen by searching nearby. Therefore, the speaker says, *"Do you see that boat out there in the lake? There's a duck swimming right next to it"* (Langacker 2008: 83, his example (25a); italics in original).

Reference-point relationships do not designate specific linguistic phenomena, but rather represent special conceptual-mental organization. These relationships, similar to other cognitive abilities, regard a variety of linguistic manifestations. Reference point (R) and Target (T) in a reference-point relationship (Figure 1) are salient entities that can be recognized separately. A sequential mental access is built from R to T.

Possessive constructions are one of the typical manifestations of a reference-point relationship in a language's grammar. Langacker (1991: 169–172, 2013) analyzed the possessive morpheme *-'s* in English as profiling a reference-point relationship where one entity (the possessor) is invoked as a reference point for the purpose of making mental contact with a target entity (the possessed) which is within the dominion of the possessor. For instance, *'s* in *Sally's dog* invokes a reference-point relationship in order to identify the target entity *dog*. It builds a mental path from a salient entity, here *Sally*, a known person to the addressee as the reference point (R) to make the target entity (T), *dog*, accessible. Other possessive components such as English possessive pronouns function similarly. Other manifestations of a reference-point relationship in grammar are pronominal anaphora and topic. Thus Langacker suggests that the "intrinsic salience of R and T is therefore not to be identified with the kinds of prominence imposed by grammatical constructions. The same reference point relationship can be reflected in multiple expressions involving alternate choices of profiling and trajector/landmark alignment" (Langacker 2008: 507).

In example (1), *the kid* is the trajector (here, the grammatical subject) of the process 'winning'. *The kid* is first identified as the target (T) by the process 'winning' which is a reference point. Then in the second stage, *the kid* serves as the reference entity for making the process 'talk to' accessible (Figure 2). By conceptualizing this reference-point relation, the landmark of the process in the main clause, and consequently the entire profiled relation, becomes accessible. As illustrated in Figure 2, the mental process of conceptualizing a construction with an embedded relative clause includes two stages of reference-point relationship scanning.

The head noun in a relative clause that serves as a reference point (Langacker 2013: 446) is one of the focuses of this study which will be discussed more with examples from ZEI relative clause structures.

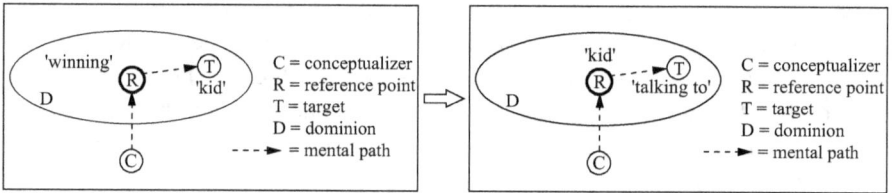

Figure 2: Conceptualizing a relative clause construction through two stages of a reference-point relationship (adapted from Ronald W. Langacker, "Reference-point constructions"; in *Mouton Classics: From Syntax to Cognition. From Phonology to Text*, Berlin/Boston: de Gruyter Mouton, 2013, p. 418, fig. 2).

3 Relative clause structure and NMMs in signed languages

One of the first studies on relative clause constructions in signed languages was carried out by Liddell (1978, 1980) on American Sign Language (ASL). He showed that raised brows, a backward head tilt, and a raised upper lip are non-manual markers of relative clauses in ASL. These NMMs serve as the manifestation of syntactic structure in the subordinate clause.

A decade later, Fontana (1990) determined that head internal relative clause constructions in ASL can be considered as two connected sentences formed similar to topic-comment structures. Fontana based his claim on the evidence that the facial expressions in relative clauses and topics in ASL are similar and that they both occur in sentence-initial position. There are other studies in which the similarities between the non-manual markers in topic and relative clause construction have been reported. In fact, some have suggested that non-manual markers used for topicalization and relativization in ASL are not distinguishable (Liddell 1978; Coulter 1983). I argue in the present study that both topic-comment structures and relative clause structures are manifestations of reference-point relationships conceptually, and this might explain the similarities in the markers associated with these constructions.

Facial markers have been discussed as important parts of relative clauses in other signed languages as well. In their study on German Sign Language (Deutsche Gebärdensprache, or DGS), Pfau and Steinbach (2005) showed that DGS relative clauses are externally headed, appear post-nominally, and use clause-initial relative pronouns. NMMs in DGS co-occur only with the relative pronoun. Perniss, Pfau and Steinbach (2007) analyzed relative clauses among various signed languages and showed that NMMs such as raised brow are common with relative clauses in DGS, Italian Sign Language (Lingua dei Segni Italiana, or LIS) and ASL. Squinted eyes in Israeli Sign Language (Shassi) is shown to be one of the markers of relativization and is associated with 'shared knowledge' (Dachkovsky and Sandler 2009). Moreover, Dachkovsky and Sandler claim that the eye squint in Israeli Sign Language expresses restrictivity by marking restrictive relative clauses as opposed to non-restrictive relative clauses. Eye squinting has a pragmatic significance which is related to retrieving information that is accessible for both interlocutors. Squinted eyes marks mutually retrievable or shared knowledge but it also typically characterizes relative clauses, remote past and other structures (Dachkovsky and Sandler 2009).

According to Kubus (2016) and Kubus and Nuhbalaoğlu (2018) a headshake has an important role in relative clause constructions in Turkish Sign Language (Türk İşaret Dili, or TİD). Kubus (2016) also identifies squinted eyes as a predominant marker of relative clauses in TİD (2016: 208) and claims that if the squint occurs simultaneously with the head noun then the relative clause is internally headed, whereas if the head noun is not accompanied with the squint, then the relative clause is externally headed. According to Kubus (2016) raised brows might signal topicalization of either the head noun or the relative clause. A cheek raise and tensed upper lip are mentioned as other markers in TİD relative clauses which along with an eye squint indicate shared knowledge.

Raised eyebrows and tension of the eyes and upper cheeks as markers of relative clauses in LIS is reported in Branchini (2006) and Branchini and Donati (2009). The NMMs appear along with a specific sign they label as PE. PE is a relative clause marker in LIS characterized manually with the index finger stretched out and shaken downwards, which co-occurs with the silent articulation of a labial stop. PE is co-referential with the nominal in the relative clause, and this co-referentiality can be realized through agreement in space (Branchini and Donati 2009: 7).

The significance of non-manual markers in the structure of subordination, especially relative clauses, has been reported in Hong Kong Sign Language (HKSL) (Tang and Lau 2012) and DGS (Pfau and Steinbach 2016) as well as LIS (Branchini and Kelepir 2017). According to Mosella Sanz (2011) the NMM cluster including raised eyebrows, a body lean and squinted/tensed eyes is the syntactic marker of relative clauses in Catalan Sign Language (Llengua de signes catalana, or SLC).

In sum, data from a limited number of signed languages (ASL, DGS, LIS, Israeli Sign Language, SLC, HKSL, and TİD) show that non-manual markers, specifically facial displays, accompany relative clause constructions. The reported non-manual markers in these studies is summarized in Table 1. These studies show that these languages clearly mark the clause (or relative pronoun) with an identifiable and grammatical facial expression and, interestingly, that raised eyebrows and squinted eyes are the most common facial markers (cf. Wilbur 2017: 28).

Table 1: Non-manual markers in relative clause constructions.

Signed Language	NMMs
ASL (Liddell 1978, 1980)	raised brows, backward head tilt, tensed upper lip
DGS (Perniss, Pfau and Steinbach 2007)	raised brow
LIS (Perniss, Pfau and Steinbach 2007; Branchini 2006; Branchini and Donati 2009)	raised brow, tension of eyes and upper cheek
ISL (Dachovsky and Sandler 2009)	squinted eyes
SLC (Mosella Sanz 2011)	raised brows, body lean, squinted eyes
HKSL (Tang and Lau 2012)	raised brows
TİD (Kubus 2016; Kubus and Nuhbalaoğlu 2018)	headshake, squinted eyes, raised brows, cheek raise, tensed upper lip

4 ZEI Relative clauses

There are manual and facial markers in ZEI that accompany relative clauses as shown in example (2). A point, sometimes glossed as INDEX or IX (Wilbur 2017), is the prominent manual marker, which is produced right after the pivot, i.e., the nominal with a semantic role in each clause.[4]

(2) [WOMAN PERSON point CITY BUSHEHR KNOW]-BR/ES ENROLL
'The woman I knew from Bushehr had enrolled (in the group).'

Example (2) is taken from a previously public video in which a deaf teenage girl tells a true story about her life. She has been a ZEI signer since early childhood and attended a school for deaf children in south Iran. The relative clause in (2) modifies WOMAN which is its landmark. At a higher level of organization, the complex nominal [WOMAN PERSON point CITY BUSHEHR KNOW] is the subject of ENROLL, i.e., it elaborates the trajector of ENROLL, which is the woman. The 'point' as it is coded in the gloss is produced right after the nominal expression, where the index finger points toward the signer's right. A very common nominal grounding element in signed languages is pointing (Wilcox and Occhino 2016; Martínez and Wilcox 2019), which is common in relative clause constructions as well. Nominal grounding pertains to identification (Langacker 2016; Martínez and Wilcox 2019). By nominal grounding the signer or speaker directs the interlocutor's attention to the intended discourse referent, here, the woman in Bushehr.

The main correspondence in the relative clause in (2) connects the profile of WOMAN to the landmark CITY BUSHEHR KNOW. The result of this correspondence profiles the woman rather than the idea of the signer knowing her. At a higher level of organization, then, the composite expression is the trajector of ENROLL. Therefore, the higher structure of the sentence as a whole shows WOMAN as having two roles: it participates in both the knowing and the enrolling processes.

In addition to the point, raised eyebrows and squinted eyes also occur with the relative clause in (2). These are multifunctional facial displays that are common in relative clause constructions. In following sections, each of the three markers is described in order to analyze their functions and schematic meanings in ZEI relative clause constructions.

4.1 Pointing

A point (as in Figure 3) appears to be an obligatory marker in ZEI relative clause constructions, occurring in all ZEI examples in the present paper. Pointing has also

---

[4] The facial markers brow raise (BR) and eye squint (ES) are discussed in sections 4.2 and 4.3 below. See also the transcription key following the chapter.

been reported to be obligatory in relative clause constructions in DGS (Pfau and Steinbach 2005), LIS (Branchini and Donati 2009), and HKSL (Tang, Lau and Lee 2010). By pointing, the interlocutor provides mental access to an entity in the discourse space, which is a previously established conceptual domain. In fact, pointing is a very common human communicative behavior for allowing mental access to an intended referent (Wilcox and Occhino 2016; Kendon 2010). Different studies on the function of pointing in signed languages (Coppola and Senghas 2010; Cormier, Schembri, and Woll 2013; Meier and Lillo-Martin 2013; Wilcox and Occhino 2016; Morford et al. 2019) show that signers make use of pointing to direct attention, to specify referents, locations and directions, to indicate verb arguments, and as demonstratives.

The point in ZEI relative clauses appears right after the 'type noun', i.e., the nominal expression that defines a basic type. Another example of a relative clause construction with a point is shown in example (3).

(3) [BEFORE YOU ONE KILO STONE SALT **point** SELL HOUSE STONE]-BR/ES

   point STAY
   'The one-kilo saltlick stone you sold (me) earlier is still there at home.'

Figure 3: The point.

Example (3), from which Figure 3 is taken, is from a public video in which the signer tells an anecdote about two neighbors. The signer is a deaf man from north west Iran who regularly published ZEI videos on his Telegram Channel for the deaf community in Iran. Here, he first establishes the location of the two neighbors, one to his right and the other to his left. Example (3) is what one of the neighbors is saying to the other.

The first point in (3), which is in the relative clause, is toward the space to the signer's left where the sign STONE was produced, and the second point in the main clause is toward the signer's right side specifying the HOUSE location. Similar to the point in (2), here too the point after SALT assures that the entity is understood as a particular instance of a type noun with a particular location in space. The function of pointing is very similar to that of a definite article which profiles an instance of some type and indicates its discourse status. Pointing has been shown to be a grammatical strategy of nominal grounding in signed languages (Wilcox and Occhino 2016; Martínez and Wilcox 2019). Nominal grounding refers to strategies by which the signer or speaker directs the addressee's attention to the intended discourse referent. Wilcox and Occhino (2016), in their analysis of pointing in ASL, show that the focus of attention in pointing is a function of a 'Place' symbolic structure. The phonological pole of Place is a spatial location in the current ground. The schematic semantic pole of Place is a 'thing'.[5]

One can analyze the point in ZEI relative clause constructions as a relative pronoun. However, more investigation on points and their characteristics in relative clauses is needed in this regard. In her study on the development of a relative pronoun from a demonstrative marker in Israeli Sign Language, Dachkovsky (2020) shows that demonstratives have gone through grammaticization processes and grammatical "degradation" (2020: 163). The evidence presented in Dachkovsky's study is that pointing signs in a newer generation of ISL signers are no longer toward the physical locations and these have become more entrenched in the grammar. Pointing in all ZEI cases in the present study is toward a space already introduced in the discourse context and is associated with the head-noun entity. More data are needed, however, to examine different behaviors and functions of points in relative clauses, and to provide more evidence for the hypothesis of a point as a relative pronoun in ZEI.

---

5 Two broad classes of elements on which interlocutors strive to achieve intersubjective alignment are things and occurrences. An occurrence or event is "something that occurs (happens), a relationship that exists in time" (Langacker 2016: 77). A thing is "something conceived as a single entity — intrinsically (like a point of light) or as the result of grouping (like a team)" (Langacker 2016: 63). Clauses profile occurrences; nominals profile things.

4.2 Brow raise

One prominent facial marker in ZEI relative clause constructions is raised eyebrows (see Figures 3, 5, 6, and 7). Pointing accompanied by a brow raise has been observed in relative clause structures of other signed languages as well (e.g., DGS, LIS and ASL (Perniss, Pfau, and Steinbach 2007); LIS (Branchini and Donati 2009); SLC (Mosella Sanz 2011); HKSL (Tang and Lau 2012); TİD (Kubus and Nuhbalaoğlu 2018)).

The brow raise is produced simultaneously with the nominal expression and is often held over the entire relative clause as in (2) and (3). Another example is (4) from a video in which the signer tells the 'pear story'. The signer is a young deaf man from west Iran who participated in the ZEI documentation project.

(4) [MAN point FRUIT_PICKING]-BR/ES CLIMB_DOWN
'The man who was picking fruit came down (the tree).'

Along with the point that identifies the subject of a finite clause, i.e., the agent of the event 'pick', a raised brow is produced. The raised brow is held over the entire relative clause and the brow lowers right at the beginning of the main clause GOING_DOWN.

Here we have a nominal that functions as a reference point with a scope bigger than a single clause. MAN refers to an entity activated in the conceptual dominion from which mental access is subsequently available to two events: picking the fruit and going down the tree. The man who was picking fruit previously in the story is the same one who now, in the present sequence in (4), came down the tree.

As Verhagen (2001) argues, a relative clause cannot function as a separate discourse segment, because the relative clause is required to complete the conceptualization of some part of another clause. In his analysis of conceptual dependency in relative clause structures, Verhagen emphasizes the discursive nature of relative clause structures and suggests that a restrictive relative clause is required to complete the conceptualization of some part of another clause, and hence cannot function as a separate discourse segment (Verhagen 2001: 341). According to Wilbur (2017: 14), ASL internally headed relative clauses cannot stand alone (i.e., are not main clauses) as long as the brow raise is present. This suggests that, at least for ASL, conceptual dependency is marked by raised eyebrows.

In example (4), MAN point FRUIT_PICKING constitutes a conceptual grouping which refers to an event previously introduced in the discourse, i.e., the man who was picking fruit, but this needs to be comprehended as part of a bigger conceptual group. The two conceptual groups are construed in relation to one another by means of identifying the nominal referent. This conceptual grouping containing the nominal is marked by a brow raise. As long as the raised eyebrows are held, it is necessary that in order for the comprehension to be completed, a second conceptual grouping that includes another clause must be perceived.

MAN plus the point activates the man as a reference point entity and simultaneously as the trajector for both the relative clause (the first conceptual grouping) and the main clause (the second conceptual grouping). 'The man' is the reference point for reaching the target which is the proposition profiled in the main clause 'came down the tree', and so is internal to the target proposition of the main clause as well.

4.2.1 Relative clauses and topic constructions: Some similarities

A brow raise in ZEI has various functions including topic marking. According to Gundel (1988: 210), topic is what the utterance is about or is something the speaker intends to increase the addressee's knowledge about. It is thus a manifestation of reference point relation with a discourse scope (Langacker 2008). As Janzen (2017: 521) states, a topic is chosen as a reference point from which to view the assertions made in the comment that follows, and topic choice is subjective. According to Janzen (1998, 1999, 2017), in his study on topic-comment structures in ASL, raised eyebrows mark the topic and the eyebrows return to neutral position at the beginning of comment phrase. A raised brow has been reported as a common marker of topic in other studies and other signed languages as well (ASL (Liddell 1980), Sign Language of the Netherlands (Nederlandse Gebarentaal) (Coerts 1992), HKSL (Sze 2009, 2011), and Russian Sign Language (Russkii Zhestovyi Yazyk) (Kimmelman 2015)).

Topic represents a particular kind of reference point organization, distinguished from others by the nature of the target. In contrast to possessives and pronominal anaphora, where the target is a thing, for topics the target is a proposition (P), i.e., a grounded process (Langacker 2008: 513). Figure 4 shows Langacker's basic configuration of topic constructions.

The conceptualizer (C) apprehends the target (T), which is a proposition (P) through the reference point (R), which is the topic. The small circle connected to

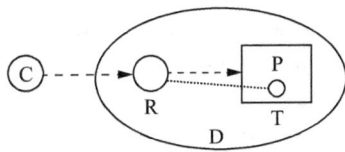

Figure 4: Topic (Langacker 2008: 513, his Figure 14.3; reproduced with permission from Oxford Publishing Limited through PLSclear).

R by the dotted line in Figure 4 represents the manifestation of R within P, that is, the element of P that R corresponds to. "A topic is a reference point in discourse, directing the hearer to the proper realm of knowledge for interpreting the target proposition" (Langacker 2008: 516). Subject, as a trajector of a profiled process, is also a reference point through which the process is conceptualized.

4.3 Squinted eyes

Another common facial display in ZEI relative clause constructions is squinted eyes (fourth photo from the left in Figure 5: MARRY). The signers in the ZEI examples discussed so far produce squinted eyes while signing the head noun of the relative clause. A somewhat different case is in example (5), which is evident in Figure 5 as well. Example (5) is taken from a video by a deaf girl who has been a ZEI signer since early childhood. The video is a love story about a man who could not forget his first love.

(5)   [S-U-S-A-N point GIRL]-BR [MARRY]-ES DIVORCE
      'Susan, the girl who had gotten married got divorced.'

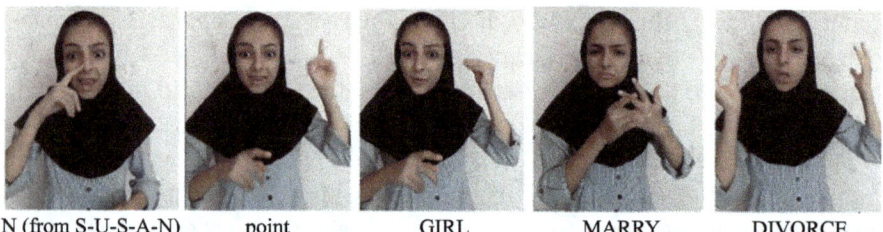

| N (from S-U-S-A-N) | point | GIRL | MARRY | DIVORCE |

Figure 5: Squinted eyes in the relative clause.

As Figure 5 shows, the eye squint appears only with the sign MARRY. Susan had been introduced in the story earlier, and her marriage was also one of the earlier sections of the story. Now, in this section, Susan is mentioned again with new information: her divorce. One can interpret the squinted eyes as a tense marker or a marker of remote past because this is a common marker when ZEI signers talk about remote past. However, squinted eyes like other facial displays is a multifunctional marker. Referring to some entity as old information in the discourse and referring to some event happened in the past both are marked by squinted eyes. In (5) the two meanings are overlapped: the marriage had happened years before and also this is old information in the discourse which is now connected to new information profiled by DIVORCE.

What Dachkovsky and Sandler (2009) report on the association of squinted eyes with the retrieval of shared knowledge in the discourse in Israeli Sign Language also seems to be the case in ZEI relative clause constructions. Squinted eyes in relative clause constructions is a marker of directing the interlocutor's attention to a previously identified entity or event in the discourse. In example (4) for instance, the entity 'man' and the event 'picking fruit' have been introduced in previous episodes of the story. Squinted eyes signal intersubjectively that some entity or event which has been introduced in the discourse earlier in relation to the time of speaking. In (5), it indicates that the process 'marry' is to be understood as old information in the discourse because it was mentioned previously in the story.

Similar to the brow raise, squinted eyes end with the relative clause, just before the beginning of the main clause. These two markers indicate the dependency of the relative clause, and the onset and offset of the two are good criteria for determining clause boundaries.

4.4 Other markers

Apart from pointing, raised eyebrows, and squinted eyes that are prominent markers in relative clause structures in ZEI, three other markers are observable in some relative clause structures: tension of the upper cheek muscles (a smile-like face), body shifting, and a head shake. However, unlike raised brows, squinted eyes, and pointing, they are not present in all the data studied.

Muscle tension in the cheeks is more observable when both raised brows and squinted eyes are pronounced strongly. Thus, it might be an inevitable tension of facial muscles because of the squinted eyes and raised eyebrows. An anatomic investigation of facial muscles might be needed to test this hypothesis. More semantic-discursive analysis also is needed for understanding this marker in relative clause constructions. This takes place in example (3) (the saltlick stone) above, from which Figure 6 is taken.

Another example is (6), from which Figure 7 is taken.

(6) [**BOY point FALL**]-BR/SE/CHEEK-TENSION SIT point
 'The boy who fell before is sitting now.'

Similar facial marking on relative clauses has been mentioned by Liddell, who observed that ASL relative clauses are marked with the brow raised, a co-occurring

Figure 6: Tension of the cheeks as a marker of the relative clause in (3).

Figure 7: Tension of the cheeks in (6) as a marker of the relative clause.

backward tilt of the head, and muscle contraction that raises the cheek and upper lip (Liddell 1978, 2003).

Another observed marker in ZEI relative clauses which sometimes appears along with pointing is a body tilt toward the opposite side of the direction of the point. Then, following the relative clause, the body tends to lean to the other side or to a neutral position to produce the matrix clause. This results in a spatial division: one side for each clause. The body tilt seems to indicate the dual function of the nominal, as being both the trajector of the main clause and the landmark or trajector of the relative clause. The signer specifies two active locations in the signing space, one for the relative clause and the other for the main clause. The body tilt serves to distinguish the two locations and thus the events based on conceptual features of the discourse. However, a body tilt is not observed in all relative clause cases in this study, and more in-depth analysis is needed to investigate its grammatical role in various relative clause constructions.

5 Discussion

Whereas an adverbial clause modifies another clause, a relative clause modifies a nominal expression (Langacker 2008). Relative clauses are processual noun modifiers. Relative clauses traditionally have been categorized as subordinate clauses along with adverbial clauses and complement clauses. The head noun in relative clause constructions serves one function in the main clause and another in the relative clause. Another way to put this is that a relative clause modifies a nominal expression and furthermore, it provides a conceptual context which is larger than a dominion with only one trajector and one landmark.

Relative clauses can be analyzed as cases of a reference-point relationship in which an entity is activated in the conceptual domain to reach a proposition target that is sequentially activated. The first element activated is a nominal expression by attributing it to an event (which is the relative clause). The event is part of shared knowledge, and that is the reason for being selected as the first reference point. The next sequence is the target in another reference-point relationship: the activated element has another event to be attributed to (the main clause).

The relative clause and the main clause are conceptually dependent and there is normally a participant in the relative clause responsible for this dependency. The trajector or landmark of the relative clause plays a conceptual role in the main clause in that this participant functions as a pivot to make the matrix clause understandable as the larger conceptual dominion.

One of the key characteristics of the relative clause as the modifier of a nominal is that the point is a tool or marker indicating that the nominal is definite. As evidence, Guity's (2022) analysis of the 1-handshape point as an index in ZEI (what he refers to as *Esharani*) shows many examples in which the point serves different grammatical functions such as pronouns, definite articles, and demonstratives. The video data in Guity's study was gathered through fieldwork as he spent a summer travelling across Iran, interviewing deaf signers from different regions. The topics of the interviews cover many issues including the signers' daily lives and their linguistic ideologies. When the point functions in the role of a definite article, it appears after the nominal.

The definiteness of the head noun is comprehended from the mental contact established by pointing. The point indicates that the signer and addressee both have access to the identity of the relevant nominal. As Langacker (2016) states, pointing has a directive force: it directs the interlocutors' conceptual attention "to follow its direction, so that both interlocutors end up focusing attention on the same entity, the gesture's intended referent" (2016: 110).

A prominent multifunctional facial display that occurs in ZEI relative clauses is raised eyebrows. Raised brows occur in relative clauses as well as in topics and conditional clauses. In these ZEI grammatical structures, raised brows may best be characterized as designating a reference-point relationship. A reference-point relationship is based on a conceptual ability by which an entity or event is mentally accessible through a mental path built from another entity (Langacker 2013: 417). The structural similarity in these constructions is compatible with Fontana's (1990) analysis of ASL relative clauses in which he compared relative clause constructions with topic-comment structures and found similarities between the facial markers of the two constructions. However, Fontana claims that relative clause constructions in ASL are a type of topic, whereas my claim is that relative clause and topic constructions are both types of reference-point relationships.

Raised brows have been shown to be a common marker of topic in signed languages (Liddell 1980; Coerts 1992; Janzen 1998, 1999, 2017; Sze 2009, 2011; Kimmelman 2015). My argument is that similar to topics, relative clauses are cases of reference-point relationships with an *event* as their target. Topic represents a particular kind of reference-point organization, distinguished from others by the nature of the target. In contrast to possessives and pronominal anaphora, where the target is a thing, for topics the target is a proposition, i.e., a grounded process (Langacker 2008: 513).

In a relative clause construction, we deal with two phases of focused awareness with a temporal sequence. The first phase activates an entity in the conceptual domain serving as the reference point: the nominal expression which is placed in focus. Its activation sets the conditions for accessing elements of the reference point's dominion, one of which is focused as the target. Unlike other reference-point relationships (e.g., possessives and pronominal anaphora), the target in a relative clause construction is not another entity but an event. For instance, in example (2) the target is the event 'enroll'. This target event becomes accessible via identification of its trajector, 'woman', the entity which has been activated in the relative clause in the first phase: 'the woman I know from Bushehr'.

The proposition in the main clause becomes accessible through mental scanning from an entity that serves as the reference point. This forms the second phase in completing the comprehension of the matrix clause. The initial phase, marked by the raised brow, is when an entity (thing) becomes accessible via the first event, and then in the second phase, another event is accessible via the very same entity. Raised brows serve to establish the first reference-point relationship and to ensure that the entity is recognized by the addressee. As focus shifts to the target (the event profiled in the main clause), the reference point—having served its purpose—fades into the background and the eyebrows return to their neutral position. In the ZEI relative clause examples analyzed here, the eyebrows return to their neutral location right after the relative clause and at the beginning of matrix clause.

Raised eyebrows seem to associate with the restrictivity of an relative clause in ZEI. Restrictivity refers to the semantic feature of an relative clause by which the nominal is singled out from other members of a group. The conceptual composite of the two clauses will not be understood as a whole until the eyebrows return to their neutral position and the signer signs the matrix clause content. Thus, not only are raised brows a marker of a relative clause, but also the duration this marker is held is a boundary marker of the clause. This eyebrows up and eyebrows down sequence is essential for understanding the relations profiled in the matrix clause as a whole. As has been discussed for some other grammatical markers in signed languages, there is a symbolic co-equality between the degree of muscle tension and the degree of grammatical meaning (Wilcox and Wilcox 1995; Siyavoshi 2019b: 24–25): the more connected the two clauses to be comprehended, the clearer raised eyebrow is pronounced. This can be associated with the prosodic function of facial displays in the grammar. No raised eyebrow at all may be an indication that clauses occupy separate windows of attention and are apprehended independently, although more research is needed to confirm this.

Along with raised brows accompanying the relative clause, another facial display occurs which is squinted eyes. Squinted eyes, also sometimes labeled as "tensed eyes" has been reported to be the marker of relative clauses in different signed languages (Branchini and Donati 2009; Dachkovsky and Sandler 2009; Brunelli 2011; Mosella Sanz 2011; Kubus 2016). Like other facial displays, the eye squint is also a multifunctional marker and appears in various grammatical constructions. It has been discussed as a marker of modality in ZEI (Siyavoshi 2019b) with the meanings of probability and doubt. It is also a common marker for adverbials expressing remote past. Squinted eyes profiles some event as being at a distance from the immediate reality. The distance that squinted eyes profile can be discursive: to refer to an entity that has been introduced in the discourse before the present utterance.

According to Brunelli (2011) "tensed eyes" is the primary marker of relative clauses in LIS, and as well, raised brows mark topics and conditionals, but not specifically relative clauses unless they are also topics. As discussed in the present study, restrictive relative clauses and topics can both be analyzed as manifestations of reference-point relationships and this might explain the phonological similarities. As described above, when raised eyebrows mark a topic, the head noun is profiled as the reference point.

Directing the interlocutor's attention to the fact that what is expressed (here a nominal) has been mentioned before in the discourse, squinted eyes indicate a conceptual distance that is discursive. Squinted eyes seem to be associated with bringing conceptually distant ideas or propositions into focus: the entity has been introduced in the discourse earlier and is not new information. The co-occurrence of squinted eyes and raised brow in a relative clause might be explained by overlapping two notions: the notion of a reference point relationship in the relative clause which profiles an entity in order to make a mental contact with a target, and the notion of distance, i.e., the entity has been introduced in the discourse earlier and is not new information.

6 Conclusion

This chapter presents a Cognitive Grammar analysis of relative clause constructions in Iranian Sign Language (ZEI), claiming that these constructions can be characterized as manifestations of a reference-point relationship. A manual marker (pointing), and two facial markers (raised brows and squinted eyes) were described and analyzed as important markers of ZEI relative clause constructions.

Relative clauses are part of a larger conceptual context which is the matrix clause. The trajector or landmark of one process functions as the trajector or landmark of another process as well, and the two processes together need to be comprehended as a whole. Thus the grounded nominal expression in a relative clause construction has a dual grammatical role in the utterance.

Pointing, as the necessary manual marker of ZEI relative clauses, has a directing force to establish a mental contact with an entity—the head noun—and to indicate its definiteness. It has a reference-point function and establishes mental contact with the head noun as a pivot, because it is the participant with a semantic role in both the relative clause and the matrix clause. A reference-point relationship allows for a sequential scanning mental process by which an activated entity in the first conceptual domain functions as the reference point to lead the conceptualizer to a target. Activation of the nominal head as the reference point in the relative clause is marked by raised eyebrows which are held through the entire relative clause. This forms the first phase of a relative clause construction in which an entity becomes accessible via an event. In the second phase, a second event (the main clause) is accessible via the very same entity. The eyebrows raising and then returning to their neutral position indicates the boundary between the two phases. In this way the relative clause and the main clause are construed to be in relation to one another.

Another facial display for identification of the nominal referent is squinted eyes. Accompanying raised brows and the point, squinted eyes evoke old information and indicate that the nominal has been previously mentioned in the discourse. The interlocutor's attention is thus directed toward this previously identified entity in the discourse by squinted eyes in the relative clause.

Analyzing the remaining relative clause markers (upper cheek tension, body shifting, and a head shake) is beyond the scope of this study, therefore these are left for future studies. Also, more in-depth study is needed for categorizing different relative clause constructions in ZEI along with a more fine-grained semantic analysis of each marker in these various relative clauses.

Transcription key

English words are glosses for ZEI signs. If more than one word is used to gloss a sign, the words are separated by an underscore. Letters separated by dashes indicate fingerspelling. Relative clauses are in bold. Square brackets indicate a phrase accompanied by one or more NMMs: [. . .]-BR refers to raised brows; ES means eye squint; CHEEK-TENSION means the cheek muscles are raised and tensed.

References

Andrews, Avery D. 2007 [1985]. Relative clauses. In Timothy Shopen (ed.), *Language Typology and Syntactic Description. Vol. 2: Complex constructions*, 2nd edn., 206–236. Cambridge: Cambridge University Press.

Branchini, Chiara. 2006. *The grammar of Italian Sign Language with a study about its restrictive relative clauses*. Venezia: Università Ca' Foscari MA thesis.

Branchini, Chiara & Caterina Donati. 2009. Relatively different: Italian Sign Language relative clauses in a typological perspective. In Anikó Lipták (ed.), *Correlatives Cross-linguistically*, 157–191. Amsterdam/Philadelphia: John Benjamins.

Branchini, Chiara & Meltem Kelepir. 2017. Coordination & subordination. In Josep Quer, Carlo Cecchetto, Caterina Donati, Carlo Geraci, Meltem Kelepir, Roland Pfau & Markus Steinbach (eds.), *SignGram Blueprint: A Guide to Sign Language Grammar Writing*, 404–490. Berlin/Boston: de Gruyter Mouton. https://doi.org/10.1515/9781501511806

Brunelli, Michele. 2011. *Antisymmetry and sign languages: A comparison between NGT and LIS*. Amsterdam: University of Amsterdam dissertation.
Chafe, Wallace L (ed.). 1980. *The Pear Stories: Cognitive, Cultural, and Linguistic Aspects of Narrative Production*. Norwood, NJ: Ablex.
Coerts, Jane. 1992. *Nonmanual grammatical markers: An analysis of interrogatives, negations and topicalisations in Sign Language of the Netherlands*. Amsterdam: University of Amsterdam dissertation.
Comrie, Bernard. 1989. *Language Universals and Linguistic Typology: Syntax and Morphology*. Chicago: University of Chicago Press.
Coppola, Marie & Anne Senghas. 2010. Deixis in an emerging sign language. In Diane Brentari (ed.), *Sign Languages*, 543–569. Cambridge: Cambridge University Press.
Cormier, Kearsy, Adam Schembri & Bencie Woll. 2013. Pronouns and pointing in sign languages. *Lingua* 137. 230–247.
Coulter, Geoffrey R. 1983. A conjoined analysis of American Sign Language relative clauses. *Discourse Processes* 6(3). 305–318.
Dachkovsky, Svetlana. 2020. From a demonstrative to a relative clause marker: Grammaticalization of pointing signs in Israeli Sign Language. *Sign Language & Linguistics* 23(1–2). 142–170.
Dachkovsky, Svetlana & Wendy Sandler. 2009. Visual intonation in the prosody of a sign language. *Language and Speech* 52(2–3). 287–314.
de Vries, Mark. 2018. Relative clauses in syntax. In *Oxford Research Encyclopedia of Linguistics*. https://dx.doi.org/10.1093/acrefore/9780199384655.013.56
Fontana, Josep M. 1990. Is ASL like Diegueño or Diegueño like ASL? A study of internally headed relative clauses in ASL. In Ceil Lucas (ed.), *Sign Language Research: Theoretical Issues*, 238–255. Washington, DC: Gallaudet University Press.
Guity, Ardavan. 2022. *Esharani grammatical sketch: An initial description of the lexicon and grammar*. Washington, DC: Gallaudet University dissertation.
Gundel, Jeanette K. 1988. Universals of topic-comment structure. In Michael Hammond, Edith A. Moravcsik & Jessica Wirth (eds.), *Studies in Syntactic Typology*, 209–239. Amsterdam/Philadelphia: John Benjamins.
Janzen, Terry. 1998. *Topicality in ASL: Information ordering, constituent structure, and the function of topic marking*. Albuquerque NM: University of New Mexico dissertation.
Janzen, Terry. 1999. The grammaticization of topics in American Sign Language. *Studies in Language* 23(2). 271–306.
Janzen, Terry. 2017. Composite utterances in a signed language: Topic constructions and perspective-taking in ASL. *Cognitive Linguistics* 28(3). 511–538.
Kendon, Adam. 2010. Pointing and the problem of 'gesture': Some reflections. *Revista di Psicolinguistica Applicata* 10(3). 19–30.
Kimmelman, Vadim. 2015. Information structure in Russian Sign Language and Sign Language of the Netherlands (dissertation abstract, University of Amsterdam, 2014). *Sign Language & Linguistics* 18(1). 142–150.
Kubus, Okan. 2016. *Relative clause constructions in Turkish Sign Language*. Hamburg: Universität Hamburg dissertation.
Kubus, Okan & Derya Nuhbalaoğlu. 2018. The challenge of marking relative clauses in Turkish Sign Language. *Dilbilim Araştırmaları Dergisi*, 29(1). 139–160.
Langacker, Ronald W. 1991. *Foundations of Cognitive Grammar*, vol. 2: *Descriptive Application*. Stanford, CA: Stanford University Press.
Langacker, Ronald W. 2008. *Cognitive Grammar: A Basic Introduction*. Oxford: Oxford University Press.

Langacker, Ronald W. 2009. *Investigations in Cognitive Grammar.* Berlin/New York: De Gruyter Mouton.
Langacker, Ronald W. 2013. Reference-point constructions. *Mouton Classics: From Syntax to Cognition. From Phonology to Text*, 413–450. Berlin/Boston: de Gruyter Mouton.
Langacker, Ronald W. 2016. *Nominal Structure in Cognitive Grammar.* Lubin, Poland: Marie-Curie Skłodowska University Press.
Liddell, Scott K. 1978. An introduction to relative clauses in ASL. In Patricia Siple (ed.), *Understanding Language Through Sign Language Research*, 59–90. New York: Academic Press.
Liddell, Scott K. 1980. *American Sign Language Syntax.* The Hague: Mouton.
Liddell, Scott K. 2003. *Grammar, Gesture and Meaning in American Sign Language.* Cambridge: Cambridge University Press.
Martínez, Rocío & Sherman Wilcox. 2019. Pointing and placing: Nominal grounding in Argentine Sign Language. *Cognitive Linguistics* 30(1). 85–121.
Meier, Richard P. & Diane Lillo-Martin. 2013. The points of language. *Humana.Mente Journal of Philosophical Studies* 24, 151–176.
Morford, Jill P., Barbara Shaffer, Naomi Shin, Paul Twitchell & Bettie T. Petersen. 2019. An Exploratory Study of ASL Demonstratives. *Languages* 4(4), 80. doi:10.3390/languages4040080
Mosella Sanz, Marta. 2011. The position of fronted and postposed relative clauses in Catalan Sign Language. Paper presented at Formal and Experimental Approaches to Sign Language Theory (FEAST), Venice, 20–22 June 2011.
Perniss, Pamela M., Roland Pfau & Markus Steinbach. 2007. Can't you see the difference? Sources of variation in sign language structure. In Pamela Perniss, Roland Pfau & Markus Steinbach (eds.), *Visible Variation: Comparative Studies on Sign Language Structure*, 1–34. Berlin/New York: Mouton de Gruyter.
Pfau, Roland & Markus Steinbach. 2005. Relative clauses in German Sign Language: Extraposition and reconstruction. In Leah Bateman & Cherlon Ussery (eds.), *Proceeding of the Thirty-Fifth Annual Meeting of the North East Linguistic Society (NELS 35), Vol. 2*, 507–521. Amherst, MA: Graduate Linguistic Student Association.
Pfau, Roland & Markus Steinbach. 2016. Complex sentences in sign languages: Modality – typology – discourse. In Roland Pfau, Markus Steinbach & Annika Herrmann (eds.), *A Matter of Complexity: Subordination in Sign Languages*, 1–35. Berlin/Boston: De Gruyter Mouton.
Schilperoord, Joost & Arie Verhagen. 1998. Conceptual dependency and the clausal structure of discourse. In Jean-Pierre Koenig (ed.), *Discourse and Cognition: Bridging the Gap.* 141–163. Stanford, CA: CSLI.
Siyavoshi, Sara. 2019a. *The expression of modality in Iranian Sign Language (ZEI).* Albuquerque NM: University of New Mexico dissertation.
Siyavoshi, Sara. 2019b. Hands and faces: The expression of modality in ZEI, Iranian Sign Language. *Cognitive Linguistics* 30(4). 655–686.
Sze, Felix. 2009. Topic constructions in Hong Kong Sign Language (dissertation abstract, University of Bristol 2008). *Sign Language & Linguistics* 12(2). 222–227.
Sze, Felix. 2011. Nonmanual markings for topic constructions in Hong Kong Sign Language. *Sign Language & Linguistics* 14(1). 115–147.
Tang, Gladys, Prudence Lau & Jafi Lee. 2010. Strategies for relativization in HKSL. Paper presented at Theoretical Issues in Sign Language Research (TISLR) 10, Purdue University, West Lafayette, IN, 30 September – 2 October, 2010.
Tang, Gladys & Prudence Lau. 2012. Coordination and subordination. In Roland Pfau, Markus Steinbach & Bencie Woll (eds.), *Sign Language: An International Handbook*, 340–364. Berlin/Boston: De Gruyter Mouton.

Verhagen, Arie. 2001. Subordination and discourse segmentation revisited, or: Why matrix clauses may be more dependent than complements. In Ted J. M. Sanders, Joost Schilperoord & Wilbert Spooren (eds.), *Text Representation: Linguistic and Psycholinguistic Aspects*, 337–357. Amsterdam/Philadelphia: John Benjamins.

Wilbur, Ronnie. 2017. Internally-headed relative clauses in sign languages. *Glossa: A Journal of General Linguistics*, *2*(1), 25. 1–34. https://doi.org/10.5334/gjgl.183

Wilcox, Sherman & Corrine Occhino. 2016. Constructing signs: Place as a symbolic structure in signed languages. *Cognitive Linguistics* 27(3). 371–404.

Wilcox, Sherman & Phyllis Wilcox. 1995. The gestural expression of modality in ASL. In Joan Bybee & Suzanne Fleischman (eds.), *Modality in Grammar and Discourse*, 135–162. Amsterdam/Philadelphia: John Benjamins.

VI Concluding commentary

Adam Kendon
Language in the light of sign and gesture

1 Introduction

As Penny Boyes Braem and Virginia Volterra show in their chapter (this volume), developments in understanding signed languages are having important consequences for the notion of "language". Doctrines considered fundamental in linguistics such as "duality of patterning" (see Pietrandrea, this volume) or the "arbitrariness of the linguistic sign" are now in doubt (see Russo and Pietrandrea, and especially, Langacker, this volume), claims about "language autonomy" are also being questioned.

This is not only because of newer understandings of signing; spoken language students have raised these issues too. Research on signing has raised them more urgently, perhaps because of worries about whether signing is properly linguistic or not. The fear was that, if signing depended upon "gesture" or "pantomime", it could not qualify as linguistic and those who advocated its use in deaf education would find this difficult to justify. Whereas in the early decades of the nineteenth century signing was widely used and admired in deaf education on both sides of the Atlantic, it came under severe attack at the infamous 1880 Milan conference of deaf educators (Facchini 1985). Thereafter, using signing in deaf education was suppressed, with unfortunate consequences for deaf persons; academic interest in signing also declined, and what little there was mainly aimed to confirm its shortcomings (Baynton 1996). After 1960 all this changed. In that year William Stokoe showed that signing among the deaf had structural features like those of spoken languages. It is our understanding of signed languages gained from this insight and from research that followed it that now challenges some long held notions in linguistics.

Much more recently (onwards from the 1980s) "gesture studies" emerged (Kendon 2007). These made it clear that the body movements speakers make when speaking are integral to their utterance productions and how these utterances achieve meaning. Does this mean that these movements are a part of language? Further, since these bodily expressions of speakers are often similar in function (and sometimes also in form) to those used by signers, does this have implications for understanding signed languages in relation to spoken languages? What follows is a commentary on these matters, prompted in part by some of the chapters in this book.

Adam Kendon, Cherry Hinton, Cambridge, United Kingdom

https://doi.org/10.1515/9783110703788-017

2 How signing came to be regarded as "linguistic"

When, in the late 1950s, William Stokoe saw that the visible bodily actions his deaf students used for communication must be serving them as talking serves the hearing, he decided to see if these had structural features comparable to those of spoken language. To do this, he analyzed the patterns of communicative manual action observed among his deaf students by applying the framework developed in American structural linguistics as expounded by Trager and Smith (1951). He demonstrated, to the satisfaction of many, that the units of expression being used could be seen as if they were composed of contrasting features, in much the way that this had been shown for spoken words. He called these features *cheremes*, since, according to his analysis, they were functionally parallel to *phonemes*. Stokoe thus demonstrated that signing had *duality of patterning*, a property considered criterial for a system to be considered as language.[1]

Once Stokoe's work (Stokoe 1960) came to be more widely known, signed language research began to expand. In its early stages, much was undertaken to establish further features of signing showing it to be linguistic. No one disputes this today, yet, as Boyes Braem and Volterra (this volume) show, there is much in signing that does not fit the structural linguistic framework. This is important in the debate about what can and cannot count as "language".

3 Origins of a linguistic conception of "language"

Although language has been an object of fascination and reflection since ancient times, and was, in Ancient Greece, an important object of inquiry, the idea that its study should constitute a separate branch of learning in the modern sense only emerged in the middle of the nineteenth century. Before then, the study of language was pursued because understanding it was useful in philosophical inquiry and in historical and antiquarian studies. Language practice was also studied, as in rhetoric, or in teaching a language. The idea that it should be studied for its own sake only developed after Europeans had encountered Sanskrit. Sanskrit had been shown to have features in common with languages in Europe, including Greek, Latin and the Germanic tongues. This was interpreted to mean that these languages, including Sanskrit, had all differentiated from an earlier common ancestral language (later called Indo-European). This prompted the beginning of comparative philology

---

[1] Maher (1996) is a history and assessment of Stokoe's work and reactions to it. For American structuralism see Hymes and Fought (1981) and Andresen (1990).

which investigated historical changes in languages with a view to understanding their genealogical relationships.

The work in comparative philology led to the discovery that the changes that languages undergo with time, at least in respect to their phonology, were governed by fixed laws internal to these languages. Languages thus seemed to be autonomous systems, organized according to their own principles. This suggested that there could be an independent "science of language" which, by the end of the nineteenth century was called "linguistics".[2]

For this new "linguistics" to become an independent science it was necessary to show that its object of inquiry was distinct and would be investigated according to its own methods. Various definitions were put forward stating that the task of the language scientist was to explain the general principles or laws of language, but there was one formulation that came to be very influential and was widely accepted as clarifying what the "new linguistics" was all about.

This was put forward by Ferdinand de Saussure in his posthumously published *Cours*.[3] A distinction was drawn between *diachronic* studies of how languages change historically, and *synchronic* studies, which investigate the systemic organization of a language as used by speakers in a language community in a current period: the aim is to account for how linguistic signs operate in relation to one another as if within a unified system which does not change with time.

The unified system of language here envisaged, or *langue*, as Saussure called it, is an *abstraction*, it is important to remember. It can never be directly observed, but only inferred from observations of actual utterances—Saussure called this *parole*—but also from the judgements of native speakers about the correct way to say things.

4 The importance of a conceptual boundary for language

Saussure's idea of *langue* as the proper object of inquiry for the new "linguistics" appears to have "crystallized" for many language scientists what was distinctive

---

[2] There are many histories of linguistics. Morpurgo Davies (1998) and Turner (2014) have been useful for me. Alter (2005) gives details about the establishment of "linguistics" as a new scientific discipline.
[3] Ferdinand de Saussure's *Cours de linguistique énérale* was edited by Charles Bally and Albert Sechehaye from notes left by Saussure and by some of his students, published in Paris in 1916 with several subsequent editions. I rely on the annotated translation by Roy Harris (Saussure 1983). Sanders (2004) is a useful guide.

about the object of their work. This was first felt in Europe. In the early decades of the twentieth century linguistics grew vigorously with different schools emerging, such as in Prague, in Copenhagen, and in London, who all acknowledged Saussure although diverging from him in various ways. They all were dedicated to investigating the properties of language as an a-historical system.

In America, the analysis of language at first developed separately from Europe, largely because linguists in America were dealing with Indigenous languages, unwritten and unknown, and they were not, like their colleagues in Europe, inheritors of the older historical philological tradition. The pioneering work of Boas, Sapir, and Bloomfield, which established the American structural linguistic approach, also implied that general principles operated in language systems. By the 1950s the importance of Saussure was also recognized, and there, too, if only retrospectively, the idea of *langue* as the object of linguistic inquiry was acknowledged.[4]

Thus it was agreed on both sides of the Atlantic that the science of language was after an account of the *language system*, whether viewed as *langue* in Saussure's terms, as the *patterns* that were the guidelines for speakers for utterance construction as the American structuralists might have put it (e.g., Gleason 1961), or the *competence* or "I-Language" as members of the Chomsky school would come to say.

One implication of this notion of a language system is that speakers are considered to have a sense of the *correctness* or *incorrectness* of linguistic expressions. That is, there are ideal patterns which *ought* to be followed. The idea of the language system is thus also ideological and normative, despite the claims of the new linguists that this was not so. This idea of the language system is thus something quite different from a regularity of nature arrived at inductively.

For this reason, the boundary between what can be "in" as linguistic and what is "out" was doubly important. It was important because linguists wanted to establish that they studied something separate and autonomous, with its own methods and theory. It is also important because there are always pressures on individuals to "speak correctly". The boundary between what is correct and what isn't needs to be clearly maintained.

So far as spoken languages are concerned, being clear about what belongs as "language" and what not seems clear enough. Linguists need concern themselves only with speech and much of what is speech can be written down. As Harris (1980, 1981) and Linell (2005), among others, have pointed out, it is largely what can be written down that is the actual material that linguists study. Writing, developed

---

4 See Morpurgo Davies (2004), Falk (2004), and Puech (2004), all referenced in Sanders (2004). See also Graffi (2013). For the Americans, see Andresen (1990).

over the course of millennia, provides a convenient abstraction from spoken language, so the question of whether something is or is not what a linguist should be interested in is, one might say, already settled.

For linguists dealing with signing, however, where only the kinesic medium is involved, it is much less clear where the language boundary is. No generally accepted writing system for signed languages yet exists,[5] so there is no pre-established guide as to what might or might not belong in a language that is signed. As a result, there is room for debate about what aspects of signing can be considered properly "linguistic". In the early post-Stokoe era, when the claim for the linguistic status of signing still had to be justified, there was a strong inclination to disattend or play down the importance of features that could not be accommodated in the structuralist framework, especially iconicity and facial expressions and movements involving the body beyond the hands (Wilcox 2004). The volume edited by Lynn Friedman (1977), in which the importance of iconicity in ASL was asserted, was considered "controversial" (Siple 1979). Whereas in Klima and Bellugi (1979) iconicity in signing was acknowledged, it was regarded as "paradoxical" and studies therein were described that showed that it was not important for the production or the understanding of signing (Todd 1980).

5 Criterial features of language in the structural tradition

In the structural tradition there are four features commonly regarded as criterial for a code system to be counted as a "language".[6] These are: (1) the arbitrariness of the linguistic sign, (2) its discrete or particulate character and (3) its segmental structure, from which follows (4) the possibility of "double articulation" or "duality of patterning". Before discussing these I first will remark on Saussure's point that linguistic signifiers signify categories created by the language and not by things in the external world. It is because of this that the linguistic sign is arbitrary. The doctrines of the signifier's discreteness, segmentability and duality of patterning, were given emphasis later. We shall see how developments in understanding signing may call for some reassessment of these features.

---

5 See Antinoro Pizzuto and Garcia (this volume).
6 See Hockett's (1960) design features.

5.1 Saussure on the nature of the "signified"

In regard to the Saussurean notion of the *linguistic sign* it is important to note that Saussure insisted that the *signified*, inseparably linked as it is to its *signifier*, is a *concept*, a humanly created *category*, not something that exists in the external world, independent of human judgement. It is important to understand this, for then we can properly appreciate an important aspect of his doctrine of the arbitrariness of the linguistic sign. Saussure argued that there is no motivated or causal relation between signifier and signified. This follows from the idea that the concepts or categories that are discriminated as a language is established are discriminated by the language users, and are not determined by external properties in the outside world. Saussure's well known example establishing this point is the way in which, in English, there is a word for a certain animal, the *sheep*. When the meat of that animal is to be eaten the English speaker talks of *mutton*. In French, in contrast, there is only one word, *mouton*, which means both "sheep" and its meat, when it is to be eaten. The French language is free, as is the English language, to categorize things in whatever way it likes. Doubtless, we might investigate the history of how this difference between English and French came about, but there is nothing about sheep and the meat we get from it that will determine this difference in categorization. As we shall see, arbitrariness of this nature, which Pietandrea (this volume) terms "radical arbitrariness", implies nothing about the *forms* signifiers may have. As we shall see, these can be iconic without compromising this principle.

5.2 The doctrine of arbitrariness and the problem of iconicity

Saussure also maintained that the arbitrariness of the linguistic sign meant that the form of the sign is not constrained by features of what it signifies. For example, in regard to the signifier for the animal "dog", there is nothing "doggy" about the word *dog* any more than there is anything "doggy" about *chien*, or *cane*, or *Hund* (French, Italian, German, respectively), and he regarded apparent exceptions, as in names for birds, as in *cuckoo*, or onomatopoetic forms such as *bang* or *crash* or *quack*, to be too few to be important. Today we know that, on the contrary, signifiers in both signed and spoken languages often have features which can be seen as "mapping on" to features of what they signify. Furthermore, they can vary in the degree to which they do so. No matter the degree to which a signifier has an iconic character, however, it still remains arbitrary in relation to its signified, insofar as what is signified is a concept or category which is established by the language, and not constrained by what is external to it.

In the light of this, the worry that students of signing had when they saw that signs were often iconic was a worry that they need never have had. Signs can be blatantly iconic, but how they categorize the world, thought, experiences, is determined by the makers of the language, not by what is external to them. Signifiers that are iconic therefore do not violate the doctrine of arbitrariness. There never was any need to play down the iconicity of the signifier or to try to find ways in which it could be denied linguistic significance.

Iconicity in signed language, it is agreed, is pervasive and no longer upsets signed language linguists. Iconicity in spoken signifiers, on the other hand, has been a matter of debate since the days of Plato (Genette 1995), but since the beginning of the "new linguistics" it has usually been dismissed, as Saussure did himself, as being too occasional to be of interest from a linguistic point of view. At least since the publication of *Sound Symbolism* (Hinton, Nichols and Ohala 1994), however, much work has now shown that iconicity of various kinds is widespread in spoken signifiers, as may be seen in the collection edited by Raffaele Simone (1995), the work of Janis Nuckolls (1996, 1999), the recent review by Perniss and Vigliocco (2014), Dingemanse, et al. (2015), and a recent study by Blasi et al. (2016), among much else. The work of Marcus Perlman and colleagues is also important, demonstrating the extensive depictive potential of the human voice (Perlman 2017; Ćwiek et al. 2021). Iconicity in grammar, at least since Haiman (1985), is also widely acknowledged (cf. Langacker, this volume).

Highly pertinent, also, is the work on ideophones or expressives. These are words that function as *depictions*. They are phonologically different from the other elements of the languages they occur in, and seem extra-grammatical. An illuminating treatment is Dingemanse (2011), and see also Voeltz and Kilian-Hatz (2001), Haiman (2018), and Akita and Pardeshi (2019). Long overlooked in Western linguistics, perhaps because they are sparse in Indo-European languages, ideophones are now considered a major word class in many languages. They are abundant in languages of Africa, of the Pacific, and of Asia, for example in Japanese and Korean.

Given this, it seems reasonable to conclude that creating signifiers that in some way depict what they signify is a fundamental process of language, whether vocal or kinesic. Talmy Givón was right in declaring: ". . . we ought to consider iconicity the truly general case in the coding, representation and communication of experience, and symbols a mere extreme case on the iconic scale" (Givón 1985: 215).

5.3 Segmentation and the doctrine of duality of patterning

As we have already noted, Stokoe claimed to have shown that signs used in the signed language he studied could be analyzed as if they were composed from a limited repertoire of kinesic forms, which could be considered as discrete segments.[7] Signs, Stokoe showed, are composed of sub-sign units, meaning that they had *double articulation* or *duality of patterning*. According to prevailing linguistic doctrine, this was a key feature that any code must have if it was to be regarded as a "language". Stokoe's demonstration was important in convincing skeptics that signing was truly a *linguistic* form of expression.

Yet it was not so very many years later that some began to see that these "sub-sign" units, or *cheremes* (now usually called "phonemes"[8]), had features that reflect the sign's meaning. If one grouped together different signs which shared some aspect of their meanings, they were often found to have form characteristics in common. For example, signs related in meaning to mental activities tend to have in common a locus of articulation in space close to the side or front of the head; signs that related in meaning to horizontal flat things, a table, a sheet of paper, a floor, would use an open palm-down or flat handshape; signs with meanings related to power or grasping used a closed or closing hand or a fist; and so on. As shown by Friedman (1977), Boyes Braem (1981) and others (Occhino's chapter, this volume, provides a review), these aspects can be indicative of properties of whatever it is that is being signified.

Stokoe also recognized this, and later proposed "semantic phonology" (Stokoe 1991) according to which signs are not considered to be compositions of separable kinesic segments, but as actions which, in virtue of how the hand is shaped and what it does as the signer moves it about, can represent in kinesic form features of the concept it signifies. They do not have a "phonology" in the sense understood in spoken language linguistics and do not show "duality of patterning" in the way that spoken meaning units are said to do. As Occhino herself notes, signers see meaning in aspects of the sign which calls into question their meaninglessness.

The attempt to establish a sign "phonology" that matches "phonology" for spoken language was an attempt to align observations to a preconceived conception of language structure. Once signing was seen as functionally just like talking, there was an incentive to elevate it to the status of a *language*. Within the theoretical framework prevailing at the time the way to do this was to show an equivalence to spoken language, not functionally but in formal or structural terms. Stokoe's demonstration that signs could be analyzed into separately identifiable features meant that in signing we had something equivalent to a structural feature con-

---

[7] Stokoe recognized an important difference between *cheremes* and *phonemes*, namely that cheremes are present in the sign simultaneously, in a spoken morpheme phonemes are successive. This is still roughly correct, but later work suggests some modifications.
[8] Mistakenly, in my view.

sidered essential for a system to be a language. On this view, signs were judged as equivalent to morphemes in spoken language.

As work on signed language has proceeded, and with the recognition that iconicity in signs is a core feature, and that enactment and depiction and expressive modification are also integral to signing, it seems clear that the way most signs are formed and become established is an *emergent* process. Depictive bodily configurations and movement patterns undergo performative abbreviation and form modification as they are adjusted to fit within an already established pattern of sign making. The "duality of patterning" that we can perceive in signed language is a consequence of a theoretically inspired analytic procedure. It is not an account of how signs come about, nor of how they work in practice within the language when in use by signers.

Similarly in spoken language, as Albano Leoni's (2009) historical review shows, many spoken language phonologists now understand that speakers do not construct their words, nor do recipients apprehend them, as if they are composites of discretely separable units with no meaning. Speakers produce words as complex action configurations and listeners apprehend them as acoustic gestalts. When there is doubt about something that was said, speakers and listeners may decompose an uttered word, typically down to the level of the syllable, rather less often to the level of minimal sound segments. An existing unit of speech or sign can be analyzed into segments, but these segments result from a *post hoc* analysis and are probably not really there in the unit as produced by the speaker or signer.[9]

6 "Gesture" and "sign"

Before the linguistic status of signed languages had been proposed and accepted, no clear distinction was made between "sign" and "gesture". If one was talking about expressive bodily actions, especially of the forearms and hands, the terms "gesture" and "sign" were used almost as if they were synonyms.[10] The deaf were said to be using "gesture language" or using "signs", and this meant much the same thing. After signing gained recognition as linguistic, however, the bodily actions used for talk among the deaf were called "signs" while "gesture" was to mean only the visible bodily actions of hearers. "Signing" was declared to be a form of lan-

---

[9] The analytic procedure showing minimal segments and duality of patterning historically depends upon alphabetic writing. See Aronoff (1992).
[10] Earlier discussions are Kendon (1988, 2004: Chapters 1 and 2, 2008, 2013). See also Goldin-Meadow and Brentari (2017), Dotter (2018) and Müller (2018).

guage, whereas "gesturing" was something speakers did and it was not a part of "language". Between signing and gesturing a "cataclysmic break" was declared (Singleton, Goldin-Meadow and McNeill 1995).

After the publication in 1992 of David McNeill's book, *Hand and Mind*, the question was asked: if such visible bodily action was a part of using language in speakers, should we not also expect this for signers? Signers ought to gesture when signing, just as speakers gesture when speaking. A paper about this appeared in 1999, in which signers were described as inserting emotional displays into their discourse, or moving their bodies expressively, while making lexical signs with their hands (Emmorey 1999). A paper called "Gesture in Signing" (Duncan 2005) described users of Taiwanese Sign Language (Táiwān Shǒuyǔ) re-telling episodes from an animated cartoon.[11] In using a "small animal" classifier when describing the actions of the cat in this cartoon, it was observed how the signers sometimes modified the handshape away from the standard version, for example, adding features showing how the cat changed his body posture when he was to climb inside a drainpipe. The way the modifications were done, it was noted, was different for each signer. These seemed to be idiosyncratic and thus were deemed to be "gestural" rather than linguistic. Duncan suggested that this illustrated how a signer can gesture while signing, just as a speaker can gesture while speaking. She writes that signs can have a gesture "overlay", following an expression from Emmorey and Herzig (2003) who, she reports, suggest that iconic gestures may occur as "gradient variation on a handshape morpheme" (Duncan 2005: 284).

Duncan also reviews other studies, which show how signers use other forms of expression not regarded as linguistic, such as work by Liddell (2003), Emmorey and Herzig (2003), Liddell and Metzger (1998) and others. She refers to the phenomena they describe, including what is observed in classifier constructions and constructed action, again as analog or gradient, but she also calls it "gestural". For instance, she discusses Schembri, Jones, and Burham's (2005) study which compared speakers and signers as they enacted classifier constructions depicting movement trajectories of animals or vehicles. They found that both groups did this in very similar ways (although, unsurprisingly, the signers used standard "classifier" handshapes while the non-signers did not). Duncan writes that the authors "interpret these results as evidence for an analogic, gestural dimension of patterning in the movement and location components of these classifier constructions..." (Duncan 2005: 283).

---

[11] The "Tweety Bird" cartoon in which the cat Sylvester is always trying to catch the little canary Tweety Bird, but is always outwitted. This animated film has been much used by McNeill and his students. People were filmed re-telling it and often used depictive hand movements while doing so.

It seems to me that, in all these accounts, it is not only not necessary to add the epithet "gestural"; there are also drawbacks to doing so. In all of these examples it is surely sufficient just to write of these movements and sign performance modifications, as analogic or gradient, or to explain, as Duncan also sometimes does, that the movements referred to are mimetic. To say, in addition, that they are "gestural" does not further clarify our understanding of what these movements are like or how they are expressive. On the contrary, such usage can make understanding less precise and it may introduce theoretical problems, as well.

In Duncan's paper, as in the chapter by Emmorey (1999) we have cited, "gesture" is being used in opposition to "sign". This is in accordance with the practice that developed, as I earlier indicated, once signing had been shown to have linguistic credentials. However, if "gesture" is used in this way it leads to the idea that there is a separate "gesture system", categorically distinct from "language" and I think this is a mistake.

For example, Duncan claims that observations of handshapes being expressively modified away from their standard forms can be understood as signs being "overlaid" by gesture, thus she implies that the "sign" is held to be a discrete, fixed unit and the expressive modification of it is an "add-on". It is difficult see how this is justified. There is no separate "gesture" being made here. It is enough to say there is a modification of the signing action which shows something of how the cat adjusted his posture to meet the odd situation in the cartoon. Modifications like this are widely used in signing (see Brennan 1992, especially pp.79–91). There is no need for any sort of separate concept of "gesture." It is much more straightforward to say that the signer is altering the manner in which the unit of expression is being done, adjusting it to suit current expressive requirements and expectations.

Other studies of sign modifications similar to Duncan's have been published which are interpreted in this other way, rather than saying that signs can have gestures added to them or can be overlaid by them. In a study by Orit Fuks (2014), Israeli Sign Language (Shassi) users were asked to sign several different scenarios in which there was something referred to that differed in shape, size, or number, from one part of the scenario to another. It was observed that, in all the examples, the signers modified the lexical sign used for the object or objects that changed in size, shape or number in the scenario, so as to depict the change in the referent's features from its first mention to the second.

These depicting modifications, similar to the alterations Duncan had observed, Fuks regards as showing that in signing the signer may manipulate a sign "when constructing the utterance to enhance or enrich the unit's meanings in discourse" (2014: 210). She argues for an approach which would examine "how different types of semiotic features [i.e., gradient, dynamic, more static, discrete] are reciprocally synchronized in the utterance construction stage to achieve efficient unified semantic ensembles" (2014: 211).

Another study, somewhat similar, is reported by Lindsay Ferrara and Rolf Halvorsen (2017), who observed users of Norwegian Sign Language (norsk tegnspråk). Here signers were telling the story of *Frog, Where Are You?* (Mayer 1969).[12] They describe how a signer, re-telling a part of the story where the boy falls in a pond and has to swim to the shore, shows aspects of the boy's effort in doing so, by modifications in how the "swimming" sign is performed. In another episode, where the boy falls asleep with his pet dog, another signer uses modifications to show the boy's relief at getting rest and how he sleeps "peacefully". These are done by modifying how the lexical signs are performed, and also by elements of facial actions and head positions. In their conclusion they say "Our goal with these examples was to shift the discussion away from distinctions between the conventional and the non-conventional or the linguistic from the gestural. Instead we hope to promote languaging as a dynamic mode of interaction that recruits from a semiotically diverse repertoire that is manipulated creatively in context to describe and depict meanings" (Ferrara and Halvorsen 2017: 390).

In both these publications we see expressed a view that, in signing, the signer uses a diverse repertoire of elements which can be manipulated in context to adjust nuances of meaning, through depiction and other means, which are integral components of the signing performance. In this performance the signer can draw from the full range of their expressive resources, which are orchestrated, attuned, modified and adjusted according to whatever the communicative aim of the utterance might be. The word "gesture" can thus be done without when describing these phenomena.

The word "gesture" can also be a problem because it has (at least in English) so many different but connected meanings that it is difficult to use it precisely. Unless writers are prepared to be explicit about which meaning they intend and can stick to this, the word can leave a reader confused. For example, an article by Goldin-Meadow and Brentari (2017) seeks to explain the interrelationships between gesture and sign, reviewing much recent work. If the different uses of "gesture" found therein are compared, one is left uncertain as to just what the authors mean by it. Thus, they first define "gesture" as "manual movements that speakers produce when they talk" (introductory section, paragraph 3, p. 1), then later they say that forms in signing that are "analog and gradient" are "gestural" (4.2, paragraph 3, p. 8). Then again, they say that hearing non-signers "can invent gestures that resemble signs" (4.2, paragraph 6, p. 8). They also add that "there is gesture in the oral

---

12 This story, told in pictures, shows the adventures of a small boy when he goes out looking for his pet frog which had escaped from his house.

modality" (7.2, paragraph 6, p. 15). One is left wondering just what is meant (see Kendon 2017 for additional commentary).

In the Oxford English Dictionary (second edition, 1989) the first meaning of "gesture" as it is used in our current era (Definition 4) is given as "a movement of the body or any part of it that is expressive of thought or feeling".[13] If it were agreed in linguistic and related discussions to use "gesture" in just this way, to say that it means any visible bodily movement used as intended or wilful expression, either on its own, or in conjunction with vocal expression, then "sign" in a signed language becomes a *specialized variety* of "gesture". This leaves us with the problem of explaining in what ways it is specialized, but it does not seem so very difficult to do so.

This approach, which is implied in Kendon (1988) and which I used in my book, *Gesture: Visible Action as Utterance* (Kendon 2004), does not send us into investigations looking for gesturing in signing, worrying about whether an item is a "gesture" or a "sign", nor does it suggest that "gesture" is a separate system which "interfaces" with sign (Brentari 2019: 101–111). Rather, it invites us to undertake careful descriptions of the different kinds of semiotic forms we find, as signers (or speakers) use visible bodily action when they are *languaging*, as we might say. More generally, *languagers* make signifying use of visible bodily action in many different ways, one of which is to fashion conventionalized forms and, if only the kinesic modality is in use, then repertoires or vocabularies of conventionalized forms will develop which can be part of a shared communication system which, if it reaches a certain level of complexity, may be called a signed language.

7 Conclusion

At the end of his book *Grammar, Gesture and Meaning in American Sign Language* Liddell writes that "spoken and signed languages both make use of multiple types of semiotic elements in the language signal" and suggests that "our understanding of what constitutes language has been much too narrow" (Liddell 2003: 362). The concept of language he refers to here is the one that linguists have used in their discipline ever since it emerged in the nineteenth century, following the achievements of comparative philology, as already described. Of necessity, the comparative philologists only worked with languages in their written form. As already mentioned,

---

13 See https://www-oed-com.uml.idm.oclc.org/view/Entry/77985?rskey=iUiRIy&result=1&isAdvanced=false#eid

as Harris (1980, 1981) and Linell (2005) have argued, using written language as the first data for analyzing language has deeply infected linguists' thinking.

From the time when linguistics became a separate discipline, many writers have expressed dissatisfaction with the concept of language implied when (in effect) admitting only what can be written determines what is linguistic. Scott Liddell is certainly not the first to do so. Edward Tylor (1832–1917), important in the history of cultural anthropology and deeply knowledgeable of comparative philology, saw that the conception of language this work promoted would not accommodate features he believed important. In his book *Researches in to the Early History of Mankind and the Development of Civilization* ([1865] 1878) he devotes six chapters to language which, as he says, gives humans the power to utter their thoughts. It is a central element that makes human civilization possible. However, for him *uttering* is not only a matter of words. He says when we use this word we must attach to it "a sense more fully conformable to its etymology. . . . To *utter* a thought is literally to put it outside us, as to *express* it is to squeeze it out." This is "the wonderful process by which man, *by some bodily action* can. . .make other men's minds reproduce almost exactly the workings of his own. . ." (Tylor 1878: 14, my italics).[14] That is, for Tylor, uttering can be done not only by words but by visible bodily actions and by graphically inscribed pictures. He shows this by devoting chapters both to "gesture language" and to "picture language", in which he discusses what was then known of "picture writing" among the Indigenous North Americans and the Maya and Aztec of central America.

In volume one of his *Primitive Culture* (1871), there are two chapters on language where he gives his view of what it includes, and he warns against the view held by those who eliminate from speech "all the effects of gesture, of expression of the face, and of emotional tone". Doing so will take us "far towards reducing [language] to that system of conventional articulate sounds which the grammarian and the comparative philologist habitually consider as language." (Vol. I, p. 167). Language, he says, includes "gesture, expressions of the feature [i.e., the face], emotional tone, emphasis, force, speed, etc. of utterance, musical rhythm and intonation, and the formation of vowels and consonants which are the skeleton of articulate speech" (Vol. I, p. 163) and adds that if we do not take these into consideration it becomes inexplicable: If we consider only the "articulate words of the dictionary", he continues, if we insist on regarding language to be only that which is considered by the grammarian and the philologist, "language then comes to be looked upon as a mystery, and either occult philosophical causes have been called in to explain its phenomena, or else the endowment of man with the faculties of thought and utter-

---

[14] It is in Tylor's sense of "utterance" that I use this word in this essay.

ance has been deemed insufficient, and a special revelation has been demanded to put into his mouth the vocabulary of a particular language" (Vol. I, p. 232).[15]

Tylor, thus, starts with the observation that humans have a capacity to make their thoughts available for others. Doing this is to *utter*. He then goes on to distinguish the different ways in which uttering can be done and it is these different ways that make up his view of language. He sees it as a dynamic, continuously emerging means of "putting out thoughts", incorporating the materials of expressive calls, gestures, and imitative actions, both vocal and kinesic, and transforming them by processes of conventionalization. He maintained that, in order to understand the nature and origin of language, we cannot exclude these components from the purview of linguistic science. However, since it was the triumphs of comparative philology that were behind the idea that language could be studied as a scientific object, it was the materials that the comparative philologists focused upon—words and syntax—that came to be the focus of study in this newly independent discipline.

In studying words and syntax and finding regularities in how these seemed to change over time, language came to be regarded as a system that could be defined in terms of its formal properties. The Tylorian view, on the other hand, is one whose starting point is function, it is what gets done by utterance action. Starting here, one then proceeds to look at the different ways of doing utterance, and seeks to formulate how these are interrelated and how their different properties may make possible somewhat different but complimentary kinds of outputs.

It is something like this that seems to be emerging in revisions to thinking about language that both signed language studies and gesture studies are bringing about, although these revisions have also been afoot for some time among students of spoken languages. The division that Trager (1958) initiated between "language" and "paralanguage" has been questioned by many, who feel that the role of the voice (and of bodily movement) in spoken language needs to be given much more attention. Intonation has always occupied a rather uncertain place in the structuralist framework and writers such as Bolinger (e.g., 1983) have long maintained that its gradient character cannot be denied, yet insisting it is a central feature of language. Hockett (1987: 140) admitted that the sharp division that attempted to preserve the "linguistic" from gradient features of the many different aspects of the voice, and also from kinesics, was the product of "wishful thinking", that there are no sharp boundaries but only "zones of transition" (1987: 27). More recent is the critique of the language/paralanguage division by Albano Leoni (2009, 2017) who concludes a review of this problem with these words: "these things [i.e., para-

---

15 Chomsky (2010: 59) provides a modern "occult philosophical explanation" for language.

linguistic phenomena] are a part of signification, of connotation, and contribute to determine the linguistic mode in which we stand in the world together with our conspecifics. Therefore the linguist must consider them: they enter legitimately among his *objets*." (Albano Leoni 2017: 22–23, translation mine).

Tylor's broad view of what ought to be included within the purview of the linguist, his idea that "language" must include all those aspects of the activity of uttering that the "grammarian and the philologist" had stripped away, thus is more widely accepted today; as we have seen, research in signed language and gesture studies have contributed much to this.

A fully coherent theoretical framework to accommodate this broader view of "what is language" may not yet have arrived. On the other hand, there are some promising beginnings, including chapters of many of the authors found in this volume along with their recent work. Sherman Wilcox and his associates are prominent in developing this view (see especially Wilcox and Xavier 2019). Others are Ryan Lepic and Corrine Occhino (2018), who show very nicely how a speaker's use of kinesics for an act of depiction can be treated in an integrated manner along with speaking within a linguistic framework ("construction morphology") that applies as well to signed discourse. I mention one more approach, the approach to signed language developed by Christian Cuxac (see, for example Cuxac and Sallandre 2007), which deserves much more attention than it has received among anglophones so far. Cuxac begins his analyses of French Sign Language (LSF) with the recognition that signers, in their discourses, fully integrate various kinds of depictions and enactments with lexical signs. It would be very interesting to show how his approach could as well be adapted for the analysis of languaging with speaking. Here might be another starting point for the integrating framework being sought after.

References

Akita, Kim & Prashant Pardeshi (eds.). 2019. *Ideophones, Mimetics and Expressives*. Amsterdam/Philadelphia: John Benjamins.

Albano Leoni, Federico. 2009. *Dei suoni e dei sensi. Il volto fonico delle parole*. Bologna: Il Mulino.

Albano Leoni, Federico. 2017. Qualche riflessione sulla dicotomia linguistico/paralinguistico. In Anna De Meo & Francesca M. Dovetto (eds.), *La Comunicazione Parlata/Spoken Communication. Napoli 2016*, 13–26. Canterano: Aracne.

Alter, Stephen G. 2005. *William Dwight Whitney and the Science of Language*. Baltimore, MD: Johns Hopkins University Press.

Andresen, Julie Tetel. 1990. *Linguistics in America 1769–1924: A Critical History*. London: Routledge.

Aronoff, Mark. 1992. Segmentalism in linguistics: The alphabetic basis of phonological theory. In Pamela Downing, Susan D. Lima & Michael Noonan (eds.), *The Linguistics of Literacy*, 71–82. Amsterdam/Philadelphia: John Benjamins.

Baynton, Douglas C. 1996. *Forbidden Signs: American Culture and the Campaign Against Sign Language.* Chicago/London: University of Chicago Press.
Blasi, Damián E., Søren Wichmann, Harald Hammerström, Peter F. Stadler & Morten H. Christiansen. 2016. Sound-meaning association biases evidenced across thousands of languages. In Anne Cutler (ed.), *Proceedings of the National Association of Sciences* (*PNAS*) 113(39), 10818–10823.
Bolinger, Dwight. 1983. Intonation and gesture. *American Speech* 58. 156–174.
Boyes Braem, Penny. 1981. *Significant features of the handshape in American Sign Language.* Berkeley, CA: University of California, Berkeley dissertation.
Brennan, Mary. 1993. The visual world of British Sign Language: An introduction. In David Brien (ed.), *Dictionary of British Sign Language/English*, 1–133. London/Boson: Faber and Faber.
Brentari, Diane. 2019. *Sign Language Phonology.* Cambridge: Cambridge University Press.
Chomsky, Noam. 2010. Some simple evo devo theses: How true might they be? In Richard K. Larson, Vivian Déprez & Hiroko Yamakido (eds.), *The Evolution of Human Language: Biolinguistic Perspectives*, 45–62. Cambridge: Cambridge University Press.
Cuxac, Christian & Marie-Anne Sallandre. 2007. Iconicity and arbitrariness in French Sign Language: Highly iconic structures, degenerated iconicity and diagrammatic iconicity. In Elena Pizzuto, Paola Pietrandrea & Raffaele Simone (eds.), *Verbal and Signed Languages: Comparing Structures, Constructs and Methodologies*, 13–33. Berlin/New York: Mouton de Gruyter.
Ćwiek, Aleksandra, Susanne Fuchs, Christoph Draxler, Eva Liina Asu, Dan Dediu, Katri Hiovain, Shigeto Kawahara, Sofia Koutalidis, Manfred Krifka, Pärtel Lippus, Gary Lupyan, Grace E. Oh, Jing Paul, Caterina Petrone, Rachid Ridouane, Sabine Reiter, Nathalie Schümchen, Ádám Szalontai, Özlem Ünal-Logacev, Jochen Zeller, Bodo Winter & Marcus Perlman. 2021. Novel vocalizations are understood across cultures. *Scientific Reports* 11(10108). 1–12.
de Saussure, Ferdinand. 1983[1959]. *Course in General Linguistics, edited by Charles Bally and Albert Sechehaye, translated and annotated by Roy Harris.* London: Duckworth and Co.
Dingemanse, Mark. 2011. *The Meaning and Use of Ideophones in Siwu.* Nijmegen: Max Planck Institute for Psycholinguistics Series No. 64.
Dingemanse, Mark, Damián E. Blasi, Gary Lupyan, Morten H. Christiansen & Padraic Monaghan. 2015. Arbitrariness, iconicity and systematicity in language. *Trends in Cognitive Sciences* 19(10). 603–613.
Dotter, Franz. 2018. Most characteristic elements of sign language texts are intricate mixtures of linguistic and non-linguistic parts, aren't they? *Colloquium: New Philologies* 3(1). 1–62.
Duncan, Susan. 2005. Gesture in signing: A case study from Taiwan Sign Language. *Language and Linguistics* 6(2). 279–318.
Emmorey, Karen. 1999. Do signers gesture? In Lynn S. Messing & Ruth Campbell (eds.), *Gesture, Speech and Sign*, 132–159. Oxford: Oxford University Press.
Emmorey, Karen & Melissa Herzig. 2003. Categorical versus gradient properties of classifier constructions in ASL. In Karen Emmorey (ed.), *Perspectives on Classifier Constructions in Sign Languages*, 221–246. Mahwah, NJ: Lawrence Erlbaum Associates.
Facchini, Massimo G. 1985. An historical reconstruction of the events leading to the Congress of Milan in 1880. In William C. Stokoe & Virginia Volterra (eds.), *SLE '83: Proceedings of the 3rd International Symposium on Sign Language Research, Rome, June 22–26, 1983*, 356–362. Silver Spring, MD: Linstok Press.
Falk, Julia S. 2004. Saussure and American Linguistics. In Carol Sanders (ed.), *The Cambridge Companion to Saussure*, 107–123. Cambridge: Cambridge University Press.
Ferrara, Lindsay & Rolf Piene Halvorsen. 2017. Depicting and describing meanings with iconic signs in Norwegian Sign Language. *Gesture* 16(3). 371–395.

Friedman, Lynn A. (ed.). 1977. *On the Other Hand: New Perspectives on American Sign Language*. New York: Academic Press.

Fuks, Orit. 2014. Gradient and categorically: Handshape's two semiotic dimensions in Israeli Sign Language discourse. *Journal of Pragmatics* 60. 207–225.

Genette, Gérard. 1995. *Mimologics* [*Mimologiques: Voyage en Cratylie*, Thaïs E. Morgan, Translator]. Lincoln/London: University of Nebraska Press.

Givón, T. 1985. Iconicity, isomorphism and non-arbitrary coding in syntax. In John Haiman (ed.), *Iconicity in Syntax: Proceedings of a Symposium on Iconicity in Syntax, Stanford, June 24–26, 1983*, 187–219. Amsterdam/Philadelphia: John Benjamins.

Gleason, H. A. 1961. *An Introduction to Descriptive Linguistics*. New York: Holt, Rinehart and Winston.

Goldin-Meadow, Susan & Diane Brentari. 2017. Gesture, sign and language: The coming of age of sign language and gesture studies. *Behavioral and Brain Sciences*, doi:10.1017/S0140525X15001247, e46

Graffi, Giorgio. 2013. European linguistics since Saussure. In Keith Allan (ed.), *The Oxford Handbook of the History of Linguistics*, 469–484. Oxford: Oxford University Press.

Haiman, John (ed.). 1985. *Iconicity in Syntax: Proceedings of a Symposium on Iconicity in Syntax, June 24–6, 1983*. Amsterdam/Philadelphia: John Benjamins.

Haiman, John. 2018. *Ideophones and the Evolution of Language*. Cambridge: Cambridge University Press.

Harris, Roy. 1980. *The Language Makers*. Ithaca, NY: Cornell University Press.

Harris, Roy. 1981. *The Language Myth*. Ithaca, NY: Cornell University Press.

Hinton, Leanne, Johanna Nichols & John J. Ohala (eds.). 1994. *Sound Symbolism*. Cambridge: Cambridge University Press.

Hockett, Charles F. 1960. Logical considerations in the study of animal communication. In Wesley E. Lanyon & William N. Tavolga (eds.), *Animal Sounds and Communication*, 392–430. Washington, DC: American Institute of Biological Sciences.

Hockett, Charles F. 1987. *Refurbishing Our Foundations: Elementary Linguistics from an Advanced Point of View*. Amsterdam/Philadelphia: John Benjamins.

Hymes, Del & John Fought. 1981[1975]. *American Structuralism*. The Hague: Mouton.

Kendon, Adam. 1988. How gestures can become like words. In Fernando Poyatos (ed.), *Cross-Cultural Perspectives in Nonverbal Communication*, 131–141. Lewiston, NY: C. J. Hogrefe.

Kendon, Adam. 2004. *Gesture: Visible Action as Utterance*. Cambridge: Cambridge University Press.

Kendon, Adam. 2007. On the origins of modern gesture studies. In, Susan D. Duncan, Justine Cassell & Elena T. Levy (eds.), *Gesture and the Dynamic Dimension of Language: Essays in Honor of David McNeill*, 13–28. Amsterdam/Philadelphia: John Benjamins.

Kendon, Adam. 2008. Some reflections on 'gesture' and 'sign'. *Gesture* 8(3), 348–336.

Kendon, Adam. 2013. Exploring the utterance roles of visible bodily action: A personal account. In Cornelia Müller, Alan Cienki, Ellen Fricke, Silva Ladewig, David McNeill & Sedinha Tessendorf (eds.), *Body-Language-Communication*, 7–28. Berlin/Boston: Mouton de Gruyter,

Kendon, Adam. 2017. Languages as semiotically heterogeneous systems. Open Peer Commentary, for Goldin-Meadow and Brentari (2017), *Behavioral and Brain Sciences*. doi:10.1017/S014052X15001247, e46

Klima, Edward A. & Ursula Bellugi. 1979. *The Signs of Language*. Cambridge, MA: Harvard University Press.

Lepic, Ryan & Corrine Occhino. 2018. A construction morphology approach to sign language analysis. In Geert Booij (ed.), *The Construction of Words: Advances in Construction Morphology*, 141–172. Cham, Switzerland: Springer International AG.

Liddell, Scott K. 2003. *Grammar, Gesture and Meaning in American Sign Language*. Cambridge: Cambridge University Press.
Liddell, Scott K. & Melanie Metzger. 1998. Gesture in sign language discourse. *Journal of Pragmatics* 30. 657–697.
Linell, Per. 2005. *The Written Language Bias in Linguistics: Its Nature, Origins and Transformations*. London/New York: Routledge.
Maher, Jane. 1996. *Seeing Language in Sign: The Work of William C. Stokoe*. Washington, DC: Gallaudet University Press.
McNeill, David. 1992. *Hand and Mind: What Gestures Reveal about Thought*. Chicago: Chicago University Press.
Mayer, Mercer. 1969. *Frog, Where Are You?* New York: Dial Press.
Morpurgo Davies, Anna. 1998. *History of Linguistics, Volume IV: Nineteenth-Century Linguistics*. London/New York: Routledge.
Morpurgo Davies, Anna. 2004. Saussure and Indo-European Linguistics. In Carol Sanders (ed.), *The Cambridge Companion to Saussure*, 9–29. Cambridge: Cambridge University Press.
Müller, Cornelia. 2018. Gesture and sign: Cataclysmic break or dynamic relations? *Frontiers in Psychology* 9(1651). doi:10.3389/fpsyg.2018.01651
Nuckolls, Janis B. 1996. *Sounds Like Life: Sound Symbolic Grammar, Performance and Cognition in Pastaza Quechua*. New York/Oxford: Oxford University Press.
Nuckolls, Janis B. 1999. The case for sound symbolism. *Annual Review of Anthropology* 28. 225–252.
Perlman, Marcus. 2017. Debunking two myths about the vocal origins of language: Language is iconic and multimodal to the core. *Interaction Studies: Social Behaviour and Communication in Biological and Artificial Systems* 18(3). 376–401.
Perniss, Pamela & Gabriella Vigliocco. 2014. The bridge of iconicity: From a world of experience to the experience of language. *Philosophical Transactions of the Royal Society of London, Series B, 369: 20130300*. https://doi.org/10.1098/rstb.2013.0300
Puech, Christian. 2004. Saussure and Structural Linguistics in Europe. In Carol Sanders (ed.), *The Cambridge Companion to Saussure*, 124–138. Cambridge: Cambridge University Press.
Sanders, Carol (ed.). 2004. *The Cambridge Companion to Saussure*. Cambridge: Cambridge University Press.
Schembri, Adam, Caroline Jones & Denis Burnham. 2005. Comparing action gestures and classifier verbs of motion: Evidence from Australian Sign Language, Taiwan Sign Language and Nonsigners' gestures without speech. *Journal of Deaf Studies and Deaf Education* 10(3). 272–290.
Simone, Raffaele (ed.). 1995. *Iconicity in Language*. Amsterdam/Philadelphia: John Benjamins.
Singleton, Jenny L., Susan Goldin-Meadow & David McNeill. 1995. The cataclysmic break between gesticulation and sign: Evidence against a unified continuum of gestural communication. In Karen Emmorey & Judy S. Reilly (eds.), *Language, Gesture, and Space*, 287–311. Hillsdale, NJ: Lawrence Erlbaum.
Siple, Patricia. 1979. Review of Lynn A. Friedman (ed.), *On the Other Hand: New Perspectives on American Sign Language*. *American Anthropologist* 81(1). 138–139.
Stokoe, William C. 1960. *Sign Language Structure: An Outline of the Visual Communication Systems of the American Deaf* (Studies in Linguistics Occasional Papers 8). Buffalo, NY: University of Buffalo.
Stokoe, William C. 1991. Semantic phonology. *Sign Language Studies* 71. 99–106.
Todd, Payton. 1980. Interpreting *The Signs of Language*. *Sign Language Studies* 28. 217–238.
Trager, George L. 1958. Paralanguage: A first approximation. *Studies in Linguistics* 13. 1–12.
Trager, George L. & Henry Lee Smith. 1951. *An Outline of English Structure* (Studies in Linguistics: Occasional Papers 3). Norman, OK: Battenberg Press.

Turner, James. 2014. *Philology: The Forgotten Origins of the Modern Humanities*. Princeton, NJ: Princeton University Press.

Tylor, Edward Burnett. 1871. *Primitive Culture: Researches into the Development of Mythology, Philosophy, Religion, Art, and Custom* (Two volumes). London: John Murray.

Tylor, Edward Burnett. 1878 [1865]. *Researches into the Early History of Mankind and the Development of Civilization*. Boston: Estes and Laurent [London: John Murray].

Voeltz, F. K. Erhard & Christa Kilian-Hatz (eds.). 2001. *Ideophones*. Amsterdam/Philadelphia: John Benjamins.

Wilcox, Sherman E. 2004. Hands and bodies, minds and souls: What can signed languages tell us about the origin of signs? In Morana Alac & Patrizia Violi (eds.), *In the Beginning: Origins of Semiosis*, 137–167. Turnhout, Belgium: Brepols.

Wilcox, Sherman E. & André N. Xavier. 2019. A framework for unifying spoken language, signed language and gestures. *Todas as Letras U* 15(1). 88–110.

Index

Access 11, 12, 55, 108, 121, 161, 228, 426, 434
Acquisition 25, 27, 28, 86, 146, 160, 384
American English 181, 189, 190, 205–206
American Sign Language (ASL) 5, 33–34, 83, 131, 166, 211, 243, 330, 357, 392, 422, 447
Annotation 30, 50
- Gloss-based annotation 56, 64, 336
Arbitrariness 3, 33–35, 38–39, 77, 82–84, 94, 105, 113, 120, 131, 215–216, 447–449
- Radical arbitrariness 84, 94, 95
Argentine Sign Language (LSA) 187, 389–390, 397, 407, 413
Articulation 84, 187, 212–214, 262, 368, 450
- Articulators 60, 128, 132, 149, 260, 265, 309, 333
- Articulatory gesture 2, 132, 203
- Co-articulation 64

Blending 6, 313–314, 320
- Blending Theory 276, 304, 311, 322
- Conceptual blending 265, 316, 321
- Conceptual integration 6, 231, 277, 321, 420
- Real Space blending 164–173, 231, 275
- Surrogate blend 277, 281, 284, 286, 291–292, 299
- Token blend 276, 281, 284, 289, 292, 299
Body 4, 9, 26–27, 37, 82, 87, 149, 150, 157, 185, 213, 218–219, 244, 247–248, 255, 267, 277, 310, 350, 431, 443, 447, 455
- Body action 9, 165, 167, 265, 268
- Bodily expression 443
- Bodily meaning 158–159, 169, 444, 451–452, 455, 456–457
Brazilian Sign Language (Libras) 389–390, 395–401, 406, 413–414
Brow raise 330, 333, 334–335, 340, 350–351, 418–419, 422–424, 428, 429, 431, 434–437

Categorization 30, 92, 111–112, 183, 448
Chereme 33, 81–82, 134, 444
Chunking 280, 282, 358–360, 384
Classifier(s) 27, 59, 61, 282, 306–308, 452
- Classifier handshape 32, 318, 379
Cognition 92–93, 111, 146, 268
- Embodied cognition 128, 149

Cognitive linguistics 1, 6, 8–9, 26, 97, 125, 127, 276, 362, 417
- Cognitive Grammar 105–106, 111, 122, 124, 125, 127, 149, 183, 206, 266, 419
- Cognitive Iconicity 7, 83, 128, 130, 145, 149
- Cognitive Phonology 135, 149
Collocations 357, 367–369, 375
Complex symbolic unit 168, 263, 266–268, 269
Conceptual distance 83, 211–212, 218, 222, 230, 234, 236–237, 436
Constituency 85, 122–123
Construal 117, 129, 148, 158, 230
Construction Grammar 149
Constructions 59–63, 123, 129, 137–138, 142, 183, 192, 199, 206, 357, 417, 458
Constructed action 27, 59, 61, 63, 217, 244–245, 252, 256, 277, 299, 357, 452
Contiguity 76, 87–89
Conventionality 106, 146, 258, 263–264
- Conventionalization 105, 124, 352, 366, 382, 457
Corpus 51, 63, 65, 190, 245, 304, 360
- Corpus linguistics 97, 362
Cyclic assembly 196–198

Danish Sign Language (DTS) 329
Deixis 159, 164
Depiction 38, 164, 167, 170, 176, 255, 259, 298, 381, 449, 451, 454, 458
Design features 34, 76, 137
Diachronic 83, 85, 86, 348, 393, 445
Discourse complexity 275, 279, 297, 299–300
Distal space 211–212, 218, 222, 225, 228, 230, 236
Duality of patterning 50, 77
- Double articulation 447, 450
Dynamic 4, 35, 105, 106, 121, 237, 305–308, 310, 320, 382, 454

Emblem 175, 182, 247, 256, 259, 329–330, 333, 344, 348
Embodied; Embodiment 26, 127–129, 135, 141, 149–150, 160, 162, 167, 221, 223, 265, 268
Enactment 27, 164, 170, 172, 243, 277, 451
Entrenchment 105–106, 111, 124, 145, 218–219, 266–267, 310, 367, 382

https://doi.org/10.1515/9783110703788-018

Evidentiality 390, 415
- Evidential 230–231, 233, 238

Face-to-face language 32, 39, 53, 65, 163, 172, 181, 305, 322, 359
Facial consent 329
Facial display 418, 424–425, 434–435
Fixed expression; fixed form 277, 333, 357–358, 361, 367, 453
Force dynamics 144–145, 158, 169
French Sign Language (LSF) 56, 61, 389, 394, 458

Gesture space(s) 158, 160, 163, 188, 189, 193, 212, 223–225, 234
Grammaticalization (Grammaticization) 4, 329, 330, 391–394, 397, 414, 427
Graphic representation of signed language 32, 49–51, 54, 57, 63, 133

Hierarchy 107–108, 121, 122

Iconicity 2–3, 25, 33, 80, 82–84, 105, 109, 135, 148, 164, 303, 305, 447–449
- Diagrammatic iconicity 110, 114, 116
Ideophone 449
Indexing 198, 236, 237, 238
Indicating act; indicating strategy 187, 198
Interaction 53, 57, 85, 94, 110, 127, 130, 144–145, 165, 168, 172, 173–175, 181, 263, 304, 312, 322, 346, 351, 359, 373, 384, 394, 415, 454
Interpersonal Place 181
Iranian Sign Language (ZEI) 335, 336, 394, 418
Irish Sign Language (ISL) 211
Italian Sign Language (LIS) 30, 36–37, 49, 60–61, 65–66, 67, 81–83, 94–95, 96, 304, 336, 390, 397, 423–424, 428

Joint action 181, 182, 197–199, 201–202, 203, 205–206

Language origins 1–2, 28, 87
Languaging 28, 29, 38, 455, 458
Layering 107–108, 118, 119, 121, 305, 322
Linguistic status 62, 76, 80, 81, 84, 109, 330, 348, 351, 447, 451

Linguistic system 76, 84, 94, 183, 262, 303, 310, 320, 329, 394

Mental space(s) 164–165, 168, 231, 276–277, 316, 318, 320
Metaphor 36–37, 39, 119, 139, 146, 158–159, 167–170, 184, 211–212, 218–219, 221, 227, 228, 230, 260, 303, 371
- Source domain 167, 170, 222, 303, 308–309, 315–316, 319, 322
- Target domain 167, 222, 303, 309–310, 311–312, 315–317
Metonymy 36, 92, 138, 147, 158–159, 166, 167, 203, 307, 310, 314, 319
Milan congress/conference 3, 443
Mirror neurons 25, 87, 165, 172
Modality (linguistic) 338–339, 343, 389, 390, 392–395, 397, 414, 435
- Deontic modality 391, 398, 411
- Epistemic modality 335–336, 351, 390, 395, 397
- Modal 218, 329, 335, 392, 394–396, 399–401, 406, 412, 415
- Non-epistemic modality 390, 395, 400–401, 412, 413, 415
- Possibility 335–336, 389–392, 395, 400, 404
Mouth action 349–351
- Mouth gesture 350–351
- Mouth shrug 329
Multi-word expressions 358, 363, 370
Multimodality 29, 32
- Multimodal 25, 29, 31, 32, 39, 158, 182, 190, 202, 204, 233, 305, 320, 322

Nominal grounding 425, 427
Non-dominant hand 132, 142, 143–144, 219, 277, 290–292, 407
Non-manual 30, 56, 61, 62, 65, 164, 184, 252, 261, 318, 320, 330, 340, 345, 346, 349, 392, 397, 398, 412, 418, 422–423, 424

Openness 76, 77, 79, 85–86, 90, 93, 95

Partitioning 166, 175, 217, 257, 265, 277–278, 284, 304
Perspective 216–217, 220, 222–223, 237, 243, 247, 252, 255, 260, 261, 268, 282, 284, 297–298

Phonology 33–35, 81, 88, 128, 134–135, 137, 149–150, 358, 445, 450
– Phoneme 33, 81, 131, 133, 134–135, 146, 444, 450
Place 186–187, 188, 199, 206
Plasticity 79, 91–94, 96
Point, pointing 57–58, 158, 160, 163–164, 172, 176, 186–187, 198, 215, 256, 277, 290–291, 336, 375–376, 418, 424–425, 426–427, 428, 434, 436
Polysemy 392, 393, 397, 414
Processing activity 105, 106, 109, 111, 129
Profiling 122, 311, 312, 321, 417, 421, 422
Pronoun 212, 225, 228, 238, 261, 282, 290, 338, 339, 372, 373, 375, 418, 421, 423, 427, 433
Prosodic grouping 123–124
Proximal space 214, 223–224, 230, 232, 233, 235, 237, 238
PUOH assembly 191–192, 194, 196, 199–200, 202, 205

Quebec French 243, 246, 248, 250, 251, 253, 257, 268
Quebec Sign Language (LSQ) 243, 245–248, 250–252, 255–257, 261, 263, 266, 268–269

Recursion 78–79, 85, 90, 96
Recycled utterances 357, 360, 361–362, 368, 373, 375, 378, 379, 380–381, 382–385
Referencing 214, 237
– Reference point 420–422, 428–430, 433, 434–436
Reflexive 77, 93, 95, 96
Relative clause 417

Schema; schematic 119, 121, 123, 141–144, 166–167, 187, 198, 203, 205, 227, 263, 267–268, 312, 329, 359, 361, 366, 375, 379–381, 383–384, 427
– Schematization 311, 357, 371
Semiological Approach 60, 61, 65
Seriality 107–108, 121
Signed language discourse 49–50, 52, 54, 61, 62, 66, 67, 322
SignWriting 11, 31–32, 52, 64–66, 67, 96
Simultaneity 132, 255, 261
Structural tradition 447
Suppletion 414
Swedish Sign Language (STS) 136, 216, 275, 346, 362
Symbolization 59, 88, 109–111, 114–115, 121, 122, 124, 266
– Symbolic strategies 27, 28
– Symbolic structure 88, 105, 128–129, 183–184, 186, 189, 194, 199, 202, 205, 362, 427
Systematicity 134, 138, 145

Topic 32, 169, 173–174, 184, 189, 191–194, 198, 200, 204–205, 277, 288, 303, 306, 308, 330, 341, 343, 365, 375, 421, 422–423, 429–430, 434, 436
Transcription 50, 157, 280
Transfer(s) 27, 60–63, 65–66, 308
Transitive construction 143–145
Typology 175

Vision 161, 262, 371
Visual perception 160

www.ingramcontent.com/pod-product-compliance
Lightning Source LLC
Chambersburg PA
CBHW051552230426
43668CB00013B/1829